Social Welfare in Canada

UNDERSTANDING INCOME SECURITY

THIRD EDITION

For Vaida, Justin, and Kristina

For the liberation of all people and communities from institutionalized greed, ill will, and unawareness.

Social Welfare in Canada

UNDERSTANDING INCOME SECURITY

THIRD EDITION

STEVEN HICK
CARLETON UNIVERSITY

THOMPSON EDUCATIONAL
TORONTO

Information on how to obtain copies of this book is available at:

Website: http://www.thompsonbooks.com
E-mail: publisher@thompsonbooks.com
Telephone: (416) 766-2763
Fax: (416) 766-0398

Library and Archives Canada Cataloguing in Publication

Hick, Steven F. author
Social welfare in Canada : understanding income security / Steven Hick. — 3rd ed.

Includes bibliographical references and index.

ISBN 978-1-55077-230-2 (pbk.)

1. Social security—Canada—Textbooks. 2. Income maintenance programs—Canada—Textbooks. I. Title.

HV105.H523 2013 362.5'820971 C2013-902368-2

We acknowledge the support of the Government of Canada through the Canada Book Fund for our publishing activities.

Printed in Canada.

1 2 3 4 5 18 17 16 15 14 13

Brief Contents

Contents

Acknowledgments

Crafting works such as this one, and its sister publication *Social Work in Canada: An Introduction*, involves the work of a large number of people. From the outset, I have intended to make these books accessible to a wide audience—providing information and analysis in a clear and succinct manner. This would not have been possible without the generous feedback of students in my social work and social welfare courses. I thank them for their generosity and insight.

The first edition of this book owes a debt of gratitude to Allan Moscovitch and Keith Thompson. The idea for the first edition came from Allan, and it was Keith who believed that it could be done. I would also like to thank the graduate students that provided feedback and ideas, including Cheryl Parsons, Amy McGee, Kate Belcher, Teresa Raposo, Monica Reinvall, Carole Bourque, and Erin Brown. I would also like to thank the editorial team at Thompson Educational for their persistent and excellent work.

A Special Thanks

Thanks must go to Purnima Sundar at Carleton University for her contributions to the previous edition ("The Social Welfare of Immigrants"). The racialization of immigrant poverty is something that this country cannot afford to ignore. A special thanks too to Roy Haynes for his contribution to the second edition ("Disability and Social Welfare").

A special thanks to Alvin Finkel at Athabasca University for substantially re-working the chapter on the early history of income security (Chapter 2) and developing an entirely new chapter on the recent history (Chapter 3) for this edition. Special thanks as well to Peter Graefe at McMaster University for his policy-making chapter (Chapter 5) and telling us how all this comes about, politically.

The significant changes to this edition were inspired by several anonymous peer reviewers. The book is greatly improved due to their feedback and I thank them all for their astute suggestions.

My family—Vaida, my partner, Justin, my son, and Kristina, my daughter—must certainly be acknowledged. The early phases of the "second edition" occurred while I was recovering from a serious head injury and their support kept me going forward. They also provided ideas that contributed directly to the work.

Preface

This text is intended for students who are relatively new to social policy analysis, social work, and other human service disciplines who need a broad survey of the field. It is also appropriate for students in public administration, social work, economics, political science, or sociology who may not be familiar with the various income security programs in Canada.

While providing an historical background, the book also gives a overview of the many programs that exist in Canada today. Combined with information and data on the socio-economic and political context of social welfare, this book enables readers to form their own views about the nature and character of social welfare in Canada.

The Third Edition

This is a very substantially revised edition, called for by the momentous changes that have occurred in income security policy and programs since the last edition. The data have been updated, of course. But there is more to this new edition than simply data updates.

We have tried to capture the complex changes that have occurred since the new Conservative government was elected in 2006 (and re-elected with a majority in 2011). This period also coincided with the global economic downturn that began in 2008 and painfully lingers on today. This edition attempts to understand the implications of this new period for the welfare and income security of Canadians.

This new edition is divided very simply, as follows.

- Chapter 1 introduces the field.
- Chapters 2 and 3 provide a detailed overview of the early and recent history of social welfare.
- Chapters 4 and 5 look at welfare approaches and policy formation.
- Chapters 6 and 7 focus on poverty and on employment/unemployment, respectively.
- Chapter 8 deals with families and Chapter 9 with children.
- The next four chapters (10, 11, 12, and 13) deal with specific policy issues (immigrants, Aboriginal peoples, the disabled, and the elderly).
- The final chapter (Chapter 14) looks at global issues in social welfare today.

My Philosophy

This book does not dictate a particular standpoint on the nature of Canadian social welfare. Although I do not hesitate to state my views and take a stand, my philosophy is that people should explore all the issues and discover this world for themselves, eyes wide open.

I have seen the suffering and pain that people experience because of the inadequacies of our social welfare systems, and at the same time, I have been involved—through social activism, policy work, and research—in trying to move governments toward action that might ameliorate this. I have also met with people in other countries who were dying—or seeing their family members and neighbours die—due to war or the lack of the basic necessities of life. Throughout all of this, I have come to the conclusion that our current social and economic systems are extremely unhealthy, oppressive, and unjust to both people and the planet.

But this is only my conclusion. While I personally believe that only major changes will relieve our society, I would like students to question and discuss all the issues, and with the facts at hand arrive at their own conclusions and above all act on them. I hope that this book might be a small part of that journey.

Any and all suggestions

We, of course, welcome any and all suggestions for improving future editions of this work and look forward to hearing from you: publisher@thompsonbooks.com.

Graphs, Charts, and Tables

Graphs and Charts

List of Tables

Introducing Social Welfare

Understanding Income Security

Social welfare is a defining feature of Canadian society. The social services and income security programs available to Canadian citizens affect nearly every single member of the population at some point in his or her life. Indeed, given the scope and importance of social welfare, it is surprising that so few citizens are aware of the history of social welfare in Canada, how it all works, or the issues and concerns surrounding it.

This chapter examines the role of income security in our society and economy and reviews the current state of affairs. It will enable you to become familiar with the income security concepts and issues in Canada today.

"We're in a giant car heading towards a brick wall and everyone's arguing over where they're going to sit."
— DAVID SUZUKI

The "Social Safety Net"

Income security programs are at the centre of the welfare state in Canada. These programs are designed to protect Canadian citizens from unforeseen economic events that cause disruption in their lives. Income security programs are used by all sectors of society. They capture Canada as we know it, as a caring society.

Defining Canada

Over the course of our lives, almost everyone benefits from Canada's income security system. People retire and draw retirement benefits, some become incapacitated and draw on income support benefits, while others may become unemployed temporarily and require Employment Insurance (EI) to carry them over. In short, income security programs provide protection for all Canadians, if and when they need it.

Unfortunately, our **social safety net**, as it has come to be called, has seriously eroded in recent years. The causes for this weakening are many and varied. But it has happened so quietly, intentionally or unintentionally, that staunch advocates of the welfare system have described it as a form of "social policy by stealth." The intense debates over social welfare—whether it is needed at all or how extensive it should be—are important. In many ways, the outcome of these debates will define Canada in the years to come. All the more reason to know the history of social welfare and how it works in practice.

The Canadian Welfare System

Taken as a whole, the **social welfare system** consists of a combination of income security programs and social services. Although it is not always easy to distinguish between an income security provision and a social service, there is a difference.

- **INCOME SECURITY PROGRAMS** provide monetary or other material benefits to supplement income or maintain minimum income levels (e.g., Employment Insurance, Social Assistance, Old Age Security). If everyone could meet his or her income needs, the need for income security programs would be drastically reduced or eliminated. Without income security programs, Canadians would be much more financially vulnerable.
- **SOCIAL SERVICES** (personal or community services) help people by providing non-monetary aid to those in need. Offered by social workers, these services include probation, addiction treatment, youth drop-in centres, parent-child resource centres, child care, child protection services, women's shelters, and counselling.

Income security programs and social services are provided to citizens through social policies. **Social policies** are the rules and regulations, laws, and other administrative directives that set the framework for social welfare activity. These policies are then implemented through **social programs** (or targeted initiatives) that put these social welfare policies into practice.

The Saskatchewan health plan was the first step towards universal health care in the province. Here, Tommy Douglas presents the first hospital card to a pensioner in 1946.

The Welfare State Today

Taken together, the range of programs and services available to Canadian citizens is commonly referred to as the **welfare state.** This is a system in which the state protects the health and well-being of its citizens, especially those in social and financial need. The key functions of the welfare state are (1) using state power to achieve desired goals (powers include government, bureaucracy, the judiciary, and political parties); (2) altering the normal operation of the private marketplace; and (3) using grants, taxes, pensions, social services, and minimum-income programs such as Social Assistance ("welfare") and Employment Insurance (EI).

The basic purpose of Canada's social welfare system is to help people through the difficult times until they can rebuild their lives themselves. The system helps people face a variety of contingencies or difficulties—retirement, unemployment, loss of income, disability, illness, violence, homelessness, addiction, racism, warfare, death, separation, divorce, aging of family members, and responsibilities associated with additional children. These contingencies can be grouped into three interrelated categories: (1) contingencies that threaten economic survival, (2) contingencies that threaten the integrity of the person, and (3) contingencies that affect the family.

To help individuals and families face contingencies that may affect their income, Canadian governments at various levels (federal, provincial, and municipal) provide a wide range of income security programs. These are the subject of this volume.

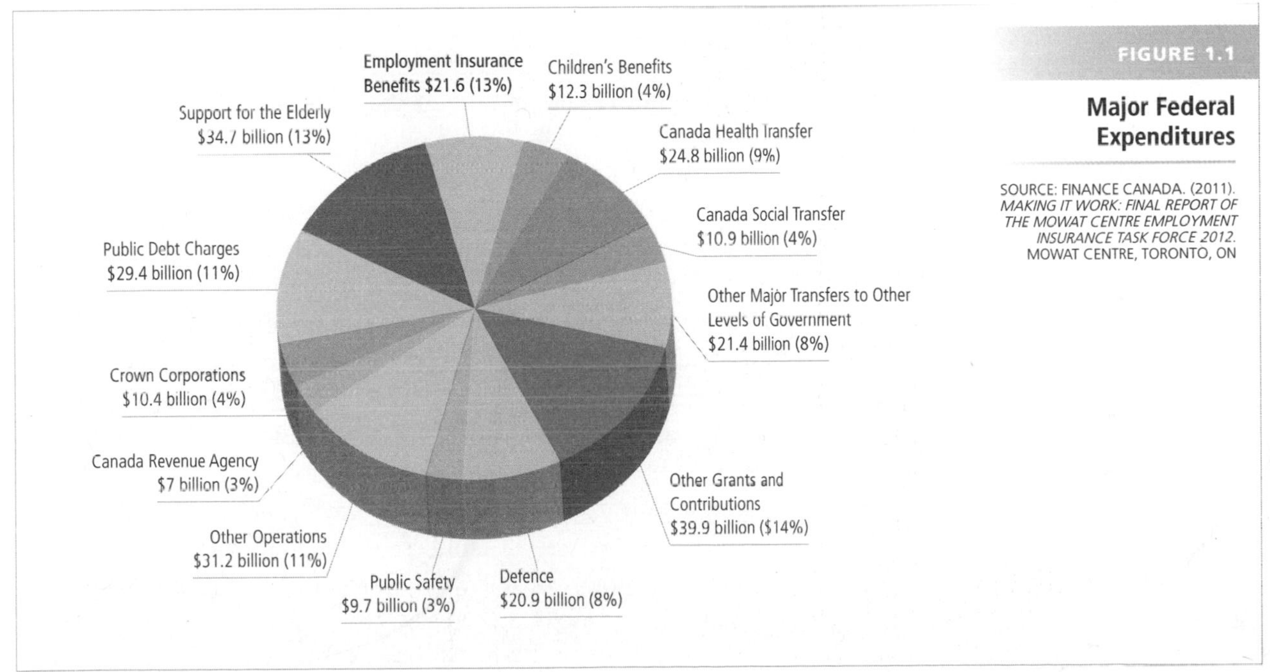

FIGURE 1.1

Major Federal Expenditures

SOURCE: FINANCE CANADA. (2011). *MAKING IT WORK: FINAL REPORT OF THE MOWAT CENTRE EMPLOYMENT INSURANCE TASK FORCE 2012.* MOWAT CENTRE, TORONTO, ON

Tax expenditures

Revenue returned to taxpayers for various exemptions, deductions, and credits (RRSP contributions, GST refund, etc.) should be viewed as part of the income security system.

Tax Expenditures as Social Welfare

Textbook treatments of income security in Canada often miss the tax expenditure side of the public system. **Tax expenditures** are foregone tax revenues resulting from special exemptions, deductions, rate reductions, rebates, credits, and deferrals that reduce the amount of tax that would otherwise be payable. The principal function of the tax system is to raise the revenues necessary to fund government expenditures. However, the tax system is also an instrument of policy that serves to advance a wide range of economic, social, environmental, cultural, and other public policy objectives.

Tax expenditures include deductions for pensions, and Registered Retirement Savings Plan (RRSP) contributions, credits for charitable donations, and benefits for families with children. Tax expenditures are often designed to encourage certain kinds of activities or to serve other objectives, such as providing assistance to lower-income or elderly Canadians. While this is not often thought of as income security, it can dramatically affect the income of Canadians. By not collecting taxes from those who have a taxable income, an individual's income is effectively increased.

Redistribution of Wealth

The use of tax expenditures for income security purposes is increasing in Canada. For example, the Canada Child Tax Benefit (CCTB), a tax-free monthly payment available to eligible Canadian families to help with the cost of raising children, is an income security program that uses the tax system to redistribute income.

The main benefits of using the tax system are that (1) the programs do not bring the stigma of collecting welfare benefits, as the money is redistributed anonymously; (2) eligibility is determined on the basis of income as reported on the income tax return rather than through an intrusive "needs test"; (3) tax-based income-tested programs are less costly to administer, as they use an already existing administrative structure (the tax system) and do not require the hiring of social workers and others to implement a needs test; and (4) the programs have a low profile and therefore may be more secure and less likely to be removed for political reasons.

Tax-based income security programs do not only benefit low-income Canadians. The programs also have an appeal for higher-income Canadians who appreciate the low profile and non-stigmatizing nature of this type of income security. For example, the CCTB provided $10.3 billion in benefits to 3.1 million families, or 82 percent of all families in Canada, in the government's 2011/12 fiscal year. And almost 6 million people contributed $33.9 billion to their RRSPs in 2010, an increase of 2.6 percent from the year before.

Analyzing Social Welfare Problems

Finding Lasting Solutions

Many people view social problems as being too complicated with no clear solutions. Social problems are indeed usually very complex, but a systematic analysis can often lead to positive and lasting solutions.

A social problem is a situation that is incompatible with some standard or norm held by a significant number of people in society, who agree that action is needed to alter the situation. In many cases, this standard is already expressed in human rights codes or social policy legislation. Armed with a basic knowledge of social issues and how society works, it is possible to analyze social problems and point to possible solutions.

Consider the social problem of homelessness. If you try to list all the factors that cause or contribute to homelessness, you would end up with a long and varied list. The causal factors could be categorized according to "internal factors" and "external factors." Internal factors are personal or internal to the individual. External factors exist out there in society and are of a policy, systemic, or structural nature.

When looking for solutions, certain things may be emphasized over others. Typically the focus will be on the individual factors, as they are somewhat easier to address. In relation to homelessness, for example, which is often associated with alcohol or drug addiction, individual counselling might seem like a practical solution.

However, it is easy to understand that a comprehensive program of affordable housing (a possible external factor) would have a much larger impact in the long run than a one-on-one counselling activity with a homeless individual, as important as this is. When seeking solutions, usually it is necessary to address both the internal and external factors simultaneously.

Table 1.1 offers a typical list of factors that are likely to contribute to homelessness. Some could be said to be individual problems, whereas some pertain more to the way our society operates.

Table 1.1

External Factors
Low income, unemployment, economic recession
Lack of affordable housing, low vacancy rates
Discrimination
Low rates of income assistance
Lack of social support systems, cutbacks in social services
Lack of educational opportunities
Internal Factors
Mental illness
Alcohol and drug addictions
Disabilities, physical or mental
Lack of job skills
Laziness
Family trouble

There are several factors that lead to the social problem of homelessness and various social welfare programs that attempt to alleviate it.

Approaching Social Welfare

Residual approach: In this view, social welfare is a limited, short-term, and temporary response to human need. The approach is based on the idea that individuals' needs should be met through the market and the family.

Institutional approach: This approach holds that social welfare is a necessary measure to help all people attain a minimum standard of living. It is based on the idea that individuals cannot always meet all of their needs through family and work.

Structural approach: This approach considers market-based economic structures to be essentially exploitative and oppressive and argues that while social welfare is necessary for survival, it also perpetuates the current system.

Approaches to Social Welfare

The idea of providing support to citizens in need is no longer a controversial one in Canada. Pretty well everyone concurs. Major disputes do arise, however, in determining which groups are in need and to what extent they need state assistance. The varied approaches capture the controversies surrounding social welfare today. Each approach conveys a different sense of what social welfare is and how extensive it should be.

Successive Canadian governments have moved back and forth essentially between two approaches to social welfare: the residual view and the institutional view. A third approach, the structural approach, also needs to be considered.

The Residual Approach

In the **residual approach**, social welfare is a limited, temporary response to human need, implemented only when all else fails. It is based on the premise that there are two "natural" ways through which an individual's needs are met: through the family and through the market economy. The residual model is based on the idea that the government should play a limited role in the distribution of social welfare. The state should only step in when these normal sources of support fail and individuals are unable to help themselves.

Residual social welfare is highly targeted to those most in need. Additionally, it tends to provide benefits at a low level in order to discourage use and make welfare undesirable. Canadian public social welfare programs, from early history at least up to the Depression of the 1930s, can be characterized as essentially residual in nature. In the past two decades, we have tended to move back to this view.

The Institutional Approach

In the **institutional approach**, social welfare is a necessary public response that helps people attain a reasonable standard of life and health. Within this view, it is accepted that people cannot always meet all of their needs through family and work. Therefore, in a complex industrial society, it is legitimate to help people through a set of publicly funded and organized systems of programs and institutions. For many who hold this approach, these institutions are the bulwarks of a democratic and caring society.

The institutional model attempts to even out, rather than promote, economic stratification or status differences. The period after World War II saw the beginning of the rise of the institutional view not only in Canada but throughout the industrialized world. There was an enormous expansion of the welfare state during this period. More recently, the welfare state apparatus has contracted and many of the older ideas of limited, temporary (residual) support have re-emerged.

The Structural Approach

Proponents of the **structural approach** to social welfare view the "system" as essentially exploitative. They focus on the injustices that arise from the normal operation of the market and the perpetuation and further advancement of private concentrations of ownership and wealth. While social welfare provides benefits for people in need, it does not directly address the exploitative nature of capitalist markets.

This approach sees social problems and inequalities as a built-in feature of society. It calls for society itself, including its major institutions, to change radically. In particular, many proponents of the structural approach believe that economic globalization, as well as Canada's economic and social structures, are exploitative and oppressive. Within this approach, feminist, gay and lesbian, and anti-racist critiques have drawn attention to the ways in which social policies and programs stereotype and control the lives of people in ways that negatively affect their lives and their livelihoods.

The structural approach has never underlined Canada's official social policy, but it is increasingly being vocalized by a variety of groups and organizations. They advocate system-wide change. Many focus on localized changes that can materially improve the living conditions of the individuals and groups. Others advocate wholesale re-distribution of income and wealth by pursuing legal and political initiatives that will help to bring about this structural change in Canadian society. The Occupy movement is an example, as is the Idle No More movement which focuses on Aboriginal poverty.

The Supreme Court of Canada recently upheld the right of federal and provincial governments to collect social service payments from the sponsors of immigrants.

The Provision of Social Welfare

Direct government benefits alone do not reflect the entire spectrum of income security expenditures. There are many other forms. There are several different ways of categorizing social welfare provisions, and one useful distinction is between public and private welfare.

Public and Private Welfare

Public welfare takes place at the three levels of government: the federal or national government, the provincial and territorial governments, and the regional and municipal governments. These various levels of government fund and deliver monetary benefits and services. The government also enforces employment-related policies and legislation, such as labour standards and minimum wage legislation, as well as policies that affect the quantity and distribution of employment and employment equity programs. These policies and legislation can affect the income of Canadians and therefore can be considered a part of our income security framework.

Private welfare can be non-profit or for-profit. Organizations that provide these benefits are usually registered and clear rules and regulations govern their activities. Typically, these agencies are incorporated as *non-profit* organizations and often receive funds from the government and from private sources. These non-profit agencies rarely charge money, given that they generally are providing support services to those without resources to pay. Most often, they provide "in-kind" benefits to those lacking income—food, emergency shelter, and other bare necessities. Consider the Salvation Army. It receives its principal funding from individual donations, and it also receives funds to support its community activities from different levels of government. It is registered as a non-profit organization, and its boards of directors are composed of private citizens who are elected annually.

Income security is also provided by *for-profit* organizations in areas such as retirement pensions, dental and optical plans, and private long-term disability insurance. These for-profit companies provide insurance, but their purpose is also to generate a profit for themselves in the course of doing so. Countries such as Norway, the Netherlands, and Denmark, have substantial mandatory employer-paid income security programs. Canada does not.

With government cutbacks in recent years, more and more sources of income security protection are being provided by **non-profit and for-profit welfare agencies**. Food banks and emergency shelters are increasingly helping people with low incomes, while people with more material means are turning to private (for-profit) pensions and insurance programs to ensure their economic security in the future. All three organizations—public, private non-profit, and for-profit—are part of the income security system in Canada today.

Four Types of Programs

Most income security programs are filed under the category of public welfare. These programs are delivered by all three levels of government—federal, provincial, and municipal—and include the following categories:

- **MINIMUM-INCOME PROGRAMS** provide monetary assistance to those with little or no other source of income. The amount tends to be determined by a "needs test." Social Assistance ("welfare" or "workfare") is a minimum-income type program.
- **INCOME SUPPLEMENTATION PROGRAMS**, as the name suggests, supplement income obtained elsewhere, whether through employment or other income security programs. These programs may have a broad entitlement or they may be targeted to those in need. The National Child Benefit Supplement and the Guaranteed Income Supplement are examples of such programs.
- **SOCIAL INSURANCE PROGRAMS** follow the principle of shared risk. Those who contribute become eligible for benefits should the need arise. Employment Insurance, Workers' Compensation, and the Canada/Quebec Pension Plan are social insurance programs.
- **DEMOGRANTS** are flat-rate payments to individuals or households on the basis of demographic characteristics (e.g., number of children or age). The Universal Child Care Benefit is Canada's only universal program. Old Age Security (OAS) was a universal program before a clawback was implemented.

"... it's fair and simple ... walk through it and if you are indeed handicapped and unemployable you will show no blisters..."

Income Security Programs

Universal: programs available to everyone in a particular category, such as seniors.

Selective: programs limited to those people who are determined to be in need based on a "means test" or a "needs test."

"Universal" vs. "Selective" Programs

When designing income security programs, a key distinction is made as to whether they are "universal" or "selective." Over the years, Canada has had a mix of both.

- **UNIVERSAL PROGRAMS** are available to everyone in a specific category (such as people aged 65 and over or children) on the same terms and as a right of citizenship. The idea is that all persons are equally eligible to receive program benefits, regardless of income and financial situation.
- **SELECTIVE PROGRAMS** target benefits at those who are found to be in need or eligible based on a means test (sometimes called an income test) or a needs test. The test determines eligibility based on the income and assets of the prospective recipient. The benefit is reduced accordingly, and there is always a level at which no benefit is granted.

In the post-war era, universal programs were seen as a way to build national solidarity. More recently, they have been viewed as too expensive and have all but disappeared.

The Case For and Against

The foremost objection to universal programs is their cost. Giving a benefit to everyone, regardless of income, means that even the wealthy get a benefit. On the other side of the issue, universal programs tend to be less expensive to administer, as government workers are not required to scrutinize each person's situation.

Universal program supporters, on the other hand, maintain that universal income security promotes a sense of citizenship, solidarity, and nationhood. They claim that selective programs for the needy tend to be punitive and stigmatizing, are more susceptible to cutbacks, and lack necessary mass public support. If services are only for the poor, they argue, then the services are likely to be poor services. Finally, many believe that universal income security programs can fulfill various economic functions, such as economic stabilization, investment in human resources, and development of the labour force.

Increasingly, social policy experts are seeing that some selective programs are necessary for tackling poverty and inequality. Selective programs are often viewed as more efficient and less costly in the long run, as the government provides benefits only to those individuals most in need. However, identifying eligible recipients using means or needs tests can be administratively complex and costly, and can take money out of the system that could be directed towards benefits. In some cases, the higher administrative costs are partially avoided by using the tax system as a method of determining eligibility and as a means of dispensing benefits.

Income Redistribution

A key objective of the Canadian social welfare system is **income redistribution** that is fair. What exactly is "fair" and which programs are the most effective means to achieve this is what is at issue. With the introduction of the Universal Child Care Benefit (UCCB), for example, Canada now has one officially universal income security program, much like the Family Allowance program available from 1944 to 1993. Other programs such as the Canada Child Tax Benefit approach universality in their coverage but contain an income test.

All of Canada's other income security programs have complex selection criteria based on income, work history, or the willingness to find a job. Employment Insurance, for example, is based on eligibility tied to past employment and income levels. Everyone pays into the program, and in this sense it is comprehensive, but a strict set of criteria determines who is eligible to receive benefits, and the benefits level depends on prior contributions.

Other programs are more selective still. To be eligible for Social Assistance, one must pass a means test, proving that income and assets fall below a certain level. In provinces with workfare, such as Ontario and Alberta, applicants must also comply with an employment or training placement. Those wishing to access these programs must complete forms and possibly have an interview with a caseworker in order to prove that they are in need and do not have the means to meet their needs.

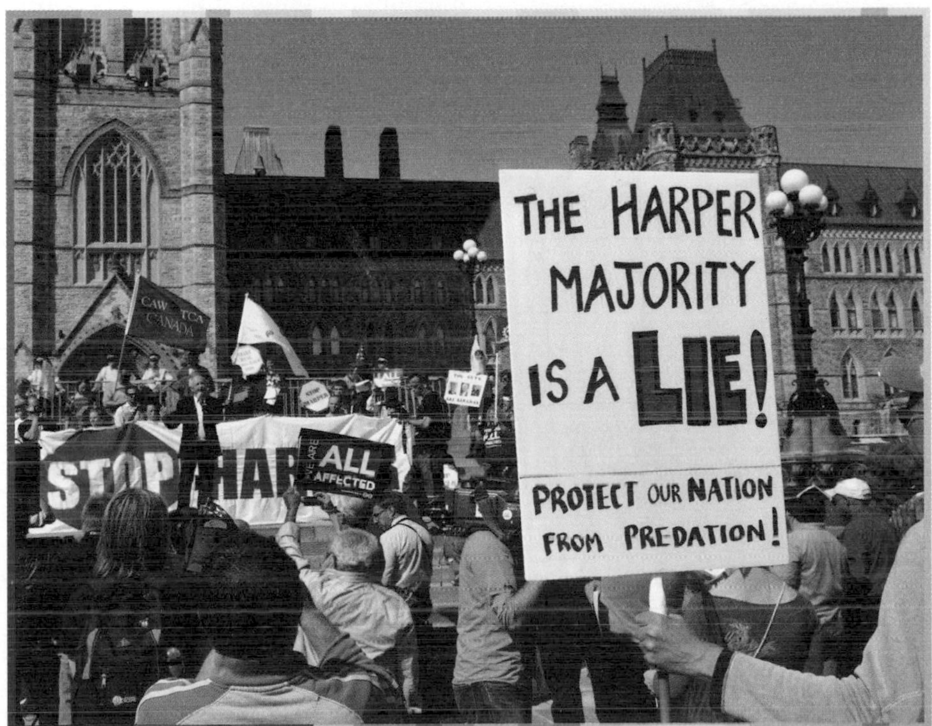

Sid Ryan of the Ontario Federation of Labor speaks at a protest to on Parliament Hill on September 17, 2012

Human Resources and Skills Development Canada

www.hrsdc.gc.ca

For more information on the income security programs offered in Canada, see the Human Resources and Skills Development website.

Public Income Security Programs

Nowadays, Canada's income security programs are in the newspaper headlines almost on a daily basis, and the effectiveness and affordability of such programs are frequent topics of discussion. The emphasis is often on the need to cut spending and to reduce the deficit, but the host of benefits that these programs bring to families, society, and the economy are often downplayed. Yet, many Canadians rely on these income security programs to bring some economic stability to their lives, and without them they would not be able to regroup and again be able to participate fully in society. Here are some of the key income security measures that help Canadians get back on their feet.

EMPLOYMENT INSURANCE. This federally administered program, originally called Unemployment Insurance (UI), dates back to 1940. Since then, UI has undergone numerous changes. EI provides a level of income replacement to workers who are temporarily unemployed and meet strict eligibility conditions. Sickness, maternity, and parental benefits are included in this program. Also included in EI are benefits for those whose livelihood depends on the fishing industry. Claimants are eligible for a range of skills development programs. EI is paid for through employer and employee contributions. Recently, the program has become restricted, providing coverage for fewer and fewer workers.

WORKERS' COMPENSATION. Workers' Compensation provides provincially administered benefits to protect individuals against income loss due to workplace injury or disease. Employers fund the programs. In return for participation in the provincial programs, workers waive their rights to sue their employers in the case of a work-related injury or disease. Worker's Compensation was the first type of social insurance program in Canada (instituted in Ontario in 1914).

SOCIAL ASSISTANCE (OR "WELFARE"). Social Assistance programs have their roots in early municipal and provincial relief programs that provided only minimal support to the "deserving poor" or those deemed unable to work because of age or infirmity. Gradually expanded to include those in need but without resources, Social Assistance has remained a residual program of last resort for those with no other source of income or savings. Social Assistance programs, also called *welfare* or *workfare*, have remained a provincial responsibility with some funding coming from the federal government. The provinces are free to design their own programs and set the level of benefits. In some provinces, "employable" recipients must participate in work placements. This is known as *workfare*. In 2007, the federal government introduced the Working Income Tax Benefit (WITB). The benefit aims to offset the disincentives of moving from welfare to work, for example, higher income taxes and the loss of social benefits such as drug plans.

CANADA CHILD TAX BENEFIT, NATIONAL CHILD BENEFIT SUPPLEMENT, UNIVERSAL CHILD CARE BENEFIT. There is a long history in Canada of providing benefits to families with children. Some of these benefits are delivered through the tax system in the form of tax credits and exemptions, and others have been direct cash transfers. In 1944, a universal benefit called the Family Allowance was instituted, and this benefit went to all families with children, regardless of income. Over time, this benefit became targeted towards middle- and low-income families. In 1993, the Family Allowance benefit was eliminated completely.

The Canada Child Tax Benefit (CCTB) includes two aspects: the CCTB basic benefit and the National Child Benefit Supplement (NCBS). The CCTB provides a tax credit to those who qualify, based on an income test, for low- and middle-income families with children. Currently, up to 80 percent of families receive some portion of the CCTB. Some low-income families are eligible for an additional benefit—the NCBS. An interesting aspect of this federal benefit is that provinces are allowed to claw back the benefit from families on Social Assistance. With the monies taken, the provinces are expected to reinvest in programs to help alleviate child poverty and its effects.

In 2006 the newly elected federal Conservative government announced the Universal Child Care Benefit (UCCB). The UCCB payment is paid on behalf of children under the age of 6 years in installments of $100 per month per child. It is a taxable benefit (unlike the CCTB, which is a tax credit).

Human Resources Minister Diane Finley is shown announcing changes to Employment Insurance in Ottawa in May of 2012.

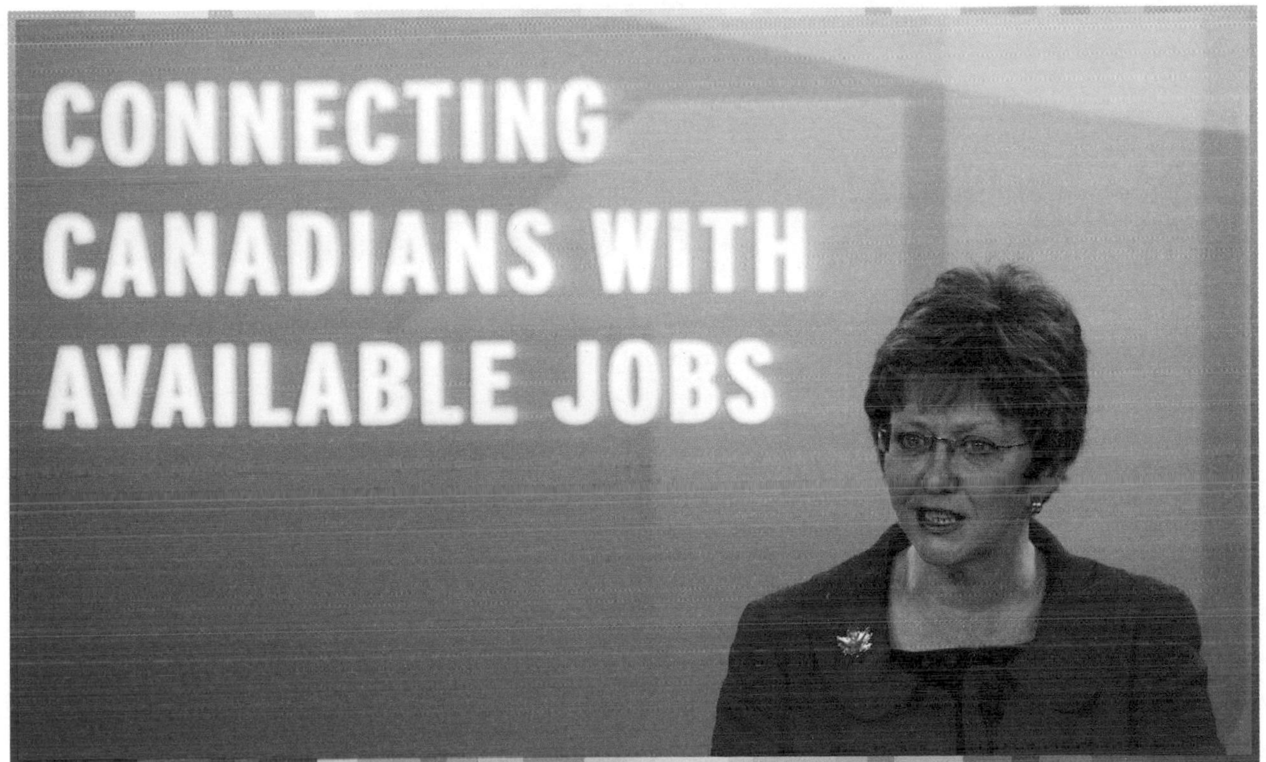

CANADA/QUEBEC PENSION PLAN. The Canada/Quebec Pension Plan (C/QPP) is a national contributory and earnings-related pension program introduced in 1966. It provides benefits in the case of retirement, death, and long-term disability. Employees and employers jointly finance the CPP and QPP, with current contributions supporting current beneficiaries. In this sense, the plan is a pay-as-you-go system. Any funds not paid out are invested for the purpose of creating a larger reserve fund. Eligibility for this benefit currently begins at 60 years of age, with maximum benefits paid out after age 65. The plan consists of Retirement, Disability, and Survivor's and Orphan's Death Benefits. The pension is earnings-related, so there is a maximum amount for which claimants are eligible. It should also be noted that periods of low earnings because of caring for young children, illness, unemployment, or retraining, are considered exempt from the calculation. This provision is particularly significant for women, who often take time out of the labour force to provide caregiving.

DISABILITY. Severe and prolonged disability resulting in the inability to participate in the labour force qualifies one for a disability pension. There is an earnings-related portion and a basic flat-rate portion, which is unrelated to the earnings. Recipients may also qualify for supplemental child benefits if there are dependants. People with disabilities may be eligible to receive benefits through provincial Social Assistance programs, Workers' Compensation, the Canada/Quebec Pension Plan, and, in some cases, through the Veterans Disability Pension.

Nortel pensioners rally to protest the handling of their pension funds by the Ontario government at Queen's Park in Toronto on Wednesday, September 15, 2010.

OLD AGE SECURITY, GUARANTEED INCOME SUPPLEMENT, SPOUSE'S ALLOWANCE, REGISTERED RETIREMENT SAVINGS PLAN. As noted earlier, between 1952 and 1989, all elderly Canadians received a universal monthly benefit called Old Age Security (OAS)—an income security program financed and administered by the federal government. Prior to 1952, this benefit was targeted to the very low-income elderly population. Since 1989, the benefit has again become targeted, with only those who qualify because of low or modest income being eligible for benefits. OAS benefits are quite low in relation to the cost of living. Without another source of income upon retirement, such as C/QPP or Registered Retirement Savings Plans (RRSPs), many seniors would live in poverty. To assist those who do not have access to these programs, there are two related programs: the Guaranteed Income Supplement (GIS) and the Spouse's Allowance (SPA). The SPA is now called "The Allowance." These benefits supplement the OAS for the low-income elderly. From 1966 until today, the GIS has provided a popular add-on to the OAS for those pensioners with little or no other income. The OAS is the basic building block of retirement for Canadians. It is a flat-rate monthly benefit that goes to everyone providing they meet certain residency requirements. It is paid to individuals and does not depend on previous paid employment, nor on the income of the spouse or partner. As a result, women who have not worked outside the home receive the benefit in their own name. The OAS is clawed back from individuals whose income reaches $69,562, with the entire amount clawed back once income reaches $122,722.

What's Happening to Old Age Security?

In the federal budget of 2012, the Conservative government announced changes to the eligibility for the Old Age Security benefit. Critics accused the government of cutting tens of millions of dollars from pensions and placing the welfare of seniors in jeopardy.

SURVIVOR AND DEATH BENEFITS. In the case of a contributor's death, surviving family members may be eligible for benefits. These are intended to provide support to the surviving spouse and children.

VETERANS DISABILITY PENSION. Income security programs for veterans specifically recognize the service of war veterans. A Veterans Disability Pension is available to those who apply to Veterans Affairs Canada, provided they have a service-related permanent disability resulting from an injury or disease. Income and assets are not considered as eligibility criteria; the benefit is based solely on the extent of the disability and the fact that it is military service-related. As is the case with disability benefits, what constitutes a disability and its extent is not always easily determined or agreed upon by all interested parties.

OCCUPATIONAL BENEFITS. In addition to publicly administered benefits, private benefit plans also exist. These plans may be directly tied to one's workplace and include both retirement plans and other insurance-based benefits such as dental and drug plans, or they may be savings plans with tax-supported provisions, such as RRSPs. While individuals save and invest this money for future use, the government foregoes the collection of tax on this saved money. The deferred revenue not collected by government amounts to billions of dollars per year.

Caledon Institute of Social Policy

www.caledoninst.org

The **Caledon Institute of Social Policy** is an independent, non-profit organization that completes research and analysis to help encourage public awareness and debate on the role of social policy in Canadian society.

Government Spending on Income Security

The expenditure for government-funded income security benefits covers just over one-quarter of government expenditures at all levels of government. Statistics Canada figures for 2009 show that the total expenditure for all levels of government on income security programs was $190.3 billion out of the total government expenditure (all levels) of $631 billion. In their publications, the government refers to this expenditure as a social security expenditure, which equates to what we are calling income security.

Clearly, by any measures, the various levels of government in Canada spend a considerable amount on income security.

Behind the Numbers

These figures only include direct government spending on pensions and benefits for the elderly, Employment Insurance, Social Assistance, child benefits, and Workers' Compensation. The figure does not include mandatory private social benefits provided by employers, voluntary private social benefits provided by charities, or tax breaks for social purposes. It is interesting to note that the government social security statistics also do not include RRSPs, which primarily benefit the more well-off.

In 2011-12, there were $54.5 billion in transfer payments to other levels of government and another $60.2 billion in direct transfers to individuals (Government of Canada, 2012). Most of the transfer payments consisted of the Canada Health Transfer ($27.0 billion), fiscal equalization ($14.7 billion), and the Canada Social Transfer ($11.5 billion). Of the transfers to individuals, most involved pensions and benefits for the elderly ($38.1 billion), followed by Employment Insurance ($19.4 billion) and the Universal Child Care Benefit ($2.7 billion). Demographic trends show that the elderly population in Canada will increase in the years ahead, which will no doubt increase government income security expenditures.

At first glance, these big numbers suggest that Canada is a rather generous welfare state, but, in fact, our social security contributions are lower than those for many developed countries. A 2011 ranking of social security contributions for single individuals without children places Canada twenty-second among thirty-four countries (OECD, 2012). We fall well behind some social welfare regimes in Scandinavia (Norway, Denmark) and even some countries in continental Europe (Germany, Belgium, the Netherlands). At the same time, our income taxes are relatively low, ranking eighteenth for the same group of countries, and our income tax rate as a percentage of gross wage earnings is lower than for the selected countries mentioned above, all of which have been relatively successful in terms of economic growth and stability.

Do High Taxes Stifle Economic Growth?

Is Canada Becoming More Unequal?

The role of taxation policy underlies many social welfare policy debates, with arguments forcefully advanced on all sides. The prevailing view is that tax cuts will automatically lead to economic growth. This view is held not so much by practitioners on the front lines as by governments, economists, and policy makers. It is highly oversimplified. Canada is often portrayed as one of the most overtaxed nations in the industrialized world. It is argued that a decrease in taxes will make consumers consume more and investors invest more. The economy will grow, and this will result in more jobs and prosperity—or so the argument goes.

The underlying premise of this argument is highly questionable. For one thing, Canadians are not taxed more than residents of most other advanced industrialized countries, and a reduction in taxes does not automatically affect the economy in some magical way. Evidence from the OECD shows that Canada's economic growth rate was lower than that of countries with a higher tax load.

The Beneficiaries of Income Security

Moreover, there are studies that suggest that tax policy and public spending on programs such as income security can have a greater impact on economic growth than tax cuts. This is because much of the revenue from a tax cut would flow into personal savings and an increased reliance on imports.

To be sure, income security programs are key factors in shaping income distribution in Canada. These cash benefits are an important source of income for at least 60 percent of the population and have become even more so since 1980.

Beyond mere cash benefits, however, such programs help both the federal and provincial governments provide economic stability and foster economic growth. The view that we are somehow over-taxed and that tax reductions will automatically stimulate economic growth minimizes the importance of tax revenue in regulating the economy and providing security for all citizens.

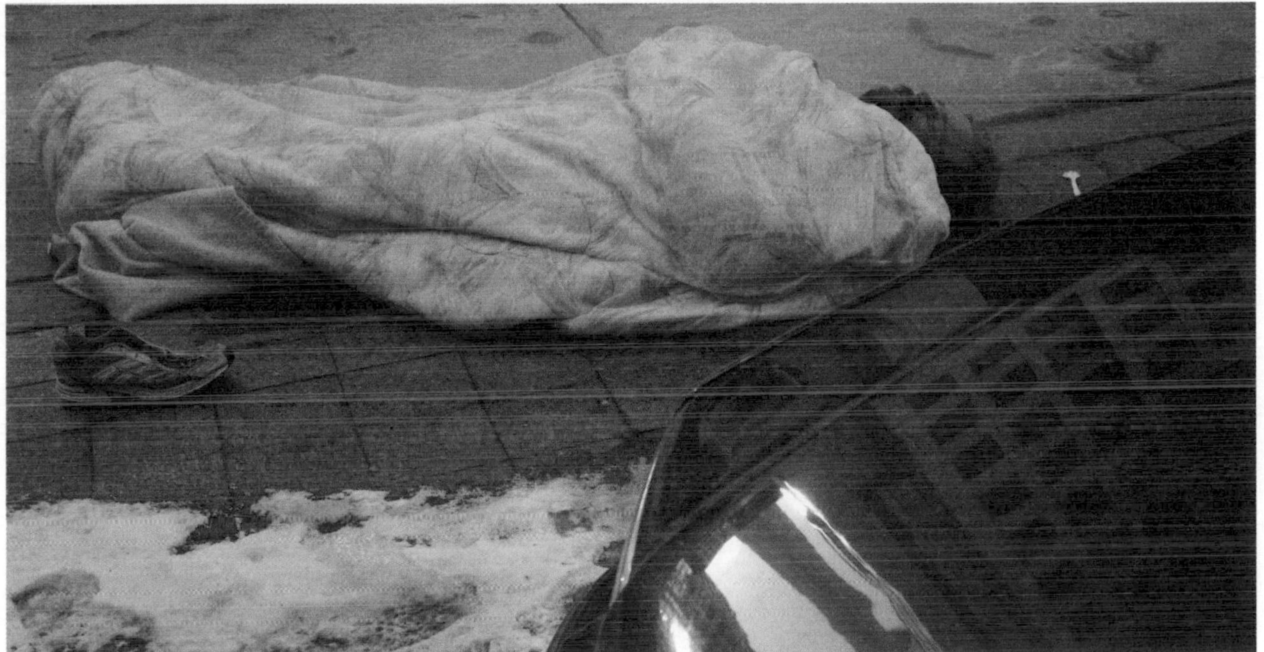

Canadian Federalism

Federalism is a system of government in which a number of smaller states (in this case, provinces and territories) join to form a larger political entity while still retaining a measure of political power.

Canadian federalism has always influenced income security policy in Canada.

Canadian Federalism and Income Security

When Canada was formed in 1867, social welfare was largely a private responsibility of the individual, family, and church. The *British North America Act* (1867) said little about jurisdiction over income security or social services.

Political wrangling, side-deals between the federal government and the provinces, and non-stop constitutional amendments over the subsequent years and decades eventually formed the basis for our income security system. Throughout this process, income security slowly emerged as a central area of federal authority. The provinces, on the other hand, largely prevailed in the delivery of programs and services. The *Constitution Act* of 1982 did not change these arrangements but rather codified them.

An important point to note, however, is that the federal government has always been responsible for services and programs for "registered Indians," as defined by the *Indian Act*. The provision of social welfare to Aboriginal people is, therefore, somewhat different than for the rest of the population and amounts to a race-specific program. At times, the two jurisdictions intersect and overlap, but essentially the federal government retains responsibility for the welfare of Aboriginal peoples (see Chapter 11).

Reforms to the Social Welfare System

Prior to 1996, federal government contributions to Social Assistance and social services had been funded through the **Canada Assistance Plan (CAP)**, which was established in 1966. One of the most significant changes to Canada's social welfare system arose with the introduction of the **Canada Health and Social Transfer (CHST)** in 1996. Under the CAP, federal government contributions to health care services and post-secondary education had been funded through **Established Programs Financing (EPF)** since 1977. Both CAP and EPF were replaced with the CHST.

The Canada Assistance Plan (1966-1996) was a 50/50 cost-shared program—the federal government shared 50 percent of the cost of eligible Social Assistance and social services spending with the provinces. With the CAP, federal transfers rose as provincial social welfare expenditures increased, so the CAP provided an economic stabilizing function. Federal transfers increased in economic recessions, thereby stimulating the economy through social spending. Conversely, CHST is a fixed per-capita or per-person amount based on the population of the province, which means federal transfers are not necessarily connected to either the needs of the people or the state of the economy. Many believe that it is the economic stabilizing effect of social spending that has prevented a depression-style drop-off in the Canadian economy since the Great Depression of 1930. Under the CHST, it is argued, this stabilizing effect is greatly reduced.

The Search for National Standards

National standards, as were set out in the CAP, are almost absent in the CHST. The CAP stipulated that the provinces must establish eligibility for Social Assistance based on need, make services available regardless of when recipients established residency in the province, establish an appeals procedure, and require no service or other work (also known as *workfare*) in return for social benefits. Many policy analysts have feared that, with the removal of national standards, provinces will establish very different benefit levels and eligibility criteria.

A more recent welfare reform was the **Social Union Framework Agreement (SUFA)** of 1999 between the Government of Canada and the provinces and territories (with the exception of Quebec). This initiative is the umbrella under which governments agreed to concentrate their efforts to renew and modernize social policy. The agreement recognized a number of principles, including a common quality for social programs and that health care in particular should be "comprehensive, universal, portable, publicly administered, and accessible." Most commentators have applauded SUFA, but there have been criticisms. Perhaps the most common are the lack of inclusion of Aboriginal governments and the lack of a role for municipal governments.

In 2004, the CHST was divided into the **Canada Health Transfer (CHT)**, in support of health, and the **Canada Social Transfer (CST)**, in support of post secondary education, Social Assistance, and social services (including early childhood development).

Reforms to Social Welfare

Canada Assistance Plan (CAP), 1966

Canada Health and Social Transfer (CHST), 1996

Social Union Framework Agreement (SUFA), 1999

Canada Health Transfer (CHT) and Canada Social Transfer (CST), 2004

TABLE 1.2

Federal Transfers to Individuals and Other Levels of Government

	2011-12 (millions of dollars)	
Transfers to Other Levels of Government		
Canada Health Transfer	$27.0	
Fiscal Equalization	$14.7	
Canada Social Transfer	$11.5	
Other	$1.3	
Total Transfers to Other Levels of Government		$54.5
Transfers to Persons		
Elderly Benefits	$38.1	
Employment Insurance	$19.4	
Universal Child Care Benefit	$2.7	
Total Transfers to Persons		$60.2
Total Major Transfer Payments		$114.7

Note: Totals may not add due to rounding. **Source:** Government of Canada (2012). *Public Accounts of Canada: Volume 1: Summary Report and Consolidated Financial Statements.* Ottawa: Minister of Public Works and Government Services Canada.

Organisation for Economic Co-operation and Development

www.oecd.org

Founded in 1960, the Organisation for Economic Co-operation and Development (OECD) is a global organization committed to furthering democratic government and the market economy across the globe. Canada is among the 34 member states and is one of the founding members.

Globalization and Social Welfare

Canada does not exist apart from the rest of the world. Behind all the debates over social welfare and income security is the new economic context of globalization.

Economic globalization refers to the growing integration of international markets for goods, services, and finance. It involves the considerable expansion of trade in goods and services between countries, the geographical expansion and increase in power of transnational corporations (TNCs), and the use of formal agreements between nations and international bodies such as the World Trade Organization (WTO) to protect the rights of TNCs.

Globalized Social Welfare

In many nations, especially poorer ones, economic restructuring and cutbacks to social programs have been imposed by international agencies in the form of "structural adjustments" (see Chapter 14 for details). The Canadian government is not immune to these pressures and adjusts its own income security programs to meet the new economic order and to battle with other nations to be among the most "investor friendly" nations.

The impact of globalization on Canada's income security programs is being felt mainly by the most disadvantaged in our society, and they are also the ones who are least able to fight back. The rise in the number of people who are homeless, the growing number of food banks, and the persistence of child poverty are signs of this. But it is not only the very poor that suffer. The middle class is increasingly finding that high-paying jobs are moving offshore to corporate tax havens or export-processing zones. Globalization affects them as well with respect to job security. Moreover, working Canadians may not be able to depend fully on the income security protections offered by such programs as Employment Insurance and Old Age Security.

Globalization generally means that national and local governments increasingly have less freedom to act exclusively on behalf of their citizens, especially on big economic and social questions of the day. In view of this, in the future, income security provisions aimed at creating greater equality of income and opportunity among individuals will likely become intertwined with the issue of global human rights.

The UN's **Social Protection Floor Initiative** is an example of positive work being done along these lines. The initiative is aimed at bringing agencies, NGOs, development banks and other organizations together to support countries committed to building national "social protection floors" for their citizens. The initiative aims to make governments responsible for the promotion of essential and universal guarantees, which in turn would set the ground for a more comprehensive social protection system.

Conclusion

The multi-faceted area known as social welfare has two major components: *income security* (programs that provide financial or material assistance) and the *social services* (personal and community services to help people improve their well-being). This text deals mainly with income security side of the welfare system. A companion volume entitled *Social Work in Canada: An Introduction* examines the social services side.

Most citizens of Canada will face social or economic difficulties at some point in their lives. Nowadays, and especially with the economic downturn after 2008, job security is an ever-present concern for many Canadians. And with downwards pressure on wage and salaries, a job itself is not a guarantee of income security. Income security programs are a kind of social insurance—the idea is that citizens all pay into it and then share the risk of unexpected events such as poverty, unemployment, disability, and economic insecurity in old age. At the macroeconomic level, income security programs also help to put money into the hands of consumers, which in turn stimulates demand in the economy.

Generally, there is broad consensus on the need to help the disadvantaged members of our society. However, there is less agreement about whether income security programs should be extended and strengthened, or whether they should perhaps be reduced. At the root of the debate are political ideologies, economic theories, and basic notions about how our society works or how it should work. These debates are continuing, and are even heating up.

In recent years, federal, provincial, and municipal governments have been making far-reaching changes to our social welfare system. These changes are eroding many safeguards that have been built up over the years. The changes involve a new vision of where Canada is and where it is going. Many such changes have been justified on the grounds of economic necessity—that Canada no longer can afford comprehensive welfare programs if we want to maintain a competitive advantage in the global marketplace.

This is one course Canadians can take, but it is not the only course open to us. Other countries in Europe, notably Denmark and Finland, have continued to fund and even expand their social welfare commitments, and they continue to have good productivity and economic growth. As we look ahead, it is important to have this debate and decide which direction we want to take.

World Trade Organization

www.wto.org

Founded in 1995, the World Trade Organization deals with the rules of trade between nations.

CHAPTER 1 REVIEW

LEARNING OBJECTIVES

After completing this chapter, you should be able to:

- Explain the critical role income security programs play in the lives of all Canadians.
- Explain the term "welfare state."
- Understand how wealth is redistributed.
- Identify the potential causes of social problems.
- Explain the "residual," "institutional," and "structural" approaches.
- Explain the distinction between "public" and "private" welfare and between the four types of public programs.
- Make the case for and against "universal" and "selective" welfare programs.
- Have an understanding of the different income security programs available to Canadians.
- Understand the importance of federalism and national standards.
- Explain how globalization affects social welfare on the world scale.

KEY CONCEPTS

- Caledon Institute of Social Policy
- Canada Assistance Plan (CAP)
- Canada Health and Social Transfer (CHST)
- Canada Health Transfer (CHT)
- Canada Social Transfer (CST)
- Demogrants
- Economic globalization
- Established Program Financing (EPF)
- Federalism
- Income redistribution
- Income security
- Income supplementation programs
- Institutional approach
- Minimum income programs
- Non-profit and for-profit welfare agencies
- Private welfare
- Public welfare
- Residual approach
- Selective programs
- Social insurance programs
- Social policies
- Social programs
- Social safety net
- Social services
- Social Union Framework Agreement (SUFA)
- Social Protection Floor Initiative
- Social welfare system
- Structural approach
- Tax expenditures
- Universal programs
- Welfare state

REVIEW QUESTIONS

1. What are the main components of the social welfare system in Canada? What is the underlying purpose of the welfare system?
2. Define and compare the following sets of terms: (1) "social policy" and "social program," and (2) "public welfare" and "private welfare."
3. What is meant by the "residual" and "institutional" approaches to welfare? And by the terms "universal" and "selective" programs?
4. What are the four types of public welfare? Briefly summarize each.
5. What is the division of responsibilities between the federal and provincial governments with respect to income security for Canadians, and what are the major changes brought about by the CHST of 1996 and the SUFA of 1999?

EXPLORING SOCIAL WELFARE

1. As discussed in the chapter, social problems are due to a combination of internal and external factors. Research the social problem of "addiction" (or "substance abuse"), and create your own list of internal and external causal factors. Discuss a social policy that might reduce the problem at both levels.
2. Pick one social welfare "problem" that is of interest to you. Define the issue and discuss the major groups and organizations (including governments) that are working towards a solution. Explore the challenges in resolving the issue.

CRITICAL THINKING

What is your first recollection of there being a social welfare system in Canada, and what ideas or feelings do you associate with the memory?

How do you think you and other Canadians benefit from having an income security system?

WEBSITES

Canadian Centre for Policy Alternatives
www.policyalternatives.ca
The Canadian Centre for Policy Alternatives (CCPA) is an independent, non-partisan research institute concerned with issues of social, economic, and environmental justice. Founded in 1980, the CCPA is one of Canada's leading, progressive voices in public policy debates. Whether it's the push to privatize our health care system, the growing gap between the rich and poor, or gas companies gouging at the pump, the CCPA sets out to set the record straight on behalf of Canadians across the country.

Canadian Council on Social Development (CCSD)
www.ccsd.ca
CCSD is one of Canada's most authoritative voices promoting better social and economic security for all Canadians. A national, self-supporting, non-profit organization, the CCSD's main product is information, and its main activity is research. It focuses on concerns such as income security, employment, poverty, child welfare, pensions, and government social policies.

Statistics Canada
www.statcan.gc.ca
Statistics Canada is the federal government's agency commissioned with producing and disseminating statistics to help better understand Canada and its citizens. Statistics Canada was established in 1971, replacing the Dominion Bureau of Statistics. Internationally, the agency is held in the highest regard for the quality of its data and its research methodology. *The Daily*, a free subscription service issued by the agency Monday to Friday, provides the most recent information released by the agency.

2 The History of Social Welfare in Canada

Emergence of the Welfare State

The welfare state evolved gradually during the twentieth century, both as a response to the vicissitudes of capitalist economy and the protests of workers and farmers for a greater share of the country's wealth. Following World War II, a consensus eventually was reached on a welfare system that would ensure minimum incomes and services for all citizens.

Income equality significantly improved in the post-World War II period and that period itself witnessed unparalleled economic growth. This chapter reviews social welfare in Canada up to the early 1970s, after which time the welfare system in Canada began to face more serious challenges (outlined in Chapter 3).

"People must know the past to understand the present and face the future."
—NELLIE MCCLUNG, (1873–1951), CANADIAN WRITER AND EARLY WOMEN'S RIGHTS ACTIVIST

The Rise of Income Security in Canada

The rise of income security in Canada can be divided into four periods, coinciding with major political, social, and economic changes.

- **Phase 1**: the colonial period to 1867
- **Phase 2**: the industrialization period, 1867–1940
- **Phase 3**: the welfare state period, 1941–74
- **Phase 4**: the era of erosion, 1975–present

This chapter deals with the first three periods, while Chapter 3 deals with the fourth. But first, let's remind ourselves what came earlier and set the broader historical context for the rise of income security in Canada.

Before the Europeans

The most egalitarian period of Canada's past not only preceded the welfare state period but the existence of Canada and of its predecessor colonial provinces. For 13,000 or more years before Europeans began to settle in what is now Canada, Aboriginal groups had established complex civilizations throughout every region.

The social structures within these societies varied, from the strict equality found in semi-nomadic Northern hunting First Nations to the stratified, sedentary societies on the West Coast engaged in fishing and gathering in an area with plentiful resources. On the whole, these societies had developed mechanisms for sharing wealth and insuring collective responsibility for the weakest. Custom, rather than law, dictated the responsibilities of members of Aboriginal societies.

Performers representing the diverse Aboriginal peoples of Canada dance during the opening ceremonies at the BC Place for the XXI Winter Olympic Games February 12, 2010 in Vancouver.

Canada's Unique Social History

www.socialpolicy.ca/cush
This website offers an overview of social history in Canada with audio and video clips, as well as links to activities and supplemental readings.

The Transition from Feudalism to Capitalism

In Britain, by the early 1600s, when France was establishing New France, feudalism had largely disappeared in favour of a new system of relations based on capitalism. Under **feudalism**, the lords' returns were restricted by how much the peasants could produce surplus to their own subsistence needs. But erosion of the soil in England resulting from poor farming methods made subsistence difficult and reduced lords' returns as early as the 1300s. The Black Plague of 1348-49, which reduced the population of Europe by as much as one half, temporarily also dramatically reduced the number of peasants whom English lords could exploit. Their income in long-term decline, lords looked for ways of making their lands more productive and of reducing their dependence on the number and productivity of peasants.

Origins of Social Welfare

A rise in international demand for wool in the mid-1400s provided English landowners with a rationale for ending the system of mutual obligations between lord and peasant. They removed subsistence plots of land from hundreds of thousands of peasants, giving much of the land over to sheep and small numbers of hired shepherds. Remaining land, instead of being left as small peasant plots, was allotted as larger plots to those peasants regarded as more productive. Gradually the feudal ethic, with its emphasis on gaining wealth by having more and more peasants owing some portion of their production to the lord, gave way to an emphasis on "improving" one's lands. Lords no longer viewed peasants as having a right to their plots of land; instead, one only had a right to land if one used it to make it as productive as it could potentially become. As for the former peasants, branded as surplus and lazy, they lost their land and livelihood and became available to be the workforce in towns and cities. Their labour, extracted by strict entrepreneurial employers, could then become the means to increase national income further.

In the wake of the Black Death, many serfs and town labourers who survived the pestilence attempted to take advantage of the labour shortage by taking to the roads and demanding decent wages from potential employers. The king and parliament, determined to preserve feudal relations, passed the **Statute of Labourers** in 1351, which required workers to return to their former masters whenever possible and to take whatever employment others offered them if their former master had died, leaving no heir to employ them. Wages were also frozen at 1346 levels for all forms of work. And, for good measure, to emphasize that no one had a right to avoid work or to refuse whatever work was offered them regardless of wages or working conditions, provision of alms to individuals deemed capable of seeking employment became a legal offence punishable by imprisonment.

The Poor Laws

Such legislation temporarily maintained, however shakily, feudal relations. As population levels were restored and landlords, adopting a more capitalist viewpoint, shed unnecessary labourers, the concerns of the king and parliament turned from merely forcing workers to stay with a particular employer towards dealing with the new phenomenon of mass unemployment.

Many of the expelled farm labourers who flooded the towns were unable to find work, particularly when market conditions were weak. They often resorted to riots to gain the attention of the authorities. The latter used force to suppress riots, and indeed executed many rioters. They also recognized that the long-term maintenance of order required some means of satisfying those unable to find work during periods of economic crisis, while at the same time reinforcing earlier laws that required all able-bodied men to take whatever work was on offer to them.

The result was a revision of the Poor Law in 1601, often referred to as the Elizabethan Poor Law.

The First Poor Law, 1536

A Timeline

In 1536, during the reign of Henry VIII, the first Poor Law had been devised to distinguish between able-bodied beggars, who were viewed as undeserving of aid, and the deserving poor, chiefly the sick and elderly, the disabled, and sometimes widowed and deserted mothers and orphans. They constituted about five percent of the overall population, and responsibility for their care was placed in the hands of parishes.

The law's formal title, *An Act for the Punishment of Sturdy Vagabonds and Beggars*, made clear the state's hostility towards anyone who was capable of working remaining without work. But the Act also made provisions for parishes to intervene, where necessary, to help the deserving poor.

Previously, the deserving poor might have taken refuge in the Catholic monasteries, but the King, in the process of creating the Anglican Church, disbanded the monasteries and seized their assets. He also tried to separate the church and state as much as possible, and giving the latter control over poor relief served that aim.

Over the next 65 years, various laws would refine the initial Poor Law, provide cottages for the disabled (also called poorhouses) and provide for destitute children aged between five and fourteen. There also were experiments with different funding models, from voluntary donations to a national tax on property to local taxation.

But thanks to the growth in numbers of the landless poor, another 20 percent of the population barely scraped by. Deemed employable, these individuals and families could eke out a living when the economy was buoyant but earned too little to have savings for times when employment was unavailable.

Insofar as it kept people on the edge of destitution, the poor law policy seemed to be designed to encourage those living on the edge to take any job available.

The Elizabethan Poor Law

The **Elizabethan Poor Law** refined earlier versions of the Poor Law, defining principles for worthiness of state aid that would remain in place until the early 1900s, not only in Britain but also in Britain's former colonies, including Canada.

1. The employable poor were divided into two groups: the deserving poor and the undeserving poor. The deserving poor were those unable to work plus those who were fit for work and willing to take any job on offer at rates determined by the employer.
2. The state recognized no responsibility for the undeserving poor and made provision to place them in Houses of Correction, which would attempt to change their attitude toward work, or in prisons if they appeared unruly.
3. The state recognized only limited responsibility for the deserving poor. To provide them with any more, the government argued, would discourage them from ever seeking work again and would encourage others not to take jobs on offer that offered low pay and unsafe or otherwise unbearable working conditions.
4. In determining the bare minimum that poor relief recipients could receive, the state must always insure that minimum was lower than the minimum wages that day labourers were receiving. This principle, often called, "less eligibility," insured that those in work would always be terrified to lose their employment and forced to live an unspeakably miserable life.
5. To make assistance stigmatizing and reduce costs of administration, the authorities were empowered to build workhouses for recipients of aid. They could implement so-called "**indoor relief**," which involved forcing poor individuals and families into the workhouse, making them earn their aid through work or by work performed for employers to whom the workhouse contracted them out. But local authorities could also provide "**outdoor relief**" for those who remained in their own homes. In practice, outdoor relief was common because of the building costs.
6. Families, regardless of income, were made responsible for care of indigent parents or children so as to relieve the state of that responsibility. That meant the state only had responsibilities for those without blood relations who could be forced to help out.
7. The parish had the right and the duty to separate children aged five to fourteen from destitute parents and find jobs or apprenticeships for them.
8. Tax collection and administration of poor relief occurred at the parish level (Britain was made up of about 1500 parishes in 1601) with overseers of the poor appointed to weed out deserving from non-deserving applicants for relief.

Britain's North American Colonies

This was the system of social welfare that Britain's North American colonies adopted. When Britain eventually defeated France and extended its colonization to areas that form today's Canada, the jurisdictions that were created adopted the philosophy and model that guided state policies towards those in need of help.

In short, under this system, the purpose of social welfare was to provide the minimum assistance necessary to keep the non-dissolute unemployed alive while still tacitly blaming them for their failure to find work and putting maximum pressure on them to take whatever jobs might come available. Only members of society deemed unemployable and without relatives to support them were exempted from such pressure, but they too received only modest state aid and were often placed in institutions.

Until the late 1800s, such state institutions were generally undifferentiated, and the mentally ill, orphans, the unemployed, and the frail elderly were often under one roof.

Punishment for Illegal Begging

Whipped, Beaten, and Caged

During the sixteenth century, hysterical and cruel laws were passed to eliminate the largely imaginary explosion in the number of potential workers choosing to beg as an alternative to seeking and accepting work. There was no recognition of the role that the new capitalist social relations played in creating widespread unemployment.

Henry VIII

Before the institution of the Elizabethan Poor Law of 1601, King Henry VIII, father of Elizabeth I, licensed begging to ensure that the undeserving poor, or those people who were considered able to work, would not be able to beg. In 1530, Henry VIII, copying other European jurisdictions, introduced licensing of beggars to limit begging to unemployables.

He also instituted severe punishment for unlicensed and therefore undeserving beggars. Such a beggar was to be "tied to the end of a cart naked and beaten with whips ... till his body be bloody ... after which [he] shall oath to return to the place he was born ... and there put himself to labour."

Edward VI

In 1547, King Edward VI, the son of Henry VIII, seemed intent to outdo his infamous father. He increased the punishment and decreed that on their first offence, idlers and wanderers would have a " 'V' marked with a hot iron in the breast" and be enslaved for two years.

On their second offence, they would be marked with an "S" on the forehead and be enslaved forever. The third offence would result in the death sentence.

While in practice justices of the peace were rarely willing to impose such heinous penalties, they often sentenced unlicensed beggars to being whipped, beaten, caged, or given hard-labour prison sentences.

Poor Law Amendment Act, 1834

During the Industrial Revolution of the 1800s, which produced a great deal of social dislocation, families affected either by unemployment or below-subsistence wages relied on the Poor Law authorities. The taxes required to pay poor relief increased twofold between 1803 and 1818 and threefold by 1832 (Webb & Webb, 1927).

Parliament appointed an investigative commission that unsurprisingly, given the continued exclusion of those without property from the franchise, supported the elite theory that blamed the existence of poverty on dissolute workers and the unemployed rather than on the workings of an uncontrolled capitalist system. Following the recommendations of the commission, Parliament enacted the **Poor Law Amendment Act of 1834** to make the seeking of relief as unattractive as possible. Rates were cut and the able-bodied were only to receive relief in a workhouse. However, placing the poor in workhouses or poorhouses proved difficult, as it was expensive—costing almost twice as much as outdoor relief.

Reformation Theology

The dominant beliefs at the time were anchored in Reformation Protestant theology. Pauperism was thought to be a result of family defects, and individuals were seen as responsible for their poverty. Idleness, worldly temptations, and moral decline resulted in poverty. At the same time, the Protestant work ethic dictated that people could lift themselves out of poverty through discipline and hard work.

This hard-line and rather self-interested viewpoint resulted in many deaths, particularly during the Irish famine from 1845 to 1851 that resulted in the death by disease or starvation of over a million of Ireland's people and the migration of a similar number. The ideologies of free-market superiority and racism joined here. Britain could have insured that the class of prosperous farmers in Ireland who exported most of their crops to England and Wales fed their own people instead. But, motivated by free-market ideology and a view of Irish inferiority, they instead limited and at times banned outdoor relief.

In 1846, justifying a decision to end all outdoor relief, the British Treasurer Sir Charles Edward Trevelyan wrote to Sir Randolph Routh, chairman of the Relief Commission: "The only way to prevent the people becoming habitually dependent on the government is to bring the operations to a close. The uncertainty about the new crop only makes this more necessary." (Burke, 1987, p. 112). More workhouses were built and their inmates were required to perform labour within and without the workhouses, often dying because they were already weakened by hunger.

Malthus, Smith and Bentham

John Graham, Karen Swift, and Roger Delaney, three prominent Canadian social policy professors, outline how the ideas of several key theorists of the day reinforced Poor Law ideas: Thomas Malthus, Adam Smith, and Jeremy Bentham (Graham, Swift, & Delaney, 2003).

- Malthus believed that if the poor were coddled, they would multiply too swiftly and threaten society's limited material wealth. He called for the poor laws to be abolished.
- Smith, known as the ideologue of capitalism, believed that the pursuit of individual self-interest would benefit everyone.
- Finally, Bentham's utilitarian beliefs promoted the greatest possible good for the greatest number of people. He called for monetary expansion and for minimum wages but also promoted the placing of paupers in workhouses where their attitudes could be reshaped so as to slot them better into an industrial society.

Jeremy Bentham (left) and Adam Smith (right)

Key Historic Welfare Debates

There are ongoing debates, centuries old, about the best way to accomplish social welfare goals. These debates can be captured in a few points.

Deserving vs. Undeserved Poor

Codified in the Poor Laws and reasserted in colonial practices, the notion of **deserving and undeserving poor** remains a fundamental argument behind income security. The premise is that those physically able to work can find work and should be ineligible for most forms of state aid when they do not work. People who are not physically able to work are considered the uncontentiously deserving poor.

Those who are physically able to work but fail to find employment are regarded suspiciously and viewed as the undeserving poor. When they are not turned down altogether for state assistance, they are subjected to "work tests," "workfare," and the like—that is, made to do some work for the state that does not actually constitute a job in return for minimum income security. Failure to perform the work test means being cut off from state support.

Economic Security vs. Disincentives to Work

The principle of "**less eligibility**" meant that the pauper received less from relief than the labourer received from wages, usually substantially less. The intention was to stigmatize relief.

The principle of less eligibility has remained implicit with the rise of income security in Canada. Programs insure that a recipient of assistance receives less than the lowest-paying job yields.

Bare Subsistence vs. Adequate Standard of Living

To determine which applicants should receive bare subsistence levels of income, income security programs use either a means test or a needs test. A means test looks at the income and assets of applicants—the applicants' means of supporting themselves. It is sometimes called an income test when only income (not assets) is considered. A needs test involves an assessment of the person's resources and budgetary needs. When first implemented in 1956, it was thought that this would provide assistance that would allow for a social minimum or an adequate standard of living.

Of course, determining "need" can be difficult—does it include only the very bare necessities of life for oneself and one's family or does it go beyond that to include a better quality of food and housing, for example, or even important things such as cultural activities or leisure time activities?

Fact of Need vs. Cause of Need

Early income security and welfare programs assumed that the unemployed were personally defective. This came from the mindset of the early settlers—rugged individualists with a frontier mentality. They were glad to help a hard-working neighbour who fell on hard times but felt no responsibility beyond their immediate communities. Receiving relief had to carry the stigma of failure attached to it, and if need be it would involve humiliating inquiries into the personal affairs of the receiver. Typically, the person who had fallen on tough times was regarded as defective, since that was assumed to be the only logical cause for her or his inability to succeed.

The fact-of-need approach establishes that the person is indeed experiencing problems making ends meet and indeed may well be having difficulty just surviving. The person is therefore assumed in the first instance to be in need, and benefits are paid without much intrusive personal inquiry. The cause of the need was important in determining eligibility.

In the post-war period, with the expansion of the welfare system, there was a gradual shift away from the "blaming the victim" approach towards establishing an actual need and then providing the appropriate support. More recently, there has been a shift back towards earlier notions that involve built-in disincentives (e.g., rigorous means tests or other intrusive inquiries) that are designed to discourage those who might want to take advantage of welfare services.

This man would have been eligible to beg under Elizabethan poor laws that distinguished between the "deserving" and "undeserving" poor.

Phase 1: 1604-1867

This period was characterized by:

- Local and limited relief for the poor
- Social welfare as a private service (little role for government)
- Aversion to taxes
- Gradual imposition of a reserve system on the First Nations.

Phase 1: The Colonial Period, 1604-1867

This first phase in the emergence of income security in Canada spans the arrival of settlers from France and England to Confederation and the proclamation of the *British North America Act* of 1867. In this era, social welfare was local and private, and economic security was a matter for the family first and the community second, not the government. The state's role, whether or not a Poor Law was in place in a given colony, was initially limited to supporting charities, though it gradually expanded to include building workhouses and implementing public health measures. Both the state and charities approached poverty by regulating and providing aid to the poor rather than by addressing the causes of poverty.

French and English Models

Two different but often parallel models produced this state of affairs: Quebec's church-based model that had its origins in New France and that persisted after the British conquest; and a Poor Law model (even where no Poor Law as such existed, as in Ontario) supplemented by private charity in the rest of the colonies.

The Quebec model, in which the church rather than the state provided social services, included an array of institutions from schools and hospitals to shelters for the poor, foundlings, prostitutes, and the aged. But it had shared Poor Law ideology to a large degree and placed more importance on cause of need than fact of need. The Church, which had owned a significant portion of the land during the period of New France and benefited from land sales afterwards, defended inequalities in the distribution of wealth and property. Funds and services were denied to able-bodied individuals even when unemployment was rife, particularly if they were judged as dissolute and sporadic in their church attendance. Single mothers were forced to give up their babies to the nuns. By contrast, the Soeurs Grises (Grey Nuns), beginning in 1858, opened daycares in working-class areas to care for children of working or ill mothers. And the Church, while its shelters often seemed similar to workhouses and poorhouses, always provided a portion of its help as outdoor relief.

In English Canada, which, like French Canada, was mainly rural, charitable organizations, both female and male, took on many of the same responsibilities that the Church assumed for Catholics in Quebec. These organizations were organized on a local basis. Though Nova Scotia introduced a Poor Law in 1758 and New Brunswick in 1786, charities rather than the state provided most of whatever assistance reached those in need. Villages and small towns often proved generous in helping local families who fell upon hard times, but outsiders who arrived at the town gates were jailed or even publicly auctioned to the lowest bidder in an effort to prevent strangers from taking advantage of whatever charitable instincts existed in the area.

The Workhouse

Both population increases and immigration created a growing underclass dependent on wages. The gradual rise of industry created many of the same problems that had occurred earlier in Europe: private charities were overwhelmed and the state, which often provided subsidies to the charities, was forced to play a bigger role. As in Britain, that role followed the punitive model of the **workhouse**. Saint John opened the first in 1835, followed within two years by Montreal, Quebec, Toronto, and Kingston.

Families were often separated within the workhouse and the children hired out to whatever employer was willing to provide room and board in return for work. There was no supervision to insure that the children were safe at work, not overworked, and free of physical and sexual abuse. Within the workhouse all men had to perform the "workhouse test": physical labour that proved that they were not in the workhouse as a means of avoiding the search for paid work. The cost of building and maintaining workhouses caused both Ontario and Quebec, with their growing populations, to agree over time to rely more on outdoor relief than indoor relief. But a work test was instituted to replace the workhouse test: a person would stay at home but be required to perform jobs such as cutting wood or breaking rock. New Brunswick and Nova Scotia, which experienced slow growth after the 1850s, resisted moves towards outdoor relief. They did not shut down their workhouses until the second half of the 1950s.

Expropriating First Nations Peoples' Lands

Destroying Aboriginal Cultures

Neither the workhouse nor traditional outdoor relief applied to First Nations, who lost much of their land base in the eastern half of what is now Canada before 1867.

British North American colonial governments were determined to parcel out most of the First Nations people's lands to settlers. Claiming that they were trying to protect First Nations from being chased out altogether by the new arrivals, the governments established reserves for First Nations peoples. But in practice they did little to stop settlers from encroaching on the better reserve lands.

Aboriginal people found themselves marginalized in the lands that they had inhabited for many millennia. (For more, see Chapter 11: Aboriginal Social Welfare.) The ruling political and economic elites refused to see the economic structural conditions that had caused poverty for many European-descended working people, and they were blind to the causes of First Nations penury.

The very people who dispossessed First Nations of the resources that had always provided for their well-being claimed that they were saving them from lives of savagery and paganism. Instead of viewing First Nations destitution as the result of colonial theft and racism, they blamed the First Nations peoples for holding on to their ancient ways as the reason for their poverty. So public policy towards Aboriginal "welfare" focused on destroying Aboriginal cultures and assimilating Aboriginal peoples into the European world, always however as a racially inferior group meant to serve the needs of their conquerors.

Phase 2: 1868-1940

This period was characterized by:

- The beginnings of a transition from private to public social welfare
- World War I, protest and social unrest
- Industrialization and urbanization
- Economic hardship of the Great Depression
- The emergence of Keynesian economic ideas

Phase 2: The Industrialization Period, 1868-1940

This second phase of the history of income security in Canada covers the post-Confederation period up until World War II. After 1867, Canada industrialized rapidly. This drew both people from abroad and people from rural communities into towns and cities. Many people left the security of the family to look for greater economic opportunity, sometimes ending up with insecure factory or mining jobs.

Popular sentiment still favoured charity and local volunteer decision-making with close scrutiny of the supposed help-worthiness of an individual. Most poverty was still seen as the product of individual failings, and relief was minimal and carried stigma. The numbers of both reformers and socialists grew, but conservatives seemed largely to hold sway until the severity of the Great Depression caused a massive shift away from conservative beliefs that individuals were the cause of their own poverty.

Workers' Compensation

Before World War I, despite growing labour unrest after the turn of the twentieth century, governments did little to alter the Poor Law inheritance of "less eligibility" and almost exclusive local control over Social Assistance. The one major exception was the establishment of a universal provincial-level program of Workers' Compensation (initially called Workmen's Compensation) in Ontario in 1914, with other provinces stepping on board in later years.

Supported both by many employers and by the rising labour movement, workers' compensation, paid for by employers' contributions, provided both short-term and long-term financial support for injured workers and their families without assessing blame for injuries on the job. Previously, workers who were injured on the job had to depend on charity or attempt to sue the employer in court for liability for the injury. The occasional generosity of courts in awarding huge damages to injured workers caused many employers to prefer a no-fault, state-run system of compensation.

While Quebec had established a state system of Workmen's Compensation in 1909, it was voluntary for businesses to participate and compensation was only provided in cases where the worker was deemed blameless. Ontario, following most American states, chose the no-fault, universal model, which eventually all provinces and territories, including Quebec, adopted. Six provinces had legislated programs based on the Ontario model by 1920, followed by Quebec in 1928, Saskatchewan in 1930 and Prince Edward Island in 1949. In 1950, one year after joining Canada as a province, Newfoundland and Labrador also legislated Workers' Compensation. Yukon did not pass legislation until the 1958 Workmen's Compensation Ordinance.

Mother's Allowance/Pensions

As compensation's original name implied, the program was mainly designed for men. Shortly after several provinces had instituted Workmen's Compensation, a number of provincial governments responded to campaigns from women's rights activists and introduced Mothers' Allowances to aid women who were raising children alone and without an adequate income. Manitoba acted first in 1916, followed by Saskatchewan in 1917, Alberta in 1919, and British Columbia and Ontario in 1920. The eastern provinces did not follow suit until later: Nova Scotia in 1930 and Quebec in 1937, while New Brunswick enacted legislation in 1930 but did not implement it until 1944.

Unlike Workmen's Compensation, which applied universally and did not make moral judgments, Mothers' Allowances were infused with conventional judgments of "good women" versus "fallen women." Widows, wives with husbands too ill to work, and sometimes deserted wives were eligible for mothers' allowances. But every province excluded single mothers from receiving a Mother's Allowance and they all hired workers to make inquiries about how well the mothers were running their homes, cutting off women who appeared to have a man in their lives or who were judged to be lacking in virtue.

The campaign for mothers' pensions picked up during the First World War, too. The federal government extended pensions to the widows and children of soldiers who gave their lives. In practice, Mothers' Allowances were low and most needed to work, at least part-time, to make ends meet.

Crowds of unemployed men outside the Bowery Mission in 1935

Women and the Right to Vote

The focus on respectable motherhood reflected the conservative strategies of early twentieth century feminists. A mostly middle- and upper-class movement at the time, its activists and the movement emphasized motherhood as they campaigned to end women's political and social inferiority. Questioning the gender division of labour as such would have led to a backlash and to a smaller movement for incremental changes of benefit to women. The first priority of the movement at the time was **women's suffrage**, and the movement proved to be highly successful.

Women obtained the right to vote in federal elections in 1918, and between 1916 (Manitoba, Saskatchewan, Alberta) and 1940 (Quebec), the provinces extended voting rights to women. With voting rights in hand, reform-minded women, focusing on motherhood, turned their attention to Mothers' Allowances, a program that some male social reformers had also supported before the war.

Women's Right to Vote

The Famous Five "Persons"

Canadian women's suffrage, or the right to vote, is less than one hundred years old, although the late 1800s saw many extensions of suffrage to women in various colonies, states, and territories in the western world. Women in Canada first gained the right to vote during World War I; those women with male family members fighting in Europe were extended the right to vote to help pass the *Conscription Act*. But after the war Canada extended the right to all women.

Women in Canada were still not considered persons under the law until the "Famous Five"—Emily Murphy, Nellie McClung, Irene Parlby, Louise McKinney, and Henrietta Muir Edwards—challenged the status quo. Several of these women held powerful positions in Canadian society, but their authority was challenged because they were not considered persons.

The Supreme Court of Canada decided that the word "person" in the *British North America Act* did not include women. The Famous Five took their fight to the Privy Council in England, which at the time was Canada's highest court. They won both their case and the right for women to serve in the Senate and other public offices.

When Could Women Vote?

1916	Manitoba
1916	Saskatchewan
1916	Alberta
1917	British Columbia
1917	Ontario
1918	Nova Scotia
1918	Canada
1919	New Brunswick
1919	Yukon
1922	Prince Edward Island
1925	Newfoundland and Labrador
1940	Quebec
1951	Northwest Territories

Income Security for the Elderly

The *Government Annuities Act* of 1908 gave another option to those who had the private funds to prepare for their old age; this was done by making payments into a government-operated voluntary scheme. After retirement, the individual would receive payments representing the return of the original funds plus accumulated interest. The federal government had offered this program as an alternative to the across-the-board old-age pensions, which New Zealand and several Australian states had introduced in the decade preceding 1908. But between 1908 and the passage of the federal *Old Age Pensions Act* in 1927, only about 7,713 annuities were issued (Guest ,1999).

Neither Liberal nor Conservative governments seemed keen to pursue federal income security programs despite recommendations for old-age pensions in several post-war reports on labour unrest in Canada. In the 1921 federal election, the first two Labour members of Parliament were elected: J.S. Woodsworth, a former Methodist minister and social worker in Winnipeg; and William Irvine, a Unitarian minister in Calgary. Working with a sub-set of radical Progressive Party members, the Labour members formed a "Ginger Group" in the House of Commons who pushed for progressive reforms. Led by Woodsworth, the Ginger Group created the **Co-operative Commonwealth Federation (CCF)** in 1932, the forerunner of today's New Democratic Party. When Prime Minister Mackenzie King was reduced to a minority after the 1925 federal election, he met with the Progressive and Labour members of Parliament to learn their price for support of his government. Woodsworth demanded old-age pensions and King conceded. His government fell anyway, but when his Liberals received a majority in 1926, he kept his promise to Woodsworth.

The *Old Age Pensions Act* of 1927 was the first foray by the federal government into the provision of a minimum income program. The act provided federal funds of up to ten dollars per recipient per month to provinces that were prepared to set up a public pension and match the federal donation. But only Canadian citizens over the age of 70, who had been British subjects for at least twenty years, and who could pass a means test that demonstrated that they had almost no other means of support (the maximum allowable annual income was $365) were eligible for a pension. First Nations and Inuit were ineligible, though Métis were included. Led by British Columbia in 1927, the five most westerly provinces had all implemented provincial programs before the Depression started. Quebec and the Maritime provinces followed only after the federal government increased its contribution to 75 percent of the pension in 1931, but these provinces set the pension well below the maximum twenty dollars per month. Like Mothers' Allowances, Canada's first old-age pensions supplied too little income to allow recipients to survive unless they had some other source of income. But they helped to keep many people from poorhouses and workhouses.

Pre-Depression Programs

Some key programs passed in this period were:

***Government Annuities Act*, 1908**: an early example of a government retirement savings program

Workmen's Compensation Acts: provided standardized compensation for injured workers, while taking away their right to sue employers

Mothers' Allowances: the first allowances were developed to deal with war widows and to encourage women to leave the workforce after World War I

***Old Age Pensions Act*, 1927**: the first major income security program in Canada

The 1929 Crash

In 1929, the American stock market crashed, and this, along with other economic problems, led to a complete collapse of economies across the world, including in Canada. The **Great Depression** was a time of economic stagnation, and many people lived in great poverty. The Prairie provinces were also affected by a widespread drought that left many farmers without a crop.

In 1930, R.B. Bennett's Conservatives defeated the laissez-faire King government, promising to spend lavishly on relief. But he shared the view common at the time that deficit spending would drag down the economy. Protests against government inaction became widespread. In 1932, the government announced that single, homeless, unemployed men would only receive relief if they moved to relief camps under the authority of the Department of National Defence. In the camps, inmates were paid only 20 cents a day for such mandatory work as clearing bush, building roads, and planting trees.

The New Deal in the United States

Putting Americans Back To Work

Franklin D. Roosevelt was elected president in 1932. Roosevelt's response to the Depression was called the New Deal: a series of programs between 1933 and 1937 with the goal of relief, recovery, and reform of the United States economy.

The programs included the Federal Emergency Relief Administration (FERA), which provided funds to depleting local relief agencies; the Civil Works Administration (CWA), which employed men to build or repair roads and airports; the Civilian Conservation Corps (CCC), which put 2.5 million unmarried men to work maintaining and restoring forests, beaches, and parks; and the Works Progress Administration (WPA), which put eight million Americans to work in several different areas, including an arts program designed to employ entertainers and provide inexpensive entertainment to the public. The emphasis of Roosevelt's New Deal was to put Americans back to work, and it had the added side effect of developing infrastructure across the country.

In 1935 Roosevelt introduced the Social Security Act, which in addition to several provisions for general welfare created a social insurance program designed to pay retired workers aged 65 or older a continuing income after retirement in the form of a single, lump-sum payment. Social Security continues today in the United States.

The United States also introduced unemployment insurance in 1935. But, unlike Canada, the American version of unemployment insurance gave the states control over the program. Southern congressmen, anxious to keep African-Americans in their place in the segregated South, were unwilling to give the federal authorities the right to create universal rules for eligibility for unemployment insurance.

On to Ottawa Trek

In the United States, by contrast, Roosevelt's **New Deal** was putting people to work in public works projects. Taking a cue from this and growing Canadian social unrest, Prime Minister Bennett went on the radio in January of 1935 and told Canadians he would bring in his own New Deal, which would include Unemployment Insurance. The unemployed were not impressed.

The "On to Ottawa Trek" in June 1935 and "Regina riot" on July 1 that brutally ended the trek made Bennett appear still more interested in repression than reform. The trek was prompted by the poverty, dismal working conditions, and poor benefits in the unemployment relief camps—and by the federal government's inaction in getting people back to work. Unwilling to yield to the trekkers' demands that he close the camps and provide either work or relief payments equivalent to wages for their inmates, Bennett ordered the RCMP to stop the trekkers when they reached Regina.

The trekkers had gained adherents as they moved eastwards from Vancouver, and Bennett feared that their numbers would swell when they reached radical Winnipeg, home of the country's most famous general strike in 1919. RCMP arrests of trek organizers in Regina on July 1 led to an all-out battle with unarmed trekkers that the armed Mounties eventually won, though not before one man was killed and hundreds were injured. The Mounties then ordered the trekkers to return to their camps, providing transportation to get them there.

Unemployed workers in the west joined the "On to Ottawa Trek" in June 1935; the trains were stopped in Regina.

The Great Depression

The Great Depression was a turning point for Canada. Before 1930, the government intervened as little as possible, believing that the free market would take care of the economy, and that churches and charities would take care of society. But in the 1930s, a growing demand arose for the government to step in and create a social safety net with a minimum hourly wage, a standard work week, and programs such as medicare and Unemployment Insurance.

Employment and Social Insurance Act, 1935

Bennett did get Parliament to pass the 1935 *Employment and Social Insurance Act*. But King's government referred the legislation to the courts, which struck it down in 1937 because it represented federal intervention in the broad area of civil rights that the *British North America Act* reserved for the provinces. The Liberal government quickly responded by forming the Royal Commission on Dominion-Provincial Relations to inquire whether the division of powers entrenched in 1867 when Canada was a dominantly rural society needed changes. Among its conclusions was that provincial governments should retain responsibility for unemployed people who were unemployable, seniors, single parents, and the disabled, and that the federal government should take responsibility for employables.

With World War II having just begun and all provinces being temporarily on board—the provincial Liberals had defeated the Union Nationale in Quebec in late 1939, removing the major threat to a federal program—King obtained provincial agreement and obtained an amendment to the *British North America Act* that gave Canadians a federal unemployment insurance system.

With the *Unemployment Insurance Act* of 1940, Canada became the last industrialized country to adopt a contributory-based unemployment insurance program. But that program, at its inception, excluded seasonal workers along with most women workers and Aboriginal peoples from benefits.

TABLE 2.1

Key Events in Social Welfare in the 1940s and 1950s

Canada and World Events	Social Welfare
1940s	
War-related state controls	Universal social legislation
Crown corporations	*Unemployment Insurance Act* (1940)
End of World War II	Marsh Report (1943)
High labour unrest	Family Allowance (1944)
International revolutions	Veterans benefits (1944)
Emergence of Keynesian economic ideas	White paper on employment (1945)
Beginning of transition to public social welfare	Hospital construction
Economic hardship of Great Depression	Organization of provincial of social services
Urbanization and rapid industrialization	End of federal grants for relief
1950s	
Economic prosperity	Expanded social programs
High levels of employment	Old Age Pension for all at age 70 (1952)
Cold War propaganda	Means-tested pension at age 65 (1952)
Low level of unrest	*Disabled Persons Act* (1955)
Liberal government	*Unemployment Assistance Act* (1956)
Expansion of education	Allowances for blind disabled
Acceptance of government intervention	Hospital care coverage (1957)

Changing Perceptions: The Depression and Its Aftermath

The Depression was so financially devastating that people were shocked into changing long-held beliefs about why people are poor and what the state should do to help. People began to see that poverty and unemployment were not the results of individual inadequacy or laziness but were common and insurable threats to everyone's livelihood. Public perception of the poor began to shift.

Massive numbers of people were unemployed, and Canadians began to see that this could not possibly be due to individual fault but had more to do with the operation of the economy and the lack of government policies to correct for the ups and downs within a market-directed economy. As both families and municipalities went broke trying to cope with massive unemployment, the notion that help for the poor should be a local or family responsibility was replaced with the idea that the government should be responsible for providing relief to the unemployed.

The Limits of a Market Economy

King's Liberals were re-elected in 1945, and King, who remained a fiscal conservative, made what could perhaps be interpreted as a half-hearted attempt to implement his promises. He proposed a comprehensive set of federally funded social programs to the provinces at a federal-provincial conference shortly after his re-election. But, though he knew that it was a deal-breaker, he proposed that the provinces give the federal government the exclusive right to levy income and corporate taxes so that it would have sufficient funds to finance its new programs while insuring that neither individuals nor companies were overtaxed. The provinces, as King expected, indicated that they needed sources of funding to fulfil their own obligations to their voters, but King, who privately did not want to implement a large number of new programs, would not budge (Finkel, 2006). Federal-provincial disputes would continue to plague efforts to achieve social reform in the years that followed, with each side blaming the other for lack of progress.

Supporters of comprehensive social programs tended to be adherents of the ideas of the British economist John Maynard Keynes. As outlined in Chapter 4, Keynes's theory provided the foundation for demand-management through government spending and other fiscal and monetary policies. While King himself remained largely unconvinced by Keynes's ideas, the Department of Finance and the Bank of Canada were persuaded that a modest application of Keynes's theory was acceptable for Canada. The government, they believed, could use a combination of tax policy, social programs, and the timing of public works to correct problems inherent in a market economy and to insure that all citizens received at least a minimally adequate income.

Phase 3: 1941-1974

This period was characterized by:

- A post-World War II desire for security
- Rapid industrialization and urbanization
- A remembrance of the lessons of the Depression
- An acceptance of government intervention
- An acceptance of Keynesian economics
- A variety of landmark income security programs and legislation
- The 1966 Canada Assistance Plan (CAP)
- A growth of the socialist and reform movements (CCF-NDP)
- The Cold War with the communist Soviet Union

Phase 3: The Welfare State Period, 1941-1974

The depth of the Great Depression haunted policy-makers as World War II endured. They feared that, if a recession occurred at the end of the war, ordinary people would revolt. The CCF's success in opinion polls and its forming the government of Saskatchewan in 1944 after almost winning the 1943 Ontario elections, plus militant unionization campaigns, drove home the point that a return to pre-1939 economic and social norms was not feasible. Though many politicians and business people remained deeply conservative and created organizations to return to pre-war values, a "**welfare state consensus**" emerged after the war and lasted for about thirty years.

The Post-War Consensus

The consensus held that economic growth and social programs could be partner policies rather than enemies and that in fact, the redistribution of wealth that socialists proposed could be avoided by simply growing the economic pie and insuring, via state policies, that shares of the bigger pie remained similar to shares of the previous smaller pie. That would allow those at the bottom of the income scale to achieve a bit more prosperity but not at the expense of the wealthy. The state's role then was not to redistribute existing wealth but to help industry increase overall wealth and then insure that the tendency of unregulated markets to create ever greater maldistribution of wealth was checked by government programs.

The "welfare state" thus became the successor to the "warfare state," in which the Canadian government had become the largest employer of labour and created large Crown corporations to deal with both military and domestic needs. Much of the population had hoped to see the wartime economic model applied in peacetime.

By 1971, social programs had reached a point where they were touching the lives of most Canadians. But important business and professional interests fought the implementation of many of these programs, including universal medical insurance and the Canada/Quebec Pension Plan. Before the 1970s, most Canadians rejected the arguments of these special interests as the product of greed and old-fashioned ideological thinking. Unfortunately, by the mid-1970s many changes affected Canada—inflation and unemployment grew, oil prices went up, and the global economy changed. This began a downward spiral in terms of government revenue and expenditures, along with more sophisticated campaigns from the right-wing against universal social programs and in favour of a resumption of Poor Law ideology.

Following is a brief summary of the developments between 1941 and 1974, the period before the backlash against the welfare state became politically important.

The Beveridge Report and the Marsh Report

The Need for Universal Social Welfare

The Beveridge Report came out of Britain in 1943, the same year as the subsequent Canadian Marsh Report. These reports established the baseline for the rapid expansion of social welfare.

Sir William Beveridge wrote a comprehensive report on post-war social security for Britain. It included comprehensive health insurance and income security. This crucial report was followed by a Canadian equivalent written by Dr. Leonard Marsh (pictured at right). Marsh was born in England and attended the London School of Economics, graduating in 1928. After completing his schooling, Marsh studied wages and housing and spent some time conducting research for Sir William Beveridge. In 1930, Marsh moved to Canada, where he had accepted the position of Director of Social Research at McGill University. While at McGill, Marsh published several books on the state of employment in Canada.

In 1940, Marsh became the research director for the Committee on Post-War Reconstruction, and it was in this position that he would write his *Report on Social Security for Canada*, which became commonly known as the **Marsh Report**. The report was written in just one month and received extensive media attention. In it, Marsh detailed the need for comprehensive and universal social welfare programs. His report sparked debate over universal income security benefits versus targeted income security benefits.

The report was presented to the committee for which Marsh was working and was also presented to the federal government, which at that time was led by William Lyon Mackenzie King. It was largely ignored at the time, but many now consider the Marsh Report to be the most important report in the history of the Canadian welfare state.

Marsh suggested that the country should establish a "social minimum"—a standard aimed at protecting the disadvantaged through policies such as social insurance and children's allowances. Despite initially being largely ignored, by 1966, most of Marsh's recommendations had become law. His work served as the blueprint for the modern Canadian social security system. Marsh himself viewed his report as the natural outgrowth of the decade of social studies he had directed at McGill University.

In the report, Marsh established the concept of a desirable living minimum income. He went on to outline proposals that meet the principal types of contingencies that characterize industrial society, coining the three categories of contingencies which are still used today to describe social welfare. He proposed a two-pronged system of social insurance to cover both employment risks and universal risks: the first covered wage-earners, and the second covered all persons for old age, disability, and death. He also proposed children's allowances and health insurance. Finally, he emphasized the importance of training and placement programs to help people, especially youth, prepare for employment.

The report made headline news as the media spoke about the proposed social spending of billions of dollars. People sensed the beginning of a new era in which they would have medical insurance coverage and protection from unemployment. These were new ideas to most people, and they sparked debate about what this would mean for Canadian society. While some stressed the positive impacts on citizenship and responsibility for one another, others spoke of the onset of communism. Some social workers at the time, such as Charlotte Whitton, spoke negatively about the idea of social insurance. She advocated for social assistance, in which trained social workers supervised and counselled people needing assistance.

After writing The Marsh Report, Leonard Marsh would go on to work for the League for Social Reconstruction, act as a welfare adviser to the United Nations Relief and Rehabilitation Administration, and spend twenty-five years at the University of British Columbia's School of Social Work. He retired and was named Professor Emeritus in 1972.

Welfare-Expansion Era Programs

This era marked the arrival and development of many of Canada's social welfare programs. These programs include:

- *Family Allowance Act*, 1944
- The *Old Age Security Act*, 1951
- The *Old Age Assistance Act*, 1951
- The *Unemployment Assistance Act*, 1956
- The Canada/Quebec Pension Plan, 1965
- The *Unemployment Insurance Act*, 1971

The Era of Social Welfare Program Expansion

From simply looking through this list of social welfare programs, you can see how important this period was in establishing the Canadian welfare state. Total expenditures on social welfare, health, and education grew from 4 percent of gross domestic product (GDP) in 1946 to 15 percent of GDP by 1976 (Moscovitch & Albert, 1987, p. 31).

The first piece of government legislation for this period was the *Family Allowance Act* of 1944. It was the first federal universal (that is, not means-tested) income security program in Canada, and when it was introduced, considerable debate took place over the desirability of a universal program. The goals of this important piece of legislation were to maintain purchasing power when the war ended and demonstrate the government's commitment to the upcoming generation. The legislation also fit in with the government's efforts to send Canadian mothers, whom the government had encouraged to work during the war because of labour shortages, back home. Both economic and social conservative motives were at work here: the government was skeptical that work could be found for all who wanted it and hoped to insure one job per household by excluding married women from most employment, and it also believed that the traditional model of households in which women were dependent on men was worth preserving. The family allowance, however, made a concession to married women who were going to be losing their jobs after the war: the family allowance would be delivered in their names rather than those of their husbands, giving them some money in the household over which they alone could exercise discretion.

Following provincial agreement and an amendment to the *British North America Act* to permit the federal government to operate a pension plan, the *Old Age Security Act* (OAS) of 1951 provided a universal pension, or demogrant, of $40 per month to everyone beginning at the age of 70. Pension payments began in 1952 and were taxable.

At the same time, the *Old Age Assistance Act* of 1951 provided a means-tested amount of $50 per month for those aged 65 to 69. This program was cost-shared 50-50 by the federal and provincial governments but was administered by provincial welfare departments who used a means test to determine eligibility. It was viewed by the elderly as a personally invasive and stigmatizing program. Meanwhile, in 1955, a slow broadening out of coverage of workers for unemployment insurance began with a revised *Unemployment Insurance Act*.

The Canada/Quebec Pension Plan of 1965 provided a wage-related supplement to OAS and was the first program to be indexed to inflation, or the cost of living allowance (COLA). It provided wide coverage and advanced the concept of a social minimum.

The Canada Assistance Plan

In 1966, the **Canada Assistance Plan (CAP)** was introduced (see Appendix B). CAP was instrumental in standardizing and funding Social Assistance nationwide and was in effect between 1966 and 1996. This program was the consolidation of federal-provincial programs based on means tests or needs tests. Half the costs of all shareable items were assumed by the federal government, provided a needs test was given. Assistance was possible for the working poor, and the public was given the right to appeal decisions. It also forbade the use of workfare in Social Assistance.

The historic debate concerning "fact of need" versus "cause of need" peaked when CAP was introduced. CAP was intended to simply meet needs regardless of the cause for need. This was a strong effort to reverse the long-held belief that those in need were somehow defective. Others debated this misguided notion. This fact-of-need concept, combined with a needs-assessment procedure, was first introduced with the *Unemployment Assistance Act* in 1956.

CAP was the basis for cost-sharing, not only for income security programs but also for a wide range of social services and programs that included health services, children's services, Social Assistance, disability allowances, old-age assistance, services for the elderly, and institutional care. This program was the cornerstone of Canada's social service funding until 1996, when it was replaced by the Canada Health and Social Transfer. The CHST will be discussed in more detail in Chapter 3: Challenges to Social Welfare.

TABLE 2.2

After-Tax Comparisons of Incomes Received by Quintiles of the Canadian Population, 1951 and 1972

	1951 (%)	**1972** (%)
Top 20%	41.1	39.1
2nd 20%	22.4	23.7
3rd 20%	17.4	18.3
4th 20%	12.9	12.9
5th 20%	6.1	5.9

Source: Adapted from Statistics Canada, Income Distribution by Size in Canada, Selected Years: Distribution of Family Incomes in Canada, 1972.

First Nations' Welfare

By 1966, the relief system for First Nations peoples had collapsed and was replaced with access to mainstream social welfare programs (Moscovitch & Webster, 1995).

This turnaround was the result of a recognition by the government that it was failing in its attempts to assimilate or to eradicate the Métis, the Inuit, and the First Nations.

For a more in-depth discussion of the history of Aboriginal social welfare, see Chapter 11.

The 1969 Senate Committee on Poverty

The 1969 Senate Committee on Poverty reported high poverty levels and recommended an income supplementation scheme for the working poor, but the plan was rejected by the provinces as being too costly. In 1970, the federal government undertook a major review of income security programs, which resulted in two important reports: the White Paper entitled Income Security for Canadians and the White Paper on Unemployment Insurance. The former report called for greater emphasis on anti-poverty measures and stated that resources should be concentrated on those with the lowest incomes. In other words, it recommended that selective benefits replace universal programs. The debate between supporters of universal and targeted programs was re-ignited. The reports also advocated for benefits that would provide an adequate standard of living, rather than poverty- or subsistence-level benefits. For the first time, significant government reports recommended benefit levels that addressed poverty and provided adequate standards of living. This ignited debate about the role of income security programs in Canadian society.

These reports were followed by program expansion and increases in old-age benefits and Unemployment Insurance. The *Unemployment Insurance Act* of 1971 extended Unemployment Insurance to cover more people and eased qualifying conditions. Benefits were raised to two-thirds of wages. These income security program changes created benefits that neared the level of an adequate standard of living.

TABLE 2.3

Key Events in Social Welfare in the 1960s and 1970s

Canada and World Events	Social Welfare
1960s Grassroots unrest—growth of anti-poverty, First Nations, labour, student, and peace organizations Founding of NDP Quebec separatism Economic growth and employment	*General Welfare Assistance Act* (Ontario) (1960) *National Housing Act* (1964) Canada/Quebec Pension Plan (1965) Canada Assistance Plan (1966) *Medicare Act* (1968)
1970s Fiscal crisis of state Conservative business ideas prominent Shift to residual concept of social welfare Rise of U.S. influence in Canada Rise of women's movement Rise in women's employment	Cutbacks begin in health, education, and welfare programs More law and order Rise of contracting out NGOs funding militant groups *Unemployment Insurance Act* (1971) Established Program Financing (EPF) legislation to finance education and health

Conclusion

The ideas underlying Canada's earliest income security programs had their roots in the English Poor Laws and their adoption in British North America in the colonial period. The Elizabethan Poor Laws were enacted to address the large numbers of desperately poor people, and to control workers entering the new, wage-based labour market. The laws also gave rise to the conceptions of the deserving and undeserving poor. Those considered deserving were people who were very old, sick, or severely disabled. Able-bodied poor were thought to be capable of working and therefore deserving only of temporary assistance when work was unavailable, and even then only at rates "less eligible" than the lowest rates of pay on offer for common labour, and after the performance of a "work test."

The emergence of our current system breaks down into four periods: the colonial period, 1840-67; the industrialization period, 1868-1940; the welfare state period, 1941-74; and the period of erosion, 1975-present. The colonial period is characterized by limited and local charity, and harsh notions of who was deserving of assistance, both on the part of charities and the state. The industrial period saw a gradual shift from private to public social welfare, the emergence of Keynesian ideas, and a shift from blame-oriented beliefs to socially-oriented beliefs (in order to explain poverty during the Great Depression).

After World War II, Canada saw the development of the welfare state, as we have come to know it. In this period, the reach of the federal government changed dramatically. Following the war effort, there was general acceptance of government intervention in the economy and society, and Poor Law notions of targeting the most deserving of the poorest of the poor gave way, at least in part, to notions of social minimums for everyone and universal social rights.

Of course, those who had opposed the expansion of welfare programs did not entirely disappear. Chapter 3 will explain why their ideas were able to reassert themselves so effectively after 1975. After that date, we began to see the erosion of many of the major reforms achieved during the welfare state period.

CHAPTER 2 REVIEW

LEARNING OBJECTIVES

After completing this chapter, you should be able to:

- Understand the rise of social welfare in the transition from feudalism to capitalism.
- Understand the thinking behind the Elizabethan poor laws.
- Explain the role of the "workhouse" in the early history of social welfare.
- Understand the key themes underlying the historic debates over social welfare.
- Explain the differences between the French and English models of social welfare.
- Distinguish the four main phases in the history of social welfare and income security in Canada.
- Explain the significance of the 1929 crash and its aftermath on the development of social welfare.
- Explain the significance of the Beveridge Report and the Marsh Report.
- Explain what is meant by the "post-war consensus" in relation to social welfare.

KEY CONCEPTS IN CHAPTER

- Beveridge Report
- Canada Assistance Plan (CAP)
- Capitalism
- Co-operative Commonwealth Federation (CCF)
- Deserving and undeserving poor
- Elizabethan Poor Law
- Feudalism
- Great Depression
- Indoor Relief
- Marsh Report
- New Deal
- Outdoor Relief
- *Poor Law Amendment Act* of 1834
- Principle of less eligibility
- Statute of Labourers
- Welfare state consensus
- Women's suffrage
- Workhouse

REVIEW QUESTIONS

1. What are the four phases in the rise of income security in Canada? Map out these phases in a timeline, and include a list of the major developments in each period.
2. In what different ways did Aboriginal societies in Canada, New France, and British North America deal with issues of income security?
3. What factors led to the emergence of income security in conjunction with the rise of the economic system of capitalism?
4. How do our current conceptions of social welfare remain linked to the ideas of early English post-feudal society?
5. What are the principal ideas behind the English Poor Laws, and how do they compare with the ideas underlying economic security for the poor in each of the first three phases in the rise of income security in Canada?
6. What were the three pieces of broad federal legislation that affected all income security programs in Canada, and what were the specific impacts?
7. The economic crash of 1929 ushered in the Great Depression. Describe the effects of this period on the lives of Canadians at the time and on political developments during the inter-war period.

8. What is meant by the "Postwar Consensus?" What income security programs were created during this period?

CRITICAL THINKING

What do you think are the "big" historical developments that have influenced social welfare in this country?

If any of these factors were removed, how do you think the social welfare system might have evolved?

EXPLORING SOCIAL WELFARE

1. How has history and politics shaped the social policies that we have today? Pick an income security program and trace the history of the program, using a variety of sources.
2. Many of the welfare and income security programs available today are premised on underlying ideas about why people fall into difficulty and, accordingly, what they need to do to get themselves out. Select a program (e.g., employment insurance, workers' compensation, child benefits, workfare, etc.) and critically examine it from the point of view of the premises underlying the program.

WEBSITES

The Canada Assistance Plan: A Twenty Year Assessment, 1966–1986
www.canadiansocialresearch.net/allanm.htm
This article by Allan Moscovitch originally appeared in the 1988–89 edition of *How Ottawa Spends* (Carleton University) and provides an excellent critical analysis of CAP's history.

Canada's Unique Social History
www.socialpolicy.ca/cush
Canada's Unique Social History is an interactive online course which provides an overview of different aspects of the history of social welfare in Canada, including a glossary, photos, and additional resources.

Health Canada
www.hc-sc.gc.ca
Health Canada is the department of the federal government responsible for helping Canadians maintain and improve their health, while respecting individual choices and circumstances. The Health Canada website provides information about the working of the department itself, a vast amount of information relevant to healthy living for Canadians, and information about legislation and commissions of inquiries. Health Canada works collaboratively with the provinces and territories to test ways in which the Canadian health care system can be improved and ensure its sustainability for the future.

3

Challenges to Social Welfare

Income Security Under Siege

From 1945 to 1975, as we saw in Chapter 2: The History of Social Welfare in Canada, there was a historic social compromise among capital, labour, and the state to create an embryonic "welfare state." After 1975, that compromise was almost constantly at risk.

The period after 1975 was characterized by a shift away from the institutional conception of social welfare, accompanied by increases in economic integration and globalization. Along with it came widespread cuts to income security expenditures and greater restrictions in the design of social welfare programs. This chapter examines the changes that ensued in the second half of the twentieth century and likely challenges to social welfare in the twenty-first.

"Like slavery and Apartheid, poverty is not natural. It is man-made and it can be overcome and eradicated by the actions of human beings."

— NELSON MANDELA, ANTI-APARTHEID ACTIVIST, REVOLUTIONARY, AND POLITICIAN WHO SERVED AS PRESIDENT OF SOUTH AFRICA FROM 1994 TO 1999, THE FIRST TO BE ELECTED IN A FULLY REPRESENTATIVE, MULTIRACIAL ELECTION.

Why the Post-War Compromise Ended

After 1975, the "welfare states" in the advanced capitalist countries began systematically to be dismantled. There was a shift towards individual and family responsibility, rather than community responsibility, for the well-being of community members. The term "**neo-liberalism**" was coined to signify this return to pre-WWII social values (or, as critics described it, towards "anti-social" values).

The Profitability Crisis

Why did conservative forces turn against the "post-war compromise" with respect to social welfare? The short answer is that, by the late 1970s, after-tax corporate profits were beginning to erode and rates of economic growth were slowing down. In the years to follow, the corporate sector placed a great deal of pressure on governments everywhere. They called for both fiscal (expenditures and taxes) and monetary (financial/money) policy to emphasize belt-tightening. In their view, the Keynesian policies, with their focus on demand, gave too little incentives to industry.

In short, the corporate community in Canada was united by the late 1970s in making demands for a reduced state presence and lower taxes, and they seemed to encounter a less organized, or less prepared labour force.

TABLE 3.1

Spending on Social Programs: International Comparisons

Country	1960	1981
Belgium	17.0	38.0
Netherlands	16.3	36.1
Sweden	14.5	33.5
Germany	20.5	31.5
Italy	16.5	29.1
Denmark	10.2	29.0
Austria	17.9	27.9
Ireland	11.7	27.1
Norway	11.7	27.1
United Kingdom	13.9	24.0
France	13.4	23.8
Canada	**12.1**	**21.7**
United States	10.9	21.0
New Zealand	13.0	19.6
Australia	10.2	18.6
Japan	8.0	17.5

Source: OECD Bulletin, No. 146 (Jan. 1984), reprinted in Andrew Armitage, *Social Welfare in Canada: Ideas, Realities and Future Paths*, 2nd ed. (Toronto: McClelland and Stewart, 1988), 22.

The Guaranteed Annual Income Debate

The debate over the idea of a **Guaranteed Annual Income** best illustrates this shift in values. The Report of the Special Senate Committee on Poverty in 1970 called for a guaranteed annual income (GAI) for all Canadians set at 70 percent of the minimum income required to get out of poverty. It was one of many recommendations that would not be implemented, including a national daycare plan, minimum wages to be set at 60 percent of average wages, and community-operated clinics offering integrated health and social services.

The Trudeau government at the time, though responding positively to pressures to extend unemployment insurance coverage to all unemployed Canadians, was increasingly concerned about rising inflation. It was reluctant to consider a potentially costly guaranteed annual income program in addition to the UI reforms. A White Paper in late 1970 suggested that a guaranteed annual income program should only occur if family allowances and old-age pensions, (universal programs), became means-tested programs, with the monies thus saved being applied to GAI. Opposition was almost unanimous.

National Anti-Poverty Organization (NAPO)

In 1971, a national conference of local organizations of the poor met in Ottawa and decided to form a national organization. The result was the **National Anti-Poverty Organization (NAPO)** (formed in 1972, now called Canada Without Poverty). It made the struggle for a GAI with an above-poverty level its fundamental demand. But they received a cool response from the federal and most provincial governments—both inflation and unemployment were continuing to rise.

In the federal election of October 1972, the Liberals under Trudeau lost their majority and relied on the NDP to win confidence votes in the House. The new Minister of Health and National Welfare, Marc Lalonde, came forward with a proposal in 1973 that included a modest GAI. But the Minister of Finance, John Turner, opposed new social spending, and only the three NDP premiers—in British Columbia, Manitoba, and Saskatchewan—expressed much interest in a GAI.

The Trudeau government dropped all talk of a GAI in 1978 in favour of a modest Refundable Child Tax Credit that did provide modest benefits, but that involved far less government expenditure (and therefore far less social impact). The government was not only cautious about legislating new programs of social welfare but also began to make cuts in existing programs. In 1977, it shelved equal federal-provincial sharing of medicare and postsecondary education spending. Beginning in 1982, the federal government's limited increases for postsecondary education began the process of a federal pullback from its earlier commitment to match provincial spending on medical care and postsecondary education.

Mincome in Manitoba

Guaranteed Annual Income Experiment

Hoping to keep the GAI debate alive and to appeal to the NDP provincial governments, Trudeau agreed to a request from Manitoba premier Ed Schreyer (below) to run an experiment to provide research that would either prove or disprove the claims by conservatives that a GAI would provide disincentives for people to work. The program was labeled **Mincome**, short for Minimum Income.

From 1974 to 1978, randomly chosen modest to low income Manitobans received a GAI in one of three formulations combining a particular level of guaranteed income with a particular level of clawback of any income that a Mincome recipient received beyond the GAI. Ironically, by 1978, the antagonism to new national social spending had reached a point where the data assembled through the Mincome experiment was not even tabulated.

When social scientists later gained access to the data, they found that the impact of receiving the Mincome GAI on individuals' seeking and finding work was minimal. In Dauphin, a city of over 12,000, where instead of random selection of participants, all residents with incomes below the minimum income for eligibility for Mincome—about a third of households in the town—were allowed to participate, there were startling results.

Evelyn Forget, of the University of Manitoba's Department of Community Health Sciences, reported "an 8.5 percent reduction in the hospitalization rate for participants relative to controls, particularly for accidents and injuries and mental health. We also found that participant contacts with physicians declined, especially for mental health, and that more adolescents continued into grade 12. We found no increase in fertility, family dissolution rates, or improved birth outcomes. We conclude that a relatively modest GAI can improve population health, suggesting significant health savings." (Forget, 2011)

Forget focused on the social determinants of health and demonstrated that guaranteeing people's incomes, even at a very modest level—people in Dauphin were only guaranteed 60 percent of the income required to beat the poverty level for the size of their household—actually saved money in the short term and promised longer-term savings.

However, despite the success of the Mincome program in terms of health and well-being of the individuals involved and the wider community, the decision-makers of the late 1970s were not interested in major social experimentation.

The Conservatives Under Mulroney, 1984-1993

The Trudeau government followed tight-money policies after 1975 that ran counter to Keynes's prescription for expanding the money supply during periods of recession. They also made a number of cuts in social programs. Still bigger changes in social policy would take place during the prime ministership of Progressive Conservative Brian Mulroney from 1984 to 1993.

By that time, both the United Kingdom (Margaret Thatcher, 1979) and the United States (Ronald Reagan, 1980) had elected governments committed to rolling back the welfare state. Their Canadian counterparts now had a chance to implement their agenda at a much faster pace. Mulroney, upon becoming PC leader in 1983, denounced the "socialism of business regulation" and allegedly high taxes of the previous government.

Because the Canadian economy was so closely tied to the American economy, the Reagan experiment had a major impact on unemployment in Canada, which rose from 8 percent in 1981 to almost 13 percent in 1982. Mulroney recognized that Canadians were not yet prepared to follow the American and British examples, so he focused his election appeal on a denunciation of Liberal cronyism rather than Liberal economic and social policies. He called Canada's social programs a "sacred trust" that he felt sworn to uphold and even joined the leaders of both the Liberals and the NDP in promising a national daycare program. But the ink was barely dry on the ballots before he attempted to reduce the value of old-age pensions. (He beat a quick retreat in the face of an unexpected militant response from seniors.)

Free Trade

The Mulroney government would make its mark both on the Canadian economy and on social programs in Canada by negotiating an agreement, the **Canada-United States Free Trade Agreement**, that became the centrepiece of its re-election bid in the federal election of 1988 and was implemented early the following year.

Supporters of free trade argued that in the new globalized economy, protection of local industries was old-fashioned and kept alive uncompetitive firms while deterring innovation and the establishment of firms with a global reach. Opponents of free trade argued that it would worsen the problems Canada already faced from runaway firms looking for the cheapest place to operate and would result in downward pressures not only on wages but on social programs.

Mulroney denied a connection between social programs and free trade. But once he had won the election, he quickly changed his tune. Canadians, he argued, could not compete internationally if they taxed corporations and wealthy individuals too much. Social programs, he claimed, were at the root of Canada's deficits and debts.

Cuts, Cuts, and Still More Cuts

The Mulroney government began to cut grants for medicare and post-secondary education by 2 percent per year in 1986. In 1990, they announced sped up cuts that would eliminate Established Programs Financing altogether by 2004. They also de-indexed child benefits from inflation, cut supplements for hiring and training workers, and withdrew from any role in low-income housing.

Mulroney also ended universality in family allowances and OAS, later announcing the end of the universal family allowance program altogether. The Child Care Tax Benefit (CCTB), introduced in 1989 as a means-tested modest supplement to the family allowance for low-income and middle-income families, would replace the universal family allowance. While the CCTB would contribute to reducing poverty for families, the rate was too low to be of significance. Meanwhile, CAP expenditures were also cut. Rules for collecting unemployment insurance were toughened and payments were reduced.

This period was characterized by a significant retreat in government spending on social programs and income supports. The Conservatives claimed they needed to stay aligned with Reagan's policies in the U.S.

Key Dates

Mentioned in This Chapter

International

1973 OPEC policies push up oil prices in Western countries

1979 Election of Margaret Thatcher's Conservatives in the United Kingdom.

1980 Election of Ronald Reagan as president of the United States

National

1972 Establishment of National Anti-Poverty Organization

1973 Establishment of C.D. Howe Institute; the federal government proposes a modest Guaranteed Annual Income program to the provinces

1974 Establishment of Fraser Institute; Mincome experiment begins

1977 Established Programs Financing begins

1981 Conference Board of Canada established

1984 *Canada Health Act* legislated

1989 Canada-United States Free Trade Agreement passed; Canada Child Tax Benefit introduced

1992 Family allowances discontinued by the Mulroney government

1996 Canada Health and Social Transfer (CHST) replaces Canada Assistance Plan

2002 Romanow Report tabled

2004 CHST split into Canada Health Transfer and Canada Social Transfer

2005 Proposals for a national daycare plan and for the Kelowna Accord placed before Parliament

2006 National daycare plan and Kelowna Accord die with the election of the minority Conservative government; Universal Child Care Benefit introduced

2012 Harper government changes the minimum age for receipt of Old Age Pensions and Guaranteed Income Supplement from 65 to 67

Across Canada

In Ontario, a one-term NDP government from 1990 to 1995 largely resisted cuts in social spending. But the election of Mike Harris's Progressive Conservatives in 1995 resulted in Alberta-style cuts.

Similarly in British Columbia, NDP governments from 1991 to 2001 made only minor cuts, while the Liberal government that followed them in office in 2001 wasted little time in carrying out the sorts of cuts that had occurred in other provinces.

Only Quebec, with the introduction by the Parti Québécois government of a universal public, five-dollar-a-day daycare program in 1997, which was only slightly modified by the provincial Liberals when they replaced the PQ in 2003, could claim a major social policy advance in the period after 1975.

The Liberals Return to Power, 1993-2006

Paradoxically, the continued high deficits and debts caused a significant group of Conservatives to feel that the Mulroney government was insufficiently conservative. They formed a new party called the Reform Party which was pledged to cut social programming far faster and indeed to cut taxation at the same time, all while reducing deficits and debts.

Reform spoke about "starving the beast," that is the state, by depriving it of revenues and yet insisting on it breaking even. While the strength of Reform helped to reduce the once mighty Progressive Conservatives to a mere two seats in the 1993 federal election, the major benefactors of the split on the right were the federal Liberals led by Jean Chrétien.

Yet the Liberals in power during their first term from 1993 to 1997 were at least as neo-liberal in their economic policies as their Tory predecessors. They cut transfers to the provinces, refused to reverse the Conservative decision to gut family allowances, and also got rid of the Canada Assistance Plan. Monies that had gone to CAP for Social Assistance were combined with funds for medicare and postsecondary education and then shrunk to create the **Canada Health and Social Transfer (CHST),** which was implemented in 1996. Though the provinces would be receiving less money overall, their compensation was that the federal government would not tell them what to do with any of it. Notions of universality and federally supervised standards simply went out the window. Under CAP, provinces could be penalized for failing to provide income support for someone who was in need; but under CHST, there was no mechanism for dealing with provinces that decided to exclude groups and individuals whom they wished to label as having caused their own poverty.

Low-income housing, ended by the Mulroney Tories, was not revived by the Chrétien government. The Liberals renamed Unemployment Insurance as Employment Insurance (EI) and went well beyond what the Conservatives had done to toughen eligibility requirements for Employment Insurance. While 96 percent of the unemployed were eligible to collect from the insurance program after the Trudeau reforms of 1971 and 85 percent were still eligible in 1989, only 41 percent of the unemployed were eligible to collect by 1997. Those who did collect saw their rates reduced. But EI premiums did not come down and the government used money from the program for retraining programs, which should have been funded from general revenues.

All this cutting predictably left low-income Canadians more vulnerable to falling into poverty. The national after-tax poverty rate was just over 10 percent in 1989 but had risen to 16 percent in 1996. More and more, the vulnerable in Canadian society would be dependent on the ups and downs of the economy rather than on social guarantees from the federal and provincial governments.

The Shrinking State

Governments that insisted on neo-liberal policies claimed that they had no option. Canada, they claimed, was pricing itself out of world markets because of its allegedly Cadillac social services. But the numbers did not support this claim.

For example, social expenditures as a percentage of Gross Domestic Product in the year 2000 were: Canada, 17.3%; United Kingdom, 21.3%; France, 28.3%. The percentage point change in social expenditure as a percentage of GDP in 1990-2000 was: Canada, -1.3%; United Kingdom, +1.8%; France, +1.7% (CCSD, 2005).

For Canadians, the dropout of the state from its previous level of social involvement would result in a growing income gap between the wealthiest and the poorest Canadians. According to OECD figures, the after-tax incomes of the wealthiest ten percent of Canadians increased by 1.6 percent annually on average from 1985 to 2007; for the bottom ten percent, the increase was 0.9 percent. Real disposable incomes for the bottom decile had fallen to less than one-tenth of the disposable incomes of the wealthiest decile: $10,260 to $103,500. The ratio between the top and bottom deciles in 1980 had been 8.

While disparities were even worse in the United States, where the top decile received 14 times the income of the bottom decile, the ratio in Germany and the Scandinavian countries was a far more modest 6 to 1. "Taxes and benefits reduce inequality less in Canada than in most OECD countries," reported the OECD (Grant, 2011).

Tax Reform

Statistics Canada offered a different perspective.

"It was not the explosive growth in program spending that caused the increase in deficits after 1975, but a drop in federal revenues ... and rising debt charges ... This partly reflects tax reform which shifted the tax burden from corporations to persons, and from income taxes to consumption taxes."

EDMONTON JOURNAL, JUNE 20, 1991

Though at arms-length from government, the Mulroney government forced Statscan to scrub this report from the official record.

The Conservatives Return, 2006

After making huge cuts to social programs in their first term of office, the Liberals, presiding over an economy that was on the upturn once again, were able to turn the former deficits into annual budget surpluses. But apart from reinvesting in medical care, they proved unwilling to either refinance social programs that had suffered cuts or introduce new programs. Their focus instead was on tax cuts, and they campaigned on a program of income and corporate tax cuts in 2000 that favoured the wealthy and knocked the sails out of the campaign of the latest installment of the Reform Party, the Canadian Reform Conservative Alliance, usually just called the Canadian Alliance.

The Liberals' success as a centrist party had been fuelled from 1993 onwards by the split between the Reformers and Progressive Conservatives. In 2003, those two parties fused to form the Conservative Party of Canada and in 2004 chose Stephen Harper, the former leader of the Canadian Alliance, as the leader of the merged party. Early polls suggested that the merged party would do poorly against the Liberals, who had chosen Paul Martin as their new leader to replace Jean Chrétien in 2003 and were popular because the economy remained in good shape. But a scandal involving federal sponsorship money for cultural and sporting events during the Chrétien period erupted in early 2004. Martin came out of the election with a minority of parliamentary seats and was dependent on the NDP, which had won only 19 seats under its new leader Jack Layton but had regained a greater share of the popular vote than it had since the early 1990s.

In 2005, Martin tabled a budget that included almost $5 billion in cuts to taxes for big corporations. Layton announced that the NDP would agree to vote for the budget if Martin cancelled the corporate tax cuts in favour of additional monies for social spending, the environment, and foreign aid. The proposed social programs included $1.6 billion for affordable housing, which the federal government had stopped supporting in the Mulroney era.

Martin, not wanting to face an early election and hoping to win back voters who had switched to the NDP in 2004, agreed to Layton's proposal. Attempting to replace his party's association in the public image mainly with the sponsorship scandal and sitting on a comfortable budget surplus, Martin soon attempted to move his government away from neo-liberalism and to embrace social reform. He negotiated a daycare accord with the provinces that had the potential to finally create the elusive national daycare policy that politicians had been promising Canadians since the televised debates of the national party leaders in 1984. He also negotiated a deal called the Kelowna Accord with the provinces and the major national Aboriginal organizations that would invest $5 billion into housing, education, and economic development on Canada's much-neglected reserves.

The Conservatives Win a Majority, 2011-

By the fall of 2005, the NDP, whose support was rising in the polls, tired of supporting the Liberals in the face of criticism that they were allowing a corrupt government to stay in power. All three opposition parties voted against the government in a confidence vote and an election was set for January 2006.

From 2006 until 2011, Stephen Harper led minority governments. The federal election in May 2011 gave Harper a parliamentary majority. During his years in power there has been a steady acceleration in cutbacks of social programs that were in place to limit the inequalities and social dangers that a marketplace economy creates.

In common with many leading politicians of the pre-World-War-II period, the Conservative government believes that the marketplace, left alone, will distribute goods and services to those who have worked for them and, in turn, incentivize those who do not work hard enough or smart enough. The Conservative government after 2006, and especially after 2011 when it gained an outright majority, took this philosophy to heart. We look now at the policies in a number of areas to demonstrate how this social conservative outlook translates into public policy.

Grants to Provinces for Health and Social Welfare

Changes Over Time

Canada Assistance Plan (1966-96)
The Canada Assistance Plan (CAP) involved federal grants to the provinces to finance half of all Social Assistance expenditures in return for which provinces agree not to turn down any needy person.

Medicare Grants (1968-77)
These medicare grants involved federal grants to provinces to finance half of all medicare expenditures in the country, using a formula that takes into account the higher needs of poorer provinces.

Established Programs Financing (1977-96)
Established Programs Financing (EPF) gave grants to provinces to help finance medicare and post-secondary education. These consisted of federal block grants to the provinces that included a direct grant plus a percentage of federal taxes rather than a guarantee of half of expenditures.

Canada Health and Social Transfer (1996-2004)
CHST replaced both CAP and EPF. Direct grant from the federal government plus tax points; that is, a percentage of federal taxes. No limits on how provinces divide this money between health and social spending but must meet conditions of *Canada Health Act* and must provide social support to people from other provinces who move to their province.

Canada Social Transfer (2004-present)
The CST is a $19.8 billion federal block transfer (2011-12) to provinces and territories in support of post-secondary education, Social Assistance, and social services, including early childhood development and early learning.

Canada Health Transfer (2004-present)
The CHT is a $30.3 billion (2012-13) block transfer for healthcare.

Fiscal Policy

The Conservative government has made deep cuts in government revenue, arguing that individual consumers and investors can make better decisions in almost every area of spending than governments. The **Goods and Services Tax (GST)** was cut, first to six percent in 2006 and then five percent in 2008. The GST cut deprived the federal treasury of about $13 billion annually. The government also followed its predecessors in introducing sharp cuts in corporate taxes. The Liberals had cut the tax rate to 22 percent after the 2000 election, and the Conservatives went further with an additional 7 percent cut between 2006 and 2012. On January 1, 2012, the corporate tax rate was down to 15 percent, compared to 29.1 percent in 2000, or about $27 billion less in potential taxes.

To a large degree the Tory philosophy was to "starve the beast," that is to cut taxes to the point where governments could argue that they simply lacked the revenues to fund major social programs.

FIGURE 3.1

Canadian Corporate Tax Rate, 2000–2012

SOURCE: CANADIAN MANUFACTURERS AND EXPORTERS. (2011). THE ECONOMIC IMPACT OF CORPORATE TAX RATE REDUCTIONS.

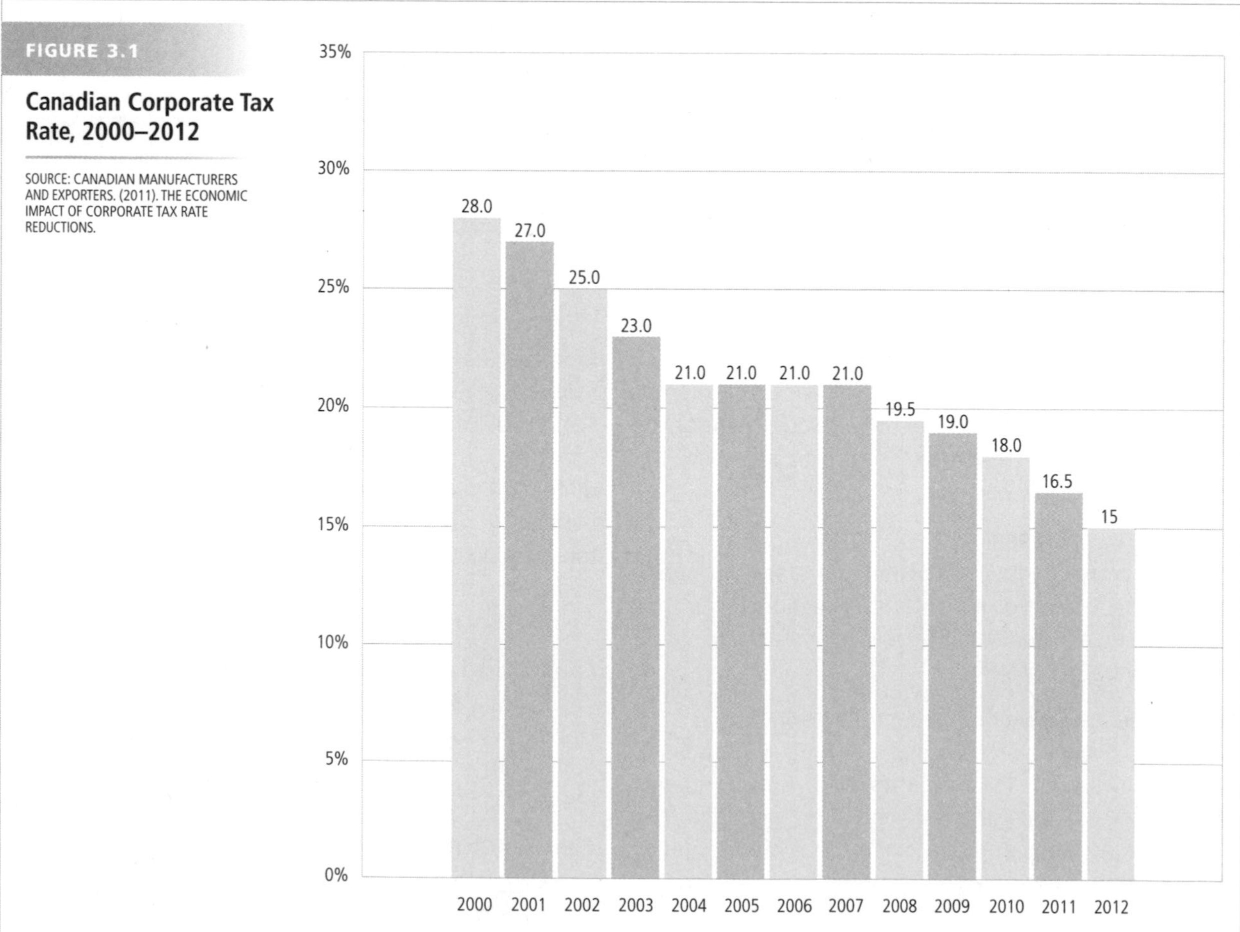

Child Poverty

One of the first casualties was daycare. The **national daycare plan** proposed by the federal Liberals and NDP, as well as the provinces, was dropped after the 2006 election and never revived.

The 2006 budget gave a taxable tax allowance of $1200 a year, called the **Universal Child Care Benefit (UCCB)**, to all parents of children under 6 years of age as an alternative to a child care program. Though the new government expanded spending in a number of areas, such as the military, it also chose to cut federal spending in a number of social program areas, including adult literacy, youth unemployment, and social development.

The widespread cutbacks in program spending and rising family and child poverty levels angered many Canadians, those relying on income assistance and those not. In 2012, the government even terminated the National Council of Welfare, whose task was to provide advice to government on poverty issues.

FIGURE 3.2

Child Poverty Report Card, Selected Countries

SOURCE: THE CONFERENCE BOARD OF CANADA

REPORT CARD

Child Poverty

	1980s	1990s	2000s
Australia	C	C	C
Austria	n.a.	n.a.	A
Belgium	n.a.	n.a.	B
Canada	C	C	C
Denmark	A	A	A
Finland	A	A	A
France	A	B	B
Germany	A	B	B
Ireland	n.a.	n.a.	B
Italy	B	D	C
Japan	B	C	C
Netherlands	A	B	B
Norway	A	A	A
Sweden	A	A	A
Switzerland	n.a.	n.a.	B
U.K.	B	C	B
U.S.	D	D	D

Source: The Conference Board of Canada.

How has Canada performed historically on this indicator?

- Canada, like Australia, has received steady "C"s since the 1980s for its child poverty rate.
- Four Nordic countries have been consistent "A" performers—Denmark, Finland, Norway, and Sweden. The US has been the only consistent "D" performer.

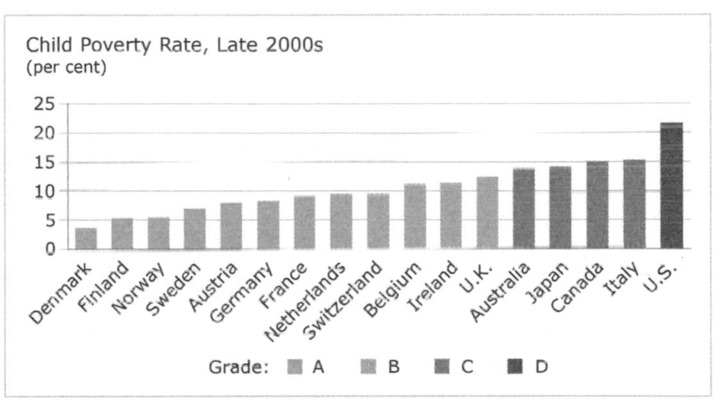

First Nations Policies

The Conservatives also cancelled the **Kelowna Accord**. The Accord represented a series of agreements between the federal government, provincial premiers, territorial leaders, and the leaders of five national Aboriginal organizations. The Accord had sought to improve the education, employment, and living conditions for Aboriginal peoples through governmental funding and other programs.

Meanwhile, programs for Aboriginal peoples continued to be piecemeal and underfunded, leaving more and more reserves unable to provide basic human services. The government continually blamed the leadership on the reserves for whatever failures were occurring, denying that there was insufficient money in the system to deal with deficiencies in infrastructure and in staffing for health, housing, education, and sanitation programs. So, for example, on Attawapiskat Reserve in northern Ontario, it was revealed in 2011 that many of the 2000 residents lived in shacks with mould on the walls, and used plastic buckets for toilets, continuously dumping waste outside. A local elementary school had been contaminated by diesel fumes that made both staff and students ill, and a privately owned diamond mine abutting the reserve paid only token royalties while contaminating local water supplies and threatening the local hunting and fishing economy. But, as Jim Foulds, MPP for Port Arthur from 1971 to 1987, explained, "With little evidence Prime Minister Stephen Harper charged that the funds that the federal government had transferred to the reserve over several years had been mismanaged. With no consultation he put the band under third party management." (Foulds, 2011)

Reserve schools, according to research conducted for the federal government, receive between $2000 and $3000 less per student than provincially-funded schools. It shows in the lack of computers and other technology in those schools and in their inability to hire and keep teachers. There are too few schools, and many of the schools need repairs. While government reports suggest that about $3 billion needs to be spent to create parity between First Nations schools and provincial schools, the Harper government in 2012 committed only $275 million to deal with the problem over a three-year period.

Similarly, while federal reports suggest that $490 million a year needs to be spent over a 10-year period to provide clean water on reserves, the federal government committed only $165 million a year for two years in its 2011-12 budget. At the same time, the Harper government closed down the National Aboriginal Health Organization, whose task was to advise the government on culturally sensitive ways of delivering health programs, to save five million dollars. It also terminated the Métis Health Funding Program. Such cuts suggest that Aboriginal people were especially targeted by the Harper government for cuts, but other groups such as the elderly were not to be spared.

Pension Reform

The 2012-13 budget comments: "To ensure that Old Age Security (OAS) remains sustainable and reflects demographic realities, the Government will adjust the age of eligibility requirement for OAS, which will begin to be implemented in 2023 and will be fully implemented in 2029." The age of eligibility for both **Old Age Security (OAS)** and the **Guaranteed Income Supplement (GIS)** was raised from 65 to 67. The government argued that because Canadians were living longer and having fewer children, the costs of providing government funding guarantees to all or most of them when they turned 65 would become prohibitive for a younger generation which was smaller in number.

Kevin Page, the parliamentary budget officer, challenged those claims. He noted that the increase in recipients resulting from the size of the Baby Boom generation would be short-term and that in the long run the OAS and GIS budgets were sustainable. But the Conservative government under Stephen Harper, having decided to reduce taxes on corporations and the wealthy and hoping to continue to cut taxes, had developed a notion of "sustainability" that required compressions in most social programs.

The government also announced plans to cut the pensions of federal workers, partly by forcing them to pay a larger share of the payments towards those pensions. But it also intended to impose "defined contribution" plans in which pensioners' earnings would be determined by the market value of the investments that the pension fund had made. Such plans would replace the existing "defined benefit" plans in which the pensioner was guaranteed a fixed annual return. In better economic times, defined benefits plans had been viewed favourably by employers because they could use the pool of funds provided by the workers for pensions and invest it in markets that often gave the employer benefits beyond the monies needed to pay the employer's pension obligations. As markets wobbled in the 1980s and afterwards, employers imposed defined-contribution pensions in which workers, not the employers themselves, were at risk for any bad investments that pension managers made on their behalves.

Efforts by the trade union movement and the NDP to double Canada Pension Plan (CPP) deductions and thereby fund a doubling in CPP payments were rejected by the Conservatives. The government sided with the private insurance industry and investment companies, which claimed that it was up to individuals and groups to make private arrangements to insure that they had enough money to live on after retirement. Increasingly, they made the same argument about how those unable to find work should deal with their plight.

Growing Income Inequality

The Gini coefficient, an international accounting figure for distribution of wealth in which 0 means perfect distribution of wealth and 1 means that one person controls all wealth. Income inequality has increased over recent decades. In the 1980s, it was as low as .281. It roes in the 1990s and has remained in the low to mid .30s since 2000 and beyond.

Employment Insurance

During the recession of 2008-10, the government reluctantly agreed to demands from the other parties in Parliament to extend **Employment Insurance (EI)** benefits for about 190,000 recipients facing a cutoff of their benefits. But with a majority in hand after the 2011 election, the Conservatives decided to limit expenditures on employment insurance while forcing more workers to leave their home regions to seek employment in regions with labour scarcities.

The 2012-13 budget document noted ominously: "Along with providing relevant and timely job information, the Government will introduce legislation to strengthen and clarify what is required of claimants who are receiving regular EI benefits and are looking for work. In the coming months, the Minister of Human Resources and Skills Development will announce fair and transparent guidelines for compliance, which take into account local labour market conditions and an individual's past history with the EI program."

The four Atlantic premiers quickly denounced what appeared to be a thinly veiled attack on seasonal workers unable to find work in their areas during the winter months. If they were to be forced to work far from home for part of the year, the concern was that they might pull up stakes altogether and leave many industries without a labour force. But the federal government's focus on cutting costs and on finding workers for expanding industries dominated its agenda not only in employment insurance policy but also in immigration policy.

Seasonal fishing industry workers in towns like this one in Nova Scotia could be affected by the 2012/2013 federal budget.

Immigration Policy

With respect to **immigration policy**, the Conservative government has made an employer's need for a particular individual or set of individuals a higher priority than family reunification. It also gave priority to wealthy individuals who might become investors in Canada over skilled tradespeople and professionals as potential immigrants.

For decades, skilled workers had been able to apply for immigration to Canada, and depending on how they scored in a "points system" meant to determine their suitability as immigrants to Canada, could hope to be allowed to immigrate. But cutbacks in immigration staff and the changing priorities regarding immigrants had led to a queue of about 280,000 individuals in the skilled workers column by 2012. Though many of those workers had been waiting for more than four years for their chance to demonstrate why they should be allowed to come to Canada, all of the applications were thrown out. Individuals would have to start all over again with their applications and there would be no priority given to those who had been in the former queue.

The government also seemed more and more to want to focus on **temporary foreign workers (TFWs)** rather than landed immigrants with a chance of becoming citizens. The Temporary Foreign Workers Program allowed employers to bring in needed workers for jobs that Canadians allegedly could not fill. Between 2004 and 2008, the number of TFWs had doubled from 125,000 to over 250,000 and included workers in the Alberta oilsands, farm labourers, restaurant help, and caregivers, among others. A survey by an immigration lawyer for the Alberta Federation of Labour demonstrated that three in five were violating either or both of the *Employment Standards Code* and the *Occupational Health and Safety Act*.

Demand for TFWs fell during the recession from 2008 to 2010 but picked up once the economy began to revive in 2011. The government announced plans to make it easier for employers to hire TFWs; in some fields, an employer would not need to make an argument that they needed to hire TFWs while in others their requests would be expedited. In 2012, the number of fields for which an employer need not make an argument for hiring TFWs was expanded, while the incentive to hire them was magnified: the Temporary Foreign Workers Program was amended to allow employers to pay a TFW only 85 percent of what a Canadian citizen or landed immigrant would receive for the same work.

Refugees from "designated countries of origin" were also declared ineligible for medical benefits while awaiting adjudication of their applications. Approved refugees, who had all received supplementary medical coverage since the 1950s, including pharmaceuticals, vision care, and dental care, would lose that coverage. Such apparent callousness to refugees reflected the Tories' focus on those deemed most likely to contribute to Canada's economic growth.

Environmental Policy

While **environmental policy** is distinct from social policy, the government's cuts to environmental programs demonstrated the overall philosophy that regarded government intervention in the economy, except when it benefited industry, as taboo. In 2012, Environment Canada's budget was cut 6 percent, while the Canadian Environmental Assessment Agency took a 40 percent cut, with most environmental assessments devolved entirely to the provinces.

Likewise, the Experimental Lakes Program, which had played a key role in Canada's efforts to cut acid rain, was terminated, likely because its scientists were studying the long-term effects of oil sands operations. The scientists associated with this program were among 2000 scientists and professionals involved in protecting the environment and the food supply who were dismissed by the government. The National Roundtable on the Economy, an advisory body which advised the government on sustainability issues, was also shut down.

The government stridently supported the Northern Gateway Pipeline Project, despite safety concerns and disregarding the fact that the pipeline, carrying bitumen from the Fort McMurray oil sands, would pass through the lands of Aboriginal peoples who opposed the project. British Columbia worried that a project, which the federal government extolled as a national project, would actually mainly benefit one province—Alberta—while leaving BC to clean up the inevitable messes once an oil spill occurred.

The Conservative government supports the idea of a pipeline that would transport bitumen from the Fort McMurray oil sands in Alberta through British Columbia.

Federal Downloading to Provinces

Not only did the program cuts affect the services that Canadians could expect from the federal government, they also had an impact on the services that they might be able to expect from their provincial governments.

In late 2011, Harper warned the premiers that when the existing Canadian Health Transfer, which increased annually by 6 percent, expired in 2014, it would be extended for only two years at that rate and then replaced for ten years by a grant that would tie health spending not to need but to the rate of productivity growth plus inflation in Canada. That was estimated to be about 4 percent per year. Increases in the Canada Social Transfer would be fixed at 3 percent, reflecting their smaller importance in Canadian political debate compared to the Health Transfer. Since the rate of inflation for 2011 was 2.9 percent, there was no guarantee that a rate of 3 percent would cover off inflation, much less increased need. The provinces would be expected to pick up the increasing tab for health expenditures. The premiers and territorial leaders estimated that the plan would cost them $36 billion over 10 years relative to what the previous ten-year plan had provided.

Social Welfare Legislation

Canada Social Transfer and Canada Health Transfer (CST/CHT): CST is a $16.3 billion (2006/07) federal block transfer to provinces and territories in support of post secondary education, Social Assistance and social services, including early childhood development and early learning and child care; CHT is a $33 billion (2006/07) transfer for healthcare

Social Union Framework Agreement (SUFA): intended to smooth out relations between levels of government, this agreement determines how programs such as medicare, social services, and education are to be funded, administered, and delivered

TABLE 3.2

Key Events in Social Welfare in the 1980s and 1990s

Canada and World Events	Social Welfare
1980s Monetarist economics Deepening poverty Globalization on the rise Conservative policies U.S. dominance in Canada Cold War tensions Third World unrest Waves of refugees Rise in militancy and popular coalitions	Major contracting out, cutbacks, workfare Period of cost control for social programs with significant spending cutbacks Increases in punitive programs Women's issues (daycare, reproductive choice, pay equity, violence) discussed but little progress Rise of food banks, role of charities increases Rise of free trade (NAFTA) *Young Offenders Act* (1984)
1990s Economic stabilization Rising militancy of First Nations, women, visible minorities, disabled, etc. Agenda: Jobs and Growth report (1994) Environmental movement strong Polarization of rich and poor Popular demands for real social justice Rising labour militancy at grassroots Rise of information and communications technology (ICT) and knowledge-based economy Labour market restructuring	Attempts to transfer costs to provinces, cities CHST and SUFA Canada Child Tax Benefit and National Child Benefit (1998) The new *Employment Insurance Act* (1995) Cuts in corporate taxes Free trade Privatization of universal programs Cuts to women's, immigrants', and Aboriginal rights and programs Move to workfare and privatization

A Brief History of the Health and Social Transfers

A Timeline

1966 The Canada Assistance Plan (CAP) was introduced, creating a cost-sharing arrangement with the provinces for Social Assistance programs. Conditions were attached to federal funding.

1977 The federal government introduced Established Programs Financing (EPF) to fund provincial educational programs.

1982 It was announced that a GNP per capita escalator would be applied to the total EPF, including both cash transfers and transfer tax points.

1983 The post-secondary education portion of EPF was limited to 6 percent and 5 percent growth for 1983/84 and 1984/85 under the "6&5" anti-inflation program.

1984 The government enacted the *Canada Health Act* (CHA). Funding was conditional on respecting the five criteria of the CHA (universality, accessibility, portability, comprehensiveness, and public administration), and provisions for withholding were introduced.

1995 Effective in 1996, EPF and CAP programs were to be replaced by a Canada Health and Social Transfer (CHST) block fund. For 1995/96, EPF growth was set at GNP—3 percent, and CAP was frozen at 1994/95 levels for all provinces. CHST was set at $26.9 billion for 1996/97 and $25.1 billion for 1997/98. CHST for 1996/97 was to be allocated among provinces in the same proportion as combined EPF and CAP entitlements for 1995/96.

1996 The federal government announced a five-year CHST funding arrangement (1998/99 to 2002/03) and provided a cash floor of $11 billion per year. For 1996/97 and 1997/98, total CHST funding was maintained at $26.9 billion and $25.1 billion respectively. Thereafter, the transfer was set to grow at GDP—2 percent, GDP—1.5 percent, and GDP—1 percent for the next three years.

1998 CHST legislation put in place a $12.5 billion cash floor beginning in 1997/98 and extending to 2002/03.

1999 The federal government announced increased CHST funding of $11.5 billion over five years, targeted only for health care.

2000 Provincial first ministers agreed on a plan for renewing health care and investing in early childhood development. The federal government committed to invest $21.1 billion of additional CHST cash, including $2.2 billion for early childhood development over five years.

2003 Early learning and child care (ELCC) was a priority, with $900 million over five years in increased federal support announced.

2004 First ministers agreed to the 10-Year Plan to Strengthen Health Care, resulting in $41.3 billion in additional federal funding to provinces and territories for health. The CHST was divided into two separate funds called the Canada Health Transfer and the Canada Social Transfer, effective April 1.

2007 Budget 2007 restructured the CST to provide equal per capita cash support to provinces and territories. Additional investments were made for post-secondary education programs for children and other social programs. Total CST cash levels were also set to grow by three percent annually. The CHT was legislated to move to equal per capita cash in 2014-15.

2009 The Budget Implementation Act 2009 legislated an adjustment to ensure that Ontario receives the same per capita CHT cash as other Equalization-receiving provinces.

2011 The Government announced in December 2011, that the CHT will continue to grow at six percent until 2016-17. From 2017-18, the CHT will grow in line with a three-year moving average of nominal GDP growth, with funding guaranteed to increase by at least three percent per year. In addition the CST will continue to grow at its current rate of three per cent annually in 2014-15 and beyond. Both the CHT and the CST will be reviewed in 2024.

In a number of other important areas, federal downloading seriously jeopardized the provinces' abilities to provide key services:

- A federal Omnibus Criminal Justice bill increased minimum mandatory sentences for many crimes, made the punishment of juvenile offenders more punitive, and otherwise increased the costs of operating and maintaining prisons. The bill reflected the government's view that crime was best dealt with through harsher punishment rather than programs aimed at improving conditions that helped to create criminals. But the increased costs of operating prisons were downloaded to the provinces.
- The government's killing of the national child care strategy, which involved federal help to provinces that increased child care spaces, made it less attractive for provinces to expand their child care programs.
- The federal government ended its participation in former federal-provincial programs for housing the poor and the elderly. It also announced its intention to shut down the Canada Mortgage and Housing Corporation.
- The failure to establish clear greenhouse gas emissions programs downloaded this responsibility to the provinces, resulting in a hodgepodge of programs across the country.
- Raising the age for granting Old Age Pensions and the Guaranteed Income Supplement to 67 meant that the provinces' tab for people requiring Social Assistance would now include people who were 65 and 66.

Conclusion

The long retreat on social programs after 1975 eroded the redistribution of wealth that Canada experienced during the welfare state period. The Conference Board of Canada reported that between 1976 and 2009, "Most gains have gone to a very small group of 'super-rich.'" And those gains were huge. "The richest Canadian 1% has almost doubled its share of the national pie—from 7% to almost 14%—over the last three decades. The average top 100 CEOs' compensation was $6.6 million in 2009, 155 times the average worker's wage. The 61 Canadian billionaires have a combined wealth of $162 billion, twice as much as the bottom 17 million Canadians." (Campbell, 2011)

While the idea of the welfare state era did not die completely, and the election of the NDP as the official opposition in the federal election of 2011 suggested that many Canadians remained unconvinced by neo-liberal arguments, Canada had in power the most determined government since the Second World War. Cutbacks carried out by earlier governments more or less came with promises that, when deficits had disappeared, and public debt was reduced, the government would look to improve social programs once again. No such implied promises have been made by the Conservative government. The intention was to shrink the role of government, permanently.

CHAPTER 3 REVIEW

LEARNING OBJECTIVES

After completing this chapter, you should be able to:

- Explain why the "post-war compromise" in relation to social welfare ended.
- Understand the significance of the debate over the "guaranteed annual income."
- Describe the "Mincome" experiment in Manitoba.
- Describe the main developments in social welfare under the Conservative governments of Brian Mulroney from 1984 to 1993.
- Explain the main developments under the Liberal governments from 1993 to 2006.
- Explain the main developments under the Conservative government from 2006 to the present.

KEY CONCEPTS IN CHAPTER

- Guaranteed Annual Income (GAI)
- Canada-U.S. Free Trade Agreement
- Canada Health and Social Transfer (CHST)
- Employment Insurance (EI)
- Environmental policy
- Goods and Services Tax (GST)
- Guaranteed Income Supplement (GIS)
- Kelowna Accord
- Immigration policy
- Mincome
- National Anti-Poverty Organization (NAPO)
- National Daycare Plan
- Neo-liberalism
- Old Age Security (OAS)
- Temporary Foreign Workers (TFW)
- Universal Child Care Benefit (UCCB)

REVIEW QUESTIONS

1. What changing circumstances caused corporations to increase pressure on governments to scale back social programs?
2. How did the Guaranteed Annual Income debate in the 1970s demonstrate the shift that was occurring in government attitudes towards social programs?
3. What contradictory policies regarding social spending were evident in the second half of the Trudeau years in government?
4. What policies, implemented first the Mulroney government and then by the Chrétien government, eroded Canada's social programs?
5. How did the change from the Canada Assistance Plan to the Canada Health and Social Transfer, and then the Canada Social Transfer, weaken the federal government's commitment to protect the poor in Canada?
6. What changes have recent Conservative governments introduced with respect to income security for Canadians?

EXPLORING SOCIAL WELFARE

1. Negotiations over federal funding for income security programs have at times been intense. Research the Canada Assistance Plan, the Canada Health and Social Transfer, and the current Canada Social Transfer and Canada Health Transfer. Write a report that discusses the major differences among these transfer methods.
2. Assess the extent to which the income security programs created during the "welfare state period" counteracted the values of the preceding period (which focused on the "deserving versus the undeserving poor" and notions of "less eligibility"). To what extent has the recent period of "welfare state erosion" reinstated some of the values associated with the earlier period.

CRITICAL THINKING

Political developments affect what happens and how things happen, by definition. If federal elections had turned out differently, what do you think might have been the effect on social welfare provision?

Do you think it makes sense for young people to get involved in politics? Can individuals actually make a difference?

WEBSITES

Caledon Institute of Social Policy
www.caledoninst.org
Established in 1992, the Caledon Institute of Social Policy is a private, non-profit organization. The Institute does not depend on government funding and is not affiliated with any political party. Its goal is to "inform and influence opinion and to foster public discussion on poverty and social policy." Caledon's high-quality research and analysis covers a broad range of social policy areas.

Canada Without Poverty
www.cwp-csp.ca
Canada Without Poverty is a non-partisan, organization dedicated to the elimination of poverty in Canada. Since its inception, the organization has been governed by people with direct, personal experience of poverty. Acting from the belief that poverty is a violation of human rights, the organization's work includes raising awareness, participating in research, and influencing public policy to prevent and alleviate poverty.

Human Resources and Skills Development Canada
www.hrsdc.gc.ca
Human Resources and Skills Development Canada (HRSDC) is a department of the Government of Canada. Its mission is to build a stronger and more competitive Canada, to support Canadians in making choices that help them live productive and rewarding lives, and to improve Canadians' quality of life.

Social Welfare Theory

Values, Ideology, and Beliefs

Canadians disagree about the nature and importance of social welfare programs. Some of the disagreement is based on common myths about the natures of social welfare programs as well as the people these programs are designed to help. However, if it were just a matter of getting to the facts, then the arguments could be settled easily.

Compounding the problem is the fact that much of the disagreement stems from factors such as differing political ideologies, values, and understandings that people hold, either implicitly or explicitly. This chapter explores some of these different types of political ideologies as well as the varying economic theory approaches.

"Practical men, who believe themselves to be quite exempt from any intellectual influences, are usually the slaves of some defunct economist."
— JOHN MAYNARD KEYNES

Why People Differ on What to Do

Government officials, academics, and welfare activists differ widely about the role social welfare should play in our society. The social policies that flow from each viewpoint determine how social welfare is delivered and how comprehensive it is.

Four Approaches

This chapter outlines four approaches to social welfare:

1. The **political ideology approach** situates social welfare in the context of economic, social, and political theory—conservative, liberal, social democratic, and socialist beliefs.
2. The **economic theory approach**, as its name implies, focuses on the influence of economic theories—Keynesian economics, monetarism, and political economy.
3. The **welfare state regimes approach** classifies welfare states according to how welfare is provided in various societies.
4. The **gender-based approach** to social welfare identifies two regime types based on an analysis of the family and unpaid labour: the male-breadwinner regime and the individual earner-carer regime.

Social welfare can also be examined within a **social inclusion** framework. Social inclusion takes a wider perspective on income security, incorporating non-monetary issues such as education, community life, access to health care, and political participation.

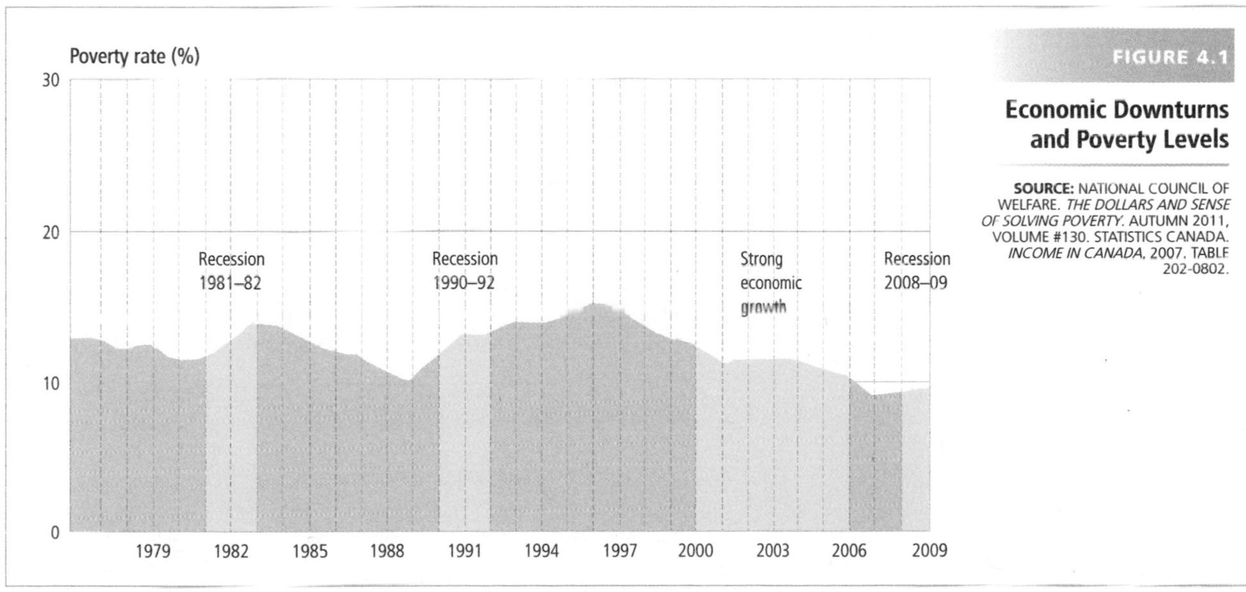

FIGURE 4.1

Economic Downturns and Poverty Levels

SOURCE: NATIONAL COUNCIL OF WELFARE. *THE DOLLARS AND SENSE OF SOLVING POVERTY.* AUTUMN 2011, VOLUME #130. STATISTICS CANADA. *INCOME IN CANADA*, 2007. TABLE 202-0802.

FIGURE 4.2

Four Approaches to Social Welfare Theory

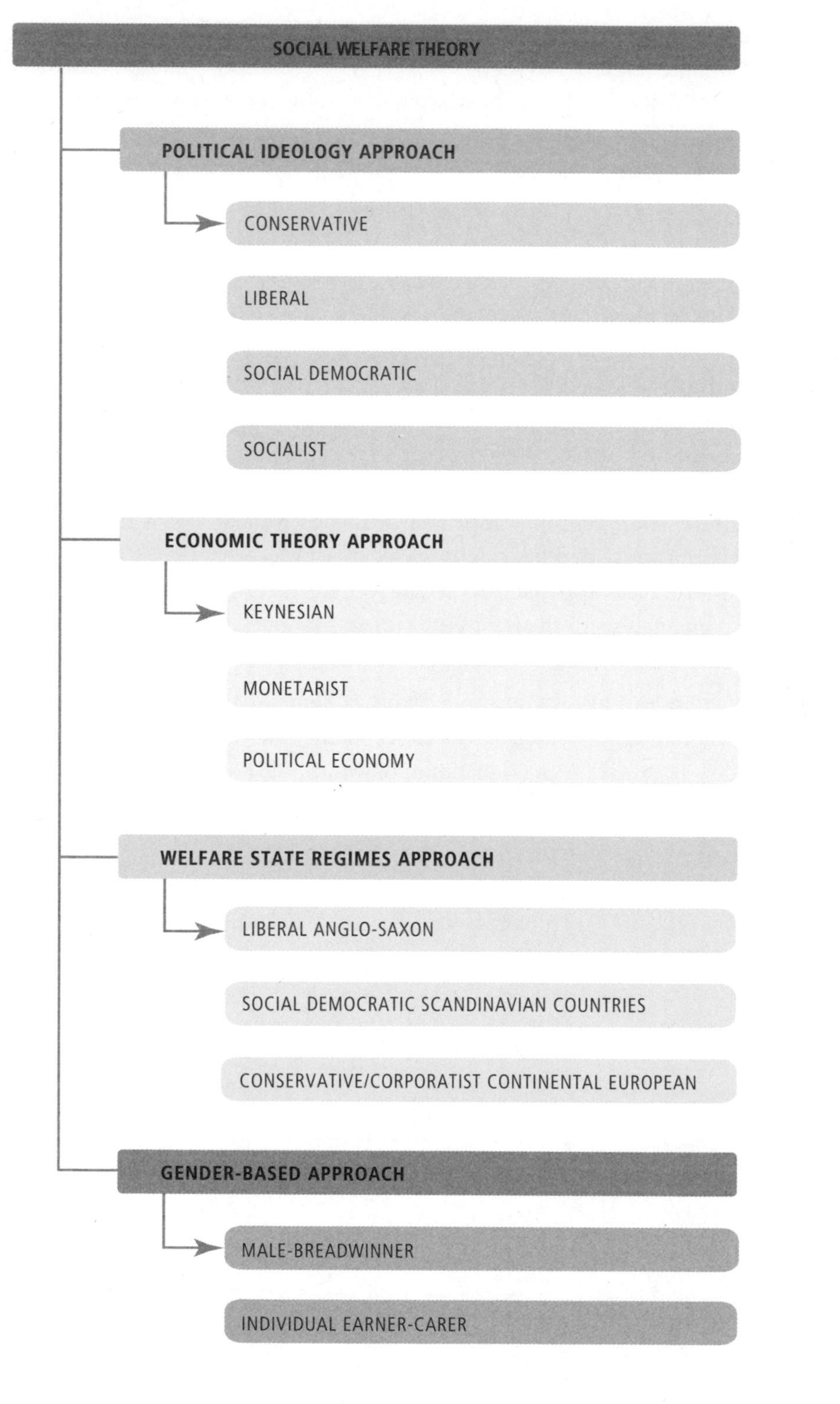

Political Ideology Approaches to Social Welfare

One way to look at the different approaches to social welfare is to examine the political ideologies underlying the approaches. These are normally divided according to conservative, liberal, social democratic, and socialist belief systems. Most people present these ideologies in terms of "right wing" or "left wing," with the former referring to the conservative ideology and the latter referring to social democratic or socialist beliefs. Liberals are often referred to as "centrists," that is, somewhere between the right and left.

Conservative Ideology (Anti-Collectivists)

Conservative ideology holds that each person knows best what he or she wants, and therefore the individual should have the maximum opportunity to pursue his or her own self-interests. According to this approach, the role of government (including interference in the free market economy) should be limited, and the role of private property and private enterprise should be paramount. Adherents to this view accept that this may lead to inequality in terms of wealth and power but see this as a necessary aspect of society.

The basic values of conservative ideology are:

- Freedom
- Individualism
- Inevitability of inequality

Conservatives believe that the best government is the one that governs the least. In other words, governments should establish the rules of the game (e.g., the pursuit of self-interest) but not be a primary actor—there should be a limited number of laws and regulations, and political institutions should not be involved in economic activity. Instead, conservatives say, the best system is a private system in which everything is bought and sold through the market.

In accordance with this underlying philosophy, conservatives believe that social welfare interferes with the labour market and creates a dependency on government. They believe that much of social welfare is misguided and creates the opposite of freedom and individualism. They believe that many social programs hinder the operation of the market and thereby limit efficiency and wealth creation. In their view, social welfare expenditures often lead to inflated demands on the public purse. Insofar as welfare is necessary, they argue that private social welfare is better—it reduces social services and targets social program benefits to only the very needy. George and Wilding refer to these people as "anti-collectivists" (1993, p. 19) due to their adherence to individualism and inequality. According to this "anti-collectivist" ideology, competition is at the root of modifying the behaviour of irrational and imperfect citizens and is the surer road to progress.

The Conservative Party of Canada

For most of the 1980s, the Progressive Conservative (PC) Party ran a majority government in Canada, but in 1993 it lost all but two of its seats. While many conservatives voted with the Liberal Party in that election, much of the conservative vote went to a new party from Western Canada, the Reform Party, which later became the Canadian Alliance. The Conservative Party of Canada began in 2003 with the merging of the Canadian Alliance and Progressive Conservative parties. While the two parties often disagreed on key policy issues, especially social issues, with the Canadian Alliance Party having a more socially conservative ideology, the two parties recognized that the right would never win an election if they continued to split the conservative vote. In 2006, the Conservative Party of Canada won a minority government under Prime Minister Stephen Harper. In 2011, Stephen Harper succeeded in winning an outright majority.

The Liberal Party of Canada

The Liberal Party of Canada embraces the values of the liberal ideology. Its philosophy is that the dignity of each individual man and woman is the cardinal principle of democratic society. The Liberals led majority governments throughout the 1990s under Jean Chrétien, but after his retirement, the party was only able to secure a minority government under Paul Martin in 2004 and was forced to call another election in 2005, losing to the Conservative Party. In 2006, the Liberal Party elected a new leader, Stéphane Dion.

After the Liberals were again defeated in the 2008 general election, Dion resigned as leader but remained in Parliament.

The Liberal Party took a drubbing in the 2011 election when it was reduced to only 34 federal seats. The party's newest leader, Michael Ignatieff, resigned after the election, forcing a new leadership race.

In April of 2013, Justin Trudeau easily won the leadership, taking over from interim leader Bob Rae.

Liberal Ideology (Reluctant Collectivists)

Not to be confused with the "Neo-Liberals" (see box on next page), this group is more difficult to define. The liberals endorse the private (free) enterprise system, but at the same time, they believe that the market needs a degree of government regulation.

The primary values of a **liberal ideology** are:

- Pragmatism
- Liberty
- Individualism
- Inevitability of inequality
- Humanism

Pragmatism means that, as a government or an individual, you do what needs to be done. Liberals have often been described as less ideological, which means they are willing to do things that suit the circumstances. There is an acceptance of the basic tenets of conservatism—such as liberty, individualism, and social inequality—but the inclusion of two other values, pragmatism and humanism, differentiate liberalism. Liberty, individualism, and social inequality are tempered by a bottom line of social justice for the poor.

The liberal view is that the government should regulate the free market to a degree and provide a minimum of income security benefits. George and Wilding refer to this group as the "reluctant collectivists" (1993, p. 44). Liberals firmly believe that governments should intervene to ensure that the economy and society remain stable and grow over time—private markets require regulation, and it is legitimate to restrict the freedom of the market in order to establish a social minimum and to preserve society by avoiding unrest.

Liberals are strong proponents of the insurance principle, particularly the idea of social insurance. They believe that the risk of unemployment and other interruptions in earnings—social contingencies—should be spread evenly across society. Everybody pays, and everyone benefits if and when they need to. At the same time, liberals advocate a social minimum program, such as basic welfare, to provide benefits for those who may not be covered by social insurance.

Liberals advocate a mix of targeted programs as well as universal programs, such as medicare, that are available to all Canadians. In many ways, the famous interwar economist John Maynard Keynes epitomized the liberal ideology. He believed in the free market economy but also that there must be a way to organize it in order to avoid unemployment and poverty. Writing in the depths of the 1930s recession, concern about unemployment was at the root of Keynes's work, and it had a lasting effect on postwar economic and social policies in the West. (Keynes's ideas are described more fully later in this chapter.)

The "Neo-Liberalism" and Its Critics

Searching for Another Way

The term Neo-Liberalism is itself not hard to define, or at least it is not hard to describe the way the term has come to be used in recent years. Nowadays, "Neo-Liberalism" essentially refers to a political philosophy that gives priority to the belief in the free operation of a market economy without much state involvement.

Most often, the label is used as a term of opprobrium, a criticism of "right-wing" political and ideological views. Those who adhere to this philosophy are more likely to refer to themselves, or be referred to by others, as Neo-Conservatives ("Neo-Cons") or simply Conservatives.

Return to Market Fundamentalism

When the term first came to prominence in the 1930s, the Neo-Liberal doctrine was associated with a "modern" interpretation of classical economics insofar as it asserted a stronger role for the state in economic affairs. That part of the "Neo" has now receded and Neo-Liberalism, at least in its boldest assertions, nowadays more closely resembles the philosophy of laissez-faire found in classical economics. In economics, the principal theorists behind the return to "market fundamentals" were Fredrick Hyak and later Milton Friedman.

The "Washington Consensus"

The thinking behind the so-called "Washington Consensus" of the 1990s (see Chapter 5), is a good representation the Neo-Liberal policies:

- Governments should not run large deficits.
- Marginal tax rates should encourage innovation and efficiency.
- International trade should be liberalized to encourage competition and growth.
- Goods and services that the government cannot provide as effectively or efficiently, such as telecommunications, should be privatized to encourage choice and competition.
- Property rights should be protected in law.
- Regulations that impede market entry and restrict competition should be eliminated.

Neo-Liberal and Its Critics

The Neo-Liberal approach is widely criticized from the left and the centre. The criticism is that there is an important role that governments can play in ameliorating the harmful effects of the market and globalization on the welfare of ordinary citizens and the harmful effects of the invisible hand of the market on national economies generally.

Indeed, some liberal and labour critics of Neo-Liberalism argue that the state is necessary to "save the market economy from itself." The Labour Party's "Third Way" under Tony Blair perhaps best captures this view. The Third Way itself was a criticism of Margaret Thatcher's staunchly pro-market policies.

Many critics of Neo-Liberalism, some "liberal" rather than socialist in outlook, refer to instances where the Neo-Liberal economic policies led to devastating results. They point in particular to the economic crisis of 2008 (the so-called "Great Recession") as definitive proof that the unfettered market does not work and leaves only devastation in its wake.

The New Democratic Party

The New Democratic Party is Canada's social democratic party, and its origin is in several labour and agrarian organizations formed before and during the Great Depression. According to their official mission statement, the New Democratic Party seeks fundamental change and seeks to focus government efforts on equality and social justice.

Under its charismatic leader, Jack Layton, the NDP significantly increased its number of MPs in Ottawa in the federal election of 2011, reaching an all-time high of 103 and becoming the official opposition. The party also made a major breakthrough for the first time in the province of Quebec (59 seats). Many see these NDP gains as a major turning point in Canadian politics.

Tragically, Jack Layton became seriously ill and died in August 2011 at the age of 61 from an undisclosed type of cancer. Thomas Mulcair was elected as the new leader of the NDP in March 2012.

Social Democratic (or New Democratic) Ideology

The ideology of the social democrat (or, in Canada, the New Democrat) is a middle ground between liberalism and full-fledged socialism ("Socialist Ideology", see next section). It is characterized by belief in the democratic process and adamant support for public social welfare programs.

The key values of **social democratic ideology** are:

- Social equality
- Social justice
- Economic freedom
- Fellowship and cooperation

To the social democrat, social inequality wastes human ability and is inefficient in its distribution of resources. In an unequal society, issues of class, gender, and race determine opportunities in the labour market. Social democrats argue for social justice on the basis that in "natural law" everybody has an equal claim to the wealth of society, and no one has a claim to immense wealth. Freedom for social democrats is not only political, it is economic—the kind of freedom that results from government intervention in maintaining a stable economy and stable employment.

Finally, social democrats believe in cooperation and the common good. This is a very different understanding of what governments should be doing, particularly in the area of social welfare. Markets must be regulated, and they believe that government enterprise has a substantial role. The economy itself should be a mixture of public and private companies, hence their notion of the "mixed economy."

The income security provisions of a social democratic government would highlight universal programs, full employment, and citizenship engagement. Full employment, the social democrats believe, should be a matter of government policy. Social democrats also support the use of national income for social programs. They feel that this kind of development represents a positive expansion of the idea of citizenship, encompassing not only voting, freedom of expression, and access to the court system, but a range of universally provided social services and income security provisions. Social democrats de-emphasize income testing and income targeting and use these only when necessary. They believe that unemployment and under-employment are a waste of the talents and capacities of citizens and a socially and economically destructive drain on our productive potential.

The social democrats feel that they are part of a greater national and international movement that seeks to challenge the dominant political agenda of market globalization and the resulting environmental, social, and economic problems.

Socialist Ideology

Karl Marx

Modern socialist ideology has its roots in the influential writings of Karl Marx (1818-1883). Marx believed that socialism was a transitional state between capitalism and communism—a transition that would come about by means of a social and political revolution.

The **socialist ideology** could be described as emphasizing:

- Freedom
- Collectivism
- Equality

Marx's saying, "From each according to their abilities, to each according to their needs," summarizes this view. In short, production should be organized according to social criteria and distributed according to need. Socialists believe that people cannot truly be free unless they are free from poverty and have the opportunity to develop as human beings—in other words, political and civil rights cannot be separate from economic and social rights.

Socialists promote a view of society where the proletariat, or the workers, own the means of production (productive enterprises) through their own state. While supporting social welfare as a way of surviving under a market economy, the socialists view state-instituted social welfare programs as mechanisms of social control—mechanisms that can foster inequality by regulating and controlling the subordinate classes.

Karl Marx (1818–83)

"Workers of the World, Unite."

Karl Marx is the most influential socialist thinker in history. He is widely known for authoring the *Communist Manifesto* with Friedrich Engels in 1848, which argued that class struggle was the basis of all history and which ends with the famous adage: "workers of the world, unite."

Marx wrote many other works on philosophy and political economy, including *Theory of Surplus Value* (1862) and *Capital* (1867–94), a work in several volumes that examined the capitalist process of production.

Marx is often misrepresented by both Marxists and non-Marxists, who focus solely on his revolutionary ideas. However, his revolutionary theories were rooted in his analysis of the capitalist mode of production, how it came to be, and how it works.

Marx predicted an end to capitalism, that the workers would rise up against this exploitative system, which was destined to have crisis after crisis and therefore could not continue. He advocated the overthrow of capitalism and the establishment of a "workers' state."

Marx is perhaps best known for his theoretical works. Lesser known is the active role he and his collaborators played in the intense political struggles and debates at the time within the emerging labour movement.

Marx's theories have inspired generations of workers to fight for reforms, and generations of politicians, theorists, and activists to fight for social equality. Many of his ideas are now part of mainstream political and economic thought, though perhaps not acknowledged as such.

Fiscal Policy Versus Monetary Policy

Fiscal policy: the use of government expenditure to manage the economy

Monetary policy: the process of controlling interest rates and the money supply to manage the economy

Economic Theory Approaches to Social Welfare

Another way to look at social welfare and social welfare systems is from the point of view of the economic theory that underlies them—the **economic theory approaches**.

Certainly, economic theory has had a profound impact on the development of social welfare programs. In fact, social policy analysts would generally agree that without the theory of Keynes himself, we would not have developed a welfare state in the postwar period. Some even refer to this period as the "Keynesian Welfare State."

The Keynesians, the monetarists, and the political economy theorists have fundamentally different views on the role of government in the social and economic sphere. They also have contrasting views on unemployment, the causes of poverty, and the impact of social spending on society. Let us look at each in more detail.

The Keynesians

Keynesian is the adjective used to describe a follower of the economic theory of the British economist John Maynard Keynes (1883–1946). Much of Keynes's important work took place during the Great Depression in the 1930s, and his best-known work is *The General Theory of Employment, Interest and Money*, published in 1936. His theories, culminating in the publication of *The General Theory*, precipitated the "Keynesian Revolution," as it came to be known. His economic theories provided the intellectual rationale for the intervention of governments in economies and the transformation of social policy. Keynes's ideas were considered radical at the time, and some mistakenly called Keynes a socialist in disguise.

Aggregate demand is the total spending of consumers, business investors, and public agencies. Keynes believed that any increase in aggregate demand in the economy would result in an even bigger increase in national income. Any increase in aggregate demand leads to more people being employed; if more people are employed, more people are spending their income, and more spending leads to even more employment. With more income there is even more spending, and so forth. Keynes referred to this as the *multiplier effect*.

Keynes argued that markets would not automatically lead to full-employment equilibrium but that the economy could settle into equilibrium at any level of unemployment. In other words, the economy could reach equilibrium even with high unemployment and impoverishment. Unemployment, according to Keynes, is a result of the overproduction of goods—that is, the previous output of products cannot be sold because those who would buy them are now unemployed and impoverished. This results in a general economic depression.

According to Keynes, classical economic policies of government non-intervention in the economy would not work. Economies need prodding, and this means active intervention by the government to manage the level of aggregate demand.

Keynes's theory appealed to economists and governments of the day because it provided an alternative to the traditional view that unemployment can and should be eliminated by a drop in wage rates. Keynes's theory was much more politically palatable. According to Keynes, the solution to unemployment was a growth in government spending, with the government purposely taking on budget deficits. Government spending to stimulate the economy was part of what Keynes called fiscal policy. Fiscal policy takes place when the government gets actively involved in the economy through spending in order to manage the level of demand.

Demand management means adjusting the level of demand to ensure that the economy arrives at full-employment equilibrium. If there is a shortfall in demand, such as in a recession (a deflationary gap), the government will need to reflate the economy. If there is an excess of demand, such as in a boom, the government will need to deflate the economy.

Keynes also believed that unemployment decreases savings, as the general population withdraws money from savings in the struggle to survive. Without savings, Keynes said, there is no investment; without investment, no employment; without employment, there is no spending; without spending, there is an overproduction of goods that cannot be sold.

Reflationary policies to boost economic activity may include:

- Increasing the level of government expenditure
- Cutting taxation to encourage spending
- Cutting interest rates to discourage saving and encourage spending
- Allowing some money supply growth

Deflationary policies to dampen the level of economic activity may include:

- Reducing the level of government expenditure
- Increasing taxation to discourage spending
- Increasing interest rates to encourage saving and discourage spending
- Reducing money supply growth

Keynesian economics had a direct and major influence on the policies of most governments, including Canada's, in the period after World War II. Governments accepted the maintenance of a high and stable level of employment as one of their primary aims and responsibilities after the war to promote maximum production and purchasing power.

John Maynard Keynes (1883–1946)

Keynes was a British economist who revolutionized economics with his classic work, *The General Theory of Employment, Interest and Money* (1936), which is regarded as one of the most influential pieces of writing in the twentieth century.

Heavily influenced by the Great Depression, Keynes argued for government intervention to help mitigate the effects of economic recessions and booms. His theory quickly and permanently changed the way the world looked at the economy and the role of government in society.

Milton Friedman

The Monetarists

The term monetarism was coined in 1968 by Karl Brunner, and it refers to the macroeconomic theories and doctrines most closely associated with University of Chicago economist Milton Friedman. Although "born" in 1956, monetarism only became a powerful intellectual force in the late 1960s and early 1970s and had to wait until the late 1970s and early 1980s to be channelled into economic policy.

The **monetarists** advocate the use of monetary policy to stimulate the economy. Monetarist theory asserts that managing the money supply and the cost and availability of credit or interest rates (monetary policy), rather than focusing on government expenditure (fiscal policy), is the key to managing the economy. According to the monetarists, the government should not stimulate the economy through government spending but should maintain a steady money supply. Market forces will then adjust inflation, unemployment, and production automatically and efficiently.

Modern monetarist theory was developed to try to explain a new economic phenomenon during this period—stagflation. Stagflation was an expression coined to try to explain two simultaneous economic problems: stagnation and inflation. Much of the monetarists' work revolved around the role of expectations in determining inflation, and a key part of their theory was the development of the expectations-augmented Phillips curve. The Phillips curve showed a trade-off between unemployment and inflation (more of one led to less of the other). Friedman argued that there were a series of different Phillips curves for each level of expected inflation, hence the theory of the expectations-augmented Phillips curve. The theory asserts that full employment is bad for the economy because it leads to inflation. If workers see other unemployed workers as ready and willing to take their jobs, they are less likely to seek wage increases. Therefore, according to monetarist theory, some unemployment is good because it helps to control inflation caused by wage demands.

Monetarist economists formulated the idea of *natural unemployment* or NAIRU (non-accelerating inflation rate of unemployment). They believe that there is a natural, acceptable, and beneficial level of unemployment. Attempts to lower unemployment below NAIRU will result in the risk of accelerating or increasing inflation. This is in sharp contrast to the Keynesian idea of full employment.

The other aspect of the theory is control of the *money supply*. Money refers to anything that serves as a generally accepted medium of exchange, a standard of value, and a means of saving or storing purchasing power. The money supply is the total quantity of money in the economy. Governments can directly affect the money supply by printing or destroying currency, bills, and coins, or indirectly by adjusting interest rates.

The key to monetarist policy is to control consumer and business spending by raising and lowering interest rates. The Bank of Canada (a government agency) controls prime interest rates. Lowering interest rates can stimulate the economy and slow money supply growth. Lower interest rates, for example, tend to increase spending (aggregate demand) and reduce savings. Conversely, higher interest rates tend to curb domestic spending. Strong demand for Canadian goods and services puts upward pressure on prices if the demand is larger than the economy's capacity.

Since the work of monetarists is mainly limited to their view of inflation, their policy is controlling the money supply to control inflation. They believe that the economy will automatically tend to the natural rate of unemployment. Rather than spending money to stimulate the economy, the government should not intervene except to reduce taxes, to maintain a steady money supply and rate of inflation, and to provide financial incentives to businesses. The end result, according to the monetarists, is more business activity and therefore more employment.

Supply-side economic policies may include:

- Reducing taxes (which leads to more business profits, creates more businesses, or creates more personal incentive to work)
- Lowering interest rates (which encourages more consumer spending and business expansion)
- Privatizing government-owned companies (which removes unfair competition in the marketplace)
- Deregulating the economy (which creates more cash flow in businesses and a more flexible business environment)
- Providing financial incentives to businesses, such as direct grants of money, low interest loans, or deferred taxes (which encourages businesses to maintain or expand production and increase employment)
- Improving education and training (which makes the workforce more occupationally mobile)
- Making people more geographically mobile by scrapping rent controls or simplifying house buying
- Reducing the power of trade unions

For the past two decades, Canadian governments have largely adhered to monetarist economics, in practice if not always in theory. Monetary policy has been emphasized over fiscal policy, taxes have been cut, and government social spending has decreased. Rather than viewing income security spending as part of demand management policy, Canadian governments have increasingly viewed it as a negative influence on work incentives. Governments at all levels have abandoned the notion of increasing spending during recessions in order to stimulate the economy.

Milton Friedman (1912–2006)

Milton Friedman, widely regarded as the leader of the "Chicago School" of monetary economics, which stresses the importance of the quantity of money as an instrument of government policy and as a determinant of business cycles and inflation, is the twentieth century's most prominent economist advocate of free markets. In his 1962 book, *Capitalism and Freedom*, Friedman argued that the role of government in a free market should be minimal. Friedman was also a supporter of many libertarian policies, such as the decriminalization of drugs and the end of the American military draft.

Political Economy Theorists

Among the economic theories of social welfare and its role in modern society, the third variant has wide-ranging political and cultural components. **Political economy theorists** believe that the operation of economic markets is tied to private concentrations of ownership and is essentially exploitative. This perspective has never been a central tenet of government social policy, but it has nevertheless shaped many of the critiques of the present-day welfare state.

Most adherents to the political economy perspective would argue that social spending serves to prop up and justify an unjust economic system. The welfare state, in their view, is one of the contradictions of capitalism: it increases well-being, particularly for the rich countries of the world, but it also frustrates the pursuit of a truly just society. It reinforces the very institutions and values that the welfare state was established to do away with.

Political economy policies attempt to decrease the inequality by transferring the ownership of main sectors of production to ordinary workers and by expanding and developing high-quality and accessible health, education, and social services. Political economy theorists would opt for nationalizing the major economic sectors and for pursuing community economic development and worker-owned and state-owned enterprises. A well-developed social infrastructure—including free education, health care, and other services—would also be central to this vision.

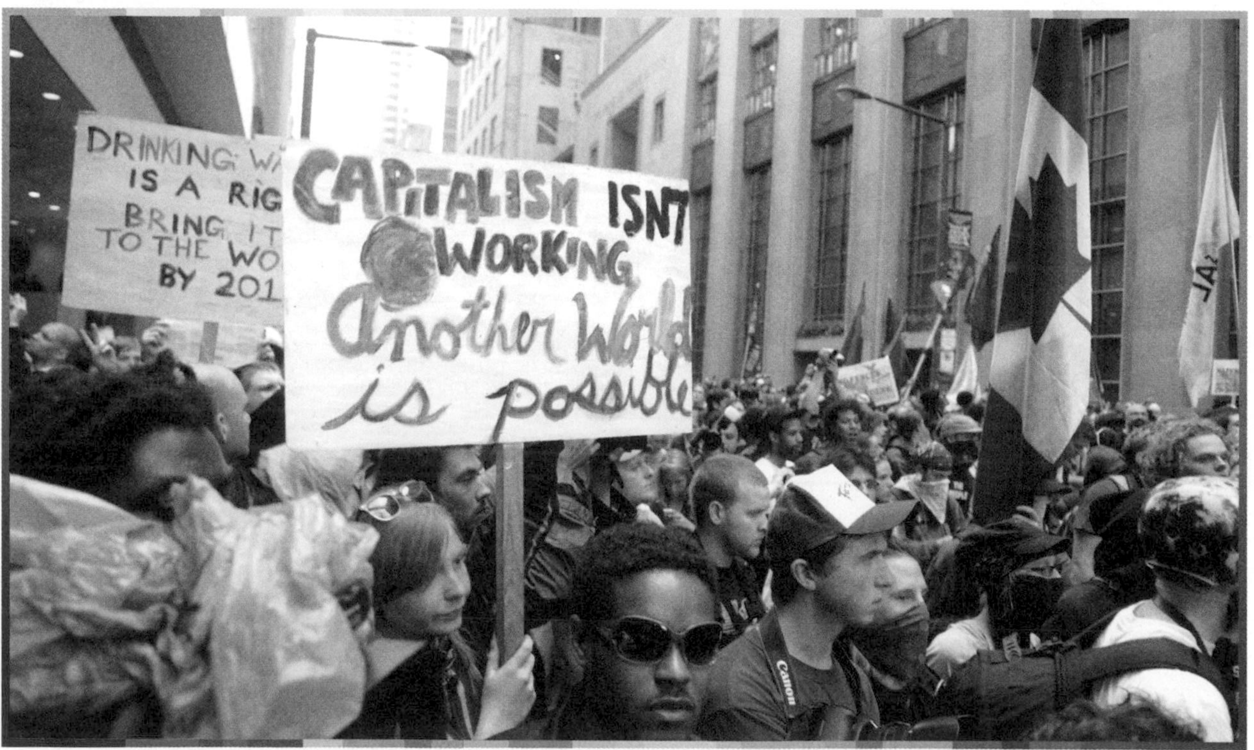

Activists, and protestors march down King Street in Toronto during the G20 summit in June 2010.

Social Citizenship

Right or Investment?

Underpinning social welfare is the idea of **social citizenship**. T.H. Marshall's lecture, "Citizenship and Social Class," has influenced social welfare thinking for decades. In it, he outlines the history of social rights, beginning first with the rights and obligations in feudal society.

In feudal society, each person had a status (noble, commoner, or serf) that accorded certain rights and duties. With the transition to capitalism, these rights were dissolved. Struggles over rights resulted in the acquisition of civil rights in the eighteenth century, political rights in the nineteenth century, and social rights in the twentieth century. This culminated in the notion of citizenship rights and the postwar mindset that underlies the welfare state.

According to Marshall, citizenship rights are best fulfilled through a welfare state and through that state's involvement in economic and social affairs. A key component of Marshall's citizenship rights are social rights, which include the right to economic welfare and security, the right to share in social heritage, and the right to live according to the standards prevailing in society.

Social Investment Framework

Social rights underpinned the development of post-World War II welfare states in Western industrialized countries, including Canada. The period was typified by a shift from a residual approach (seeing social welfare as a form of stigmatizing charity) to an institutional approach to social welfare (seeing social welfare as a right or entitlement). Social rights were placed on the agenda beside civil and political rights.

In the past few years, social policy analysts have begun to outline social welfare within a "social investment" framework—the "third way," or "removing the bar." The goal of social investment is social inclusion. It therefore requires change at multiple levels—change that goes beyond meeting basic needs.

The new approach has merit because it underlines the multidimensional aspect of social welfare. Others argue that the introduction of social investment and social inclusion may obscure the difficult issues of poverty, racism, and other forms of inequality and powerlessness.

TABLE 4.1

Comparison of Social Rights and Social Investment Frameworks

	Social Rights Framework	Social Investment Framework
Vision	Social welfare is a right of citizenship	Social welfare is achieved by giving people equal opportunity
Time Horizon	Meeting social welfare needs in the present	Improving the present to prepare for the future
Strategy	Provide income protection	Provide equal opportunity
Problem Identification	Lack of income	Multi-dimensional nature of problems
Target	Raising the bar	Removing the bar

Welfare State Regimes Approaches

- Liberal Anglo-Saxon welfare states
- Social democratic Scandinavian countries
- Conservative/corporatist continental European welfare states

Welfare State Regimes Approaches to Social Welfare

To this point, we have examined social welfare systems from the point of view of ideologies and economic theories. A third classification is based on how welfare is actually practised in different countries. The **welfare state regimes approach** classifies nations or welfare state regimes according to established patterns of income security provision in these countries.

Building on the work of Richard Titmuss (1958), Gøsta Esping-Anderson (1999) has identified three types of social welfare state: (1) liberal Anglo-Saxon welfare states, (2) social democratic Scandinavian countries, and (3) conservative/corporatist continental European welfare states. It is important to point out that these were conceived as "ideal types" and that no welfare state exists in this pure sense.

Esping-Anderson classifies welfare states according to three criteria: (1) the public/private sector mix, (2) the extent of decommodification of citizens, and (3) the extent of inequality reduction or reinforcement. Decommodification occurs when a social program is delivered as a matter of right and when a person can maintain a livelihood without reliance on the market. People are decommodified, so to speak, when, due to the existence of income security programs, they do not need to rely on selling their labour as a commodity to survive.

Many social welfare theoreticians have added to or changed the Esping-Anderson dimension. In particular, many feminist scholars have focused on gender-relevant dimensions, and others have examined racial dimensions. Fiona Williams, a British social welfare scholar, for example, has pointed out how the discipline of social welfare as a whole has marginalized gender and race. She developed a framework that accounts for patriarchy, imperialism, and the international division of labour (Williams, 1989).

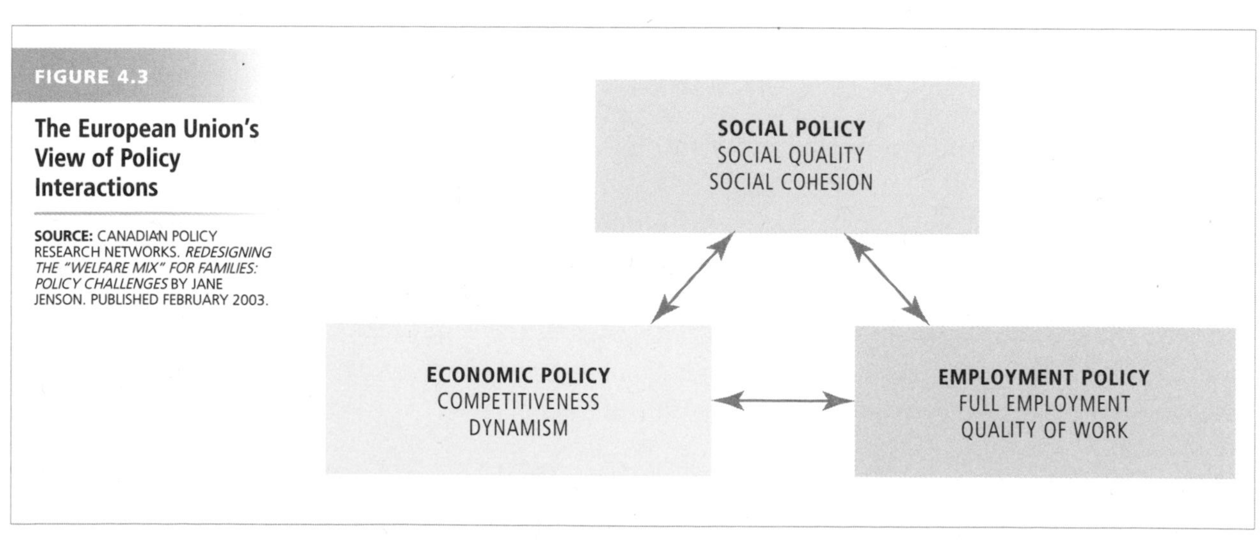

FIGURE 4.3

The European Union's View of Policy Interactions

SOURCE: CANADIAN POLICY RESEARCH NETWORKS. *REDESIGNING THE "WELFARE MIX" FOR FAMILIES: POLICY CHALLENGES* BY JANE JENSON. PUBLISHED FEBRUARY 2003.

Liberal Anglo-Saxon Welfare States

Esping-Anderson's **Liberal Anglo-Saxon Welfare Regimes** include countries such as Canada, the United States, Australia, the United Kingdom, and Ireland. He used the term *liberal* to refer to the classical liberalism that is concerned with laissez-faire economics and minimal government interference (which is different from the use of the term *liberal* as a political ideology). Welfare regimes of this type emphasize minimal benefits in order to discourage people from choosing public assistance instead of work. Overall, benefits are residual, available only as a last resort and only to those in need. Income security programs have low benefit levels and are limited, needs-based, and selective. Private sector delivery of programs is encouraged.

The central principles of this model are privatization and the targeting of benefits. In many of the countries with this model, the desire to reduce taxation and expenditures is paramount. Over the past decade, these aspects of this model have taken hold in many countries. Middle classes have opted for an increased level of private welfare, and the government has sought to shift benefits to the most needy. In addition, there has been increased concern with ensuring that work incentives are strong.

Social Democratic Welfare Regimes

The **Social Democratic Welfare Regimes** model is focused on optimum conditions for the citizen as a right. It resembles an institutional approach to social welfare. Full employment, the elimination of poverty, access to high-quality and well-paying jobs, comprehensive health care, a safe working environment, and a decent retirement are basic rights that are guaranteed (Olsen, 2002, p. 75). This model emphasizes citizenship rights and the creation of a universal and comprehensive system of social benefits. Despite significant economic problems in the 1990s in Sweden and Finland, Scandinavian countries have fundamentally maintained, and even strengthened, their welfare states during the last decade.

The principle underlying this model is that benefits should be provided to all, regardless of their employment or family situation. Government authorities provide most of the income security benefits, and churches or charities fulfill a limited role. Intertwined with these comprehensive and universal income security benefits is a wide range of health and social services. These are either free or subsidized.

Such programs, however, are expensive and require a high level of personal and corporate taxation to function. The combination of high taxes and generous benefits results in the redistribution of income from high-income earners to low-income earners. Because of these programs, citizens of these countries are more "decommodified" than citizens in other advanced capitalist nations. In other words, they do not need to rely on income from the labour market to survive.

Conservative/Corporatist Continental European Welfare States

Germany, Austria, and France typify the **Conservative/Corporatist Continental Welfare States** model. Esping-Anderson has referred to these welfare states as "conservative" or "corporatist" at different times in his writing. Both terms refer to the basic principles of authority, tradition, and resistance to change.

Welfare states following this model provide income maintenance to uphold the status quo and maintain income difference between classes. They are less concerned with eradicating poverty or creating a more egalitarian society. Employment-linked social insurance programs financed through employee contributions are directed at income maintenance and do not seek to redistribute income between the classes. Germany provided the ideas behind the first legislation on social insurance, according to which social benefits are given only to those who have been in the labour market. This evolved into the conservative or corporatist model, which emphasizes the protection of people with stable, lifelong employment. People with a tenuous connection to the labour market, such as workers with irregular careers, face difficulties in being eligible for benefits.

Continental welfare states have developed a variety of family support and income security programs. However, this approach often provides little leeway for addressing the specific concerns of women, immigrants, and racial minorities.

In the traditional patriarchal family, women were responsible for child care. Within the individual earner-carer regime, men are just as likely to be caregivers and therefore have access to social welfare programs previously reserved for women.

Social Inequality and Social Well-Being

The Spirit Level

In their book, *The Spirit Level: Why More Equal Societies Almost Always Do Better* (2009), Richard Wilkinson and Kate Pickett describe in detail how greater equality contributes to the health and well-being of societies. Their research links inequality to a wide range of social issues, including mental and physical health, drug use, obesity, educational performance, teenage births, violence, imprisonment, and social mobility.

Their conclusion is that societies with the greatest inequalities in income and wealth are those most afflicted by serious social ills. The greater the inequalities, the greater the stress on people all along the income spectrum, and the worse the outcomes are for a society overall, and not just for those at the bottom of the income ladder.

Furthermore, more wealth does not, in itself, tackle social ills. The United States is an example—it is one of the wealthiest countries, but it has a very great distance between the top and bottom of the income ladder.

The US also has much higher rates of crime, violence, teen births, health problems, and poverty than less wealthy nations.

Most other wealthy nations, including the Nordic countries, France, Germany, and Japan, are generally closer together with less inequality and fewer social ills. Canada falls in the middle, which suggests that we are doing some things well.

A number of recent studies of inequality, however, indicate that we are slipping in some areas. For example, recent figures on child material wellbeing illustrate that the Canadian situation is actually regressing rather than improving. The same is true for recent immigrants and seniors.

For well-being to improve significantly in Canada, it looks like we will need to both learn from and build on the policies that have been able to achieve good outcomes elsewhere—namely, that have found a way to reduce inequality levels.

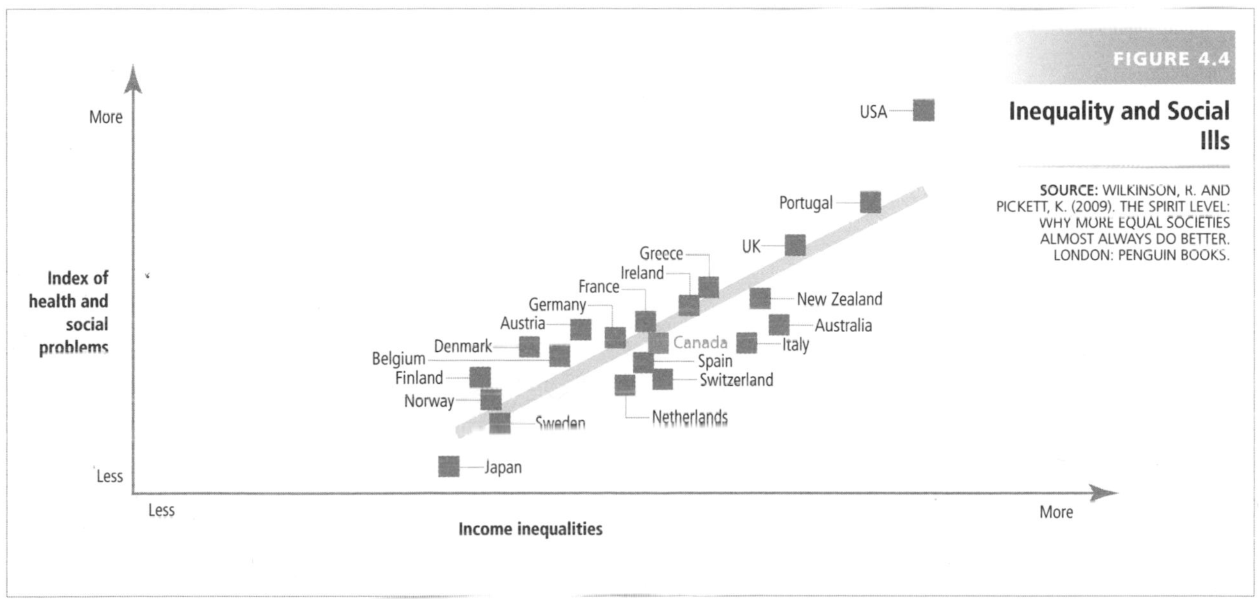

FIGURE 4.4

Inequality and Social Ills

SOURCE: WILKINSON, R. AND PICKETT, K. (2009). THE SPIRIT LEVEL: WHY MORE EQUAL SOCIETIES ALMOST ALWAYS DO BETTER. LONDON: PENGUIN BOOKS.

Gender-Based Approach to Welfare State Regimes

Male-breadwinner regimes
Individual earner-carer regimes

Gender-Based Approaches to Social Welfare

Patricia Evans and Gerda Wekerle, two Canadian social work scholars, view Esping-Anderson's "welfare state regimes" framework as flawed insofar as it only considers the state-market dimension in meeting needs and subsumes women within the family. According to Evans and Wekerle, this approach ignores the distribution of labour within the household and between the family and state (1997, p. 11). Many other feminist scholars have developed theories (or variations) that take into account the very specific and unique contexts in which women, children, and families find themselves.

Many aspects of social welfare policy and delivery can and certainly should be examined in conjunction with gender concerns. In particular, there needs to be a recognition that the demands of the family and the unpaid work of women leads to stratification along gender lines. The definition of decommodification can be refashioned to include the capacity of women to maintain an autonomous household, free from the dictates of the market.

Social welfare theorists can also appreciate Sheila Neysmith's discussion of how the separation of family life, the labour market, and state responsibilities into separate domains has hampered social welfare advancement. Her analysis demonstrates that public and private labour—or production and reproduction—need to be connected to achieve a complete understanding of the social welfare system (Neysmith, 1991).

Diane Sainsbury of the University of Stockholm, a prominent author in gender and welfare studies, has outlined a gender approach to welfare state regimes. Her model is different from Esping-Anderson's in that it distinguishes regimes on the basis of ideologies that describe actual or preferred relations between men and women, principles of entitlement, and notions of caring. She distinguishes between the male-breadwinner regime and the individual earner-carer regime.

Male-Breadwinner Regimes

Male-breadwinner regimes are characterized by an ideology of male privilege based on a division of labour between the sexes that results in unequal benefit entitlements (Sainsbury, 1999, p. 77). Men are seen as the family providers and thereby are entitled to benefits based on their labour force participation or their position as "head of the household." In such regimes, marriage is the preferred family form. Women are viewed primarily as wives and mothers and receive their entitlements as such—their primary role is to care for their husbands and children in the form of unpaid work. There is little state involvement in caregiving. Unmarried mothers and divorced women fall outside the confines of the "normal" policies of this type of regime.

Individual Earner-Carer Regimes

The **individual earner-carer regimes** approach is in sharp contrast to the male-breadwinner regimes approach. The individual earner-carer regimes approach focuses on the shared roles between men and women leading to equal rights (Sainsbury, 1999, p. 79).

In this model, both sexes have equal rights to social entitlements as earners and caregivers. Paid work in the labour market and unpaid caregiving work have the same benefit entitlements, thereby neutralizing gender differentiation with respect to social rights. Both men and women are seen as equals. The state plays a central role in the provision of services and payments, whether it be caring for children, elderly relatives, the sick, or people with disabilities.

The gender-based approach to welfare state regimes provides a useful lens for analyzing social welfare. This approach focuses on how entitlements are awarded and how these are often based on an ideology that supports a gendered division of labour, with men as breadwinners and women as caregivers. This approach goes beyond looking at relations in the market and takes into account relations within the family and relations between men and women. "Gender-equality friendly policies do not support the traditional division of labor between women and men," note Kerstin Sörensen and Christina Bergqvist. "On the contrary, they encourage women as well as men to abandon their traditional roles and identities by, for example, encouraging women's labor market participation and men's care work" (Sörensen & Bergqvist, 2002).

The increasing economic independence of women has weakened the traditional patriarchal division of labour with in the family and put personal relationships on a more equal footing.

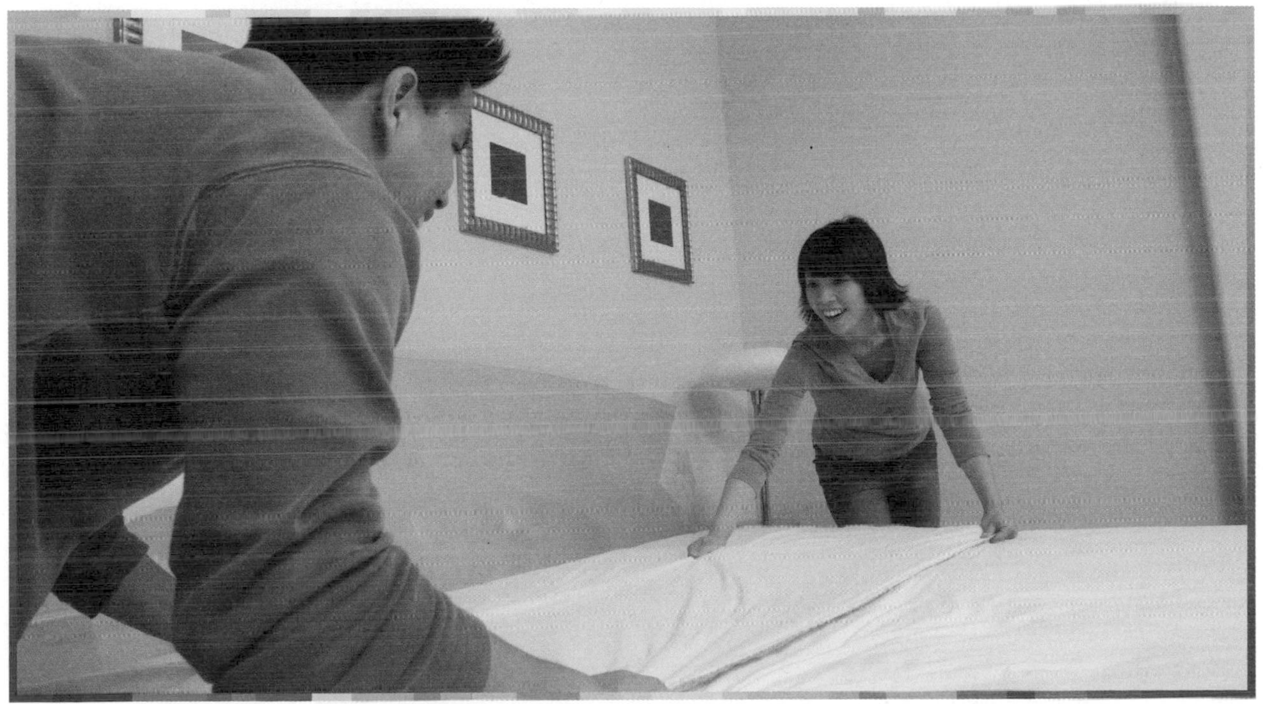

Social Investment Bonds?

Debate

An Investment in the Public Good

EDITORIAL, *THE GLOBE AND MAIL*, MAY 8, 2013

The idea of investing in protecting children at risk, or housing the homeless. Or educating Aboriginal youth is a tough one to wrap one's mind around. It sounds a bit like capitalism gone haywire. Or, a cynic would say, like government trying to offload its costs and responsibilities.

But the social finance program announced this week by the Canadian government appears to be offloading in the best sense. It is an attempt to create partnerships among government, non-profit or charitable groups and the private sector, thereby unlocking the creativity and entrepreneurship in each. Maybe it is capitalism gone haywire, but so what if it works?

The 15 social-impact projects announced by Human Resources Minister Diane Finley sound promising. Boys and Girls Clubs of Canada would run a program to introduce young people to the skilled trades. The government expects to save money because fewer people will be dependent on the state; success will be measured by the numbers who enter the trades. Pathways to Education would work with Aboriginal teens to help them reach postsecondary school. The Social Finance for Supportive Housing Working Group would create 10,000 homes for people with mental illness. JVS Toronto would work with young people at risk of conflict with the law.

In a social-impact bond, an investor supports a social service and makes a profit—paid by government—if the service meets its goals. The investor bears the risk. It is a staple of British Prime Minister David Cameron's Big Society approach to community issues. One British program set up a five-year bond for children in care that funded intensive supports for 380 teens and their families. If 100 children are diverted from care, investors received the pre-arranged return. The United States and Australia are also moving ahead with similar programs.

There is no evidence that social finance is meant to replace traditional social services. It's an experiment in how new financial tools can supplement existing social programs, relieving government of some of the cost burden and developing more effective ways of doing things. Some may roll their eyes at the new buzzword—social innovation—but if it brings in new sources of money, new incentives and new players, it deserves a chance.

Private Money, Public Programs? There Will Always Be Strings

SHERRI TORJMAN, THE CALEDON INSTITUTE

In response to the perpetual shortage of funding for a wide range of social needs, Ottawa just announced its commitment to the use of social impact bonds.

In theory, the announcement is a positive development in Canada, which has fallen behind the rest of the world in the creative use of capital for social purposes. In practice, its use will have to be carefully monitored.

The emerging sphere of social finance opens many new fiscal doors. Social finance is a term that refers to a range of instruments, including social impact bonds, which blend public and private money to tackle tough social problems.

Social impact bonds were first introduced in Britain in 2010 to finance a project at a prison for short-term male offenders. Its purpose was to help prevent recidivism among former prisoners.

Under the social impact bond model, the private sector or a social organization finances and delivers services under contract to the government against a bond issued by that government. The private sector or social agency promises to accomplish certain objectives within a designated time frame.

If successful, the private sector or social agency cashes in the bond and receives reimbursement of its costs plus a rate of return. Social impact bonds are therefore not bonds in the traditional sense of the term, but a form of public-private partnership.

The potential problem with social impact bonds is not the fact that they bring private capital into the social equation—it's the obsession with quantifiable performance outcomes.

There is nothing wrong with achieving outcomes; that's what social investments are all about. The potential problem is the unreasonable pressure that the funding formula can create to achieve outcomes that may not be attainable within the time frame set out to provide investors with the return they expect.

The requirement to achieve the numbers can inadvertently skew an entire program. For example, in order to attain designated quotas (and get paid), employment training programs often accept participants with few employment barriers. The programs are essentially "creaming"—selecting the candidates most likely to succeed. Individuals who need more assistance or more time to achieve the designated employment goals may fall by the wayside.

Another question arises from the perspective underlying this approach. Whose benefits will they seek to achieve? Typically, the lens of success is created by the funding body—in this case, governments. But sometimes, the outcomes governments desire may not produce positive outcomes for the participants. Take, for instance, welfare reform.

There is no shortage of government programs that seek to move recipients off welfare. It is assumed that if they leave the program, they will have escaped poverty and their lives will improve.

The reality is that many people are worse off than before. They may have gained paid work but often get a job that pays only minimum wage or that offers only part-time work. In fact, many households are worse off leaving welfare for work because they may lose access to a range of benefits—child care, subsidized housing, health services, medications, disability supports—that may be worth hundreds or even thousands of dollars a year.

It's not a bad thing to help move recipients off welfare. But it is incorrect to assume that paid work alone will improve their lives. There needs to be a range of associated reforms, including health and dental care, improved earnings supplements and lower income taxes for these households. Any initiative supported by social impact bonds must take into account the broader context and, where possible, incorporate related reforms.

Finally, positive outcomes in the social field often take several years to achieve—sometimes even a generation. Social impact bonds must allow sufficient time for achieving the stated objectives. Private investors will have to be patient with their capital if these bonds are to become serious instruments to support real social change.

The federal government needs to proceed with caution when it comes to social impact bonds. Money always comes with strings. It will be important to ensure that these strings don't strangle.

Canadian Centre for Policy Alternatives (CCPA)

http://www.policyalternatives.ca/

The CCPA is a non-profit research organization founded in 1980 to promote research on economic and social policy issues from a progressive point of view. Under the heading "research and publications" the CCPA has a wide variety of reports on relevant social welfare issues, such as the report entitled *The Rich and the Rest of Us*.

Social Inclusion Approach to Welfare

The concept of **social inclusion** emerged in Europe during the 1980s as a means of addressing growing social divides, and it is now a central topic in Canadian social policy discussions. The concept challenges social welfare scholars to consider the non-economic aspects of society that lead to social disadvantages or social exclusion, such as education, community life, health care access, and political participation. The concept is often referred to as being about "removing the bar" rather than "raising the bar"—the need to remove barriers and sources of exclusion.

Beyond Income

In a market-based economy, income and other material resources are key to facilitating opportunities or capacities. The social inclusion perspective challenges us to move beyond income and material resources to consider other items that affect well-being and human development. For example, the United Nations' well-known Human Development Index (HDI), on which Canada has consistently scored high, measures more than just income. The index also includes life expectancy, adult literacy, and the student enrollment ratio. It measures items that shape future opportunities, such as basic and advanced education and health, taking a social inclusion viewpoint on inequality.

Mitchell and Shillington, two Canadian social policy researchers, define *social inclusion* as a process of investments and actions that will ensure that all children and families are able to participate as valued, respected, and contributing members of society by closing the physical, social, and economic distances that separate people (2002, p. 6). Social welfare programs organized according to this perspective would go beyond providing material or income benefits. They would also include (1) developing the capacities of people to earn their own income; (2) the direct participation of people in the decisions that affect them; (3) respecting and valuing of differences; and (4) reducing the social and physical distance between people (i.e., mixed-income neighbourhoods and integrated classrooms).

Overall, the concept of social inclusion as a solid framework for social welfare is still a work in progress. Some scholars and social welfare activists have cautioned that it may be too vague a concept, thereby letting governments off the hook concerning issues such as poverty, racism, and historical exclusionary practices such as the colonization of First Nations. This book focuses on welfare programs that further income security, one of the pillars of social inclusion. But this is not meant to minimize other aspects of social inclusion. These other aspects are the basic building blocks for survival, and they develop opportunities and the capacities of individual members of society. All of these work together to form social inclusion.

Conclusion

There are different ways to categorize the diverse ideas that underpin social welfare and income security provision in Canada. This chapter provided a brief overview of some of the main approaches. Clearly, no one approach can capture all the aspects of the welfare state—but together they can help us understand how it works.

This chapter examined four basic approaches to social welfare: the *political ideology* approach (conservative, liberal, social democratic, and socialist); the *economic theory* approach (Keynesian economics, monetarism, and political economy); the *welfare state regimes* approach (Liberal Anglo-Saxon, Social Democratic, and Conservative/Corporatist); and the *gender-based* approach (male-breadwinner regimes and individual earner-carer regimes). A final model or approach—*social inclusion*—has gained support in recent years. This approach underscores the importance of non-economic factors—education, community, health, and political participation—in the welfare of citizens.

While general approaches and models can provide a framework for understanding and critiquing social welfare policy, it is also important to keep sight of the particular government policies and programs in force at any given time, which may or may not fall neatly into any one category. The chapters that follow examine income security in the context of addressing each of the following areas: poverty, employment, the rights of women, children and families, immigration and immigration reform, the plight of First Nations, Métis, and Inuit peoples in Canada, the rights of persons with disabilities, the elderly and retired, and the overall problem of social welfare in an era of globalization.

When reading these chapters, keep in mind that behind these social programs may well be the ideas of "some dead economist" (to repeat Keynes's words quoted at the beginning of this chapter). In other words, try wherever possible to identify the social welfare theory that stands in the background. As you move through these chapters, draw upon some of the material presented in this chapter to see where the ideas and debates that guide these programs may have originated.

CHAPTER 4 REVIEW

LEARNING OBJECTIVES

After completing this chapter, you should be able to:

- Describe the influence of Keynesian economics on the development of social welfare.
- Describe the influence of monetarist ideas on the development of social welfare.
- Describe the influence of socialist ideology on the development of social welfare.
- Explain what is meant by the term "neo-liberals."
- Explain the idea of "social citizenship" as a right and investment.
- Describe the "political ideologies," "economic theories," "welfare state regimes, and "gender-based" approaches to welfare.
- Understand what is meant by the term "social inclusion" in relation to social welfare.

KEY CONCEPTS

- Conservative ideology (anti-collectivist)
- Conservative/corporatist continental welfare states
- Economic theory approaches
- Gender-based approaches to social welfare
- Individual earner-carer regimes
- Keynesians
- Liberal ideology (reluctant collectivist)
- Liberal Anglo-Saxon welfare regimes
- Male-breadwinner regimes
- Monetarists
- Neo-liberalism
- Political economy theorists
- Political ideology approaches
- Social citizenship
- Social democratic ideology
- Social democratic welfare regimes
- Social inclusion
- Socialist ideology
- Welfare state regimes approaches

REVIEW QUESTIONS

1. What are the four approaches to social welfare, and how do they differ?
2. What is an ideology? What political ideologies exist in Canada, and how do they differ in their views of social welfare?
3. Keynesianism and monetarism are two different approaches to economic management. Define each approach and discuss two ways in which the two approaches differ.
4. Explain the political economy perspective, and discuss how its policies would differ from the other two economic approaches.
5. What are the welfare state regime types? Discuss two differences between them.
6. What dimensions are added by the gender-based approach to welfare state regimes? Based on this, what two types of welfare state regimes emerge?

EXPLORING SOCIAL WELFARE

1. Each political party in Canada has a unique platform in relation to social welfare and income security. Pick one federal or provincial political party, and on its website, locate its views on social welfare in its platform. How does the party's platform with regard to social welfare relate to the political ideologies discussed in this chapter?
2. Social welfare debates are greatly influenced by economic theory. Research the issue of "minimum wage" and discuss the economic arguments for and against raising it in the context of the different economic approaches to welfare.

CRITICAL THINKING

Why do you think there are so many different ways to conceptualize something so seemingly straightforward as "social welfare?"

Reflect on the following statement: "The role of social workers is to do social work, not to change society." How does this statement relate to ideology?

WEBSITES

Canadian Association of Social Workers (CASW)
www.casw-acts.ca
Founded in 1926, CASW is the national voice for Canadian social workers. It produces and distributes timely information for its members and initiates and sponsors special projects on their behalf. CASW representatives serve on coalitions and participate on a host of affiliated, nationwide committees. A Code of Ethics for the profession, a series of national policy and position papers, research projects, reports, and selected books are also available from CASW.

Canadian Association for Social Work Education (CASWE)
www.caswe-acfts.ca
CASWE-ACFTS is a voluntary national charitable association of university faculties, schools, and departments offering professional education in social work at the undergraduate, graduate, and post-graduate levels. Their website offers research reports, news, and school information.

International Council on Social Welfare (ICSW)
www.icsw.org
The International Council on Social Welfare (ICSW) was founded in Paris in 1928 under the original name of International Conference of Social Work. The Council gathers and disseminates information, undertakes research and analysis, convenes seminars and conferences, draws on grassroots experiences, strengthens non-governmental organizations, develops policy proposals, engages in public advocacy, and works with policy-makers and administrators in government and elsewhere. The International Council on Social Welfare represents national and local organizations in more than 70 countries throughout the world.

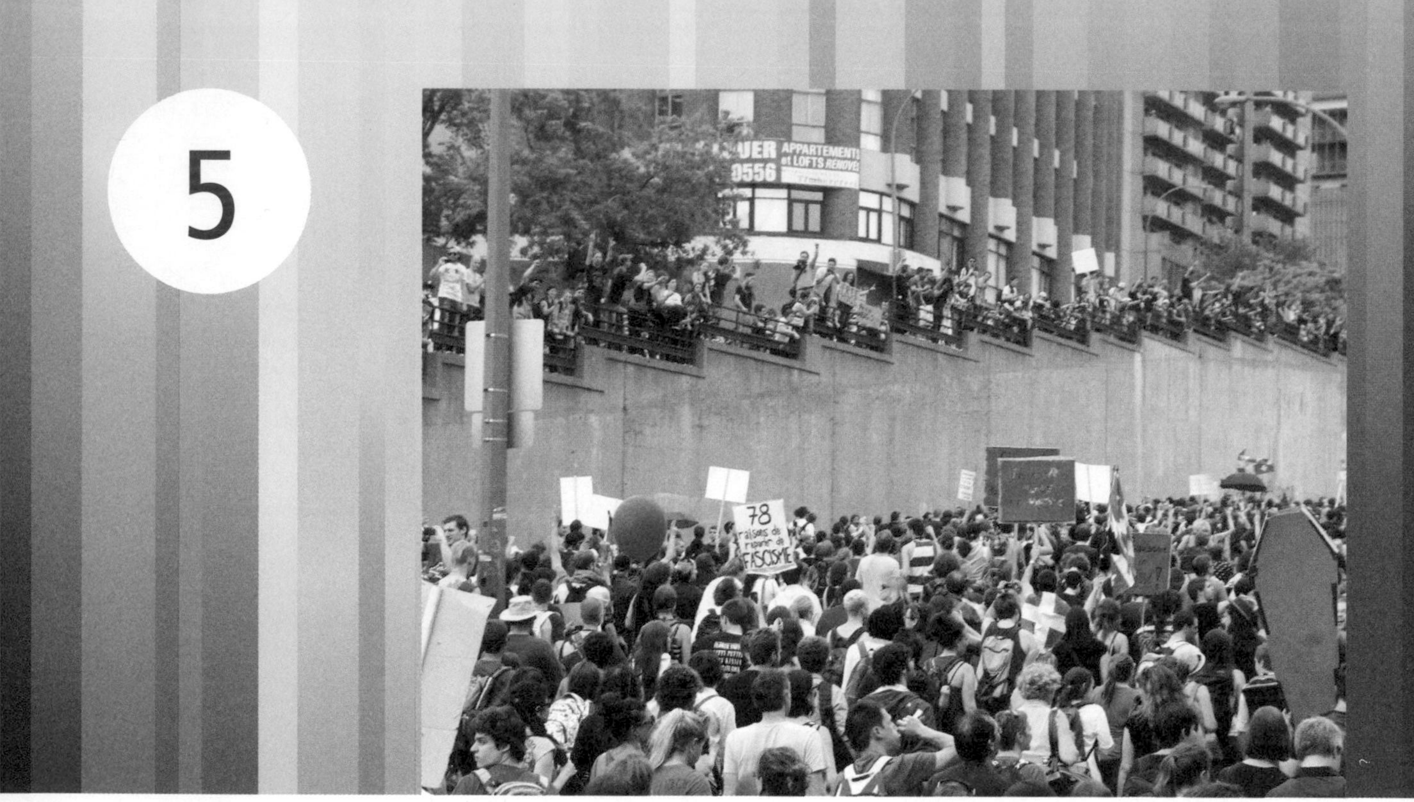

5

Making Social Policy in Canada

How Things Get Done ... or Not Done

If social workers, or Canadian citizens more generally, wish to affect social policy, it may be useful to examine concretely the way in which policy is made. The key question is how groups of ordinary citizens acting together can intervene in the policy-making process and make a difference to the kinds of social policies that are adopted by federal, provincial, and municipal bodies.

The answer to the question "How do things get done (or not get done?" is complicated. This chapter attempts to answer the question by examining the division of powers between the various levels of government and then looking at the different stages of policy development and the way in which policy is made in real time.

"People must know the past to understand the present, and to face the future."

— NELLIE McCLUNG (1873–1951), CANADIAN WRITER AND EARLY WOMEN'S RIGHTS ACTIVIST

Federal, Provincial, Territorial, and Municipal Responsibilities

Policy-making in Canada takes place under a constitution that spells out the responsibilities of the federal and provincial governments. In the realm of social policy, the division is messy and not always straightforward.

The **Constitution Act, 1867** gives the provinces the responsibility for making social policy in most areas, reflecting the nineteenth century view that these are largely of a local and private nature. The federal government's main social policy powers are employment insurance, pensions (shared with the provinces), and Aboriginal peoples living on reserves. At times, it has used other powers to affect social policy, such as in relation to immigration, or the labour market and employment to influence training, parental leave, and compassionate care policy. For example, the government justified extending parental benefits in the early 2000s under its employment insurance powers.

This exact division of powers and responsibilities is therefore a little confusing. After all, is there not a *Canada Health Act*, placing conditions on the delivery of health services in provinces, not to mention federal housing policy? Doesn't the federal government deliver tax benefits related to child care or disability supports? The reason for this confusion is that, over time, practice has muddied the formal constitutional division.

The provincial Premiers share a laugh at a typical meeting of the annual Council of the Federation.

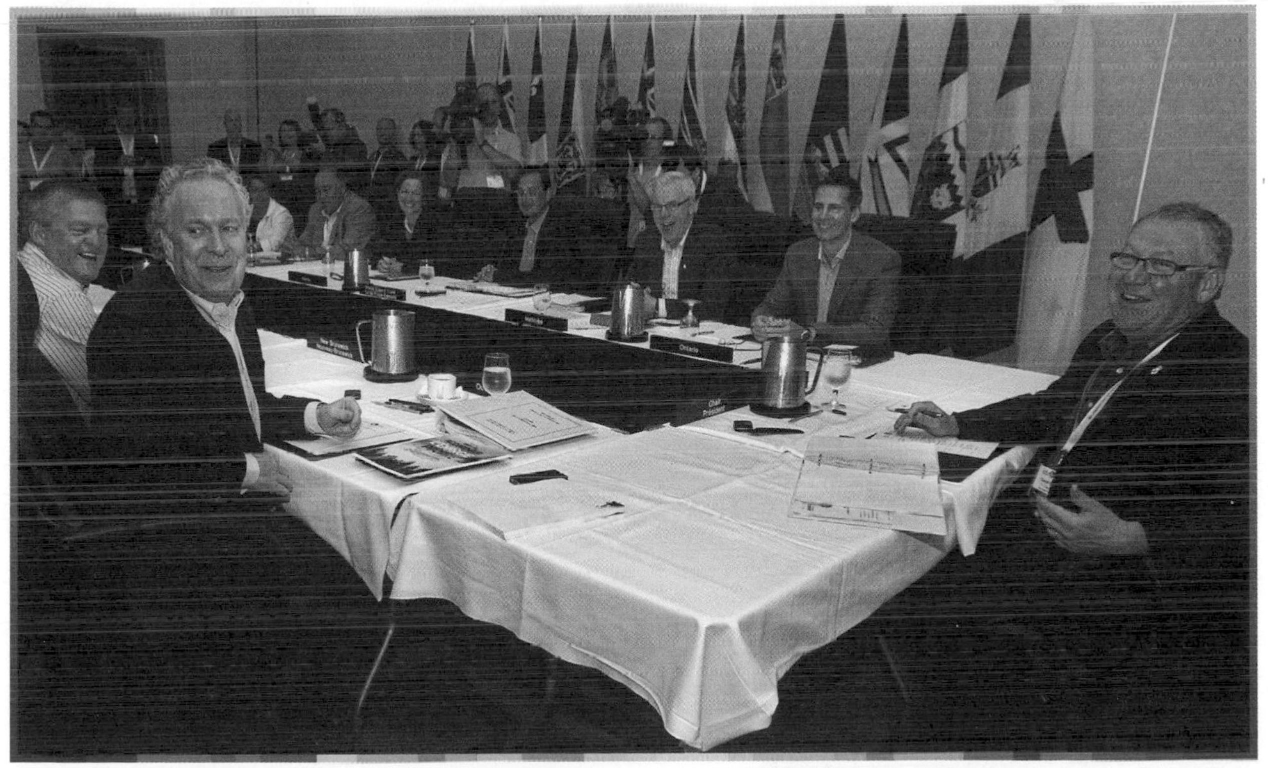

Canada Assistance Plan

Under the **Canada Assistance Plan** of 1966, the federal government committed to paying half the cost of provincial Social Assistance, provided provinces put in place a social assistance system that provided financial assistance on the basis of need, that it not limit eligibility on the basis of residency (i.e., it cannot discriminate against newcomers to the province or to Canada), and that an appeals system be put into place.

Federal Spending Power

Two important practices have enabled the federal government to impinge on the jurisdictions of the provinces. They are both based on the idea of the **federal spending power**. These involve (1) transfers to provinces and (2) transfers to individuals.

Federal "spending power" refers to the ability of the federal government to spend money outside of its immediate jurisdiction. It was on the basis that the federal government got involved in a wide range of policies after the Second World War, including social assistance, housing, social services, and disability programming. It was able to do so by offering to pay a percentage of the cost of a provincial program in a given area (e.g. vocational rehabilitation for people with disabilities or child care services for individuals on Social Assistance), provided that the provincial program met certain "national standards."

Federal/Provincial Negotiations

Indeed, federal spending power was the engine driving the post-1945 Canadian welfare state. What provinces did was largely to negotiate with the federal government to provide more flexibility in defining national standards, to allow more provincial voice in policy design and delivery.

Since the 1990s, the federal spending power has changed form (Graefe, 2008). The federal government no longer offers to pay a percentage of provincial costs. Instead, it offers to share costs up to a maximum amount. This approach has meant far less capacity to set standards, and indeed recent agreements do not constrain provinces beyond commitments to spend in fairly broadly defined areas (housing, child services, etc.) and to report to citizens on outcomes. For instance, the 2003 Labour Market Agreement for Persons With Disabilities had the federal government promising to share costs of employment programming for persons with disabilities up to a maximum of $223M per year. In return, the provinces had to share plans on what programs they were going to offer and provide annual reports on programs, such as the number of clients served, the number who completed programs, and the number who found jobs.

However, in reality the provinces are increasingly bypassed by the federal government through direct transfers to individuals, such as with the Universal Child Care Benefit, tax credits for childhood physical activity, or the purchase of supports for persons with disabilities. In these cases, the federal government either sends money directly to individuals (the child care benefit) or provides a credit at tax time (childhood physical activity) on the grounds that services like child care or physical activity will increase if people have the money to pay for them.

The Municipalities

Municipalities also make social policy, but their role is harder to define. They are sometimes called "creatures of the provinces" because the provinces set municipal powers and responsibilities.

Some provinces, like Quebec, have adopted centralized policy-making and delivery models. By contrast, Ontario has, at least until recently, tasked municipalities with significant roles in funding and delivering social assistance, child care, and housing programs. Where there is a larger service delivery role for municipalities, there is often also more space to innovate and change policies at the provincial or federal level. For instance, experimentation in child care in Toronto in the 1970s and 1980s pushed the provincial and federal governments to consider new models that better responded to women's growing presence in the paid work force.

More recently, municipal interest in community economic development has led to a greater social policy role, as have federal programs in areas like community housing. The powers that municipalities exercise around planning and land-use are increasingly called upon to deal with concentrated poverty, as in the case of the Urban Development Agreements in the Lower East Side of Vancouver and the North End of Winnipeg.

The Constitution Act, 1867

The Division of Powers between Different Levels of Government

The division of federal and provincial responsibilities is set out in sections 91 and 92 of the *Constitution Act, 1867*. Here are the main social policy powers and some of the programs built on them (shown in brackets).

At that time, the problems now addressed with social policies were seen as personal and familial responsibilities with a residual role for private charity. As such, important responsibilities often hide under strange language.

Federal Responsibilities:

- **s. 91(2A)** Unemployment Insurance (Employment Insurance) [added in 1940]
- **s.91(11)** Quarantine and the Establishment and Maintenance of Marine Hospitals
- **s.91(24)** Indians, and Lands reserved for Indians (social welfare policies for on-reserve Aboriginal peoples)
- **s. 94a** Old age pensions and supplementary benefits, if not in conflict with provincial law (Canada Pension Plan, Old Age Security, Guaranteed Income Supplement) [added in 1964]

Provincial Responsibilities:

- **s. 92(7)** The Establishment, Maintenance, and Management of Hospitals, Asylums, Charities, and Eleemosynary Institutions in and for the Province (medical and hospital Insurance, Social Assistance and social services)
- **s. 92(8)** Municipal Institutions in the Province (municipal social policy)
- **s. 92(16)** Generally all Matters of a merely local or private Nature in the Province (family policies, social policy more generally like housing)
- **s. 93** Education (primary, secondary, post-secondary)

Federalism and Social Policy Development

The division of responsibilities between the federal and provincial governments affects social policy development in a variety of ways. In areas where the provinces and territories have more autonomy and responsibility, there may be differences in the social policies across Canada. This has come to be referred to loosely as "**weak federalism**," though in itself it is not without some strengths as well.

For example, many have pointed to Quebec's universal, low-cost child care system, or its initiatives in mental health and housing, as social policy experiments not found elsewhere in the country. Similarly, a number of provinces have recently adopted poverty reduction strategies (Newfoundland, Nova Scotia, Quebec, Ontario, Manitoba), while others have not.

Experimentation and Community-Building

This provincial variation gives rise to one positive effect of "weak" federalism on social policy—namely, it allows for experimentation with new programs, thereby reducing the risk for other provinces if the policy adopted subsequently proves to be neither effective nor politically popular. Perhaps the best positive example here are the early adoption of universal public hospital and medical insurance in Saskatchewan, innovations that were then spread Canada-wide in the late 1950s and late 1960s respectively.

That said, the presence of a successful policy or set of policies in one provinces does not automatically lead to imitation: Quebec's universal low-cost child care program has been both political and social policy success but has yet to be replicated in another province. Even with studies showing that the government gets back as much in taxes (from more parents working and paying tax) as the program costs, no other province has followed suit.

A related effect of federalism has been competition between the federal and provincial governments for the loyalties and allegiances of Canadian citizens. Social policies are not only about solving problems but also about whether the "sharing community" is a provincial or pan-Canadian one. In some instances, the difference can be important. For example, when Quebec nationalism was on the rise, as it was in the 1970s and again in the 1990s, the federal government has tended to increase social policy initiatives, such as those around child benefits or community programming, in a bid to maintain Quebecers' allegiance to Canada.

Likewise, the extension of parental benefits from 22 to 50 weeks was at least in part the response of the federal government to the family policy plans of the Parti Québécois government, which included a new parental leave program.

Problems With Federalism

Social policy scholars in Canada generally take the view that federalism slows and limits social policy development rather than facilitates it. When policy relies on the federal spending power, some degree of federal-provincial negotiation and coordination is required, with the possibility of the policy being blocked, delayed, or diluted in the process. In addition, the nature of debate turns from "what is the best means of solving the policy problem" to one of "which government is legitimately allowed to do what," making it difficult for policy advocates to openly debate options. The social policy ideal is compromised by what is feasible in intergovernmental negotiations.

There are additional problems associated with federalism. For instance, the division of powers makes it difficult for social policy advocates to identify which government, federal or provincial, to lobby, particularly in cases where action by both is needed (for instance, a change in provincial disability policy may require changes to the Canada Pension Plan's disability benefits). This confusion can likewise be used to "pass the buck." For instance, when the UN Special Rapporteur on the Right to Food criticized Canada's performance in ensuring the right to food to all, the federal government brushed off the reprimand by claiming that responsibility for ensuring that right fell to the provinces. Representatives of the Canadian women's movement used to speak of the need to be skilled in the "federalism fox-trot": dancing with multiple governments is complicated!

"The Premier's conference comes up with a unity strategy."

United Nations Organizations

United Nations Children's Fund (UNICEF), created in 1946, and a permanent part of the United Nations since 1953. Beginning with work to fight famine and disease among children, it now acts broadly on behalf of children's rights to protection, education, health care, shelter, and good nutrition.

Food and Agriculture Organization (FAO), established as a United Nations agency in 1945. Its core mission is tied to ensuring people have regular access to enough high-quality food to lead active, healthy lives.

International Labour Organization (ILO), created in 1919, and part of the United Nations since 1946, with an emphasis on policies around work, be it labour standards, social security, worker health and safety, and economic and social development.

United Nations Organization for Education, Science and Culture (UNESCO). Founded in 1945, its work relates to such diverse issues as education, development goals, migration, and multiculturalism.

The Global Context

In the late 1990s, there was much debate about whether "**globalization**" signalled the end of national diversity in social policy and a move towards ever "leaner and meaner" policies. Were all countries going to be pushed to cut social policies to the bone? (Mishra, 1999)

There were many different arguments for why this might be, but three important factors were: (1) the heightened corporate power provided by increased capital mobility; (2) the influence of the ideas of international organizations; and (3) the restrictions imposed by international free trade agreements. Fifteen years later, the conclusion of cutting to the bone appears perhaps to be a little strong, but if we look at these three factors we can see that those concerns continue to exert some effect on social policy.

International Organizations

Many international organizations provide advice and expertise on public policy. What makes them international is that the members of these organizations are national governments. These organizations are also quite diverse. Some, like the **World Bank (WB)** or the **International Monetary Fund (IMF)**, are financial organizations. When countries require access to these organizations' loans to finance investment or their credit to deal with balance of payments imbalances, these organizations have leverage to persuade countries to adopt their advice. Other organizations like the **Organization on Economic Cooperation and Development (OECD)** or the **United Nations (UN)** and its agencies (such as the **United Nation's Children Fund (UNICEF)**, the **International Labour Organization (ILO)**, the **Food and Agriculture Organization of the United Nations (FAO)**, and the **United Nations Educational, Scientific and Cultural Organization (UNESCO)** do not have financial leverage. They must use other means to affect policy in their member states.

This can involve networking with officials, but also issuing reports and opinions that praise and shame governments in terms of their performance or the extent to which they adopt the views of international organizations. In recent years, the OECD has produced report cards on child care that have shamed Canada, which regularly ranks at the bottom of the member countries for its investments and outcomes.

In the 1990s, research looked at how international organizations were encouraging "one size fits all" policies. It was argued that social and economic policies must encourage the free play of market forces, and that the state's role should be to ensure that markets worked effectively. For the IMF and the World Bank, this took the form of what has been dubbed the **Washington Consensus**, which encouraged the privatization of public services and a limited role for governments in ensuring social rights.

For the OECD, the key document was the 1994 *Jobs Study*, which argued that governments should reduce labour market regulation and unemployment support in order to increase labour market flexibility and, by extension, rates of employment. This way of thinking had clear echoes in the remaking of Canadian Unemployment Insurance into Employment Insurance in 1996, with attempts to discourage repeated use of the program and other changes at the time.

There is also a recognition that the organizations themselves are internally divided over policy options and thus change their views over time. For instance, looking at the family policies of international organizations, Rianne Mahon (2008) has noted how the OECD has over time moved from not challenging gender roles to making that part of their preferred policy template. The World Bank has likewise come to underline the importance of the state in ensuring development and the possibility of policies aimed at the poor having extra impacts (as the poor spend their money in local economies).

Multinational consulting firms likewise act globally. For instance, a number of Canadian provinces, such as Ontario and New Brunswick, hired Andersen Consulting to help them toughen the administrative controls and screening tools in their social assistance systems in the 1990s. Of course, different consultancies and different networks are known for their respective expertise and leanings. As a result, in the choice of a consultant, governments often have a pretty good idea as to what sort of advice they are going to be receiving at the end of the process.

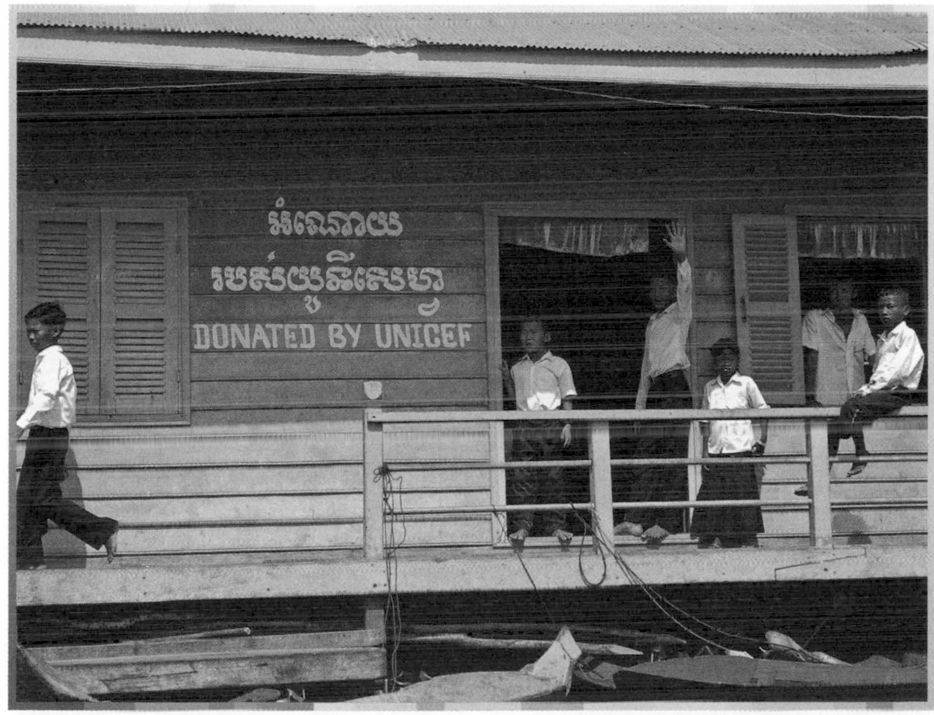

Children attend a school built by UNICEF in Battambang, Cambodia.

International Economic Organizations

The **World Bank** was created in 1944. Its current mandate is worldwide poverty alleviation and supporting development through providing loans for investments in education, health, infrastructure, public administration, and financial and private sector development.

International Monetary Fund (IMF), created in 1944. It works to foster global growth and economic stability through providing advice as well as conditional loans for countries in financial difficulty. The advice and loans often touch budgetary choices about which social policies should be offered and how they should be delivered.

Organization for Economic Co-operation and Development, established in 1961. It provides a forum of policy exchange between governments on a wide range of issues, including labour market and social policies.

Corporate Power and National Policy

Beyond the influence of the many organizations that act on a global scale, particular attention has been given to the influence of the global economy and the manner in which global capitalism has shaped policy-making by enhancing the power of corporations.

We can think of corporate power in two forms or levels, namely *structural* power and *agency* power (Farnsworth & Holden, 2006). The **structural power of business** is bound up in the organization of the system itself. Under capitalism, firms need to be profitable to survive and so make decisions with an eye to competitiveness and profitability. Social policies that affect profitability by imposing greater costs on firms (higher taxes, wages, and greater administrative oversight) are likely to lead firms to invest elsewhere, resulting in a drop-off of economic activity. As a result, policy-makers are likely to exercise self-restraint, anticipating the likely economic impact of their decisions. This impact has famously been likened to a "prison"—policy-making is limited by what is consistent with profitability.

This does not mean that social policy will not get made: indeed, the costs associated with policies like quality health care, housing, and education may generate net benefits to firms by improving the quality of the labour force. There are also cases where policies, such as minimum wages, may hurt the profitability of some sectors, like retail stores (which pay their staff at or near the minimum wage), while being deemed broadly beneficial for others, such as the financial industry (who want workers to be wealthy enough to afford their products and services). Nevertheless, the concern for business profitability is built centrally into policy-making without any business owners or managers needing to flex a muscle or pick up a phone. It is for this reason that it is called *structural*, because it is built into the normal workings of our economic system.

Despite this structural power, business interests do feel a need to organize to affect both the general direction of public policy and specific pieces of legislation. To do so, they have invested time and resources into a range of activities, from directly lobbying, to creating industry associations (e.g, Canadian Federation of Independent Business, the British Columbia Business Summit, and the Canadian Chamber of Commerce) to lobby on their behalf, to funding think tanks (the Conference Board of Canada, the C.D. Howe Institute, the Fraser Institute, the Atlantic Institute for Market Studies) in order to promote a particular way of thinking about policy options. This is the **agency power of business**. Business enjoys a number of advantages on this front compared to most other policy-makers, ranging from greater financial resources, knowledge about likely economic impacts of policies, and the fact of already being an organization (as compared to many public interest organizations that may need to build an organization from scratch).

The structural and agency power of business interests in social policy is not new, but it has been enhanced in a period of globalization with greater trade and capital mobility. In terms of *agency*, corporations can draw on global networks of policy thinking and policy development to strengthen their own domestic cases. More significantly, increased competitive pressures and greater opportunities to move investments to other countries increases the leverage that corporations have in negotiating with governments. In this context, it is easy to make dire predictions about cutting social protection and social policy to the bone, as corporations play countries off against each other.

While critics often liken the threat of leaving to blackmail, some times no doubt correctly, it is worth remembering the *structural* limits in which corporations act. If they truly are unable to compete with other countries, or if their Canadian production is far less profitable than their production abroad, the result is a loss of profitability. Over time, this makes it more difficult to modernize and update their production facilities, with likely impacts in terms of lower employment, lower wages, and more pollution. In other words, the social policy demands of business organizations, often presented as necessary for global competitiveness, may not always identify the correct remedies. However, behind them is a set of real competitive imperatives that cannot be wished away as long as our economic well-being is organized around market competition.

The example of Caterpillar closing down its locomotive factory in London, Ontario and moving its production to the United States after its workers refused to take a 50% pay cut serves as a telling symbol of the ability of firms to drive hard bargains and to punish places that refuse to make concessions.

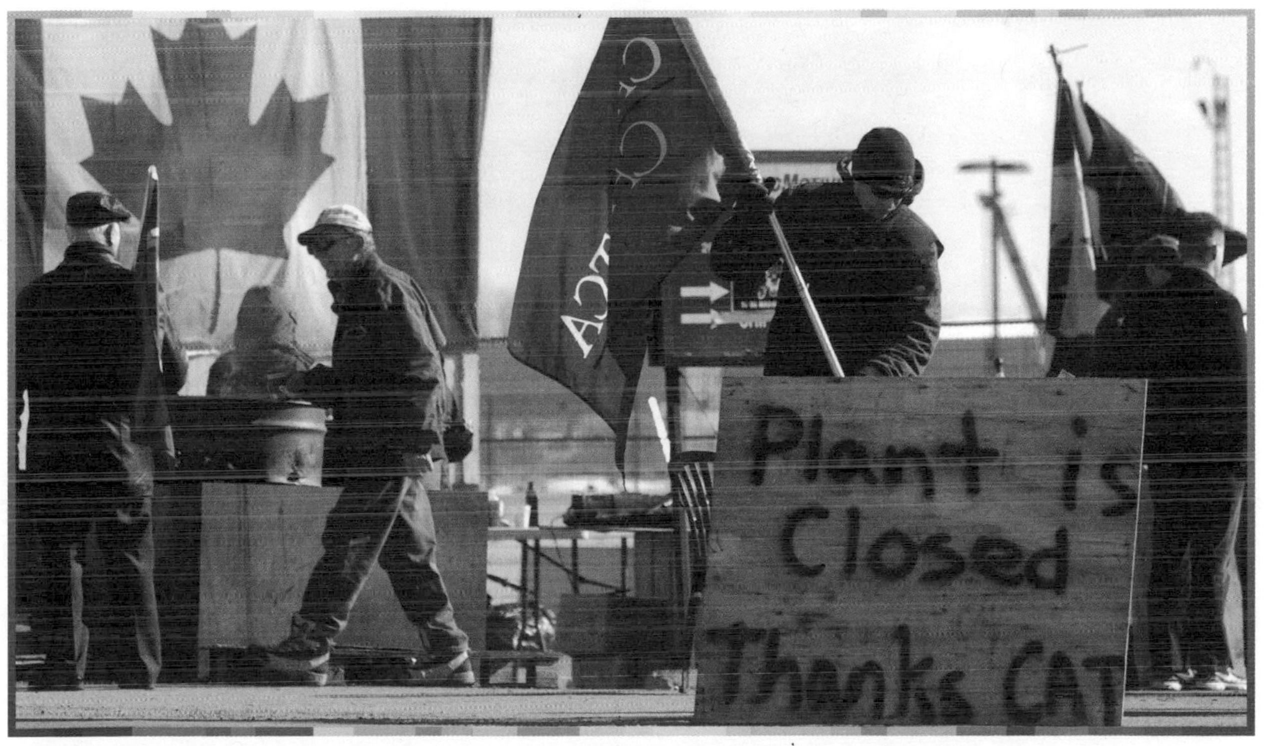

A Race to the Bottom?

Globalization and Its Effects

The prediction that the intensification of global competition, and the heightening of structural power that this entails, will lead to a race to the bottom where each country tries to outdo the next in cutting programming (so as to keep costs low for internationally mobile businesses) has not entirely been borne out by the literature on the welfare state.

Certainly, spending on social policy has increased in the developed countries and in many cases consumes a slightly higher percentage of the national product than 20 years ago (Castles, 2004). While inequality in labour market earnings has increased, in most countries, social policies have managed to limit inequality after taxes and transfers. In that sense, social policies are doing more work than previously.

In addition, welfare states in the Global North have also seen new social policy initiatives developed around new social risks, such as child benefits, child care, and income supplementation for low-wage workers (Bonoli, 2005). This is a story of welfare state adaptation and survival rather than of the welfare state being cut to the bone.

On the other hand, some scholars argue that given population aging and greater unemployment, one might expect much greater expenses. As such, the relative stability of social expenditure as a percentage of the national economy hides the reality of social policy cutbacks. Indeed, looking at specific programs such as unemployment insurance and sickness and injury benefits for workers, there have been significant reductions in the rates paid in these programs.

In this view, while corporate power has not led to a race to the bottom, it has changed what social policy does. Rather than providing security from the risks of losing their jobs, it is instead directed at pushing people back into the labour market (Korpi, 2003). Corporate power is thus less about getting rid of social policy than about getting social policy to help maintain a flexible labour market and to supply a high-quality labour force.

Globalization may not have cut the welfare state to shreds, but it has reduced the protection that individuals receive when faced with enduring risks of unemployment, low-pay, injury, sickness, and old age.

"...and the winner of this week's "Race to the Bottom" is..."

Free Trade Agreements and Policy-Making

Free trade and investment agreements, such as the North American Free Trade Agreement or the rules agreed through the World Trade Organization, also affect social policy-making. These agreements regulate the actions of governments in a variety of ways.

Important provisions include "non-discrimination" and "national treatment," meaning that governments must not discriminate between firms on the basis of the nationality of ownership (for instance, in giving preference in bidding to domestic firms or in only providing subsidies to citizens buying goods and services from domestic companies), or impose additional "performance requirements" (be it maintenance of employment levels or the transfer of technology) on foreign investment.

In terms of social policy, there are also concerns that national governments could be subject to paying damages for lost profits if they introduced public social programs in fields already occupied by private providers based in other countries. This might be a possibility in cases, for example, where foreign child care or home care firms had managed to gain significant market share in advance of government plans to introduce a universal public system. Alternatively, if existing public programs such as Medicare were privatized, there is a fear that governments would be unable to make them public again without having to compensate the private providers (Grieshaber-Otto & Sinclair, 2004).

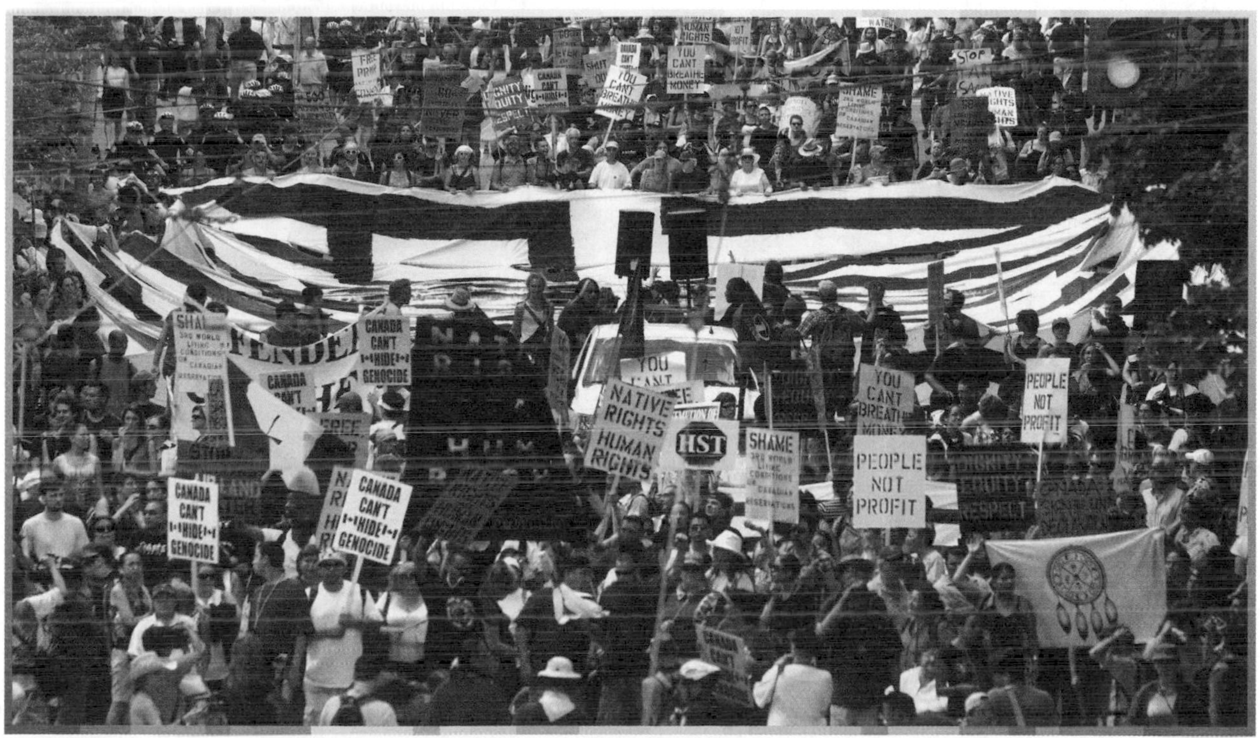

Protesters march during a demonstration for indigenous sovereignty ahead of the G8 and G20 summits in downtown Toronto, June 24, 2010.

Policy-Making as It Actually Happens

From the foregoing, it is clear that social policy-making is affected by a large number of factors and features. Two similar (but different) models have been used to describe the policy-making process as it actually happens.

Model 1: The Stages Model of Policy-Making

A common model for simplifying policy-making is the "**stages model**" perspective (see Table 5.1). This is based on seeing policy-making as a rational and incremental exercise in problem-solving that follows a predictable process.

In the stage model, policy moves from identifying a problem through to setting the agenda for government action by showing how policy could address the problem. The various options for dealing with the problem are then analyzed thoroughly and assessed against a set of criteria (efficiency, effectiveness, equity, cost, etc.). Upon implementing a policy, policy-makers then carefully evaluate the outcomes of the policy with any observed problems or shortcomings serving as the starting point for a new cycle of policy-making.

The idea that policy-making follows such a rational process reflects how many people think policy is made. In most cases, the policy-makers have a reasonably good understanding of the effects of policies. If they persist with a policy, it is because they are happy with the configuration of goals and winners served by a policy. For instance, city councillors know that cutting funding for after-school programs is likely to hit poor kids the most, lower school attendance, reduce the effectiveness of crime prevention, and thus cost more in the long run. But they may decide that they prefer to do so because in the short term it saves money, reduces taxes, and thus increases their chances for re-election. Provincial and federal politicians may also come to accept much of the evidence about the benefits of better public child care but still oppose it because of an ideological aversion to "the state" looking after two and three year olds.

TABLE 5.1

The Stages Model of Policy-Making

Problem Definition	What is the problem?
Agenda-setting	Can the problem be addressed through government policy? What are the different ways that the government could address the policy?
Adoption	What is the best option in terms of the selection criteria being used?
Implementation	How can the policy best be put into effect?
Evaluation	How effective is the policy in addressing the problem? Are changes needed? Does the presence of the policy create or unearth new problems?

This is consistent with what has been written in other chapters. There are different understandings of how the world works, and more importantly, different understandings of what counts as fair, just, and efficient. These are reflected in different ideologies (such as liberalism, socialism, etc.; see chapter 3), and are translated through different political parties, interest groups, and social movements. In this view, evidence and rationality is still important—it does a disservice to your values if the solutions you propose end in failure. But rather than seeing policy-making as evidence-based, it is more appropriate to see it as a power-based process that is evidence-informed.

Another criticism of the stages model is that it is overly linear. In the "real world," there may be developments simultaneously or indeed cases where the process seems to work backwards. An example would be when Ontario Education Minister John Snobolen mused that the government needed to "create a crisis" in order to build momentum for its proposed policy changes. On the other hand, the stages model has some descriptive/analytical value in breaking policy-making into discrete activities that can then be understood and analyzed.

What CEOs are Asking of Jim Flaherty

Boardroom Confidential

2011 Asks		2012 Actions	
Reduce pay of Canadian workers	>	EI changes, temporary foreign worker program changes	✓
Reduce public sector pay (esp. in lower ranks) Reduce size of the public sector	>	2012 Budget cuts 19,000 public sector jobs, pledges to reduce salaries and eliminate severance pay	✓
Limit union power through right-to-work (issue: creates productivity differentials with U.S.)	>	Ontario PCs open issue of right-to-work, as does Conservative MP Pierre Poilièvre Union power limited via back-to-work legislation at Air Canada and Canada Post	✓
Higher retirement age	>	Increase in age for receiving Old Age Security	✓
Open shipping, telecom, and airlines to more foreign competition	>	Changes to ownership restrictions in telecom act	✓
Two-tier health care (efficiencies)	>	No action; privatization continues	

Model 2: The Funnel of Causality Model

A model that does provide more space for considering power and influence is the "**Funnel of Causality**" (see Figure 5.1). In this model, the policy decision (the point at the bottom) can be seen as the result of a wide range of factors. Certainly, those involved and strategies employed by bureaucrats, politicians, and lobbyists directly affect the policy choice. However, those individuals are there in part because of an institutional order (electoral system; type of legislative system; type of bureaucracy; constitutional division of powers) that makes them legitimate deciders, and their choices are partially explained by what they think serves their longer term interest.

A different set of institutions would change who was present in making policy and what their strategies were. For instance, some have explained the much earlier and fuller development of public medical insurance in Canada as compared to the United States as largely the result of differences in the legislative institutions (the American Congressional system provides many more opportunities for opponents to block change than the Canadian Parliamentary system) and in the way federalism works in the two countries (Canadian provinces have more autonomy and financial resources to try new things).

The model takes into account "structural" factors, which are often taken for granted and usually change quite slowly—for example, how the economy is organized, industry structure, and the geography of employment (adjustment programs for workers in declining industries look different in a country where it is forestry in decline). Another structural factor is demography. For instance, there is a great deal in the media about population aging and the policy challenges it presents or the question of policy responses required for a diverse, multicultural country. As with the economic factors, they are also affected by institutions and the individuals involved.

FIGURE 5.1

The Funnel of Causality

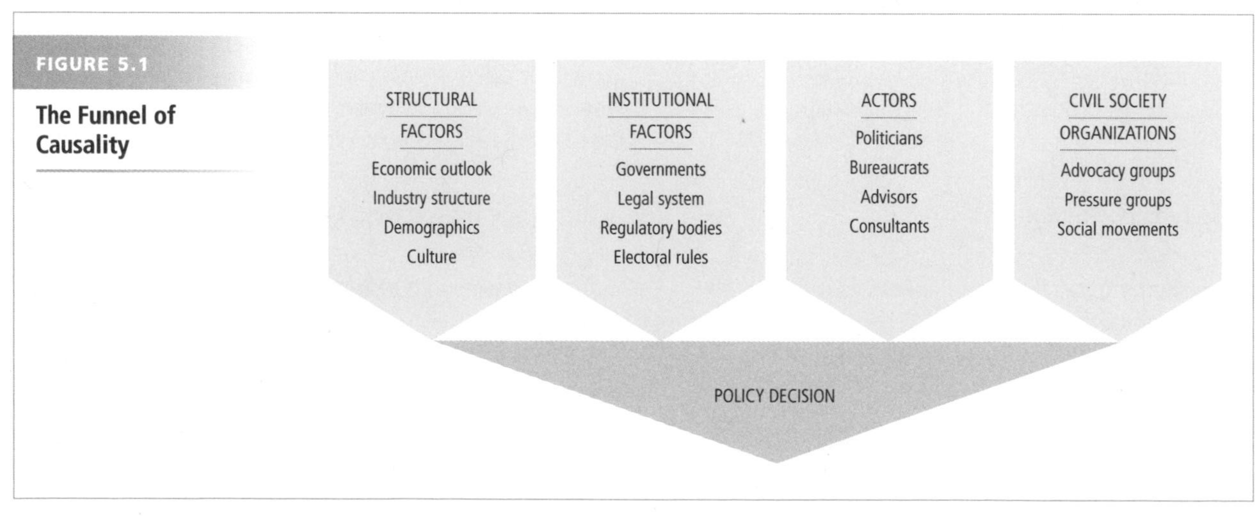

Another significant structural influence is culture. Feminist analysis has long made clear how understandings of the roles of women and men has affected both program design and who has access. When women's roles were seen as closely tied to mothering, social assistance systems supported women to stay out of the labour market until their children were grown. Now, women on Social Assistance are actively encouraged to seek work, usually when their youngest child reaches age two. Similarly, views about sexuality affect how same-sex couples are treated by social policies like survivor benefits in pensions.

Cultures have variable understandings of the extent to which people in distress deserve help. For instance, the evidence that low social assistance rates are socially and economically counterproductive given the high costs of poverty is often brushed aside by cultural understandings that those on Social Assistance deserve their fate and that higher rates would make them less likely to find paid work.

The funnel of causality captures influences on policy that have been discussed in this chapter. On the other hand, this model has been criticized for being more descriptive than analytical: it identifies a range of possible influences without necessarily always clarifying which influences are most important in particular situations.

Combining the models

Just as the stages model has value in breaking policy-making down into constituent activities, the funnel of causality approach has value in providing an inventory of influences on policy. Putting the two together can provide a sense of possible times/places to intervene, the sorts of intervention that might be successful, and a map of the constraints weighing on other actors.

Why Does Quebec Excel?

Child Care in the Funnel of Causality

The strength of the "funnel of causality" model can be seen if applied to why Canada, outside Quebec, consistently finishes at the bottom of the rankings for public investment in early childhood education and care.

A causal story must look at the interactions, not just single elements.

Structure

Canada operates under relatively free-market capitalism, which creates resistance to raising taxes to introduce new social programs. Quebec largely shares Canada's economic constraints.

Culturally, Canadians tend not to support the development of universal child care services so much as subsidizing parental choice. This is not so different in Quebec, although there has historically been a "pro-natalist" element to Quebec nationalism.

Institutions

Federal-provincial disputes have slowed the development of child care policy in most parts of Canada, yet federalism has played little role in the development of Quebec's child care program. The regular presence of majority governments, both federally and the provinces, should have aided policy progress.

Actors

There have been networks of women's organizations, child development experts, bureaucrats, and supportive politicians pushing for child care policy, coming close to significant federal policy development in the 1980s and early 2000s, as well as in certain provinces at times (e.g., British Columbia).

Quebec differs from the rest of Canada as it has both a strong women's movement and a family movement.

The Death of Evidence

Being able to provide evidence in support of policy claims has become increasingly important in the past two decades. Yet, recent events question if the power of evidence is on the wane when it contradicts government priorities.

The 2012 federal budget cut the budget of Statistics Canada and Library and Archives Canada, reduced regulatory oversight of fisheries to stocks of fish that are of "human value," and closed important evidence-generating organizations (the National Council of Welfare, the First Nations Statistical Institute, and the National Roundtable on the Environment).

Former Progressive Conservative pollster Allan Gregg wryly noted:

"This was no random act of downsizing, but a deliberate attempt to obliterate certain activities that were previously viewed as a legitimate part of government decision-making—namely, using research, science, and evidence as the basis to make policy decisions."

Role of Civil Society in Shaping Social Policy

Civil society organizations have an impact at various stages of the policy process and affect policy in many ways. We can think of how women's organizations and queer rights organizations have transformed deeply held understandings of appropriate gender roles or of how we define a family. As we get into the realm of institutions and persons, the role of these organizations and individuals becomes more directly observable.

At the level of problem definition and agenda-setting, organizations contribute in two ways. The first relates to the role of civil society organizations in transforming individual hardships into collective problems through forms of community organizing and mobilization. Organizations themselves act as sites where people come to identify shared problems and indeed are often places where new problems are identified and named. Out of this process, the possibilities for collective responses through the state begin to be identified, and actions are taken to alert politicians and bureaucrats about the need for action. In sum, they begin to set the agenda.

In the past 20 years, this mobilization function has proven less effective than in the past in terms of getting a hearing from institutional policy-makers. More recently, influence has been closely linked to the ability to provide expertise and technically sophisticated advice about policy problems and solutions. The consultants and advisors are playing a bigger role, or at least seem to be.

Policy Advisors, Bureaucrats, and Politicians

At the level of policy formulation, the role of civil society organizations is less clear. This type of policy-making usually takes place within the bureaucracy itself, involving a mixture of political input from the policy advisors of the government of the day and the technical and policy expertise of the permanent bureaucracy and their consultants. Sometimes these individuals work in close dialogue with trusted organizations (or individuals associated with those organizations) to ensure that the policy finds willing public supporters or at least heads off unnecessary opposition. At other times, these organizations are largely shut out.

There are a variety of factors that explain the extent of involvement of civil society organizations, including the extent of technical knowledge held by these organizations, their "closeness" with the governing party, the extent to which they are trusted with sensitive information, and their capacity to mobilize their membership behind compromise solutions. For groups that are not "inside" the process, the main channel of influence is to prod the governing party and educate the public so that the politicians remain aware of the possible risks in terms of lost public support if they adopt particular policy solutions.

The PMO and the Privy Council Office

Throughout the stages discussed here, civil society organizations, particularly those that are likely to employ social workers, are unlikely to be central players. The agenda priorities flow largely from the Prime Minister (or provincial Premier) and their partisan advisers in the **Prime Minister's Office (PMO)** and from the permanent bureaucracy as organized by the **Privy Council Office**. The key decisions are generally made within government departments, with a keen eye on getting the support of the Ministry of Finance and ensuring the Prime Minister's Office and the Privy Council share their vision and solution enough to bring it forward for approval by Cabinet or Parliament.

This is not to say that civil society does not make a difference, but that it is often not at the level of debating the fine details. Indeed, questions of fine detail are usually the result of a long-term process of discussion between government and non-government experts about the relative worth of different ways of solving the problem. Influence on the shorter time-scale is often more broadly political: of making it costly for a government not to act, either by embarrassing it by highlighting the failure to engage with a serious problem or by making it clear that a certain line of action will cost votes in a future election.

Policy-making is in part a political act, and so successful policy participation involves determining who has the power to decide at specific points of the policy process and developing strategies that reward those people for making the desired choices.

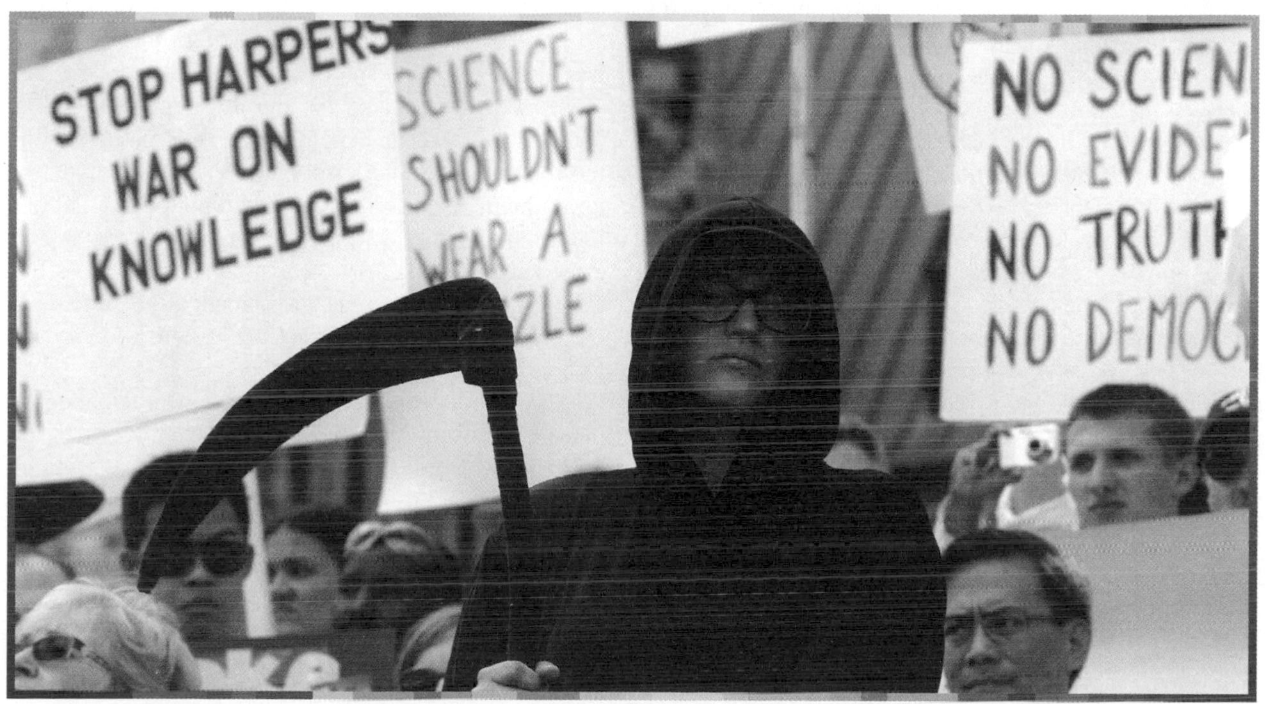

Scientists and academics gathered on Parliament Hill to protest what they coined the "death of evidence," Conservative budget cuts they say will undermine science in Canada and with it good policy-making based on sound research.

Policy in Real Time
The Ontario Poverty Reduction Strategy

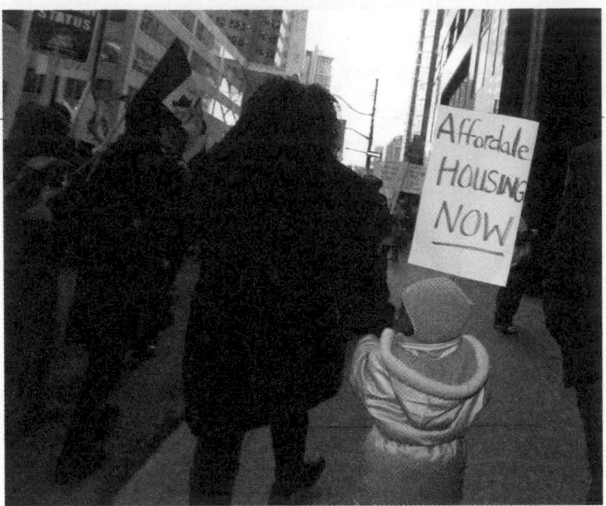

One way of thinking about policy models and policy actors is to use them to understand the adoption of a specific policy, such as the 2008 Poverty Reduction Strategy adopted by the Ontario government (see Hudson & Graefe, 2011).

Certain structural factors helped set the stage for making poverty an issue. Changes in the economy and the labour market had created a pool of citizens who worked and yet remained in poverty. At the same time, even with the economic growth of the late 1990s, the number of children growing up in poverty in Ontario did not drop noticeably. These trends offended some underlying cultural values, such as the idea that those who work should not be poor or that even a basic equality of life chances is denied to children who grow up in poverty. This concerned not only social advocates but also some members of the business community.

The Liberal government elected in 2003 was aware of these issues. The New Democratic Party managed to win a couple of by-elections by emphasizing the need to raise the minimum wage so as to reduce working poverty. Organizations within the Liberal party, such as the organization of Liberal women, were also pushing for the government to do more. A number of organizations in Toronto closely linked to the Liberals, such as the Daily Bread Food Bank or staff at the Atkinson Foundation, were pushing the same way. In the 2007 election, the Liberals responded by promising a poverty reduction strategy if re-elected. When they were re-elected, the agenda was set.

The issue then became what policy would be adopted. The government's initial focus was on the problem of child poverty. The government Cabinet ministers responsible for the file insisted that the policy not bind the government to any targets so they would not be embarrassed if they missed one. The child focus would also restrain the cost of the strategy by limiting the size of the group to be affected. Community organizations, by contrast, wanted a broader policy that addressed the poverty of adults as well as children, one with firm poverty reduction targets and timelines.

These organizations drew on the experience of the governments of Quebec and especially Newfoundland, which had adopted policies such as targets and timelines, and set up a network of organizations called "25-in-5" to lobby the government. This group attracted a group of antipoverty organizations, and it also had tacit support within the Toronto business community, who worried that poverty reduced the quality of the labour force and made Toronto less attractive for foreign investment.

The government's own canvassing of poverty reduction elsewhere (including Britain, Ireland, and New York City), its own modelling of how its antipoverty policies (including a new child benefit) would reduce poverty, and the success of 25-in-5 in rallying public opinion, led the government to change its mind and adopt a target and timetable to reduce child poverty by 25 percent in 5 years in December 2008. This commitment nevertheless had the caveat that the federal government also had to do its part by enriching the National Child Benefit and Working Income Supplement.

Given poor economic conditions and large budgetary deficits since the Strategy was announced in 2008, it is unlikely that Ontario will meet its target in 2013 and indeed has slowed the implementation of its child benefit. Community organizations, including those that were in the 25-in-5 network, continue to push for the full implementation of the strategy as well as its expansion to deal with adult poverty and Social Assistance.

Conclusion

It has been said that making policy is like making sausages: you probably do not want to know how it is done. The saying probably reflects a distaste for the exercise of power and persuasion in policy-making, which is felt to add a kind of impurity to what should ideally be a rational process.

Policy-making is complicated, as this chapter has shown. Evidence and knowledge matter in policy-making, but the constraints of economic organization, the individuals and organizations of those involved (be they community organizations, parties, or business associations), the constitutional division of roles and responsibilities (federal-provincial negotiations), and cultural preferences (such as around gender roles) play a big part. Indeed, social policy may also be like sausage in a more literal sense—it results from a complex mix of ingredients, and the exact mixture is unlikely to be *exactly* the same from one sausage to the next.

While policy may be too complex to be reduced to a simple story, there are enough regularities in terms of causal factors and stages of development that allow informed citizens and social welfare activists to make sense of what is happening. This chapter reviewed two such models of policy-making—the "stages model" and the "funnel of causality" model. In each case, policy must be understood in its full details, since the full list of ingredients that go into the process are many and varied.

There is enough predictability in policy-making that groups of citizens can themselves develop strategies and make decisions that affect policy outcomes. All that is required is to take into account the bigger picture, the individuals and institutions involved, while at the same time not to forget the smaller items—where exactly things are at that point in time and what is achievable. For, in policy-making and elsewhere, the devil is always in the details.

CHAPTER 5 REVIEW

LEARNING OBJECTIVES

After completing this chapter, you should be able to:

- Explain the division of responsibilities between the different levels of government.
- Understand the notion of "federal spending power" in relation to social welfare.
- Discuss the advantages and disadvantages of a federal system of government.
- Identify the many types of international organizations that offer advice and expertise on public policy.
- Understand the notions of "the structural power of business" and "the agency power of business."
- Explain the effects of globalization on social welfare policy.
- Understand the effects of free trade and investments on social welfare programs.
- Explain the "stages model" and "funnel of causality model" of policy formation.
- Explain the role of "civil society organizations" in social policy formation.

KEY CONCEPTS IN CHAPTER

- Agency power of business
- Civil society organizations
- *Constitution Act of 1867*
- Federal spending power
- Food and Agriculture Organization of the United Nations (FAO)
- Free trade
- Funnel of causality model of policy-making
- International Labour Organization (ILO)
- International Monetary Fund (IMF)
- Organization for Economic Co-operation and Development (OECD)
- Prime Minister's Office (PMO)
- Privy Council Office
- Stages model of policy-making
- Structural power of business
- United Nations (UN)
- United Nation's Children Fund (UNICEF)
- United Nations Educational, Scientific and Cultural Organization (UNESCO)
- Washington Consensus
- "Weak federalism"
- World Bank (WB)

REVIEW QUESTIONS

1. Explain the basic division of powers between the federal, provincial, territorial, and municipal levels of government. Give examples.
2. Discuss the advantages and disadvantages of federalism in the Canadian context in relation to social policy formation.
3. Describe the influence of globalization, international trade organizations, and transnational corporations on policy formation.
4. Describe the "stages model" of policy-making and the "funnel of causality" model and discuss the merits of each in understanding how policy is actually made in Canada today. Give examples.
5. What is the role of civil society shaping social policy in Canada. Discuss the influence of policy advisors, bureaucrats politicians, and laypersons in social policy formation.

EXPLORING SOCIAL WELFARE

1. Identify a social policy issue that is of interest to you. Using the tools explained in this chapter, try to assess the factors and organizations involved in trying to influence policy in this area. Put yourself in the position of a social policy advisor and indicate what you might recommend to bring about a significant policy change In this area.
2. Get involved in a local community initiative that is of interest to you. Do your best to try to understand the issues, context and the individuals and organizations involved. Use the models discussed in this chapter. If there is an opportunity, you can offer advice if you think you may have something useful to contribute.

CRITICAL THINKING

To what extent is the division of powers between the federal, provincial, and municipal levels of government a good thing or a bad thing in terms of actually getting things done?

Can you imagine a more efficient way of running a country?

WEBSITES

The United Nations (UN)
www.un.org
The United Nations (UN) is an international organization founded in 1945 at the close of World War II by 51 countries committed to maintaining international peace and security, friendly relations among nations, and promoting social progress, better living standards, and human rights. Due to its unique international character and the powers vested in its founding Charter, the organization can take action on a wide range of issues and allow its 193 member states to share their views.

The World Bank (WB)
www.worldbank.org
The World Bank (WB) is not a bank in the ordinary sense. It is comprised of two institutions managed by 188 member countries: the International Bank for Reconstruction and Development (IBRD) and the International Development Association (IDA). The IBRD aims to reduce poverty in middle-income and creditworthy poorer countries, while the IDA focuses exclusively on the world's poorest countries.

The World Trade Organization (WTO)
www.wto.org
The World Trade Organization (WTO) is the only global international organization dealing with the rules of trade between nations. At its heart are the WTO agreements, negotiated and signed by the bulk of the world's trading nations and ratified in their parliaments. The goal is to help producers of goods and services, exporters, and importers conduct business.

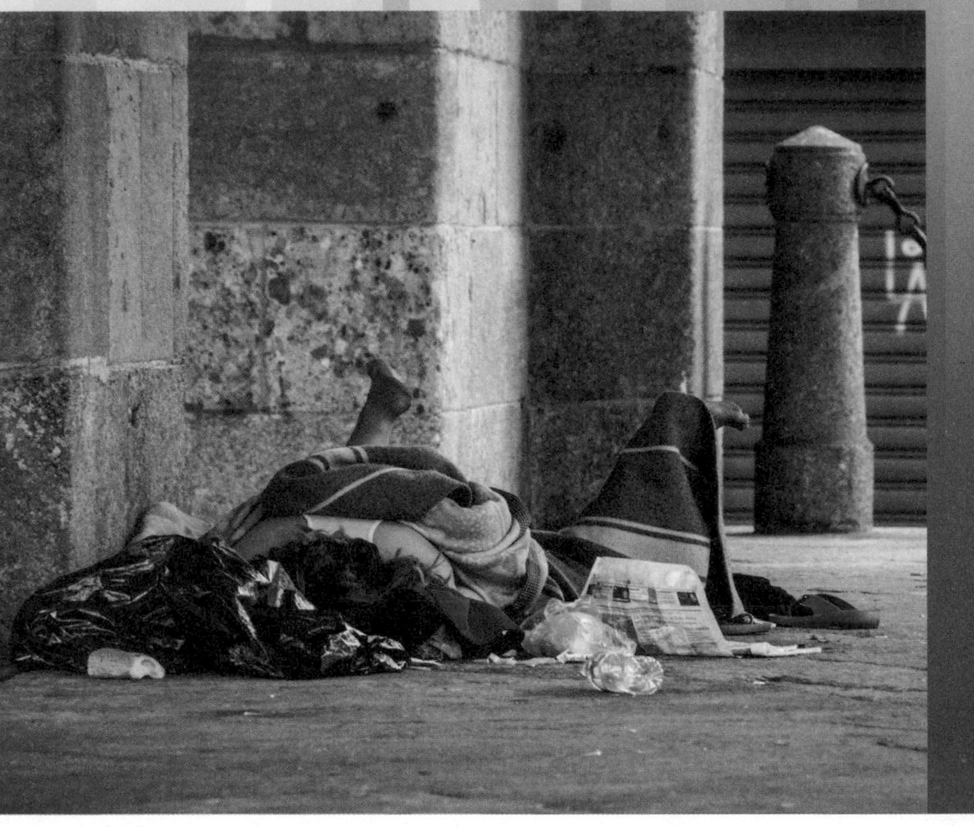

6 Canadians Living in Poverty

In Need of Social Assistance

> "Today, 826 million people are chronically and seriously undernourished although the world can nourish 12 billion human beings—twice its present population—without any problem."
>
> — SHUKOR RAHMAN, WORLD FOOD PROGRAMME

About one in six Canadians lives in "straitened circumstances," the government's euphemism for poverty. Statistics are only part of the story—most Canadians would be shocked if they knew how much the poor must struggle to make ends meet. One of world's great failures is the perpetuation of poverty. Poor nutrition, poor health, a lack of shelter, and in some cases death are directly related to poverty and contribute to the degradation of our social structures.

The different approaches to addressing poverty have a long history in Canada and in the international community. This chapter explores the different aspects of poverty—how it is defined, its extent, diverging explanations for its continued existence, and what to do about it.

The Persistence of Poverty

The United Nations Development Programme (UNDP) describes poverty as "a denial of choices and opportunities for living a tolerable life." The World Bank speaks of "income poverty" as living on less than $1 per day. Recently, the UN itself has created a new index—probably the most accurate yet—that captures the "multidimensional" aspect of poverty and allows for international comparisons.

Clearly, poverty has been discussed, defined, and measured in an infinite number of ways, and yet it persists. What to do about it?

Dollars & Sense

Dollars & Sense reviewed a number of studies in the areas of health, justice, human rights and human development, work and productive capacity, and child development (National Council of Welfare, 2011). The report found that reducing inequality, and especially helping the extremely poor, has positive individual and societal effects.

1.7 Billion People in Poverty Worldwide

The UN's new **Multidimensional Poverty Index (MPI)** will replace the UN's traditional Human Development Index (HDI). The MPI identifies deprivations across three dimensions and shows the number of people who are "multidimensionally poor." The MPI can be examined by region, ethnicity, and other groupings as well as by dimension, making it an ideal tool for policy-makers and for comparing countries worldwide.

According to the MPI measure, about 1.7 billion people in the 109 countries covered by the MPI—about a third—live in "multidimensional" poverty (at least 33 percent of the indicators reflecting acute deprivation—health, education, and standard of living). This number exceeds the estimated 1.3 billion people in those countries who live on $1 a day or less. Clearly, world poverty is a very serious problem.

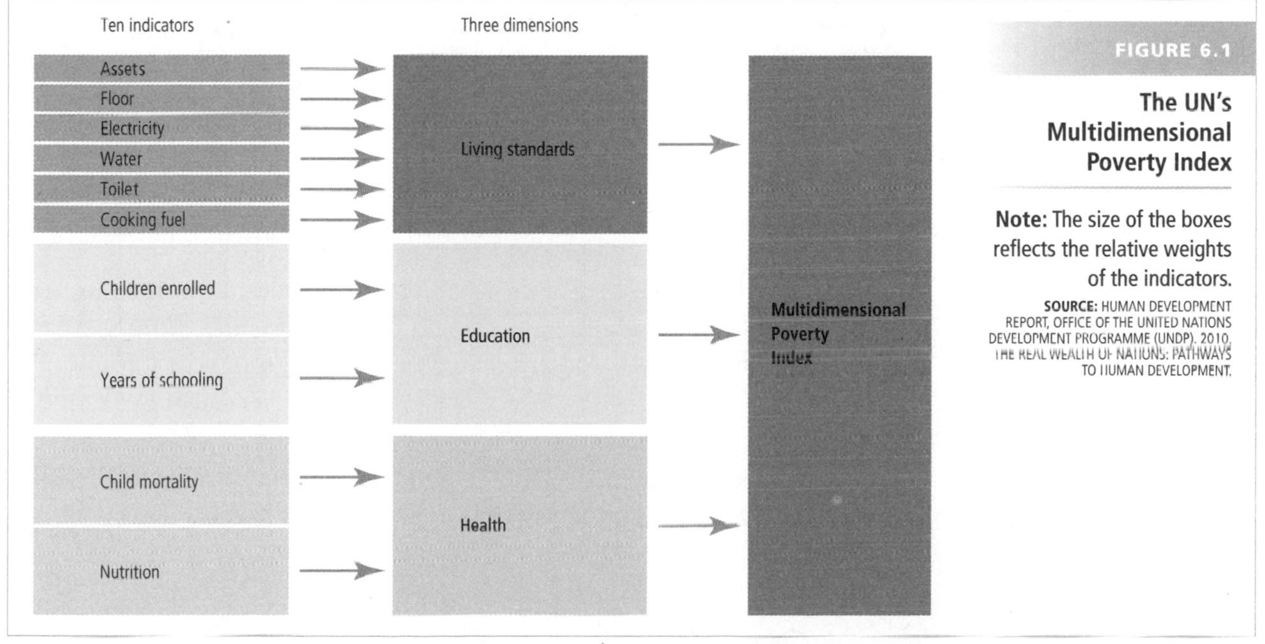

FIGURE 6.1

The UN's Multidimensional Poverty Index

Note: The size of the boxes reflects the relative weights of the indicators.

SOURCE: HUMAN DEVELOPMENT REPORT, OFFICE OF THE UNITED NATIONS DEVELOPMENT PROGRAMME (UNDP). 2010. THE REAL WEALTH OF NATIONS: PATHWAYS TO HUMAN DEVELOPMENT.

Absolute Measure of Poverty

Based on an essential basket of goods and services deemed necessary for survival or well-being relative to cultural context and value judgements.

Open for debate because people do not agree on what should be included in the "basket."

Measuring Poverty

In Canada, poverty has traditionally been defined using two different types of indices or measurements. *Absolute measures of poverty* are based on an essential basket of goods and services deemed necessary for survival or well-being. *Relative measure of poverty* are based on how low one's income is relative to that of other members of society.

"Absolute" and "Relative" Poverty

Absolute measure of poverty are based on the costs associated with a basket of "essential" goods and services. Of course, the issue then is determining what is "essential" to survival. Critics of this type of measure say the basket of goods and services should include items that bring a household beyond mere physical survival—adequate space, cooking facilities, storage for fresh food, furniture, transportation, and even recreation and leisure. Others would place strict boundaries on what should be included, based on the absolute approach. For example, Christopher Sarlo, a senior analyst with the Fraser Institute, believes that poverty figures may be exaggerated. He developed a measure of absolute poverty by limiting the basket of goods and services to those deemed necessary (Sarlo, 1992; 2001; 2008).

On the other hand, **relative measures of poverty** focus on the number and proportion of persons and households whose incomes fall below some fixed percentage of the average or median for the same household size and configuration. This measure essentially reflects the differences in income between the poor and the majority of society, rather than being an fixed standard. Relative poverty is established by setting a poverty line that is some fraction of either the mean or median income for another reference group (or another country).

Other jurisdictions use poverty measures of their own. For example, the European Commission sets an explicit poverty measure at a poverty line of 60 percent of the national mean income. The United States, on the other hand, still uses an absolute measure of poverty, and the World Bank, as noted earlier, defines absolute poverty as living on less than $1 per day.

Some measures of poverty, such as Statistics Canada's **Low Income Cut-off (LICO)**, are based on both absolute and relative measures. This combined measure is often referred to as a "relative necessities" approach. LICO is not explicitly put forth as a poverty line by the Canadian government but rather as indicating a level of low income.

While there is no consensus on which measure to use, and while the exact magnitude varies depending on the measure used, the research suggests that the variations among the various measures is not pronounced.

Low Income Cut-Off Measures

One of the key challenges when estimating poverty is to ensure that, whichever measure is used, it is reliable, consistent, and accurately captures the extent, duration, and depth of poverty. There are three measures frequently found in the poverty literature:

- **LOW-INCOME CUT-OFF (LICO).** Statistics Canada's LICOs represent the income level at which a family may find itself in "straitened circumstances" because it has to spend a greater proportion of its income on necessities than the average family of a similar size. Statistics Canada has cut-offs for seven family sizes and five community sizes.
- **MARKET BASKET MEASURE (MBM).** MBMs calculate the amount of income needed by a household to meet its needs, defined not just in bare subsistence terms but also with respect to what is expected by community norms. Human Resources and Skills Development Canada (HRSDC) places MBM somewhere between subsistence and a more generous social inclusion basket.
- **LOW-INCOME MEASURE (LIM).** LIM is the most common index for international comparison. It defines low income as being below one-half the median income of an equivalent household.

Unlike the United States and some other countries, Canada has no official, government-mandated poverty line. Of these three indices, the most widely used poverty measure in Canada is LICO, which is calculated and released yearly by Statistics Canada.

Measure for Measure

One of the challenges is to ensure that, whichever poverty measure is used, the measure allows for reliable estimates, consistent trending, and is accurate in capturing the extent, duration, and depth of poverty.

While the exact magnitude may vary, research suggests that the variations among the different measures is not pronounced and the trend lines are consistent.

TABLE 6.1

Before-Tax LICOs 2011

	Community Size			
	Census Agglomeration (CA)		Census Metropolitan Area (CMA)	
Family Size	Less than 30,000 inhabitants[1]	Between 30,000 and 99,999 inhabitants[2]	Between 100,000 and 499,999 inhabitants	500,000 inhabitants or more
1 person	$18,246	$19,941	$20,065	$23,298
2 people	$22,714	$24,824	$24,978	$29,004
3 people	$27,924	$30,517	$30,707	$35,657
4 people	$33,905	$37,053	$37,283	$43,292
5 people	$38,454	$42,025	$42,285	$49,102
6 people	$43,370	$47,398	$47,692	$55,378
7 or more people	$48,285	$52,770	$53,097	$61,656

1. Can include some small population centres. 2. *Includes population centres with less than 10,000 inhabitants.

Source: Statistics Canada Low income cut-offs before tax, 2011 (1992 base)

Social Exclusion

A person living in poverty is not only lacking in basic resources—food, shelter, clothing—but also has limited opportunities to participate in the social, economic, and cultural activities of his or her society, thereby experiencing social exclusion.

Beyond Income

Many scholars, particularly in Europe, are increasingly conceptualizing poverty in terms of **social exclusion** rather than absolute or relative poverty per se. The concept refers to marginalization—having limited opportunities or abilities to participate in the social, economic, and cultural activities of society.

Social Exclusion

The use of social exclusion is an attempt to broaden the definition of poverty beyond simple income-level calculations. It includes measuring the extent to which people have freedom of choice. Social exclusion views poverty not as a low level of income but as the inability to pursue well-being because of the lack of opportunities.

How people define poverty varies by gender, age, culture, and other social aspects. A young person may define poverty as a lack of job opportunities, while an elderly person may see it in terms of food security or health care. Poor people themselves are acutely aware of their lack of power, voice, and independence. Many poor people speak of poverty in terms of humiliation, isolation, safety, and inhumane treatment. They often speak about these aspects of poverty as being worse than the lack of income.

Clearly, poverty is more than simply a lack of income, and broader measures are needed. Increasingly, the solutions to poverty are viewed in the context of basic human rights. (See Chapter 14 for more about welfare and human rights.)

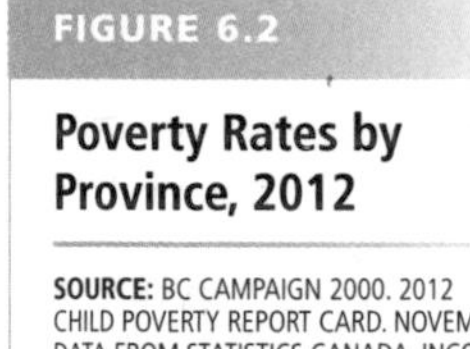

FIGURE 6.2

Poverty Rates by Province, 2012

SOURCE: BC CAMPAIGN 2000. 2012 CHILD POVERTY REPORT CARD. NOVEMBER. DATA FROM STATISTICS CANADA. INCOME IN CANADA 2010, TABLE 802, CAT. NO. 57-202-X

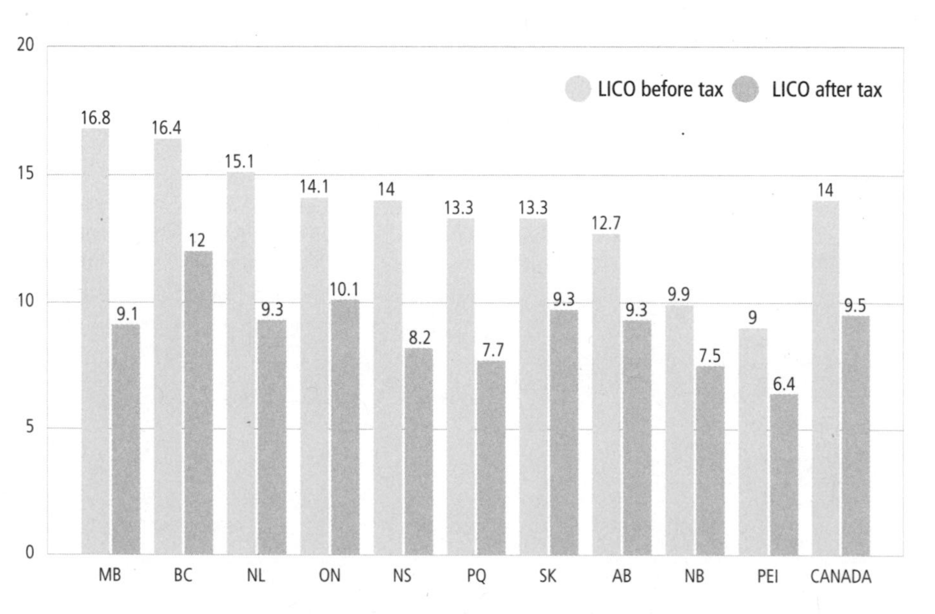

Living on Welfare

Bare numbers do little to illuminate the challenges facing people on Social Assistance. The following cases may reveal what life on welfare or disability benefits is actually like.

Case Studies

Women Surviving and the Educated Poor

Mary, Amira, and Marie: Women Surviving

Mary, a single woman, spends $350 per month on rent for her bachelor apartment. She spends a further $30 per month on utilities. Since Mary lives in Ontario, she will receive a maximum per month for basic living expenses and a maximum per month for rent, even though her rent exceeds this. She will receive a total of $626 per month—this is the provincial maximum (or the maximum barring exceptions—more money could be possible if a physician recommended a special diet or if Mary lived in the far north of Ontario, for example). After rent and utilities, this leaves Mary with $140 each month with which to pay for food, clothing, transportation, and other expenses.

Amira, a single mother, has one five-year-old daughter. Their one-bedroom apartment costs $450 per month and their utilities cost a further $50 per month. Amira receives $446 per month as a basic needs allowance and another $500 to pay for shelter. Amira also receives a back-to-school allowance for her daughter each July. She receives $69 for this allowance because her daughter is under age 13—when she is over age 13, Amira will receive $128 to pay for her school-related costs. Each November, Amira receives $105 as a winter clothing allowance for her child. For all other expenses, including child care, Amira must rely on the $446 dollars per month she has left after paying her rent.

Marie is homeless. Although she is eligible for the basic needs allowance, in order to receive her shelter allowance, Marie must provide receipts to prove she is using the money to pay for shelter.

Carlos: Educated Poor

Carlos is 26 and came to Canada as a refugee five years ago, settling in Toronto. His homeland had been completely destroyed and he fled for his life. His younger sister is developmentally challenged, and she lives with him. Any job that he gets just barely covers the cost of paying for someone to take care of his sister. She needs special care and does not speak English, so it is very difficult to find care.

Carlos is a well-educated man who previously worked as a physician in his home country. When he arrived in Canada, he found that the Canadian Medical Association did not recognize his medical degree, and he was forbidden to work in his profession. He was immediately placed on Social Assistance and encouraged to "upgrade his skills." He was unable to find a way to gain Canadian medical credentials, so he enrolled in a college nursing program.

He was enrolled as a full-time student but found it impossible to dedicate himself to full-time work and full-time study. He did get a $2,500 Special Bursary, but that made him ineligible for the Ontario Student Assistance Program (OSAP) loans. Eventually, Carlos changed to part-time studies. His job pays $7.50 per hour—that is only $14,625 per year without holidays. He found that it was impossible to live in Toronto on that money and pay tuition on top of it. He was left with no choice but to postpone his studies.

The Feminization of Poverty

Poverty affects over three million Canadians, including six hundred thousand children. Figure 6.3 shows the trend for recent immigrants, off-reserve Aboriginal people, and persons within disabilities. However, across all these groups, and across mainstream Canadian society as well, women in particular represent a disproportionate percentage of the poor.

Here are the percentages of those living in poverty in the following groups:

- Aboriginal women, (First nations, Métis, Inuit), 36%
- Visible minority women, 35%
- Women with disabilities, 26%
- Single-parent mothers, 21%
- Single senior women, 14%

The term "feminization of poverty" is widely used to capture this troubling phenomenon.

Source: Canadian Women's Foundation. (2013). "Factsheet: Moving Women Out of Poverty." Toronto: CWF.

Myths About the Poor

Income security programs for the poor are been based on myths about the poor and what it means to be poor. Many anti-poverty organizations, including the Canada Without Poverty (formerly the National Anti-Poverty Organization) and the Canadian Council on Social Development (CCSD), have documented a variety of such myths. The following are widespread today:

- **POVERTY IS THE FAILURE OF THE INDIVIDUAL.** This stereotype has a long history. The reasoning is that paupers are being punished for hidden sins. This idea blames the victim and says that people with energy and ability can make their way in life and that incompetence and poverty are clear signs of biological and social inferiority.
- **THE MAJORITY OF WELFARE RECIPIENTS ARE ABLE-BODIED MEN WHO ARE SIMPLY LAZY.** There is a straightforward rebuttal to this myth—examine the demographic characteristics of individuals on Social Assistance. Studies have found that less than 15 percent of Social Assistance recipients are "employable" men. Many more are children (in the range of 30–40 percent) or people with a disability (25–30 percent).
- **THE POOR DO NOT WANT TO WORK.** More than half of those on welfare do work full- or part-time if they are able to do so. If we look at people who are on welfare, we see that about 30-40 percent are children. Another 16 percent are single mothers, many still caring for young children. If we look at the number of welfare cases, we find that about 27 percent are disabled people (National Council of Welfare, 2002).
- **POOR PEOPLE DO NOT PAY TAXES.** In a report for NAPO, Andrew Mitchell and Richard Shillington found that low-income people paid over $4 billion dollars in annual federal taxes in 2004. Of this, approximately 70 percent would come from federal commodity taxes. The remainder was from income taxes (12 percent), C/QPP contributions (12 percent), and EI contributions (5 percent; Mitchell & Shillington, 2004).
- **THE WELFARE SYSTEM IS RIFE WITH CHEATING AND FRAUD.** A study conducted by a national auditing firm estimated fraud to be within the range of 3 percent of the welfare budget (on the other hand, there are estimates that income tax fraud is in the order of 20 percent). The Ontario government reports that $46 million was saved due to catching people committing welfare fraud. Analysis of the government's claim (see the discussion later in this chapter) reveals that, of the 15,680 reductions or terminations due to "fraud," very few were actually convicted of fraud. Most of what is reported as fraud is actually administrative error.

- **WE CANNOT AFFORD THE SOCIAL PROGRAMS NEEDED TO ELIMINATE POVERTY.** Canada is a very prosperous country with high rates of economic growth and a high gross domestic product (GDP) per capita. Yet in Canada, all "social protection" government transfers add up to only 18 percent of the GDP, whereas France transfers 29 percent, Germany transfers 27 percent, the Netherlands transfers 33 percent, Finland transfers 36 percent, and Sweden transfers 40 percent (Bohácek, 2002, p. 26).
- **ALL CHILDREN IN CANADA ARE ASSURED A DECENT START IN LIFE.** Studies show strong links between poverty on the one hand and poor health and poor academic achievement at school on the other. Children in poor families are more likely than other children to suffer chronic health problems. They are almost twice as likely to drop out of school. Many studies have also found that "higher income is almost always associated with better outcomes for children" (Statistics Canada, 2006a, p. 4). The CCSD examined 31 outcomes and living conditions and, not surprisingly, found a strong statistical association with family income levels and overall health and well-being.
- **WELFARE RATES ARE TOO GENEROUS.** All welfare rates are well below LICO and always have been. Some provinces are worse than others. Welfare benefits for single employable people are the least adequate (see Table 6.2).

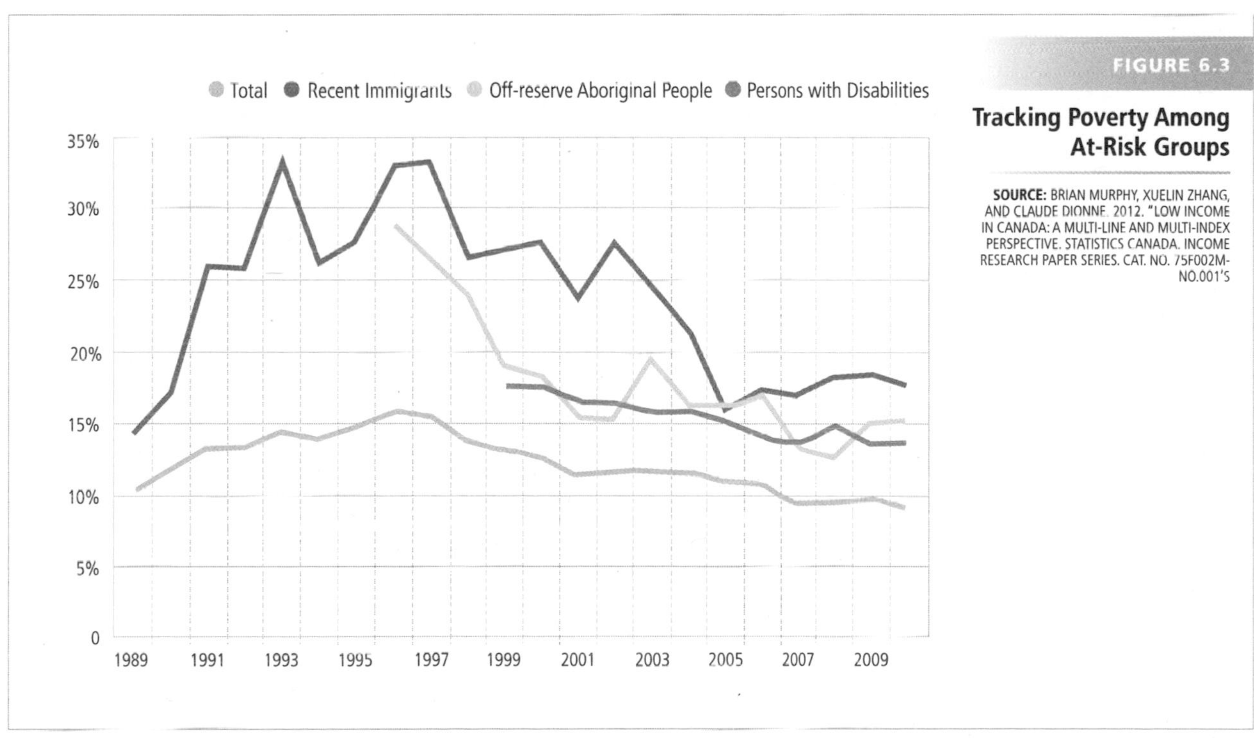

FIGURE 6.3

Tracking Poverty Among At-Risk Groups

SOURCE: BRIAN MURPHY, XUELIN ZHANG, AND CLAUDE DIONNE. 2012. "LOW INCOME IN CANADA: A MULTI-LINE AND MULTI-INDEX PERSPECTIVE. STATISTICS CANADA. INCOME RESEARCH PAPER SERIES. CAT. NO. 75F002M-NO.001'S

Dual Labour Market Theory

Analysts using **dual labour market theory** separate the labour market into two broad categories:

Primary labour market: unionized or professional employment with high wages, benefits, good working conditions and opportunities for advancement, and a relatively small number of qualified workers.

Secondary labour market: low-wage jobs with few benefits, part-time hours, lack of job security, and competition between the large pool of available workers, all of which help keep wages down.

Three Explanations for Poverty

There are three explanations for poverty. Each takes a different viewpoint on how the economy and society interact and on how people end up in poverty.

Human Capital Perspective

The **human capital perspective** focuses on the labour force characteristics of individuals. Thus, low earnings that lead to poverty can result from factors such as lower levels of education, fewer job skills, old age, poor health, and low geographic mobility. Beyond this, differences in earnings are ascribed to differences in preferences between income and leisure. This is known as the *income-leisure choice theory:* the view is that people will choose between paid employment and unpaid leisure. Those with lower incomes are said to have chosen the latter.

With this approach, it is thought that income distributions depend largely on the interaction of supply and demand in the market for labour. As such, in a sense, workers receive what they contribute. This approach places emphasis on education and job training in order to break the poverty cycle.

Market Economy Perspective

In the **market economy perspective**, the focus is on the broader economy and society rather than the individual. Its historical basis is in Keynesian economics, as outlined in Chapter 4. It takes into consideration the barriers people face as a result of location, discrimination, and lack of demand in the economy. This explanation emphasizes that economic conditions and the characteristics of the labour market affect income levels.

Adherents to this perspective believe that market conditions are crucial. Market conditions shape employment and therefore income security, and these markets may also be limited or constrained by institutional factors, social norms, and other non-economic factors, such as:

- **SOCIALIZATION.** People may be conditioned to believe certain things about themselves and their position in society.
- **DISCRIMINATION.** Negative stereotypes, racial discrimination, and employment barriers may limit employment opportunities.

In today's society, for example, there are fewer primary jobs and significantly more secondary jobs. The primary jobs are knowledge based; secondary jobs are less skilled and more unstable. One explanation for low incomes, therefore, is the growth of secondary labour markets. Similarly, the Canadian labour force is being pitted against workers in other low-wage countries, driving Canadian wages and benefits down.

Political Economy Perspective

Three Explanations for Poverty

Human capital perspective
Labour market perspective
Political economy perspective

The **political economy perspective** focuses on the close relationship between politics and economics (see Chapter 3). The large concentration of ownership of major corporations affects the way governments operate in the regulation of industry and the labour market. Those who control large corporations influence social policy-making. This perspective has its roots in the labour and socialist movements

Within this perspective, labour markets are segmented into competing camps. Stratification in the labour market is useful, it is argued, because employers can pay some workers less than others and create a group of flexible low-paid workers who can be moved in and out of employment as needed. Examples are not hard to come by. Many women, for example, are trapped in low-paying "women's work" in the labour market which is viewed as an extension of their domestic work in the home. The full value of their work is unrecognized

Similarly, discrimination based on **ethnicity**, both at interpersonal and at institutional levels, negatively affects immigrants and especially people of colour. Some researchers have found that, even when immigrants are highly educated, their achievements are not recognized in the local labour market.

Increasingly, social policy analysts are advocating an approach that considers all three perspectives—one emphasizing accessible and quality education and training, job creation, employment equity, and public participation in labour policy discussion and development.

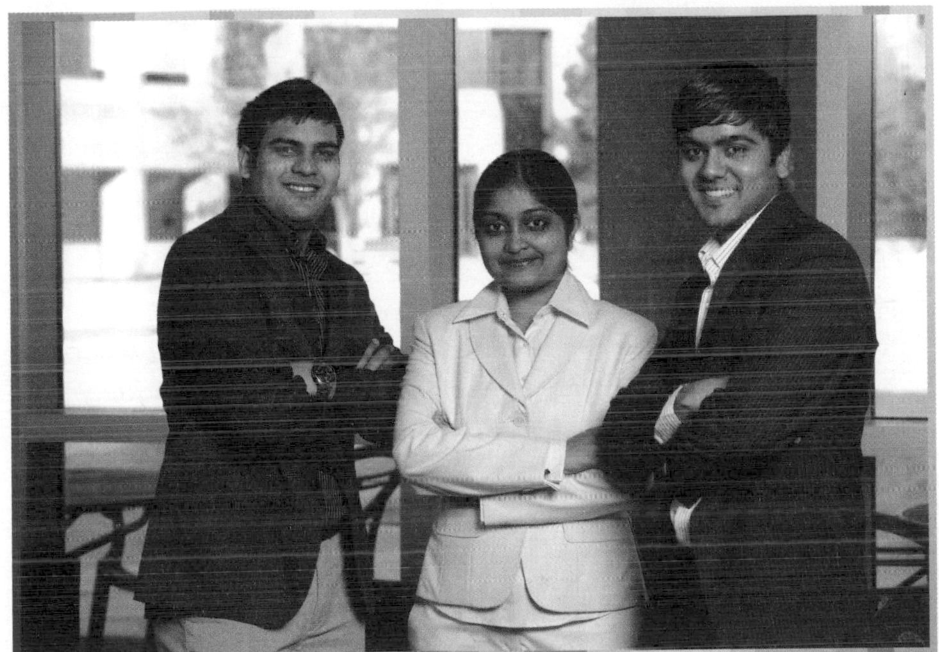

Discrimination based on ethnicity and race is a factor contributing to poverty in Canada today.

The National Council of Welfare

The National Council of Welfare (NCW) was an important citizen's advisory body to the Minister of Human Resources and Skills Development Canada and the public generally on matters of concern to low-income Canadians. The Council was first formed in 1962 and then substantially broadened in scope by the Government Organization Act of 1969.

Funding for the Council was cut in the federal budget of 2012, resulting in the agency being dissolved without any alternative advisory body operating within the government and focusing specifically on matters concerning low-income Canadians.

How Much Poverty?

In discussing how much poverty exists, three dimensions need to be considered: (1) how many people are poor (the headcount measure); (2) by how much they fall below the poverty line (the poverty gap measure); and (3) for how long they are poor (the poverty duration measure). Social policy analysts need to examine all three aspects of the problem to develop coherent and comprehensive income programs.

Poverty Headcount

Poverty is much more widespread than most people realize. The **poverty headcount** measures the number and proportion of persons in poverty. Based on the 2010 LICOs, there are 3.5 million people living in poverty, or 9 percent of the total population. These numbers are an underestimate, as they exclude Aboriginal peoples on reserves, residents of Yukon, Nunavut, and the Northwest Territories, and people who live in homes for the aged or other institutions.

Provincial poverty rates for 2010 also vary. British Columbia has the highest rate (11.5 percent) and Prince Edward Island has the lowest (3.9 percent). Because so many Canadians reside in Ontario and Quebec, more than half of Canada's poor can be found in these two provinces. To determine whether these rates are high or low, it is useful to compare them with those of different countries using a comparable measure. With poverty defined as 50 percent of the median income (adjusted), we find that Canada (9.4 percent) ranks 16th out of 133 countries. All continental European countries rank ahead of Canada with the exception of Italy. Canada ranks ahead of the United States, Australia, and the United Kingdom (indexmundi.com).

Depth of Poverty

Another dimension of poverty is the total shortfall from the poverty line—that is, the depth of poverty. Poverty rates do not always show whether poor people are living in abject poverty or merely a few dollars below the poverty line. To determine this, we need to measure the poverty gap.

The **poverty gap** is a measurement of how much additional income would be required to raise an individual or household above the agreed poverty level. Statistics Canada refers to this as the "average income deficiency." Statistics Canada has tracked the poverty gap over the last 30 years by age, family type, and different poverty measures. The gap is different for different groups, of course. For example, for lone parent families, the poverty gap was $2,789 (i.e., living at 85 percent of LICO) in 2009. For a couple with two children, on the other hand, it was substantially more at $9,680 (or 67 percent of LICO; Human Development Council, 2011).

Poverty Duration

Finally, it is important to consider **poverty duration**, or how long people experience low income. Statistics Canada's Survey of Labour and Income Dynamics (SLID) follows the same set of people for six consecutive years and is designed to capture changes over time. This data shows that, over the long term, poverty affects a greater number of Canadians than yearly poverty rates suggest. Clearly, vulnerable groups, such as persons with disabilities, those with lower levels of education, racialized communities, lone parents, recent immigrants, and Aboriginal peoples all face the risk of longer-term poverty.

How long do people stay in poverty? According to a 2012 report released by the Citizens for Public Justice, 17.3 percent of Canadians experienced poverty for one or more years over the period 2005-2010 (CPJ, 2012). In addition, 4.1 percent were in low income for at least four of the six years, and 1.5 percent were persistently poor over the period. Overall, the average time spent in low income declined from the duration of poverty in the mid 1990s (from 2.7 to 2.4 years); however, for vulnerable groups, the risks of long-term poverty are much higher

People also experienced greater difficulty exiting low-income since the "Great Recession" (as it has been called) that began in 2008. The massive downturn triggered an increase in poverty and, according to the CPJ, the "immobility rate" rose from 60.2 in 2006-07 to 65.9 in 2008-09, falling back to 63.1 in 2009-10 (CPJ, 2012). Again, the rate for vulnerable groups would have been higher during and following on from the recession.

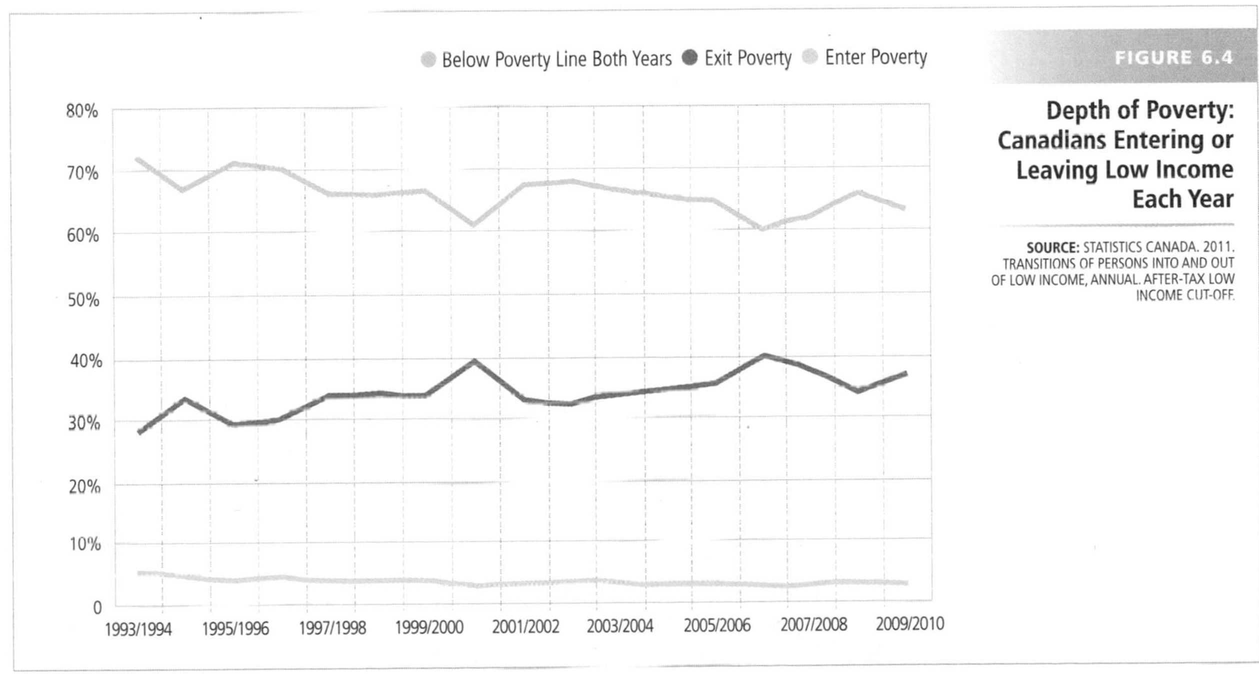

FIGURE 6.4

Depth of Poverty: Canadians Entering or Leaving Low Income Each Year

SOURCE: STATISTICS CANADA. 2011. TRANSITIONS OF PERSONS INTO AND OUT OF LOW INCOME, ANNUAL. AFTER-TAX LOW INCOME CUT-OFF.

The $tate of the World's Children

www.unicef.org/sowc

UNICEF produces an annual report called *The State of the World's Children* that compares, among other items, child poverty rates throughout the world.

Inequality and Poverty

Poverty and inequality are related concepts, but they should not be confused.

- **Poverty** refers to some benchmark standard and how many people live below that standard.
- **Inequality** refers to the differences between income groups.

The way in which total income is divided between households is a measure of inequality (also known as income distribution). Two common measures of inequality are quintile distributions and Gini coefficients, as explained below.

Quintile Distributions

Quintile income distribution is one way to look at inequality. A quintile represents one-fifth (20 percent) of the total number of people being studied. If you take all Canadians and ranked them according to income, you could then divide them into five equal quintiles. The top quintile is the one-fifth of people with the highest incomes. The fourth quintile is the one-fifth with the second-highest incomes, and so on down to the one-fifth of Canadians with the lowest incomes.

If the Canadian population is divided into five sections (quintiles), in 2010, the richest 20 percent (the richest fifth) of Canadians had an average income 9.3 times that of the bottom 20 percent and 2.6 times that of the middle 60 percent (HRSDC, 2013).

FIGURE 6.5

The Changing Income Gap between Richest and Poorest Quintile Groups in Canada

DATA SOURCE: STATISTICS CANADA, CANSIM TABLE 202-0701

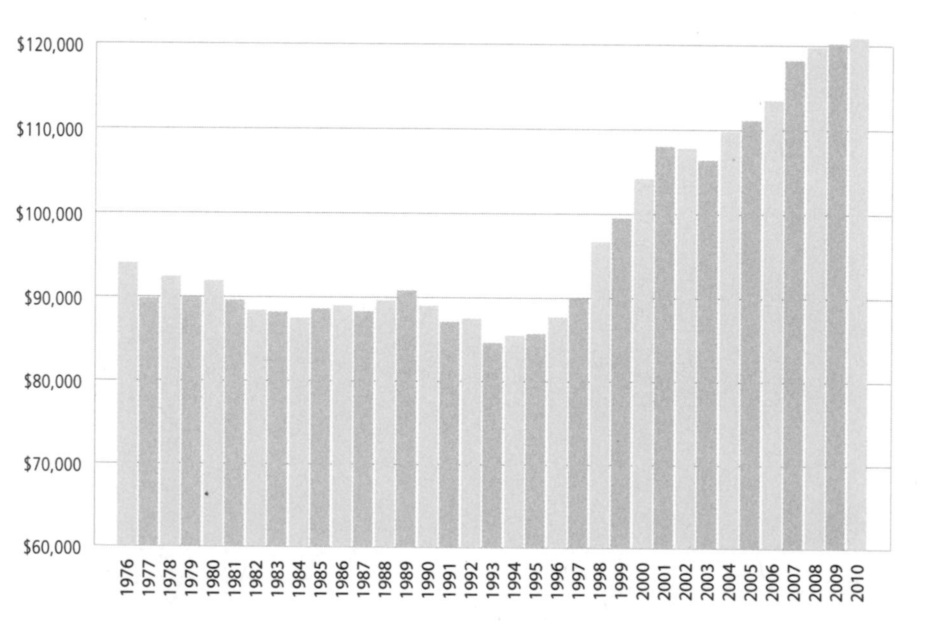

Gini Coefficient

A second measure of income inequality is the **Gini coefficient**, named after the Italian statistician Corrada Gini. This measures the degree of inequality in the overall income distribution. Values can range from 0 to 1. A value of 0 indicates that income is equally divided among the population, with all units receiving exactly the same amount of income. At the opposite extreme, a Gini coefficient of 1 denotes a perfectly unequal distribution, where one group possesses all of the income in the economy. A decrease in the value of the Gini coefficient can therefore be interpreted as reflecting a decrease in inequality and vice versa.

By this measure, income inequality is higher in Canada than in 11 similar countries (Conference Board of Canada, 2013). Although income is distributed more equally in Canada than in United States, for example, Canada nevertheless ranks 12th, suggesting that it is doing a rather mediocre job of ensuring income equality. The Conference Board of Canada also notes that Nordic countries are the clear leaders on the income equality report card. United States, on the other hand, is the worst performer.

Using the Gini coefficient as the indicator, income inequality in Canada has increased over the past 20 years. Canada reduced inequality during the 1980s, when the Gini coefficient reached a low of 0.281 in 1989. Inequality rose in the 1990s, but it has so far remained around 0.32 in the 2000s (Conference Board of Canada, 2012).

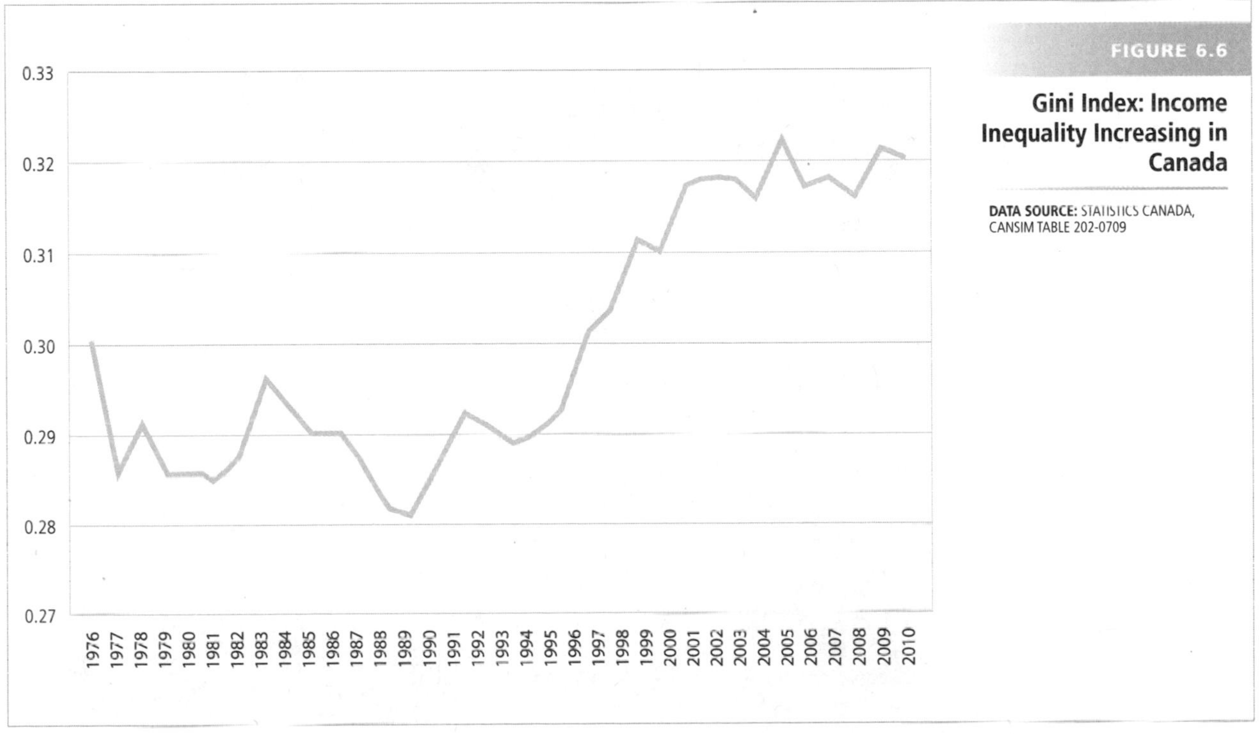

FIGURE 6.6

Gini Index: Income Inequality Increasing in Canada

DATA SOURCE: STATISTICS CANADA, CANSIM TABLE 202-0709

Social Assistance—When All Else Fails

Many families and individuals experience difficult life events, challenges, or changes that may affect their capacity to function effectively in their private and public lives. This can happen to anyone unexpectedly. When a person has no source of income, he or she is entitled to what is commonly known as **Social Assistance (SA)**, often referred to simply as *welfare*.

Social Assistance is a province-based minimum income program for people who are defined as "in need." Strict eligibility criteria, known as *needs tests*, are applied to determine whether people are in need. Social Assistance is a program of last resort with roots in early charity relief and the English Poor Laws.

The Social Safety Net

Each of Canada's 10 provinces and three territories designs, administers, and delivers its own Social Assistance program. Entitlement is based on a test, which takes into account the assets and income of the applicant's household and its basic needs (food, clothing, shelter and utilities, household necessities, and personal needs) as defined in provincial legislation. Generally, Canadians access Social Assistance only when all other public and private means of support are exhausted.

Each province also establishes its own administrative and eligibility requirements for those applying for benefits.

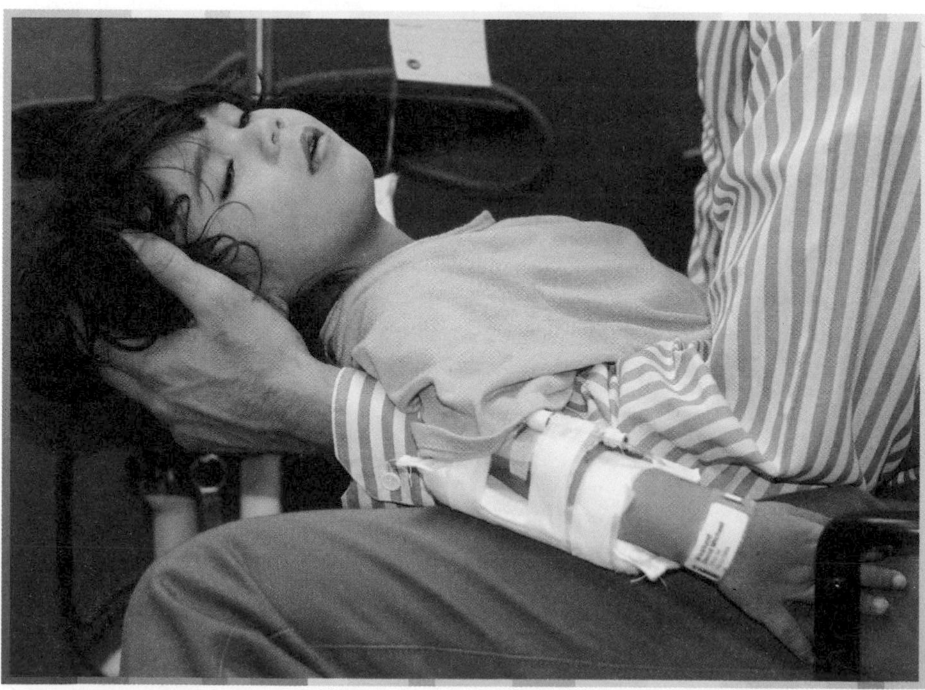

Children who grow up in poorer families are more likely to suffer chronic health problems and drop out of school.

Thirteen Provincial/Territorial Welfare Systems

As noted in Chapter 1, Social Assistance is referred to as a "minimum income" program. It transfers income to people who have little or no employment or other income, but it supplies only a bare minimum of funds for survival. The transfer is also conditional insofar as it is based on a needs test.

There are 13 different Social Assistance systems across the country. There are also municipal responsibilities in some regions. Aboriginal Affairs and Northern Development Canada (AANDC) is responsible for the Social Assistance for Registered Indians living on reserves. Such programs are delivered either by the provincial or territorial government or by an Aboriginal agency (depending on the province or territory) in accordance with the prevailing Social Assistance rules and regulations of that province or territory. AANDC covers the entire cost of such assistance.

International Council on Social Welfare (ICSW)

www.icsw.org

Founded in Paris in 1928, the ICSW is a non-governmental organization that represents organizations in more than 50 countries around the world. The ICSW undertakes research and organizes consultations to help analyze social problems and develop policies.

Determining Eligibility

Provincial and territorial jurisdictions classify their welfare clients according to a general classification scheme. The categories are:

- Employable Persons
- Lone Parent Families
- Persons with Disabilities
- Persons with Multiple Barriers to Employment, and
- Aged Persons

Applicants must meet the administrative requirements—that is, provide documentation first with respect to his/her financial situation—in order to determine their eligibility. The **eligibility rules** regarding this process vary by jurisdiction.

- Applicants must be of a certain age (usually between 18 and 65).
- Full-time post-secondary students may qualify for assistance in some provinces and territories if they meet stringent conditions. In some provinces and territories, students must leave their studies to apply for assistance.
- Parents must try to secure any court-ordered maintenance support to which they are entitled.
- People who are disabled require medical certification.
- People on strike are not eligible in most jurisdictions.
- Immigrants must try to obtain financial assistance from their sponsors.

After this administrative requirement is met, the applicant must then undergo a needs test. This involves looking at the individual's assets and income in relation to their needs.

How Effective is Social Assistance?

One way to evaluate the effectiveness of Social Assistance benefits in addressing poverty levels is to compare the welfare dollar amounts to after-tax LICO levels. The difference between the two is a fair indicator of the **effectiveness of Social Assistance** in at least ameliorating the situation of the poor in our society.

A discrepancy between the incomes of those relying on Social Assistance and basic needs puts the health and well-being of these Canadian families and children at risk.

What the Data Show

Prior to being dissolved in 2012 by the Conservative government, the National Council of Welfare released up-to-date monitoring data on welfare incomes across the country in a series of regular reports. Table 6.2 shows the provincial poverty gaps by household type. When adjusted for inflation, welfare incomes were consistently below adequacy level (Statistics Canada's after-tax LICOs).

The most vulnerable group, consistently across all provinces, is single unattached individuals. Their welfare income was at best 62 percent of after-tax LICOs and at worst 21 percent. The comparable figure for MBM measure was 64 percent and 24 percent. Only BC, Newfoundland and Labrador, and Saskatchewan breached the poverty lines.

TABLE 6.2

Welfare Incomes Compared With After-Tax Low-Income Cut-Offs (LICO, A.T.)

	Welfare Income	LICO (A.T.)	Poverty Gap	Welfare % of LICO
Newfoundland and Labrador				
Single Employable	$9,593	$15,579	$5,986	62%
Person With a Disability	$11,123	$15,579	$4,456	71%
Lone Parent, One Child	$19,297	$18,960	$337	102%
Couple, Two Children	$22,339	$29,455	$7,116	76%
Prince Edward Island				
Single Employable	$6,906	$15,384	$8,478	45%
Person With a Disability	$9,067	$15,384	$6,317	59%
Lone Parent, One Child	$16,531	$18,725	$2,194	88%
Couple, Two Children	$24,045	$29,089	$5,044	83%
Nova Scotia				
Single Employable	$6,359	$15,579	$9,220	41%
Person With a Disability	$9,197	$15,579	$6,382	59%
Lone Parent, One Child	$14,992	$18,960	$3,969	79%
Couple, Two Children	$20,967	$29,455	$8,488	71%

	Welfare Income	LICO (A.T.)	Poverty Gap	Welfare % of LICO
New Brunswick				
Single Employable	$3,773	$15,579	$11,006	24%
Person With a Disability	$8,665	$15,579	$6,914	56%
Lone Parent, One Child	$16,171	$18,960	$2,790	85%
Couple, Two Children	$19,775	$29,455	$9,680	67%
Quebec				
Single Employable	$7,312	$18,421	$11,109	40%
Person With a Disability	$10,881	$18,421	$7,540	59%
Lone Parent, One Child	$17,583	$22,420	$4,837	78%
Couple, Two Children	$22,614	$34,829	$12,215	65%
Ontario				
Single Employable	$7,501	$18,421	$10,920	41%
Person With a Disability	$12,905	$18,421	$5,516	70%
Lone Parent, One Child	$17,372	$22,420	$5,048	77%
Couple, Two Children	$22,695	$34,829	$12,134	65%
Manitoba				
Single Employable	$6,815	$18,421	$11,606	37%
Person With a Disability	$9,423	$18,421	$8,998	51%
Lone Parent, One Child	$14,829	$22,420	$7,592	66%
Couple, Two Children	$21,476	$34,829	$13,353	62%
Saskatchewan				
Single Employable	$8,780	$15,579	$6,799	56%
Person With a Disability	$10,902	$15,579	$4,677	70%
Lone Parent, One Child	$17,923	$18,960	$1,037	95%
Couple, Two Children	$24,001	$29,455	$5,454	81%
Alberta				
Single Employable	$7,241	$18,421	$11,180	39%
Person With a Disability	$9,433	$18,421	$8,988	51%
Person With a Disability/AISH	$14,297	$18,421	$4,124	78%
Lone Parent, One Child	$15,749	$22,420	$6,671	70%
Couple, Two Children	$22,101	$34,829	$12,728	63%
British Columbia				
Single Employable	$7,778	$18,421	$10,644	42%
Person With a Disability	$11,392	$18,421	$7,029	62%
Lone Parent, One Child	$16,899	$22,420	$5,521	75%
Couple, Two Children	$21,179	$34,829	$13,650	61%

Source: Welfare Incomes 2009, National Council of Welfare, 2010, Reproduced with the permission of the Minister of Public Works and Government Services Canada, 2013.

The Working Poor

There is a widespread perception that the only people who are poor are those who are unemployed, and that many of those who are unemployed are single parents staying at home with children. The truth is that, today, paid work itself is not a guarantee of an adequate family income. Many of the poor are actually employed.

Working Families in Poverty

Human Resources and Skills Development Canada (HRSDC) provides operational definitions of the **working poor**. Working poor individuals, they say, are those persons aged 18–64 who have worked for pay a minimum of 910 hours in the reference year, who are not full-time students, and whose family income falls below LICO. Working poor families include at least one working poor individual.

A large portion of those living with low incomes are employed, but they are working at jobs that provide such a low wage that they remain in poverty. Two-parent families with one earner, for example, have a poverty rate well above the rate for two-earner families. As governments cut back on income security programs and tighten eligibility requirements for income supports, many find that the job opportunities do not provide an income sufficient for their family's well-being or even survival. This has forced increasing numbers of working Canadians into the category of the working poor.

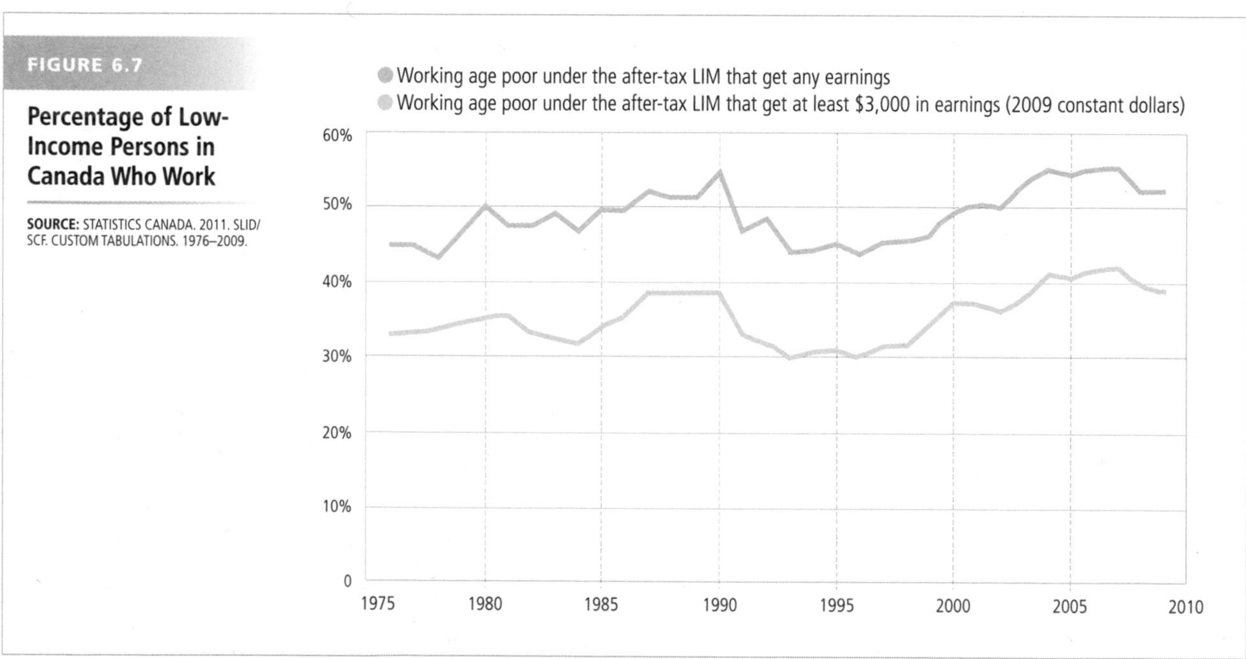

FIGURE 6.7

Percentage of Low-Income Persons in Canada Who Work

SOURCE: STATISTICS CANADA. 2011. SLID/SCF. CUSTOM TABULATIONS. 1976–2009.

More on the Working Poor

Work alone, then, is not an assured route out of poverty. Indeed, one in three low-income children has a parent who works full-time throughout the year, and many adult full-time workers earn less than $10 per hour. There were 881,100 people working in part-time jobs in October 2010 because they could not find full-time work, up from 682,900 two years prior. This works out to an increase of 29 percent in involuntary part time workers (Diaconal Ministries of Canada, 2012).

There is a widespread and deep-seated myth that the poor are idle and somehow "deserve what they get." The **Metcalf Foundation** study, the first of its kind in Canada, documented the changing face of Toronto's workforce and looked specifically at the working poor population. They found that even during times of economic prosperity (early 2000s), the number of working people unable to make ends meet grew by 42 percent (Stapleton et al., 2012). According to the study, working people living in poverty are younger than average, are more likely to be immigrants, and are more likely to be single (if they have a family, chances are that they are a single parent or that there is only one breadwinner in the home). With the exception of many well-educated immigrants unable to find appropriate employment, their education levels also tend to be, on average, lower than working people who aren't poor.

According to the research, the working poor are actually working, on average, almost as many hours as people who are employed and making a decent living (Stapleton et al., 2012; Paperny, 2012).

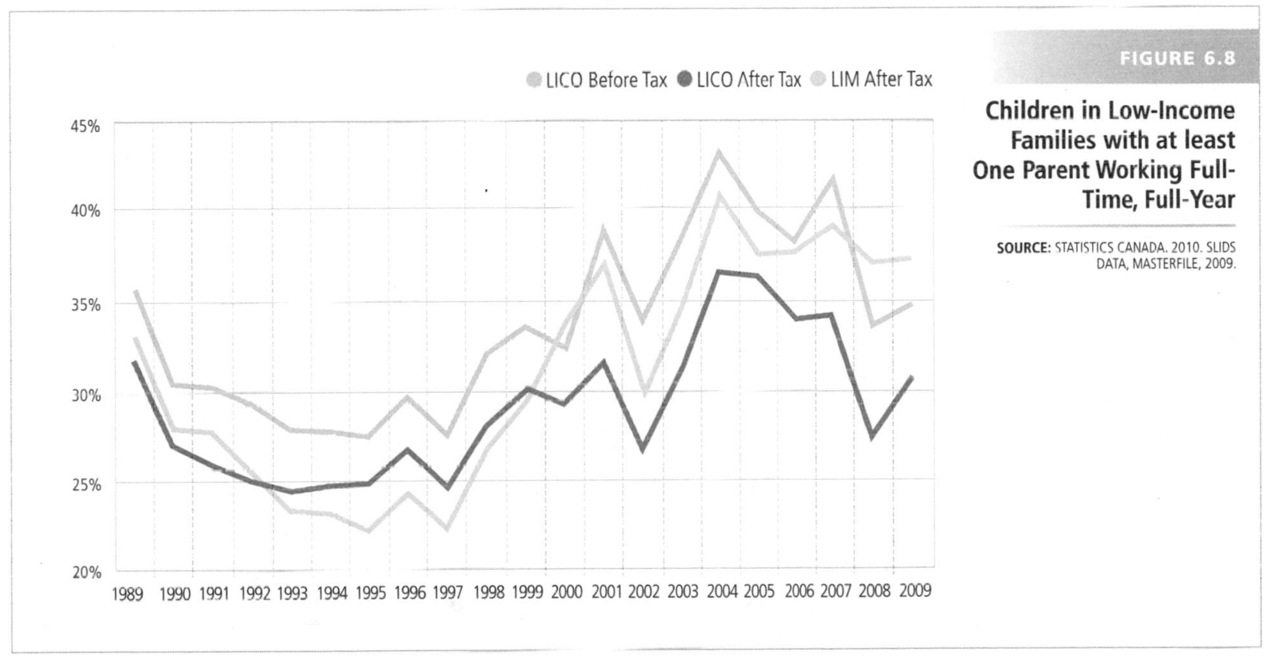

FIGURE 6.8

Children in Low-Income Families with at least One Parent Working Full-Time, Full-Year

SOURCE: STATISTICS CANADA. 2010. SLIDS DATA, MASTERFILE, 2009.

The Real Costs of Homelessness

$1,932 / mo.
Shelter Bed

$4,333 / mo.
Provincial Jail

$10,900 / mo.
Hospital Bed

$701 / mo.
Rental Supplement

$199.92 / mo.
Social Housing

Homelessness

Symptomatic of the growing problem of poverty in Canada, homelessness is on the rise. Simply defined, **homelessness** is the absence of a place to live. A person who is considered to be homeless has no regular place to live and stays in an emergency shelter, in an abandoned building, in an all-night shopping area, in a laundromat, outdoors, or any place where they can be protected from the elements.

Reasons for Homelessness

Two types of homelessness can be distinguished: absolute homelessness and relative homelessness. **Absolute homelessness** is a situation in which an individual or family has no housing at all or is staying in a temporary form of shelter. **Relative homelessness** is a situation in which people's homes do not meet the United Nation's basic housing standards, which are that a dwelling must:

- Have adequate protection from the elements
- Provide access to safe water and sanitation
- Provide secure tenure and personal safety
- Not cost more than 50 percent of total income
- Lie within easy reach of employment, education, and health care

Homeless people seen on the streets are long-term or "chronically" homeless people who represent less than 20 percent of the homeless. The rest are families and individuals who find themselves without a place to live for a period of time.

People become homeless for a variety of reasons. The major reasons appear to be economic crises due to unemployment or low income, mental health problems, other severe health problems, violence or abuse in the home, eviction, a lack of support from family and friends, and substance abuse problems. In some cases, these factors can overlap and are precipitated by unemployment, health problems, or a family crisis. Changes to government policy, such as the *Tenant Protection Act* in Ontario, have removed rent controls and made it easier to evict tenants. When combined with a decrease in affordable housing, homelessness becomes a growing problem.

According to Statistics Canada, about two-thirds of Canadians own their own homes—half without a mortgage. This is a testament to the wealth in Canada, for some. The problem, however, is for those with low incomes. Only 40 percent of households in the lowest quintile (the bottom 20 percent of income recipients) own their own homes, compared to 85 percent for the highest quintile (Lefebvre, 2002). The number of families living in shelters is dramatically increasing. While the majority of people staying emergency shelters are still single men, the number of families living in these homeless shelters is growing steadily.

The Hidden Homeless

However, the raw numbers on homelessness do not capture the full desperation experienced by those living on the streets. They do not include women in emergency shelters, people who are living in substandard situations (a relative's basement), or women who use sexual contracts to find shelter.

Homelessness has increased over the past decades, in large part as governments have cut back on social housing. In many cases, people simply cannot afford the available housing in their community. What is called for is a "Housing First" strategy, according to a recent policy report from the **Mowat Centre at the University of Toronto**, with greater responsibility at the provincial level and a program of investment in low-cost affordable housing (Hughes, 2012).

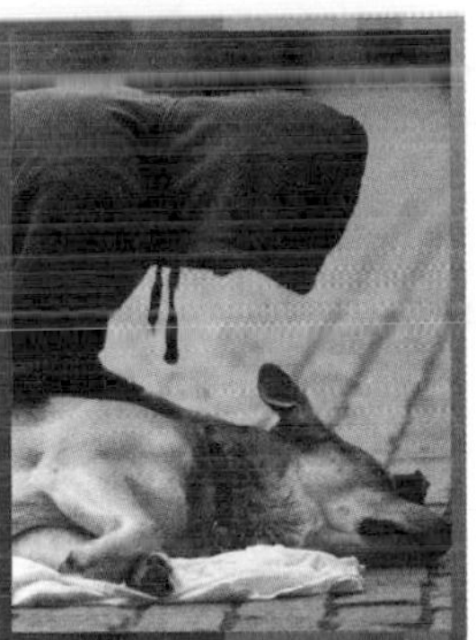

Homelessness is on the rise in Canada.

People at Imminent Risk of Homelessness

Many factors can contribute to individuals and families being at imminent risk of homelessness. Though in some cases individual factors (such as those listed below) may be most significant, in most cases it is the interaction of structural and individual risk, that in the context of a crisis, influence pathways into homelessness. In other words, what separates those who are at risk of homelessness due to *precarious housing* from those what are at *imminent risk*, is the onset of a crisis, a turn in events, or the increase in acuity of one or more underlying risk factors. Factors that may contribute (as singular or co-occurring factors include:

Precarious employment. Many people have unstable employment and live paycheque to paycheque. Precarious employment describes non-standard employment that does not meet basic needs, is poorly paid, part time (when full time work is desired), temporary, and/or insecure and unprotected. An unanticipated expense, increases in cost of living or a change in employment status may undermine their ability to maintain housing and lead them into homlessness.

Sudden unemployment with few prospects and little to no financial savings or assets, or social supports to turn to for assistance.

Supported housing with supports that are about to be discontinued. Some Housing First models provide supports, but on a time-limited basis. If such resources (aftercare, services) are withdrawn, individuals and families may be at imminent of re-entering homelessness.

Households facing eviction, lacking the resources needed to afford other housing including social supports/ living in areas with low availability of affordable housing.

Severe and persistent mental illness, active addictions, substance use and/or behavioural issues. Homeless rates have multiplied with the downsizing of mental health facilities and reductions in substance use resources for communities

Division of household—caused by situations (such as separation, divorce, conflicts between caregivers and children, or roommates moving out) where the affected are unable to keep existing housing.

Violence/abuse (or direct fear of) in current housing situations, including (1) people facing family/gender violence and abuse; (2) children and youth experiencing neglect, physical, sexual, and emotional abuse; (3) seniors facing abuse; and (4) people facing abuse or discrimination caused by racism or homophobia or misogyny.

Institutional care that is inadequate or unsuited to the needs of the individual or family.

Food Insecurity

With cutbacks in many income security programs, many more Canadians are also having to rely on **food banks and feeding programs** in order to survive. In 2012, there were over 1,900 food programs in Canada, and 882,188 people received emergency food from these food banks in a one-month period (Food Banks Canada, 2012). The number who utilize food banks is 31 percent above the levels before the 2008 economic crisis. According to Food Banks Canada, over 38 percent of those helped are under the age of 18.

A Helping Hand

Feeding programs provide cooked meals at specified times during the day. They often operate out of shelters or church basements and provide two meals per day. Such programs are operated by volunteers and by those who use the service. For example, The Well in Ottawa does not start providing meals until enough people volunteer to help. Many feeding programs are run in conjunction with emergency shelters.

Feeding programs often also provide additional services, such as free laundry facilities, telephone access, newspapers, and clothing. In certain instances, access to computers and the Internet is also available. At most times, social workers are available and may even work directly from within the program.

FIGURE 6.9

Relying on Food Banks

SOURCE: FOOD BANKS CANADA (2012). *HUNGERCOUNT 2012.* TORONTO: FOOD BANKS CANADA

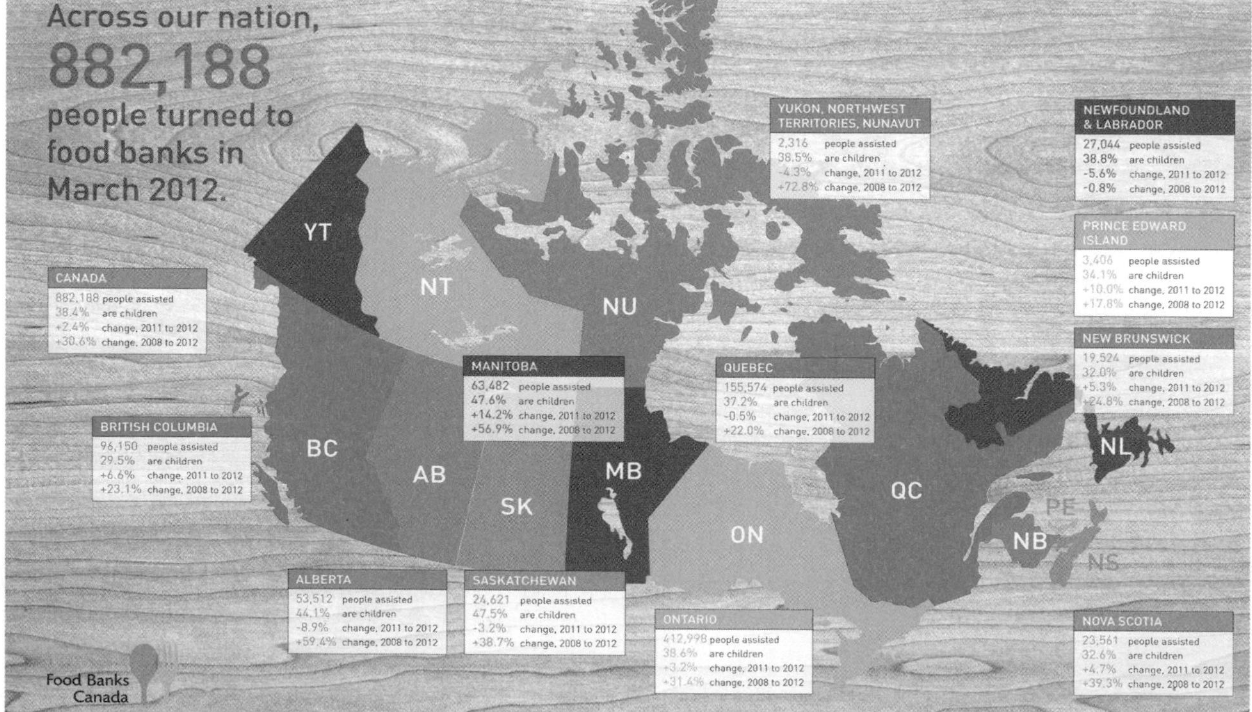

Unable to Keep Up With Demand

Of those Canadians using food banks, the majority also rely on income security programs as their income source. As Social Assistance rates decrease and eligibility requirements for EI tighten, it is estimated that food bank usage by Canadians will continue to increase.

Yet, there is difficulty in keeping pace with demand. Over half (55 percent), of food banks report that they have had to cut back the amount of food provided to each household (Food Banks Canada, 2012). Many believe that the unravelling of the social safety net means that access to basic food is in jeopardy.

"It is shocking that, in a country as prosperous as Canada, hundreds of thousands of children rely on food banks to have enough to eat each month," said Katharine Schmidt, Executive Director of Food Banks Canada, in a news release in October 2012. "Though food banks do what they can to fill the need, too many kids are still going to school on empty stomachs."

"Hunger saps you physically and emotionally, particularly if you don't know where your next meal is coming from," continued Schmidt. "It has negative long-term health impacts, and prevents Canadians from contributing to their full potential."

Hunger Counts

The HungerCount 2012 study found that:

- 11% of those receiving food each month (93,000 people) are accessing a food bank for the first time.
- 1 in 5 households assisted by food banks have income from current or recent employment.
- 21% of households helped are living on an old age or disability pension.
- Half of households receiving food are families with children.

TABLE 6.3

Food Bank Use In Canada by Province

Province/Territory	Total Assisted, March 2012	Percent Children, March 2012	Total Assisted, March 2011	Total Assisted, March 2008	% Change, 2011-2012	% Change, 2008-2012
British Columbia	96,150	29.5%	90,193	78,101	6.6%	23.1%
Alberta	53,512	44.1%	58,735	33,580	-8.9%	59.4%
Saskatchewan	24,621	47.5%	25,432	17,751	-3.2%	38.7%
Manitoba	63,482	47.6%	55,575	40,464	14.2%	56.9%
Ontario	412,998	38.6%	400,360	314,258	3.2%	31.4%
Quebec	155,574	37.2%	156,279	127,536	-0.5%	22.0%
New Brunswick	19,524	32.0%	18,539	15,638	5.3%	24.8%
Nova Scotia	23,561	32.6%	22,505	16,915	4.7%	39.3%
Prince Edward Island	3,406	34.1%	3,095	2,892	10.0%	17.8%
Newfoundland & Labrador	27,044	38.8%	28,642	27,260	-5.6%	-0.8%
Territories	2,316	38.5%	2,420	1,340	-4.3%	72.8%
Canada	882,188	38.4%	861,775	675,735	2.4%	30.6%

Source: Food Banks Canada (2012). *HungerCount 2012*. Toronto: Food Banks Canada.

From Welfare to "Workfare"

Several reforms of Social Assistance have been tried or considered over the past few decades. In some cases, these reforms have sparked controversy. Three of these reforms will be discussed here: workfare, the zero-tolerance rule concerning welfare fraud, and the "spouse-in-the-house" rule,. Many of the recent reforms have been directed at increasing work incentives or decreasing eligibility.

Canadian Council on Social Development

www.ccsd.ca

The CCSD is a non-governmental, non-profit organization founded in 1920; it seeks to develop and promote progressive social policies through research, consultation, public education, and advocacy. The publications catalogue provides an extensive list of publications that analyze poverty in Canada.

Workfare

Some provincial welfare programs require applicants to work as a term of eligibility. This is commonly known as **workfare**, and it has drawn sharp criticism from social welfare advocacy groups. Refusal to participate in the program results in some sort of penalty. For example, workfare could require people to work at specific jobs in order to get a government cheque, or it could mean that people receive a smaller cheque if they refuse to accept work through a government program. It might also require applicants to select retraining or pursue self-employment programs. Workfare placements could involve working in a community or social service agency. Applicants may also choose community work placements as a workfare option for the purposes of increasing skills, knowledge, and networks in the labour market.

Critics equate workfare as a return to the "work test" of the Elizabethan Poor Laws (see Chapter 2). Others cite research to show its failure in other countries—particularly the United States. It has also been criticized for being expensive to administer and for taking away jobs from the paid labour force.

The first Canadian food bank opened in 1981 in Edmonton as a temporary measure. Toronto's Daily Bread Food Bank, pictured here, is an organization that advocates for welfare reform and eliminating the need for food banks.

Others see workfare as a "blame-oriented" approach that ignores job creation, arguing that people want to work but that there are not enough good jobs.

It is important to distinguish between two types of workfare: formal workfare and de facto workfare.

- *Formal workfare* is officially prescribed in policy and procedures. It states that employable benefit recipients must work for a specific minimum number of work units (usually measured in hours per week) in a job that is approved by the welfare authority.
- *De facto workfare* is more common and occurs when provinces stringently enforce job-search and training requirements for employable people. The government pays monthly supplements to people who actively train for and find employment. Some provinces pay extra benefits to recipients who are participating in an approved training program or job-search activity. Other provinces deduct benefits from those who do not participate in mandated employment-related programs.

Workfare is hotly debated, and a variety of terms are used to describe it, such as formal or de facto workfare, welfare-to-work, and even trainfare. Most provinces like to call their programs, rather euphemistically, "welfare-to-work" programs.

Terminology aside, it is clear that across the country, a more coercive and disciplinary approach is being used towards welfare recipients. The programs are defining increasing numbers of people as "employable." For example, in many provinces, single parents with children are now considered employable depending on the ages of their children. In addition, these programs have mandatory participation requirements and sanctions for non-compliance, and they generally operate with the mindset of "any job is a good job."

Most workfare schemes, whether de facto or formalized, rely on the same myths that have always plagued Social Assistance: that the average user will stay on Social Assistance indefinitely if not forced to do useful work. However, Christopher Clark, a policy analyst for the Canadian Council on Social Development, points out that the reasons for the increased welfare rolls are that many households are finding it impossible to meet basic needs while working in low-income jobs (Clark, 1995).

Consider, for example, a single mother with a young child who is offered a minimum-wage paying job. In order to take the job, she must find child care and pay for her own transportation. She must deal with the stress of not being with her child, the expenses related to child care, likely loss of access to a drug plan, and the discouragement of making the same or less income than she was receiving from assistance.

As Clark writes, "if the alternative for most people on Social Assistance is a minimum-wage job, the labour market offers little hope for avoiding the poverty trap."

Prosecuting "Welfare Fraud"

Welfare fraud is not defined in provincial Social Assistance policies, but the courts have defined it generally as the deliberate attempt to deceive the government to obtain or increase welfare benefits. The data on reported cases and successful prosecutions of welfare fraud are scarce. The *Ontario Welfare Fraud Control Report 2001–2002* shows 38,452 fraud investigations (Government of Ontario, 2002). This resulted in 12,816 terminations of assistance and 393 criminal convictions. The government report says that $46 million was saved as a result of reducing or terminating assistance. They do not state the cost of tracing these missing funds.

Perpetuating Myths

Several problems become evident when one analyzes the Ontario welfare fraud statistics. First, the most prevalent reason for the reduction or termination of assistance is listed as "incarceration" (45.5 percent of cases in 1999–2001 and 43.6 percent in 2001–02). This means that most of the savings comes from terminating people who were receiving assistance while in prison. Other reasons include "spouse not declared" (10.9 percent), "undeclared income" (14.8 percent), "undeclared earnings" (9 percent), and "not at a stated address" (8.5 percent). Many of the other reported frauds were overpayments and administrative errors or cases where documents were missing.

The rules surrounding social welfare are so complex, unrealistic, and difficult to follow that recipients are likely to be in a situation where they are always breaking some rule. And it is not only recipients breaking the rules—welfare workers cannot possibly know or follow all of the rules and are left breaching key ones daily. The use of the term "fraud" to cover a wide range of non-criminal conduct builds upon and perpetuates myths about welfare recipients as criminals who prefer to rip off the system rather than work.

TABLE 6.4

Welfare Fraud in Ontario

Year	Convictions	Investigations
2001–2002	393	38,452
2000–2001	430	52,582
1999–2000	557	43,900
1998–1999	747	49,987

Source: Government of Ontario Ministry of Community and Social Services, Welfare Fraud Control Reports from 2001–02, 2000–01, 1999–00, 1998–99.

Kimberly Rogers, R.I.P.
The Welfare System at Its Worst

While the statistics on abuses within the welfare system are hard to come by, the full ramifications for individual recipients accused of fraud can be harrowing. Consider the case of Kimberly Rogers.

Sudbury resident Kimberly Rogers died on August 11, 2001, while confined to her overheated apartment; she was eight months pregnant. She had been convicted of welfare fraud for not declaring the student loans she received while collecting Social Assistance. She was sentenced to:

- Six months under house arrest
- Only three hours per week could be spent outside of her apartment
- Repayment to welfare of $13,648.31
- Eighteen months' probation
- Loss of the right to have part of her student loan forgiven
- No income at all for three months

Clearly, Kimberly's death was a case of the welfare system gone completely out of control. The public outcry against the injustice was overwhelming.

Coroner's Inquest

A coroner's inquest was called and the jury made a large number of recommendations to avoid repeat catastrophes going forward. For example, they concluded that the zero-tolerance lifetime ineligibility for Social Assistance as a result of the commission of welfare fraud pursuant to the *Ontario Works Act*, s. 36 should be eliminated.

The inquest also recommended that suspension and prosecution should not necessarily be automatic—each case should be evaluated to determine the most appropriate response. The jury also recommended that drug benefits should not be suspended even when regular benefits were and that the government should review social assistance rates, which until then had not been raised even to take account of increases in the cost of living. As well, the jury made several recommendations to other government ministries.

Most of the coroner's inquiry recommendations have yet to be implemented. One can only hope there will be no more such cases.

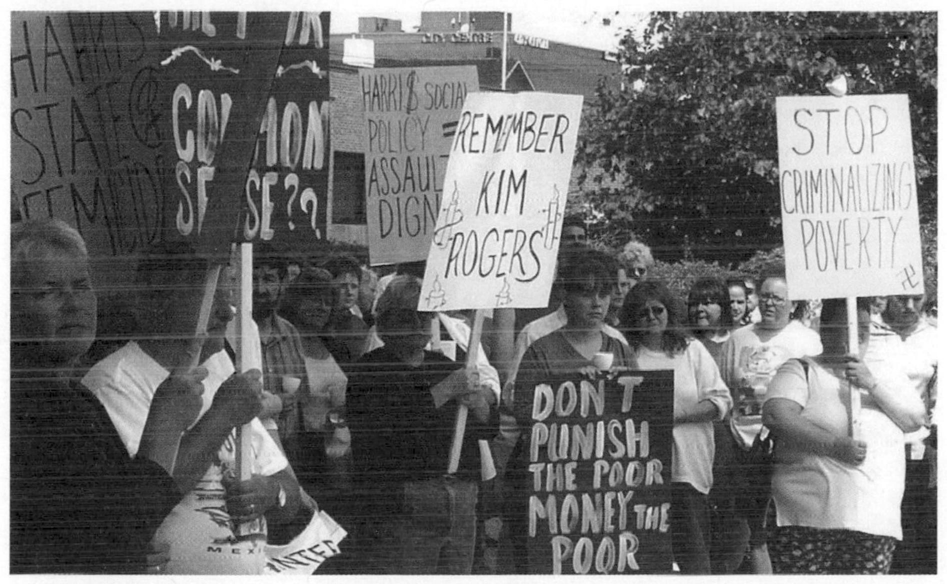

In August 2001, Kimberly Rogers died while under house arrest for committing welfare fraud. At a rally to remember Kimberly Rogers outside the provincial building in Sudbury, Ontario, protesters call for changes to welfare policies.

The "Spouse-in-the-House" Rule

A Successful Charter Challenge

Social workers and welfare advocacy groups have long been critical of the so-called "**spouse-in-the-house rule**." In some cities, welfare workers were trained to determine whether a person of the opposite sex had stayed overnight at a welfare recipient's home (they looked for things such as an extra toothbrush or shoes).

If it was determined that there was someone staying in the home, that person could have been deemed financially responsible for the person receiving welfare support. The rule is still applied (as described below) in a modified way.

Charter of Rights Challenge

Until 1986, the definition of "spouse," under Social Assistance legislation required a determination of whether opposite-sex co-residents were living together as "husband and wife." A Canadian *Charter of Rights and Freedoms* challenge to this definition prompted the Ontario government to bring in a new definition in 1987. Under the 1987 definition, an individual welfare recipient cohabitating with a person of the opposite sex had a grace period of up to three years before being considered a spouse.

In 1995, the Ontario government replaced the 1987 definition of spouse with a new definition. A person could be a spouse in one of four ways.

Three of those ways were similar to the previous definition: a person could be a spouse by self-declaration, by being required to pay support under a court order or domestic contract, or by having a support obligation under the *Family Law Act*. The Ontario government defined the fourth way to be a spouse more expansively than it had in the past. Under this provision, economic interdependence is deemed to exist as soon as there is evidence of cohabitation.

The new definition of "spouse" is overly broad, and captures relationships that are not spousal or marriage-like. This is the provision that is at issue.

Unconstitutional

The new policy was deemed unconstitutional in 2000 by the Ontario Divisional Court and again in 2002 by the Ontario Supreme Court. The 2002 court decision has ruled that citizens on welfare cannot be discriminated against just because they collect Social Assistance. The Ontario government began to appeal the case to the Supreme Court, but it dropped the appeal in 2004.

While the government has abandoned the appeal, welfare departments are still enforcing a variant of the spouse-in-the-house rule. A welfare recipient's benefits are reassessed after he or she has lived with an income-earner for three months.

This is a shift from previous policy that terminated benefits. It appears that the revised policy might be unconstitutional as well.

LEAF

This is an issue that has been debated by social policy analysts for decades, and it seems that whenever governments aim to cut spending on Social Assistance, they turn to this rule.

The Women's Legal Education and Action Fund (LEAF) is a national, non-profit organization working to promote equality for women and girls in Canada. LEAF maintains that the "spouse-in-the-house" rule directly affects single mothers who may want to form relationships.

They maintains that the law forces women and their children to be economically tied to a man or that women must give up having live-in relationships or even sharing accommodations with men.

The Charter Committee on Poverty Issues, an anti-poverty organization, also argues that Canada falls short in a number of areas stipulated in international human rights law, and the "spouse-in-the-house" regulation is just one example.

Conclusion

People can unexpectedly find themselves in poverty for a wide variety of reasons—lack of employment, employment that pays too little, a serious disability, major family responsibilities, or simply by being a member of a disadvantaged group. Policy-makers have put forth different explanations for the existence of poverty. Over the past few decades, the emphasis has been on developing programs—and indeed penalties—that would encourage people to seek gainful employment and move back into the labour force. This approach has not always worked.

Social Assistance programs intend to provide a minimum income as a last-resort measure. The levels are often not enough to allow people and families to find their way out. With the 1996 discontinuation of CAP and its replacement with the CHST, and with the 2004 CHT/CST split, the federal government has effectively cut much of the transfers to the provinces that would otherwise cover welfare programs. This has weakened the provinces' ability to handle the welfare rolls and weakened national standards and the protections available to citizens in need. It has also made welfare provision more uneven between the provinces and, in some provinces, has opened the door to more coercive programs such as "workfare," or one of its variants, as provinces attempt to deal with expenditure shortfalls.

Poverty is a serious issue in Canada. Today, Social Assistance rates in all provinces are below LICO levels. Rates in some of the provinces and territories, especially rates for "single employables," often reach only one-fifth or one-third of LICO. The situation of lone-parent families and unattached individuals is also particularly dismal. The ranks of the "working poor" are rising, as is the number of people who are homeless and those individuals and families accessing food banks.

Poverty causes not only individual hardship and lost opportunities, but it weakens the nation's economic performance. At the societal level, these benefits include better management of health care costs, reduced crime, a more productive labour force, overall advances in citizens' well-being, and greater social cohesion and public confidence. At the individual and family levels, welfare and income security can literally be a matter of life and death.

CHAPTER 6 REVIEW

KEY CONCEPTS IN CHAPTER

- Absolute measures of poverty
- Dual labour market theory
- Effectiveness of Social Assistance
- Eligibility rules
- Ethnicity
- Food banks and feeding programs
- Gini coefficient
- Homelessness (absolute and relative)
- Human capital perspective
- Inequality
- Labour market perspective
- Low Income Cut-off (LICO)
- Low Income Measure (LIM)
- Metcalf Foundation
- Market Basket Measure (MBM)
- Mowat Centre at the University of Toronto
- Multidimensional Poverty Index (MPI)
- Political economy perspective
- Poverty duration
- Poverty gap
- Poverty headcount
- Poverty
- Quintile income distribution
- Relative measures of poverty
- Social Assistance (SA)
- Social exclusion
- Spouse-in-the-house rule
- Welfare fraud
- Workfare
- Working poor

REVIEW QUESTIONS

1. What is meant by the terms "relative" and "absolute" measures of poverty? Give examples of each.
2. How does Social Assistance work? How are eligibility criteria applied?
3. What is the Poverty Gap? How is it calculated and how extensive is the poverty gap across the country?
4. What are the two types of homelessness? What do you think can be done to solve the homelessness situation?
5. What is the extent of food insecurity in Canada today? How many individuals and families depend on food banks?
6. What is meant by the term "workfare?" Research how workfare is applied in several provincial jurisdictions across the country. Compare each.

LEARNING OBJECTIVES

After completing this chapter, you should be able to:

- Distinguish between "relative" and "absolute" poverty.
- Distinguish between LICO, MBM, and LIM as measures of poverty.
- Understand the three dimensions of poverty.
- Understand "quintile distributions" and "Gini coefficients" as indicators of inequality.
- Understand how inequality has changed over time.
- Describe the three main explanations of poverty.
- Explain the flaws behind common myths about the poor.
- Understand how Social Assistance works and how eligibility criteria are applied.
- Understand the extent of the "working poor."
- Understand the extent to which food banks are depended upon.
- Understand the idea behind "workfare" in all its forms.
- Appreciate the inherent difficulties identifying and prosecuting "welfare fraud."

7. Explain the "spouse-in-the-house" rule. How is it interpreted? What's wrong with it?

CRITICAL THINKING

Why do you think that still, at the beginning of the twenty-first century, there is so much poverty in the world (and in Canada)?

What do you suppose it would be like if everyone was assured a decent standard of living and, effectively, there was no poverty?

EXPLORING SOCIAL WELFARE

1. Engage your friends and family in a discussion about poverty and the poor. Assess whether their views in any way might be influenced by prevailing myths about the poor.
2. Research the issue of the working poor in Canada. Why has the number of working poor increased in the past five years? What income security program(s) may be partially responsible for this?

WEBSITES

Food Banks Canada
http://www.foodbankscanada.ca
Food Banks Canada is the national charitable organization representing and supporting the food bank community across Canada. Food Banks Canada strives to meet the short-term need for food and find long-term solutions to hunger in order to reduce the need for food banks and emergency food services in Canada.

The Metcalf Foundation
www.metcalffoundation.com
The goal of the George Cedric Metcalf Charitable Foundation is to enhance the effectiveness of people and organizations working together to help Canadians imagine and build a just, healthy, and creative society. The Foundation focuses its resources primarily on three areas: the performing arts, the environment, and poverty reduction.

Centre for Equality Rights in Accommodation
www.equalityrights.org/cera/
The Centre for Equality Rights in Accommodation (CERA) is dedicated to promoting human rights in housing and ending housing discrimination. CERA carries out this work through public education, research, law reform, human rights casework, test case litigation, and using international human rights law and mechanisms.

PovNet
www.povnet.org
For people involved in anti-poverty work, this site has up-to-date information on a variety of pertinent issues related to the persistence of poverty in Canada.

Employment, Unemployment, and Workers' Compensation

Canadians in the Labour Market

> "Annual income twenty pounds, annual expenditure nineteen six, result happiness. Annual income twenty pounds, annual expenditure twenty pounds ought and six, result misery."
> — CHARLES DICKENS, CHAPTER TWELVE, *DAVID COPPERFIELD*

Many difficult social problems in our society can be attributed, to a large extent, to the repercussions of unemployment (or low wages). Without a job, a person faces the likely prospect of declining social status, less access to quality health care, loss of housing, and a multitude of other problems.

Two key income security programs provide insurance against a possible interruption in earnings: Employment Insurance (EI), which is delivered by the federal government, and Workers' Compensation (WC), which is offered by the provinces. This chapter examines the Canadian labour market, these two employment insurance programs, and the implications for the welfare and income security of Canadians.

Employment and Unemployment

In the nineteenth century, the concept of unemployment did not really exist. People who were physically able to work, but did not work, were assumed to be lazy. Nowadays, some form of "wage labour" is the norm. In our economy, the possibility of losing wage income is a frightening prospect for individuals and their families.

Employment includes any legal activity carried out for pay or for profit. It also includes unpaid family work when it is a direct contribution to the operation of a farm, business, or professional practice owned or operated by a related member of the household. Official **unemployment** (as it is counted in the unemployment statistics) is made up of people in the labour force who do not have paid employment, are available to take work, and are actively looking for a job.

Some employed people are employed part-time (less than 30 hours per week) and others are self-employed. Many people prefer to work part-time or be self-employed; others possibly have been put in a situation where that may seem to be the best option for them. Part-time employment and self-employment are becoming more prevalent, particularly if full-time work is less of an option in difficult economic times. Self-employed people rely on their own initiative and skills, and undertake the risks of starting and operating their own businesses.

However, paid work of some kind, sometimes involving more than one job, is the most common form of employment for most people.

The Working Income Tax Benefit (WITB)

The **Working Income Tax Benefit** (WITB) is designed to provide minimal income support to those low-income individuals and families who are already in the workforce and to encourage other Canadians to enter the workforce.

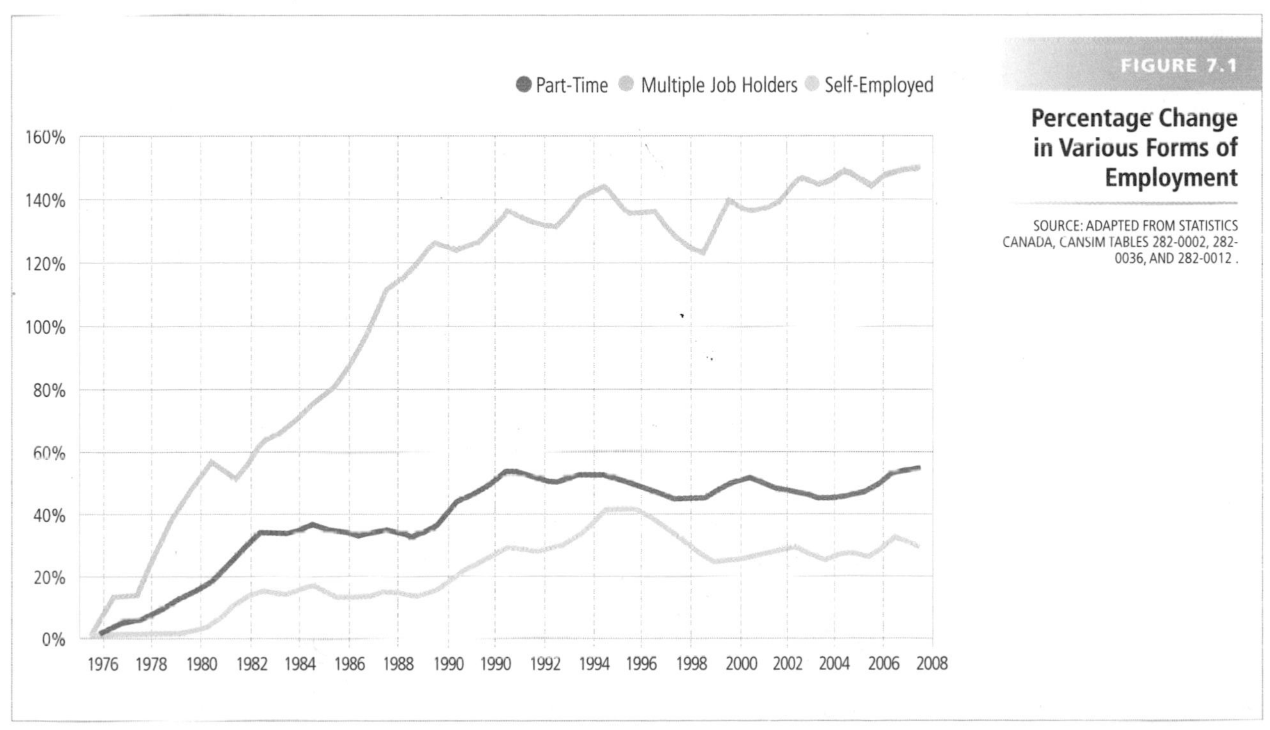

FIGURE 7.1

Percentage Change in Various Forms of Employment

SOURCE: ADAPTED FROM STATISTICS CANADA, CANSIM TABLES 282-0002, 282-0036, AND 282-0012.

Labour force

The number of people in the country 15 years of age or over who have jobs or are looking for jobs

Labour force participation rate

The percentage of the working-age population included in the labour force

Unemployment rate

The percentage of the labour force that is unemployed

Employment Ratios

The official definition of the **labour force** is the number of people in the country 15 years of age or over who either have a job or are actively looking for one. A number of key ratios are used to capture the labour force activity of Canadians. The two key ratios are the Labour Force Participation Rate and the Unemployment Rate.

The Labour Force Participation Rate

The ratio of the labour force to the working-age population (age 15 or over) is referred to as the **labour force participation rate.** It is calculated as follows:

$$\textit{Labour Force Participation Rate} = \frac{\textit{Labour Force}}{\textit{Working-Age Population}} \times 100$$

In 2012-13, the labour force participation rate was 71.3 percent for men and 62.2 percent for women (Statistics Canada, 2013). This means that 71.3 out of every 100 men and 62.2 out of every 100 women aged 15 years and over were part of the labour force. The rate varies widely between provinces. A high participation rate means that a large proportion of the working-age population is either employed or actively looking for work. A high participation rate can reflect optimism about the availability of jobs.

The Unemployment Rate

The **unemployment rate** is the percentage of the labour force that is unemployed. The rate of unemployment can be determined by the following calculation:

However, not all unemployed people are counted as unemployed. As noted earlier, if you are unemployed but have given up your search for a job, you are no longer counted as unemployed.

$$\textit{Unemployment Rate} = \frac{\textit{Number of Unemployed People}}{\textit{Number of People in the Labour Force}} \times 100$$

The rate of unemployment in Canada has varied over the years. During the Depression, the rate was around 25 percent. In the 1960s, the rate was as low as 3.4 percent. Since the mid-1970s, unemployment has risen to 10 percent and has stayed just above or below this level most of the time. Unemployment rates are higher for youth, women, persons with disabilities, and Aboriginal persons. Unemployment rates also differ widely between provinces.

The Employment-Population Ratio

Employment population ratio

The percentage of the working-age population that is employed

A third ratio worth noting is the employment-population ratio. The **employment population ratio** represents the share of employed persons as a percentage of the total population and is as follows:

$$\textit{Employment Population Ratio} = \frac{\textit{Employed Persons}}{\textit{Total Population}} \times 100$$

The employment population ratio is a fundamental indicator of the health of the labour market. The employment population ratio can be calculated for specific sub-groups and usually increases during labour market expansions and decreases during downturns.

The chart below shows the EP ratio for the 25-and-over population during the recession of 2008. Sharp declines in employment started in the final quarter of 2008 and continued well into early 2009 (with the exception of April 2009, which saw a surprising increase of 35,200 jobs, all in self-employment). In October, the unemployment rate stood at 5.1 percent and the EP ratio at 64.4 percent (69.9 percent for men and 59.2 percent for women). By May 2009, the unemployment rate increased 2.1 percentage points to 7.2 percent, and the EP ratio dropped 1.6 points, with men suffering a larger decline than women (Statistics Canada, 2012).

Factors other than the business cycle affect the employment-population ratio. The greatest long-term impact has come from the increased labour force participation of women.

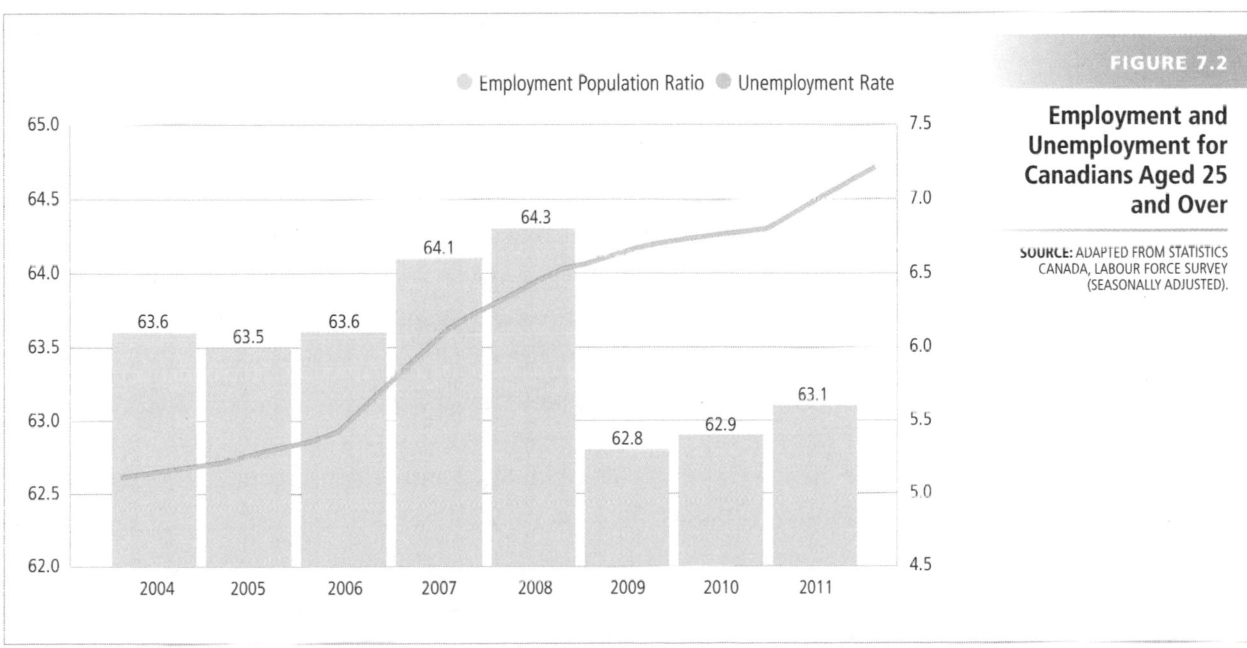

FIGURE 7.2

Employment and Unemployment for Canadians Aged 25 and Over

SOURCE: ADAPTED FROM STATISTICS CANADA, LABOUR FORCE SURVEY (SEASONALLY ADJUSTED).

Types of Unemployment

Frictional unemployment: when employees move between jobs or return to the workforce

Cyclical unemployment: results from a temporary downturn in the job market

Structural unemployment: when workers do not possess the required skills for the jobs, do not live where jobs are available, or are unwilling to work at the offered wage

Types of Unemployment

Anyone can lose his or her job, often when it is least expected. The Employment Insurance system is designed to help people through these stressful periods.

As noted earlier, if a person has given up searching for a job, he or she is not considered to be part of the labour force and is not included in the official unemployment statistics. From a narrow labour market point of view this may make sense, but from a social inclusion point of view there is something unsettling about the calculation.

As noted earlier, many Canadians also face **underemployment**—when the education and training required for the job is less than the education and training of the worker who is doing the job. Underemployment is generally not measured in Canada. Underemployment increases as higher quality jobs become relatively fewer in number.

Frictional, Cyclical, and Structural Unemployment

Some unemployment is unavoidable, due to people moving between jobs and mismatches between the skills of the unemployed and the requirements for available jobs. Employees who move between jobs cause what is known as **frictional unemployment**. This includes new labour force entrants, such as those returning to the labour force after completing school or raising children.

Cyclical unemployment occurs due to a temporary downturn in the job market. The most common form of cyclical unemployment occurs when workers are temporarily laid off.

If, on the other hand, unemployed people do not have the skills that are required for the available jobs, do not live where jobs are available, or are unwilling to work at the wage rate offered in the market, this form of unemployment is known as **structural unemployment**. The extent of structural unemployment will depend on various things:

- **MOBILITY OF LABOUR.** If people quickly switch jobs from a declining industry to a rapidly growing one, there will be less structural unemployment.
- **THE PACE OF CHANGE IN THE ECONOMY.** If demand, supply, and people's tastes change at a fast rate, industry has to adapt quickly to change. This leads to more structural unemployment.
- **THE REGIONAL STRUCTURE OF INDUSTRY.** If declining industries are heavily concentrated in one area, this may make it much more difficult for people to find new jobs (e.g., shipbuilding). Some areas have taken many years to adapt to and reduce the level of structural unemployment.

The Full Employment Debate

In 1945, the Canadian government's *White Paper on Employment and Income* made a commitment to **full employment**, accepting the argument that unemployment results mainly from the unregulated operation of labour markets. The government was committed to intervening in the economy to create jobs and control job losses. This was a recognition that the government could reduce unemployment by directly generating economic activity and assisting the private sector. At the time, this commitment was a strong break from the past, when individuals had essentially been responsible for their own employment.

Some still believe that we should reorganize our economic system to ensure that everyone who wants to work has a suitable job. However, the notion of full employment as a government policy objective has largely been abandoned. During the 1970s, in the US and other industrialized countries, the traditional trade-off between unemployment and inflation became less clear (stagflation). Monetarist economists, led by Milton Friedman, came up with the notion of the Non-Accelerating Inflation Rate of Unemployment (NAIRU), which refers to an "acceptable" level of unemployment at which inflation rises.

The *Unemployment Insurance Act* of 1971 addressed the idea of full employment and established that 4 percent unemployment was henceforth to be considered "full" employment. Subsequent to this, the idea of "full" employment has been rarely mentioned in government circles in the context of Canadian social policy.

NAIRU

A combination of frictional and structural unemployment results in what is referred to as natural unemployment or NAIRU (Non-Accelerating Inflation Rate of Unemployment). According to monetarist economists, attempts to lower unemployment below NAIRU will risk the acceleration or increase of inflation.

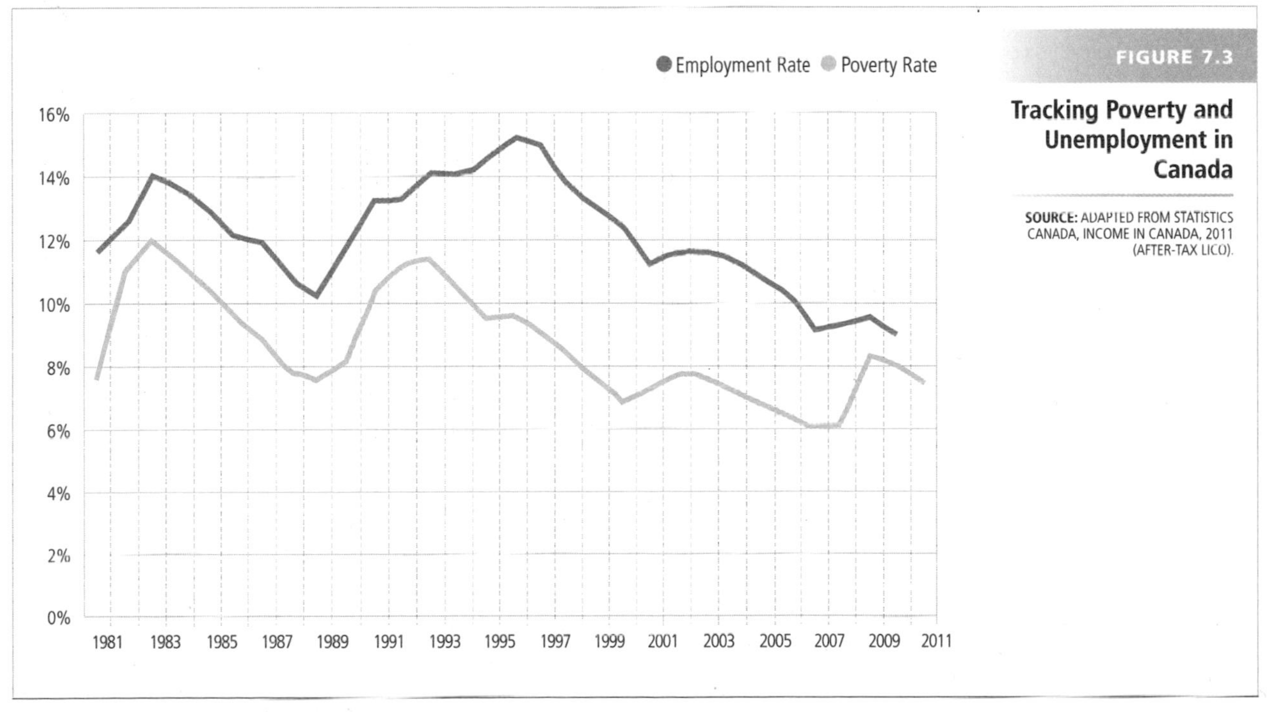

FIGURE 7.3

Tracking Poverty and Unemployment in Canada

SOURCE: ADAPTED FROM STATISTICS CANADA, INCOME IN CANADA, 2011 (AFTER-TAX LICO).

Recessionary Effects

In the first two months of 2009, 240,000 Canadians lost their jobs. By 2010, there were still 102,000 fewer jobs than in 2008.

The average duration of unemployment increased from 14.8 weeks before the 2008 crisis to 21.1 weeks in 2011 (Statistics Canada, 2012).

Factors Influencing Unemployment

Unemployment generally occurs when the supply and demand for workers or labour are out of synch. Supply and demand, in turn, are influenced by a range of forces created by the interaction of economic, structural, and policy factors.

Economic Factors

There is a range of more strictly economic factors that influence the supply and demand equation for jobs. Consider the following:

- **BUSINESS CYCLES.** Economists agree that market-driven economies move in cycles, and it is during the dips that unemployment may result. The cause of cycles is not as clear, but it is generally agreed that they are a function of supply and demand throughout the economy.
- **INDUSTRIAL ADJUSTMENT.** Production may move from high-wage countries to low-wage countries, from inefficient facilities to newer ones, and these moves can leave a trail of unemployed workers.
- **COST OF PRODUCTION AND PRODUCTIVITY.** Low productivity may result from obsolete plants and equipment, high cost of labour per unit, high transportation costs, bad management, and high taxes. The value of the Canadian dollar relative to other currencies, particularly the U.S. dollar, also has a major impact on business costs and competitiveness.
- **TECHNOLOGICAL CHANGES.** Increased automation can result in skills redundancies—situations in which the original workers do not have the technological skills necessary for new occupations. (However, technological change can also result in new products and markets or increased productivity.)

Structural Factors

Unemployment is also affected by a number of quasi-economic factors, which we will refer to as "structural." These include:

- **GROWING LABOUR SUPPLY.** Since 1981, Canada's labour supply has grown more than at any other time in its history. Women, persons with disabilities, and Aboriginal peoples have entered the labour force in growing numbers.
- **IMBALANCE BETWEEN SKILLS SUPPLY AND DEMAND.** People may not be able to take advantage of job opportunities because they lack the skills needed for the jobs available in their areas. The mismatching of skills in demand with those available is a common and persistent cause of unemployment. As Canada shifts to a more knowledge-based economy, the availability of jobs for those without high levels of education will shrink.

- **MOVEMENT BETWEEN JOBS.** Called *frictional unemployment*, this phenomenon refers to people who switch jobs. While they are between jobs, they are considered unemployed.
- **SEASONAL LAYOFFS.** People get laid off in seasonal occupations such as the resource industries, construction, and tourism. Canada is particularly affected by seasonal layoffs.
- **INTERNAL MIGRATION.** Rural-to-urban migration can increase unemployment until the migrating people find jobs.

Policy Factors

Government economic and social policies continue to be used as tools in effecting certain outcomes, such as the rate of inflation, deficit levels, and international trade. The following affect employment:

- **INTEREST RATES.** The use of high interest rates to combat inflation increases the cost of doing business and the cost of financing government deficits. This may lead to unemployment.
- **EXCHANGE RATE POLICIES.** The exchange rate policy of keeping the dollar artificially high may make Canadian products less competitive.
- **EDUCATION AND JOB TRAINING.** Government job-training initiatives can influence employment levels. These include job-specific training and support to schools, colleges, and universities, as well as apprenticeship programs.

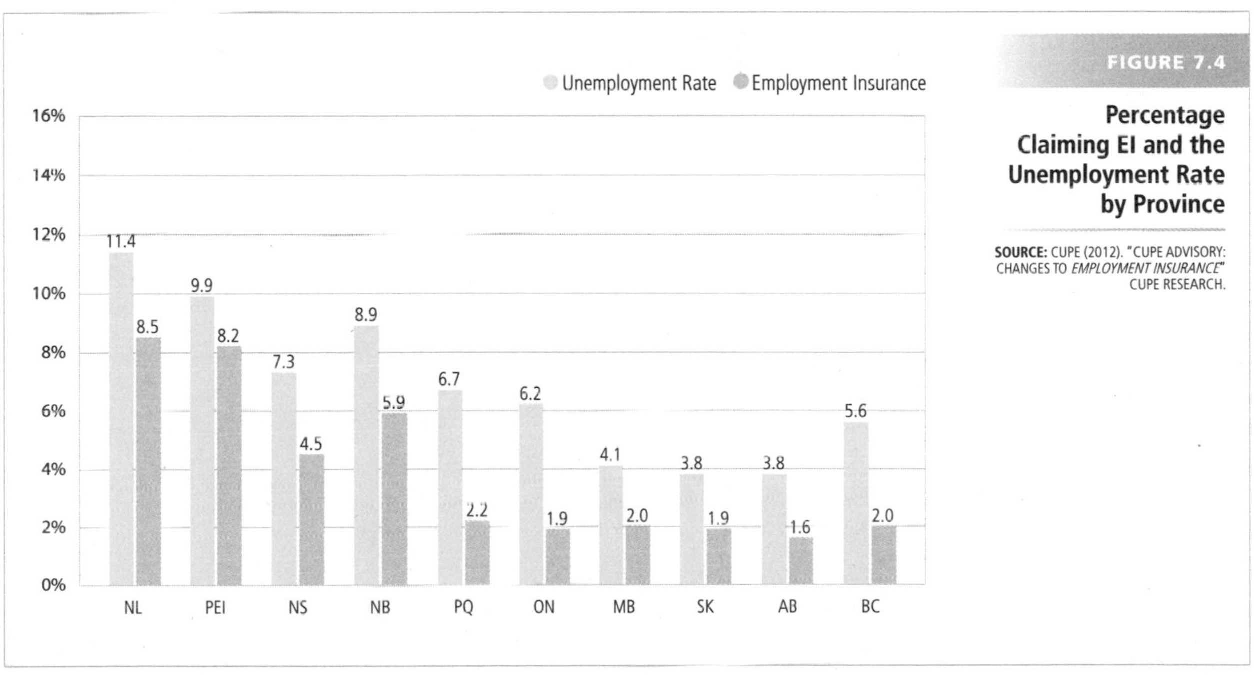

FIGURE 7.4

Percentage Claiming EI and the Unemployment Rate by Province

SOURCE: CUPE (2012). "CUPE ADVISORY: CHANGES TO *EMPLOYMENT INSURANCE*" CUPE RESEARCH.

Underemployment

When the education and training of the worker exceeds the requirements for the job

Part-Time Employment

People who have paid jobs are considered employed. However, not all employed people are employed full-time. **Part-time employment** refers to people who usually work fewer than 30 hours each week.

The *voluntary* part-time worker chooses to work fewer than 30 hours a week because he or she is a student, has personal or family responsibilities, wants to spend time in other pursuits, or may not need the income of a full-time job. The *involuntary* part-time worker prefers full-time work but can only find part-time employment.

Part-time employment has increased in the last three decades, according to Human Resources and Skills Development Canada—from 7.1 percent in 1976 to 11.83 percent in 2011. The increase is most noticeable among youth. Almost half the 47.4 percent of the employed 15-24 years olds worked part time in 2011, compared to one in four (21.1 percent) in 1976. Part-time workers are more likely than full-time workers to live under Statistics Canada's Low-Income Cut-offs (HRSDC, 2013).

Part-time workers generally experience substandard living and working conditions and a range of social problems resulting from holding several jobs while trying to balance paid work and family responsibilities.

Involuntary Part-Time Employment, 2008-2012

Many people who take part-time work do so involuntarily—they would prefer a full-time job if one were available. The increase in involuntary part-time employment is a worrisome trend because it means that the income of a growing number of Canadians is eroding.

The balance shifted dramatically beginning with the recession of 2008. In September 2008, as the recession was beginning, 20 percent of part-time workers were involuntary. That jumped to 26.3 in 2010 and back to 24.8 percent in 2011. In September of 2012, it was 25.3 percent. Today, one in four part-time employees would like to work full-time but can't find it. The trend towards short-lived and part-time jobs has made it more difficult for many Canadians to qualify for EI. Fewer full-time workers generally means fewer employees who work enough hours to qualify for Employment Insurance.

The reasons for this increase in part-time employment, and in involuntary part-time employment in particular, are many. A major difficulty, it would seem, is that, for employers, work can be added or subtracted much more easily and is much cheaper in terms of benefits. For some industries, it may be a business model that suits the post-recession world (Nazarik, 2012).

TABLE 7.1

Reasons for Part-time Work

	% Both Sexes			
	Total	**15-24**	**25-44**	**45 +**
Own illness	3.3	0.6	2.8	6.3
Caring for children	9.3	0.7	26.5	4.3
Other personal/family responsibilities	2.9	0.6	3.5	4.6
Going to school	28.7	71.0	11.8	0.8
Personal preference	26.0	4.8	15.1	55.0
Other voluntary	2.5	1.5	3.4	2.9
Other[1]	27.2	20.8	36.9	26.1
Total employed part-time (thousands)	3,311.2	1,171.5	928.9	1,210.7
% employed part-time[2]	19.1	47.4	12.4	16.4

1. Includes business conditions and inability to find full-time work.
2. Expressed as a percentage of total employed.
Source: Adapted from Statistics Canada, CANSIM Table 282-0014 and 282-0001 and Catalogue No. B9F013XIE.

Minimum Wages, 2013

These are the minimum hourly wage rates set by the provinces and territories in Canada for experienced adult workers.

Province	Wage
Alberta	$9.75
BC	$10.25
Manitoba	$10.25
New Brunswick	$10.00
Newfoundland	$10.00
NWT	$10.00
Nova Scotia	$10.30
Nunavut	$11.00
Ontario	$10.25
PEI	$10.00
Quebec	$10.15
Saskatchewan	$10.00
Yukon	$10.54

SOURCE: HUMAN RESOURCES AND SKILLS DEVELOPMENT CANADA

Minimum Wage and Social Welfare

Minimum wage laws were first instituted in Canada in 1918 in the provinces of British Columbia and Manitoba, but only women were covered. By 1920, four other provinces followed: Nova Scotia, Quebec, Ontario, and Saskatchewan. British Columbia was the first province to include men, with the *Men's Minimum Wage Act* (1925). Interestingly, the act set a higher minimum wage for men, reflecting the belief that the man should be the family's breadwinner (and therefore should be paid more).

Provincial Variations

According to Statistics Canada, approximately 5.8 percent of all employees in Canada are working at or below the provincial minimum wage. The rates vary by province and, although most provinces recently increased the minimum wage, statistics show that further increases would be required in order to raise the income of the working poor out of poverty. (Statistics Canada figures show that a full-time minimum wage earner falls well below the Low-Income Cut-Off (LICO) line.)

Young workers under 25 and women between 25 to 54 make up the majority (81 percent) of minimum wage workers. Even working 40 hours a week, many of these workers are living at or below the poverty line. Low-income single mothers are at even higher risk of living below the poverty line and not being able to provide for their children.

The rate of minimum wage work was six times higher among part-time workers in the labour force. Almost 60 percent of minimum wage workers held part-time jobs, compared with less than 20 percent for the total labour force (Statistics Canada, 2010).

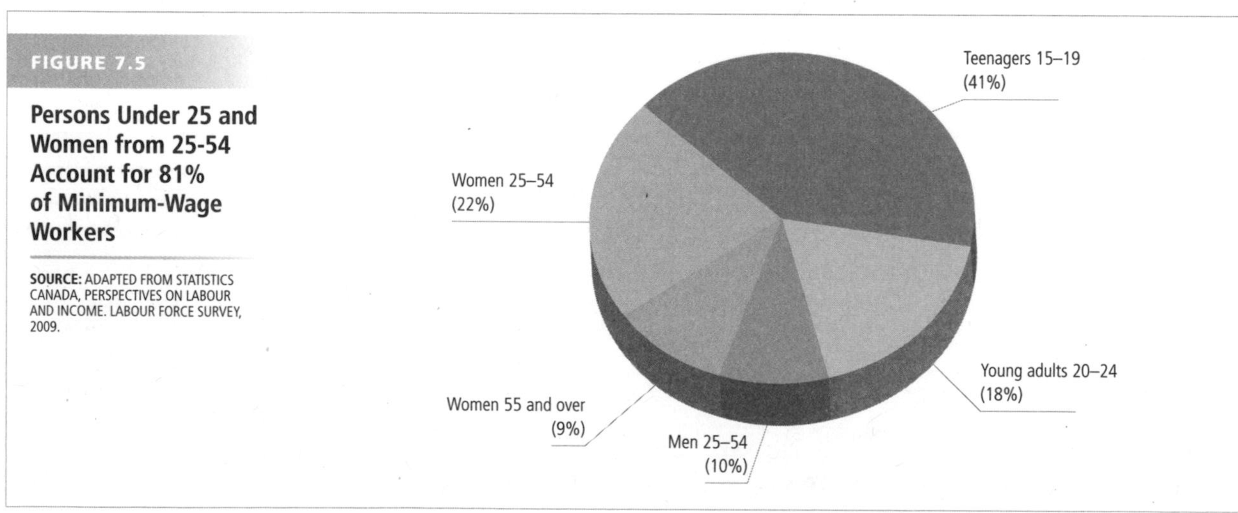

FIGURE 7.5

Persons Under 25 and Women from 25-54 Account for 81% of Minimum-Wage Workers

SOURCE: ADAPTED FROM STATISTICS CANADA, PERSPECTIVES ON LABOUR AND INCOME. LABOUR FORCE SURVEY, 2009.

Killer of Jobs?

The level of minimum wages has been the subject of considerable public and scholarly debate. Some view the minimum wage as a "killer of jobs"—hurting those it intends to help by pricing low-wage earners out of the job market. Others, specifically labour unions and anti-poverty groups, view it as a way of pursuing anti-poverty goals and greater wage equity.

With respect to the job loss argument, individual studies by economists are endlessly cited on one side or the other. However, the consensus of even the impeccably orthodox and mainstream economists at the Organization for Economic Cooperation and Development (OECD) is now that minimum wages set at "reasonable" levels do not have significant negative impacts on the employment of so-called lower-skilled adults.

Nevertheless, the debate over minimum wages continues in policy circles. Some analysts state that minimum wages should simply be set at the poverty line. Others promote a basic minimum wage as a percentage of average earnings (say, 50 percent). They believe that, in a just society, people working full-time should not find themselves living in poverty. Setting a higher minimum wage, they argue, would raise the floor for low-income earners and reduce the costs of many of our income security programs. People would then be getting their income from the labour market rather than having to turn to government transfers for help.

Many Canadians who earn minimum wage must struggle to make ends meet.

NEET

During the late 1990s, a number of European countries and the Organisation for Economic Co-operation and Development (OECD) began publishing the NEET rate—the proportion of all youth who are "Not in Education, Employment, or Training."

The term was coined in Britain after reports that an increasing number of older teenagers were leaving school and remaining jobless for long periods. Concern was raised that NEET youth would become discouraged, disengaged, and socially excluded.

Youth Unemployment

Youth unemployment—the difficulty many young people have in finding meaningful work that will enable them to make a smooth transition to adulthood—is a major problem in Canada and other rich countries, and it is unlikely to go away without policy intervention. In many European countries today, especially in Spain, Portugal, Greece, and Ireland, youth unemployment has reached catastrophic levels. Analysts are talking of a "lost generation" of youth.

Clearly, as long as they are working, young people gain valuable experience and life skills. By the same token, teens who lack job experience are at a disadvantage when competing for jobs. Research confirms that teens who have dropped out of school nowadays are having much greater difficulty finding full-time jobs than even a decade ago, and many of those who are working earn only minimum wage.

The "NEET" Generation

The importance of young people having an opportunity to acquire work experience and skills, and develop confidence, cannot be overemphasized. Policies are desperately needed to reverse this situation.

One of the problems youth face is that the economic downturn and cuts to EI forced many middle-aged and older workers with more skills and experience to accept low-income jobs. Analysts maintain that this effectively shut many employable teens and young adults out of the job market (Marshall, 2012). Indeed, it seems that many have dropped out altogether—not in employment, in education, or in training (the so-called NEET generation, see chart).

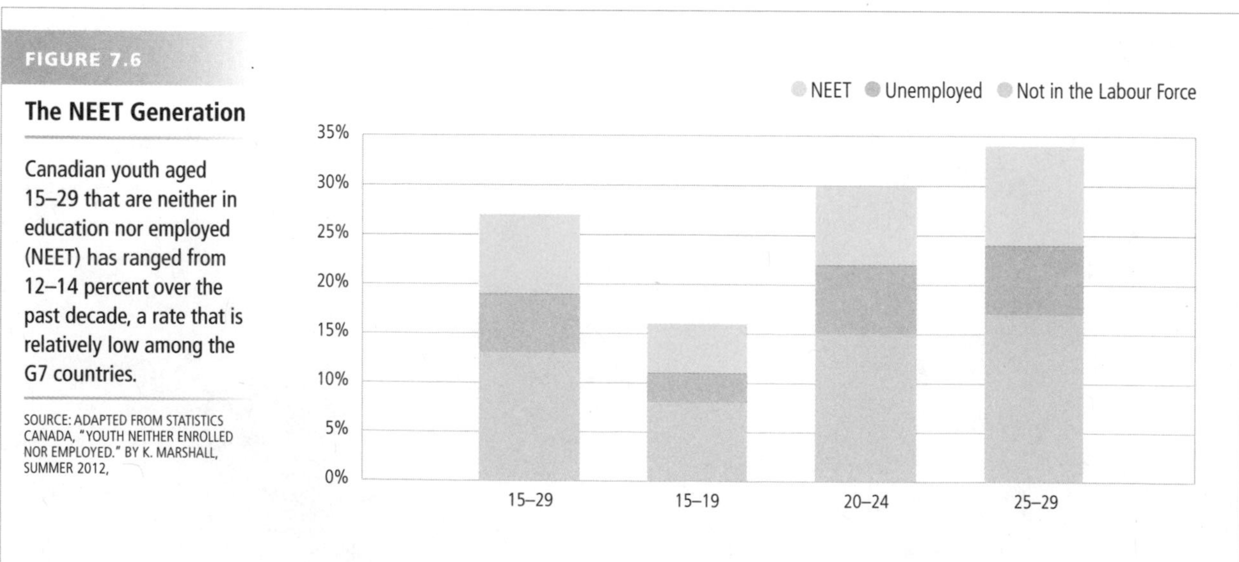

FIGURE 7.6

The NEET Generation

Canadian youth aged 15–29 that are neither in education nor employed (NEET) has ranged from 12–14 percent over the past decade, a rate that is relatively low among the G7 countries.

SOURCE: ADAPTED FROM STATISTICS CANADA, "YOUTH NEITHER ENROLLED NOR EMPLOYED." BY K. MARSHALL, SUMMER 2012,

The Plight of Younger Workers—Recessionary Effects

This trade-off was clear during the deep downturn of 2008. During and immediately after the "Great Recession," there was a surge of older workers re-entering the labour market, with massive net job losses for those aged 15-24. The recovery period has not been kind to them either. Countless youth have been discouraged by the lack of opportunity and the difficulty of finding the first serious job. Many young people have simply left the labour force; others have gone back to school to upgrade their skills and credentials still further.

A recent study by Francis Fong, released by the TD Bank, captured the plight of young Canadians during and coming out of the Great Recession of 2008. Historically, Fong noted, young workers have always been vulnerable during periods of economic downturn, and this has certainly been the case with the recent period (see chart below). In the recent recession, young people accounted for more than half the job losses, and employment still stands 250,000 below the pre-recession peak. Young workers (aged 15-19) have experienced the most difficulty (Fong, 2012).

Lack of skills and experience has always put young workers at a disadvantage when times are difficult. The unique situation today is that they are having to compete with older workers re-entering the job market, as these older workers delay retirement and thereby prevent vacancies from appearing. Fong maintained that the evidence is especially clear in the retail industries, a sector typically associated with younger workers. In this sector, the re-uptake has been slowest for younger workers as semi-retired and retired workers have re-entered the labour market (see chart below), pushing out the young.

FIGURE 7.7

Youth Employment and Job Losses by Sector

SOURCE: ADAPTED FROM STATISTICS CANADA DATA.

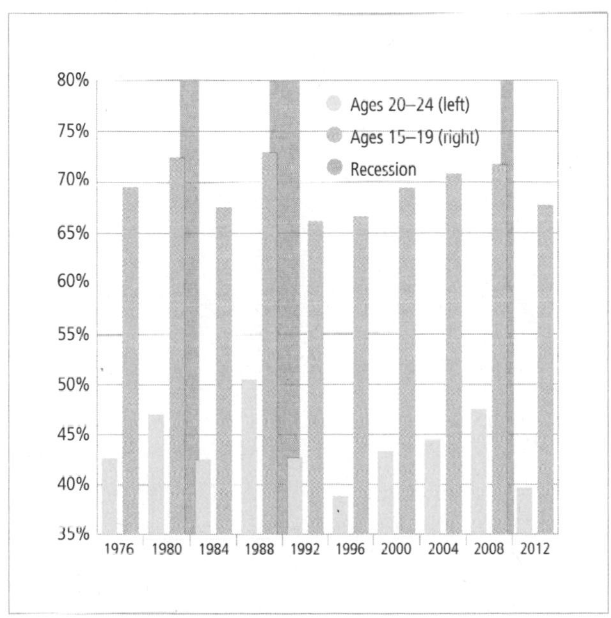

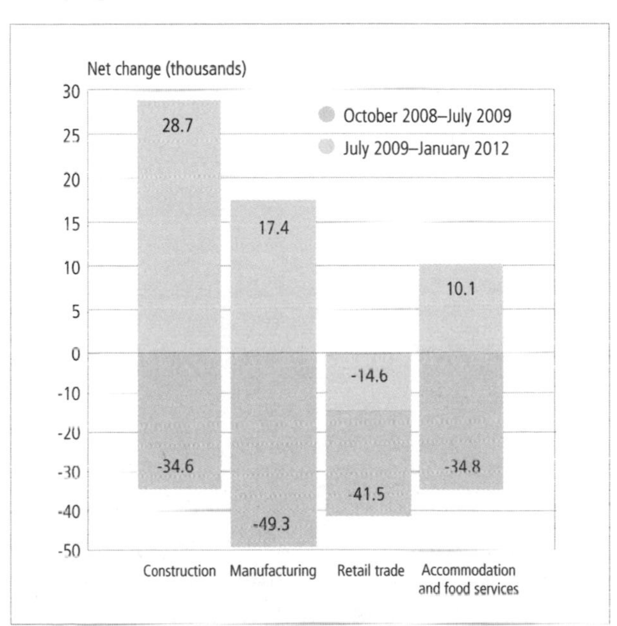

Canadian Labour Standards

The **Canada Labour Code** applies only to employment under federal jurisdiction—just 10 percent of the Canadian workforce. Provincial laws apply to the other 90 percent of workers.

The **Canada Labour Code** differs in many areas from provincial legislation. The codes deal with issues such as hours of work, minimum wage, general holidays, termination or severance pay, unjust dismissal, and various types of leave such as vacation, maternity, bereavement, or illness.

Protecting Employees—EI and WC

Two income security programs are designed to provide insurance against interruption in earnings. Employment Insurance (EI) insures against a short-term loss of employment income. Workers' Compensation (WC), on the other hand, protects the employed from the consequences of work injuries and health-related risks.

As noted earlier, EI is delivered by the federal government and WC by the provinces. Employment Insurance (previously called Unemployment Insurance) was the first national social insurance program in Canada.

Employment Insurance

Employment Insurance (EI) is a social program that contributes to the security of all Canadians by providing assistance to workers who lose their jobs. It provides temporary financial help to eligible unemployed Canadians while they look for work or upgrade their skills, while they are pregnant or caring for a newborn or adopted child, while they are sick, or while they care for a gravely ill family member. Individuals who have paid into the EI account can qualify for regular benefits of 55 percent of their average weekly insured earnings to a weekly maximum ($501 in 2013)—provided they have worked the minimum required number of insurable hours within the last 52 weeks or since the start of their last claim, whichever is shorter.

But EI does not cover all unemployed Canadians. In fact, fewer and fewer people are finding that they are eligible to draw benefits when they need them. Changes to eligibility requirements during recent years have limited the number of people who are eligible for benefits.

Workers' Compensation

Workers' Compensation (WC) is an insurance system designed to replace the tort system (the courts) in determining compensation for workplace injuries and health-related risks. Workers Compensation provides no-fault compensation. With this coverage, workers give up their right of legal action in return for certainty of compensation. Workers injured in the course of employment cannot sue employers for damages.

Roughly 85 percent of the Canadian labour force is covered by provincial WC programs. WC covers the risk of incurring costs for rehabilitation from an injury or illness contracted at or caused by the workplace or because of working. WC also provides insurance against the interruption of income or the impairment of earnings capacity, whether temporary or permanent, that arises from an illness or accident at work. This includes support for dependants in the case of the death of a worker at the workplace or arising out of work.

Case Study
Ginette and Uri

Ginette Leduc is a 32-year-old Canadian. After graduating with a communications degree from the Université de Montréal, Ginette worked for eight years with a major telecommunications company as a communications officer. She was responsible, among other things, for the publication of a company newsletter.

Four years into her job, Ginette met Uri. The two decided to get married and had a daughter, Patricia. Ginette took six months of topped-up maternity leave as provided under the collective agreement and Unemployment Insurance (as it was called in 1991).

Shortly after Ginette went on leave, Uri was laid off, and rather than look for another job, he started his own business. He and Ginette had often spoken about the advantages of a home-based business that would allow them the flexibility and autonomy to meet family needs and put their professional skills to profitable use. So, although he pursued some leads for jobs in other businesses, Uri devoted himself to getting his business started while Ginette devoted herself to Patricia.

When she went back to work, Ginette asked if she could work a four-day week in order to spend more time with Patricia. This request was granted, and as Patricia grew, the part-time arrangement provided Ginette with time to volunteer in Patricia's preschool. It also gave Ginette one day a week to devote to her sick mother.

Then, in 1994, Ginette received word that her employment was being terminated. Her supervisor explained that the company was facing stiff international competition, and all non-essential operations were being reduced or shut down. The news could not have come at a more difficult time. Ginette was three months pregnant with their second child, her mother was seriously ill, and although Uri's business was beginning to make money, he was working 50 to 60 hours a week.

The silver lining, if there was one, was that Ginette's supervisor informed her that she would be offered a contract to continue to produce the newsletter she had been writing. The supervisor could not guarantee how long this would last, but it looked reasonably secure for another year or two. Ginette could work from home. In essence, she would be doing most of the tasks she had been doing while employed, but she would have more flexibility with respect to work hours.

Ginette estimated that the work would take about 15 hours a week and thought this would be ideal, as it might give her more time to care for her mother and attend to the demands of a three-year-old and a newborn.

The difficulty, of course, was that all the benefits and advantages of paid employment were now gone. Those benefits had been crucial to the well-being of the family, because Uri, as a self-employed worker, did not have a benefits package. As an independent contractor, Ginette knew she would not have access to the maternity leave provisions of Unemployment Insurance, and she knew the extended health care plan, disability and life insurance, dental care, and employer contributions to her pension plan were gone. However, given her circumstances, Ginette felt she had no choice but to accept the contract.

The couple's combined income was about $35,000 per year when their second daughter was born. In spite of their difficult financial circumstances, Ginette felt fortunate to have the time to spend with her children and mother. In fact, she felt that were it not for the financial difficulties they were having, their lifestyle would be quite good.

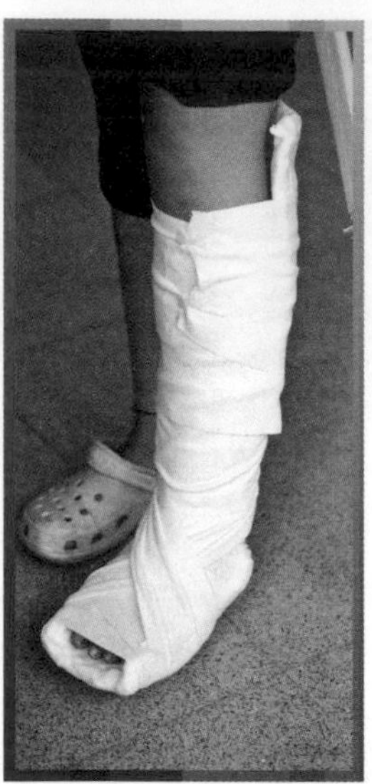

Workers' Compensation guarantees benefits to employees injured at work and protects employers from being sued.

The History of Unemployment Insurance

On August 7, 1940, the *Unemployment Insurance Act* was given royal assent and, with it, Canada became the last Western industrialized nation to institute Unemployment Insurance. Throughout the period between 1940 and 1960, numerous amendments to the UI legislation expanded eligibility and increased benefits and coverage. In general, the 1950s and particularly the 1960s saw growth in government revenues, and increased expectations from Canadians led to an expansion of the social safety net, and this included UI.

The 1970 *White Paper on Unemployment Insurance* recommended an extended and enhanced UI program, including universal coverage, increased benefits related to income, and lower contribution rates. Sickness and pregnancy benefits were also recommended. New maternity and sickness programs were also introduced, providing financial support to new mothers who worked before they had their children and to workers with short-term illnesses. In 1977, the government introduced a number of training measures for unemployed workers drawing benefits, such as work sharing and job creation programs.

During the 1990s, things began to change. The introduction of Bill C-21 in 1990 increased the number of weeks of work required to receive benefits, reduced the maximum duration of benefits for most regions, and reduced the replacement rate from 60 to 50 percent of insurable earnings for those who declined "suitable employment," quit "without just cause," or were fired. In 1993, benefits were tightened further. Bill C-113 cut the regular benefit rate from 60 percent of insurable earnings to 57 percent, and benefits for workers who quit or were fired from their jobs were eliminated.

On January 5, 1995, changes to the Employment Insurance system took effect with Bill C-12, the new *Employment Insurance Act*. The new system replaced the previous system on July 1, 1996. Beyond the name change, there were five key differences:

- **HOURS.** Benefits were based on hours worked rather than weeks.
- **EARNINGS.** Benefits were more closely tied to earnings.
- **INTENSITY RULE.** The basic benefit rate of 55 percent declined according to the number of weeks of benefits drawn in a five-year period (lowering benefits for frequent recipients).
- **EMPLOYMENT BENEFITS.** There was an increased concentration on benefits to equip an unemployed person to return to work.
- **FAMILY INCOME SUPPLEMENT.** There was enhanced protection for low-income families.

The new bill also reduced the dollar benefits payable, reduced the premiums to be paid into the EI fund by employees and employers, increased the length of work time required to be eligible, and shortened the maximum periods for which benefits can be paid.

Canada's Eroding Safety Net

Employment Insurance (at the time called UI) was successfully expanded over the postwar years and by and large fulfilled its promise. However, as a result of policy changes since the 1990s (see chart below), the EI program has been faltering. In the recession of 1982, fully 76 percent of those unemployed qualified, and in the 1990 recession, 83 percent qualified. However, EI did not hold up well in subsequent years and especially not in the aftermath of the "Great Recession" that began in 2008. In 2009, coverage was only about half of what it was in the 1990s (Mendelson, Battle, and Torjman, 2009).

The erosion began with changes to the program in the 1990s. In subsequent years, the rules governing eligibility were tightened up such that it is now more and more difficult for individuals to qualify. These changes have affected those with less stable periods in the labour force, especially women, immigrants, and youth. The amounts paid out by the program have been reduced as well.

Mendelson, Battle, and Torjman note that several other problems that have been introduced as a result of changes to the EI program. One is the funding arrangement. In the early years, the EI built up a reserve fund for servicing the next heavy draw on the system. New legislation in 2005 set premiums at a level just sufficient for the program to fund itself in the next year, leaving the program underfunded and vulnerable in the difficult times. Another problem is the regional and provincial inequities in how the program is applied across Canada's 58 "unemployment regions."

HRSDC

www.hrsdc.gc.ca

The Human Resources and Skills Development Canada (HRSDC) website provides a complete overview of Employment Insurance.

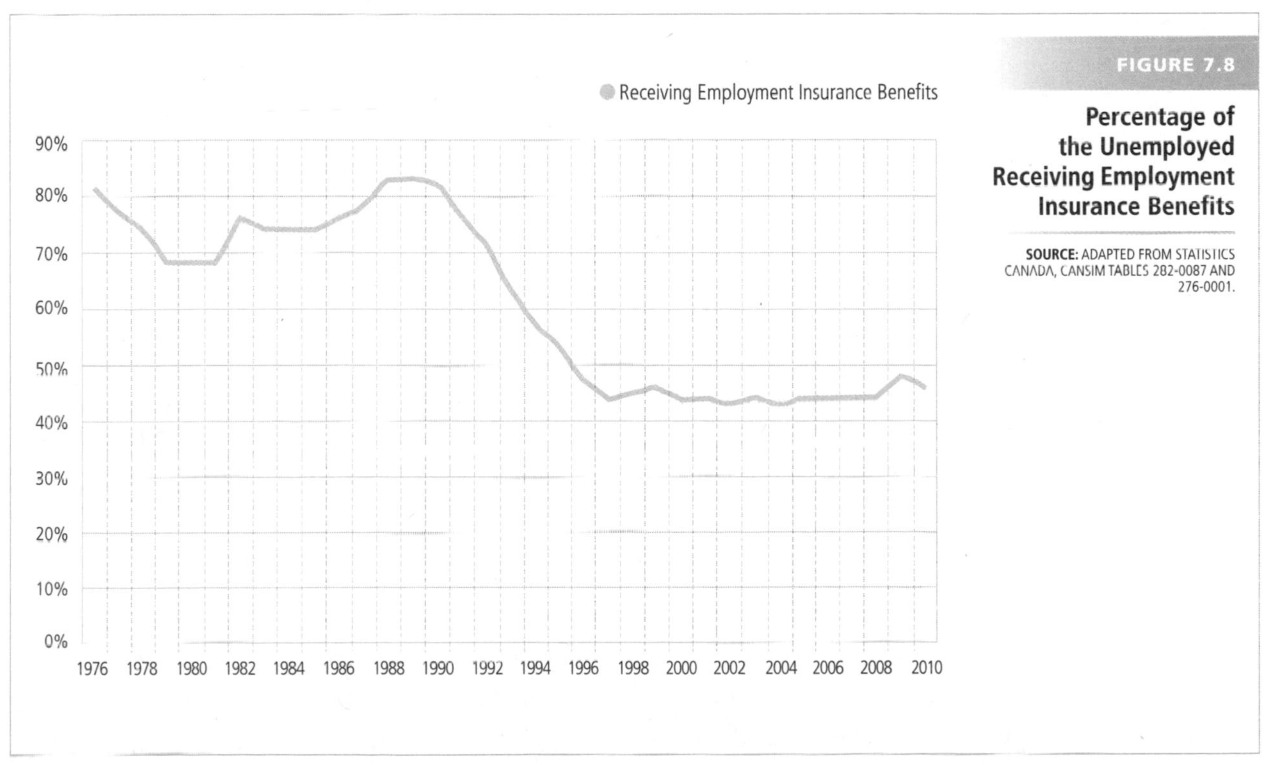

FIGURE 7.8

Percentage of the Unemployed Receiving Employment Insurance Benefits

SOURCE: ADAPTED FROM STATISTICS CANADA, CANSIM TABLES 282-0087 AND 276-0001.

Compassionate Care Benefits

In 2004, six weeks of EI compassionate care benefits (CCB) were introduced. Job protection in the federal and most provincial labour codes was simultaneously introduced. Canada is one of the few countries that has compassionate care benefits for all workers with insurable employment. Most other countries that offer such benefits restrict them to parents who are caring for sick children. Canada's program does not have these restrictions. A person can access the benefits to care for any gravely ill family member at risk of dying within 26 weeks. The definition of family member includes a wide range of people, such as grandchildren, uncles or aunts, nephews and nieces, foster parents, or even neighbours who might consider you like a family member. One needs 600 insured hours in the last 52 weeks or since the start of your last claim to qualify.

Employment Insurance: The Details

The number of insurable hours needed to qualify for EI depends on the rate of unemployment in your region. There are different **types of Employment Insurance benefits**:

- **REGULAR BENEFITS.** These are paid to people who have lost their jobs and want to return to work. To receive them, one must be actively looking for another job and be willing and able to work at all times.
- **MATERNITY/PARENTAL AND SICKNESS BENEFITS.** In addition to regular benefits, Employment Insurance provides maternity/parental and sickness benefits to individuals who are pregnant, have recently given birth, are adopting a child, are caring for a newborn, or are sick. Maternity benefits are payable to the birth mother (or surrogate mother) for a maximum of 15 weeks. A combination of maternity and parental benefits now enables women to receive up to one year of paid leave to care for their children.
- **COMPASSIONATE CARE BENEFITS.** In 2004, a new type of EI benefit was introduced called the *compassionate care benefits*. These benefits are paid to workers who have to be away from work temporarily to provide care or support to a member of their family who is gravely ill with a significant risk of death within six months.
- **FAMILY SUPPLEMENT.** The Family Supplement (FS) provides additional benefits to low-income families with children. Families with children with a net income up to a pre-determined yearly maximum have the FS benefit automatically added to their Employment Insurance payment. As income increases, the FS gradually decreases.
- **FISHING BENEFITS.** These are paid to self-employed persons engaged in fishing and who earn insufficient earnings from that activity.

The Employment Insurance program has a few other special features, such as skills development assistance, self-employment assistance, and EI for Canadian workers or residents outside Canada. The skills development assistance aims to help individuals obtain skills for employment, ranging from basic to advanced, by providing them with financial assistance to select, arrange, and pay for their own training. Self-employment assistance helps provide unemployed individuals who are eligible for EI with financial support, planning assistance, and mentoring to help them start a business.

The Employment Insurance system has a **clawback rule** which specifies that benefits must be repaid if net income is over a specific maximum. Claimants are exempt from benefit repayment (clawbacks) if they have received maternity/parental and sickness benefits. The intent of the clawback is to discourage individuals with higher annual incomes from repeatedly collecting benefits.

The Decline in Eligibility During the Great Recession

Regular benefits are 55 percent of weekly insured earnings up to a weekly maximum of $501 (as of January 2013). You may receive a higher or a lower benefit rate depending on your personal circumstances. If you are in a low-income family with children and you receive the Canadian Child Tax Benefit (CCTB), you could receive a higher benefit rate. The allowed amount of time you can be on EI, known as the **claim period**, varies depending on the number of weeks you have worked and the local unemployment rate.

To be eligible to receive regular benefits, unemployed individuals must have contributed to the EI program, they must have met the criteria for job separation, and they must have accumulated enough insurable hours. In 2011, the rate of eligibility for receiving regular Employment Insurance benefits declined to its lowest level in a decade. This was especially the case for people aged 25-44 and for women of all ages.

The main reason for the decline in the rate of eligibility was a change in the type of jobs last held by contributors with a valid job separation (*The Daily*, 2012). The share of these contributors who last worked in a permanent, full-time job—which is where one can generally have enough hours to qualify for EI—declined from 51 percent in 2010 to 45 percent in 2011. At the same time, there was an increased share of those who last worked in temporary, non-seasonal work, where one generally accumulates fewer hours.

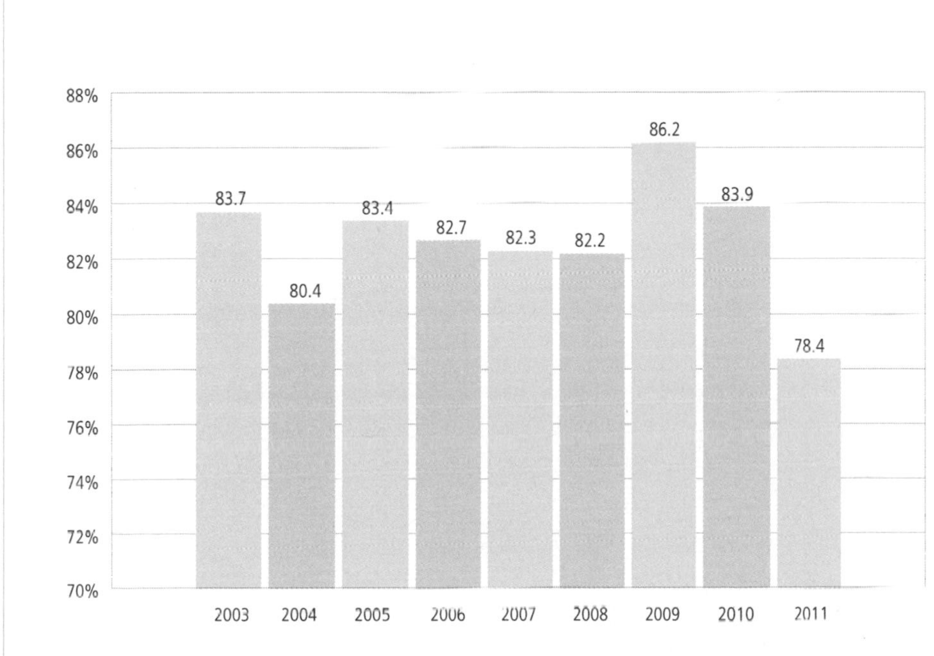

FIGURE 7.9

Employment Insurance Contributors With Enough Insurable Hours as a Share of All Contributors With a Valid Job Separation

SOURCE: ADAPTED FROM STATISTICS CANADA, EMPLOYMENT INSURANCE COVERAGE SURVEY, 2011.

EI Benefit Coverage

Statistics Canada's Employment Insurance Coverage Survey (EICS) provides the most comprehensive picture of who does or does not have access to EI benefits. The data allow three different estimates of the accessibility of the EI system.

- **B/UC RATIO.** This measures the total regular beneficiaries as a proportion of those unemployed individuals who had been contributing EI premiums in the previous 12 months.
- **R/S RATIO.** This measures the number of individuals who received regular benefits divided by the number of unemployed who had a job separation that met EI program eligibility criteria.
- **B/U RATIO.** This measures the total regular beneficiaries as a proportion of the total unemployed (both within and outside the parameters of the UI system).

By way of illustrating the difference, the three ratios are plotted in the chart below. Note that the B/UC and R/S ratios more or less follow each other and are higher. That is because the denominator is some variation of those who qualify for UI. The B/U ratio, on the other hand, measures the accessibility of UI to all the unemployed. It shows a downward tick following the 2008 recession, confirming that many became unemployed over that period but either had not paid in contributions or had not accumulated enough hours to receive benefits. In 2010, the B/U ratio was 46.4 percent, dropping from 49.0 percent in 2009.

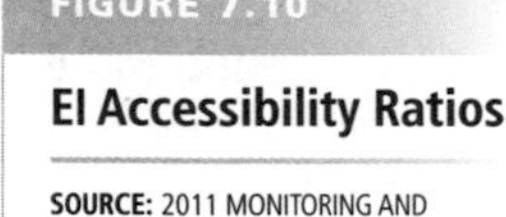

FIGURE 7.10

EI Accessibility Ratios

SOURCE: 2011 MONITORING AND ASSESSMENT REPORT, HUMAN RESOURCES AND SKILLS DEVELOPMENT CANADA, 2011 REPRODUCED WITH THE PERMISSION OF THE MINISTER OF PUBLIC WORKS AND GOVERNMENT SERVICES CANADA, 2013

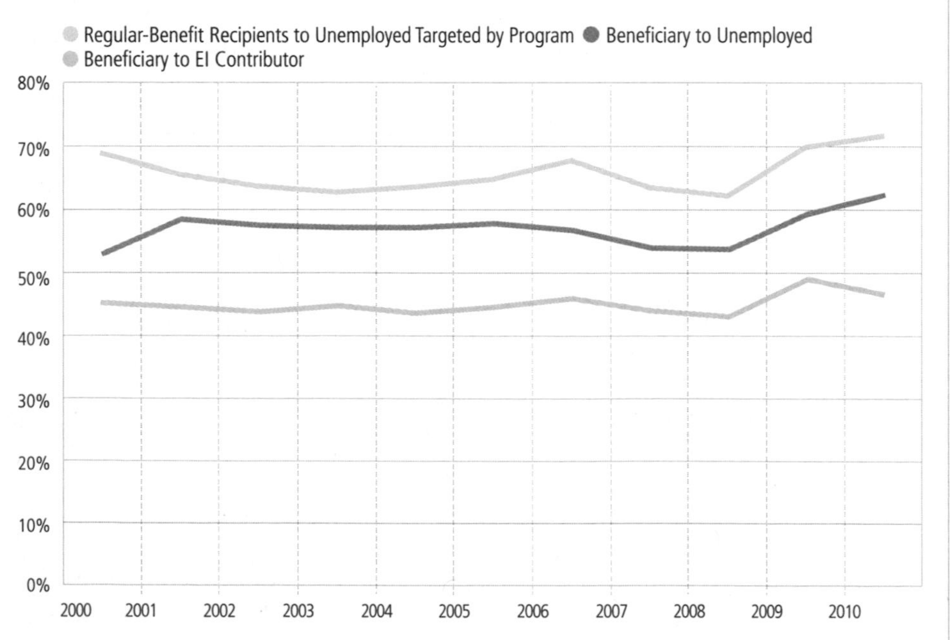

The 2012 Omnibus Bill (Bill C-38)

Radical New Changes to Employment Insurance

The Conservative government's sweeping *Omnibus Bill* (*Bill C-38*) of 2012 marked a further erosion of employment security protections for Canadians. The new changes affect regular insurance claimants but not those receiving special benefits (maternity, parental, compassionate, and sick leave). The changes place further restrictions on accessibility.

The legislation makes it still harder for workers to qualify for Employment Insurance. In particular, the changes affect the criteria as to what jobs ("suitable employment") an EI claimant will have to accept (see table below).

Capturing the essence of the changes in his announcement, the government spokesperson reportedly remarked, "Any job is a good job."

The type of work deemed suitable and the amount of reduction in wages now imposed on claimants has been lowered by the legislation. According to critics, under these new provisions, almost half of the EI claimants could be forced to accept a job with a wage that is only 70 percent of their previous job and in a position that is only somewhat matching one's skills.

The appeals system has changed as well, with cutbacks in resources, time limits on appeals, and the elimination of worker and employer seats on the appeals panels. Experts are concerned that with these restrictions, people will have to wait much longer for their claims to be heard. They may even need hire a lawyer, if this is even financially possible, to act on their behalf and argue for what they feel they deserve.

TABLE 7.2

Changes to the Employment Insurance System

Long-Tenured Workers		
Length of Time on EI	**% of Previous Wage**	**Type of Work**
0–6 weeks	90	Same
7–18 weeks	90	Same
19+ weeks	80	Similar
Occasional Claimants		
Length of Time on EI	**% of Previous Wage**	**Type of Work**
0–6 weeks	90	Same
7–18 weeks	80	Similar
19+ weeks	70	Any
Frequent Claimants		
Length of Time on EI	**% of Previous Wage**	**Type of Work**
0–6 weeks	80	Similar
7–18 weeks	70	Any
19+ weeks	70	Any

These changes affect the type of work that claimants are required to seek out and wage reductions that are now acceptable. Long tenured workers: not claimed in seven of the previous ten years and have collected 35 weeks or less of EI. Frequent claimants: three or more claims over five years totalling 60 weeks. Occasional claimants: everyone else.

Source: Government of Canada. (2013). Employment Insurance: Claimant Categories (Retrieved from: www.servicecanada.gc.ca/eng/sc/ei/ccaj/claimant.shtml)

Maternity Leave for Canadian Women

Since the extension of parental benefits in 2001, qualifying mothers are staying home longer with their newborn infants, and more fathers are claiming benefits. Canada is tied with Denmark as the fifth-best country for parents wanting time off, following Sweden, Norway, New Zealand, and Australia.

Canada offers one year of maternity leave for mothers to raise their newborns, but Canada ranks 15th when it comes to the amount of benefits offered.

Maternity and Parental Benefits

Only women can claim **maternity benefits**, which are administered in the same way as parental leave, for 15 weeks. However, the combination of maternity and parental benefits now enables parents to receive up to one year of paid leave to care for their infants. **Parental benefits** are payable either to the biological or adoptive parents while they are caring for a newborn or an adopted child. To receive either benefit, one is required to have worked 600 hours in the last 52 weeks or since the last claim.

In 2006, Quebec implemented the **Quebec Parental Insurance Plan (QPIP)**, replacing similar EI benefits. The QPIP is an expanded parental benefits plan. It is designed to support new parents in their desire to have children and support them as they devote more time to their children in their first months. The QPIP pays benefits to all eligible workers—salaried or self-employed—taking maternity leave, paternity leave, parental leave, or adoption leave. The QPIP replaced the maternity, parental, or adoption benefits previously provided to Quebec parents under the federal employment insurance plan. The QPIP is an "income replacement" plan—to be eligible for parental insurance, one must have received work income (Gouvernement du Québec, 2013).

Coverage and Eligibility for Benefits

In the rest of Canada, there has been little change in the coverage and eligibility of mothers for maternity or parental benefits since 2003. According to Statistics Canada, in 2011, 76.6 percent of all recent mothers (with a child aged 12 months or less) had insurable employment, compared with 78.9 percent in 2010. Among these insured mothers, 88.6 percent were receiving maternity or parental benefits, unchanged from 2010 (Employment Insurance Coverage Survey, 2011). On the other hand, Quebec, which has the Quebec Parental Insurance Plan (QPIP), had the highest share of recent mothers with insurable employment (86.2 percent) and the highest share of insured recent mothers receiving maternity or parental benefits (97.9 percent). For all provinces combined, only 29.3 percent of recent fathers took parental leave in 2011, little changed from both 2009 and 2010.

Interestingly, the QPIP, which was introduced in 2006, has had and continues to have a significant effect on the number of fathers who claimed or intended to claim benefits. The QPIP permits leave that applies exclusively to fathers and, as might be expected, this has altered the statistics for that province considerably. Statistics Canada report that the percentage of fathers in Quebec who took or intended to take parental leave has tripled since the introduction of the plan, from 27.8 percent in 2005 to 83.9 percent in 2011. Outside Quebec, only 11.0 percent of recent fathers took or intended to take parental leave in 2011, virtually unchanged from 2010 (Employment Insurance Coverage Survey, 2011).

Making Ends Meet on Employment Insurance
A Case Study

Kate and her daughters Taylor and Jordan live in Vancouver. Kate lost her job in 2009.

Because the Vancouver economy has been struggling throughout the recession, Kate has not been able to find new work. Fortunately, because she had worked full-time since Jordan started kindergarten two years ago, she had enough hours to qualify for Employment Insurance benefits. She even qualified for the maximum of forty-one weeks. Kate's former retail sector job paid $540 a week, or $28,080 a year, which was a modest but decent income. But now her weekly EI benefit is only $270 a week. Because it runs out after 41 weeks, Kate will actually be on her own, and potentially struggling financially for the last two months of the year.

Kate also receives $650 a month in child benefits, the BC Earned Income Supplement, and the GST and BC climate action credits. This brings her total monthly income to $1,730 for the months that she receives EI. Kate's income for the whole year, $19,950, is $7,894 below the after-tax LICO.

The average rent for a two-bedroom apartment in Vancouver is $1,169 a month. This would take up 67.5 p of Kate's monthly income, leaving her $561 a month to spend on food, clothing, utilities, transportation and other necessities for her family. This means that Kate would have to spend well below the $522.86 a month on food that the Dieticians of Canada calculate that it would cost for a nutritious food box for her family.

In comparison, if Kate lived in Montreal, she would qualify for 45 weeks of benefits, almost an extra month. Child benefits (federal and provincial) plus the GST credit would give Kate an additional $883 a month, bringing her total monthly income to $1,963 for the months that she receives EI. Kate's income for the whole year would be $22,746, $5,098 below the after-tax LICO.

Across the country, many Canadians like Kate are struggling to make ends meet on EI benefits that are simply not high enough to keep them and their families out of poverty.

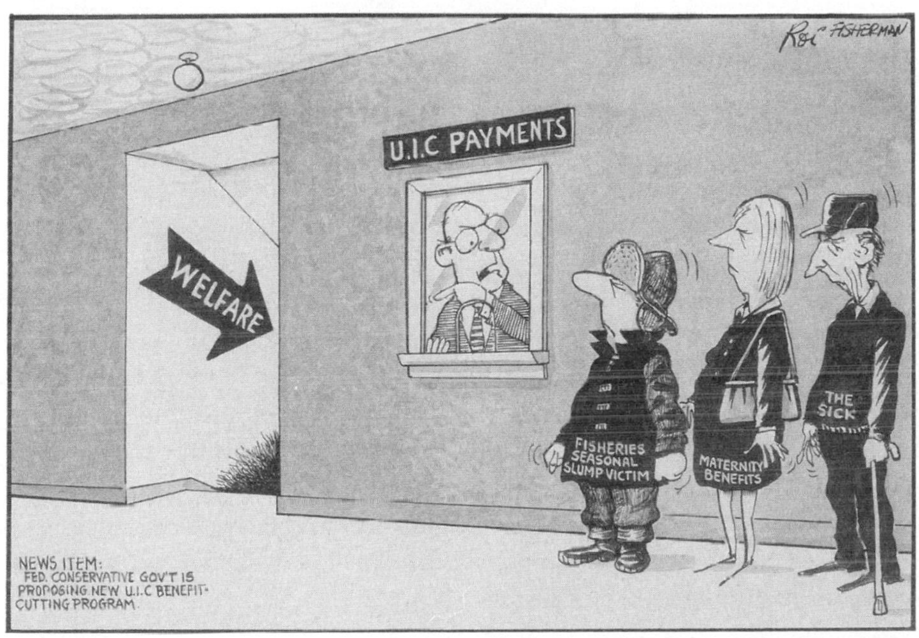

"You're all on the wrong floor, try the basement"

The History of Workers' Compensation

Workplace Safety and Insurance Board

www.wsib.on.ca

The WSIB administers the Workers' Compensation system in Ontario and advocates for workplace safety, health, and injury prevention.

The idea of **Workers' Compensation** originated in England and the United States in the late 1800s and early 1900s. Early laws in England made it extremely difficult for workers to sue an employer successfully for negligence. The employers' defences, which developed earlier in the nineteenth century, were based on the assumptions that contracts between workers and their employers were the same as commercial contracts between people of equal bargaining power. If workers did not like the employers' terms and conditions, they could simply find work elsewhere.

By the end of the nineteenth century, the situation began to change. Unions were becoming more powerful, and political parties of the day competed for the labour vote. The government passed legislation that slightly loosened the hold of employers' defences, and it became somewhat easier for workers to succeed in the courts. A spate of successful lawsuits concerning the dangerous factories of the era put many employers in a panic. Employers began to push for legislation that protected them from these lawsuits.

Royal Commission, 1913

To some extent, this was a worldwide problem, and it resulted in England's 1897 *Workmen's Compensation Act* and numerous state acts in the United States between 1908 and 1915. Germany enacted the first Workers' Compensation law in 1884, followed by Poland the same year, and England, Czechoslovakia, and Austria in 1887. The new laws were the first instance in history of a compulsory social insurance program. The German program was based on a non-profit system that required employers, through trade associations, to operate a collective liability system of insurance which was guaranteed by the government.

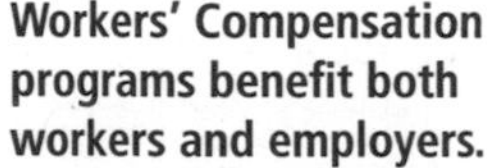

Workers' Compensation programs benefit both workers and employers.

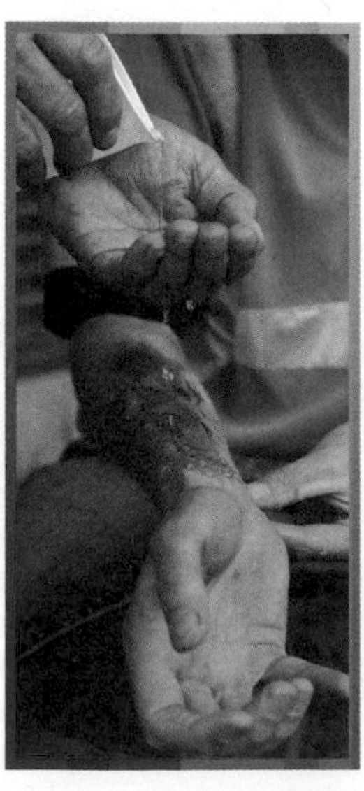

In Ontario, increasing accident rates and pressure from labour unions led the government to appoint a Royal Commission, headed by William Meredith, to study the matter. The Royal Commission report was submitted in 1913 (Meredith, 1913). Meredith rejected the assumptions underlying employers' legal defences. He maintained that workers had few choices concerning their places of work. He condemned the fellow servant rule as a "relic of barbarism." Meredith recommended abolishing what he called "this nuisance of litigation" and proposed the "historic compromise" that became known as the *Meredith principle*.

The **Meredith principle** is a compromise in which workers give up the right to sue for work-related injuries, irrespective of fault, in return for guaranteed compensation for accepted claims.

Provincial Legislation

Meredith Principle

A 1913 compromise in which workers give up their right to sue employers for work-related injuries in exchange for guaranteed compensation.

Every province has its own Workers' Compensation program, but eligibility criteria, benefit levels, and coverage all vary considerably between the provinces. Some provinces and territories, such as the Yukon, the Northwest Territories, Nunavut, and Newfoundland and Labrador have added both workplace health and safety to the titles of their organizations. Other provinces, such as Manitoba, Alberta, Nova Scotia, and British Columbia, work exclusively in injury compensation, and they have retained the title of Workers' Compensation Board.

When Workers' Compensation systems first began, far less was known about the intricate relationship between one's work and health. In the early days, work injuries were usually readily identifiable as traumatic incidents. Today, many claims relate to occupational diseases or hazards. For example, claims for items such as occupational cancer due to prolonged exposure to chemicals at the workplace are more common today than they used to be.

The Meredith Principle, 1913

Guaranteed Compensation for Accepted Claims

The Meredith principle still forms the basis of Workers' Compensation systems across Canada. It was the first legislative challenge to the idea that free enterprise without government interference would be just and fair.

As a result of Meredith's report, *Ontario's Workmen's Compensation Act* received royal assent in 1914 and was implemented in 1915. The *Workers' Compensation Act of Manitoba* quickly followed suit in 1916. British Columbia's *Workmen's Compensation Act* was passed in 1902, but it did not come into force until 1917, when the Workmen's Compensation Board was created.

Legislation followed in all other provinces and territories over the next 40 years. Yukon did not institute legislation until the 1958 Workmen's Compensation Ordinance; Saskatchewan's legislation came in 1930, PEI's in 1949, and Newfoundland's in 1950.

The passage of these early acts in Ontario, BC, and Manitoba was revolutionary. At the time, no social welfare programs existed in Canada—nor did the income taxes to fund them. These programs were also revolutionary in that they broke away from the principle of individual fault and prescribed a collective responsibility.

Expanded Coverage

Until the 1960s, changes to programs consisted mostly of revising benefit levels and clinical rating schedules to enable the boards to more easily determine benefit rates and prevent litigation. The use of schedules provided a kind of rough-average justice but also provided benefits based on a presumed wage loss related to the nature and extent of the injury—rather than the impact of the injury on one's earnings.

In the 1960s, compensation was expanded to include injuries that developed over time, as long as they were work-related. This means that conditions such as occupational cancer and chronic stress could now be claimed. Conditions such as these are currently giving the boards difficulty because it is hard to be sure whether or not such conditions are work-related.

Some governments are removing such items from their lists and refusing to accept related claims. The problem with this approach is that it merely places the problem back into the courts, and employers find themselves in litigation—situations that Workers' Compensation Boards were created to avoid.

Many people living in poverty are participating in the workforce. In most places in Canada, people working full-time in minimum wage jobs would be below the Low Income Cut-off for their area.

The Efficiency/Equity Debate

The **efficiency/equity debate** is at the heart of many social policy discussions and debates over employment and unemployment in particular.

Economic efficiency generally refers to economic growth with a flexible and increasingly productive labour market. Social equity, on the other hand, refers to the existence of adequate levels of health and security for all people and a reasonably equal distribution of income and wealth. Statements such as "Canada cannot afford generous social programs" or "more taxes will just kill the economy" contain ideas about trade-offs between economic efficiency and social equity.

Some argue that social spending undermines competitiveness by channelling valuable resources away from making business firms more competitive. Others counter that social spending helps improve employee skill levels, employee health and confidence, and family security, thereby making Canada more competitive. So what is the relationship between economic efficiency and social equity? Is there a direct trade-off, as many would have us believe?

The issue is complex, to be sure. The largest collection of research on the issue seems to be the Luxembourg Income Study (LIS) project, a database of household income surveys. These surveys provide demographic, income, and expenditure information on three different levels (household, person, and child), from twenty-five countries on four continents (Europe, America, Asia, and Oceania). The LIS data generally shows that the "efficiency-equality trade-off associated with welfare state economies does not hold" (Bohácek, 2002, p.1).

From Welfare State to Social Investment State

In the last decade, governments worldwide have started to recognize that a new policy mix is required to respond to changing labour markets, an aging population, worsening inequality, poverty, and a knowledge-based economy. Governments in the European Union are now considering social policy, economic policy, and employment policy in a new way—as being interrelated. Rather than seeing an inverse trade-off, they see each area reinforcing one another.

With this in mind, they put forward a social welfare policy mix that addresses employment support, income support (especially for families with children), and service support (such as housing and child care). They call this an "activation for social inclusion strategy."

The social investment state and its variations focus on:

- Partnership investments in lifelong learning and training;
- Encouragement for family-friendly workplaces; and
- Support for innovation, entrepreneurship, and expansion of existing enterprises.

Conclusion

Like other developed economies, Canada is shifting to an information- and knowledge-based economy and, whether we like it or not, Canada now competes in a world market.

To do so effectively, above all we need a highly competent and highly confident workforce, and we need employment and social programs that help us get there. Rather than viewing these programs as a drain on the economy, there is a need to look more closely at the interactions between the economy, employment, and social policy. Employment and social programs can be better designed to ensure that every Canadian has the opportunity to participate actively in all aspects of community life and that Canadians are ready to meet the challenges of employment and living in the twenty-first century.

A strong EI program is one of the keys to competing on a world scale. It can facilitate the transition period. Many social welfare analysts are now calling for a change in outlook premised on the idea of social inclusion rather than exclusion. The concern is that too many people—particularly young people and minorities—have been shut out of the system, and recent EI changes are making it even more difficult to qualify. Rather than forcing people off the system, the idea is for EI to be more inclusive, and to see it playing a bigger part in preparing Canadians for the challenges they will face in the twenty-first century.

This approach is more in line with the policies of several Scandanavian countries that have been able to use social programs to propel their economies forward. The idea is to use employment and social programs pro-actively to help build a confident workforce and encourage people, especially young people, to gain the knowledge, skills, and experience in order to meet future challenges. It is an inclusive strategy that ultimately will reduce the number of individuals and families requiring social welfare assistance in the first place.

CHAPTER 7 REVIEW

LEARNING OBJECTIVES

After completing this chapter, students should be able to:

- Describe the main employment ratios used to capture economic activity.
- Discuss the "full employment" debate.
- Describe the main causal factors leading to unemployment.
- Understand the many factors associated with part-time work.
- Discuss the pros and cons of "minimum wage" legislation.
- Discuss the state of youth unemployment.
- Outline the history of EI and WC.
- Understand the main components of the EI system.
- Explain the possible effects of the new changes to EI.
- Understand paternity and parental benefits.
- Describe the history of Worker's Compensation.
- Understand the debate over "efficiency vs. equity" with respect to employment.

KEY CONCEPTS IN CHAPTER

- B/U ratio, B/UC ratio, R/S ratio
- Claim period
- Clawback rule
- Cyclical unemployment
- Efficiency/equity debate
- Employment
- Employment rate
- Employment Insurance (EI)
- Employment population ratio
- Frictional unemployment
- Full employment
- Labour force participation rate
- Maternal benefits
- Meredith principle
- Minimum wage laws
- NAIRU (Non-Accelerating Inflation Rate of Unemployment)
- Parental benefits
- NEET Generation (Not in Employment, in Education, or in Training)
- Part-time employment
- Omnibus Bill (Bill C-38)
- Quebec Parental Insurance Plan (QPIP)
- Self-employment
- Structural unemployment
- Underemployment
- Unemployment
- Unemployment rate
- Workers' Compensation (WC)
- Youth unemployment

REVIEW QUESTIONS

1. Why are people who have stopped looking for a job not counted in the official unemployment statistics? What other ways are there to measure labour force activity?
2. What is the B/U ratio, and how has it changed over the past decade?
3. Do you think minimum wage laws are a good idea? Explain why you think this way.
4. Describe the labour market experiences of youth, and explain possible reasons for these experiences.
5. What was the primary impetus for the introduction of Workers' Compensation in the industrialized countries of the world, including Canada? Explain.
6. What is the "Meredith Rule?" What was the compromise reached by this rule?

7. Define what is meant by the concepts of "economic efficiency" and "social equity," and explain why some might regard the two as being in a trade-off relationship.

CRITICAL THINKING

If everyone had a good job and was earning a good income from it, and was contributing usefully to society, would this be a bad thing?

What's "wrong" with the idea of full employment? Why have governments not pursued it?

EXPLORING SOCIAL WELFARE

1. Visit the Government of Canada's Youth Employment Strategy website (www.youth.gc.ca/eng/common/yes.shtml). What are the major components of the strategy? Write a brief overview of the strategy outlining your opinion on how it will affect young Canadians.
3. Examine closely a recent news item concerning changes to employment insurance. Describe the change and how this will affect eligibility levels among the unemployed.

WEBSITES

Canadian Labour Congress
www.clc-ctc.ca
The CLC is the umbrella organization for dozens of affiliated Canadian and international unions, as well as provincial federations of labour and regional labour councils. The Canadian Labour Congress represents the interests of more than three million affiliated workers in every imaginable occupation from coast to coast to coast. The CLC conducts research and publishes employment- and labour-related reports, many of which are available online.

Canadian Policy Research Networks (CPRN)
www.cprn.org
Founded in 1994, CPRN's mission is to create knowledge and lead public debate on social and economic issues important to the well-being of Canadians. It currently has four themes or networks in the areas of family, health, public involvement, and work.

Perspectives on Labour and Income
www.statcan.gc.ca/pub/75-001-x/
This publication from Statistics Canada brings together and analyzes a wide range of labour and income data. Topics include youth in the labour market, pensions and retirement, work arrangements, education and training, and trends in family income. One section highlights new products, surveys, research projects and conferences. Another section uses charts and text to describe a variety of subjects related to labour and income.

Women and the Family

Changing Roles and Emerging Household Trends

"Most people do not understand sexism or if they do they think it is not a problem ... Their misunderstanding of feminist politics reflects the reality that most folks learn about feminism from patriarchal mass media."
— BELL HOOKS, AFRICAN-AMERICAN SCHOLAR, WRITER, AND SOCIAL ACTIVIST

Over the decades, social policy analysts have examined income security and have paid special attention to women and families—and for good reason. A gendered division of labour exists in Canadian society that has resulted in women earning less than men and working in low-wage industries. In addition, many women bear the primary responsibility of caregiving for dependent family members.

While there are income security programs in place to assist women and families, they are often based on outdated conceptions and can help perpetuate women's disadvantaged position. This chapter explores the changing roles and emerging household trends and the implications for income security of Canadians.

Labour Force Participation of Women

One of the defining social characteristics of the second half of the 20th century has been the increasing labour force participation of women. Indeed, the participation rate for Canadian women more than doubled in a 30-year period, from 29 percent in 1961 to almost 60 percent in 1991. Today it stands at 62.2 percent.

The social implications of this remarkable economic shift were phenomenal. Among other things, it gave rise to the dominance of the two-earner family, increased the demand for child care, increased the need for part-time work and flexible work arrangements, and heightened the pressure for legislation that would foster and ensure equality between men and women (Gunderson, 1998).

The Gender Gap

Nevertheless, by virtue of the primary role they are expected to play in caregiving and their disadvantaged position in the labour market, more women than men still live in poverty. In the case of lone-parent families, the burden is even greater. Despite all the legislative changes in the area of pay equity and employment equity, there is a continuing need for social policy-makers and social work practitioners to be aware of the economic problems women still face as women.

This chapter examines the role that income security programs play in perpetuating or alleviating the challenging conditions that Canadian women and families face.

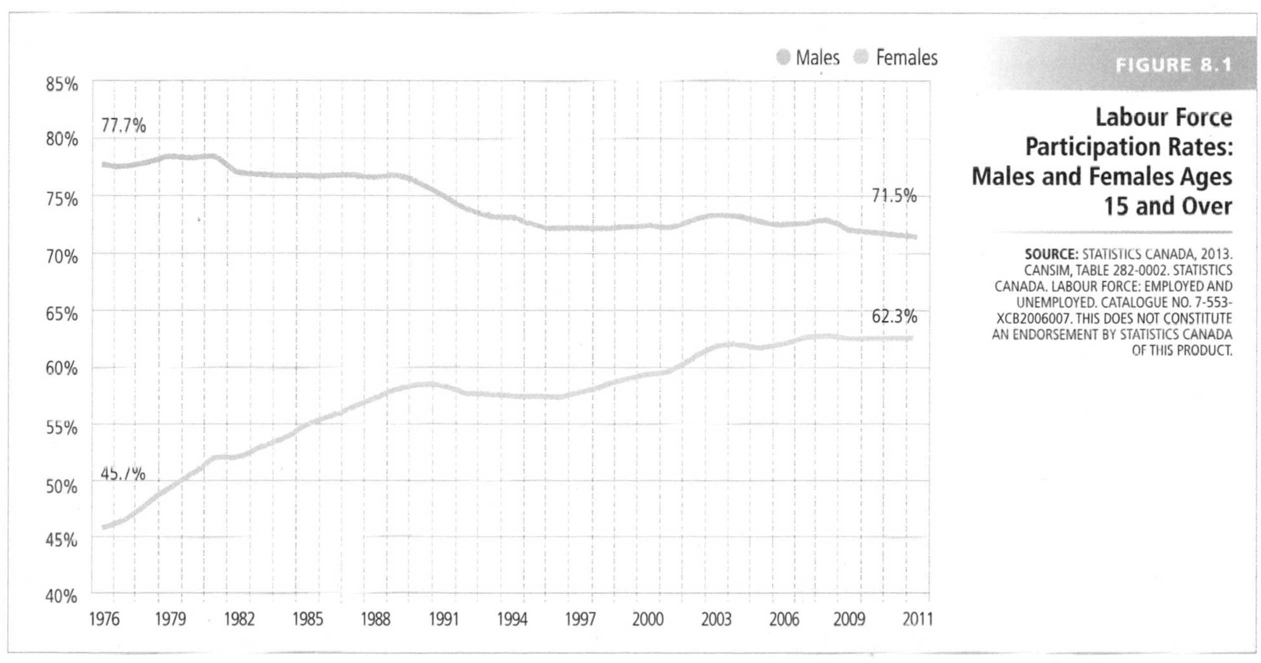

FIGURE 8.1

Labour Force Participation Rates: Males and Females Ages 15 and Over

SOURCE: STATISTICS CANADA, 2013. CANSIM, TABLE 282-0002. STATISTICS CANADA. LABOUR FORCE: EMPLOYED AND UNEMPLOYED. CATALOGUE NO. 7-553-XCB2006007. THIS DOES NOT CONSTITUTE AN ENDORSEMENT BY STATISTICS CANADA OF THIS PRODUCT.

Employment Equity

Since the 1970s, increasing numbers of women have entered the labour force. As a result, there has been a shift in the policy representation of women from "stay-at-home mothers" to "worker-mothers." This shift has helped to reverse the economic dependency of women. However, it has by no means completely altered the disadvantages that women face in the workplace or in the home.

In the economic sphere, there were many legislative changes in the post-World War II period, and especially in the 1970s and beyond, aimed at fostering greater gender equality at work. Among these policy initiatives were the following:

- **Equal pay policies** (including pay equity or equal pay for work of equal value) designed to improve women's pay
- **Equal employment policies** (including employment equity) to help women's employment and promotion opportunities
- **Other facilitating policies** (e.g., child care, parental leave) to put women on an equal footing with men in the labour market (Gunderson, 1998).

Nevertheless, although more and more Canadian women entered the labour force in this period, they seldom did so on equal terms with men. The industries and occupations initially open to women were the less-prestigious ones. Women's incomes were far inferior to those of men in the same occupations, and all sorts of sexist justifications for this fundamental inequality were readily available. In addition, many women ended up doing double duty—working and taking on primary responsibility for child care and elder care at home.

TABLE 8.1

Average Hourly Wage by Sex and Occupation

Occupation	Males ($)	Females ($)	Ratio
Management occupations	36.50	29.11	0.80
Business, finance, and administrative occupations	23.86	20.29	0.85
Natural and applied science and related occupations	31.43	27.66	0.88
Health occupations	25.78	25.19	0.98
Occupations in social science, education, government service, and religion	30.68	26.69	0.87
Occupations in art, culture, recreation, and sport	24.14	23.89	0.99
Sales and service occupations	19.72	14.33	0.73
Trades, transport and equipment operators, and related occupations	22.59	16.81	0.74
Occupations unique to primary industry	21.53	14.97	0.70
Occupations unique to processing, manufacturing, and utilities	20.95	14.83	0.71

Source: Adapted from Statistics Canada, "Labour Force Survey estimates, wages of employees by type of work, National Occupational Classification for Statistics (NOC-s), sex and age group, annual (current dollars unless otherwise noted

Male Jobs and Female Jobs

Much of the gender wage gap can be explained by differences in the typical workplaces of women and men. Research consistently indicates that "women are concentrated in low-paying occupations, industries, establishments, and occupations ... and that gender segregation accounts for a sizable portion of the overall gender wage gap" (Drolet, 2002). For example, men have higher levels of representation in manufacturing industries as well as in construction, transportation, wholesale, and trade. On the other hand, women are more concentrated in retail services, education, and health. In fact, 56 percent of women work in sales and service, business, finance, and administration.

The Economic Importance of Women's Earnings

Paradoxically, gender inequality in employment is increasingly out of step with changes in household incomes. For many families today, the income of women is much more than just "pin money." In fact, many two-parent families are reliant on the income of both working parents. Indeed, in close to 28 percent of Canadian families, the female contributes more than the male to the total employment income of the family.

In the past 30 years, there has also been a dramatic increase in lone-parent families and also in women living on their own. In such cases, women's employment is likely to be the main or only source of income. For single parents and women living on their own, wage inequality makes their lives even more precarious.

TABLE 8.2

Contribution of Wife to Employment Income of Husband-Wife Families

		Number of Children in Family (% Families)			
Percentage of Employment Income Contributed by Wife	**Percentage of All Families**	**0**	**1**	**2**	**3+**
0	19.71	23.63	16.98	15.31	21.52
1-25	19.63	14.27	21.40	23.98	25.40
26-50	32.69	29.14	34.23	36.97	32.45
51-75	14.68	15.07	14.98	14.86	12.15
76-99	5.10	6.09	5.03	4.16	3.76
100	8.19	11.80	7.37	4.72	4.73
More then 50	27.96	32.97	27.38	23.74	20.63

Source: Adapted from Statistics Canada, "Family characteristics, husband-wife families, by wife's contribution to husband-wife employment income, annual," Table 111-0021, CANSIM (database), Using E-STAT (distributor), February 2010

Equal Pay for Equal Work

One of the fundamental issues facing women in the labour force is pay inequality—women being paid less than men for work of the same value. **Pay equity** is now policy in most of Canada's provinces and territories, as well as several countries of the European Community, the Scandinavian countries, Australia, New Zealand, and many American states. The goal is to prevent discrimination related to the under-evaluation of work traditionally performed by women.

Pay equity legislation relies on comparisons between jobs that have a similar overall value. The jobs themselves are objectively evaluated, not the individuals holding those jobs. If jobs have the same value, discrimination in wages is not permitted, and this is regardless of how many male and female employees are doing those jobs.

Why the Gap?

The gender wage gap is to some extent a legacy of past social policies and attitudes. Minimum and "family" wage laws passed in the first decades of the last century set women's base salaries about a third lower than that of men. Indeed, the minimum wage in parts of Canada was lower for women as late as the 1970s.

This was based on largely prevailing perceptions about family roles at the time. Wages earned by women were regarded essentially as supplementary income. Of course, this premise has long been out of step with the reality of Canadian families. But the legacy remains.

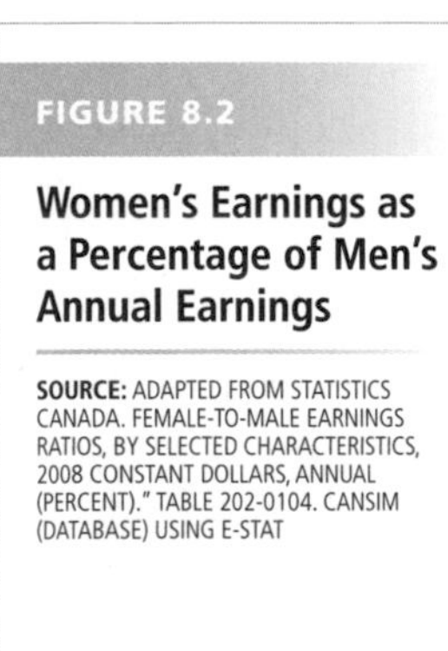

FIGURE 8.2

Women's Earnings as a Percentage of Men's Annual Earnings

SOURCE: ADAPTED FROM STATISTICS CANADA. FEMALE-TO-MALE EARNINGS RATIOS, BY SELECTED CHARACTERISTICS, 2008 CONSTANT DOLLARS, ANNUAL (PERCENT)." TABLE 202-0104. CANSIM (DATABASE) USING E-STAT

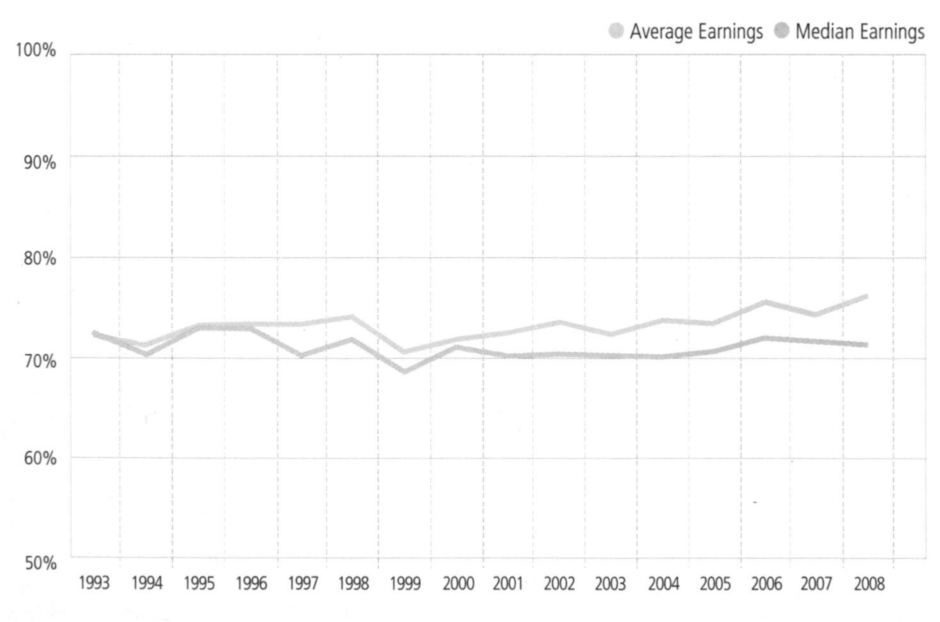

Employment Earnings for Men and Women

The Gender Gap in Earnings

Pay equity legislation has been in Canada since the 1970s. An equal value provision was first legislated in 1976 in Quebec in its *Charter of Human Rights and Freedoms*. The federal government passed its equal value provision (section 11) under the *Canadian Human Rights Act* in 1977.

Most provinces have enacted pay equity law or policy. Some provinces have passed proactive legislation that mandates employers to comply with procedures to redress gender-based wage inequities. Others are complaint-driven—employees must file a complaint to address a pay inequity.

Figure 8.2 shows changes in the average annual earnings of men and women from 1993 to 2008. The average wage earned by women has risen slightly in comparison to that of men. However, it remains substantially lower and fairly consistently so.

Of those Canadians employed full-time and full-year, women earn about three-quarters of the wage for men.

Women earn less than men even when they have the same education. Even with a university degree, the average earnings of women working full-time and full-year is less than their male counterparts.

Effects of Unionization

Pay equity legislation has certainly helped reduce the earnings gap, as has the pressure from women themselves. Interestingly, one of the biggest and perhaps least appreciated factors has been the labour movement itself and the effects of unionization.

The table below shows the difference unionization makes on male-female wage differentials. For both full-time and part-time employees, the gender wage gap is significantly less for unionized workers than for non-unionized workers, and the difference is striking. The wage ratio for unionized permanent employees is 92.6 percent whereas for non-unionized it is 78.6 percent. For temporary workers, the gap is less (93.9 percent/91.1 percent) but still present.

TABLE 8.3

Average Hourly Wage, Workers Aged 25-64

		Males	Females	Ratio
Total employees	All employees	25.91	22.00	0.849
	Employees with union coverage	26.96	25.28	0.937
	Employees without union coverage	25.42	20.18	0.794
Permanent employees	All employees	26.38	22.24	0.843
	Employees with union coverage	27.17	25.53	0.926
	Employees without union coverage	26.00	20.46	0.786
Temporary employees	All employees	21.01	19.75	0.940
	Employees with union coverage	24.85	23.29	0.939
	Employees without union coverage	18.94	17.26	0.911

Source: Adapted from Statistics Canada, "Labour force survey estimates (LFS), wages of employees by job permanence, union coverage, sex and age group, annual (current dollars)," Table 282-0074, CANSIM (database), Using E-STAT (distributor), 10 September 2010

Definition of the Family

Here is the official statisticians' basic definition of the family, which shows how hard it should be to generalize about this concept: "A census family is composed of a married or common-law couple, with or without children, or of a lone parent living with at least one child in the same dwelling. Couples can be of the opposite sex or the same sex."

Defining the Modern Family

The term **family** can be defined according to either structural criteria (what they look like) or functional criteria (what they do). Statistics Canada, for example, uses a structural definition to count the number of families for census purposes.

Statistics Canada defines a "census family" as a now-married couple (with or without never-married sons and/or daughters of either or both spouses), a couple living common-law (again with or without never-married sons and/or daughters of either or both partners), or a lone parent of any marital status, with at least one never-married son or daughter living in the same dwelling.

The definition focuses on what can be objectively measured—who lives with whom and under what circumstances. Previous definitions of the family included specific reference to marriage and ignored common-law living.

The Vanier Institute of the Family

The **Vanier Institute of the Family**, a national charitable organization dedicated to promoting the well-being of Canadian families, uses a functional definition of the family that emphasizes the activities of family members. It defines families as any combination of two or more persons who are bound together over time by ties of mutual consent, birth and/or adoption or placement, and who, together, assume responsibilities for variant combinations of some of the following:

- Physical maintenance and care of group members
- Addition of new members through procreation or adoption
- Socialization of children
- Social control of members
- Production, consumption, and distribution of goods and services
- Affective nurturance—love

The Vanier Institute's definition emphasizes the work and accomplishments of people who commit themselves to one another over time. It avoids many of the biases that have crept into definitions of the family. It acknowledges heterosexual and same-sex couples, lone-parent families, extended patterns of kinship, blended families (step-families), couples with children and those without, the commitments of siblings to one another, and the obligations and affection that unite the young and the old as their lives weave together (Vanier Institute, 2010).

Changing Expectations

Despite all the changes over the past sixty or seventy years, in many ways, our income security programs are still based on outdated, traditional notions of women and family. Although the vast majority of Canadians live in some kind of family setting, the contemporary Canadian family bears little or no resemblance to families of Canada's past. The traditional family ideal, typified in the 1950s/60s sitcom *Leave it to Beaver*, consists of two parents—a working father and a supportive non-working wife—and a couple of children. This ideal has remained dominant despite the fact that it is not really reflective of today's reality.

Over the past 30 years, the proportion of **male-breadwinner families** has decreased drastically and is now well below 25 percent of the total of all Canadian families. Currently, it is **dual-earner families** that predominate. This change has led to a complete, or near-complete, revision of family obligations in a very short time. For example, there are no clear societal expectations with regards to an individual's responsibility to care for an aunt who gets sick. At the same time, at the other end of the life spectrum, fewer children are taking responsibility for the care of their own aging parents, which has made the question of government support to the elderly an issue where it once was not.

Canadian families and family dynamics have altered significantly over the past 30 years. The chart below from the Vanier Institute reveals these changes graphically.

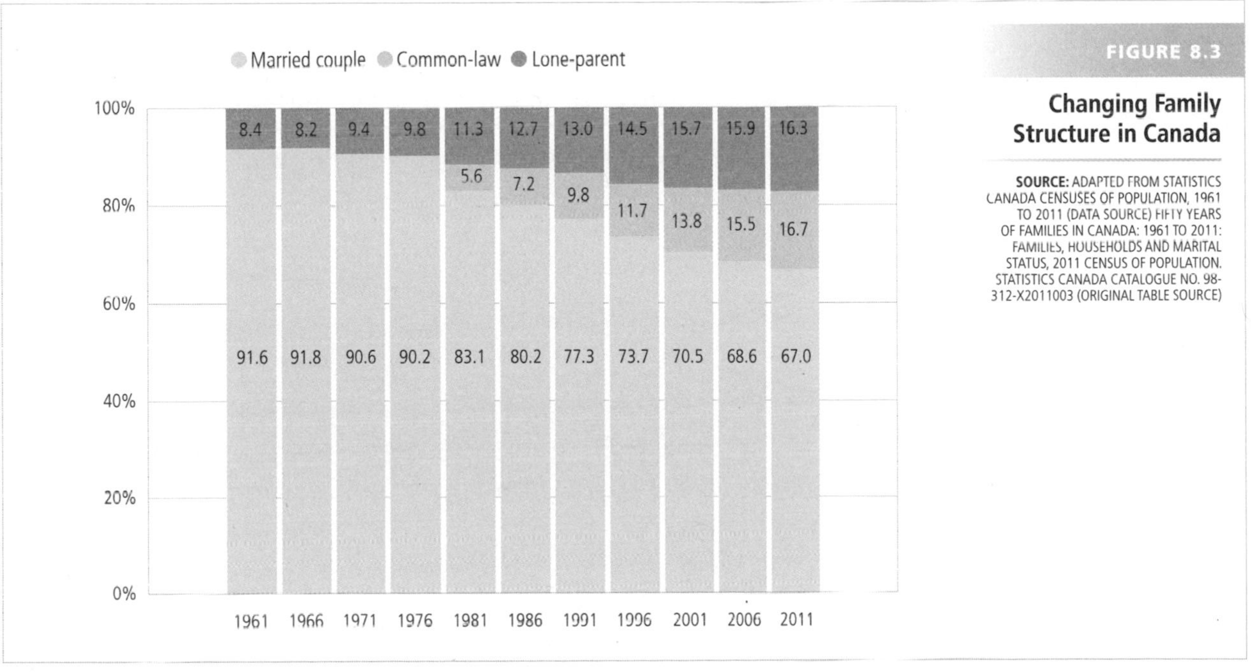

FIGURE 8.3

Changing Family Structure in Canada

SOURCE: ADAPTED FROM STATISTICS CANADA CENSUSES OF POPULATION, 1961 TO 2011 (DATA SOURCE) FIFTY YEARS OF FAMILIES IN CANADA: 1961 TO 2011: FAMILIES, HOUSEHOLDS AND MARITAL STATUS, 2011 CENSUS OF POPULATION. STATISTICS CANADA CATALOGUE NO. 98-312-X2011003 (ORIGINAL TABLE SOURCE)

Changing Families

Modern families take many different forms. The results from the 2011 Census of Population show a growing number of census families that are characterized by increasing diversity. Here are some highlights:

- There were 9,389,700 census families, up 5.5 percent from 8,896,840 families five years earlier.
- Common-law couples grew the most rapidly between 2006 and 2011, increasing 13.9 percent compared to a growth of 3.1 percent for married couples and 8.0 percent for lone-parent families.
- The predominant census family in 2011 was married couples, although they continued to decrease as a share of all families.
- For the first time in 2011, the number of common-law couples (1,567,910) surpassed lone-parent families (1,527,840).
- The share of lone-parent families edged up slightly during the decade from 15.7 percent in 2001 to 16.3 percent of all census families in 2011. About 8 in 10 lone-parent families were female lone-parent families, accounting for 12.8 percent of all families (Statistics Canada, 2012).

In the 2011 census, 64,575 couples identified themselves as same-sex common-law couples, an apparent increase of 42.4 percent. However, it seems Statistics Canada may have "inadvertently" counted some transient workers sharing accommodation (see box on page 199).

FIGURE 8.4

Households Get Smaller: Household Sizes Over the Past 50 Years

DATA SOURCE: STATISTICS CANADA, *CENSUS IN BRIEF: FIFTY YEARS OF FAMILIES IN CANADA: 1996 TO 2011*. "FIGURE 4: DISTRIBUTION (IN PERCENTAGE) OF PRIVATE HOUSEHOLDS BY HOUSEHOLD SIZE, CANADA, 1961 TO 2011. CAT. NO. 98-312-X2011003.

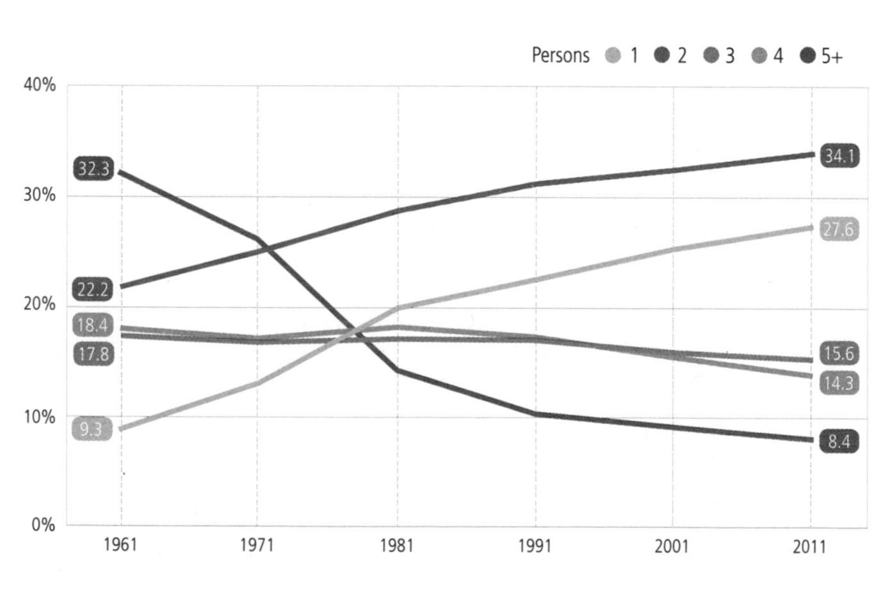

Changing the Definition of "Family" in Canada

CTV News

Traditional marriage appears to be on the decline in Canada, while same-sex couples, step-families, and common-law unions are on the rise, according to new census data from Statistics Canada.

The latest installment from the 2011 census focuses on families and marital status, as well as housing in the period between 2006 and 2011.

According to the data, the number of traditional married couples declined in Canada as a proportion of all households defined as families, but still comprised two-thirds of all family groups in the country.

Of the 9,389,700 families counted in the census, 6,294,000 were married couples—an increase of 3.1 percent from the 2006 census, but a smaller proportion than in the past, StatsCan said.

Meanwhile, common-law couples increased as a proportion of all families. There were 1,567,900 common-law families in Canada in 2011, an increase of 13.9 percent compared to five years earlier.

Single-parent families were also on the rise, up 8 percent to just over 1,527,800.

And the number of same-sex couples shot up dramatically—a change that reflects the legalization of gay marriage in Canada. In 2011 there were 64,575 same-sex couple families, a spike of 42.4 percent from the 2006 census, StatsCan said. Of those same-sex families, 21,015 were married couples, while 43,560 were common-law.

In order to qualify as a family, under StatsCan's definition, at least two people must be living under the same roof.

The release marks the third block of data to be released from the massive swath of data collected in the 2011 census. Population was covered in a February release by Statistics Canada. Age and sex were the focus in May, and the final installment in October will look at language, according to Statistics Canada.

The latest release delves deeper than ever before into how families are comprised, from the traditional two-parent family, to step-families and same-sex families.

Never before has the census parsed out blended families, a shift that revealed new insights into how those families are comprised.

The census showed that one out of every 10 children age 14 and under, living in private households, was part of a step-family in 2011. That adds up to 464,335 step-families in 2011, representing 12.6 percent of the 3.7 million couple families with children.

"One of the interesting things about a census is it gives Canadians an opportunity to see themselves across the country and to begin to see that they're not alone," said Nora Spinks, CEO of the Vanier Institute of the Family.

"And if they are going through some tough times like trying to navigate the complexities of a blended family or going through a divorce ... knowing they're not alone is a really important piece of the census experience."

While the makeup of Canadian families has changed dramatically over the last few decades, that does not necessarily mean that "traditional family values are on their way out," Jennifer Tipper of the Vanier Institute of the Family told CTV's Power Play Wednesday.

We now have "multiple variations of the family form, but families are adapting to their own and societal needs just like they've done for generations," Tipper said.

She noted that gender norms seem to be shifting in Canada—the number of single fathers raising their children has been steadily increasing. "That isn't something we would have seen 20 years ago," Tipper said.

The census also, for the first time, includes a tally of the number of foster children living in Canada—data that has so far been unknown and is prized by social workers and child welfare advocates hoping to get a better grasp on the situation.

Of the total number of children age 14 and under, 0.5 percent, or 29,590, were foster children, StatsCan said.

SOURCE: CTVNEWS.CA STAFF (SEPT. 19, 2012). "NEW CENSUS DATA ILLUSTRATES CHANGING DEFINITION OF "FAMILY" IN CANADA."

Factors Changing the Modern Family

There are several key factors that have led to changes in the family over the last 50 years. Let us look at each of these in turn.

LONGEVITY. Improved public health leads to increased longevity. The population over age 65 has increased by 60 percent over the past five decades. As well, women usually live longer than men, which has implications for pension and medical systems, as well as for relationships.

FERTILITY. Birth rates have fallen by more than half over the past five decades. In 1968, the *Criminal Code* legalized access to birth control. This has meant that women are involved in childbearing for fewer years and therefore have time for other activities.

HOUSEHOLD TECHNOLOGY. Especially since World War I, advances in technology have led to the automation of certain types of housework. Electrification, hot water, central heating, air conditioning, refrigeration, vacuum cleaners, and mass production of clothing are all aspects of the industrialization of housework.

WOMEN IN THE WORKFORCE. The proportion of women in the labour force has tripled over the past five decades. Most married women work and most contribute a significant share of total family income.

DIVORCE. The divorce rate has increased sixfold over the past five decades. This has, in turn, contributed to changes in family structures.

Women first entered the male-dominated labour force to help with the war effort during the First and Second World Wars (as depicted on the TV show *Bomb Girls*, below); today, women make up close to half of the Canadian labour force.

The Women's Liberation Movement and Other Factors

There are additional factors that have caused changes in family composition. Consider the important role of the women's liberation movement.

The first wave of the women's movement occurred in the last 30 years of the 19th century and the first 20 years of the 20th century. During this time, the movement was mainly political and was primarily concerned with the acquisition of women's right to vote. The second wave occurred in the 1960s, partly as a reaction to the rigidity of the male-dominated family structure with its fixed gender roles, and also as a result of the isolation of suburban life. The positive impact of this movement on improving women's lives, and family life in general, has been phenomenal and far-reaching.

Consider also the decline of the extended family—the family "ideal" now consists of nuclear family units that by and large live in their own homes. Thus, housing has expanded rapidly, especially the suburban single-family home. There is also the decline of religious influence. This has meant that barriers to divorce have come down, and there has been a widespread acceptance of birth control and legalized abortion (and a corresponding reduction in unwanted pregnancies, particularly among young women).

Finally, increased cultural diversity in the population has contributed to Canadians becoming more familiar with, and accepting of, different family types and household arrangements, all of which have significantly enriched Canadian society.

Mothers Are Women

www.mothersarewomen.com

Mothers Are Women (MAW) is a feminist organization that advocates for mothers as primary caregivers; it argues that until the unpaid work of women in the home is recognized as a valuable and necessary contribution, women will never achieve equality in our society.

The Policy Agenda Today

All these changes to the Canadian family obviously have, and will continue to have, a direct bearing on how social programs operate and how income security programs are delivered. In devising programs that work for women and families, social analysts and policy-makers now urgently need to take into account the following:

- Many more individuals are now living in common-law relationships while others are living alone.
- Growth in the number of lone-parent families, mostly led by women
- Growth in the number of blended families
- Growth in the number of same-sex families, some of which include children
- Growth in the number of mothers in the labour force, including women with children under the age of five
- Decline in the number of extended family members who live in one family
- Growth in the number of single-person households

The Vanier Institute of the Family

www.vifamily.ca

Founded after the 1965 Canadian Conference on the Family, convened by Governor General Georges Vanier, this organization advocates for the role of the family in Canadian society.

Seven Biases

Discussions about families are loaded with value judgements. These can be based on religious beliefs, moral beliefs, popular culture, and advertising or media representations, as well as many other social and cultural forces. According to Margrit Eichler (1997), there are **seven biases with respect to families** that have prevented social programs from keeping up with the changing nature of today's family.

1. **MONOLITHIC BIAS.** The monolithic bias suggests that there is one basic, uniform type of household—the nuclear, breadwinner-dependent family with one or more children and a woman who maintains the home: the "traditional"-type family. Nowadays, this is more of a myth than a reality.
2. **CONSERVATIVE BIAS.** The conservative bias ignores changes taking place in family structures and relationships—for example, the blended family and the same-sex family.
3. **SEXIST BIAS.** The sexist bias assumes a functional differentiation of work between men and women. Women taking care of children at home would be viewed as a natural role rather than a role that is socially constructed.
4. **MICRO-STRUCTURAL BIAS.** The micro-structural bias leads to a refusal to look outside the family to understand what is influencing it. An example occurs when people express a concern for building "self-reliance" among welfare recipients without considering the availability of jobs, daycare, and other supports.
5. **AGEIST BIAS.** This bias shows up in discussions about families when only the perspective of middle-aged adults is considered. Here, the perspectives of children and the elderly are ignored.
6. **RACIST BIAS.** The racist bias concerns a devaluing or discounting of culturally or ethnically different families. The treatment of First Nations families in Canada—where children were placed in residential schools—is a tragic example of this bias.
7. **HETEROSEXIST BIAS.** This bias treats the heterosexual family as "natural" and, therefore, the only legitimate form. Denying family status to LGBTTQ families typifies this bias.

Being aware of these societal biases helps policy-makers design social welfare programs that reflect real, existing families, not "ideal" families. Problems can arise when policy-makers bring biases into policy formation, and when practitioners continue such biases in counselling or referral. People must have access to services based on the family they live in, as opposed to the family that others thinks they should live in. Families exist outside of these biases (whether we like it or not). Acknowledging this allows practitioners to practise in a more reflective and appropriate manner.

Same-Sex Marriage in the 2011 Census

Mind the Details

Same-sex marriage was legalized across Canada by the *Civil Marriage Act*, which was enacted in 2005. Earlier provincial court decisions in eight out of ten provinces and one of three territories had already legalized same-sex marriage. Before the federal act, only Alberta and Prince Edward Island and the territories of Nunavut and the Northwest Territories had not recognized same-sex marriage.

With this legislation, to its credit, Canada became the fourth country in the world and the first country in the Americas (and the first country outside Europe) to legalize same-sex marriage nationwide.

Attempt to Restore the Status Quo Ante

In 2006, the minority Conservative government brought in a motion to the House of Commons attempting to re-open the issue and reinstate the traditional definition of marriage. However, the times had changed and the motion was decisively defeated by a vote of 175 to 123.
For now, at least, the issue is off the table.

Same-Sex Families in the 2011 Census

The most recent 2011 census provided a opportunity to re-measure the number of same-sex couple families in light of the legalization of same-sex marriage in 2005. In the 2011 census, 64,575 such families were counted, an apparent increase of 42.4 percent from the 2006 census (almost double the 2001 census when Statistics Canada started to track the numbers).

However, in its enthusiasm, Statistics Canada admitted to have inadvertently counted some transient workers who left behind their families for work in Alberta's oil fields. To be sure, these individuals were roommates and happened to be married—but just not to each other.

In the end, Statistics Canada estimated that same-sex couples account for just 0.8 percent of all couples in Canada. While not significant enough to declare the end of the traditional family, clearly there is a need for income security and other welfare programs to be constantly adjusted to the changing details of Canadian family life.

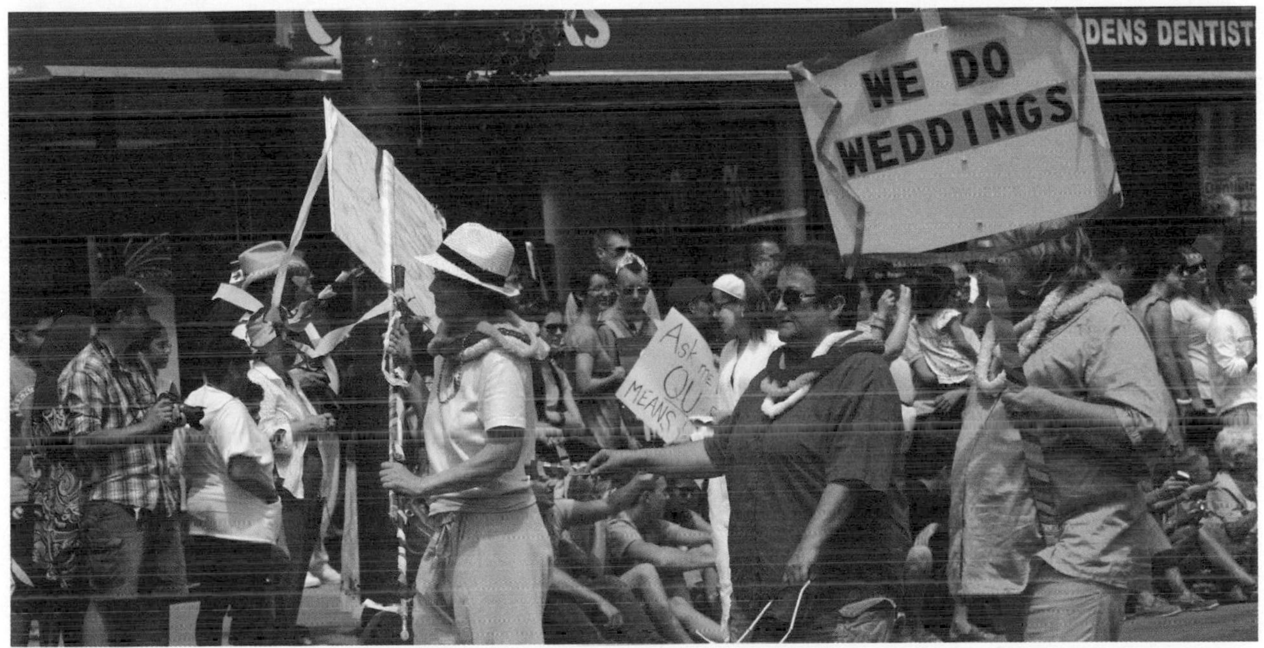

Three Models of the Family

Patriarchal: features the husband and father as the "master" of the family.

Individual responsibility: features gender equality, gender-neutral policies, and equalized caregiving.

Social responsibility: features the individual as the societal unit and views domestic tasks as socially useful service; the public shares the responsibility with both parents.

Three Models of the Family

Women are now participating in the labour force in ever-larger numbers, and many families could not survive if this were not the case. At the same time, however, government income security policy has continued to be based on the outdated assumption that women are available to care for family members and undertake domestic chores (as if they were at home all day).

Sociologist Margrit Eichler (1997) presents three conceptual models upon which new policies directed at the work-family relationship can be based. At present, the patriarchal family model perspective is losing popularity, and the individual responsibility model is gaining in influence.

Patriarchal Model of the Family

The **patriarchal model of the family** is based on perceptions that were dominant at the turn of the last century. Under this paradigm, the husband was considered the undisputed master of the family, and the wife was economically and socially beneath her husband. Children were also treated as dependants of the husband/father.

Within income security programs, this belief was reflected in the rule that a woman could not receive public assistance if her husband was alive. The wife/mother was seen as responsible for providing care and services to family members without pay. Finally, divorce did not exist (although there were separations not recognized by law) and same-sex couples were not recognized in any way.

Individual Responsibility Model of the Family

The **individual responsibility model of the family** consists of three main elements: formal gender equality, gender-neutral policies, and equalized caregiving. The *Canadian Charter of Rights and Freedoms* introduced gender equality and enshrined it in law, necessitating numerous changes in family policy. Some analysts point out that these legal gains constitute only "formal gender equality"—in other words, in the ideal world of policy, all people are treated "equally" despite continuing real-world inequalities.

Within this model, the family unit is still treated as the normal unit of administration, but the husband and wife are seen as equally responsible for the economic well-being of themselves, each other, and any children. Yet, in formulating social policy, gender neutrality ignores the differences in life experiences and caring responsibilities between men and women. Either parent is assumed to be capable of fulfilling the care and provider functions in the family. The lack of recognition that one parent cannot care for dependent children and work full-time has led to an erosion of entitlements for lone-parent families, which are predominantly led by women.

Social Responsibility Model of the Family

As an alternative, the **social responsibility model of the family** directly addresses gender inequality, gender-sensitive policies, and the social dimension of caregiving. According to Eichler (1997), this model minimizes gender inequality and stratification. She formulates the eight characteristics of this model as a set of policy goals. These include: minimizing sex stratification; collective support for dependents; collective support for caregivers; recognition to those who partially or completely support dependents, whether related or not; self-support and autonomy for every individual; and social and legal recognition to lesbian and gay families.

This model regards the individual, rather than the family, as the societal unit of administration, in the same sense that our health care system treats every citizen as an individual, and our tax system is based on individual taxation. The focus is, therefore, more on how the individual roles and responsibilities are defined within families.

Within this model of the family, familial caring and housework are seen as socially useful services (rather than privately useful services). In this context, the public shares the responsibility with both parents for the care of dependent children. Similar to child care, the costs of care for dependent adults (such as elderly family members or individuals with disabilities) are a public responsibility, although family members may also provide the care.

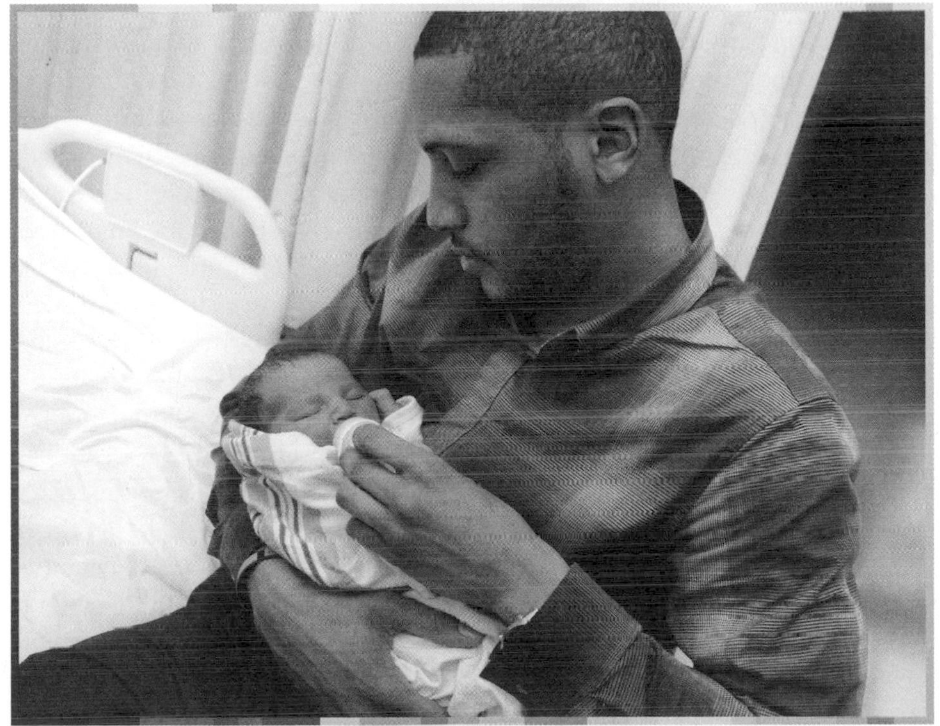

In Canada, women can claim up to 15 weeks of maternity leave when giving birth, and both men and women can claim an additional 35 weeks of parental leave for newborns or adopted children.

Women's poverty is often related to their family obligations. Many policies do not account for the complex relationship between social welfare and women's traditional responsibility for caring in our society.

Women and Caregiving

Currently, the "individual responsibility model," as identified by Margrit Eichler, underpins Canada's social welfare programs. However, this model fails to take into account momentous changes taking place in families both in Canada and around the world. In particular, it fails to recognize the critical role women play in child care and elder care tasks and the implications of this for women and their families. (Child care and elder care are discussed separately later in this chapter.)

In this context, an understanding of women's responsibility for caring and how income security programs work, or not, in the context of real families, is vital. Patricia Evans, a social work professor at Carleton University, has written extensively on why it is important to examine income security programs from the perspective and experience of women. First, she maintains that many programs are based on outdated assumptions about the roles and responsibilities of women that simply do not work. Second, it is women who dominate both sides of the social welfare encounter—as primary users of services and as service providers (Evans and Wekerle, 1997, p. 4).

Self-Fulfilling Prophecy

Generally speaking, men and women tend to access income security and other welfare programs differently. Men tend to obtain their income security benefits from social insurance-type programs, such as Employment Insurance or Workers' Compensation—and these programs tend to be less stigmatizing and more generous. Women, on the other hand, tend to draw benefits from minimum-income programs such as Social Assistance and Old Age Security—programs that are either needs-tested or means-tested, and are more stigmatizing.

Not only are women the main recipients of minimum-income Social Assistance programs, but the programs themselves can perpetuate certain biased models of the family. For example, what was once known as the "man-in-the-house" rule (now known as the "spouse-in-the-house" rule), stipulates that a woman who is living with a man is immediately not eligible for Social Assistance. The policy assumes that a man who lives with a woman should be financially responsible for her and her family, even when he is not the father of her children and has no other legal responsibility to support her or her children.

Other policies, many of which are presented as being gender-neutral, actually ignore the special circumstances of women. For example, workfare (viewing lone mothers as workers rather than as mothers) ignores the circumstances that single mothers face in relation to child care. Lack of child support and a lack of jobs that will pay sufficiently to support a family on one income are ignored by this policy. When combined with the low levels of income support through Social Assistance, it is no wonder that the majority of single mothers and their children live below most definitions of poverty.

Responsibility for Caregiving

According to Statistics Canada, women comprise three-quarters of the adults who spend more than 30 hours per week caring for children in the home. Status of Women Canada, a federal government agency, has gone as far as to say that the unequal sharing of dependant care in the family may be the most persistent barrier to gender equality.

"Family-Making"

Developing Responsive Social Policies

The idea of "family-making" was coined by Leslie Bella, a professor of social work at Memorial University of Newfoundland. According to Bella (2003), we can identify and value family, regardless of the living arrangements of family members.

Family making is defined as the processes through which we develop relationships that are enduring, caring, and intimate, and that in turn nurture and support us. According to this definition, a family relationship exists to the extent that the relationship between two or more individuals is characterized by endurance, caring, and shared domestic space.

Family making is the process through which individuals create, maintain, and strengthen relationships that constitute "family" as thus defined (Bella, 2003).

It's All About Relationships

The idea of defining a family by identifying relationships and processes rather than family composition is useful for social welfare policy-makers. Existing social policies have a tendency to disregard or invalidate non-traditional family forms and approaches to care.

Conversely, policies based on family making include the wide range of family relationships. It enables social policy-makers to address the concerns of those in diverse family forms and different cultural settings. It allows us to break away from policy based on limited or patriarchal definitions of the family.

As a result, such policies are more responsive to the diversity of family forms that actually exist in Canadian society.

The Harper Government on Child Care

In the 2007 federal budget, $1 billion of previously committed early learning and child care funding was cut and replaced with tax credits to businesses for the creation of workplace child care spaces. The budget also included a new flat child tax credit paid to parents for each child. The Code Blue for Child Care Campaign argued that this money, combined with the UCCB, would be enough to federally fund universal child care for three to five year olds.

The Need for Quality Child Care

The lack of affordable and accessible **child care** is a major barrier to full women's equality both inside the family and in the working world. Universal, quality child care would help many families and single mothers move out of poverty and away from needing to rely on social services and income security programs.

A survey by the Canadian Child Care Federation found that two-thirds of the Canadian public see child care as a developmental service and only 17 percent see it as "babysitting." The same survey also noted that almost three-quarters (71 percent) of Canadians believe that the opportunity to receive quality child care is distributed unequally, and the principal reason given for this unequal access was the absence of financial resources of the family (CCCF, 2003).

A Patchwork of Services

Relative to many peer nations in Europe, Canadian child care is "inaccessible, unaffordable, and of inconsistent quality" (Decter, 2011). To be fair, governments in Canada have increased investments directed to early childhood development. However, without a comprehensive and nationwide vision for child care, the approaches taken amount to a patchwork of services delivered through different provincial and territorial ministries. These ministries naturally have a wide range of mandates, goals, and supporting infrastructure.

TABLE 8.4

Hours per Week Spent on Unpaid Care of a Child in the Household, by Working Arrangement and Age of Youngest Child

	Women	Men
All women and men	50.1	24.4*
Working arrangement		
Dual earner couples; respondent working full-time	49.8	27.2*
Dual earner couples; respondent working part-time	59.4	40.5*
Single earner couples; respondent working	50.8	25.5*
Lone parents; respondent working	26.9	12.0*
Respondent was not working		
Single earner couples; respondent not working	81.3	36.9
Couples; neither partner working	59.5	36.3E*
Lone parents; respondent not working	30.0	8.1E*
Age of youngest child in the household		
0 to 4	67.5	30.2*
5 to 14	37.7	19.7*

E use with caution. * statistically significant difference between women and men at $p < 0.05$. **Source**: Statistics Canada, General Social Survey 2010.

Daycare Makes Good Economic Sense

Research points overwhelmingly to the positive effect of universal child care for women, children, and families. Among other things:

- Women's lifetime earnings would increase, reducing poverty rates in old age.
- More mothers would have the option of working outside the home (since Quebec introduced its child care system, twice the number of married women have entered the workforce than in the rest of Canada).
- Female lone parents would be able to train for work, get a decent job, and accept job promotions (CCAAC, 2012).

Universal child care and greater spending on early childhood education also makes economic sense in its own right and for the country as a whole. In Quebec, for example, 40 percent of the yearly costs of child care are covered by the income and payroll taxes from the increased maternal labour force participation, which helps to offset the cost of providing ECEC services (CCAAC, 2007).

Craig Alexander, the TD Bank's chief economist, in the first-ever analysis of the issue by a Canadian bank, notes that child care and early childhood education is "very much an economic topic." "If you are concerned with skills development, productivity, and innovation, you should really care about this subject," he says. Unfortunately, "at 0.25 percent of GDP, Canada ranks last among comparable European and Anglo-speaking countries," the TD report says (Alexander, 2012).

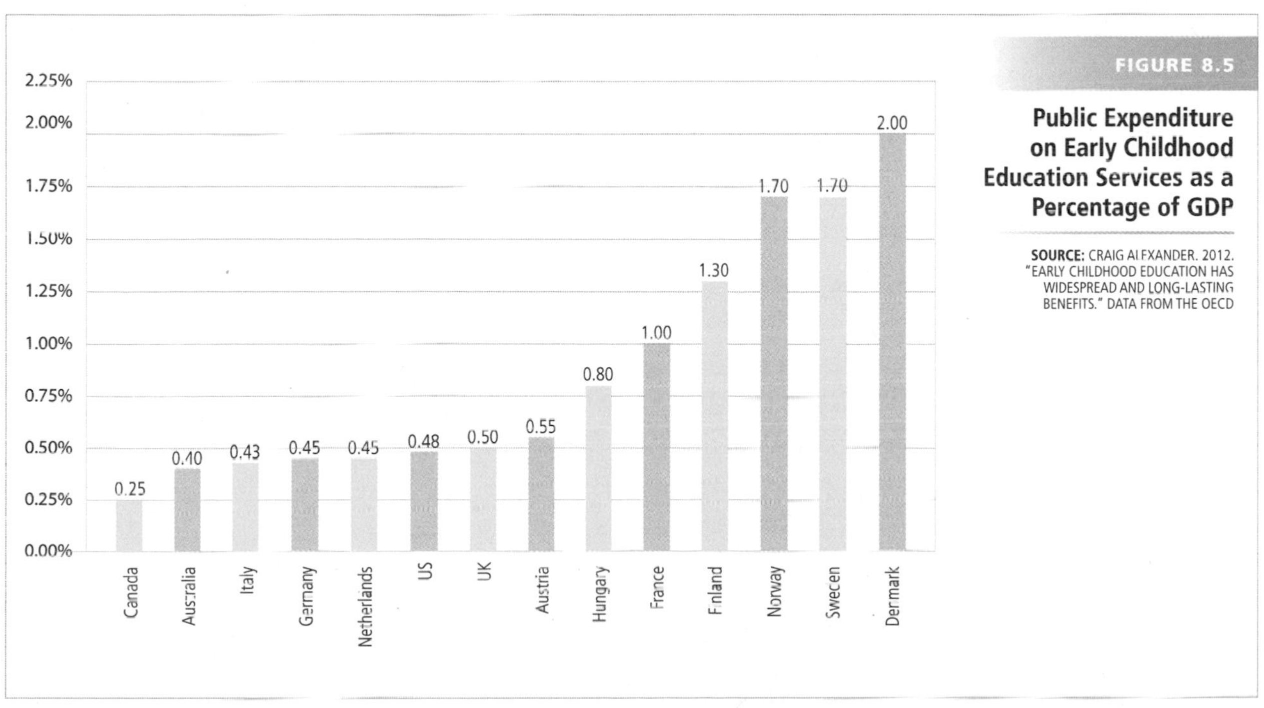

FIGURE 8.5

Public Expenditure on Early Childhood Education Services as a Percentage of GDP

SOURCE: CRAIG ALEXANDER. 2012. "EARLY CHILDHOOD EDUCATION HAS WIDESPREAD AND LONG-LASTING BENEFITS." DATA FROM THE OECD

The Need for Quality Elder Care

Families also need access to quality **elder care**, and increasingly so as the Canadian population ages. Lack of affordable, quality elder care is a major source of stress in family lives. The time and financial cost associated with providing elder care has a direct bearing on the income security of families, men and women, and especially the income security of women. For these reasons, elder care should figure prominently in income security policy and programs.

Canada's Aging Population

Canada has an aging population with a growing number of seniors with need for support and care. And the demands on caregivers increase as their family member ages. Most of the responsibility currently falls on families and friends, and again most of the responsibility within families falls on women.

Caregivers perform a range of tasks in caring for seniors: personal care, and help with tasks inside and outside the senior's house (transportation, medical care, and care management). Many seniors living in care facilities still count on family and friends for care—more than 1 in 5 caregivers provided care to seniors living in care facilities. Although 75 percent of senior care was provided by those between 45 and 65 years of age, the other 25 percent was provided by people over 65 (Cranswick & Dosman., 2008).

FIGURE 8.6

Taxonomy of Hidden Costs of Elder Care

SOURCE: FAST, J.E., WILLIAMSON, D.L., & KEATING, N. (1999). "THE HIDDEN COSTS OF INFORMAL ELDER CARE." *JOURNAL OF FAMILY AND ECONOMIC ISSUES*, 20(3), 301–326

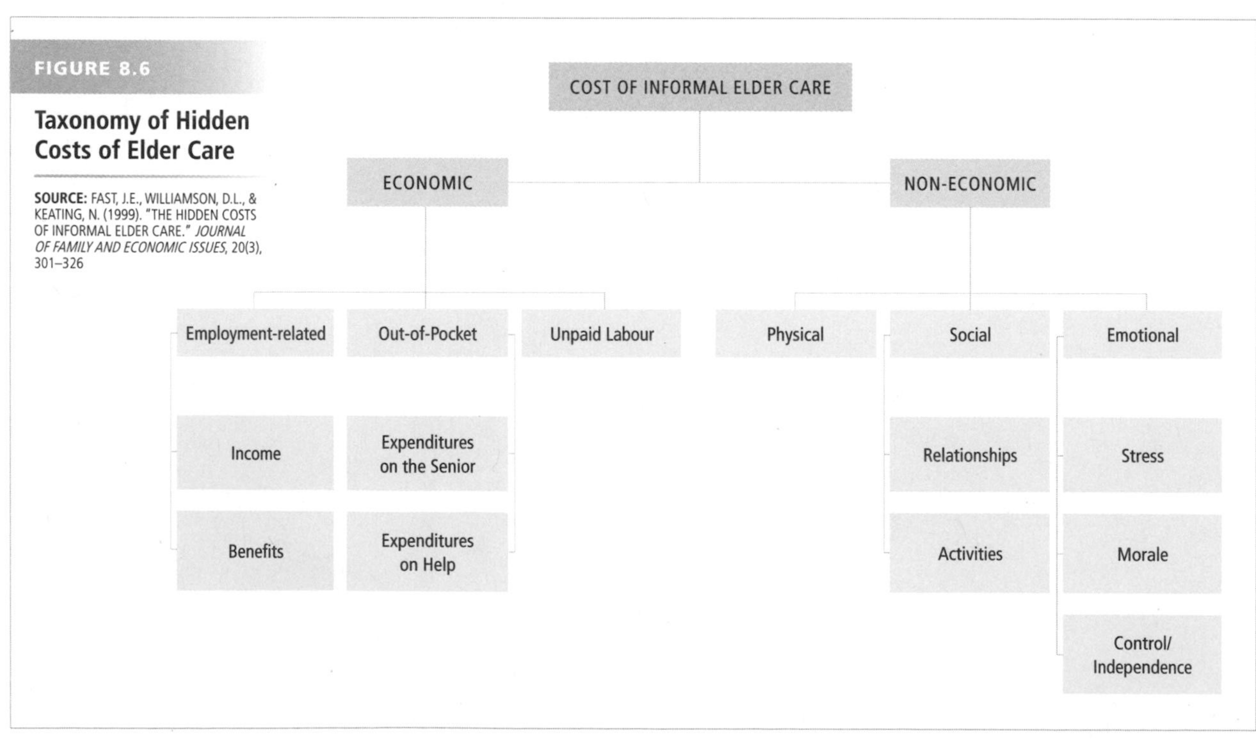

Gender, Work, and Elder Care

When examining who performs elder care tasks and how often, it is important to note that the majority of caregivers are women. While roughly equal numbers of men and women aged 45 to 64 are involved in informal caregiving to seniors, women are more likely to provide more hours (a higher intensity) of care, more personal care, and assume a disproportionate amount of responsibility for care (Cranswick & Dosman, 2008).

In 2007, nearly 40 percent of women caregivers and fewer than 20 percent of men caregivers provided personal care, which included intimate activities such as bathing and dressing.

Weakening Labour Force Attachment

Disproportionate responsibilities for elder care, as with child care, have consequences for women's status in the labour force. In a comprehensive review of the research literature, Donna Lero and Gillian Joseph found that women are more likely to take on part-time or casual labour as a way to balance work and family responsibilities. They are also more likely to require time off from work to respond to pressing family needs: on average, women lose 6.9 work days per year to family responsibilities as compared to 0.9 days for men.

In short, women incur greater non-financial and financial costs as a result of caregiving (Lero & Joseph, 2007). Financial costs include reduced wages, savings, and pensions, with implications for caregivers' long-term financial security.

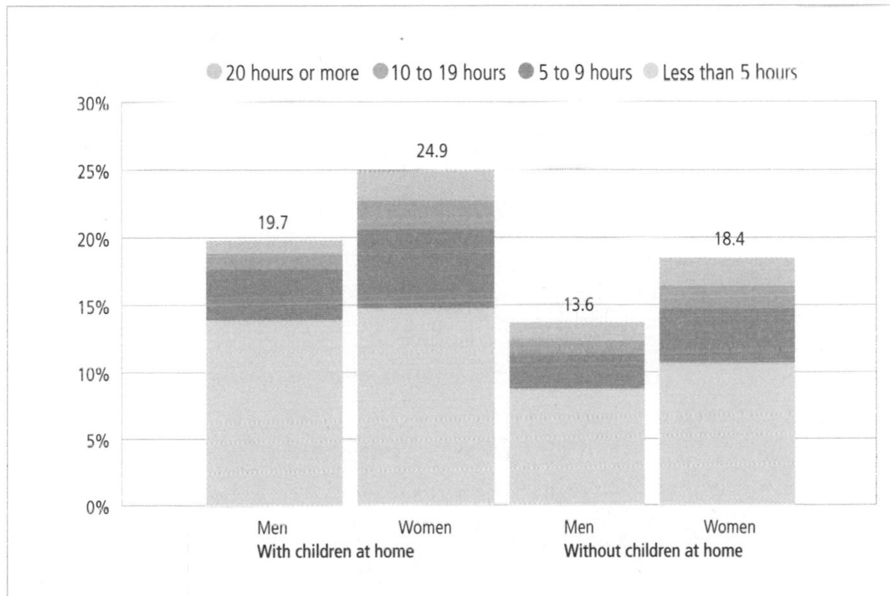

FIGURE 8.7

Unpaid Hours of Elder Care per Week by Household

SOURCE: VANIER INSTITUTE OF THE FAMILY. 2010. PROFILING CANADA'S FAMILIES IV. OTTAWA. DATA FROM STATISTICS CANADA, 2006 CENSUS OF POPULATION, CATALOGUE NO. 97-559-XCB2006007

Women and Human Rights

Canada has been a signatory to the United Nations **Convention on the Elimination of All Forms of Discrimination Against Women** (CEDAW) since 1981. In a single treaty, CEDAW brings together human rights standards for women and girls in public and in private life. The 2000 Optional Protocol to CEDAW (the "Optional Protocol") is a human rights instrument that creates new procedures to enhance oversight of compliance with CEDAW. It is hoped that the Optional Protocol will contribute to the recognition and protection of women's human rights and the promotion of gender equality in Canada and around the world.

Theorization of Women's Work and Caring

Beginning in the 1960s and throughout the following decades, a variety of theories were developed in an attempt to explain the nature and conditions of women's work and caring. Early debates were directed at rejecting the idea that women's work roles, in both the workplace and the home, were determined by biological factors, such as physical size or shape, "natural" skills or aptitudes, maternal instincts, or emotional makeup. Canadian feminist writers, such as Helen Levine, Pat Armstrong, Patricia Evans, Sheila Neysmith, and Dorothy Smith, undertook extensive research to show that gender-based work and caring divisions were socially constructed or socially organized. In fact, today's feminist theorists use the term gender as opposed to sex to highlight the socially constructed differences rather than the biological dichotomy.

Artificial Separation of Families

This chapter has drawn attention to the circumstances that contribute to the inequality of women, but more work remains to be done if we are to fully understand this relationship and be able to act on it. For example, Sheila Neysmith, a leading social work scholar at the University of Toronto, has demonstrated how social welfare progress has been hampered by the separation of family life, the labour market, and state responsibilities into separate domains or spheres. She believes that the "public" and "private" domains need to be connected in our theoretical understandings (Neysmith, 1991).

Many feminist social policy experts and women in community-based organizations believe that caregiving by mothers should be recognized as work comparable in value to the work performed in the marketplace. They believe there should be a more equal sharing of the work between men and women and of responsibilities and rewards for paid and unpaid labour within families and within society. They believe that a fundamental recognition of the unpaid caregiving work of mothers is necessary to break the feminization of poverty.

There are still many issues that need to be considered and addressed. One is the appropriate balance between professional child care and parental caregiving. Many believe that the current emphasis on supporting professional child care devalues caregiving and the women who do it, and prioritizes professionalization and the development specialist over the caregiver. These and other issues are the subjects of ongoing debates and research. What remains undisputed is that the current welfare system is not adequately addressing the range of problems faced by women and families today, and that action is urgently required to establish basic equality between the sexes.

Conclusion

It is becoming increasingly clear that income security programs are not well aligned with the changing nature of the family today. Far too many women and families fall below the poverty line. The term *feminization of poverty* depicts the phenomenon of women and families who are living in poverty in increasing numbers.

Many social programs still assume the existence of the traditional, "male-breadwinner" model of the family. In reality, this model is no longer the norm. This approach not only fails to keep up with the times, but places great strain on those, increasing in number, who do not quite align—single mothers, the working poor, and women with child care and elder care responsibilities.

The shifting of women from "stay-at-home mothers" to "worker-mothers" has decreased the economic dependency of women, but it has not significantly altered the disadvantages women face. Women still receive lower pay than men, and other issues—such as divorce and separation, and women's responsibilities as mothers, homemakers, caregivers, and nurturers—lower the earning potential of women. The problem is not that women are not working—the problem is the pay that women are receiving and the heavy responsibilities they carry in family settings for child care and elder care, which makes it difficult for them to keep up.

Of particular concern is the heavy burden placed on women in family settings for providing child care and elder care. For many women, and especially single mothers and low-wage earners, caregiving limits their full engagement in the labour market. This helps to perpetuate low-wages, precarious employment, pension shortfalls, and restricted Employment Insurance eligibility.

This is an area where social policies can make a big difference and propel the economy forward. While important gains have been made, newer programs are now needed that take into account the changing context of women and families today.

Without access to child care, some women who may otherwise be able to work are forced to go on Social Assistance.

CHAPTER 8 REVIEW

LEARNING OBJECTIVES

After completing this chapter, you should be able to:

- Understand the significance of the increased labour force participation of women.
- Understand the importance of equal pay and equal employment policies.
- Discuss the "gender gap" in earnings and the possible causes.
- Document and describe the "feminization of poverty."
- Evaluate the definition of the family provided by the Vanier Institute.
- Describe the changes in family arrangements in recent years.
- Discuss the factors that have led to changes in the modern family.
- Describe some biases that have affected how policy-makers view families.
- Describe the three models of the family.
- Appreciate the critical caregiving role played by women.
- Explain the need for quality child care.
- Explain the need for quality elder care.

KEY CONCEPTS IN CHAPTER

- Child care
- Dual-earner families
- Elder care
- Equal pay, equal employment, other facilitating policies
- Family
- Feminization of poverty
- Individual responsibility model of the family
- Male-breadwinner families
- Patriarchal model of the family
- Pay equity
- Seven biases with respect to families
- Social responsibility model of the family
- Vanier Institute of the Family

REVIEW QUESTIONS

1. The increased labour force participation of women over the past 60 years is remarkable. What factors contributed to this and what have been some of the major implications of this shift?
2. What factors have contributed to the continuing disadvantaged economic status of women in Canadian society? What are some of the solutions being proposed?
3. Describe what is meant by the concept of "feminization of poverty." Is it a useful notion?
4. Describe the structural and functional definitions of the family and how they differ.
5. Describe how families have changed over the past decades. What factors have led to these changes?
6. What are the three models of the family, and how would adhering to a social responsibility model change the way we provide income security programs in Canada?
7. Why is it particularly important to understand income security in relation to women?
8. The shift from "stay-at-home-mothers" to "worker-mothers" has not dramatically changed the disadvantaged status of women. Explain why this might be so.
9. Responsibility for child care and elder care falls disproportionately on women. Why is this the case and what can be done about it?

EXPLORING SOCIAL WELFARE

1. Identify and discuss the key factors contributing to women's lower pay situation.
2. Gender-based analysis (GBA) is a "tool to assist in systematically integrating gender considerations into the policy, planning, and decision-making processes." Read about GBA on the Status of Women Canada website (www.swc-cfc.gc.ca) in documents such as *Gender-Based Analysis: A Guide for Policy-Making* and *An Integrated Approach to Gender-Based Analysis*. Then pick one income security program and complete a basic GBA of it: the differential impact on men and women; how and why women and men are affected by the program; and make three basic recommendations.

CRITICAL THINKING

Great progress has been made in women's rights over the past fifty years. The case for gender equality seems obvious, so why do you think things have proceeded so slowly?

Fifty years from now, what might one expect to see with respect to gender equality in employment and in society generally?

WEBSITES

The Vanier Institute of the Family
www.vifamily.ca
The Vanier Institute of the Family is a national, charitable organization dedicated to providing leadership on issues affecting the well-being of Canadian families. Its work includes: collecting and analyzing information on changing patters of family formation and function; advocating social change to create more supportive environments for families; and advising government, corporations, and religious organizations on matters of family policy.

Status of Women Canada
www.swc-cfc.gc.ca
This federal government agency, which promotes gender equality and the full participation of women in economic, social, cultural, and political life, has a publications section with a large selection of online documents.

Canadian Women's Foundation
http://www.cdnwomen.org/
The foundation raises money and gives grants to help stop violence against women and build economic independence for women and their children. The website contains links to numerous publications, particularly those that deal with violence against women and girls, and women living in poverty.

Children and Families in Poverty

A Call to Action

The persistence of child and family poverty is a major threat to our country's future. What many feel is lacking today is a comprehensive and integrated approach to family income security. Without it, children and working families in Canada will continue to be in a precarious position, struggling to make ends meet financially.

While Canada does not have an official family policy, it does have a collection of income security measures directed solely at families with children, including the Canada Child Tax Benefit, the National Child Benefit Supplement, and the Universal Child Care Benefit. This chapter examines these programs and explores their impact on Canada's children.

"... while all children are born equal, they don't all have the same opportunities to flourish. This is as true for children here as it is for children in the third world."

— HER EXCELLENCY THE RIGHT HONOURABLE MICHAËLLE JEAN, FORMER GOVERNOR GENERAL OF CANADA

A World Fit for Children

Child poverty is normally thought of as something that happens in another country. However, currently 14.5 percent of Canadian children are living in poverty, and in Aboriginal communities the number is worse: 1 in 4 (Canada Without Poverty, 2012). And 38 percent of food bank users are children, according to Food Banks Canada's Hunger Count 2012 report.

Not surprisingly, social researchers are finding that the income security of children's families in the early years of life is especially important for the health, education, and personal well-being of children as they grow into adulthood. Canadian governments have long recognized that Canada's children need help—not only is it the ethical thing to do, but our economic and social well-being depends on it. In 1944, a universal benefit called the Family Allowance was instituted, and this benefit went to all families with children regardless of income. Over time, this benefit became targeted towards middle- and low-income families. In 1993, it was eliminated entirely.

Nowadays, most of the income security benefits available for families with children have been, and continue to be, delivered through the tax system in the form of tax credits and exemptions. Others are distributed through direct cash transfers. The Canada Child Tax Benefit, the National Child Benefit, and the Universal Child Care Benefit are now the principal child-related benefits for families with children. They are applied through the tax system, with eligibility determined by family income.

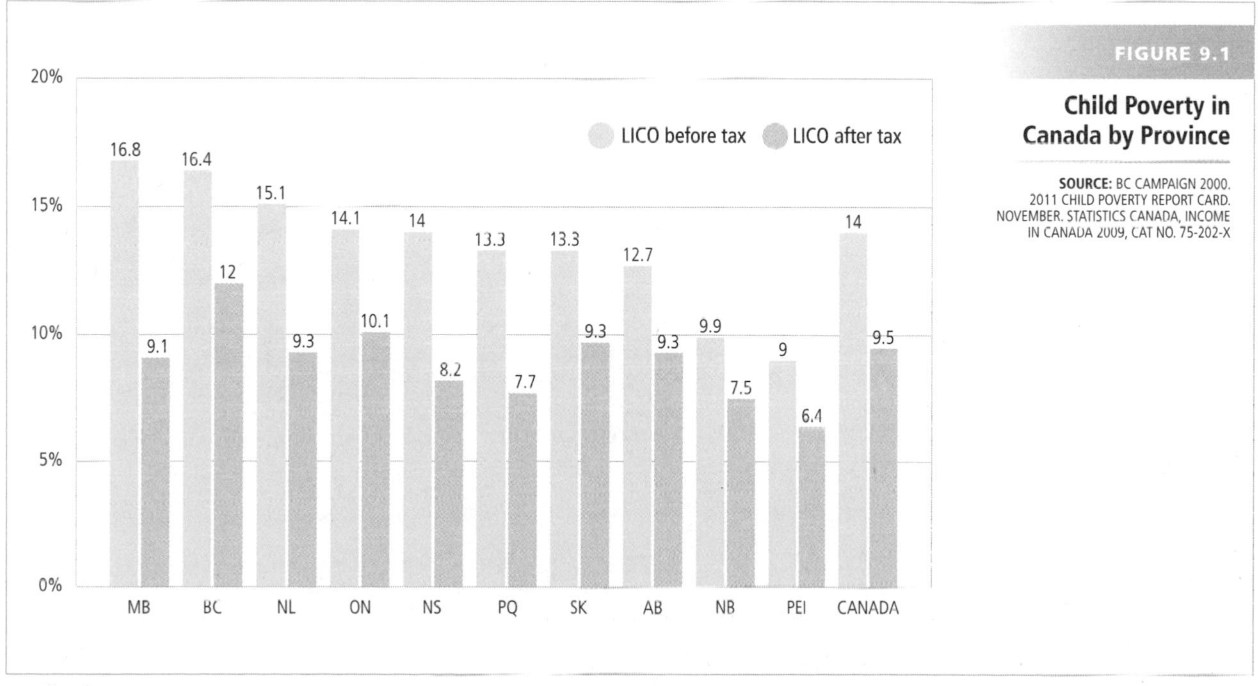

FIGURE 9.1

Child Poverty in Canada by Province

SOURCE: BC CAMPAIGN 2000. 2011 CHILD POVERTY REPORT CARD. NOVEMBER. STATISTICS CANADA, INCOME IN CANADA 2009, CAT NO. 75-202-X

Canada's Children

Good health and development during childhood are among the most important factors in making sure that individuals grow up healthy enough to learn, find work, raise families, and participate fully in society throughout their lives. Children in low-income families have higher risks of poorer health and poorer developmental outcomes than do children in middle-income and high-income families. Indeed, income is the strongest predictor of health outcomes (Mikkonen & Raphael, 2010).

Financial strain can also lead to family breakdown and contribute to social problems such as crime. As child protection teams and group homes become involved, this can translate into higher social services costs.

Campaign 2000

Campaign 2000, an across-Canada public education movement to build Canadian awareness and support for the 1989 all-party House of Commons resolution, reports yearly on the progress towards the goal of eliminating child poverty. In their report on the situation of children in the year 2000, they found that about 1.1 million Canadian children live on incomes below Statistics Canada's Low Income Cut-off (LICO), and found that many families live far below these lines.

This dire situation continues to exist despite the federal government's tax and income security policies. Many of these families and children live in modest-income households whose earnings have declined over the last decade, especially since the recession that began in 2008.

FIGURE 9.2

Child Poverty Rates With and Without Government Help

SOURCE: CHILD POVERTY REPORT CARD, 2011, BC CAMPAIGN 2000. STATISTICS CANADA, CUSTOM TABULATION, 2009

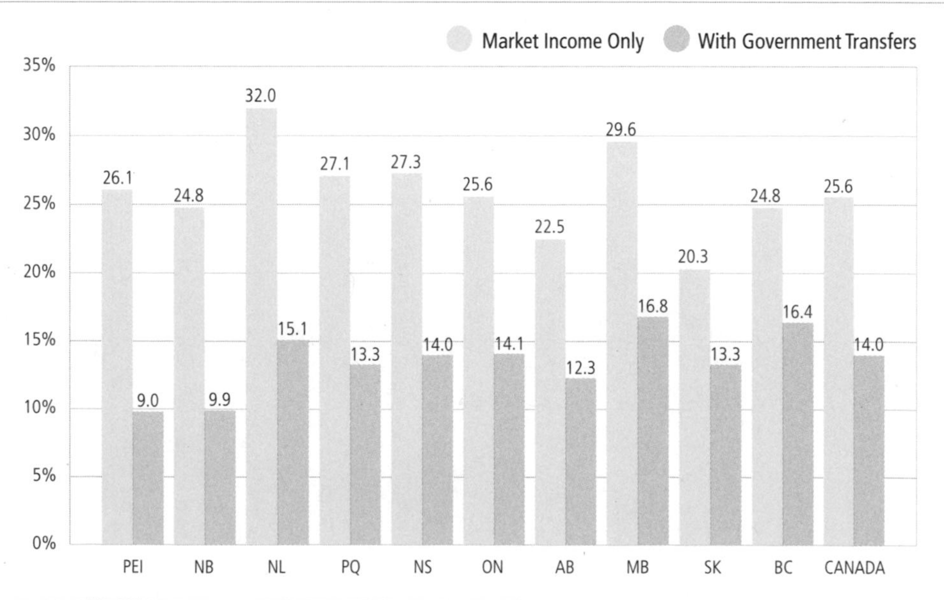

Canada and the World

One might think that in a country with enormous wealth and resources, child poverty would not be an issue. Yet, Canada's child poverty rates are higher than most other wealthy countries. Using a conservative measure of poverty to compare child poverty rates in rich countries, the UNICEF study *Measuring Child Poverty* (2012) found that Canada's rate (13.3 percent) for children is the twelfth worst, falling behind Estonia, the UK, New Zealand, and Slovakia. And this average obscures the dire situation in Aboriginal communities where close to one in four children are growing up in poverty.

The face of child poverty in Canada is also changing from the lone mother on welfare to that of the working-poor mother who is holding down at least one job. Unfortunately, single mothers who are taking up the challenge of welfare departments across the country in trading a welfare cheque for a pay stub are not finding that the transition raises them out of poverty.

The downward trend in child poverty since 1997 is an encouraging sign. To achieve a sustained reduction in child poverty, however, governments need to adopt a comprehensive and multi-pronged strategy. Delineating such a strategy would be complex, not least of which because it should include consistent and adequate income security for families with children, improvements in the availability of living-wage jobs, early childhood education and care, and affordable housing programs that provide housing for the most vulnerable families.

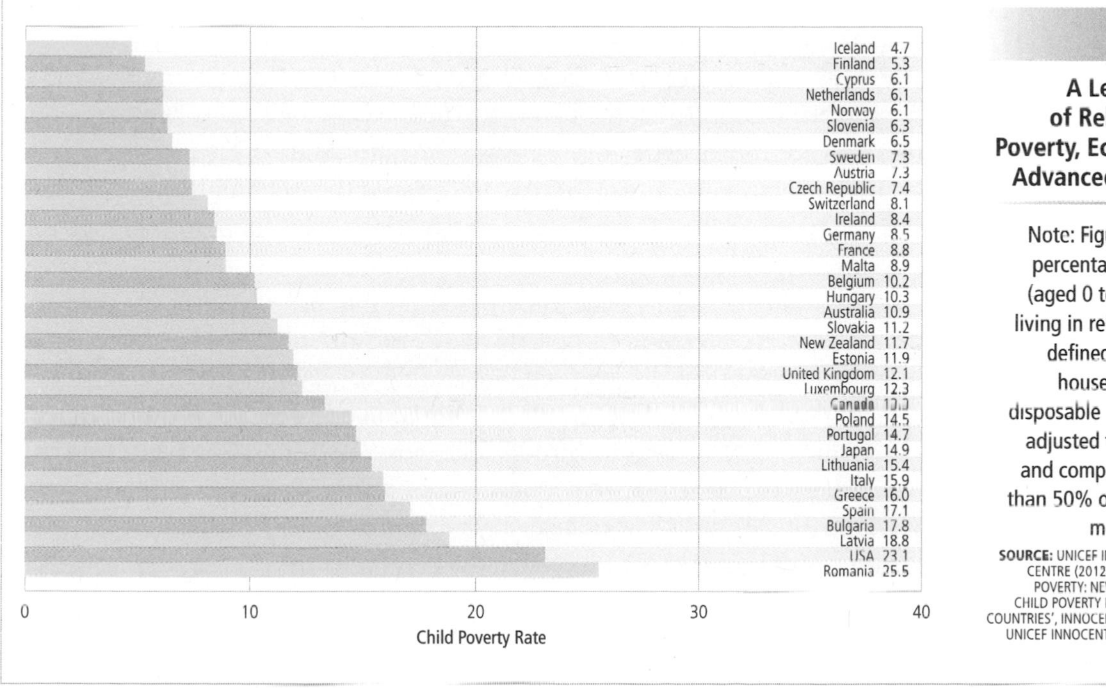

FIGURE 9.3

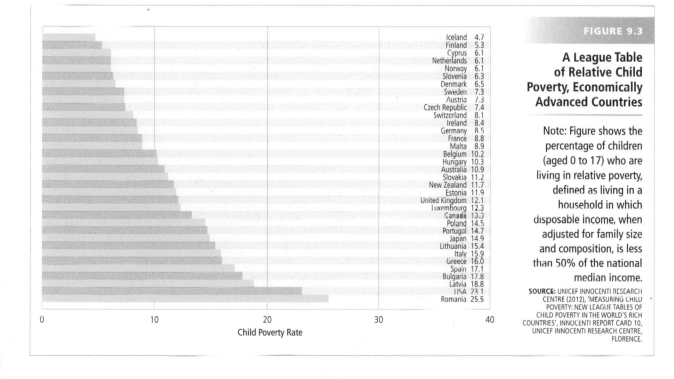

A League Table of Relative Child Poverty, Economically Advanced Countries

Note: Figure shows the percentage of children (aged 0 to 17) who are living in relative poverty, defined as living in a household in which disposable income, when adjusted for family size and composition, is less than 50% of the national median income.

SOURCE: UNICEF INNOCENTI RESEARCH CENTRE (2012), 'MEASURING CHILD POVERTY: NEW LEAGUE TABLES OF CHILD POVERTY IN THE WORLD'S RICH COUNTRIES', INNOCENTI REPORT CARD 10, UNICEF INNOCENTI RESEARCH CENTRE, FLORENCE.

Market poverty

When a household meets the characteristics of poverty despite one or more household members being employed

Market Poverty: Children in Working Poor Families

Not all children who live in families with a low income are on Social Assistance. Many parents struggling to survive on low income are employed. The problem is that the marketplace is not providing adequate income for Canadian families.

Market poverty refers to a situation in which a household remains below some measure of poverty even though one or more members of the household earn a market income or are employed. These are referred to as the "working poor." There are two obvious causes of market poverty: low wages and lack of access to the labour market. Low wages contribute to market poverty when wages do not provide an adequate income to support families. Lack of access to the labour market can be due to a lack of skills and training, for example, or particular barriers such as a lack of recognition of education, as is the case with some immigrants, or the lack of accommodation for a disability.

Self-Reliance

Increasingly, the thrust of policy-making in this area is that families should become more "self-reliant" through labour market participation, whether they are lone-parent or two-parent families. There is little consideration as to how realistic this is in terms of the level of minimum wage and the high costs of daycare for these families. For example, a single mother with a very young child that is not in school needs full-time daycare if she has a full-time job. At the general minimum wage, the cost of daycare takes up a large percentage of her earnings, particularly since full-time daycare can cost from several hundred to several thousand dollars per month depending on the daycare provider. Even when her child is in school and she works full-time during the school hours, her income is so low that the family still falls below the LICO. Two-parent families are not much better off, especially if both parents earn wages at a low hourly rate and have to pay for daycare. Even if their combined income places the family above the LICO, the cost of daycare can be enough to plunge them into poverty.

Government policies tend to be based on the idea that if people can get a job, they won't be living in poverty. However, the quality of the job is often more significant than the job itself. For example, according to Campaign 2000, in Ontario, one-third of the children from families living below the LICO have one or more parents who works full-time, and year round (see Figure 9.4).

In short, the current poverty statistics raise many questions. Why are so many working families still left with inadequate incomes? Does Canada have an official government policy that is addressing the real problem?

Four Purposes of Child-Related Income Security

Ideally, child-related income security benefits serve four main purposes:

- **TO DEAL WITH CHILD POVERTY BY PROVIDING A MINIMUM INCOME.** The first purpose is to supplement the income of lower-income families with children.
- **TO GENERATE HORIZONTAL EQUITY FOR HOUSEHOLDS WITH CHILDREN SO THAT THEY HAVE INCOME EQUAL TO THOSE WITHOUT CHILDREN.** Horizontal equity is based on the recognition that parents have heavier financial demands than childless households and single persons with the same income.
- **TO ACT AS AN ECONOMIC STIMULUS BY PUTTING MONEY IN THE HANDS OF THOSE MOST LIKELY TO SPEND IT.** This was one of the main purposes of the 1944 Family Allowance program—the idea was to provide a monthly cheque which could be spent on necessities, thereby stimulating the postwar economy.
- **TO RECOGNIZE PARENTS AS CONTRIBUTING TO THE FUTURE OF SOCIETY.** The children of today are the future. Families with children contribute something that people without children do not.

At various times, Canadian governments have implemented programs that attempt to address one or more of these goals. A nationwide approach is needed that emphasizes investing in Canada's children and addressing all these objectives simultaneously.

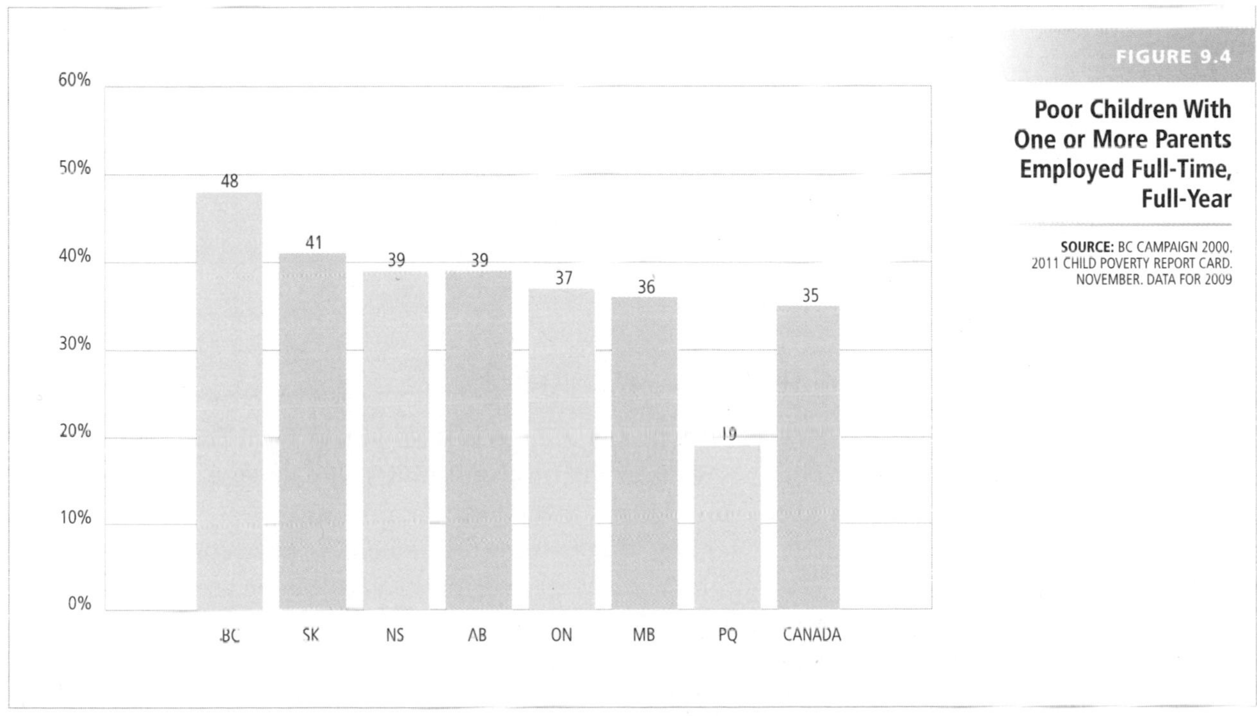

FIGURE 9.4

Poor Children With One or More Parents Employed Full-Time, Full-Year

SOURCE: BC CAMPAIGN 2000. 2011 CHILD POVERTY REPORT CARD. NOVEMBER. DATA FOR 2009

Refundable Child Tax Credit (1978)

A credit targeted for families in need of government assistance; it resulted in a decrease in Family Allowance benefits

History of Benefits for Families with Children

Our system of income security benefits directed specifically at children has a long history. In fact, when the Family Allowance was introduced in 1944, it was the first universal income security program, prior to being changed to an income-based program in 1978. The overall history can be divided into four phases.

Phase 1: Recognition of Family Needs, 1918–40

In the 1700s and early 1800s, children were treated harshly under the Common Law of England. Early legislation, such as the *Orphans Act* in 1799 and the *Apprentices and Minors Act* of 1874, gave town wardens the power to bind a child under the age of 14 as an apprentice or labourer. The *Indian Act* of 1876 demonstrated the colonizer's view of First Nations children, and many were placed in residential schools administered by Christian churches with the overriding aim of assimilation.

Income support to families with children began in 1918 with the introduction of the **Child Tax Exemption** in personal income tax. The exemption provided income tax savings that increased with taxable income. The after-tax benefit was of greatest absolute benefit to those in the highest tax brackets; the exemption provided no benefits to families that did not owe income tax. Concern about widowed mothers with small children after World War I led to Mothers' Allowances, first in Manitoba in 1916, Saskatchewan in 1917, and Ontario and BC in 1920. This provided a needs-tested monthly income support. All provinces followed suit within the next decade. Eligibility requirements varied between provinces, but one element remained steadfast—any mother deemed to be of bad character was not eligible, which was a throwback to the Poor Law concerns of distinguishing between the deserving and undeserving poor. Women's groups that wanted to avoid the stigmatizing effects of "assistance" demanded the term "pension" be used instead. They also demanded, but did not obtain, a non-discretionary pension.

Phase 2: Universal Benefits, 1941–74

Family Allowance (1944)

Known as the "Baby Bonus," the Family Allowance provided monetary benefits to all Canadian families with dependent children. It remained universal until 1973 and was eliminated in 1993

The *Family Allowance Act* of 1944 introduced the universal **Family Allowance (FA)**, providing benefits to all Canadian families with dependent children. The FA was also popularly known as the "Baby Bonus," and it was the first universal income security scheme. The FA provided a monthly payment of $5.94 to the mother of every child under the age of 16 (changed to the age of 18 in 1973). If of school age, the child had to be attending school. The stated purpose of the plan was to assure children of their basic needs and to maintain purchasing power in the postwar era.

Child welfare has changed drastically over the last century, abandoning the harsh treatment afforded children under the old common law.

The Family Allowance provision was introduced one year after the Marsh Report, which indicated that an allowance for the parents of children was central to a social security system. The majority of social workers and the Canadian Association of Social Workers strongly supported the plan. Interestingly, Charlotte Whitton, a leading social worker and director of the Canadian Welfare Council at the time, deemed the plan wasteful as both poor and wealthy families benefited. She believed that any such program should target the most needy with social utilities, such as health and housing, rather than cash. Perhaps surprisingly, many trade unions also tended to oppose the benefit, seeing it as a substitute for adequate wages.

Historians continue to debate why the Mackenzie King Liberal government introduced this universal children's benefit. Several factors have been suggested: (1) it would maintain purchasing power in the economy as a whole, (2) it was an alternative to the wage freeze that was in place at the time, (3) it would stave off the threat from the leftist Co-operative Commonwealth Federation (CCF) Party that was endorsing such a program, and (4) it would win Liberal support in Quebec where war-time conscription was unpopular.

The Family Allowance remained completely universal until 1973, when various reforms made it taxable income in the hands of the recipients. In the 1973 amendments to the act, the benefit was made taxable and was indexed to the **Consumer Price Index** (CPI). Indexation is an arrangement in which periodic adjustments are made to benefits based on changes to an index, usually the CPI. The CPI is an indicator of the consumer prices in Canada, calculated on a monthly basis using the cost of a fixed list of commodities purchased by a typical Canadian family. The CPI is used as an indicator of inflation. Why make the Family Allowance benefit taxable? The argument was that people with more income pay higher marginal tax rates and keep less of the benefit, which is the underlying idea behind a progressive income tax system. Reforms in 1989 increased the tax rate with a clawback, and the Family Allowance met its ultimate demise in 1993.

Phase 3: Erosion and Growing Poverty, 1975–90

Beginning in 1978, Finance Minister Jean Chrétien announced a merging of social security programs and income tax provisions. The Liberal government introduced the **Refundable Child Tax Credit** as a way to target families in need of government assistance. Upon the creation of the Child Tax Credit, FA benefits were reduced from an average of $25.68 per month (which would have increased to $28 with indexing) to an average of $20 per month. The stated goal of the benefit was to help families meet the costs of raising children. It was income tested and varied according to the number of children in a family.

A 2013 report on child care in Canada maintains that the number of privately run daycare spaces is growing faster than the not-for-profit spaces. Some child care experts believe that privately run daycare centres provide a lower quality of care (Commisso-Georgee, 2013).

Unlike universal benefits, the use of the tax system to target low-income families was a fundamental shift in government and policy analysts' thinking from an institutional view of social welfare to a residual view. It was also the first time that the tax system was used to redistribute income.

The tax credit provided the maximum benefit to low-income families, a declining amount to middle-income families, and no benefit to wealthy families. It provided a credit in the income tax account with the federal government. The whole credit was payable to families with a net income below a certain threshold, and it was gradually reduced until the family's income reached the national average, at which point it was reduced to zero.

If the family's tax credit was more than the amount they owed in taxes, the difference was paid to them in the form of a monthly cheque. This is what is meant by the term "refundable"—the tax credit is paid out if the taxpayer does not owe income tax.

Benefits paid in this way are called "tax expenditures." They are made up of foregone taxes, or taxes that go uncollected. In the case of a tax credit, it can become a reverse tax. This was the first major program of its type in the field of income security. Previously, it was used in the investment arena, in which governments would use it to induce certain types of investment behaviour and support various industries.

The **Child Care Expense Deduction** was first introduced in 1971 and was originally intended for lone-parent families. It was designed to offset the incremental costs of child rearing for parents in the labour force. When first introduced, the amount that parents could deduct from their personal income taxes for children was limited to $2,000 per child under the age of 14, subject to a maximum of $8,000 per family. In 1998, the deduction increased from $5,000 to $7,000 (and from $3,000 to $4,000 for children aged 7 to 16). Currently, approximately 1.2 million families use the deduction. In 1986, the FA benefit, which still existed in its reduced form, was "partially de-indexed," meaning that there were no increases in benefit levels until inflation reached 3 percent. This meant the value of the FA would lessen over time. In 1989, benefit clawbacks were introduced. The clawback came in the form of a higher tax rate for FA benefits, which meant that higher income earners would pay back their FA. This marked the end of FA as a universal program in all but name, and it eventually led to the elimination of the Family Allowance in 1993—and, many argued, to the end of universality as a principle of Canadian social security.

Convention on the Rights of the Child

Fundamental Freedoms and Inherent Rights

Since its adoption in 1989, 192 countries have signed on to the **Convention on the Rights of the Child** (which can be viewed at www.unicef.org/crc).

The basic premise of the Convention is that children (below the age of 18) are born with fundamental freedoms and the inherent rights of all human beings. Article 27 requires that governments "recognize the right of every child to a standard of living adequate for the child's physical, mental, spiritual, moral, and social development" and that when parents are unable to secure a child's standard of living, governments should assist parents "to implement this right and shall in case of need provide material assistance and support programmes, particularly with regard to nutrition, clothing, and housing."

Unfortunately, according to the Innocenti report on child poverty (UNICEF, 2005), many of the world's richest countries, including Canada, are failing to ensure that the rights outlined in the Convention are realized.

Child Tax Benefit (1993)

A monthly payment based on number of children and income level; created when government consolidated child tax credits and the Family Allowance

Included a Working Income Supplement for working poor families

Phase 4: Targeting Poverty and Work Incentives, 1991–

The idea of the "welfare wall" entered the government lexicon during this period. The term **welfare wall** refers to the disincentives that hinder the move from welfare to work because of the financial and other supports that are lost when families accept employment.

In 1993, the Government of Canada consolidated its child tax credits and the Family Allowance into a single **Child Tax Benefit (CTB)** that provided a monthly payment based on the number of children and the level of family income. In addition to a basic benefit, the Child Tax Benefit included a **Working Income Supplement (WIS)** to supplement the earnings of working poor families.

The CTB included a supplement of $213 per year for each child in a family who was under the age of seven. The maximum basic benefit was $1,020 per child per year plus an additional $75 for the third child and each subsequent child in a family. The maximum basic benefit was payable to all families with annual incomes of less than $25,921. The benefit was reduced at a rate of 5 percent of family net income in excess of $25,921 for families with two or more children and at a rate of 2.5 percent for families with one child. Families with one or two children no longer received basic benefits once the net family income exceeded $67,000.

The maximum Child Tax Benefit per child per year in 1994 was broken down as follows:

- Basic benefit: $1,020
- Supplement for third and each additional child: $75
- Supplement for children under age seven: $213
- Working Income Supplement: $500

The WIS gave an additional benefit to those working at low-income levels; the benefit was paid out at the rate of 8 percent of all earnings. This benefit was not available to unemployed parents. Families began to receive benefits from the WIS once their earnings exceeded $3,750. A maximum annual benefit of $500 was provided for families with annual incomes between $10,000 and $20,921, regardless of the number of children in the family. The WIS was reduced at a rate of 10 percent of family net income in excess of $20,921, and the benefits ceased when income reached $25,921.

In 1998 an initiative called the **Canada Child Tax Benefit (CCTB)** was introduced. The CCTB has two main elements: a Canada Child Tax Benefit (CCTB) basic benefit and the **National Child Benefit Supplement (NCBS)**. The NCBS is an additional tax credit that adds to the CCTB—it is the federal contribution to the CCTB. The NCBS provides low-income families with additional child benefits on top of the basic benefit. The terminology is confusing as the federal government, at times, refers to the overall program (CCTB and NCBS) as the National Child Benefit, instead of the Canada Child Tax Benefit (see www.nationalchildbenefit.ca). Finance Canada refers to the overall program as the CCTB.

Since 1998, the federal investment in the CCTB has risen dramatically. It is the first joint federal/provincial/territorial initiative under the Social Union Framework Agreement (SUFA) and the first national social welfare program since medicare and the Canada Pension Plan in the 1960s. The 2000 federal budget announced that CCTB funding would automatically rise with inflation.

The critics contend that the reform discriminates against welfare families in particular because they will see no net increase in their child benefits, and only the working poor and other low-income families (families not on welfare or collecting Employment Insurance) will enjoy an improvement in benefits.

In 2006, the **Universal Child Care Benefit (UCCB)** was introduced by the newly elected Conservative government. The UCCB is a taxable $1,200 per year benefit that was introduced for each child under 6 years of age. The introduction of the UCCB was widely seen as a way to scuttle the previous Liberal government's commitment to a national daycare initiative.

Universal Child Care Benefit

The Universal Child Care Benefit provides $1,200 per child under six to help offset the cost of child care. Critics argue that $100 a month is not nearly sufficient to deal with the child care concerns of the working poor.

Federal Child Benefits

Timeline and Summary

1918. Child Tax Exemption: This exemption provided income tax savings that increased as taxable income increased. It provided no benefits to families that did not owe income tax.

1944. Family Allowance (FA): This benefit was provided to all Canadian families with dependent children.

1973. Family Allowance: The benefit levels of the FA were tripled, indexed to the cost of living, and made taxable.

1978. Refundable Child Tax Credit: This more targeted and income-tested approach to child benefits provided the maximum benefit to low-income families, a declining amount to middle-income families, and no benefit to upper-income families.

1993. Child Tax Benefit (CTB): This benefit consolidated child tax credits and the Family Allowance into a monthly payment based on the number of children and level of family income.

1993. Working Income Supplement (WIS): This additional benefit was provided to supplement the earnings of low-income working families with children. Federal child benefits in 1993 totalled $5.1 billion.

1998. Canada Child Tax Benefit (CCTB) and National Child Benefit Supplement (NCBS): The NCBS replaced the WIS and was provided to all low-income families as part of the renamed Canada Child Tax Benefit.

2006. Universal Child Care Benefit (UCCB): The UCCB was introduced to provide assistance for child care expenses; it consists of a taxable benefit of $100 per month for each child under 6 years of age.

2007. Child Tax Credit announced. It provides tax relief for families with children. In 2013, it provided up to $1,000 for each child under the age of 17. Like other credits, it is reduced as income increases above $55,000 for married couples and $75,000 for single parents.

Regulated Child Care Spaces

According to a 2013 report based on a national survey by Child Care Canada, the number of regulated child care spaces nationwide has been increasing at a slower pace over recent years.

Likewise with public funding for child care, which has also increased but at a slower rate.

For-profit child care, on the other hand, continues to expand. In 2010, the number of for-profit child care spaces hit 28 percent of the total, up from 20 percent in 2004.

The report notes that the fees for child care may now be comparable to university tuition.

(Friendly and Beach, 2013)

The Canada Child Tax Benefit (CCTB)

By the end of 1997, there was a growing concern that many Canadian children did not have the opportunity for a healthy start to life and the support to reach a healthy, happy, and educated future. This growing consensus recognized that the previous child benefit system was lacking. As a result, Canada's first ministers and their governments examined various ways to improve assistance to children of low-income families.

Child Benefits for Low- and Middle-Income Families

The **Canada Child Tax Benefit (CCTB)** program is the primary mechanism for addressing child and family low income and poverty in Canada. It attempts to reduce overlap between provinces and promote labour market attachment by ensuring that families will always be better off as a result of working.

The Canada Child Tax Benefit (CCTB) is a non-taxable amount paid monthly to help eligible families with the cost of raising children under 18 years of age. The CCTB may include the Child Disability Benefit (CDB), a monthly benefit providing financial assistance for qualified families caring for children with severe and prolonged mental or physical impairments.

The CCTB has three stated objectives:

- to prevent and reduce the depth of child poverty
- to promote attachment to the labour market by ensuring that families will always be better off as a result of working
- to reduce overlap and duplication by harmonizing program objectives and benefits and simplifying administration

The CCTB program provides a tax credit to those who qualify based on an income test. Recall that a **tax credit** is an amount deducted directly from income tax otherwise payable. Examples of tax credits include the disability tax credit, the married credit for individuals, and the scientific research and experimental development investment tax credit for corporations. This is different from a **tax deduction**, which is an amount deducted from total income to arrive at taxable income. Child care expenses and capital cost allowances are tax deductions. (Tax deductions are worth more to people with higher incomes, as they are in a higher marginal tax bracket.)

The CCTB basic benefit provides child benefits to all low- and middle-income families with children. More than 80 percent of Canadian families with children receive this basic benefit. Some families are eligible for an additional benefit—the National Child Benefit Supplement. With these objectives, the CCTB aims to help low-income families by increasing federal benefits for families with children.

"Non-Stigmatizing, Inclusive, and Non Taxable"

The Canada Child Tax Benefit is the largest federal child benefit. It has many positive features, according to Ken Battle, President of the **Caledon Institute of Social Policy** and one of Canada's leading social policy thinkers. For one thing, Battle maintains, the CCTB is a non-stigmatizing, inclusive, and non-taxable program that reaches the majority of families (nine in ten)—excluding only those with the highest incomes. The CCTB is also "portable" insofar as it provides a guaranteed income supplement no matter where families live or work across Canada, and it is available to families receiving Employment Insurance, Social Assistance, or other welfare benefits (Battle, 2008a).

The Canada Child Tax Benefit is also a "progressive" program in that the payments decline as incomes rise. It provides the same amount of income support to all families with the same level of income, regardless of the source of that income, the province or territory in which they live, or their family type (Battle, 2008).

The Canada Child Tax Benefit has enjoyed substantial increases over the years, from a maximum $1,605 in 1998 to $3,436 in 2010—significant progress towards the target of $5,000 proposed by the Caledon Institute and endorsed by many family advocacy groups. The Caledon Institute maintains that the goal of a $5,000 Canada Child Tax Benefit would reduce the family poverty rate by a full percentage point and that this increment should be funded in part by abolishing the Universal Child Care Benefit. Also included with the CCTB is the National Child Benefit Supplement (NCBS), a monthly benefit for low-income families with children. The NCBS is the Government of Canada's contribution to the National Child Benefit, a joint initiative of federal, provincial, and territorial governments.

Eligibility Criteria for the CCTB

To be eligible for the Canada Child Tax Benefit, you must meet all the following conditions:

- You must live with the child, and the child must be under the age of 18;
- You must be primarily responsible for the care and upbringing of the child;
- You must be a resident of Canada; and
- You or your spouse or common-law partner must be a Canadian citizen, a permanent resident, a protected person, or a temporary resident who has lived in Canada for the previous 18 months and who has a valid permit in the 19th month.

TABLE 9.1

Annual Maximum CCTB (Including NCBS) for Families With Net Incomes Below $24,183

Number of Children	Basic CCTB	NCBS	Total	Monthly Benefit
First Child	$1,367	$2,118	$3,485	$290.41
Second Child	$1,367	$1,873	$3,240	$270.00
Third and Each Additional Child	$1,462	$1,782	$3,244	$270.33

Source: Canada Child Tax Benefit, http://www.nationalchildbenefit.ca/eng/06/cctb_children.shtml, Canada Revenue Agency, 2011, Reproduced with the permission of the Minister of Public Works and Government Services Canada, 2013

Public Spending on Families

Using United Nations data on public spending on families (cash transfers, tax breaks, and services as % GDP), we can compare the commitment of governments to the protection of children.

The UN ranks 35 countries by the percentage of GDP that each country spends on children and families. France, the United Kingdom, and Sweden lead the way, followed by Hungary, Denmark, and Belgium. Each of these spends twice as a much—as a proportion of GDP—as countries such as Canada, Spain, Switzerland, Italy, Portugal, Japan, and Bulgaria.

Canada ranks twenty-seventh out of thirty-five countries examined (UNICEF, 2012).

The National Child Benefit Supplement (NCBS)

When it created the **National Child Benefit Supplement** (NCBS), the federal government stated that the NCBS was designed to address the "welfare wall" phenomenon, a term coined by Sherri Torjman of the Caledon Institute of Social Policy (Torjman & Battle, 1993).

As has been mentioned, it is difficult for families receiving Social Assistance to make the transition from welfare to work without losing financial and other supports. For example, many low-income working families may not be eligible for benefits and services, such as the prescription drug coverage that is provided through Social Assistance for families on welfare. These barriers create the "welfare wall" effect, since some families may be discouraged from ever leaving Social Assistance since it would become difficult for low-income working families to obtain necessary support for their children.

The NCBS attempts to address this by augmenting family income only for low-income families who are not on welfare (the working poor and low-income families drawing Employment Insurance). The NCBS is designed to promote labour force participation by funding significant income supplements for low-income working families, and supports and services, such as child care and extended health benefits. In essence, it encourages and supports parents who enter and stay in the workforce (Battle, 2008a, 2008b).

An Anti-Poverty Program

The NCBS provides low-income families with additional child benefits on top of the CCTB. Over time, the supplement has increased more than the CCTB and, as a result, the NCBS now exceeds the amount of the base benefit. Though the NCBS is administered through the tax system (individuals must file a tax return to apply), the federal government says it is fundamentally an anti-poverty program. It was designed as a joint initiative with provincial and territorial governments. The federal and provincial governments, with the exception of Quebec, support the NCBS.

Until 2002, neither the CCTB nor the NCBS were indexed, which enabled the government to ignore increases in the cost of living and thereby reduce the benefit surreptitiously. The benefits are now indexed to the Consumer Price Index (CPI) (Battle, 2008b).

In 2010-2011, total annual federal support delivered through the Canada Child Tax Benefit, including the National Child Benefit Supplement, was projected to reach $10 billion. This included approximately $3.79 billion delivered through the National Child Benefit Supplement. The NCBS is not without its critics, however, especially because of how the program is administered by the provinces and territories and other limitations that diminish the benefits available to poorer Canadians.

NCBS Shortcomings

The distinctive feature of the federal National Child Benefit Supplement is that, by agreement with the provinces and territories, there is an **NCBS clawback** for Social Assistance recipients. The Ontario government, for example, claws back NCBS benefits from both Ontario Works and Ontario Disability Support Program recipients (Dawn, 2006). According to the agreement, provinces that claw back the NCBS must use the money for alternate, provincially designed and delivered programs and services for families with children. However, this rule is not always evenly applied across the provinces and territories.

There are other issues that family advocates feel limit the effectiveness of the CCTB (Battle, 2008a, 2008b). First, the CCTB calculation of benefit is based on net family income. This, of course, becomes a compelling incentive not to report oneself as part of a couple on the tax form. In the case of a single mother, for example, the tax rule stipulates that if she shares a dwelling with a person of the opposite sex for more than 12 months, her CCTB could be reduced.

Second, basing the benefit calculation on net income (before deductions), and not gross income, has negative consequences for lower-incomes families. There are many tax deductions that exist that can lower the net income (i.e., taxable income) of middle- and high-income earners. These include Registered Retirement Savings Plans (RRSPs), child care expenses, professional dues, employment expenses, interest expenses, investment losses, and even various tax shelters. Low-income families are obviously less likely to have such deductions.

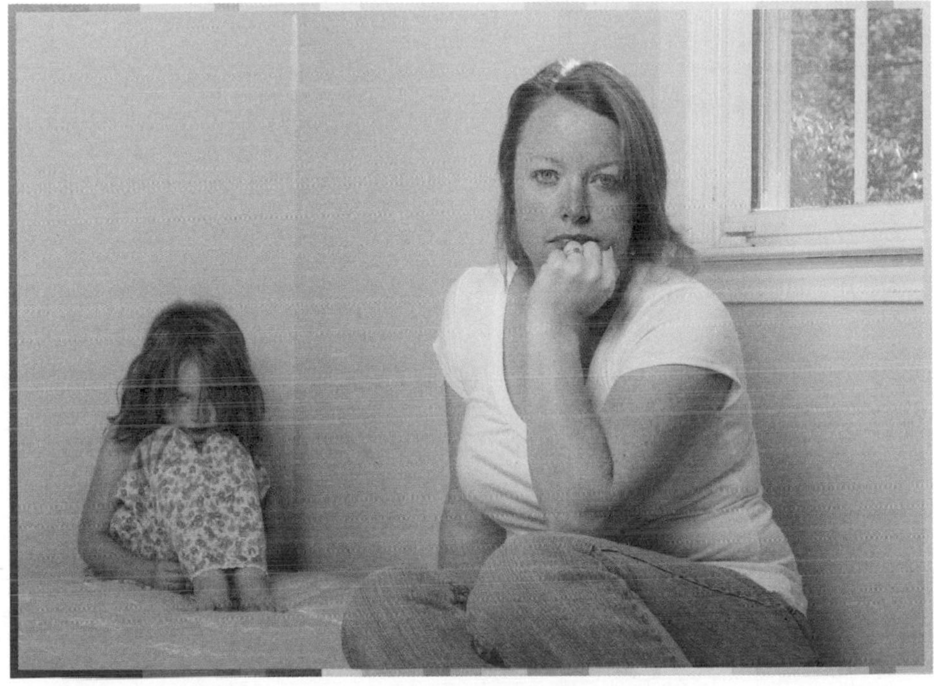

Child poverty still persists in Canada; many attribute child poverty to government policies and failure by politicians to make good on their promises.

A World Fit for Children

In 2002, the Special Session of the UN General Assembly on Children culminated in the official adoption, by some 180 nations, of the document *A World Fit for Children*. It emphasizes:

- Putting children's needs first
- Eradicating poverty and investing in children
- Committing to leaving no child behind
- Caring for every child
- Listening to children and ensuring their participation

This was the first session of the UN General Assembly to focus exclusively on issues affecting children and the first to include children as official representatives.

The Universal Child Care Benefit (UCCB)

In 2006, the newly elected federal Conservative government announced the **Universal Child Care Benefit (UCCB)**. This program was intended as a replacement for the universal child care program that the previous Liberal government had negotiated with the provinces.

Not a Replacement for a National Care Program

The UCCB payment is paid on behalf of children under the age of 6 years in installments of $100 per month per child. It is a taxable benefit (unlike the CCTB, which is a tax credit). For two-earner households, the UCCB should be declared by the spouse having the lowest net income—this means that the non-earning spouse of a millionaire could get a much larger monthly benefit from this program than a single working parent. The UCCB benefit is not taken into account, however, in calculating the CCTB or the federal goods and services tax credit. As a replacement for comprehensive child care, the UCCB payment is really intended to help cover the costs of child care.

A report by the Caledon Institute entitled *More Than a Name Change: The Universal Child Care Benefit* argues that two flaws exist in the UCCB (Battle, Torjman, and Mendelson, 2006). First, by taxing the payment in the hands of the lowest earner in a household, they punish working single parents, perhaps those who need the child care the most. Second, to help pay for the UCCB, the CCTB's young child supplement ($249 annually as of July 2006 for children under 7) was abolished. This again will be hardest felt by low-income families and single parents. The tax is complicated, and it is beyond the scope of this chapter to detail how the UCCB will affect all the different family configurations.

The **National Council of Welfare (NCW)**, a citizen's advisory body dissolved by the federal government in 2012, provided pointed analysis of the 2006 UCCB. They believe, as a taxable benefit in the hands of the lowest earner in a family, that it heightens inequities between one- and two-earner families with the same annual income and between one-earner families with two parents and employed lone parents who struggle as their family's sole or primary earner and caregiver.

Further, they do not believe that the UCCB creates child care choices to low-income families. Therefore, they see it as an inequitable child benefit and not a child care benefit. On the positive side, the NCW viewed the lack of any clawback on Social Assistance recipients by the provinces and territories as commendable.

The chart on the following pages, developed by Ken Battle, Sherri Torjman, and Michael Mendelson of the Caledon Institute, lists the many advantages of simply refocusing $1,200 to the Canadian Child Tax Credit and abandoning the Universal Child Care Benefit altogether.

TABLE 9.2

Universal Child Care Benefit Versus $1,200 Increase in Canada Child Tax Benefit

Criterion	Universal Child Care Benefit	$1,200 Increase to Canada Child Tax Benefit
Transparency	families pay back part of their $1,200 to governments	families keep what they get ($1,200 for all but high-income families)
Collateral damage to other social programs	families lose $249 per year young child support	no impact on other social programs
Progressive distribution of benefits	complex, confusing, and inequitable distribution of net benefits	progressive and straightforward distribution of benefits
Treats all family types equally	generally favours one-earner couples over single parents and two-earner couples	treats all family types the same
Coverage	covers all families with children under 6	covers all but high-income families with children under 6
Increases child benefits for poor families	poorest families end up with $951 per child under 6	poor families get and keep $1,200 per child under 6
Increases child benefits for non-poor families	increases range from $577 to $971, varying by family type and income	almost all families get and keep $1,200 per child under 6
Child care costs	pays only part of child care costs for most families	pays only part of child care costs for most families
Poverty reduction	net UCCB and CCTB total $4,400 for poor children under 6	CCTB and extra $1,200 total $4,649 for poor children under 6—close to $5,000 target
Welfare wall (disincentive to leave welfare)	many working poor families get lower net benefits then welfare families	treats all low-income families the same, so does not raise welfare wall
Impact on provincial/territorial tax and benefit	provinces/territories must decide whether to flow through the $1,200 to welfare families	provinces/territories must decide whether to flow through the $1,200 to welfare families
	increases provincial/territorial income tax revenues	no impact on provincial/territorial income tax revenues

Source: Battle, Ken, Torjman, Sherri, and Mendelson, Michael. (2006). *More Than a Name Change: The Universal Child Care Benefit.* Toronto: The Caledonia Institute.

Approaches to Children's Social Welfare

Canada's child welfare policy can best be viewed in the context of two underlying approaches to families. These are:

1. **FAMILY RESPONSIBILITY APPROACH.** According to this approach, the role of income security and social services is to facilitate decision-making and provide support when the family's ability to provide fails. This approach sees promoting labour force attachment for family members as the primary focus of any policy-making efforts.
2. **INVESTING IN CHILDREN APPROACH.** This approach holds that social spending on income supports and child education and care is an investment that benefits all of society in the long run. There is a recognition that the market is also increasingly unable to provide sufficient incomes for families and that the state must intervene pro-actively to support children and families.

Today, the Canadian government's focus on child poverty is consistent with a family responsibility approach to social welfare. Many social workers and policy analysts have been at the forefront in advocating a policy shift in the direction of the social responsibility model, recognizing that not all parents are able to work or able to find work and that they may require income assistance or child care in order to access education and attend programs to develop their skills so that they can become employable.

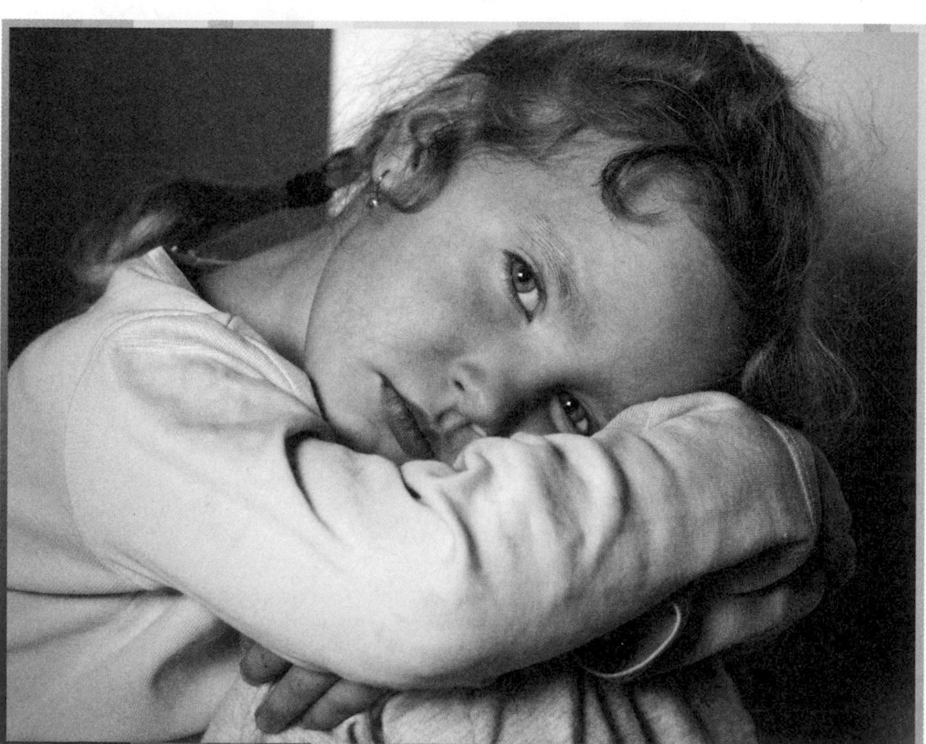

Today, many children living in poverty have parents who work in low-paying jobs.

Conclusion

Child poverty is inextricably linked with the incomes of parents or guardians, and a number of related factors appear to be keeping the child poverty rate high. First, today's families require, increasingly, the incomes of two people—the traditional "male breadwinner" model no longer works. Second, the increasing numbers of two-earner families who still cannot quite make it (the "working poor") translates into more families and children living in poverty. Third, the number of single mothers is increasing, and this vulnerable group is more likely to live in poverty. Finally, decreased levels of income security benefits, such as Social Assistance in Ontario, Alberta, and BC and restrictive eligibility criteria for Employment Insurance, have lowered family incomes and contributed to child poverty in Canada.

Canada badly needs a national family policy. At the federal level, what exists is a patchwork of federal income supports. At the provincial level, there is a an even wider range of overlapping provincial benefits schemes. The federal Canadian Child Tax Benefit and National Child Benefit Supplement were expressly directed at addressing the low-income situations of families, and the Universal Child Care Benefit was designed to help families with child care expenses. However, these programs are not without flaws. The primary program, the CCTB, is comprehensive, progressive, and portable, but needs to be substantially increased to meet the needs of families. For its part, the NCBS is intended to top up the CCTB, but the benefits themselves are subject to clawbacks and serious limitations which mitigate its effectiveness. Finally, the UCCB, which was introduced by the Conservative government in 2006 as an alternative to a national daycare program promised under the Liberal government, is a taxable benefit that works against the primary audiences for whom it was intended and it is widely regarded as a poor substitute for a nationwide child care program.

Helping children is an investment in the country's future. Without a comprehensive and integrated approach to family income policy, child care, and elder care, it is unlikely that family and child poverty will improve. Social welfare advocates and practitioners frequently witness the devastating effects of poverty on children and families. Clearly, the long-term benefits warrant the investment that can be made today.

UNICEF's Measure of Poverty

The measure of poverty used by UNICEF is different from the Statistics Canada LICO measure and therefore provides different rates.

The UNICEF measure calculates poverty as living below one-half of the median income in a country. This measure allows for easier international comparisons.

Federal Government Child Benefits

The Canadian Revenue Agency

The Canadian Revenue Agency administers the following programs that assist families and children.

CANADA CHILD TAX BENEFIT (CCTB)

The Canada Child Tax Benefit (CCTB) is a tax-free monthly payment made to eligible families to help them with the cost of raising children under age 18. The CCTB may include the

- National Child Benefit Supplement (NCBS)
- Child Disability Benefit (CDB)

NATIONAL CHILD BENEFIT SUPPLEMENT (NCBS)

The National Child Benefit is a joint initiative of the federal, provincial, and territorial governments that will:

- help prevent and reduce the depth of child poverty;
- promote attachment to the workforce by ensuring that families will always be better off as a result of working; and
- reduce overlap and duplication of government programs and services.

In July 1998, the Government of Canada enhanced the Canada Child Tax Benefit (CCTB) by introducing the National Child Benefit Supplement (NCBS). This supplement is the federal government's contribution to the National Child Benefit initiative.

CHILD DISABILITY BENEFIT (CDB)

The Child Disability Benefit (CDB) is a tax-free benefit for families who care for a child under age 18 who is eligible for the disability amount.

A child is eligible for the disability amount when a qualified practitioner certifies, on Form T2201, Disability Tax Credit Certificate, that the child has a severe and prolonged impairment in physical or mental functions, and the CRA approves the form.

The CDB is paid monthly to the Canada Child Tax Benefit (CCTB) eligible individuals and also as a supplement to the Children's Special Allowances (CSA).

UNIVERSAL CHILD CARE BENEFIT (UCCB)

The Universal Child Care Benefit (UCCB) is designed to help Canadian families, as they try to balance work and family life, by supporting their child care choices through direct financial support. The UCCB is for children under the age of 6 years and is paid in installments of $100 per month per child.

WORKING INCOME TAX BENEFIT (WITB)

The Working Income Tax Benefit (WITB) is a refundable tax credit intended to provide tax relief for eligible working low-income individuals and families who are already in the workforce and to encourage other Canadians to enter the workforce.

GOODS AND SERVICES TAX/HARMONIZED SALES TAX (GST/HST) CREDIT

The GST/HST credit is a tax-free quarterly payment that helps individuals and families with low or modest incomes offset all or part of the GST or HST that they pay.

CHILDREN'S SPECIAL ALLOWANCES (CSA)

The Children's Special Allowances (CSA) program provides payments to federal and provincial agencies and institutions (e.g., children's aid societies) that care for children. The monthly CSA payment is equal to the maximum CCTB payment plus the National Child Benefit Supplement (NCBS) plus the Child Disability Benefit (CDB) plus the Universal Child Care Benefit (UCCB) if applicable.

Additional Provincial Government Child and Family Benefits

Administered by the Canada Revenue Agency

The Canadian Revenue Agency also administers the following provincial and territorial programs that assist families with children:

ALBERTA

Alberta Family Employment Tax Credit (AFETC)
The Canada Revenue Agency administers the Alberta Family Employment Tax Credit (AFETC), which is a Canada Child Tax Benefit (CCTB) related program, on behalf of the Alberta provincial government.

The AFETC is a non-taxable amount paid to families with working income that have children under 18 years of age.

For July 2012 to June 2013, residents may be entitled to receive:

- $715 ($59.58 per month) for the first child;
- $650 ($54.16 per month) for the second child;
- $390 ($32.50 per month) for the third child; and
- $130 ($10.83 per month) for the fourth child.

The maximum is the lesser of $1,885 and 8% of a family's working income that is more than $2,760.

The credit is reduced by 4% of the amount of the adjusted family net income that is more than $34,897. Payments are made in July 2012 and January 2013. Payments are made separately from the CCTB payments.

This program is fully funded by the Alberta provincial government.

BRITISH COLUMBIA

The Canada Revenue Agency (CRA) administers the following programs on behalf of British Columbia:

Program related to the Canada Child Tax Benefit (CCTB):

- BC Family Bonus (and BC Earned Income Benefit)

Programs related to the Goods and Services Tax/Harmonized Sales Tax (GST/HST) credit:

- BC HST credit
- BC Low Income Climate Action Tax credit
- BC family bonus (BCFB)

The BCFB program includes the Basic Family Bonus and The BC Earned Income Benefit. It provides non-taxable amounts paid monthly to help low- and modest-income families with the cost of raising children under 18 years of age. These amounts are combined with the CCTB into a single monthly payment.

Basic Family Bonus
The basic family bonus is calculated based on the number of children you have and your adjusted family net income. Use our Canada child tax benefit/related provincial and territorial benefits calculator to determine the amount of your benefit.

BC Earned Income Benefit
For July 2012 to June 2013, families whose working income is more than $10,000 and whose adjusted family net income is $21,480 or less, may also be entitled to the following:

- $1.00 per month for the first child;
- $0.58 per month for the second child; and
- $5.83 per month for each additional child.

Families whose working income is between $3,750 and $10,000 or whose adjusted family net income is more than $21,480 may get part of the earned income benefit. This program is fully funded by the British Columbia provincial government.

BC HST Credit (BCHSTC)
This credit is a non-taxable amount paid to help lower-income individuals and families offset the impact of the sales taxes they pay.

For July 2012 to June 2013, the BCHSTC provides a maximum annual credit of $230 per family member. Single individuals with no children whose adjusted net income is $20,000 or less and families whose adjusted family net income is $25,000 or less will receive the maximum credit. The BCHSTC is reduced by 4% of adjusted family net income over $20,000 for singles and over $25,000 for families.

The amount is combined with the quarterly payment of the federal GST/HST credit.

Note: Since BC returned to its provincial sales tax system on April 1, 2013, the last quarterly BCHSTC payment was made for January 2013.

BC Low Income Climate Action Tax Credit (BCLICATC)
This credit is a non-taxable amount paid to help low-income individuals and families with the carbon taxes they pay.

For July 2012 to June 2013, the program provides a credit of up to $115.50 for an individual, $115.50 for a spouse or common-law partner and $34.50 per child ($115.50 for the first child in a single parent family). For single individuals with no children, the credit is reduced by 2% of his or her adjusted net income over $30,968. For families, the credit is reduced by 2% of their adjusted family net income over $36,997.

The payment is combined with the quarterly payment of the BC HST credit and the federal GST/HST credit

The BC Low Income Climate Action Tax Credit and the BC HST credit programs are fully funded by the British Columbia provincial government.

MANITOBA

The Canada Revenue Agency does not administer any benefit program on behalf of the Province of Manitoba.

PROVINCE OF NEW BRUNSWICK

The Canada Revenue Agency administers the New Brunswick Child Tax Benefit (NBCTB), which is a Canada Child Tax Benefit (CCTB) related program, on behalf of the New Brunswick provincial government. Effective July 2012, the CRA is administering a new component of the NBCTB, called the New Brunswick school supplement.

New Brunswick Child Tax Benefit (NBCTB)
The NBCTB is a non-taxable amount paid monthly to qualifying families with children under 18 years of age. The New Brunswick Working Income Supplement (NBWIS) is an additional benefit paid to qualifying families with earned income who have children under 18 years of age. Benefits are combined with the CCTB into a single monthly payment.

Residents may be entitled to a basic benefit of $20.83 per month for each child. The amount of the basic benefit is reduced if the adjusted family net income is more than $20,000.

The NBWIS is an additional benefit of up to $20.83 per month for each family. It is phased in once family earned income is more than $3,750. The maximum benefit is reached when family earned income is $10,000.

If the adjusted family net income is between $20,921 and $25,921, one may get part of the supplement.

This program is fully funded by the Province of New Brunswick.

NEWFOUNDLAND AND LABRADOR

The Canada Revenue Agency administers the following programs on behalf of Newfoundland and Labrador:

Newfoundland and Labrador Child Benefit (and Mother Baby Nutrition Supplement)
This benefit is a non-taxable amount paid monthly to help low-income families with the cost of raising children under 18 years of age. The Mother Baby Nutrition Supplement (MBNS) is an additional benefit paid to qualifying families who have children under one year of age. Benefits are combined with the CCTB into a single monthly payment.

For July 2012 to June 2013, one may be entitled to a benefit of:

- $29.58 per month for the first child;
- $31.33 per month for the second child;
- $33.66 per month for the third child; and
- $36.08 per month for each additional child.

If the adjusted family net income is above $17,397, one may get part of the benefit.

Under the MBNS, you may be entitled to a benefit of $60 per month for each child under one year of age depending on your adjusted family net income.

This program is fully funded by the Newfoundland and Labrador provincial government.

Newfoundland and Labrador Harmonized Sales Tax Credit (NLHSTC)

This credit is a non-taxable amount paid to help low income individuals and families who may be affected by the HST. Under this program, individuals or families with adjusted family net incomes of $15,000 or less receive an annual amount of $40 per adult and $60 for each child under 19. The credit is reduced by 5% of the amount of the adjusted family net income that is more than $15,000. This amount is combined with the October payment of the federal GST/HST credit.

The NLHSTC is fully funded by the Newfoundland and Labrador provincial government.

Newfoundland and Labrador Seniors' Benefit (NLSB)

This program provides a non-taxable annual amount of $946 for a single senior (65 years of age or older at any time during 2012) or a married or common-law couple with at least one senior whose adjusted family net income is $27,515 or less. Seniors will get part of this payment if their adjusted family net income is between $27,515 and $35,611.

The payment is combined with the October payment of the federal GST/HST credit.

The Newfoundland and Labrador Harmonized Sales Tax Credit and the Newfoundland and Labrador Seniors' Benefit are fully funded by the Newfoundland and Labrador provincial government.

NORTHWEST TERRITORIES

The Canada Revenue Agency administers the Northwest Territories Child Benefit (NWTCB), which is a Canada Child Tax Benefit (CCTB) related program, on behalf of the Northwest Territories.

Northwest Territories Child Benefit

The Northwest Territories Child Benefit (NWTCB) is a non-taxable amount paid monthly to qualifying families with children under 18 years of age.

You may be entitled to a basic benefit of $27.50 per month for each child.

Families who have earned income of more than $3,750 may also get the territorial worker's supplement of up to:

- $22.91 per month for one child; and
- $29.16 per month for two or more children.

If your adjusted family net income is above $20,921, you may get part of the benefit.

These amounts are combined with the CCTB into a single monthly payment.

This program is fully funded by the Northwest Territories.

NOVA SCOTIA

The Canada Revenue Agency (CRA) administers the following programs on behalf of Nova Scotia:

Program related to the Canada child tax benefit (CCTB):

- Nova Scotia Child Benefit

Program related to the goods and services tax/harmonized sales tax (GST/HST) credit:

- Nova Scotia Affordable Living Tax Credit

Nova Scotia Child Benefit (NSCB)

This benefit is a non-taxable amount paid monthly to help low- and modest-income families with the cost of raising children under 18 years of age. These amounts are combined with the CCTB into a single monthly payment. From July 2012 to June 2013, residents may be entitled to a benefit of:

- $52.08 per month for the first child;
- $68.75 per month for the second child; and
- $75.00 per month for each additional child.
- If the adjusted family net income is between $18,000 and $25,000, one may get part of the benefit.

This program is fully funded by the Nova Scotia provincial government.

Nova Scotia Affordable Living Tax Credit (NSALTC)

This credit is a non taxable amount paid to make life more affordable for Nova Scotian households with low and modest incomes. The credit offsets the increase in the HST and provides additional income for these households.

For July 2012 to June 2013, the program provides a maximum annual credit of $255.00 for an individual or a couple, plus $60.00 for each child. The credit is reduced by 5% of adjusted family net income over $30,000.

This amount is combined with the quarterly payments of the federal GST/HST credit.

The Nova Scotia Affordable Living Tax Credit program is fully funded by the Nova Scotia provincial government.

NUNAVUT

The Canada Revenue Agency administers the Nunavut Child Benefit (NUCB), which is a Canada Child Tax Benefit (CCTB) related program, on behalf of the Nunavut territorial government.

Nunavut Child Benefit (NUCB)
This benefit is a non-taxable amount paid monthly to qualifying families with children under 18 years of age. Families may be entitled to a basic benefit of $27.50 per month for each child.

Families who have earned income of more than $3,750 may also get the territorial worker's supplement of up to:

- $22.91 per month for one child; and
- $29.16 per month for two or more children.

If the adjusted family net income is above $20,921, the family may get part of the benefit.

These amounts are combined with the CCTB into a single monthly payment.

This program is fully funded by Nunavut.

ONTARIO

The Canada Revenue Agency (CRA) administers the following programs on behalf of Ontario:

- Ontario Trillium Benefit
- Ontario Energy And Property Tax Credit
- Northern Ontario Energy Credit
- Ontario Sales Tax Credit
- Ontario Child Benefit (related To the Canada Child Tax Benefit)
- Ontario Senior Homeowners' Property Tax Grant
- Ontario Sales Tax Transition Benefit

Ontario Child Benefit (OCB)
The Ontario Child Benefit (OCB) is a non-taxable amount paid to help low- to moderate-income families provide for their children.

OCB payments are delivered with the Canada Child Tax benefit in a single monthly payment. Under the OCB, for July 2012 to June 2013, applicants may be eligible to receive up to $91.66 per month for each child under 18 years of age. If your adjusted family net income is above $20,000, you may receive a partial benefit.

The OCB program is funded entirely by the Province of Ontario. The CRA administers this program for Ontario.

PRINCE EDWARD ISLAND

On behalf of the Government of Prince Edward Island, the Canada Revenue Agency administers the Prince Edward Island Sales Tax Credit, which is related to the Goods and Services Tax/Harmonized Sales Tax (GST/HST) credit.

Prince Edward Island Sales Tax Credit
The Government of Prince Edward Island announced the Prince Edward Island Sales Tax Credit (PEISTC) in its 2012 budget. This credit helps offset the increase in provincial sales tax for households with low and modest incomes.

The PEISTC provides an ongoing non-taxable quarterly payment, which will be integrated with GST/HST credit payments starting in July 2013.

QUEBEC

The Child Assistance Payments program is related to the Canada Child Tax Benefit but is not administered by the Canada Revenue Agency.

Child assistance payments: If you live in Quebec, you must file your application for child assistance payments and make any changes to your family situation directly with the Régie des rentes du Québec. However, you do not have to file an application for a child born in Quebec because the Régie is automatically notified by the Registrar of Civil Status. For more information, visit the Régie Web site.

SASKATCHEWAN

The Canada Revenue Agency administers the Saskatchewan Low-Income Tax Credit, which is a Goods and Services Tax/Harmonized Sales Tax (GST/HST) credit related program, on behalf of the Saskatchewan provincial government.

Saskatchewan Low-Income Tax Credit (SLITC)
This credit is a non-taxable amount paid to help Saskatchewan residents with low and modest incomes.

For July 2012 to June 2013, this program provides $232 for an individual, $232 for a spouse or common–law partner (or for an eligible dependant), and $90 per child (maximum of two children), or an annual credit of up to $644 per family. The credit starts to be reduced when the adjusted family net income is more than $30,465. Families with adjusted family net income between $30,465 and $62,565 may get part of the credit.

The payments are combined with the quarterly payments of the federal GST credit. The Saskatchewan Low–Income Tax Credit program is fully funded by the Saskatchewan provincial government.

YUKON

The Canada Revenue Agency administers the Yukon Child Benefit, which is a Canada Child Tax Benefit (CCTB) related program, on behalf of the Yukon territorial government.

Yukon Child Benefit (YCB)
This benefit is a non-taxable amount paid monthly to help low- and modest-income families with the cost of raising children under 18 years of age. These amounts are combined with the CCTB into a single monthly payment.

You may be entitled to a benefit of $57.50 per month for each child. If your adjusted family net income is above $30,000, you may get part of the benefit.

This program is funded by the Yukon with a contribution from Aboriginal Affairs and Northern Development Canada on behalf of Status Indian children.

CHAPTER 9 REVIEW

LEARNING OBJECTIVES

After completing this chapter, you should be able to:

- Understand the extent of child poverty within Canada and throughout the world.
- Describe the purposes of child-related income security programs.
- Discuss the history of benefits programs designed to support parents and families in Canada.
- Discuss the merits of the Canada Child Tax Benefit.
- Evaluate the National Child Benefit Supplement.
- Evaluate the Universal Child Care Benefit.
- Describe the two broad approaches to children's social welfare and how the different approaches influence policy-making.
- Identify some of the federally sponsored programs provided through the provinces and territories.

KEY CONCEPTS IN CHAPTER

- Caledon Institute of Social Policy
- Campaign 2000
- Canada Child Tax Benefit (CCTB)
- Child Care Expense Deduction
- Child Tax Benefit (CTB)
- Child Tax Exemption
- Consumer Price Index
- Family Allowance (FA)
- Family responsibility approach
- Investing in children approach
- Market poverty
- National Child Benefit Supplement (NCBS)
- National Council of Welfare
- NCBS clawback
- Poverty gap
- Refundable Child Tax Credit
- Tax credit
- Tax deduction
- Universal Child Care Benefit (UCCB)
- Welfare wall
- Working Income Supplement (WIS)

REVIEW QUESTIONS

1. What is the current poverty situation of Canada's families and children?
2. What is meant by "market poverty," and what are its basic causes?
3. What are the two general approaches to children's social welfare? What approach most closely resembles the approach followed by the Canadian government?
4. Explain the four purposes of child-related income security.
5. List and describe four key changes that took place over the history of income security for children in Canada.
6. What federal programs currently provide income security for Canadian families with children? What are the criticisms of the programs as they pertain to families on Social Assistance?
7. What is the "welfare wall?" What can be done about it to help people who are having to rely on income support and social services?

EXPLORING SOCIAL WELFARE

1. Does your province "clawback" the NCBS? If so, such monies are supposed to be spent on programs for low-income people in your province. You can find government information about reinvestments at www.nationalchildbenefit.ca. Do some research on your own and see what you can find out about the NCBS in your province.
2. Pick one of the key issues facing Canadian children and families today and locate empirical research that addresses this issue. Write a short report, complete with data portraying the issue and proposed solutions.

CRITICAL THINKING

Families count, clearly, and in general the more governments can do to support them, the better. Do you think that there are additional things that government can do today to provide practical support to Canadian families and children?

Are there any areas where you think governments are too invasive and should perhaps restrict their involvement?

WEBSITES

Campaign 2000
www.campaign2000.ca
This is an extensive site that contains report cards on child poverty, publications and other resources, and suggestions for taking action. Campaign 2000 was a cross-Canada public education movement aimed at building awareness and support for the 1989 all-party House of Commons resolution to end child poverty in Canada by the year 2000

Childcare Resource and Research Unit
www.childcarecanada.ca
The Childcare Resource and Research Unit is an early childhood education and child care (ECEC) policy research institute with a mandate to further ECEC policy and programs in Canada. It was established to: provide public education, resources and consultation on ECEC policy and research; foster and support research in various fields focusing on ECEC; carry out relevant research projects nd publish the results; support, promote and provide communication on ECEC policy and research.

Child Welfare League of Canada (CWLC)
www.cwlc.ca
The Child welfare League of Canada (CWLC) is the voice for child welfare issues across Canada. Established in 1994, CWLC is a membership-based national organization dedicated to promoting the well-being and protection of vulnerable young people.

10

The Social Welfare of Immigrants

Fostering Multiculturalism and Income Security

"We've always been a country of immigrants, waves of people from every other shore coming here to join with the Aboriginal peoples. In recent decades, we have undertaken a massive experiment in citizenship. We are learning to practice the ideals of unity in diversity, and the rich variety in our population astonishes the world."

— FORMER GOVERNOR GENERAL ADRIENNE CLARKSON AT A CITIZENSHIP CEREMONY IN 2005

Canada is one of the most ethnically and racially diverse nations in the world. It is multicultural—a place where one can live while retaining cultural traditions. Canada is also regarded as a safe haven for refugees. However, not all new immigrants are faring well in Canada—economic and social integration is increasingly difficult and the barriers to full participation in Canadian society are many.

Immigration policy itself has remained largely unchanged since the late 1960s. But all that is now changing too. Since 2008, the Conservative government has introduced changes to immigration policy at breathtaking speed. But is this what Canadians want? Have we had time to think about what they really mean? This chapter explores these issues and their long-term effects on Canadian society.

Multicultural Canada

Canada was one of the first countries to develop an explicit commitment to promoting ethnic and racial diversity through its 1971 Multicultural Policy. From this, many other policies and practices have been developed to support the growing ethno-racial and cultural mosaic.

Today, the belief in **multiculturalism** is an intrinsic part of our social, political, and even moral order. Children learn multiculturalism at school, and by and large it is practiced at work and in our local communities. However, for many new immigrants to Canada, the experience can be different from this somewhat idealized image, and perhaps increasingly so.

Changing Countries of Origin

In its early history, Canada became home to immigrants from the United Kingdom, France, and other mainly Northern European countries. In the post-World War II period, immigrants from other parts of Europe came to Canada (Italy, Portugal, Greece).

Important changes to Canadian immigration policies in the late 1960s (the "point system") resulted in the arrival of increasing numbers of newcomers from non-European countries—Asia, Africa, the Middle East, South and Central America, and the Caribbean. This resulted in a change in the ethno-racial make-up of Canadian society, bringing an exciting new dimension to the multicultural experience.

TABLE 10.1

Immigrants to Canada by Country of Last Permanent Residence

	1959/ 1960	1969/ 1970	1979/ 1980	1989/ 1990	1999/ 2000	2009/ 2010
Total Immigrants	107,880	161,245	143,825	203,357	205,710	270,512
Europe	85,512	87,228	41,284	53,457	39,984	42,151
Asia	5,263	22,958	71,574	101,174	126,142	153,308
US, West Indies	12,208	36,666	17,254	17,937	12,411	19,300
All other countries	3,132	9,784	12,122	1,585	402	410

1. Includes: England, Lesser British Isles, Northern Ireland, Scotland, and Wales. **Source:** Canada Facts and Figures: Immigration Overview Permanent and Temporary Residents, http://www.cic.gc.ca/english/resources/statistics/menu-fact.asp, Citizenship and Immigration Canada, 2011, Reproduced with the permission of the Minister of Public Works and Government Services Canada, 2013

Immigration Classes

Economic class: includes skilled workers, business owners, and entrepreneurs

Family class: requires a sponsor to provide economic and personal support for three to ten years

Refugee class: includes individuals who need protection from persecution in their home country

A Brief History of Immigration to Canada

Canadian immigration policies have always been and continue to be shaped, above all, by the economic requirements of our country. Inevitably, decisions about immigration are linked to our need for labour and the current level of population growth. When enacting these policies, however, politicians have been forced to take into account the general concerns and fears that mainstream Canadians have about the increased presence of newcomers.

Not all those concerns are rational. In their book *The Making of the Mosaic: A History of Canadian Immigration Policy*, Ninette Kelley, a member of the Canadian Immigration and Refugee Board, and Michael Trebilcock, a professor of law and economics at the University of Toronto, chart the progression of immigration policy in Canada. Their analysis showed that explicitly racist and discriminatory policies have been used in the past to control the influx of people from certain ethno-racial and cultural groups. Given Canada's commitment to diversity, equality, and freedom, many are surprised to learn that, historically, racial discrimination towards newcomers was — and still is — quite common.

Selection on the Basis of National Origin

Early in the 1900s, newcomers to Canada were sought after to help develop the country. During this time, official policies were designed to support the arrival of the "best" immigrants (for example, Germans, who were said to be "solid and hardworking") and exclude those who were less desirable. For example, the **Chinese Head Tax** (which was levied on each member of a Chinese household) and the **Continuous Journey Requirement** (which in practice prevented many South Asians from entering Canada) were deliberate attempts on the part of those in power to legally prevent individuals from particular ethno-racial groups (whom they found morally or socially unappealing) from entering the country.

During World War II (1939–45) and the two decades that followed, there was an increased demand for labour which resulted in the redesign of immigration policies to meet the growing needs of business and industry. Intense economic growth created a favourable environment for immigration: professionals and skilled workers in different trades were sought after to populate urban environments. Finding the "right" kind of immigrant was still important, and there were continued efforts to keep those from diverse ethno-racial backgrounds (as well as homosexuals, drug addicts and traffickers, Nazi-sympathizers, and communists) out of Canada. While explicitly racist policies (like the Chinese Head Tax) were no longer officially tolerated, various ethnic and racial groups were encouraged to work with the government to determine the best ways to manage and support immigration from non-European countries.

The Points System, 1967

A new policy, called the **Points System,** was introduced in 1967, which effectively eliminated nationality and race as determining factors in immigration decisions. The goal of the points system was to meet the economic and labour needs of Canada while ensuring that justice and fairness characterized the immigration process.

With the points system, individual qualities were accorded a certain number of "merit points." Higher "merit points" would increase one's chances of being granted entry into Canada. The qualities considered included level of education, personal attributes (such as adaptability, motivation, initiative), demand for the person's occupation in Canada, level of skill, the extent to which employment is already arranged, knowledge of English and/or French, the number of relatives already living in Canada, and the number of employment opportunities in their desired destination.

The points system continues to be used for **economic class** immigrants. They can be either skilled workers, business owners, or entrepreneurs. A citizen or permanent resident is also able to sponsor relatives (spouses or common-law partners, parents, grandparents, dependent children, and other family members) under the **family class**. She or he is required to assume responsibility for these family members for anywhere from three to ten years. Finally, in keeping with Canada's commitment to humanitarianism, thousands arrive under the **refugee class** each year on humanitarian grounds.

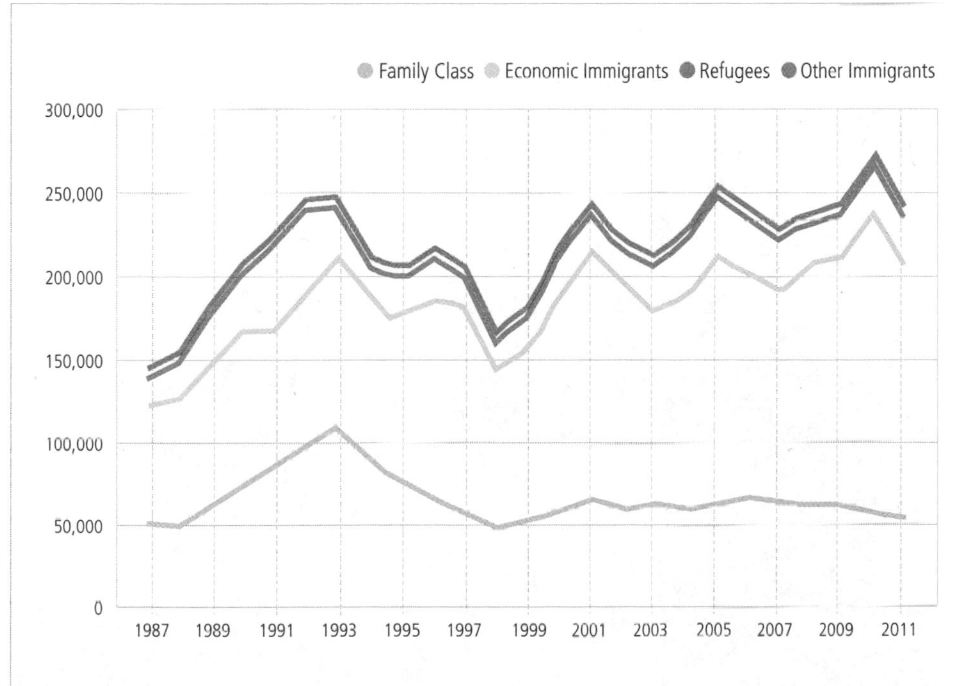

FIGURE 10.1

Immigrants by Admission Category

SOURCE: CITIZENSHIP AND IMMIGRATION CANADA. 2012. CANADA FACTS AND FIGURES: OVERVIEW PERMANENT AND TEMPORARY RESIDENTS 2011.

Multicultural Policy, 1971

Canadian Multicultural Policy was introduced in 1971. The overall goal was to reframe ethnic or racial differences as a national agenda of "unity within diversity." Its chief purposes, as described by Mahtani (2004), were first enunciated by then Prime Minister Pierre Trudeau in the House of Commons in October of 1971:

1. To assist all cultural groups that demonstrate a desire and effort to develop a capacity to grow and contribute to Canada;
2. To assist members of all cultural groups to overcome cultural barriers to full participation in Canadian society;
3. To promote creative encounters and interchange among all Canadian cultural groups in the interest of national unity; and
4. To continue to assist immigrants to acquire at least one of Canada's official languages.

This official commitment to multiculturalism is uniquely Canadian, setting us apart from other nations around the world. Indeed, according to Kelley and Trebilcock, a common sentiment among Canadians is that "racism and bigotry were European, or at least American, inventions that have little part in Canada's history, tradition, or psyche . . . Canada has a long history of welcoming refugees and dissidents" (1998, p. 441).

Canadian multiculturalism, however, is not perfect. In fact, there have been many debates about the benefits and limitations of this policy and the values and beliefs that have shaped it.

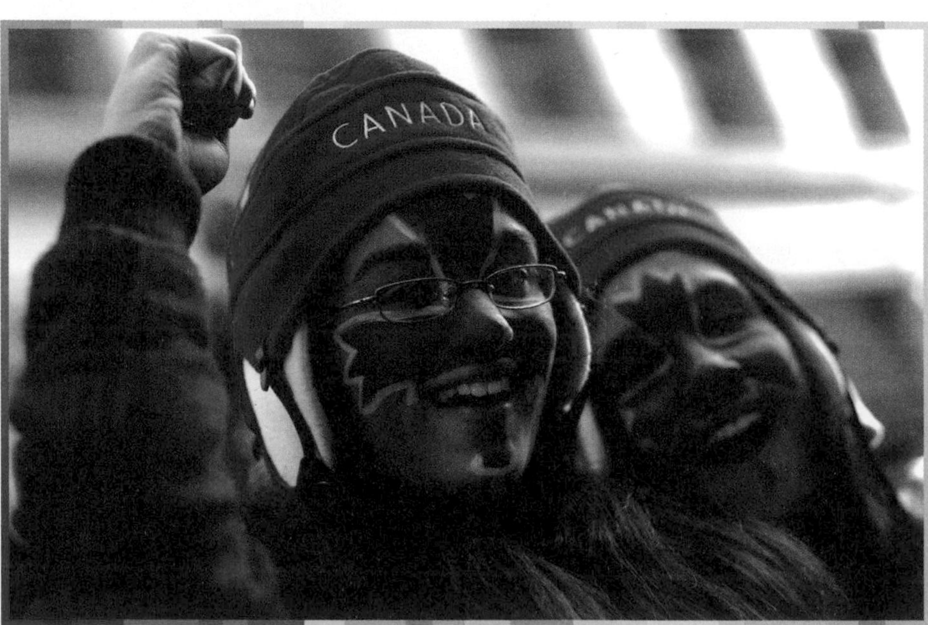

Canada boasts a very multicultural population, particularly in urban areas.

Criticisms of Multicultural Policy

Several Canadian scholars argue that multiculturalism has failed in reaching its intended goals and that aspects of multiculturalism may be detrimental to Canadian society. For example, George Dei, a professor at the Ontario Institute for Studies in Education, has suggested that multiculturalism promotes "celebrations of diversity" that divert our attention away from the disturbing effects of racial inequality in society.

This is referred to as the "saris, samosas, and steel band syndrome," and it involves displaying superficial aspects of a culture (such as ethnic trinkets, foods, and dance) to mainstream audiences at ethnic and cultural fairs and festivals. Dei argues that these celebrations do not encourage a deep and meaningful understanding of the customs and traditions of different ethnic or cultural groups. In addition, these events do not result in changes to the existing power structures that sustain inequalities between mainstream Canadians and ethno-racial minorities. Instead, these practices end up trivializing people's cultural practices and undermining the very belief in equality that Canadians claim to protect and promote (Dei, 1996).

This view is shared by Canadian writer Neil Bissoondath, who has suggested that this "celebratory" view of ethno-racial differences often ends up homogenizing people of colour. In other words, based on a limited look at certain cultural practices, all individuals who share a particular ethno-racial background are assumed to share stereotypical qualities that are different from (and less "normal" than) mainstream Canadians. Further, Bissoondath argues that by stressing the differences between people with diverse ethno-racial backgrounds and mainstream Canadians, multiculturalism threatens the cohesiveness of Canadian society (Bissoondath, 1994).

The critique is, essentially, that the emphasis on preserving traditions and customs from "back home" encourages a lack of commitment to the "Canadian" way of life that should be the uniting force for all members of society. It therefore presents a barrier to the full integration of people from all ethno-racial groups into Canadian society and instead results in their exclusion and marginalization from the mainstream. Bissoondath argues that rather than identifying ourselves as "hyphenated" Canadians (which would make him an East Indian-Trinidadian-Canadian), we should be proud to call ourselves simply "Canadian."

Such critiques of multiculturalism challenge policy-makers to reshape and improve the programs offered so that they address the real concerns of immigrants and are responsive to the needs of all Canadians, including and perhaps especially those newcomers facing economic hardship. Despite these critiques, however, it seems likely that few Canadians would deny that, over the last three or four decades and other failings aside, the experiment with multiculturalism has been anything but positive for Canadians from coast to coast.

Visible minorities

This is a category used by Statistics Canada referring to peoples who are neither Caucasian nor Aboriginal. The United Nations Committee on the Elimination of Racial Discrimination released a report in 2007 stating that Canada should reconsider using the term "visible minorities" to define people facing discrimination, suggesting that the phrase itself is discriminatory.

Chinese Head Tax

It is estimated that the federal government earned $23 million from the Chinese Head Tax policy (see feature on next page), which resulted in family separation and poverty among members of the Chinese community in Canada.

It was only in 2006 that financial restitution was made to the families of those who paid the Chinese Head Tax, and the government made a public apology for the explicitly racist and discriminatory policy.

Challenges Faced by New Immigrants

Multiculturalism notwithstanding, the challenges related to immigration and settlement, now and in the past, can include any or all of the following:

- Struggling with language and accessing educational programs
- Experiencing difficulties finding suitable and affordable housing
- Having to deal with racism, exclusion, and discrimination
- Learning to navigate complex health and social service systems

Added to these problems is the fact that many newcomers have had to leave family members and friends behind in their home countries, so they are also often dealing with concerns related to family reunification and a lack of extended kinship and social networks.

Low Incomes

Perhaps the most pressing challenge experienced by newcomers today is related to income insecurity and the problems arising therefrom. In particular, far too many recent immigrants (those who have been in Canada for five years or less) are searching for employment or are underemployed and are more likely to face low income than mainstream Canadians.

Unfortunately, this condition seems to be worsening over time. For example, recent immigrants in 1980 had a low-income rate 1.4 times greater than individuals born in Canada. By 1990, the rate for newcomers had increased to 2.1 times, or more than twice that of their Canadian-born counterparts. In 2000, these individuals were 2.5 times more likely than non-immigrants to live below the Low Income Cut-off (Picot and Hou, 2003). In 2009, nearly one-quarter (23.8 percent) of immigrants who had been in Ontario for less than five years were considered low income, much higher than the overall low income rate of 13.1 percent. Even among those in the province for less than 10 years, nearly one in five was living in poverty (19.1 percent).

According to Garnett Picot and Feng Hou at Statistics Canada, one would not have expected this trend considering that in 2000, some 42 percent of recent immigrants held university degrees compared with only 19 percent of those who arrived in 1980. The authors attempted to understand what kinds of factors might be contributing to this growing number of recent newcomers living on low incomes. Using a statistical procedure called a "regression analysis," Picot and Hou found that only half (48 percent) of the increase in the low-income rate among new immigrants could be explained by factors such as level of education, the newcomer's home country, her or his home language, the nature of her or his family structure (e.g., single- or dual-parent families), and her or his age. The question is, then, what other kinds of factors are involved?

Historical Canadian Immigration Policies

Structural Racism

The "Continuous Journey"

In the late 1800s and early 1900s, over 2,000 individuals from the Indian subcontinent arrived to work in Canada with the hope of creating a better economic situation for their families. Fear and racism among mainstream Canadians, however, led to strict policies that discouraged South Asian immigration.

As members of the British Commonwealth, Indian citizens could not be explicitly denied entry, but those arriving in Canada were required to have $200 on their person an outrageous amount, given the standard wage in India of ten cents a day. Also, the Continuous Journey Requirement permitted entry to immigrants only if they arrived "from their country of birth or citizenship by a continuous journey on through tickets purchased before leaving the country" (Kelley and Trebilcock, 1998, p. 146). On a continuous journey, a ship could not stop in any port between departure and final destination—a condition that was impossible to meet, given the distance between Indian and Canadian ports.

The Chinese Head Tax

The Canadian Pacific Railway was built in the late 1800s with mostly Chinese immigrant labour. With the influx of labourers, many believed that the number of Chinese immigrants to Canada needed to be somehow "managed." However, because of the need for labourers and the necessity of trade with China, it was not possible to restrict immigration outright. Restricting immigration from China entirely would have seriously compromised trade with China and negatively affected economic growth within Canada.

To resolve the issue, Canada developed a series of policies aimed at discouraging Chinese immigration. The most famous policy was the *Chinese Immigration Act* (1885). Under the act, a "head tax" of $50 was imposed on all incoming persons of Chinese origin with very few exceptions. The tax was eventually increased to $100 in 1900 and to $500 (the equivalent of two years of wages for a Chinese labourer) in 1903, an amount that would have been nearly impossible for many to pay.

Hire Immigrants

www.hireimmigrants.ca

Hireimmigrants.ca is a government-sponsored site that provides employers with information on hiring interns, mentoring, and community awareness programs to help skilled immigrants obtain jobs in their fields.

Barriers to Finding and Keeping Work

In a report titled *Making Work Pay*, Ron Saunders argues that recent immigrants are more likely to be employed in low-paying jobs. A quarter of newcomers who arrived in Canada during the previous five years earned less than $10/hour, compared to only one-sixth of mainstream Canadians (Saunders, 2006). This problem is further compounded when the immigrant is a member of a "**visible minority**" group, since racial discrimination results in people of colour earning less than newcomers who are white.

Skills and Training

In theory, the points system is intended to safeguard people from experiencing unemployment or underemployment and its financial consequences. It does this by ensuring that there is a need for the skills and experiences the newcomer brings to this country. The problem, however, is that for many individuals, the advanced and professional degrees granted by their countries of origin and their job skills and experiences gained prior to entry into Canada are not recognized or transferable in their current circumstances. These immigrants (referred to by those who work in this area as "foreign-trained professionals") are then required to go back to school or take intensive exams in order to become "recredentialized," a costly and time-consuming process.

TABLE 10.2

Average Weekly Earnings Lower for Landed Immigrants (Ontario)

	2006	2007	2008	2009	2010
Total	$766.16	$784.58	$814.88	$830.86	$848.00
Total landed immigrants	759.55	780.38	796.17	802.53	818.43
Very recent immigrants, 5 years or less	610.72	597.78	636.75	626.53	654.63
Recent immigrants, 5 to 10 years	714.02	706.70	747.61	734.58	733.95
Established immigrants, 10+ years	799.08	834.23	840.52	849.01	865.29
Non-landed immigrants	734.62	712.07	772.81	786.25	823.65
Born in Canada	769.62	787.98	823.12	842.75	860.04

Source: Statistics Canada, Labour Force Survey.

Language and Culture

In cases where foreign-obtained credentials are recognized, the lack of "Canadian" experience often prevents newcomers from getting the jobs they have been trained (and in some cases retrained) to do. It is difficult, however, to gain experience when not having it prevents people from acquiring appropriate employment in the first place.

In cases where people are hired in suitable positions, other factors can make it difficult to keep those jobs. Problems with the language can interfere with how work is performed and can make communicating with co-workers and managers difficult.

Something as seemingly trivial as not understanding the norms and conventions of the Canadian workplace can introduce social challenges that make it hard for newcomers to fit in with other employees. For example, in some cultures, it is not the custom to shake hands when meeting new people. In other groups, it is considered inappropriate to look superiors in the eye during a conversation. In mainstream North America, it is not only acceptable and appropriate to shake someone's hand or maintain eye contact while interacting, but it can be seen as rude or disrespectful not to do these things.

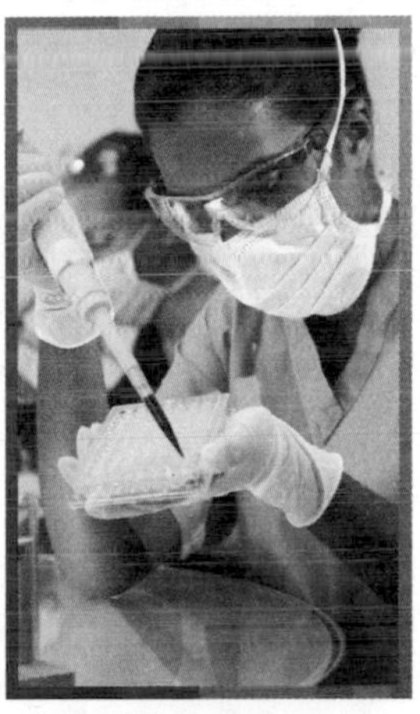

Many new immigrants find that their education and training is devalued in the Canadian job market, making it difficult for them to find jobs within their professions that make use of their skills and qualifications.

Personal Characteristics and Resources

According to sociologist and University of Toronto professor Wsevolod Isajiw (1999), immigrants who are younger often become employed more quickly than those who are older. This may reflect the general tendency in our society to value youth over age. It also may be the case that younger newcomers are typically more comfortable with the dominant language and may possess many of the personal resources described earlier. This likely enables younger immigrants to take risks and helps them to sell themselves in a potential job situation, thereby increasing their chances of gaining suitable employment.

A person's gender is also an important factor in determining how successful he or she will be in gaining suitable employment. While immigrant women deal with many of the same work-related barriers that immigrant men face, they also confront certain stressors that are unique to their gender. For example, many women must manage the added complexities of child care and family responsibilities, which can make it difficult to gain Canadian work experience. As well, immigrant women face a unique form of discrimination as a result of the combined effect of their ethno-racial background and gender.

The negative effects of age and gender on the ability to secure suitable employment can sometimes be counteracted by the presence of certain qualities in job-seekers. Aside from actual skills, a person's ability to know where to look for work, how to write a resume, how to prepare for an interview, and so on are key in determining how successful she or he will be in finding the right job.

Racism and Discrimination in Employment

Racism and discrimination related to employment can take on various forms. During the early stages of looking for work, **culturally biased hiring practices** that favour certain skills and behaviours can make it difficult for newcomers to find appropriate employment. For example, here in North America, "selling yourself" and your skills is not only desirable but necessary when searching for a new job. Members of some cultural groups, however, see this behaviour as rude and boastful and find it uncomfortable to act with such assertiveness. Also, during this stage, personal prejudices on the part of potential employers can prevent an immigrant from a visible minority group from being hired.

Workplace Discrimination

Once hired, racism within the workplace can make it difficult to stay in an employment setting. This can be overt, taking the form of discriminatory remarks or behaviours that are meant to set people of colour apart from mainstream Canadians. The expression of such personal prejudices not only creates a toxic work environment but has serious negative psychological consequences for the victims of racism.

Racism in the workplace can also take on a more subtle appearance. For example, racism might be reflected in the gross earning differentials between immigrants and their mainstream counterparts. If hired, newcomers often make less money when compared to mainstream Canadians. This is especially true for people from visible minority groups. According to Jeffrey Reitz at the University of Toronto, immigrants from non-European countries in Africa and the Caribbean, and from India, China, and the Philippines, tend to earn 15–25 percent less than (white) immigrants from Europe (Reitz, 2001). Consistent with this, researchers Ravi and Krishna Pendakur (1998) found that men from visible minority groups (both immigrants and those born in Canada) earn less than their white counterparts. While these earning differences might be explained with the argument that the skills and education acquired in European countries fit better with our employment needs here in Canada, race is a factor that is clearly at play.

Another example of subtle racism is the "glass ceiling effect." This involves allowing people of colour to advance only to a point in the organizational ranks, with top-level management positions reserved for those who are usually white and typically men. This phenomenon is referred to as the glass ceiling effect since the racial barrier is not apparent and therefore not seen as a formal obstacle. Whether obvious or somewhat hidden, acts of racism and discrimination within the work environment threaten an immigrant's emotional and psychological well-being and can result in her or him leaving the workplace.

Employment Equity

Ensuring History Does Not Repeat Itself

In 1984, **Canada's Royal Commission on Equality in Employment** introduced new legislation designed to recognize and remove the barriers that have historically characterized the Canadian employment system.

The purpose of the *Employment Equity Act* is to "achieve equality in the workplace so that no person shall be denied employment opportunities or benefits for reasons unrelated to ability and, in the fulfillment of that goal, to correct the conditions of disadvantage in employment experienced by women, Aboriginal peoples, persons with disabilities, and members of visible minorities by giving effect to the principle that employment equity means more than treating persons in the same way but also requires special measures and the accommodation of differences" (Department of Justice Canada, 1995).

Members of particular groups—women, Aboriginal people, persons with disabilities, recent immigrants, and people of colour—typically face greater challenges in finding work, are paid less, and have less job stability.

The goal of the legislation is to eliminate the barriers faced by members of these groups and to help repair some of the damage, such as chronic unemployment, poverty, etc.

In principle, Canadians support this act. They acknowledge that the history of discriminating practices has had damaging consequences both for the individuals who experienced them and for the country as a whole. They feel that such an act is a way of attempting to redress previous inequities.

Nevertheless, responses to the policy, initially at least, were somewhat mixed. Some were concerned about "reverse discrimination." Also, some people of colour were concerned that they may appear to be gaining priority access not because of merit, but because of race or gender.

Overall, however, Employment Equity legislation moves society in the right direction. Equity policies remove obstacles, begin to undo the effects of various forms of discrimination, and ensure that history does not repeat itself.

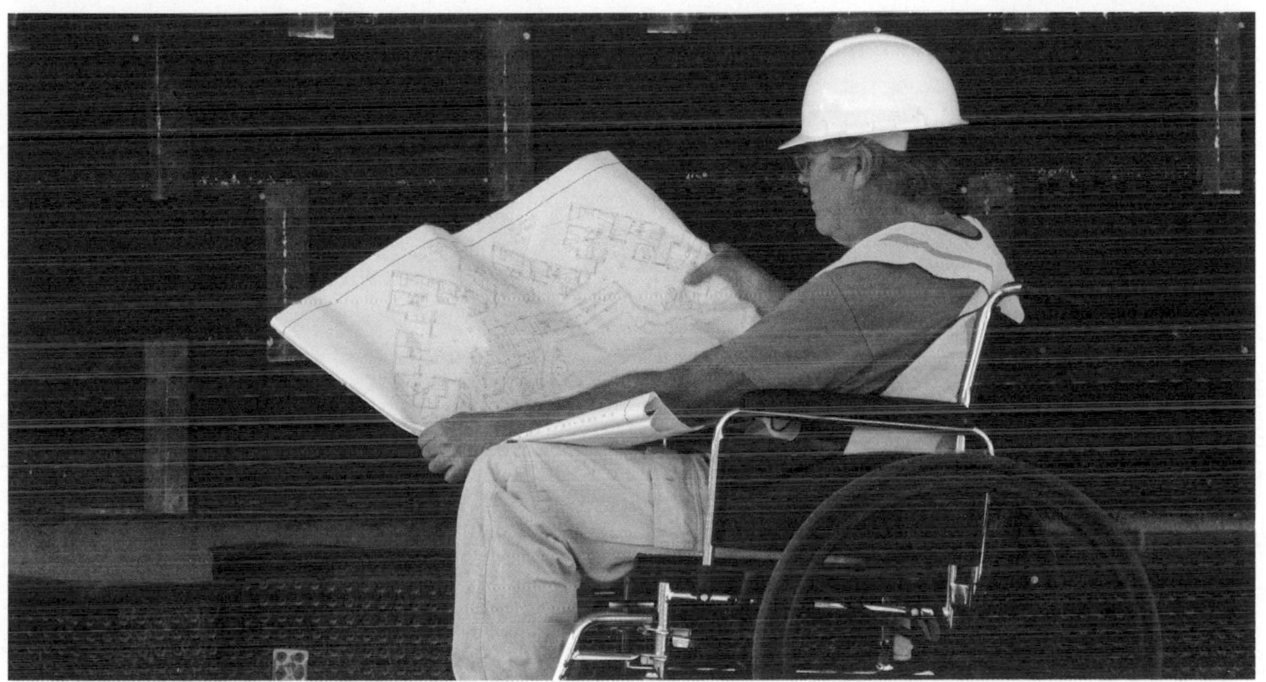

Labour market approach

Argues that the labour market dictates employment levels among newcomers

Understanding Immigration, Income Security, and Employment

There are several ways of explaining the link between immigration, income security, and unemployment or underemployment. The labour market approach focuses on the local job market and the demand for certain skills. The human capital perspective emphasizes the individual's attributes and personal resources shaping employment success.

A third way of understanding the immigration experiences of newcomers is by using an **anti-racist approach**. The anti-racist approach focuses on the role of racism and discrimination and how these factors are a part of the experience of many immigrants today.

The Anti-Racist Approach

An anti-racist perspective sees racism as an ideology that is used to justify a society in which those who are white are privileged socially, economically, and politically at the expense of people of colour. During the colonial period, white Europeans used racial distinctions to make legitimate an economic system in which people of colour were viewed as property. People of colour were seen as "less human" than the Europeans and therefore as incapable of managing themselves, their families, or their nations. Europeans, on the other hand, considered themselves to be enlightened and civilized and therefore to be the "more advanced" race. White superiority was used to justify the exploitation of people of colour and the seizing of their possessions and land. Racism was more than just the views of a small group of people with negative beliefs about another group; rather, it was used to sustain a social, economic, and political system in which people of colour are marginalized and subjugated.

Today's problem of unemployment and underemployment among immigrants would, through this lens, be viewed as the result of a system in which the majority—mainstream Canadians—enjoys certain socio-economic and political benefits, while minority groups are overrepresented in categories reflecting a lower socio-economic status and less political representation. According to this perspective, people of colour constitute a cheap labour force. Newcomers, then, are either unemployed or relegated to working in jobs that Canadians either do not want to do or will not do for the pay that is offered. Restrictions based on foreign-obtained credentials, racism and discrimination in the workplace, and the glass ceiling are effective ways of keeping people of colour out of positions of power or kept to limited numbers.

In other words, a full explanation of the situation experienced by immigrants today—especially non-white immigrants—needs to take account of all relevant factors, not the least of which is prejudice and discrimination against people of colour and "foreigners" in general.

The Live-In Caregiver Program

Opportunity or Exploitation?

We are living in a time when more and more women are working outside the home for reasons related to both personal fulfillment and financial need. There is a high demand for quality child care with various options available to parents today. An increasingly popular arrangement is in-home child care provision with babysitters or nannies working and living within the family home.

The federal Live-In Caregiver Program is designed to fill a labour market demand that is difficult to fill locally. These (mostly) women are offered full-time live-in employment prior to entry into Canada and, upon arrival, have temporary status in the country. Applicants tend to come from overseas (such as from the Caribbean, and more recently, the Philippines).

If a live-in caregiver's employment is terminated, she is subject to deportation. Otherwise, after two years, she is permitted to apply for landed immigrant status. This would provide her with full citizenship rights, except for voting or working in jobs related to national security.

Despite the protections mentioned, these women can face a range of challenges and abuses. For example, the boundaries between on-duty and off-duty times are unclear when a person lives and works in the same place. In addition, the tasks required by these women are typically not limited to child care and can include everything from running errands to walking the family pet. Finally, these women are sometimes forced into domestic situations that can result in financial, physical, and even sexual abuse. If the woman goes to the authorities before the two years are up, she risks being deported.

Although the Live-In Caregiver Program is designed to meet a particular economic need, it has several important limitations that can threaten basic human rights. Significant policy changes that address these concerns (both here in Canada as well as in the sending countries) are required, and education about how to create a respectful, productive, and caring work environment should be provided to potential employers and employees.

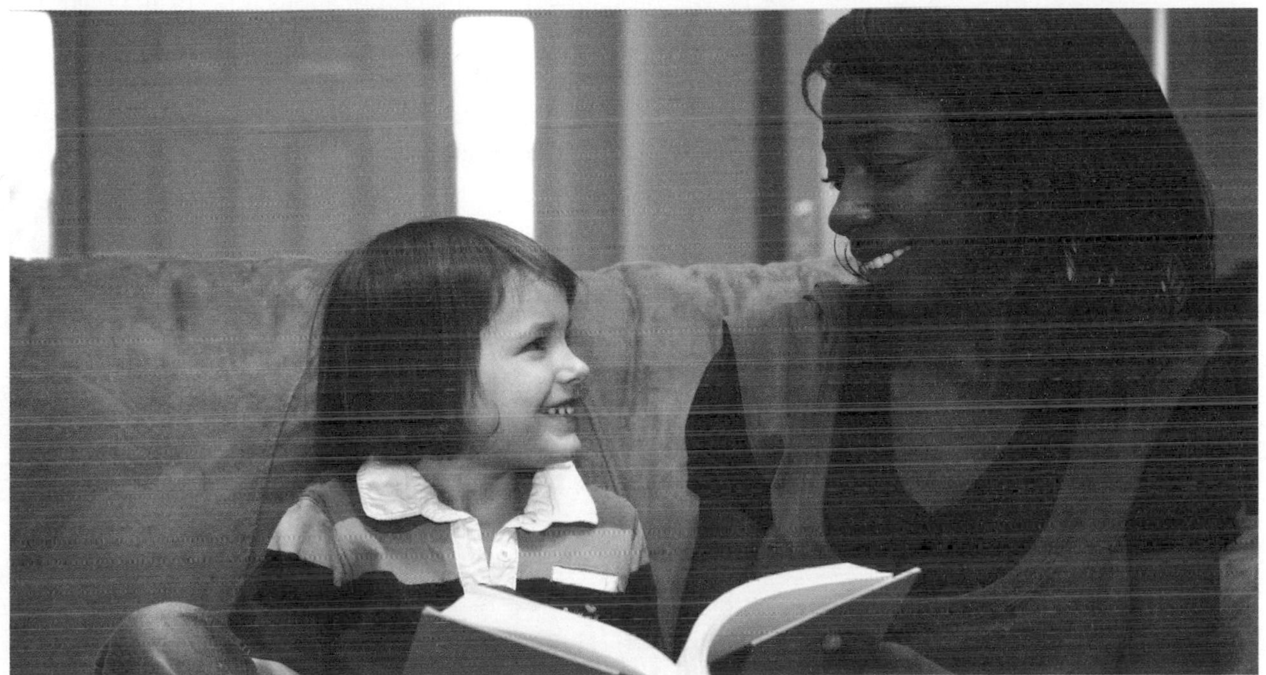

Temporary Foreign Workers

Traditionally, Canadian immigration policy has focused on bringing in immigrants on a permanent basis with a view to them quickly becoming full citizens.

The new trend favouring temporary-class workers creates a "two-step" immigration process, with new arrivals coming in on a temporary basis with reduced rights before proving themselves worthy of permanent status.

Temporary status means that workers' rights are not fully protected. In her 2009 report, the Attorney General of Canada raised concerns that temporary foreign workers are vulnerable to abuse.

Immigration Policy Reforms, 2008 ...

The immigration system that evolved to date in Canada is by no means perfect, but by and large most Canadians would likely agree that it has served them well and is widely recognized as a model around the world. Many immigrants and refugees have arrived in Canada from all parts of the world. Over time, they and their families have settled, contributed economically and socially, made the country vibrant, and generally made Canada the envy of the world.

However, the immigration system that got us to where we are today is now undergoing even more change quickly, very quickly. **Immigration policy reforms** introduced since 2008 are fundamentally altering the nature of immigration and, with it, likely the very character of our country—for better or for worse. According to Sandra Lopes, Manager, Policy and Research of the Maytree Foundation, with its new immigration policies, the Conservative federal government is beginning to change who we select to immigrate, the supports newcomers have after they arrive, and how they can become citizens. The cumulative effect, she says, will be to change Canada as we know it.

Altering the Landscape for Economic Immigration

To be sure, internationally, competition to attract immigrants is more intense than ever before. Other countries in addition to Canada are more aggressively courting immigrants as well. Indeed, many source countries for immigrants to Canada are themselves becoming immigrant destinations (e.g., China), offering greater opportunity than they did previously to people around the world seeking a better life (or at least offering them less reason to leave). For Canada to prosper and remain competitive internationally, it still badly needs more immigrants, especially skilled immigrants. To attract them, it also must ensure that programs and services are in place to facilitate settlement and integration and that equivalent foreign experience and credentials are recognized.

However, the federal government is pursuing policies that put too much emphasis on short-term and ad hoc solutions, argues Naomi Alboim, co-author of *Shaping the Future: Canada's Rapidly Changing Immigration Policies* and a **Maytree Foundation** senior fellow. "Perhaps Canadians have become complacent in thinking that there will always be a long line of people waiting to come here," she says. "But we can't take our reputation, or our past success, for granted."

Canada obviously continues to need a strong immigration program to help meet its population and labour market needs. It also needs to ensure good welfare services for immigrants when they arrive and while they fully integrate into Canadian society. However, recent federal policy shifts have altered the landscape for economic immigration to Canada, according to Alboim, and largely it has happened without public debate.

What Kind of Country Do We Want Canada To Be?

Between 2008 and the present, the federal government has made sweeping changes to immigration policy. According to the Maytree report, these have resulted in greater restrictions on "permanent" immigrants (economic, family reunification, and humanitarian), tightened rules for obtaining citizenship, and larger numbers of "temporary" workers (and therefore a "two-step" road to citizenship). There has also been a substantial increase in ministerial powers.

The authors maintain that these policy shifts have gone too far in favour of (1) short-term fixes versus long-term solutions; (2) temporary entrants versus permanent residents; and (3) reliance on provinces, employers, and educational institutions for immigrant selection. They also recommend that the public should be engaged in a national conversation on what kind of country we want and how immigration can help us get there. They list four principles to guide that discussion:

1. Immigration policy should be based mainly on long-term social and economic objectives and a commitment to citizenship.
2. Immigration policy should be evidence-based, comprehensive, fair, and respectful of human rights.
3. Immigration policy should be developed through public engagement, federal-provincial consultation, and democratic processes.
4. Immigration policy should enhance Canada's reputation around the world.

Shaping the Future

Canada's continually evolving immigration policies are thoroughly examined in an important report released by the Maytree Foundation in 2012. The report was co-authored by Naomi Alboim and Karen Cohl and is entitled *Shaping the Future: Canada's Rapidly Changing Immigration Policies.*

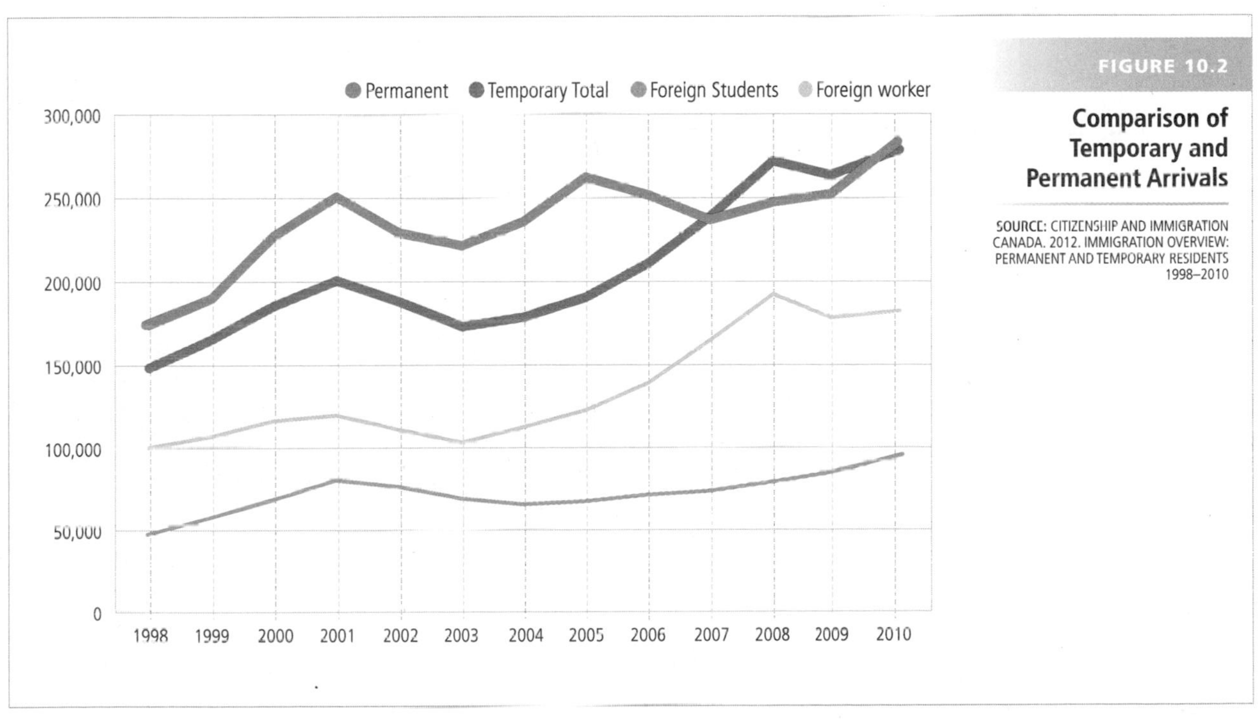

FIGURE 10.2

Comparison of Temporary and Permanent Arrivals

SOURCE: CITIZENSHIP AND IMMIGRATION CANADA. 2012. IMMIGRATION OVERVIEW: PERMANENT AND TEMPORARY RESIDENTS 1998–2010

Ottawa Toughens Immigration Sponsorship Rules

Steven Chase

The Harper government is making it tougher for people to settle foreign parents or grandparents in Canada—hiking sponsorship qualifications to make it less likely newcomers will become a financial burden for taxpayers.

Immigration Minister Jason Kenney announced more stringent requirements for Canadians or permanent residents wanting to bring their elders here under the family reunification program—new rules that will make sponsors financially responsible for these arrivals.

Changes include doubling the amount of time for which sponsors must cover any provincial social benefits incurred by their relatives. Ottawa said it is hiking the minimum necessary annual income for sponsors by 30 per cent, requiring sponsors to demonstrate they meet the new income threshold for three consecutive years instead of 12 months and extending the sponsorship responsibility period to 20 years from 10 years.

Mr. Kenney defended the changes as fiscally responsible, saying Canada has one of the most generous family reunification programs on offer.

"Why should we limit the number of parents and grandparents sponsored to Canada? Well, let me state the obvious reason. Elderly people place a much greater burden on the public health care system, a public health care system that is already in crisis, where costs are growing much faster than the economy, much faster than the population, where emergency wards are overcrowded, where wait times are enormous."

The Department of Citizenship and Immigration produced charts and figures that it said demonstrate that after the 10-year responsibility period ends, the amount of welfare usage by sponsored immigrant parents jumps significantly.

The No. 1 source for parents and grandparents coming to Canada under this program is the Punjab region of India, according to Mr. Kenney's office. The government is also moving to restrict dependent children that can accompany parents or grandparents to Canada as part of this family reunification, saying now the cutoff age will be 18 years old.

The reunification program is being overhauled in part to fix a massive backlog that had grown to 160,000 applications with a decade-long wait for approval.

Mr. Kenney said the government is on track to halve the backlog by 2014. He also said Citizenship and Immigration would take 5,000 more applications for the program in 2014. Ottawa stopped taking applications two years ago to help tackle the backlog.

Mr. Kenney also announced Ottawa will make permanent a popular alternative to the family reunification settlement program.

The recently introduced "super visa" program grants foreign parents and grandparents a multiple-entry visa good for 10 years. Citizenship and Immigration is now issuing about 1,000 super visas a month. They allow holders to remain in Canada for up to two years at a time.

The NDP accused the government of making the reunification program too expensive.

"Over 20 per cent of Canadians were born abroad. For these Canadians, Conservatives are making family reunification a more distant dream than ever," NDP immigration critic Jinny Sims said. She said the changes mean "it would cost you more to even apply to reunite with your parents or grandparents—and two decades of full financial responsibility for their care if they come. And that's only if you happen to be one of the lucky 5,000 whose applications will be accepted next year."

SOURCE: CHASE, STEVEN (MAY 11, 2013). "OTTAWA TOUGHENS IMMIGRATION SPONSORSHIP RULES" THE GLOBE AND MAIL.

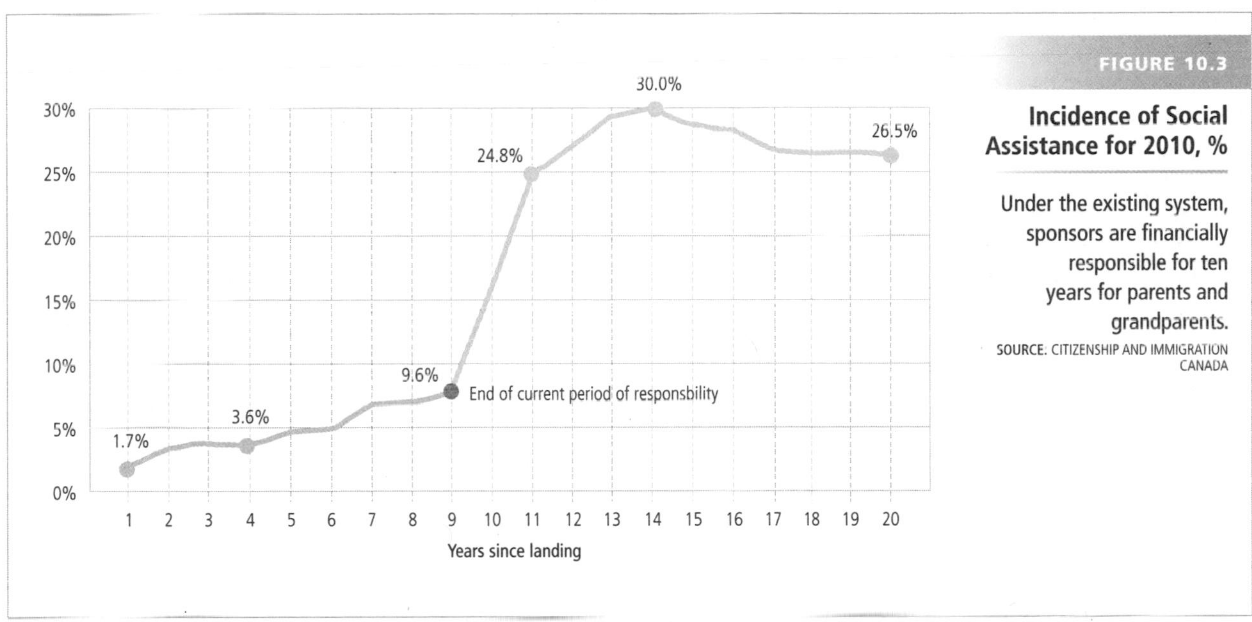

FIGURE 10.3

Incidence of Social Assistance for 2010, %

Under the existing system, sponsors are financially responsible for ten years for parents and grandparents.

SOURCE: CITIZENSHIP AND IMMIGRATION CANADA

Family Class Sponsorship

A Canadian citizen or a permanent resident of Canada can sponsor a spouse, conjugal or common-law partner, dependent child (including adopted child) or other eligible relative to become a permanent resident under the Family Class (FC). As a permanent resident, that person can live, study and work in Canada.

There are two different processes for sponsoring a family under the Family Class—one for sponsoring a spouse, conjugal or common-law partner and/or dependent children and another process to sponsor other eligible relatives.

Sponsoring a spouse, partner or children

A Canadian citizen or permanent resident may sponsor a spouse, common-law partner or conjugal partner, or dependent children to come to Canada as permanent residents.

If a Canadian citizen or a permanent resident sponsors a family member to come to Canada as a permanent resident, the sponsor must make every reasonable effort to provide for his or her own essential needs and those of the sponsor's family. The sponsor is responsible for supporting the relative financially when he or she arrives. The sponsor must also make sure the spouse or relative does not need to seek Social Assistance from the government.

Effective October 25, 2012, sponsored spouses or partners must now live together in a legitimate relationship with their sponsor for two years from the day they receive permanent residence status in Canada.

Sponsoring other relatives

A citizen or permanent resident of Canada may be able to sponsor certain relatives to become a permanent resident under the Family Class (FC).

If approved, the sponsor must make every reasonable effort to provide for his or her own essential needs and those of the relative. The sponsor is responsible for supporting the relative financially when he or she arrives. The sponsor must also make sure the relative does not need to seek Social Assistance from the government.

Permanent Residents and Refugees

Income Security and Eligibility

As a social welfare state, Canada offers a range of income security benefits to individuals who live in this country. These benefits include those for raising children (Child Tax Benefits), retirement (Canada/Quebec Pension Plan, Old Age Security, and the Guaranteed Income Supplement), job-related injuries (Workers' Compensation), the loss of a job (Employment Insurance), and longer-term unemployment (Social Assistance).

Immigrants, or "non-Canadians," are considered permanent residents if they have lived in Canada for at least two consecutive years during any five-year period. These individuals enjoy the same rights and privileges as Canadian citizens but are not allowed to vote or hold positions in public office until they are granted citizenship. Permanent residents are eligible for Child Tax Benefits and, if they have had a history of employment in this country, the various unemployment and pension programs. Depending on their particular circumstances, immigrants are also eligible for longer-term Social Assistance.

Government-sponsored refugees are eligible to receive the Child Tax Benefit and are also provided with financial resettlement assistance (for those without resources to meet their basic needs) under the Resettlement Assistance Program. This includes immediate support services (airport reception; temporary accommodations and help to find more permanent housing; help with registering for federal and provincial programs; orientation to emergency services, public transportation, education systems, and Canadian laws; support in setting up a bank account and help with budgeting; and referrals to other settlement programs), as well as a one-time, initial household start-up allowance. This is sometimes followed by monthly income support to help pay for food, shelter, fuel, clothing, prescription drugs, and other health services, with specific amounts being determined by provincial regulations.

Refugees are not, however, eligible to receive benefits for retirement, job-related injuries, or the loss of a job until such time as they gain paid employment.

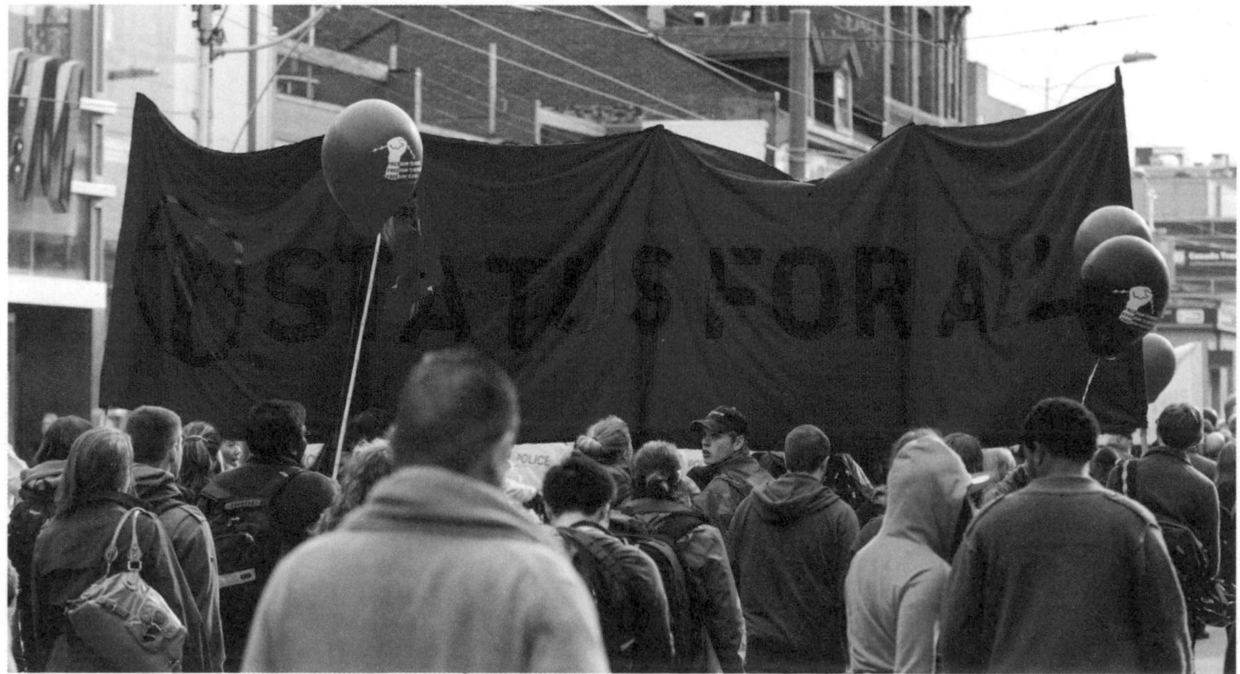

Conclusion

There was a major shift in the pattern of Canadian immigration after 1967. Prior to that time, immigration followed "national" lines, with most immigrants coming from European countries. The system was open to abuse. In the early years, racist selection policies, such as the Chinese head tax and the continuous journey requirement, limited Canada from reaching out to the world.

With the introduction of the point system after 1967, three broad classes of immigrants were created: economic, family, and refugee. Immigrants soon began coming from all over the world based on merit points awarded for age, education and skill, language fluency, and other similar criteria. These changes made the country more competitive, and also substantially altered the ethnic mix in Canada. More and more non-white immigrants arrived from Asia, Africa, and Central and South America, bringing not only their skills but adding an exciting new dimension to multicultural experience in Canada.

On the whole, the multicultural experience has worked, at least until recently. Canada is more vibrant because of it, with relatively little racial or ethnic tensions compared with many other countries. Immigrants often experienced great difficulties finding work, housing, and assimilating, especially non-white immigrants who faced, and still face, widespread racial discrimination. The process was not always smooth, but there was a sense that it was possible to create a vibrant economy and a lively cultural landscape, and to make multiculturalism work.

However, many policy analysts are concerned about the direction of immigration policy today and its likely impact on Canada's future. The changes that have been introduced, many without much public debate, reflect a much tighter approach on the part of the federal government. In particular, greater restrictions have been put on securing "permanent" status in Canada, and there have been tightened rules for obtaining full Canadian citizenship. Larger numbers are being admitted as "temporary" workers (creating a "two-step" road to citizenship). There has also been an substantial increase in ministerial discretionary powers.

Canada continues to need immigrants, but to attract them it also needs to ensure that the road to Canada, and the path to integration after arrival, is smooth. Employment and family supports are particularly important, as is family reunification. It also needs to maintain an humanitarian opening for those seeking refuge. To attract the best people, it is necessary to provide the best opportunity both before immigrants come and after they get here, so that newcomers know they will find good employment, raise healthy families, and be confident of a secure future.

CHAPTER 10 REVIEW

LEARNING OBJECTIVES

After completing this chapter, you should be able to:

- Describe the shifts over the last 60 years with respect to immigrants' "countries of last permanent residence."
- Describe the three categories of applicants created by the new "points system" in 1967.
- Discuss the pros and cons of Canada's multicultural policy.
- Describe some of the challenges faced by new immigrants.
- Describe historical instances of racism that prevented immigrants from coming to Canada.
- Evaluate the extent to which racism remains a factor in employment.
- Explain what is meant by an "anti-racist approach" to social welfare.
- Understand some of the shortcomings of the "live-in caregiver" program.
- Understand some of the major immigration policy reforms that began to take shape after 2008 and their implications.

KEY CONCEPTS IN CHAPTER

- Anti-racist approach
- Canada's Royal Commission on Equity in Employment, 1984
- Canadian Multiculturalism Policy
- Chinese Head Tax
- Continuous journey requirement
- Culturally biased hiring practices
- Economic Class
- Family Class
- Immigration policy reforms
- Maytree Foundation
- Multiculturalism
- Points System
- Racism
- Refugee Class
- Visible minority

REVIEW QUESTIONS

1. What was the significance of the shift away from the "nationality" to the "Points System" as the basis of immigrant selection after 1967.
2. Presently, what are the three categories under which newcomers can apply to immigrate to Canada? What are the criteria used in each of these categories?
3. What are the some of the main barriers that prevent these recent newcomers from finding and keeping suitable jobs in Canada?
4. This chapter provided a summary of how the labour market, human capital, and anti-racist approaches might be used to understand unemployment and underemployment among immigrants. How might a political ideology perspective (described in Chapter 4) be used to look more deeply at the economic, social, and political forces underlying this issue?
5. Describe ways in which racism, directly or indirectly, is still a factor affecting immigrant selection and a barrier in the full integration of immigrants into Canadian society.
6. Recently, there have been changes in the direction of immigration policy with respect to temporary workers and ministerial discretion. Explain what the changes have been and how they are likely to affect Canada in the future.

EXPLORING SOCIAL WELFARE

1. In your view, what are some challenges that multiculturalism introduces into Canadian society? What are some of the benefits of multiculturalism? On the whole, do you think this policy is a good one? Why or why not?
2. Use the Internet to find three community-based supports that assist foreign-trained professionals to find and keep employment. How effective are these initiatives? What do you think makes them effective (or ineffective)? How might they be made more effective?

CRITICAL THINKING

What are your ancestral roots and how were they affected by immigration policy at the time?

Going forward, how do you think future generations will look back on Canadian immigration policy reforms taking place today?

WEBSITES

Citizenship and Immigration Canada
www.cic.gc.ca
The Citizenship and Immigration Canada website offers information about the process of immigration, relevant policies and regulations, and a range of research publications focused on how today's newcomers are faring socially and economically in Canada.

Ontario Immigration
www.ontarioimmigration.ca
This particular site is the official "welcoming" website for immigrants to Ontario. Other provinces have similar portals that provide valuable information for persons wanting to immigrate to these provinces or just arriving. Typically, these portals provide information about the province before arrival, after arrival, and information on living, studying, working and doing business in the province.

Toronto Region Immigrant Employment Council (TRIEC)
www.triec.ca
TRIEC works to address barriers that prevent immigrants from participating in the labour market. Membership includes workers, employers, regulatory bodies, post-secondary institutions, assessment service providers, community organizations, and all three levels of government.

Maytree Foundation
www.maytree.ca
The Maytree Foundation is a charitable foundation that works with its many partners to fight poverty in Canada. The Foundation promotes practices that facilitate the settlement of immigrants and refugees; and offers leadership and networking opportunities. The Foundation was the sponsor of the recent report, *Shaping the Future: Canada's Rapidly Changing Immigration Policies.*

Aboriginal Social Welfare

Idle No More!

The social and economic conditions of Aboriginal peoples in Canada is dismal—many people call it "Canada's disgrace." An oppressive history of colonial government policies, broken government promises, and foot-dragging has resulted in the dire situation today. To move forward, we must understand how we got here. Healing and respect are central to the process.

"Our people are dying earlier and more often than anyone else in [this] country. We have a Third World in our front yard and our back alleys."
— PHIL FONTAINE, FORMER NATIONAL CHIEF OF THE ASSEMBLY OF FIRST NATIONS

This chapter provides an overview of the social and economic conditions of Aboriginal people today in Canada, including specific social welfare issues—poverty, health care, housing, and unemployment. It underlines the importance of respect for treaty rights and Aboriginal self-government in finally addressing the social welfare needs of Canada's First Nations, Métis, and Inuit peoples.

The First Nations of North America

The **Aboriginal peoples** of Canada are the descendants of the original inhabitants of North America. Three groups of Aboriginal people are recognized by the *Constitution Act, 1982*: Indians, Métis, and Inuit. These demarcations are often made by non-Aboriginal politicians for the purposes of governing. The term *Indian* is used in a legal capacity, where policies such as the *Indian Act* apply to **Status or Registered Indians** (persons listed in the "Indian Register"). We now generally use the term **First Nations** in place of *Indian*.

The reality is that Aboriginal peoples are a diverse population of distinct peoples with unique heritages, treaty rights, languages, cultural practices, and spiritual beliefs.

Third World Conditions

"We suffer infant mortality rates that are three times the Canadian average, an education gap that will take over two decades to close and the realization that our children are more likely to end up in jail than to graduate from high school."

National Chief Shawn Atleo, CBC News

"Third World" Conditions

Aboriginal communities have worked in good faith with successive governments to improve their overall well-being and social welfare. Yet Aboriginal people continue to live in what many have described as Third World conditions. For their part, Aboriginal people are no longer prepared to sit and wait. The broad-based "Idle No More" movement, for example, which began at the end of 2012 against what was seen as yet further intrusions by the federal government on Aboriginal rights, was part of a a continuous campaign by Aboriginal people for full equality and lasting solutions.

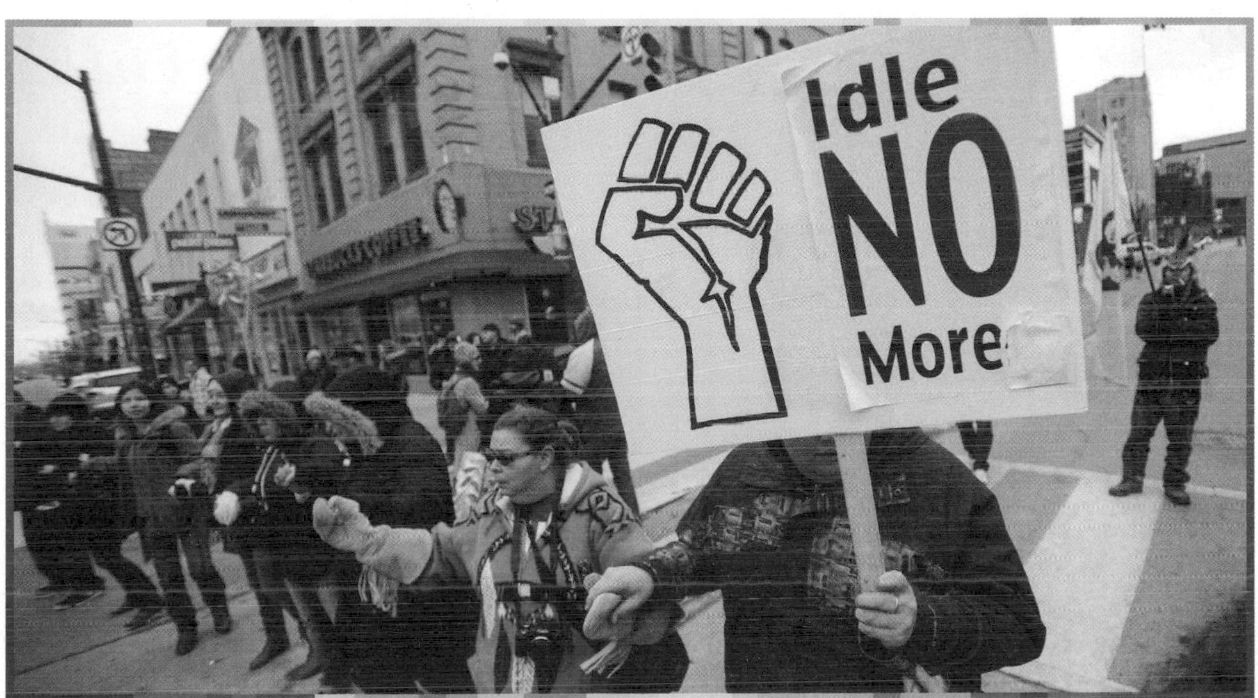

Idle No More, a grassroots movement, gathers widespread support.

The Indian Register
The Registered Indian population, also called the Status Indian population, includes individuals entitled to have their names on the Indian Register, an official list maintained by the federal government.

A Demographic Profile

The Aboriginal population of Canada consists of First Nations, Métis, and Inuit peoples. The First Nations are located primarily in Canada's western provinces—British Columbia, Alberta, Saskatchewan, and Manitoba—which contain over two thirds of the First Nations peoples. Almost three-quarters of Inuit in Canada lived in Inuit Nunangat. Inuit Nunangat stretches from Labrador to the Northwest Territories and comprises four regions: Nunatsiavut, Nunavik, Nunavut and the Inuvialuit region. The Métis represented 8 percent of the total population of the Northwest Territories, 6.7 percent of Manitoba's population, and 5.2 percent of Saskatchewan's population.

Population Growth Rates and Age Profile

The Aboriginal population is increasing at a much faster rate than the non-Aboriginal population. The Aboriginal population increased by 232,385 people, or 20.1 percent between 2006 and 2011, compared with 5.2 percent for the non-Aboriginal population (Statistics Canada, 2013). The Aboriginal share of the total Canadian population is projected to increase to 4.1 percent by 2017, up from 3.4 percent in 2001.

The Aboriginal population is also considerably younger on average than the non-Aboriginal population. In 2011, the median age of the Aboriginal population was 28 years; 13 years younger than the median of 41 years for the non-Aboriginal population.

FIGURE 11.1

Distribution of Aboriginal Population in Canada

SOURCE: STATISTICS CANADA, CENSUS OF POPULATION, 2006. AANDC TABULATIONS

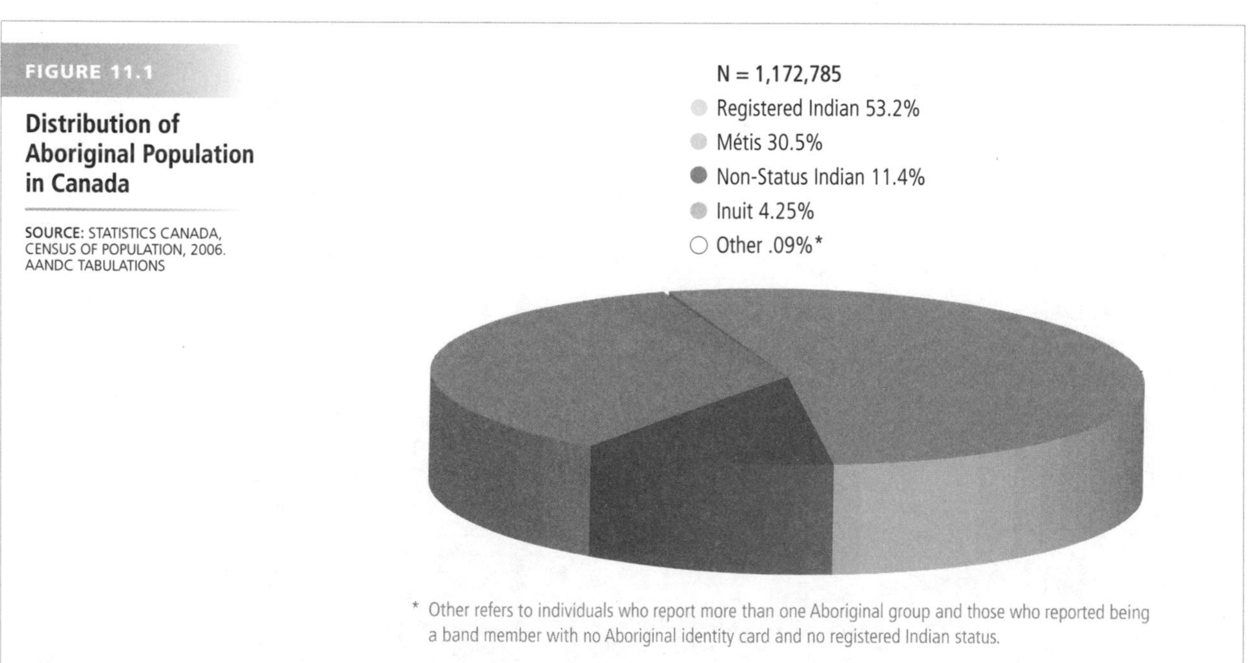

Inequalities in Income and Unemployment

The legacy of colonialism has left Aboriginal peoples among the poorest in Canada. The median income for Aboriginal peoples is 30% lower than that of non-Aboriginal Canadians, and showing very little improvement over time. What is more, the gap in earnings and employment persists regardless of community (First Nations, Métis, and Inuit), where they live (rural/urban), and despite increases in educational attainment over the past 10 years (Wilson & Macdonald, 2010).

There is one exception—Aboriginal peoples with university degrees seem to have overcome much of the income differential. However, there continues to be a significant gap in the number of Aboriginal peoples obtaining a Bachelor's degree—8 percent compared to 22 percent for the non-Aboriginal population. Below the Bachelor's degree level, Aboriginal peoples consistently make far less than other Canadians with the same level of education. Interestingly, within the Aboriginal population, women are finishing school and obtaining degrees at a higher rate than men, a trend among non-Aboriginal Canadians as well.

Higher educational alone, however, is not a "silver bullet," Wilson and Macdonald argue. Income and other disparities have historical roots and are deep-seated, and they require active intervention. They will not solve themselves. It starts by acknowledging that the legacy of colonialism lies at the heart of the problem. What is needed are new approaches and solutions that come from the Aboriginal peoples themselves based the right of Aboriginal people to self-government and control over their own communities.

Life Expectancy

The life expectancy for the Canadian population is projected to be 79 years for men and 83 years for women in 2017.

Among the Aboriginal population the Inuit have the lowest projected life expectancy of 64 years for men and 73 years for women.

Source: First Nations Comparable Health Indicators.

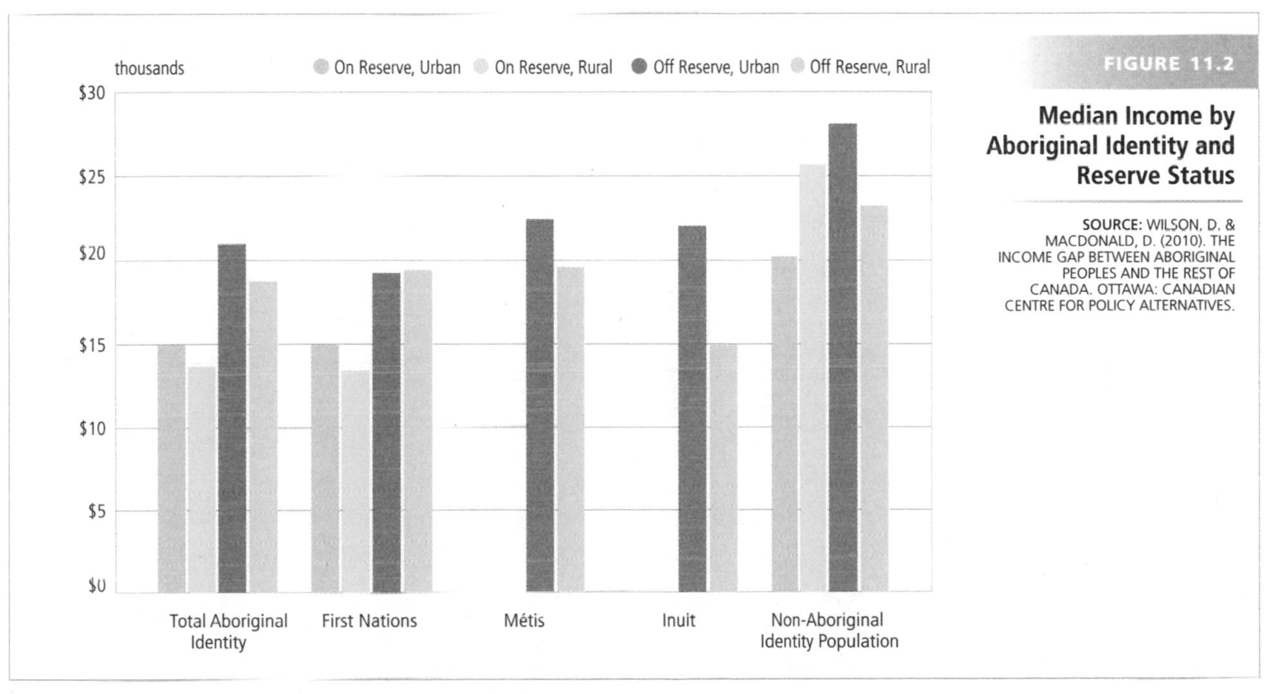

FIGURE 11.2

Median Income by Aboriginal Identity and Reserve Status

SOURCE: WILSON, D. & MACDONALD, D. (2010). THE INCOME GAP BETWEEN ABORIGINAL PEOPLES AND THE REST OF CANADA. OTTAWA: CANADIAN CENTRE FOR POLICY ALTERNATIVES.

Culturally Competent Care Environments

"When Aboriginal patients present themselves—whether it's in an emergency room or in any health centre—they're not necessarily seen for who they are and consequently they're not respected, they're not engaged as fellow human beings and as a result the care they get suffers."

John G. Abbott, CEO of the Health Council of Canada, The Canadian Press.

Urban Aboriginal People

The term *Urban Aboriginal peoples* refers primarily to Inuit, Métis, and First Nations currently residing in urban areas across Canada. Off-reserve Aboriginal people constitute the fastest growing segment of Canadian society. Although urban Aboriginal peoples are an increasingly significant social, political, and economic presence in Canadian cities, until recently, relatively little was known about these individuals' experiences and perspectives or how others view them.

Urban Aboriginal Peoples Study, 2011

The **Urban Aboriginal Peoples Study (UAPS)**, released in 2011, sought to redress this imbalance. The *Aboriginal Peoples Study* represents the first study, across major Canadian cities, to focus exclusively on First Nations, Métis, and Inuit peoples living in cities.

In many ways, the Urban Aboriginal Peoples Study was a sequel to the 1996 Royal Commission on Aboriginal Peoples (RCAP), which was established in 1991. It was a not-for-profit research endeavour supported by an arm's length group of sponsors. It provided an up-to-date picture of a population that has experienced substantial growth and change since the release of the RCAP report in 1996.

The UAPS focused exclusively on Aboriginal peoples living in 11 Canadian cities. It explored their values, identities, experiences, and aspirations. In the main survey, a total of 2,614 Aboriginal individuals participated in the UAPS survey—1,558 First Nations peoples, 789 Métis, and 265 Inuit.

Experiences of Racism

The UAPS touched on many topics, including Aboriginal peoples' communities of origin; Aboriginal cultures; community belonging; education; work; health; political engagement and activity; justice; relationships with Aboriginal and non-Aboriginal people; life aspirations and definitions of success; and experiences with discrimination.

The large majority said they were seeking to become a significant part of their urban landscape. However, participants did note that, while they have a strong sense of pride in their culture and their country, a majority continue to experience negative stereotypes. "If there is a single urban Aboriginal experience, it is the shared perception among First Nations peoples, Métis and Inuit, across cities, that they are stereotyped negatively," the report said. "Indeed, most report that they have personally experienced negative behaviour or unfair treatment because of who they are." Almost nine in 10 said they believe others behave unfairly or negatively toward Aboriginal people. Seventy percent said they had been teased or insulted because of their background.

"Idle No More is About All Canadians"

Elizabeth McSheffrey, *Grande Prairie Daily Herald-Tribune*

Grande Prairie residents gathered at the Pomeroy Hotel & Conference Centre to hear an important message from the Western Cree Tribal Council, Saturday.

The meeting discussed the implications of the federal legislation that prompted the 'Idle No More' protests and how these protests changed the way we relate to one another.

"This is about all Canadians, it isn't just about [Aboriginals]," said guest speaker and First Nations activist Tanya Kappo. Kappo was recognized as one of the original founders of the movement after she started using the Twitter hashtag #idlenomore to talk about the dangers of Bill C-45, an omnibus bill introduced to Ottawa in October 2012. "When I looked at the bill I was very worried," she said. "What I saw was an aggressive agenda of legislation that would impact directly First Nations people, lands and waters."

C-45 proposed important changes to the Indian, Environmental Assessment and Navigation Protection Acts (former Navigable Waters Act). If adopted, these changes would significantly reduce the number of federally protected waterways and open up Aboriginal land to non-Native buyers. "When we talk about it first, it's because it's going to affect us first because of where we live and our legal status in the country," said Kappo. "But it will affect every single Canadian."

Within a month, legislation gave birth to dozens of protests, rallies and meetings across the country, gaining international momentum after Attawapiskat Chief Theresa Spence went on a hunger strike in December 2012. On Dec. 14 of last year, C-45 became law and is now known as the "Jobs and Growth Act 2012." "Before C-45, there were 32,000 lakes across the country and 2.25 million rivers that had some protection as navigable waters," said Kappo.

"Now there are only 100 lakes including the Pacific and Atlantic Ocean and 62 rivers that have the same protection they had before." In Alberta, only Lake Athabasca and the Peace, Bow, North Saskatchewan and Athabasca Rivers made the list.

"What this means for everybody," said Kappo, "is that our waters are more accessible to industry and whoever else wants them." Under C-45, anyone wanting to dip into Canadian waters no longer has to go through the same process to access them. "While process can be annoying and bureaucratic, that's what protected these bodies waters before," she explained.

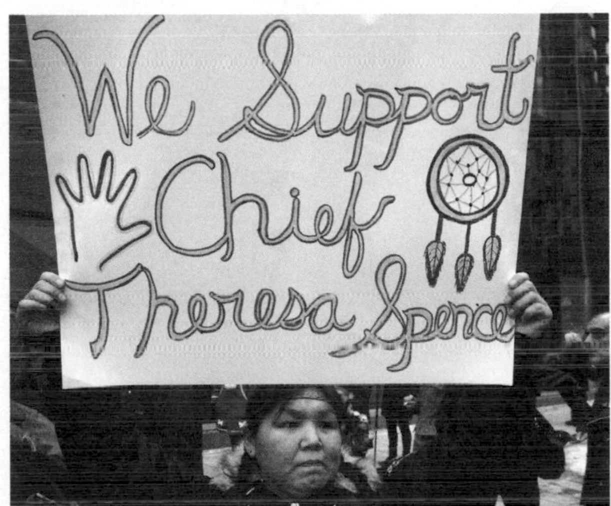

But Idle No More exposed more than controversial legislation about lakes and rivers, said Kappo. It taught Canadians how they, as a country, can respond to change. "Idle No More became about our relationships," she said, "our relationships with ourselves, our relationship with each other and our relationship with the land."

Kappo talked about how social media perpetuated the movement and quickly brought people from all across the country to the Idle No More conversation. Most importantly, Idle No More turned what started out as an "Indian issue" into a Canadian issue. "We're all here in this country together and always will be," said Kappo, "so even outside of the effects of Bill C 45, there's that relationship that we need to work on."

SOURCE: MCSHEFFREY, ELIZABETH (FEBRUARY 18, 2013). "EXAMINING THE COUNTRY-WIDE INFLUENCE OF IDLE NO MORE" GRANDE PRAIRIE DAILY HERALD-TRIBUNE (QMI AGENCY).

Aboriginal Community Well-Being

On every conceivable measure of well-being, Aboriginal communities are at a distinct disadvantage when compared to the non-Aboriginal population. The **Community Well-Being (CWB) Index** captures some of these inequalities.

The CWB Index was developed by Aboriginal Affairs and Northern Development Canada (AANDC) using Statistics Canada's Census population data. The Index incorporates elements from other sources, including the UN's Human Development Index (HDI).

Because the CWB Index results in a single score, it can provide summaries of well-being in individual communities. First Nations community scores can be compared to other Canadian community scores and across census years.

How Is the Community Well-Being Index Computed?

The CWB Index is made up of four components: Income, Education, Housing, and Labour Force. The combined CWB score ranges from 0 to 100.

- *Total income* is indicative of one's ability to purchase the necessities, comforts, and conveniences. This component is calculated using a formula based on total income per capita.
- *Higher education* makes it more likely that an individual will find a fulfilling career. The Education component includes two variables: High School Plus and University.
- *Poor housing* conditions are indicative of a lack of resources in a community. The Housing component has two variables: Quantity and Quality.
- *Labour force activity* is an indicator of an economy's health. The Labour Force Activity component consists of two variables: Labour Force Participation and Employment (ages 20-65).

FIGURE 11.3

Aboriginal Community Well-Being Index Component

A community CWB Index score is the average of its score on the four components. The four component scores are simply added together and the sum is divided by four.

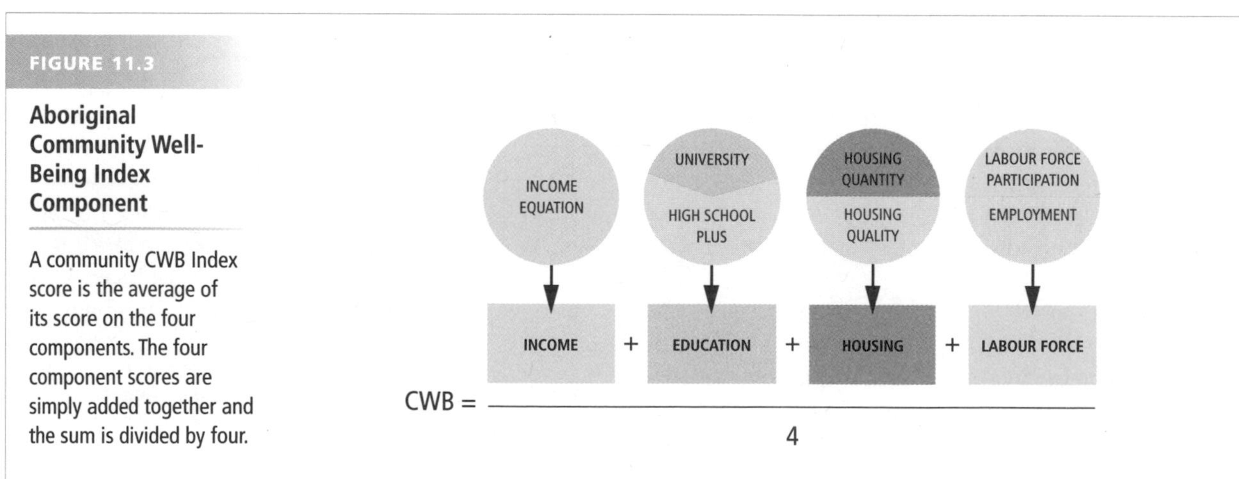

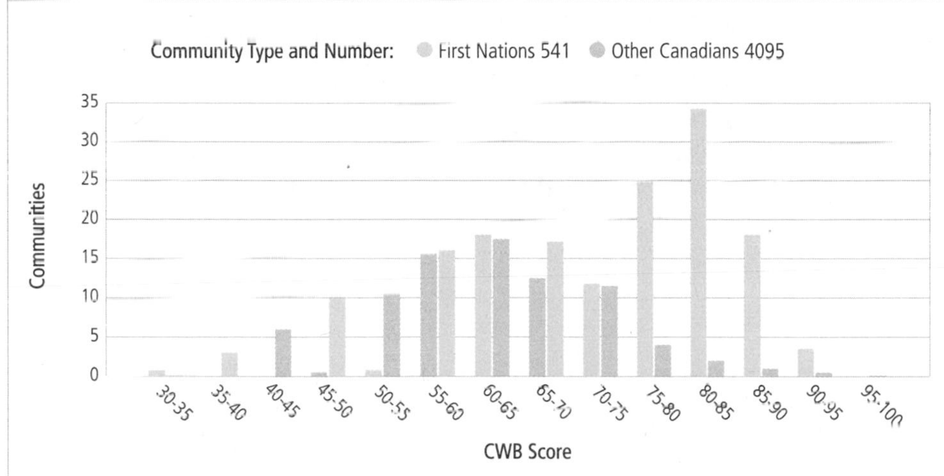

FIGURE 11.4

Aboriginal Community Well-Being Gap vs. Other Canadian Communities 2006

The distribution of the Community Well-Being scores for First Nations and other Canadian communities.

SOURCE: AANDC (2013). "ABORIGINAL DEMOGRAPHICS AND WELL-BEING." OTTAWA: ABORIGINAL AFFAIRS AND NORTHERN DEVELOPMENT CANADA

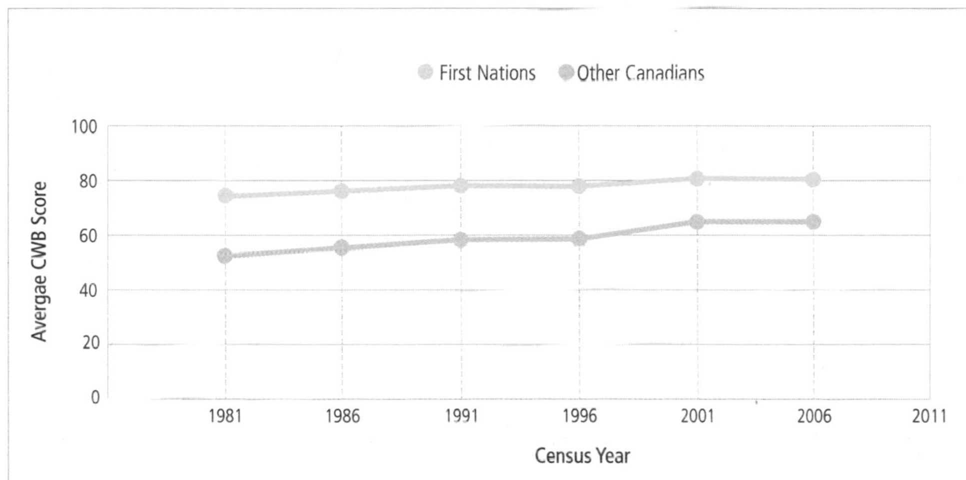

FIGURE 11.5

Aboriginal Community Well-Being Gap by Census Year

Changes in the average Community Well-Being scores for six census years for First Nations and other Canadian communities.

SOURCE: O'SULLIVAN, ERIN. (2011). "THE COMMUNITY WELL-BEING INDEX (CWB): MEASURING WELL-BEING IN FIRST NATIONS AND NON-ABORIGINAL COMMUNITIES, 1981–2006. OTTAWA: ABORIGINAL AFFAIRS AND NORTHERN DEVELOPMENT CANADA.

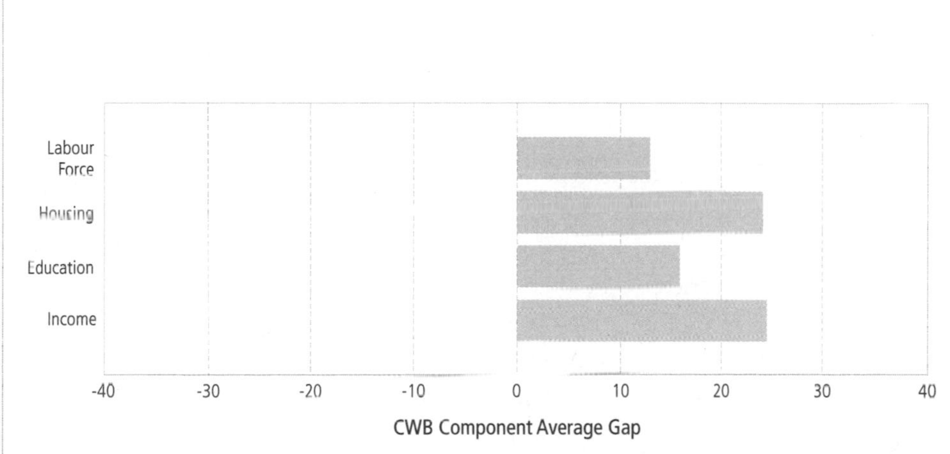

FIGURE 11.6

Aboriginal Community Well-Being Gap by Index Component 2006

The differences between average Community Well-Being Component scores for First Nations and other Canadian communities.

SOURCE: FIRST NATIONS STATISTICAL INSTITUTE (2012). OTTAWA

Aboriginal Affairs and Northern Development Canada (AANDC)
In 2011, the federal department of Indian and Northern Affairs Canada changed its name to Aboriginal Affairs and Northern Development Canada.

AANDC is responsible for maintaining and strengthening the Government of Canada's relations with organizations representing Métis, non-Status Indians, and urban Aboriginal people.

The Inuit Relations Secretariat was also created in 2004 to serve as the Government of Canada's primary point of contact for collaboration with Inuit organizations and to be an internal government source for information, advice, and expertise on Inuit matters.

In 2008, the department took on responsibilities associated with Indian Residential Schools.

Deciphering the Issues

The weight of Canadian history on First Nations peoples is overwhelming. This legacy can be captured in five key issues or themes: (1) the struggle for treaty rights; (2) the discredited *Indian Act*; (3) the effects of the reserve system; (4) the experience of the residential schools; and (5) the growing call by Aboriginal peoples for self-government.

Treaty Rights

The British government signed various treaties with Aboriginal groups before Confederation, such as the *Peace and Friendship Treaty* (1752) and the *Robinson Treaties* (1850). After Confederation, the administration of Rupert's Land (which included much of what is now Manitoba, Saskatchewan, and Alberta) went to the Canadian government. The development plan for Canada included the building of the railway and the settlement of Rupert's Land; however, because Canadian law recognized that Aboriginal people held title on that land, the government had to form agreements with Aboriginal leaders.

The **treaties** signed by the newly formed Canadian government are known as the "Numbered Treaties," beginning with Treaty No. 1 in 1871 with the Ojibway and Swampy Cree of Manitoba. Altogether, 11 Numbered Treaties were signed between 1871 and 1921, covering Northern Ontario, Manitoba, Saskatchewan, Alberta, and portions of Yukon, the Northwest Territories, and British Columbia. With the signing of these treaties, the Aboriginal peoples ceded large tracts of land to the Canadian government.

The treaties generally stipulated the relinquishment of the Indian right and title to specific land and provided for the annual payment of five dollars per person (this amount has not changed and was never indexed to inflation). These treaties also led to the creation of the reserve system; in exchange for title on the larger tract of land, the people were given smaller parcels or reserves.

Almost half of the land in Canada is not under a treaty. No treaties were signed between the Aboriginal peoples of Quebec, the Maritimes, and most of British Columbia. In fact, almost half of the population of Registered Indians did not sign land treaties. These land treaties (or in many cases, the lack of them) are currently in dispute across the country. First Nations leaders believe the notion of surrendering land was alien to their ancestors, as there was no traditional notion of land ownership in Aboriginal culture. The lands were seen as part of creation and people merely the stewards of it.

"For over 200 years, native Canadians have been relegated to the outskirts of their original land. But they have not renounced their rights and they wish to take part, too, in the country's economic life" (CBC, 2011.)

The *Indian Act* of 1876

The ***Indian Act* of 1876** was, and still is, a piece of legislation of very broad scope that regulates virtually every aspect of Aboriginal life. The *Indian Act* ("An Act respecting Indians") was enacted in 1876 under the provisions of Section 91(24) of the *Constitution Act, 1867*, which provides Canada's federal government exclusive authority to legislate in relation to "Indians and Lands Reserved for Indians." The *Indian Act* was administered in Aboriginal communities by government officials known as "Indian Agents." The act has been amended throughout the years but has remained largely intact.

The *Indian Act* strictly defines the requirements for determining who is a Status Indian. For the last century, this law has fragmented the Aboriginal population into legally distinct groups with different rights, restrictions, and obligations. Indeed, Canada is one of the few countries to have a legislative act that has separate laws for a specific group based on race or ethnicity.

The social control aspects of the *Indian Act* placed Aboriginal peoples in the position of a colonized people with limited rights. Prior to 1960 for example, Registered Indians could not vote in federal elections, but the act spelled out a process of *enfranchisement* whereby Indians could acquire full Canadian citizenship—giving up their culture and traditions and any rights to land. People could also lose their status for a variety of reasons, such as marrying non–Status Indians or non-Aboriginal individuals or by living outside the country for too long. The *Indian Act* is extremely unpopular and even many leaders and policy-makers outside the Aboriginal community feel it should be repealed.

Aboriginal Poverty

"Aboriginal peoples are among the poorest in Canada.

Aboriginal peoples also experience far greater income inequality than the rest of Canadians. They experience significantly higher rates of unemployment and lower rates of educational attainment than the rest of Canadians. And they experience higher rates of suicide, substance abuse, imprisonment, and other social ills.

This comes at enormous cost, both social and economic, to Aboriginal peoples and to Canada generally."

(Wilson and Macdonald, 2010)

This photo is from a hearing of the Truth and Reconciliation Commission, which is part of Canada's response to the Indian Residential School legacy. The commission has a five-year mandate to document the history of residential schools, inspire reconciliation, and produce a report by 2014.

The Reserve System

As the main vehicle for regulating and controlling Aboriginal movement and ways of living, the federal government established the Department of Indian Affairs, which administered the **reserve system**. Indian reserves are parcels of land that have been set aside for exclusive occupation and use by Aboriginal communities. An Indian reserve refers specifically to a parcel of land and is not synonymous with nation, community, or band; the community that occupies a reserve will often have a different name than the reserve itself. There are over 2,000 reserves in Canada with over 600 bands.

The **reserve system** is a by-product of the treaties. Aboriginal peoples were moved onto small parcels of land largely devoid of any economic potential and which could not be used as collateral to develop business ventures (land was held in trust). The Government of Canada also created reserves in regions not surrendered through treaty, such as the Wikwemikong Unceded Indian Reserve on Manitoulin Island, Lake Superior, in Ontario.

Residential Schools

Residential schools is a term used to refer to a range of historical institutions including industrial schools, boarding schools, student residences, hostels, billets, and residential schools tasked with educating Aboriginal children. The hundred or so schools were operated by various religious organizations in

Nunavut Premier Eva Aariak speaks at a celebration for the 10th anniversary of Nunavut Territory in Iqualuit in April of 2009.

partnership with the Government of Canada. In 1969, the government took over the operation of the schools; most were closed by the mid-1970s, but seven were left open throughout the 1980s, with the last closing in 1996. Over 100,000 Aboriginal children were forced into the schools, and probably 80,000 of those children are still alive today.

The residential schools prohibited the use of Aboriginal languages, traditions, and customs, and many officials were abusive. During the hearings of the Royal Commission on Aboriginal Peoples, people came forward with painful personal stories of physical and sexual abuse. Many resorted to litigation to obtain compensation, forcing the federal government to negotiate and ultimately announce the Residential Schools Settlement Agreement in 2006. The $1.9 billion agreement involved the paying of compensation and the intention to move forward with a healing process.

Part of the settlement agreement is an initiative called the Truth and Reconciliation Commission (TRC). The TRC bears the same name as the commission that heard the stories of violence and racism in South Africa after apartheid. The purpose is to give former residential school students a formal opportunity to tell their stories and to create a report that will be part of Canada's official historical record. The $60 million commission is a key component of the residential school settlement.

Mental Health
The Aboriginal communities of Canada suffer from higher rates of mental health problems such as suicide, depression, and substance abuse than the general population.

The root of these mental health issues can often be traced back to the long history of colonization, discrimination and oppression, and losses of land, language and livelihood.

Many Aboriginal families were also affected by the government's residential school policy which took many Aboriginal children from their homes. While attending residential schools, some were forced to endure violence and abuse while many others lost their first language as well as a connection the traditions of their culture and community.

(National Aboriginal Health Organization, 2011 & Health Canada, 2002)

Aboriginal Self-Government

We often think of countries in Africa or South America when we discuss colonialism, but in many ways the Aboriginal people of Canada have suffered much like indigenous people in other parts of the world. Many Aboriginal people in Canada live in so-called Third World conditions, with limited access to water, health care, education, or even a healthy diet. Treaties, the reserve system, the *Indian Act*, residential schools, and subsequent government actions are the method by which Aboriginal people were colonized, subjugated, and created as second-class citizens in their own land.

There are also political similarities. The anti-imperialist movements in Third World countries resulted in the overthrow of colonial empires. The European powers were rapidly pushed out of Africa, Asia, and elsewhere as occupying colonial powers. Internal indigenous people within settler societies are now pushing more than ever for the removal of the institutions of domestic colonialism. This is a global phenomenon and not specific to Canadian history.

The First Nations, Métis, and Inuit of Canada recognize that they are not alone, but it often appears that the Canadian government refuses to admit or does not understand that the political challenges they face are intertwined with the global struggles of colonized peoples. The call for self-government is the natural response to hundreds of years of colonial oppression, both in many Third World countries around the world and here in Canada.

"Systemic Racism" in the Correctional System

A special report to Parliament called "*Spirit Matters*," released in March 2013, gave Canada a failing grade for the fact that Aboriginal people are highly over-represented in the Canadian correctional system.

Howard Sapers, the federal correctional investigator, pointed out that the 3,400 First Nations, Métis, and Inuit prisoners account for 23 percent of inmates in federal prisons, up from 17 percent a decade ago, even though Aboriginal people are just 4 percent of the general population. And the situation is getting worse, not better.

"By any reasonable measure ... " Sapers said, "the overrepresentation of Aboriginal people in federal corrections and the lack of progress to improve the disparity in correctional outcomes continues to cloud Canada's domestic human rights record."

The report's conclusions were similar to a separate report released a week earlier by former Supreme Court of Canada Justice Frank Iacobucci.

Iacobucci said he found "systemic racism" toward Aboriginal people in the justice system.

Colonialism and Government Policy Objectives

Aboriginal social welfare needs to be viewed within the context of a colonial past. In settler nations such as Canada, colonists take administrative control from the colonized nation, thereby instituting a particular type of colonialism known as *internal colonialism*, which creates political and economic inequalities between regions or peoples.

In two works on the subject, Roger Gibbins and Rick Ponting outline the major goals or policy themes of national government public policy towards Aboriginal peoples, which are summarized in the following list (Ponting, 1997).

- **PROTECTION.** The officials developing early Aboriginal policy were very aware of the problems of alcoholism, greed, and prostitution that flourished on the frontier of Canada in the 1800s. Some had humanitarian goals and sought to protect Aboriginal people until they could be assimilated into white society. This led to laws prohibiting the private sale of Aboriginal land, the use of alcohol by Aboriginal people, and the prostitution of Aboriginal women. These officials saw the reservation system as a way to isolate and protect Aboriginal people in Canada. It can also be argued that these goals of protection were mostly illusory, glossing over the underlying goal of exploitation. For example, by isolating them on reserves, the government was free to exploit other vast Aboriginal lands.
- **ASSIMILATION.** The central pillar or thrust of federal government Indian policy was the goal of assimilation or the absorption of Aboriginal peoples into Canadian society. It was desired and expected that eventually all Aboriginals would give up their traditional customs, culture, and beliefs and become like those of the dominant society. The failure of this assimilation process can largely be attributed to barriers posed by systemic and societal discrimination. In short, the racism that facilitated the attitude of assimilation at the same time erected barriers to actual assimilation.
- **CHRISTIANIZATION.** The core assimilation policy was supported by a variety of other policies, such as the process of Christianization. To the colonial government, the civilizing of the Aboriginals was synonymous with their Christianization. Aboriginal ceremonies and cultural practices were officially discouraged or outlawed. Education through church residential schools was seen as a way to destroy the social, spiritual, and cultural systems and relations of the Aboriginals and replace them with the beliefs of mainstream Canadian society. However, because the residential schools isolated Aboriginals from the mainstream, they worked at cross-purposes to the goal of assimilation. They were the source of great antagonism in Aboriginal communities and continue to be so to this day.

- **ENFRANCHISEMENT.** As mentioned previously, this was the method envisioned for Aboriginals to obtain citizenship and thus be fully recognized as Canadians. By enfranchising, Aboriginal people lost their status and band membership, renounced their Aboriginal identity, and merged with the non-Aboriginal society. The most common reason for choosing enfranchisement was to pursue the right to vote in a federal election. Relinquishing their Indian status was the only way that Aboriginal peoples were permitted to vote in a federal election until March 1960, when the House of Commons finally gave Aboriginal people the right to vote.
- **LAND SURRENDER.** For the government, obtaining land held by Aboriginal peoples for the settlement of non-Aboriginal people was a primary goal. Reserves were seen as a way to move Aboriginals into agriculturally based communities, both to assimilate them and to free vast tracts of land for non-Aboriginal settlement. As immigration increased, the government moved to make more and more Aboriginal land available for non-Aboriginal settlement.
- **GOVERNMENT AUTHORITY.** The *Indian Act* of 1876 gave sweeping power and authority to the colonial administrators, taking away Aboriginal peoples' right to self-determination. This external political control is a fundamental aspect of colonization and is a continuing source of conflict.

The "Sixties Scoop"

The term "Sixties Scoop" refers to an estimated twenty thousand First Nation and Métis children who were taken from their families and fostered or adopted out to primarily white middle-class families starting in 1960 and continuing until the mid-1980s. The term was coined by Patrick Johnston in his 1983 report *Native Children and the Child Welfare System*.

In many instances, children were literally scooped from their homes and communities without the knowledge or consent of their families and bands. Aboriginal leaders charged that the government authorities and social workers involved acted under colonialistic assumptions that Aboriginal people were culturally inferior and unable to adequately provide for the needs of their children.

The policy was discontinued in the mid-1980s, after Ontario chiefs passed resolutions against it and a Manitoba judicial inquiry (Report of the Review Committee on Indian and Métis Adoptions and Placements, the Kimelman Report) harshly condemned it.

Jeremy Meawasige and his mother Maurina Beadle of the Pictou Landing First Nation in Nova Scotia were involved in a ground breaking Supreme Court case that has widespread implications for federal social services on reserves.

Food Security

"Among off-reserve Aboriginal households, approximately one in five (20.9 percent) households was "food insecure," including 8.4 percent with "severe food insecurity".

These rates are approximately three times higher than among non-Aboriginal households, where 7.2 percent were "food insecure," including 2.5 percent with "severe food insecurity.""

(Health Canada, 2012a)

The Historical Context of Income Security for Aboriginal Peoples

During the sixteenth and seventeenth centuries, before extensive settlement began, the relationship between Aboriginal peoples and Europeans in Canada was relatively harmonious and mutually advantageous. At first, Aboriginal peoples served as partners in exploration and trading. As the English and French became locked in an imperialistic struggle for control over the North American continent, the relationship with the Aboriginal peoples evolved into military alliances.

Then, the presence of Aboriginal peoples on lands needed for settlement became the "Indian problem" and an impediment to "civilization." This problem was addressed by land-cession treaties and assimilation policies, such as residential schools, the Indian Registry, and the reserve system. With the *Indian Act* and reserve system in place, as well as the goals of Christianization and assimilation, the colonial powers, and later the Government of Canada, were faced with the need to "take care" of the Aboriginal population—settlement interfered with traditional ways of living and effectively created a colonial underclass that persists today.

Early Relief Programs

The introduction of the reserve system was similar in many ways to the poorhouse (see Chapter 2), which was a designated place for the deserving poor. The difference, of course, is that the Aboriginal peoples' own income security had been taken away by settlement and European methods of commerce. Early relief efforts were seen as a means of easing the Aboriginal peoples' distress (often caused by starvation) and to maintain order and peace (Shewell, 2004).

The first system of income security for First Nations was a ration system based on confiscated First Nations monies that were placed in a band trust account. Annuity trusts were created with the land sales, and monetary relief was taken from the trust accounts and was granted at the discretion of the local Indian Agent. These monies were grossly inadequate and were used as much as a means to sanction behaviour or reward assimilation as for relief (Moscovitch & Webster, 1995, p. 211).

The decision to grant relief was based on the old practice of distinguishing between the "deserving" and the "undeserving" poor, and First Nations were generally considered undeserving. This system applied British Poor Law principles until the mid-1960s. "Non-registered Indians, Métis and Inuit were on the periphery of the Indian relief system although their economic circumstances were similar to, or worse than, those of the Indians" (Moscovitch & Webster, 1995, p. 212).

Inclusion in National Programs

The first Old Age Pension of 1927 excluded Indians and Inuit but was available to the Métis. (Scott, 1994). The first *Unemployment Insurance Act*, in 1940, also excluded most Aboriginal people from eligibility. The *Family Allowance Act* of 1944 did apply but only provided "in kind" rations.

The Old Age Pension exclusion remained until 1951; however, in 1948, a law was passed that allowed Registered Indians over 70 years of age to apply for a monthly allowance known as the *Allowance to Aged Indians*. In 1951, the *Old Age Security Act* and *Old Age Assistance Act* superseded the *Old Age Pensions Act* of 1927; these provisions did include all Aboriginal peoples, making it the first income security program to apply to all Aboriginal peoples.

The *Unemployment Assistance Act* of 1956 was supposed to be a cost-shared program available to Aboriginal people, but the provinces refused to pay any part of what they saw as a federal government responsibility. With the *Unemployment Assistance Act* of 1956, the federal government attempted to mirror the standards and procedures of the provincial systems. In most cases, they had lower benefit rates.

Social Assistance, or welfare, for First Nations in Canada is rife with struggle between federal and provincial governments over who should pay. Between 1951 and the early 1960s, the Indian relief system collapsed and was replaced by access to the mainstream welfare state (Moscovitch & Webster, 1995).

AIDS: Are First Nations Populations More at Risk?

"Although incidence (new HIV infections among the total population) has gone down in the Canadian population, It appears that HIV rates have been steadily increasing in First Nations and Inuit populations.

Social, economic, and behavioural factors such as poverty; substance use, including injection drug use; sexually transmitted diseases: and limited access to health services have increased their vulnerability."

(Health Canada, 2012b)

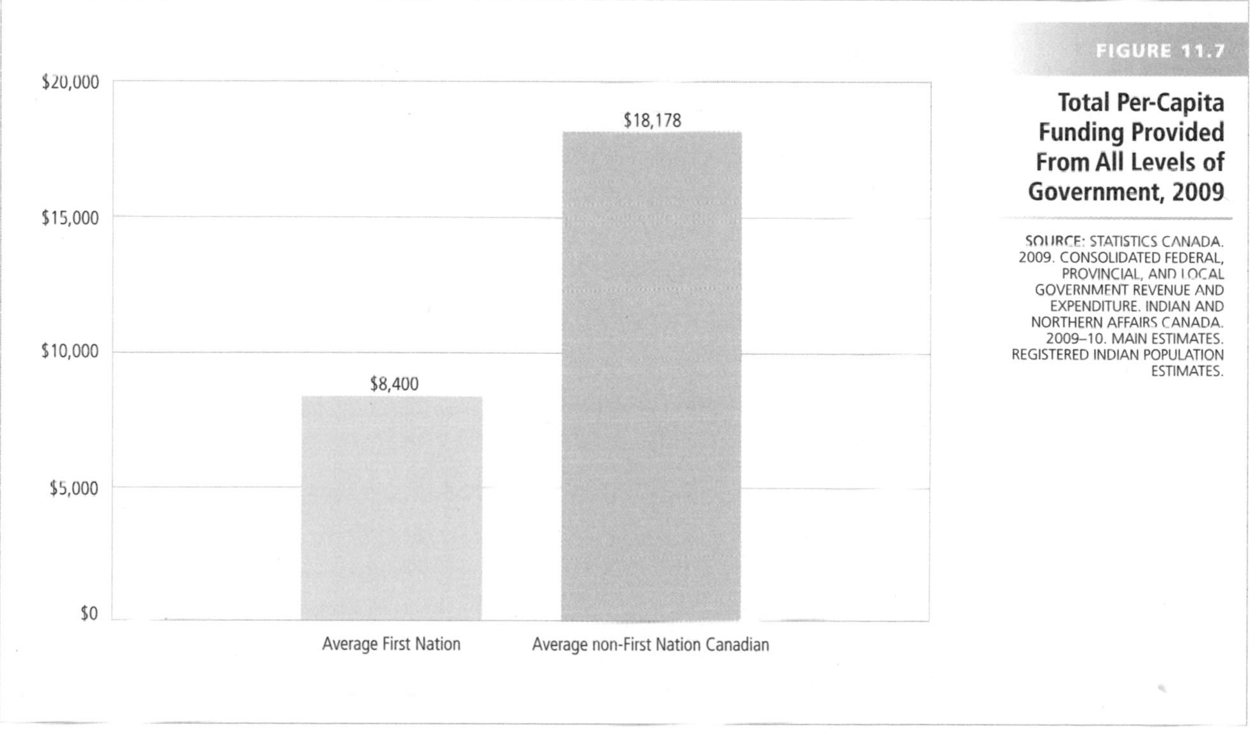

FIGURE 11.7

Total Per-Capita Funding Provided From All Levels of Government, 2009

SOURCE: STATISTICS CANADA. 2009. CONSOLIDATED FEDERAL, PROVINCIAL, AND LOCAL GOVERNMENT REVENUE AND EXPENDITURE. INDIAN AND NORTHERN AFFAIRS CANADA. 2009–10. MAIN ESTIMATES. REGISTERED INDIAN POPULATION ESTIMATES.

Assembly of First Nations (AFN)
The Assembly of First Nations (AFN) was founded in 1982 from other political organizations. It is the national organization representing First Nations citizens in Canada. There are over 630 First Nations communities in Canada, and the AFN provides them with a national voice through their leaders, advocating for issues such as Aboriginal and treaty rights; economic development; education, languages and literacy; health; housing; social development; justice; taxation; land claims; and the environment.

The Assembly is made up of chiefs who meet annually, and they elect a national chief every three years. The AFN also includes regular meetings of the Confederacy of Nations, made up of the chiefs and regional leaders, whose number is determined by population.

The Assembly of First Nations is funded mainly by Aboriginal Affairs and Northern Development Canada.

Social Assistance Today

The majority of First Nations now administer Social Assistance to members under various provincial guidelines but under the direct supervision of Aboriginal Affairs and Northern Development Canada. While the federal government continues to fund on-reserve Social Assistance, the benefits are tied to provincial rates. Some off-reserve Aboriginal communities also deliver their own programs according to provincial standards. Urban Aboriginal people receive Social Assistance through the mainstream system.

Income Assistance

The Income Assistance program is one of five social programs run by AANDC (the other social programs are the National Child Benefit Reinvestment Program, the Assisted Living Program, the First Nations Child and Family Services Program, and the Family Violence Prevention program). In 2006-2007, 534 First Nations administered their own income assistance programming. According to AANDC, the 2010-2011 on-reserve income assistance "dependency rate" was close to 34 percent, compared to about 5 percent for the rest of the Canadian population.

AANCD's Income Assistance program is designed to provide funding to assist eligible individuals and families who are ordinarily resident on-reserve with basic and special needs services that are aligned with those provided to other residents of the province or territory. The program has four main components: basic needs, special needs, pre-employment supports, and service delivery (AANDC, 2013).

The First Nations Income Assistance Working Group (FNIAWG), AANDC, and the AFN collaborate on income assistance-related programs, projects, and services for First Nations individuals, families, and communities. During 2010-2011, the AFN convened a meeting of the FNIAWG and participated in the Active Measures conference hosted by the First Nations Social Development Society in Vancouver, at which a number of priority areas were identified:

- Active measures;
- Youth issues and engagement;
- Authorities renewal; and
- A national learning event for First Nations.

The AFN has also engaged with both the Elders Council and the National Youth Council in relation to income assistance for seniors and for veterans, as well as sponsoring programs that would assist Aboriginal youth. In collaboration with the FNIAWG, the AFN social development team also worked on Old Age Security (OAS) and Guaranteed Income Supplement (GIS) programs (AFN, 2012).

Active Measures

AANDC funds "active measures" as a core component of its Income Assistance program. **Active measures** is a proactive approach to help First Nations individuals move from income assistance to more independent and self-sufficient lives with the skills and training they need to find and hold meaningful jobs (AANDC, AFN, 2013). These measures would include life skills training, child care, and training and employment incentives for employers both on and off reserve. For example, there is a growing concern about the rising number of First Nations youth that rely on income assistance as a primary source of income. Active measures programming is intended to address such problems.

An example would be access to affordable child care. As with mainstream Canadians, in order to break the cycle of poverty, First Nations' parents need ready access to affordable, quality care. Access to quality child care is crucial to early childhood development and has positive all-round benefits for parents and communities over the longer term.

Active measures programming of this kind is a focus of the joint activities of AANDC, the AFN, and FNIAWG. According to the AFN, however, a major barrier to the success of active measures are current federal budget cutbacks and restrictions. "Growing costs of administering income assistance," they maintain, "has left little room to expand the delivery of new programs."

Social Assistance
The Treasury Board implemented a policy (Treasury Board Minute Number 627879) in July 1964 establishing the provincial regulations and standards for Social Assistance programs. Authorization to administer Social Assistance on reserves was given to the Department of Indian Affairs and Northern Development (now known as Aboriginal Affairs and Northern Development Canada) upon its creation in October 1966.

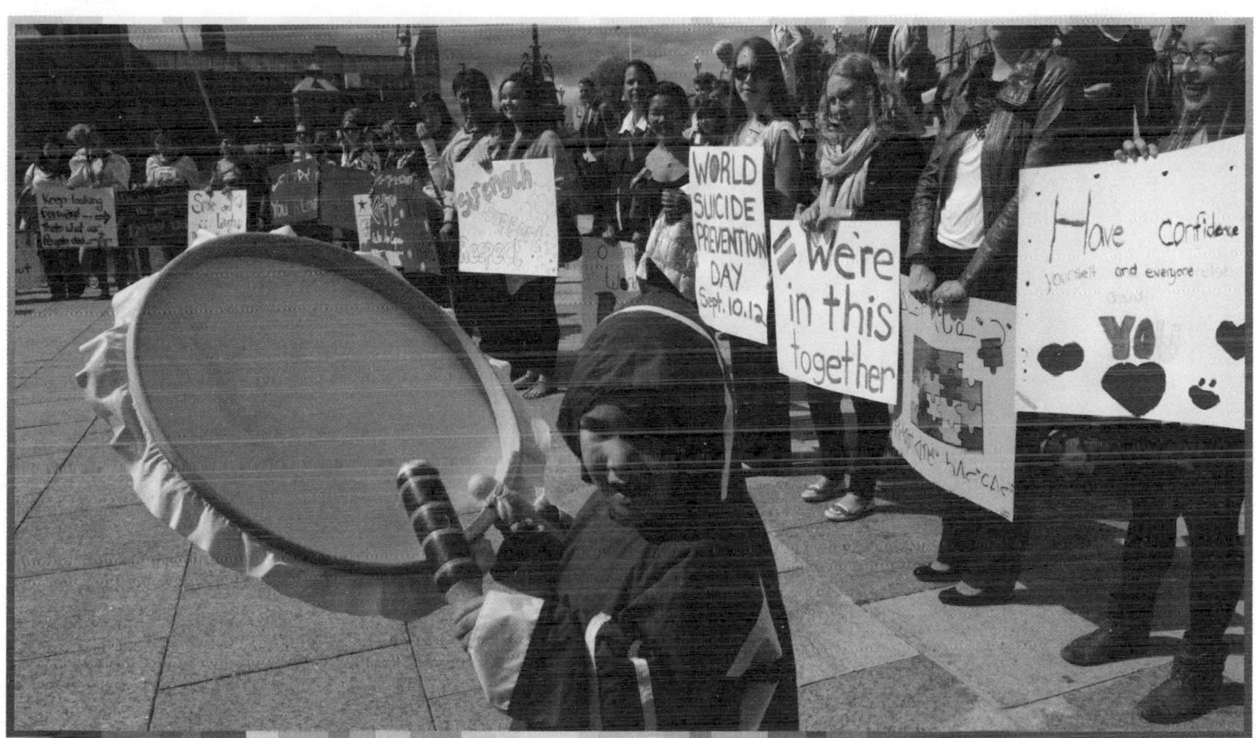

Micheal Sammortuk, 4, of Rankin Inlet joins Inuit youth as they mark world suicide prevention day with a "Celebrate Life" event on Parliament Hill in Ottawa on Monday, September 10, 2012.

Suicide Rates
The suicide rates across all age groups of Aboriginal people were three times higher than in the non-Aboriginal population.

The suicide rate was placed at 3.3 times the national average for registered Indians and 3.9 times for Inuit.

Adolescents and young adults were at highest risk. Among Aboriginal youth aged 10–19 years, the suicide rate was five to six times higher than among their non-Aboriginal peers.

(Royal Commission on Aboriginal Peoples, 1996)

Moving Towards Aboriginal Self-Government

Movement towards self-government for Aboriginal peoples has occurred in several stages. One of the earliest developments was the introduction in 1969 of the White Paper (*Statement of the Government of Canada on Indian Policy*) prepared by the then Minister of Indian Affairs, Jean Chrétien.

The White Paper argued that Aboriginal peoples should be treated as regular citizens, that they should take control of their lands, and that the Indian Affairs department should be disbanded. But the report galvanized the First Nations in united opposition, arguing that ending "the special status of the Indians" was not a solution to the problem. Harold Cardinal of the Indian Association of Alberta wrote a response titled "Citizens Plus," which came to be known as the *Red Paper*.

The report mapped out an alternative view whereby Aboriginal peoples would contribute to Canadian society while concurrently exercising rights and power at the community level.

Constitution Act, 1982

Under Sections 25, 35, and 37 of the *Constitution Act, 1982*, the Government of Canada recognized the inherent right of self-government. Building on this in the late 1990s with the Royal Commission on Aboriginal Peoples (RCAP) and *Gathering Strength: Canada's Aboriginal Action Plan* (the government's response), the approach to self-government has evolved that includes a framework for new government-to-government relationships and structures for negotiating agreements. According to AANDC, the new policy is based on "the view that Aboriginal peoples of Canada have the right to govern themselves in relation to matters that are internal to their communities, integral to their unique cultures, identities, traditions, languages and institutions, and with respect to their special relationship to their land and their Resources" (INAC, 2005, p. 78). In 2005, INAC was engaged in 72 negotiations for self-government, representing 445 Aboriginal communities (INAC, 2005).

Perhaps the most prominent example of Aboriginal self-government is the territory of Nunavut, one of the traditional homes of the Inuit in Canada. After an almost 20-year process of legal and political negotiation, the eastern half of the Northwest Territories officially became the territory of Nunavut in 1999. While Nunavut operates a democratic parliamentary system like the rest of Canada, it combines it with the practices of consensus government: all of the elected members of the legislative assembly select the premier and ministers together and decide as a group the priorities for the government. The Government of Nunavut also uses Inuit traditional knowledge and values to guide decision making and to create policies and laws that represent the territory's Inuit majority.

The Royal Commission Today

The **Royal Commission on Aboriginal Peoples** (RCAP) in 1996 was an extensive study of Aboriginal people in Canada. A central conclusion of the report was that "the main policy direction, pursued for over 150 years, first by colonial then by Canadian governments, has been wrong" (AFN, 2006, p. 1).

At the core of its 440 recommendations is a rebalancing of political and economic power between Aboriginal nations and other Canadian governments. As the Report noted: "Aboriginal peoples must have room to exercise their autonomy and structure their solutions."

The report underlined five key themes:

1. Aboriginal nations have to be reconstituted.
2. A process must be established for the assumption of powers by Aboriginal nations.
3. There must be a fundamental reallocation of lands and resources.
4. Aboriginal people need education and crucial skills for governance and economic self-reliance.
5. Economic development must be addressed if poverty, unemployment, and welfare are to change.
6. There must be an acknowledgement of injustices of the past.

In order to protect their heritage and their land rights, the need for Aboriginal self-government and one-on-one negotiations with the federal government is more pressing than ever.

Inuit Housing
Inuit in Canada are burdened with the highest hospitalization rates of children with severe lower respiratory tract infections in the world, suffer from an infant mortality rate three times that of the rest of Canada, and live with the highest levels of residential overcrowding in the country.
(Knotsch & Kinnon, 2011)

Two Inuit junior rangers unveil the territorial flag of Nunavut at the April 1, 1999, inaugural event for the new territory. The creation of an autonomous territory is one expression of Aboriginal self-government, as encouraged in the Royal Commission.

Aboriginal Peoples and the "Great Recession"

Larger Job Losses Among Aboriginal People

Aboriginal people in Canada have historically faced a much worse labour market than non-Aboriginal Canadians. Unemployment rates have been higher for the Aboriginal population, while their employment rate and average earnings tend to be lower.

The economic downturn that began in 2008 had devastating effects for the income and employment of Canadians across the board, but for some groups the effects are were significantly worse than for others.

Through the "Great Recession" and beyond, Aboriginal peoples (excluding those living on reserves or in the territories)—First Nations, Métis, and Inuit—had a harder time finding work than non-Aboriginal people. Those fifteen years of age and older experienced significantly greater declines in employment and also higher rates of unemployment than their non-Aboriginal counterparts (Statistics Canada, 2011).

The employment gap widened to 4.8 points in 2009 (from a 3.5 point gap in 2008). It was 57 percent in 2009 compared to 61.8 percent for non-Aboriginal people. Likewise with the employment rate over this period. The

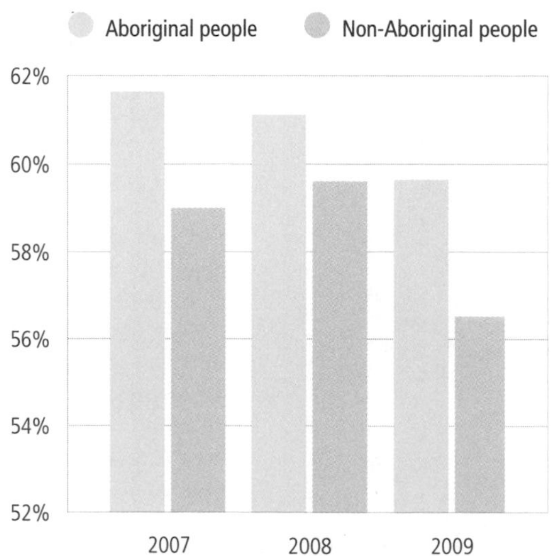

rate rose to 13.9 percent from 10.4 percent in 2009, whereas in the same period, the unemployment rate for non-Aboriginal people rose from 6.0 percent to 8.1 percent. The industry sector most affected was manufacturing where Aboriginal employment declined by 30 percent (compared to 8 percent for non-Aboriginal people).

By the end of 2010, the situation had not improved. The employment rate for Aboriginal people was then 66 percent, fifteen percentage points lower than that for non-Aboriginal people. Unemployment stood at 12.3 percent, nearly double the rate for non-Aboriginal people.

Before the economic downturn there was a economic gap in terms of employment and unemployment, but the recession had an even greater negative effect. The downturn took an especially high toll on young people, both Aboriginal and non-Aboriginal. Again, the negative effects were higher for Aboriginal youth. The employment rate was 45.1 percent for Aboriginal youth in 2009 (compared to 55.6 percent for non-Aboriginal youth. From 2008 to 2009, the youth employment rate among Aboriginal people fell by 6.8 percentage points (compared to a decline of 4.2 percentage points among non-Aboriginal youth. For both groups of youth, of course,the losses were higher than those experienced by core-age workers.

Many people in Canada and around the world were negatively affected by the economic downturn that began in 2008. The employment and unemployment effects for Aboriginal people, one of Canada's most vulnerable populations, were especially pronounced. Research subsequently prepared for the Métis National Council by the Centre for the Study of Living Standards support the findings (CSLS, 2012).

Conclusion

"Aboriginal peoples" is a collective name for the original peoples of North America and their descendants. The Canadian constitution recognizes three groups: Indians (commonly referred to as First Nations), Métis, and Inuit. These are three distinct peoples with unique histories, languages, cultural practices, and spiritual beliefs (AANDC, 2013). More than one million people in Canada identify themselves as Aboriginal persons, according to the latest census.

Since well before the time of the *Indian Act* in 1876, the Aboriginal peoples of Canada have been subjected to colonial government policies concerned mainly with seizing their land and keeping it, first for the settlers and more recently for the economic gains of resource extraction. As part of this strategy, government policies were aimed at "assimilating" Aboriginal peoples by breaking their cultural and language ties. Residential schools are perhaps the most well-known, and most disreputable, aspect of this policy. Through such policies, Aboriginal families and communities suffered immeasurable harm, such that even today many First Nations' communities experience poverty and housings conditions resembling Third World countries.

Much needs to be done to reverse the damage done to the Aboriginal communities in Canada, frequently referred to as "Canada's national disgrace." Social justice initiatives such as the Residential Schools Settlement Agreement and the Truth and Reconciliation Commission are steps in the right direction. Such measures provide opportunities for both compensation and healing. Measures to reduce the overpopulation of Aboriginal people, and Aboriginal youth in particular, in the Canadian justice system are desperately needed as well. Underlying all this is the need for Aboriginal self-government—Aboriginal control of Aboriginal affairs.

Successive federal governments have stated that the social welfare of Aboriginal people in Canada is a major priority. However, ultimately, not enough has been done and what measures have been taken often fall short of their goal. Indeed, many more Aboriginal children are in care now than there were during the residential schools era.

The survival of Aboriginal communities and culture in the face of all odds is a testament to the resilience of these communities. Most analysts now believe that top-down solutions are doomed to failure and that lasting solutions lie in Aboriginal control of Aboriginal affairs. Grassroots movements such as Idle No More, a grassroots campaign throughout Aboriginal communities that gained nationwide and even international support, point the way forward.

CHAPTER 11 REVIEW

LEARNING OBJECTIVES

After completing this chapter, students should be able to:

- Explain who the First Nations of North America are.
- Describe the major findings of the "Urban Aboriginal Peoples Study" of 1911.
- Discuss the Community Well-Being Index and its application to Aboriginal communities.
- Discuss the importance of land treaty rights and the controversies surrounding the *Indian Act* of 1876.
- Explain the reserve system.
- Describe the residential schools system and the harm it caused.
- Explain the objectives of colonial government policy towards Aboriginal peoples.
- Describe the importance of Aboriginal self-government.
- Describe the roles of AANDC and the AFN in implementing income security policy for Aboriginal peoples.
- Describe the historical significance of the Royal Commission on Aboriginal Peoples.

KEY CONCEPTS

- Aboriginal Affairs and Northern Development Canada (AANDC)
- AANDC's Income Assistance Program
- Aboriginal Peoples of Canada
- Aboriginal self-government
- Assembly of First Nations (AFN)
- Active measure
- Community Well-Being Index
- First Nations
- *Indian Act* of 1876
- Idle No More
- Internal colonialism
- Reserve system
- Residential schools
- Royal Commission on Aboriginal Peoples (RCAP)
- Status Indians (or Registered Indians)
- Treaties
- Truth and Reconciliation Commission (TRC)
- Urban Aboriginal People Study

REVIEW QUESTIONS

1. How do the social and economic conditions of Aboriginal people differ from those of other Canadians?
2. What specific factors and events in the history of the relationship between Aboriginal peoples and the governments of Canada have shaped the social welfare of Aboriginal peoples?
3. What were the six major goals of public policy in relation to Aboriginal peoples as identified by Ponting?
4. What was the residential schools system, and why did it have such a devastating effect on Aboriginal families and communities?
5. Why is Aboriginal self-government such an important idea for promoting the social welfare of Aboriginal peoples?
6. Do governments in Canada spend more or less on Aboriginal services as compared to services for the average Canadian? Are the facts regarding this question consistent with public perception? If not, why do you think this is the case?

EXPLORING SOCIAL WELFARE

1. Pick one of the social and economic conditions outlined in this chapter (such as unemployment, infant mortality, etc.). Research the issue further and write a brief report describing the situation of Aboriginal peoples as compared to other Canadians. Outline the polices that the government has undertaken to address this issue, and discuss their effectiveness or otherwise.
2. In 2006, the federal government announced the $1.9 billion Residential Schools Settlement Agreement to compensate former residential school students. The settlement agreement proposes a Common Experience Payment for all eligible former students of Indian Residential Schools, an Independent Assessment Process for claims of sexual or serious physical abuse, as well as measures to support healing, commemorative activities, and the establishment of a Truth and Reconciliation Commission. Conduct additional research and further describe this agreement. It would also be useful to obtain information from the AFN and other Aboriginal organizations.

CRITICAL THINKING

The survival of Aboriginal peoples is a remarkable testament to the power of culture and the strength of community. What can we learn from this?

What can be done within non-Aboriginal schools and communities to foster a deeper understanding that, together, we all have a stake in redressing once and for all the terrible legacy of colonial policies in relation to Aboriginal peoples?

WEBSITES

Assembly of First Nations (AFN)
www.afn.ca
The Assembly of First Nations (AFN), formerly known as the National Indian Brotherhood, is a body of First Nations leaders across Canada. The aims of the organization are to protect the rights, treaty obligations, ceremonies, and claims of citizens of the First Nations in Canada.

The Congress of Aboriginal Peoples (CAP)
www.abo-peoples.org
The Congress of Aboriginal Peoples (CAP) is an organization that represents off-reserve and Métis people. Founded in the 1970s, the organization's mission is to represent the interests of Aboriginal people who are not legally recognized under the *Indian Act*, including non-Status Indians and Métis peoples.

Aboriginal Photograph Database, Saskatoon Archives
http://scaa.sk.ca/ourlegacy
The Aboriginal Photograph Database is part of the Saskatoon Archives and is hosted by the University of Saskatoon. It provides a thematic index of photographs relevant to Aboriginal studies.

12

Disability and Social Welfare

Income Security and Full Participation

"The full participation of persons with disabilities requires the commitment of all segments of society."

— *IN UNISON: A CANADIAN APPROACH TO DISABILITY ISSUES* (HRSDC, 1998)

Disability is part of the human experience. Statistics Canada's most recent Participation and Activity Limitation Survey (PALS) found that over 14.3 percent of Canadians have a disability—that means 4.4 million people, or one in eight Canadians.

Social welfare policy is designed to promote and support the full participation of people with disabilities in all dimensions of Canadian society—a key aspect of citizenship. This support is found in a vast array of federal, provincial, and municipal programs, in tax policies, and in both the non-profit and the private sectors. This chapter highlights the social welfare issues of disability in Canada, the challenge of employment for persons with disabilities, and the various income security programs available.

Participation and Activity Limitation Survey (PALS)

The term **disability** applies to a wide range of impairments including sensory impairments, such as blindness or deafness; physical disabilities impairing mobility; and psychiatric, developmental, learning, and neurological disabilities. The provision of income and other support to persons with disabilities is complicated not only because of the range of disabilities that can exist but because needs arising from those disabilities can vary greatly, from assistance to participate in the workplace, to support when unable to work, to in-home care.

PALS Discontinued

The Participation and Activity Limitation Survey (PALS), a census-related survey that gathers statistics about disabilities, was not carried out in 2011. The government intends to replace PALS by a database culled from tax information, welfare rolls, and similar databanks.

Disabilities activists are skeptical about whether that information will be as reliable.

The Nature and Extent of Disabilities

The federal government carried out a detailed investigation into the nature and extent of disability in Canada in 2006: the **Participation and Activity Limitation Survey (PALS)**. Since the earlier PALS report in 2001, the rate of disability among adults rose from 14.6 to 16.5 percent. The most marked increase was for learning disabilities, which rose by almost 40 percent to approximately 631,000.

The overall increase in disability can be attributed partly to the aging population, but this is not the only factor. There is also evidence to suggest that the social acceptance of disability has increased. The PALS report also shows that the largest increase occurred in the number of people reporting mild disabilities.

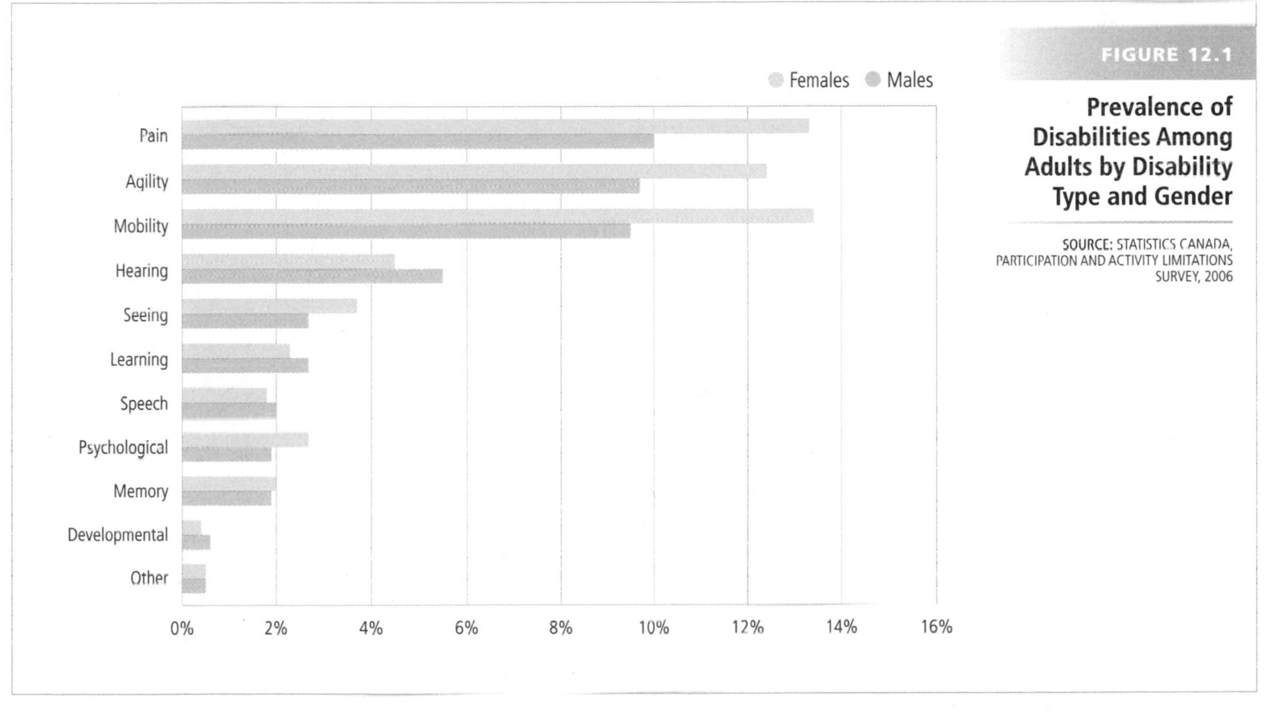

FIGURE 12.1

Prevalence of Disabilities Among Adults by Disability Type and Gender

SOURCE: STATISTICS CANADA, PARTICIPATION AND ACTIVITY LIMITATIONS SURVEY, 2006

Types of Disability

The PALS Survey

Adults

The PALS survey questions allow the identification of the following types of disabilities among adults aged 15 and over:

Hearing: Difficulty hearing what is being said in a conversation with one other person, in a conversation with three or more persons, or in a telephone conversation.

Seeing: Difficulty seeing ordinary newsprint or clearly seeing the face of someone from 4 metres (12 feet).

Speech: Difficulty speaking and/or being understood.

Mobility: Difficulty walking half a kilometre or up and down a flight of stairs, about 12 steps without resting, moving from one room to another, carrying an object of 5 kg (10 pounds) for 10 metres (30 feet), or standing for long periods.

Agility: Difficulty bending, dressing, or undressing oneself, getting into and out of bed, cutting own toenails, using fingers to grasp or to handle objects, reaching in any direction (for example, above one's head), or cutting own food.

Pain: Limitations in the amount or kind of activities that one can do because of a long-term pain that is constant or recurs from time to time, for example, recurrent back pain.

Learning: Difficulty learning because of a condition, such as attention problems, hyperactivity, or dyslexia, whether or not the condition was diagnosed by a teacher, doctor, or other health professional.

Memory: Limitations in the amount or kind of activities that one can do, due to frequent periods of confusion or difficulty remembering things. These difficulties may be associated with Alzheimer's disease, brain injuries, or other similar conditions.

Developmental: Cognitive limitations due to the presence of a developmental disability or disorder, such as Down's syndrome, autism, or mental impairment caused by a lack of oxygen at birth.

Psychological: Limitations in the amount or kind of activities that one can do, due to the presence of an emotional, psychological, or psychiatric condition, such as phobias, depression, schizophrenia, drinking, or drug problems.

Children

The PALS survey questions allow the identification of the following types of disabilities among children under 15:

Hearing[1]: Difficulty hearing.

Seeing[1]: Difficulty seeing.

Speech[2]: Difficulty speaking and/or being understood.

Mobility[2]: Difficulty walking. This means walking on a flat firm surface, such as a sidewalk or floor.

Dexterity[2]: Difficulty using hands or fingers to grasp or hold small objects, such as a pencil or scissors.

Learning[2]: Difficulty learning due to the presence of a condition, such as attention problems, hyperactivity, or dyslexia, whether or not the condition was diagnosed by a teacher, doctor, or other health professional.

Developmental delay[3]: Child has a delay in his/her development, either a physical, intellectual, or another type of delay.

Developmental disability or disorder[2]: Cognitive limitations due to the presence of a developmental disability or disorder, such as Down's syndrome, autism, or mental impairment caused by a lack of oxygen at birth.

Psychological[2]: Limitations in the amount or kind of activities that one can do due to the presence of an emotional, psychological, or behavioural condition.

Chronic condition[1]: Limitations in the amount or kind of activities that one can do, due to the presence of one or more chronic health conditions that have lasted or are expected to last six months or more and that have been diagnosed by a health professional. Examples of chronic conditions are asthma or severe allergies, heart condition or disease, kidney condition or disease, cancer, epilepsy, cerebral palsy, spina bifida, cystic fibrosis, muscular dystrophy, fetal alcohol syndrome, etc.

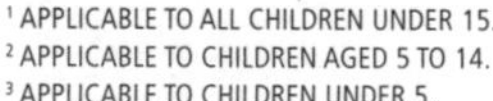
[1] APPLICABLE TO ALL CHILDREN UNDER 15.
[2] APPLICABLE TO CHILDREN AGED 5 TO 14.
[3] APPLICABLE TO CHILDREN UNDER 5.

TABLE 12.1

Prevalence of Disability by Age

Age Group	Number			Percent
	Total Population	Population With Disabilities	Population without Disabilities	Total Disability Rate
Total—All Ages	30,893,640	4,417,870	26,475,77	14.3
Total—Aged less than 15	5,471,360	202,350	5,269,010	3.7
0 to 4	1,656,040	27,540	1,628,500	1.7
5 to 14	3,815,310	174,810	3,640,500	4.6
Total—Aged 15 and over	25,422,280	4,215,530	21,206,760	16.6
15 to 64	21,373,150	2,457,940	18,915,210	11.5
15 to 19	2,102,370	96,060	2,006,310	4.6
20 to 24	2,044,710	99,440	1,945,270	4.9
25 to 34	3,942,260	239,600	3,702,660	6.1
35 to 44	4,747,62	456,930	4,290,690	9.6
45 to 54	4,912,800	740,990	4,171,810	15.1
55 to 64	3,623,390	824,920	2,798,470	22.8
65 and over	4,049,140	1,757,590	2,291,550	43.4
65 to 74	2,239,630	739,500	1,500,130	33.0
75 and over	1,809,500	1,018,090	791,420	56.3

Note: The sum of the values for each category may differ from the total due to rounding
Source: Adapted from Statistics Canada publication Participation and Activity Limitation Survey (PALS). 2006b Cat. no. 89-577-XIE.

What is Disability?

As a social category, disability is very complex because the onset varies considerably from one person to the next.

For example, a disability can be the result of sensory impairments, such as blindness and/or deafness. People can also have psychiatric disabilities, developmental disabilities, learning disabilities, or neurological disabilities. Many people have mobility as well as agility impairments, and many people with disabilities live with chronic and persistent pain.

People can be born with disabilities or people can become disabled at any age through a variety of means from illness to injury, war to famine, disease to the aging process.

History of Services for People With Disabilities

At the time of Confederation, the federal government was primarily concerned with what the *British North America Act* identified as "peace, order, and good government." The federal government was less interested in issues such as health, education, and social relief—these were assigned to the provinces. As a result, provinces developed their own unique charitable relief programs (as well as schools and institutions). Because of these provincial differences, no universal support care programs were established for people with disabilities, and no comprehensive nationwide support care policy exists in Canada to the present day (Hanes & Moscovitch, 2002).

Outdoor and Indoor Relief

Outdoor relief was a common form of assistance provided to persons with disabilities when their families could not take care of them. An early form of outdoor relief established in England, and later transported to British North America, was begging. Through the Poor Laws, the deserving poor, such as persons with disabilities, were given license to beg.

As time passed, other forms of outdoor relief supplemented begging. When families could not provide for a family member (usually an elderly person or a person with a disability), these persons were housed in private homes. Funds to cover expenses for food, clothing, shelter, and medical care were often provided through municipal taxes, charitable organizations, and religious organizations. In essence, outdoor relief meant that persons with disabilities were cared for through non-institutional methods of relief and were more or less part of the community.

By the mid-nineteenth century, outdoor relief came to be seen as a mechanism that created rather than relieved dependency, and institutions such as asylums, poor houses, and houses of industry began to replace the former methods of outdoor relief (Splane, 1965). The replacement of outdoor relief by indoor relief represents a significant shift in the philosophy regarding charitable relief.

There was a major shift in the public attitude towards social dependency and social relief as well, and the public's attitude towards the provision of relief changed. Persons with disabilities, who were once considered part of the social order, were now viewed as nuisance populations. They were to be removed from society, isolated, and placed in segregated institutions. During this time, disability was often considered a source of shame, and many persons with disabilities were often hidden away in their homes by their family members. There are numerous examples of people with various forms of disabilities being hidden or kept at home in Canada, the U.S., and the U.K. throughout the nineteenth and twentieth centuries (Hanes, 1995).

Institutionalization of the Disabled Population

The social rejection of "defective" populations was so severe that many persons with disabilities were treated as common criminals and banned from the streets of many cities. Many were charged under vagrancy laws and sent to jail. Many of those who were not sent to jail were sent to a local poor house, a house of industry, or an asylum. Provincial governments were reluctant to fund support programs for dependent populations, including people with disabilities, and very coercive means were used to provide for the relief of dependent populations (Hanes, 1995).

By the mid-twentieth century, many provinces had "special" residential schools for blind and deaf children and adolescents. Provincial institutions were established for people with psychiatric disabilities, and in many provinces, there were institutions for people with developmental disabilities. Specialized hospitals were established for many different disabled populations, including tuberculosis hospitals, orthopaedic hospitals and rehabilitation hospitals.

The **institutionalization of people with disabilities** was so widespread that it became the common belief that this was the natural order of things and that people with disabilities had always been separated from their communities (Bowe, 1978). This was to change only with the advancement of scientific medicine following World War I when the disability category increasingly fell under the domain of the medical profession. Since that time, it has tended to be medical professionals who determine the need for specialized care, income supports, pensions, educational supports, transportation supports, home care supports, and other benefits.

Persons with Disabilities Online

www.pwd-online.ca

This excellent government site provides access to a wide variety of information for persons with disabilities, family members, caregivers, and all Canadians.

Rehabilitation Services

An important era in the history of disability in Canada emerged following World War II. This period saw the massive expansion of the "welfare state," wherein social security programs (such as pensions and disability benefits) were established for a wide spectrum of people with disabilities. In addition, the post–World War II era witnessed the onset of the multidisciplinary rehabilitation team, which included the rehabilitation physician, nurse, occupational therapist, physiotherapist, and later, the social worker, psychologist, vocational counsellor, and recreologist.

The establishment of **rehabilitation services** following World War II thus laid the foundation for the modern era of medical and social services for people with disabilities. Subsequently, medical and social services were expanded to people with disabilities, including the establishment of special schools, training programs, sheltered workshops, summer camps, recreational programs, as well as the establishment of special trades and industries, and special hospitals and after-care facilities.

Models of Disability

Medical model: the view that disability is a health problem to be dealt with medically, which consequently separated people from full participation in society

Political rights model: the view that disability is a social construct, existing only as long as society maintains barriers to full participation of people who are physically or mentally different

Approaches to Disability: The Medical and Political Rights Models

The post-WWII dominance of medical professionals over the lives of people with disabilities remained unchallenged until the 1970s, when the disability rights movement developed in Canada. The rise of disability rights organizations is linked to the rise of the consumer movement, the civil rights movement, the peace movement, the gay rights movement, and the women's movement of the late 1960s and the early 1970s.

Rather than be labelled "defective" or "handicapped," disability rights advocates argued that persons with disabilities should also be seen as members of a minority group. "Many persons with disabilities," Lex Frieden suggests, "considered themselves members of a minority group related not by colour or nationality but by functional limitation and similar need" (Frieden, 1983, p. 55).

Charter of Rights and Freedoms, 1982

The **American Vocational Rehabilitation Act of 1973**, which prohibited discrimination against people with disabilities, represents a pivotal point in the history of persons with disabilities. "No otherwise qualified handicapped individual in the United States as defined by Section 7 shall, solely by reason of his handicap, be excluded from participation in, be denied the benefits of, or be subject to discrimination under any program or activity receiving federal financial assistance." Similar legislation followed in Canada at both the provincial and federal levels, and in 1982, the rights of people with disabilities were enshrined in the *Charter of Rights and Freedoms*.

Currently, two broad approaches characterize the discussions of disability. The *medical model of disability* has its roots in rehabilitation medicine, where the focus of the intervention is on the individual. It focuses on disability as an "impairment" and a "personal tragedy" and the need of the individual to adapt or otherwise to fit within mainstream society as much as possible. The *political rights model*, on the other hand, is concerned with the broader social and political context and the need for society as a whole to adapt and to address the needs of those persons with a disability.

The shift to defining disability in terms of rights, instead of medical need, was influenced not only by the disability rights movement but also by the development of disability theories that challenged the dominant medical model view of disability. The pre-eminent British disability advocate and theorist Michael Oliver coined the terms "personal tragedy theory" and "social oppression theory" of disability to describe the differences between a medical model of disability and a socio-political model of disability (Oliver, 1990). These terms perhaps better capture the different approaches for disabilities activists.

Medical Model: Personal Tragedy Theory

From the perspective of the **medical model of disability**, a disabling condition is viewed as an unfortunate life event where some form of professional and medical assistance is required (Oliver, 1990). This theory holds that disability is primarily a medical problem. The various forms of interventions are therefore introduced as a means of "curing" or "fixing" the individual.

According to this "personal tragedy" approach, persons who become disabled, as well as their loved ones, go through various stages of psychological and emotional adjustment before they can accept themselves or their loved ones as disabled. Much of the literature pertaining to the impact of disability on the individual and on the family focuses primarily on the stages of adjustment to the disability. Oliver (1996) argues that many of these explanations of adjustment to disability are based on psychological theories pertaining to or coping with death and dying—stages of shock, denial, grief, loss, reconciliation, and acceptance. Such an approach is usually based on an interpretation of coping that involves the following assumptions:

- An individual or family must move sequentially through the coping stages to become fully adjusted.
- There is but one path through the sequence.
- An individual can be placed clearly in one stage or another by analyzing their behaviour.
- There is an optional length of time for staying in each stage.

UN Report on Disabilities

The UN's *Report of the Committee on Economic, Social and Cultural Rights* (1998) questioned Canada's actions on disability, citing cuts to services such as home care, attendant care, and transportation, as well as the tightening of eligibility rules for people with disabilities.

The committee also questioned the issue of homelessness and lack of adequate support services among discharged psychiatric patients, as the Canadian government did not provide data on this matter.

Political Rights Model: Social Oppression Theory

In contrast, the **political rights model of disability** suggests that the problems faced by people with disabilities are not the result of physical impairments alone, but are also the result of the social and political inequality that exists between people with disabilities on the one hand and people without disabilities on the other (Oliver, 1990). This model thus challenges the widely prevalent view that disability is essentially an individual problem requiring individual treatment and individual solutions to problems.

The model regards people with disabilities as members of an oppressed minority population and that environmental factors—such as the lack of employment opportunities, lack of affordable housing, lack of accessible transportation, as well as the presence of negative stereotypes and prejudicial attitudes—are a primary cause of problems for people with disabilities. This, in turn, has implications with respect to resolving problems. Because many problems stem from structural and attitudinal barriers, systemic change, both social and political, is required if these obstacles are to be overcome. Among other things, this requires the incorporation of a *human rights* focus for addressing the needs of people with disabilities.

Canadian Association of Independent Living Centres

www.cailc.ca

CAILC is an organization of independent living centres across Canada; the website offers extensive resources on the movement.

The Independent Living Movement

The **Independent Living Movement (ILM)** has been a key player in the struggle to achieve human rights legislation for people with disabilities. Originating in the United States during the early 1970s and introduced to Canada in 1979, the ILM has become a dominant force in disability rights activity in Canada. The objective underlying the ILM is to encourage and help persons with disabilities achieve self-direction over the personal and community services needed to attain their own independent living.

By 1985, Independent Living Resource Centres (ILRCs) were operating in Waterloo, Winnipeg, Thunder Bay, Calgary, and Toronto. In 1986, at the first IL conference in Ottawa, the Canadian Association of Independent Living Centres (CAILC) was formed to act as a national coordinating body for the ILM, and the definition of a Canadian ILRC was developed. In 2008, a total of 26 ILRCs were operating across Canada.

The Independent Living Philosophy

The IL philosophy empowers consumers to make the choices necessary to control their community and personal resources. Consumer control means that ILRCs are governed and controlled by persons with disabilities. At least 51 percent of the members of each board of directors must have a disability, and each board must have a mix of people with and without a disability. ILRCs are non-profit and responsive to persons with all types of disabilities, including mobility, sensory, cognitive, emotional, psychiatric, and so forth. The IL philosophy believes that persons with disabilities are citizens with the right to participate in community life and advocates an alternative model of program delivery.

A 1997 CAILC study of the effects of the ILRCs found that they succeed, in large part, not simply because they provide an opportunity to learn skills, access information, or receive support, but because they do so in a way that is consistent with the independent living philosophy. The Association concluded that improvement in the quality of life for people with disabilities requires skill development as well as the removal of environmental, social, and economic barriers.

Individual empowerment was found to be a key benefit of this approach. It was particularly important in fostering competency in a variety of community living skills, as well as resulting in increased confidence and self-esteem. The Association found that individuals involved with some of the programs of the ILRC have knowledge of other IL programs as well and highly value the programs with which they are directly involved.

TABLE 12.2

Theories of Disability—Contrasting Approaches

	Rehabilitation Paradigm (Medical Model)	Independent Living Paradigm (Political Rights Model)
Definition of Problem	Physical impairment/lack of employment skills	Dependent on professionals, relatives, etc.
Locus of Problem	In the individual	In the environment and rehabilitation process
Solution to Problem	Professional intervention by physician, therapist, occupational therapist, vocational habilitation counsellor, etc.	Peer counselling, advocacy, self-help, consumer control, removal of barriers
Social Role	Patient/client	Citizen/consumer
Who Controls	Professional	Citizen/consumer
Desired Outcome	Maximize activities, living skills	Independent living

Source: Adapted from G. DeJong. 1978. *The Movement for Independent Living: Origins, Ideology, and Implications for Disability Research.* Boston: Tufts-New England Medical Center, Medical Rehabilitation Institute.

People First

"Persons with Disabilities"

In recent years, many debates have taken place in the fields of sociology, social work, political science, and disability studies with respect to the most appropriate term to be used when writing about or speaking about people who are disabled. While still used in everyday conversation, terms such as "defective," "retarded," "crippled," "lame," "handicapped," or "gimp" are now generally considered to be derogatory and certainly inappropriate.

Since the early 1980s, the term "*person with disabilities*" (or "people with disabilities") has come to be accepted as the most appropriate term to be used when referring to individuals who have disabilities. This new terminology was promoted by "people first" initiatives and the terms indicate that disability is one of many characteristics of the individual.

However, more recently, many disability rights advocates and disability theorists have challenged the "person first" conceptualizations of disability. Those who do so advocate for the replacement of the terms "people with disabilities" and "person with a disability" with the term "disabled person." The argument is that "person first" language tends to minimize and de-politicize disability rather than identify someone primarily by what differentiates them from the majority.

Both terms—"disabled people" and "people with disabilities"—are acceptable, providing the disadvantages of each term are properly acknowledged. But for the purposes of this book, the terms "people with disabilities" or "persons with disabilities" will mainly be used throughout.

The Stigma of Disability

In most Western industrialized societies, there is a growing cultural emphasis on the "body beautiful." Physical attractiveness, sexuality, and desirability have become a valued cultural norm. People with disabilities often do not meet cultural standards of physical attractiveness, and this contributes to the **stigma of disability**: that to have a disability is to be undesirable and unlovable. For the person with a disability, this has implications for developing friendships and intimate relationships, socializing, and recreational activities.

Stereotyping

It is widely believed that when people become disabled, or a loved one becomes disabled, individuals and family members go through a long period of grieving. There is a common expectation that people with disabilities should be in a continuous state of emotional distress and psychological suffering.

The social model of disability considers the disadvantages facing persons with disabilities to be caused by society, not the disability itself. Changes in society help remove those disadvantages.

A common **stereotype** is that people with disabilities are psychologically damaged in some way or other. This stems from the belief that there is an interconnection between the physical, mental, and emotional aspects of the human body. Therefore, it is theorized that if there is damage to one aspect of the system (physical disability) then there would be damage to the emotional and mental aspects as well. Of course, this is not necessarily the case.

Blaming the Victim

Sometimes the person with the disability is portrayed as deserving the disability—that is, a **blame the victim response**. Because of the influence of religious and cultural beliefs, some people believe that a disability is a consequence of sinful activities on the part of an individual or parent. An example might be a person who became disabled as a consequence of a particular lifestyle—there tends to be little public sympathy for adults who have disabling conditions because of drug use, prostitution, or through unprotected sex. Also, congenital disorders are often attributed to the risky or immoral actions or behaviours of mothers during pregnancy. There are also examples portraying persons with disabilities as evil people in folklore, literature, TV programs, and movies.

Many people without disabilities feel physically and psychologically uncomfortable when they are in the company of people with disabilities. Such fearful and negative reactions are often more common when there is a lack of exposure and a lack of contact between those without disabilities and people with disabilities. The presence of people with disabilities reminds some people that they too can, and likely will, become disabled. Such a fear may lead to avoidance, which contributes to the isolation of people with disabilities.

In Unison Report

In Unison: A Canadian Approach to Disability Issues (2000) marked the first time that Canada's federal, provincial, and territorial governments came together to express a common vision on disability issues (Social Union, 2000). This report provided Canadians with a broad view of how adults with disabilities have been faring in comparison with those without disabilities, using both statistical indicators and examples of personal experiences.

Examples of effective practices that have been implemented across Canada are also woven into the report. The situation of Aboriginal persons with disabilities is specifically highlighted.

Ableism

Many students of social work and related professions are familiar with terms such as racism, sexism, and heterosexism, but they may be unfamiliar with the term "ableism."

Ableism denotes the consequences of the belief in the superiority of people without disabilities over people with disabilities. The "PCS" model can be used to describe the essence of ableism:

- *Prejudice* towards disabled people at a personal level, which refers to revulsion, avoidance, infantilization, condescension, and other forms of prejudice.
- *Cultural norms*, which reflect a positive image of being without disability and a negative image of being disabled (people without disabilities are valued more than people with disabilities). Society's cultural norms stigmatize people with disabilities. People with disabilities are often the target of jokes and derogatory statements.
- *Social stratification and social division*, which focus on the manner in which people with disabilities are kept out of the mainstream. Social stratification and social division also explore ways in which people with disabilities are marginalized because of structural and attitudinal barriers.

Ableism

Discrimination and prejudice based on physical and mental ability towards people with disabilities, supporting the belief that people without disabilities are superior to people with disabilities.

Immigration and Disabilities

Canada's immigration laws make it difficult for people with disabilities to immigrate to Canada.

If it is determined that an individual is disabled, he or she may not be granted permission to immigrate here. And, if a landed immigrant or his or her family member is determined to be disabled, the individual as well as family could be deported.

Disability-Related Income Security Expenditures

Canada's disability income support system is based on a loosely knit set of programs. These programs have different eligibility criteria, guidelines, and procedures. Social and income security programs for disabled people are derived from private and public sources in the form of contributory or non-contributory benefits.

- **Publicly funded disability programs** are covered by federal, provincial, and municipal legislation. These programs include the Canada Pension Plan Disability Pension (a federal program), the Family Benefits plan (a provincial program), and the General Welfare Assistance plan (a municipal program in Ontario). These types of programs are funded through government taxation, and except for the Canada Pension Plan, do not require the financial contribution of recipients.
- **Privately funded disability programs** include programs that are provided through private insurance plans or through long-term disability plans as part of job benefits. These private income security programs are based on the amount of funding that the recipient has contributed directly to the plan or funding that has been contributed to a plan on behalf of the recipient.

Provincial Variations

While Canadians have a universal health care system, the benefits do not extend to providing full support for all people with disabilities. The primary similarity across the provinces is the range and types of supports and services provided. For example, provincial programs, whether in Newfoundland or British Columbia, will cover the cost of wheelchairs, canes, eyeglasses, walkers, attendant care services, home care, transportation, and so forth.

Each province has its own legislation and mechanisms for providing services to people with disabilities. The differences among the provinces are found in two areas. One is eligibility requirements; the other is the amount of funding for supports and services. As a consequence of this lack of universality, the care and treatment of persons with disabilities varies across the country. For example, some provinces, such as Newfoundland and Labrador, Prince Edward Island, Saskatchewan, and New Brunswick, have a single-tier program wherein supports and services are directly funded by the province to the individual in need. Others, such as Nova Scotia and Manitoba, have a two-tier system of support for people with disabilities—basically, the programs are funded through a system of General Welfare Assistance at the municipal and/or county level. The province provides the funding, and the money for supports and services is then transferred to the local government, which, in turn, funds the individual.

Gaining Access to Services

For people with a disability, the first step in gaining access to municipal or provincial programs, such as General Welfare Assistance or Family Benefits, is an eligibility determination carried out by a physician. The physician determines whether or not the applicant has a disability that seriously impedes his or her potential for employment. Once a person is deemed to be disabled, a Social Assistance review takes place.

First, there is an investigation of assets, which means that a person with a disability cannot have assets beyond a specific limit. Each province has its own types and levels of exemption. The next step in a Social Assistance review is a needs test. A needs test consists of three basic steps:

1. The applicant's basic requirements for living are identified (food, clothing, shelter, utilities, other household expenses, and personal allowances).
2. The applicant's available financial resources are determined.
3. The difference between total resources and total basic needs is calculated.

The amount of assistance will then be assessed according to a variety of factors, including size of family, degree of employability of the family's main decision maker, size and type of accommodation, and so on.

Employment Programs

There are eight major disability income systems in Canada.

- EI Sickness
- CPP Disability
- Veterans
- Private Plans
- Workers' Compensation
- Social Assistance
- Disability Tax Credits
- RDSP

Five of these are only available to persons who have engaged in regular salaried or wage-paid work: EI sickness, CPP-D, Workers' Compensation, Veterans' programs, and private plans (most often) do not provide benefits to people with irregular or contract employment.

(Stapleton, 2012)

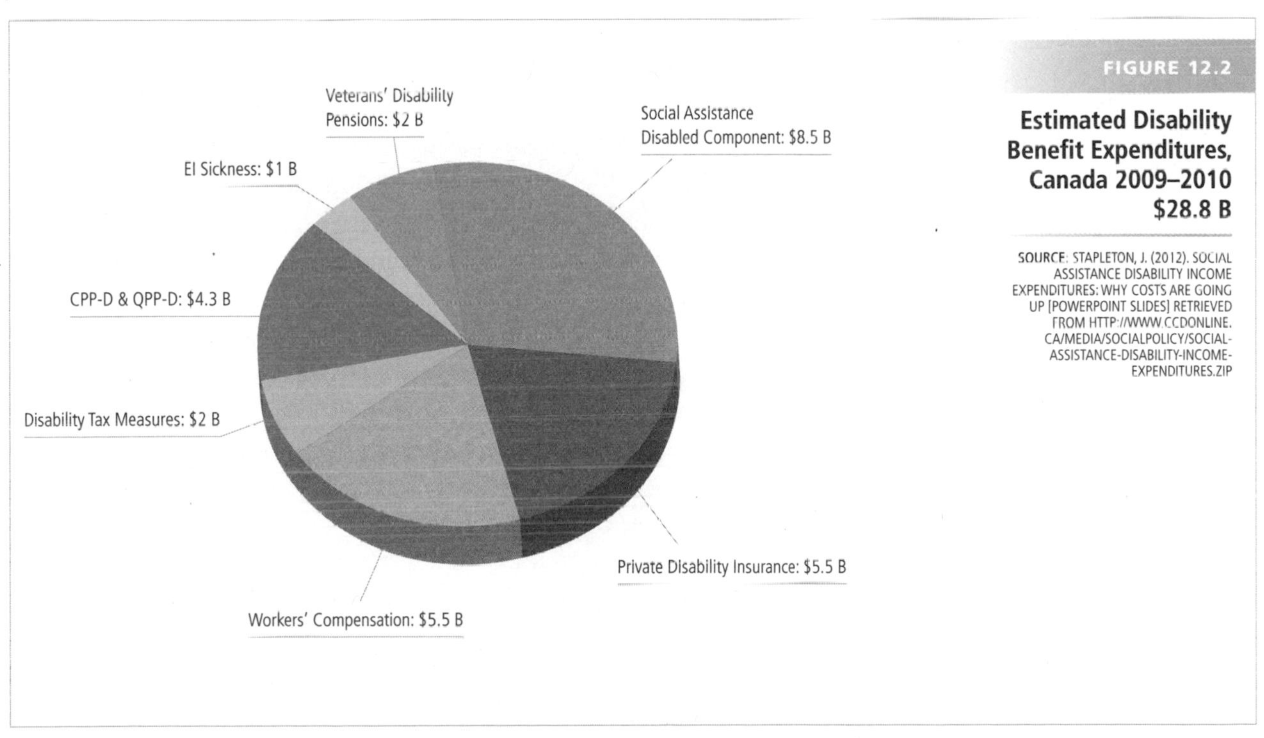

FIGURE 12.2

Estimated Disability Benefit Expenditures, Canada 2009–2010 $28.8 B

SOURCE: STAPLETON, J. (2012). SOCIAL ASSISTANCE DISABILITY INCOME EXPENDITURES: WHY COSTS ARE GOING UP [POWERPOINT SLIDES] RETRIEVED FROM HTTP://WWW.CCDONLINE.CA/MEDIA/SOCIALPOLICY/SOCIAL-ASSISTANCE-DISABILITY-INCOME-EXPENDITURES.ZIP

Federal Benefit Programs

Canada Pension Plan Disability (CPPD)
Employment Insurance (EI)
Disability Tax Credit (DTC)
Veterans Disability Pension

Federal Income Security Programs

Income security for persons with disabilities is complicated. Programs are provided by multiple layers of government, and the rules for eligibility are complicated and inconsistent. The primary program for people with labour force attachment is the Canada/Quebec Pension Plan or, if the disability was the result of a workplace accident or illness, Workers' Compensation.

Individuals who cannot participate, or are prevented from participating, in the labour force must rely on provincial Social Assistance programs that provide only minimal amounts. Disabled veterans are also eligible for a Veterans Pension. Medical expense deductions and tax credits are available through the tax system. Table 12.3 on the previous page outlines federal expenditures in various programs.

Canada Pension Plan Disability (CPPD) Benefit

The **Canada Pension Plan Disability (CPPD) Benefit** program is the largest long-term disability insurance program in Canada. The CPPD benefit caters to those with "severe and prolonged disabilities" who meet the CPP contribution requirements. The Canada Pension Plan (CPP) has been in effect since 1966 and is a national plan based on contributions from workers and employers. It is most commonly known as providing retirement pensions to workers in Canada, but it also provides survivor, death, and disability benefits to contributors and their families. Disability pensions are paid until a recipient reaches age 65, when benefits are converted to a retirement pension. Since these benefits were introduced in 1970, the CPP has seen increasing caseloads (Torjman, 2002). In 2010/11, people with disabilities received $4 billion in CPPD benefits.

In addition to having a "severe and prolonged disability," to qualify for the CPPD, you must be under 65, have earned a specified minimum amount, and contributed to the CPP while working for a minimum number of years (usually at least four of the last six years). The CPP defines "disability" as a physical and/or mental condition that is "severe and prolonged." "Severe" means that you have a mental or physical impairment that regularly makes you incapable of doing *any* type of work. This is different from most long-term disability insurance systems, which often base eligibility for benefits on incapacity to return to your former job. The CPP bases eligibility on the applicant's incapacity to do any paid work on a regular basis.

The CPPD benefit has important advantages over private insurance or most other income security programs. All working Canadians are covered by the program, including self-employed individuals who contribute. The program does not exclude people on the basis of medical history and does not charge higher premiums for contributors deemed to be high risk. Unlike many private insurance plans, the CPPD program also provides full inflation protection (Torjman, 2002).

Other Federal Supports

In addition to the CPP disability benefit, the federal government provides other income supports, such as Employment Insurance (EI) Sickness Benefits, the Disability Tax Credit (DTC), and the Veterans Disability Benefits.

- **Employment Insurance Sickness Benefits.** Intended as a temporary measure, Employment Insurance provides up to 15 weeks of benefits for people who cannot work due to short-term illness, injury, or quarantine. EI Sickness Benefits in 2010/11 was $4.2 billion (HRSDVC, 2011b).
- **Disability Tax Credit.** All Canadians with a severe and prolonged disability are eligible for the Disability Tax Credit. People that qualify claim a Disability Tax Credit on their income tax return but must have a treating physician complete a form outlining the nature of the disability. A court case (*Buchanan v. the Queen*) ruled that people with mental disabilities can qualify for the credit, and the decision was upheld in appeals. In 2010/11, $831 million in tax relief was granted.
- **Veterans Disability Benefits.** Veterans Affairs Canada administers the *Pension Act*, which provides a monthly disability pension designed to compensate veterans and their dependents. Veterans with disabilities directly related to peacetime service in the Canadian Forces are also eligible.

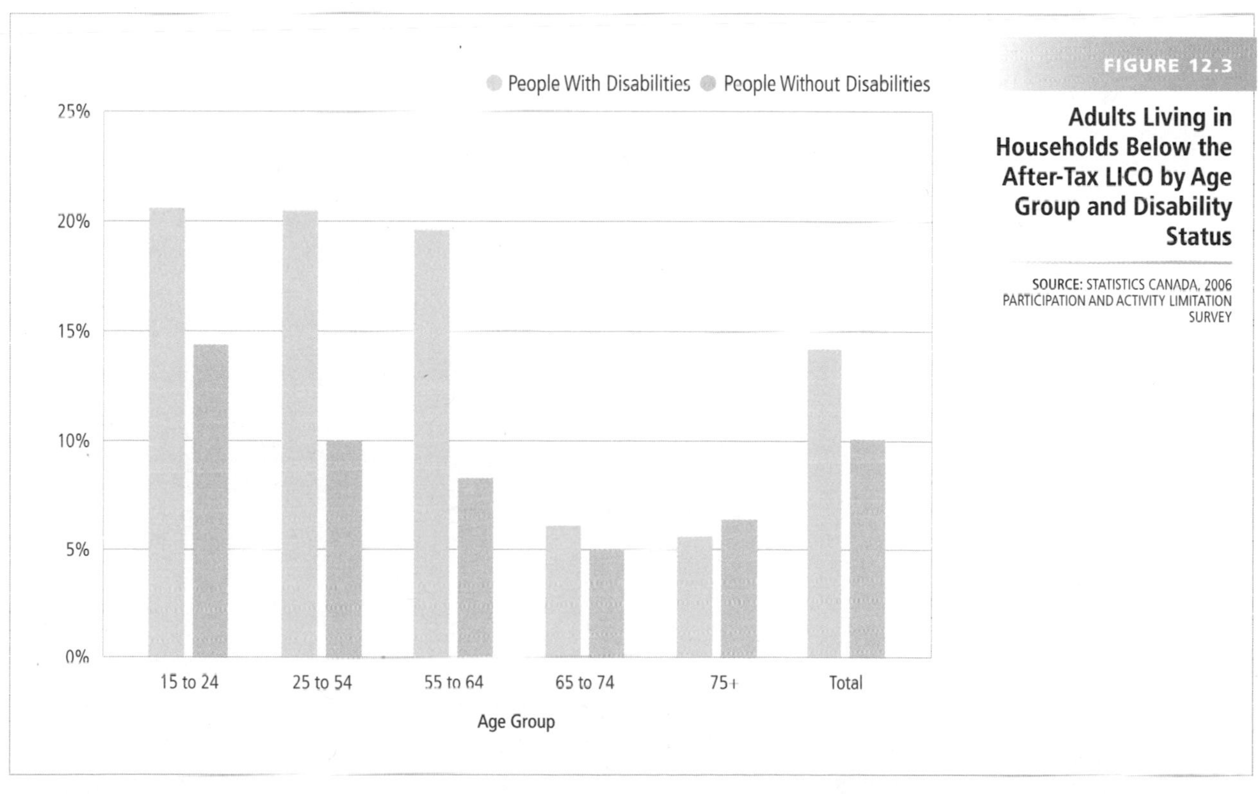

FIGURE 12.3

Adults Living in Households Below the After-Tax LICO by Age Group and Disability Status

SOURCE: STATISTICS CANADA, 2006 PARTICIPATION AND ACTIVITY LIMITATION SURVEY

Employment Programs

There are many Canadians with disabilities who are not currently employed but who nevertheless can and want to work. Through the Employment Insurance program, the federal government funds programs designed to assist people with disabilities to return to work even if they are otherwise ineligible for EI. For example, the **Opportunities Fund for Persons with Disabilities** is a $30-million-a-year employability program for people with disabilities who have had little or no attachment to the labour force.

Other initiatives include the **Labour Market Agreements for Persons with Disabilities (LMAPD)**. This is a multilateral agreement created in 2003 between the provinces and the federal government, replacing the 1998 Employability Assistance for People with Disabilities initiative. Under the agreement, the federal government provides funding to the provinces to help improve the employability of persons with disabilities. The provinces use the agreement to fund various programs such as job coaching and mentoring; pre-employment training and skills upgrading; employment counselling and assessment; and accessible job placement networks as well as post-secondary education; assistive aids and devices; wage subsidies and earning supplements; and supports for self-employment.

To help the employment situation for persons with disabilities, the federal government provides $218 million each year (HRDSC, 2011).

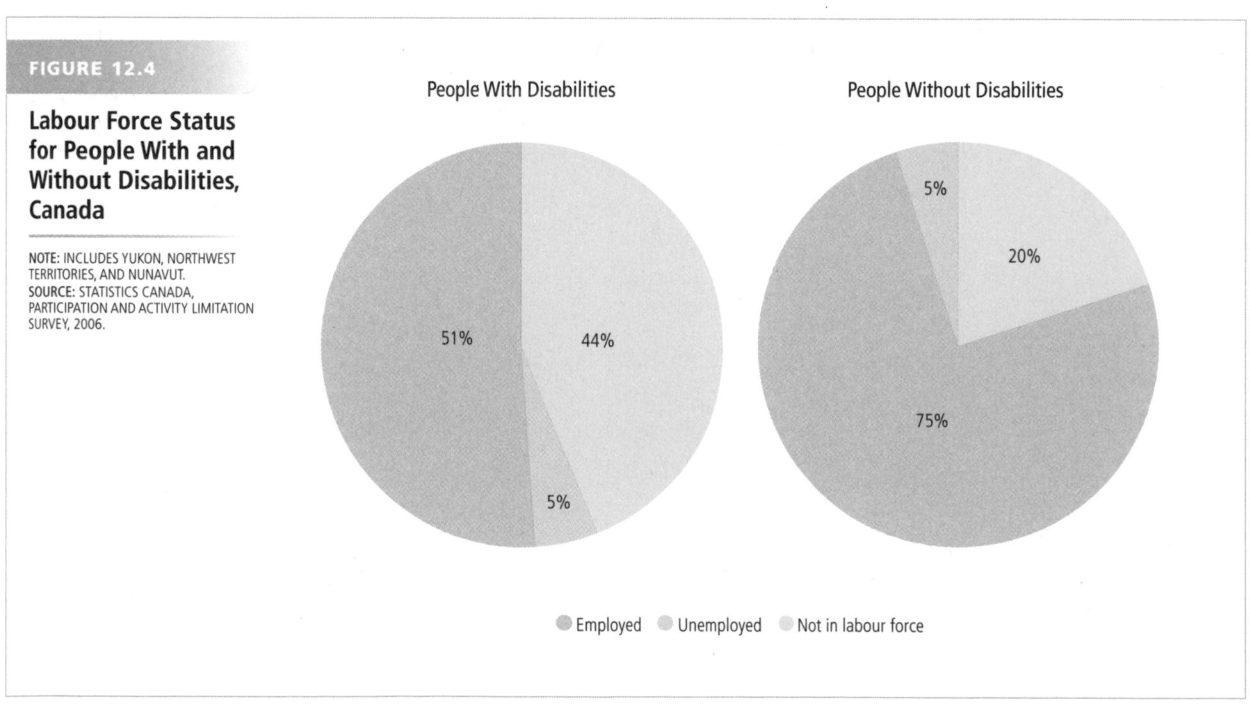

FIGURE 12.4

Labour Force Status for People With and Without Disabilities, Canada

NOTE: INCLUDES YUKON, NORTHWEST TERRITORIES, AND NUNAVUT.
SOURCE: STATISTICS CANADA, PARTICIPATION AND ACTIVITY LIMITATION SURVEY, 2006.

Workplace Accommodations

The *Canadian Human Rights Act* also ensures the right to accommodation in the workplace for people with disabilities. Beyond the legislative necessity of accommodation, ensuring access to the labour market for people with disabilities will also help alleviate an impending labour shortage caused by an aging population; making minor changes to the workplace can increase the supply of workers with individuals who would not otherwise be able to participate.

There are two million Canadians aged 15–64 with disabilities, and about 45 percent of these are in the labour force. Of those who are employed, about 35 percent have no perceived workplace limitation; the others required some kind of workplace accommodation in order for them to perform their duties at work (Williams, 2006, p. 23).

There are numerous types of workplace accommodations, and needs will be different for each individual in each context. Accommodation needs can be categorized as either job modifications or workplace modifications.

- **Job modifications** refer to the personal help that workers need to participate in the labour market.
- **Workplace modifications** are changes in the workplace environment.

Examples of job modifications could include human supports such as readers, sign language interpreters, and job coaches; technical aids such as voice synthesizers and portable note-takers; computers with Braille; communication aids; and job redesign. Workplace modifications are changes in the workplace environment.

Fifteen percent of employed people with disabilities report that they need a "modified work structure" such as handrails, ramps, accessible parking, accessible elevators, modified workstations, accessible washrooms, or accessible transportation. The highest unmet work structure need is accessible transportation; this need goes unmet 26 percent of the time. Other unmet needs are: 20 percent require handrails, ramps, accessible parking, accessible elevators, or accessible workstations, and 12 percent require accessible washrooms (CCSD, 2005).

Job redesign refers to an adjustment or modification of duties in relation to one's work. According to the Canadian Council on Social Development (CCSD), about 30 percent of persons with disabilities who are employed require a work aid or job modification. Modified work hours and job redesign are the most common types of job modification, with 19 percent requiring an adjustment in work hours and 17 percent requiring job redesign. The CCSD also reports that 29 percent of employed people with disabilities have an unmet need for "other" unspecified work aids and 27 percent for technical aids (CCSD, 2005).

Discrimination in the Workplace

According to HRSDC, more than one in five people report that they have been the victim of discrimination when trying to obtain and maintain employment. Almost 80 percent of Canadians agree that equally qualified persons with disabilities are less likely to be hired for jobs, and more than 50 percent of Canadians state that they would hide a non-visible disability from their employers (SDC, 2004, pp. 28–29).

Annual Disability Support Income as a Percentage of LICOs

Newfoundland and Labrador, 54%
Prince Edward Island, 45%
Nova Scotia, 50%
New Brunswick, 45%
Quebec, 48%
Ontario, 58%
Manitoba, 41%
Saskatchewan, 50%
Alberta, 38%
British Columbia, 51%
NWT, N/A
Nunavut, N/A
(National Council of Welfare, 2006)

Provincial Disability Programs

Individuals who do not qualify for any other public or private income security programs are left with provincially delivered Social Assistance programs. As noted earlier, these programs differ in each province and territory. The programs provide minimum income to those who pass a needs test and meet strict disability eligibility criteria. Both the benefit rates and the criteria are different in each province or territory, as indicated in Table 12.3.

Canadians with disabilities access these programs only when all other public and private means of support are exhausted. To qualify for benefits, persons with disabilities must liquidate their assets if they are over a certain value. The assets that persons with disabilities are allowed to keep while collecting benefits varies widely across Canada. The National Council of Welfare believes that having such asset limitations is bad public policy because it doesn't allow households to maintain a cushion against unforeseen emergencies. This may be even more crucial for persons with disabilities, as they may face extra financial needs, such as assistive devices or accessibility needs.

Each of Canada's 10 provinces and three territories designs, administers, and delivers its own disability income support program. In their review of welfare incomes, the National Council of Welfare (2010) outlines eligibility criteria and benefit amounts for each province and territory and compares these amounts with LICO. With a few exceptions, the annual support for a single individual is less than 50 percent of LICO, with Alberta having the lowest benefit amount.

Below are some examples of provincial programs.

- **ONTARIO DISABILITY SUPPORT PROGRAM (ODSP).** The ODSP is designed to meet the unique needs of people with disabilities who are in financial need or who want and are able to work and need support. Applicants must prove they qualify by obtaining a health status report from a registered health professional, and they must undergo a needs test. Some believe that the difference between regular welfare payments and disability payments has its origins in the Elizabethan Poor Law concepts of the deserving and undeserving poor (see Chapter 2).
- **MANITOBA INCOME ASSISTANCE FOR PERSONS WITH DISABILITIES PROGRAM.** Manitoba's Income Assistance for Persons with Disabilities Program provides financial assistance for adults enrolled in the Employment and Income Assistance program, and it also provides employment assistance. The purpose of the program is to support the additional costs associated with living in the community. The program also provides for such things as transportation passes for wheelchair users, a telephone rental allowance, a laundry allowance, and additional assistance to support employment (child care, transportation, clothing).

- **ALBERTA ASSURED INCOME FOR THE SEVERELY HANDICAPPED (AISH).** Alberta's AISH program is for adults with permanent disabilities that diminish their ability to participate in the workforce. The level of benefits depends on income and assets. There is a maximum living allowance, and additional benefits (personal income support benefits) may be provided to meet clients' special needs. The personal income support benefits can be used for such continuous costs as child care, special diets, and guide dogs, as well as one-time costs ranging from emergencies to children's school supplies. The health benefits include eye care, dental, and prescriptions; if individuals no longer qualify for AISH due to increased income, they may still qualify for the health benefits.
- **BRITISH COLUMBIA EMPLOYMENT AND ASSISTANCE FOR PERSONS WITH DISABILITIES PROGRAM (EAPD).** The Government of British Columbia has redesigned its income assistance programs. The new system, while focusing on employment for those clients who are able to work, ensures that assistance is there for persons with disabilities. This program provides qualifying persons with disabilities a higher income assistance rate, supplementary assistance, and specialized employment supports. Currently, persons with disabilities receive the highest rate of assistance available in British Columbia and the third-highest among Canadian provinces.

TABLE 12.3

Welfare Incomes for Single Person With a Disability

	Basic Social Assistance	Other P/T* Benefits	GST Credit	Other P/T* Tax Credits	2009 Total Income
Newfoundland and Labrador (NL)	$8,085	$2,700	$298	$40	$11,123
Prince Edward Island (PE)	$8,812	-	$255	-	$9,067
Nova Scotia (NS)	$8,934	-	$263	-	$9,197
New Brunswick (NB)	$7,416	$1,000	$249	-	$8,665
Quebec (QC)	$10,595	-	$286	-	$10,881
Ontario (ON)	$12,284	-	$324	$297	$12,905
Manitoba (MB)	$7,397	$1,770	$256	-	$9,423
Saskatchewan (SK)	$9,567	$840	$277	$219	$10,902
Alberta (AB-IS)	$8,244	$936	$253	-	$9,433
Alberta (AB-AISH)	$13,956	-	$341	-	$14,297
British Columbia (BC)	$10,877	$35	$303	$178	$11,392
Yukon (YK)	$14,873	$3,155	$374	-	$18,402
Northwest Territories (NT)	$17,100	$4,044	$374	-	$21,518
Nunavut (NU)	$43,592	$2,100	$374	-	$46,066

* Provincial/Territorial. **Source:** Welfare Incomes 2009, National Council of Welfare, 2010, Reproduced with the permission of the Minister of Public Works and Government Services Canada, 2013

The Disability Tax Credit

Buchanan v. The Queen

In 2006, the **Disability Tax Credit** system was revised as a result of *James W. Buchanan v. the Queen* in 2000, which determined that individuals who have mood disorders that significantly interfere with their daily activities were eligible for the Disability Tax Credit.

The *Income Tax Act* provides a credit to individuals who have a "severe and prolonged mental or physical impairment." The act requires that "the effects of the impairment are such that the individual's ability to perform a basic activity of daily living is markedly restricted." There are six basic activities defined in the act: perceiving, thinking, and remembering; feeding and dressing oneself; speaking; hearing; bowel or bladder functions; and walking. To qualify for the Disability Tax Credit, a treating physician has to complete a form, responding to questions concerning these criteria.

Mr. Buchanan was diagnosed with bipolar affective disorder and had been exhibiting symptoms of the disease for decades—while he often exhibited coping skills and above average intelligence, evidence given at court described his delusional behaviour. However, after qualifying for the credit for several years, Mr. Buchanan's doctor did not believe that he met the conditions of the tax credit and completed the tax form such that the credit would be denied. The Buchanans took the case to tax court, with Mrs. Lembi Buchanan, having power of attorney, appearing on her husband's behalf.

The physician argued that Mr. Buchanan was not impaired in the basic activities of life and asserted that, in his opinion, most patients with mood disorders don't qualify for the credit "which is intended for persons so severely disabled that they have difficulties with very basic self-care activities."

The judge in the case decided that the doctor was not offering an unbiased medical opinion when completing the tax forms for his psychiatric patients and was misinterpreting the law with his own preconceived notions of who should qualify. In her judgment, the judge explained that the doctor misinterpreted the law and misinterpreted his responsibility in determining eligibility: "He clearly did not understand that the six items defining a basic activity of daily living, as contained in subsection 118.4(1)(c) are not to be read together, but each activity is treated separately."

Evidence presented to court outlining his mood swings and delusional behaviour made it very clear that Mr. Buchanan did indeed meet the criteria of being markedly restricted in his perceiving, thinking, and remembering.

Before the judge's decision, Lembi Buchanan also submitted a brief to the Sub-Committee on the Status of Persons with Disabilities regarding her husband's situation. The overall result of this case was a recognition that individuals with mental disorders do have long-term disabilities requiring some form of life management and are therefore eligible for the Disability Tax Credit.

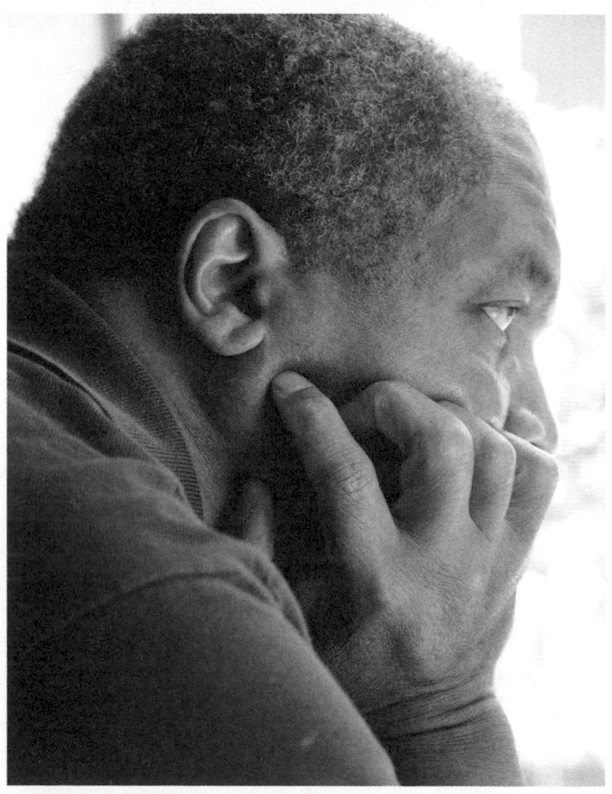

Conclusion

Disability can happen to anyone, often quite unexpectedly. The latest data suggest that 16.5 percent of Canadian have a disability. The kinds of disabilities and their severity varies enormously, which raises obvious problems in relation to social programming. But the absolute numbers of Canadians who are disabled is reason enough for policy-makers to take it seriously.

Before the program was terminated prior to the 2011 census, the Participation and Limitations Survey provided data around which serious social policies could be created for Canadians with disabilities. Researchers, policy-makers, and practitioners knew, and could track, the extent and the kind of disabilities, and the needs arising from them. That work now will be seriously hampered going forward.

The various income support programs for disabled Canadians are part of the provincial welfare or Social Assistance systems across the country. They provide extremely low benefits rates, often well below LICO. Like income assistance generally, the criteria for receiving disability benefits is strict. To receive income support as a disabled person, one must qualify (that is, document the disability and not have other means of support). If you have a disability in Canada and require income support, you can live comfortably if you are eligible for C/QPP, Workers' Compensation, or private disability insurance. Otherwise you are left with little access to income.

While great gains have been made in this area for disabled Canadians, there is still a long way to go. More and more, through the efforts of disabled persons themselves and their organizations, a new "social" model" is raising awareness about barriers that prevent the full participation of people with disabilities. This more inclusive approach, perhaps best exemplified in the Independent Living Movement, replaces medical approaches, which treated all disabilities as an illness of some kind, either to be treated with medication or shut away out of sight.

Most people with disabilities want only the same opportunities to participate as other Canadians. This involves removing barriers that exist within infrastructure, attitudes, and job design in order to achieve this goal. In the end, it is a matter of treating persons with disabilities with dignity and respect, and not discounting or preventing their potential contributions to society.

United Nations Enable

www.un.org/disabilities/
This is the website of the Secretariat for the Convention on the Rights of Persons with Disabilities, the motto for which is "full participation and equality."

CHAPTER 12 REVIEW

LEARNING OBJECTIVES

After completing this chapter, you should be able to:

- Describe the various types of disabilities and the distribution of disabilities by age group.
- Provide an overview of the history of services for people with disabilities.
- Describe the main approaches to understanding disability.
- Explain the importance of the Independent Living Movement.
- Describe the various ways in which people with disabilities are stigmatized and stereotyped.
- Explain the various disability-related income security expenditures and programs.
- Explain the various employment programs that are available for disabled persons.
- Describe some of the provincial programs available for persons with a disability.

KEY CONCEPTS IN CHAPTER

- Ableism
- Blame the victim response
- Canada Pension Plan Disability (CPPD) Benefit
- Disability
- Disability Tax Credit
- Employment Insurance Sickness Benefits
- Independent Living Movement (ILM)
- Institutionalization of people with disabilities
- Job modifications
- Job redesign
- Labour Market Agreements for Persons with Disabilities (LMAPD)
- Medical model (personal tragedy theory)
- Opportunities Fund for Persons with Disabilities
- Participation and Activity Limitation Survey (PALS)
- Persons with disabilities
- Privately funded disability programs
- Publicly funded disability programs
- Psychological disabilities
- Political rights model (social oppression theory)
- Rehabilitation services
- Stereotype
- Stigma of disability
- Veterans disability benefits
- Workplace modifications

REVIEW QUESTIONS

1. Disability refers to a range of impairments. What are some of the difficulties or impairments included under the term disability?
2. What are psychological disabilities, and how widespread are they?
3. How has our conception of disability changed since the mid-nineteenth century, and what have been the implications for social policy?
4. What are the "medical" and "social" models of disability? Compare.
5. What is the employment situation of people with disabilities, and how can employment opportunities be increased?

EXPLORING SOCIAL WELFARE

1. Go to the Canada Benefits website (www.canadabenefits.gc.ca) and look up the benefits for persons with disabilities in your region. How do the benefits in your province or territory stack up against other provinces? Consider the cost of living. How would a person with disabilities fare in your area if he or she were unable to work? Worked in a low-income job? Worked in a middle-income job?
2. Major depression can cause significant disruptions in people's lives, both financially and personally. When one compares Statistics Canada prevalence data on psychological disabilities with other research on "mental illness," it appears that major depression may be unreported. Analyze this disability, including the prevalence, types, causes, and potential treatments, by visiting the websites of the Canadian Mental Health Association (www.cmha.ca), the Mood Disorders Society of Canada (www.mooddisorderscanada.ca), and The Public Health Agency of Canada's *Report on Mental Illnesses in Canada* (www.phac-aspc.gc.ca/publicat/miic-mmac/index.html).

CRITICAL THINKING

It is only recently that persons with disabilities have begun to find a place in Canadian society. What combination of factors do you think brought this awareness about?

Think of your own personal experiences. Do you or any of your friends or family members have a disabilities? What particular social policies could be introduced that would help out?

WEBSITES

Independent Living Canada
www.ilcanada.ca
Founded in 1986 by the Independent Living Movement, Independent Living Canada is the national umbrella organization, representing an coordinating the network of Independent Living (IL) Centres at the national level.

Council of Canadians with Disabilities (CCD)
www.ccdonline.ca
CCD is a national human rights organization of people with disabilities working for an inclusive and accessible Canada. The CCD seeks to achieve its priorities through law reform, litigation, public education and dialogue with key decision-makers.

Disabled Women's Network Ontario
http://dawn.thot.net
DAWN Ontario (DisAbled Women's Network Ontario) is a progressive, feminist, and cross-disability organization dedicated to social and economic justice. The network is active in many areas of social welfare advocacy.

The Elderly and Retired

Pensions, Healthcare, and Income Security

Income security for the retired and elderly in Canada expanded rapidly throughout the 1950s and 1960s, a development which led to a large reduction in old-age poverty. However, over the coming 35 years, the percentage of persons over age 65 will double, which will place a heavy strain on the welfare of elderly Canadians. In particular, there remains the challenge of combatting old-age poverty for elderly women, for elderly people with disabilities, and for elderly Aboriginal people.

This chapter looks at the various income security programs that are currently in place for old age and retirement with a view to maintaining the best features of the current system and improving it for the challenging years that lie ahead.

"Old age pensions have been a recurring issue in Canadian politics since the beginning of the twentieth century and now have more government resources devoted to them than to any other single public program."

— KENNETH BRYDEN, AUTHOR OF *OLD AGE PENSIONS AND POLICY-MAKING IN CANADA*

Income Security for the Elderly

The median age in Canada today is 39.9 years. In 1941, it was 26.2 years. By the year 2031, 20 percent of Canada's population—one in five—will be seniors. What are the needs of these older Canadians? How will they be taken care of? What are their income security needs?

Components of the System

Canada's income security system for the elderly and retired consists of three main "pillars:"

- *Basic minimum income security allowances*, such as Old Age Security (OAS), Guaranteed Income Supplement (GIS), and Spouse's Allowance (SPA);
- *Social insurance benefits,* such as the Canada/Quebec Pension Plan; and
- *Private pensions and publicly regulated private savings plans,* such as Registered Retirement Savings Plans (RRSPs).

These programs have been significant in lowering poverty rates for the elderly and retired in the post-World War II period. The percent of elderly living in poverty fell from 36.9 percent in 1976 to 12.3 percent in 2010 (Conference Board of Canada, 2013b). Economics professor Lars Osberg at Dalhousie University in Halifax has referred to this massive income security shift as "a major success story of Canadian social policy in the twentieth century" (Osberg, 2001).

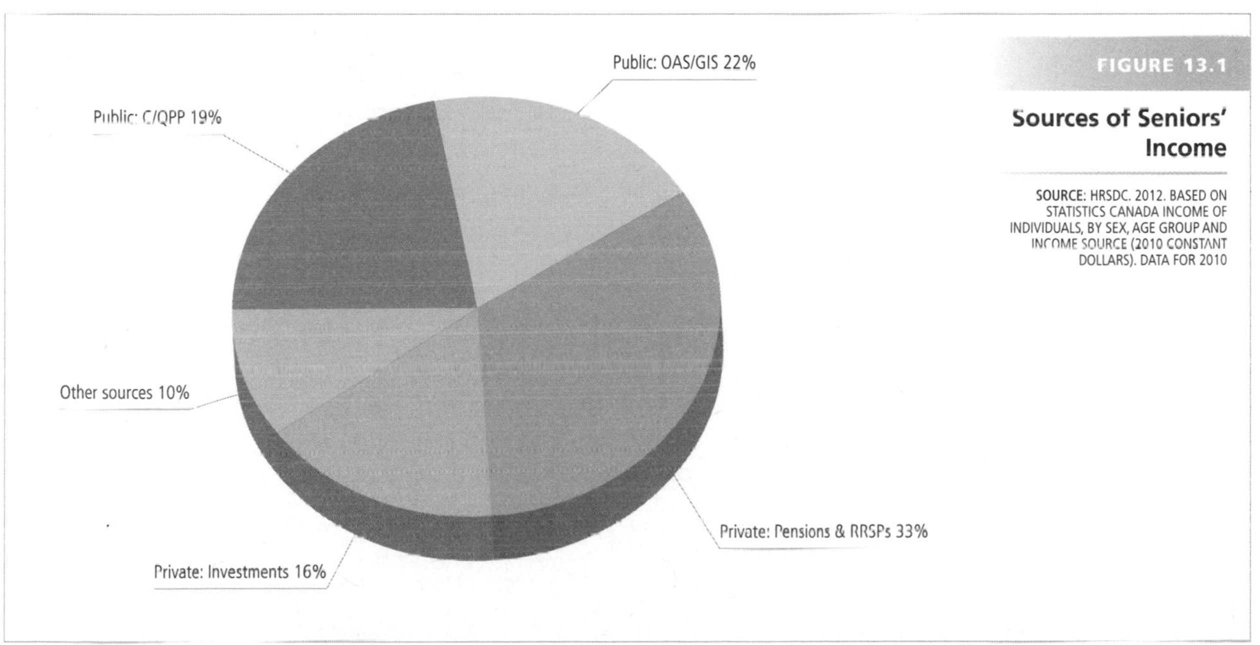

FIGURE 13.1

Sources of Seniors' Income

SOURCE: HRSDC. 2012. BASED ON STATISTICS CANADA INCOME OF INDIVIDUALS, BY SEX, AGE GROUP AND INCOME SOURCE (2010 CONSTANT DOLLARS). DATA FOR 2010

The Challenge of Aging Populations

Around the world, headlines are warning that when the "baby boom" generation starts retiring in earnest, the labour force will shrink and economic growth and material well-being will be threatened. To limit the impact, some policy analysts believe that innovative policies are needed to allow people to spread work across the full span of their lives—people can increase their leisure time in their early years and spend more time working and learning in their later years.

Canada's Seniors—Health, Finance, and Family

The latest census data (2011) put the proportion of seniors as the highest on record. Moreover, the over-65 population has actually surged by 14.1 percent since the last census—more than double the 5.9 percent increase in the population as a whole (Statistics Canada, 2012). A number of social changes have affected the composition of the retired population in Canada. These include:

- Improvement in health care and extension of life expectancy
- Long-term decline in the birth rate
- Establishment of the retirement age

These social changes have important implications for Canada's income security system. By 2030, for each person receiving income security benefits, there will only be three working Canadians to support these benefits, compared to the five of today. As the proportion of retired Canadians receiving benefits keeps increasing, economic expenditures will continue to rise steadily.

Universal Healthcare, Birth Rates, and Retirement

The first factor has been technological improvement in health care and the effect of universal health care in Canada, which has resulted in a significant extension of life expectancy. In 2011, life expectancy for Canadians was 79 years for men and 83 years for women. Life expectancy is expected to continue to grow, although more slowly, reaching 81 for men and 86 for women in 2041.

The second is the long-term decline in the birth rate. In 2001, Canada's fertility rate reached a record low at 1,512 births per 1,000 women aged 15 to 49. It now stands at less than half of the peak reached in 1959, when there were 3,935 births per 1,000 women. The 2012 fertility rate of 1.67 children per woman is expected to remain relatively constant in the near future. Combined with the extension of life expectancy, this has resulted in an increase in the proportion, or the relative size, of the older population, and these trends are expected to continue for several decades.

Third, a retirement age to leave the labour force was established in the age of industrialization. Initially, it was set at 70 years of age, and now it is set at 65. The concept of retiring from paid employment at an elderly age came about because people eventually reach an age when their level of productivity does not sufficiently maintain the demand for their labour. Whereas previously, with extended families, the elderly relied on their families for support, industrialization also changed the traditional nature of the family. There is also a widespread belief that older workers should make way for the younger generation of more productive workers, although this perception has changed somewhat in recent years as more and more people reach age 65 and, for personal or income-related reasons, continue to work past normal retirement.

Sources of Seniors' Income

Today, Canadian seniors, men and women, draw their income for retirement from multiple sources. Indeed, access to multiple sources of retirement income—public, private, and employment—has become critical for many seniors today.

According to Human Resources Skills Development Canada, in terms of public pensions, almost all seniors (96 percent) received Old Age Security (OAS) benefits and 90 percent of seniors had Canada or Quebec Pension Plan benefits (C/QPP) in 2010. In total, almost 4.2 million seniors received C/QPP pensions, and almost 4.4 million seniors had OAS pensions. In terms of private sources of income, a majority of Canadian seniors received income from investments (53 percent) and from private pensions and RRSPs (62 percent) in 2010. One-fifth of seniors (21 percent) also had earnings from employment (HRSDC, 2013).

Over the last 34 years, HRSDC reports that the proportion of Canadian seniors with private pensions, RRSPs, or C/QPP benefits has grown significantly. The proportion with income from private pensions and RRSPs more than doubled between 1976 and 2010 from 24 percent to 62 percent. Likewise, the proportion of Canadian seniors with C/QPP benefits increased from 35 percent to 90 percent during the same time period. Although they should not be taken for granted, such positive developments undoubtedly account for the greater levels of income security enjoyed by Canadian seniors today.

Seniors Canada On-line

www.seniors.gc.ca

This federal government web resource provides access to information and services that are relevant to seniors, their families, caregivers, and supporting service organizations.

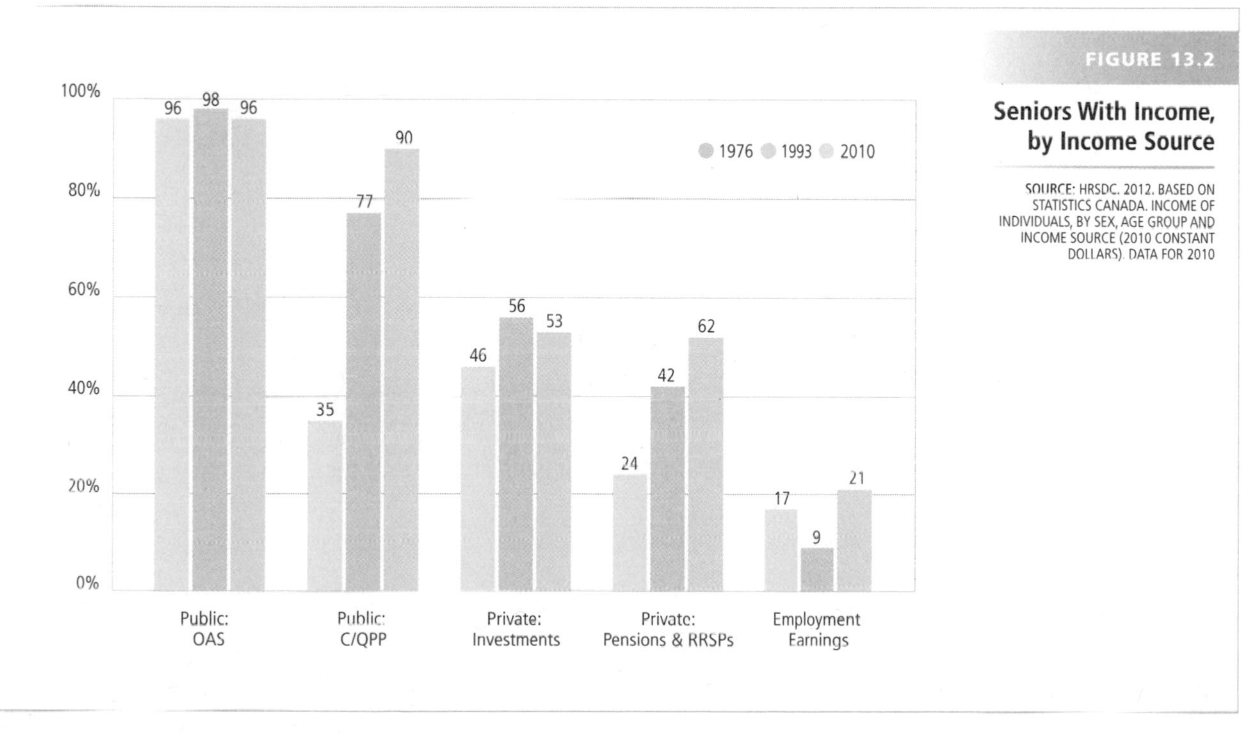

FIGURE 13.2

Seniors With Income, by Income Source

SOURCE: HRSDC. 2012. BASED ON STATISTICS CANADA. INCOME OF INDIVIDUALS, BY SEX, AGE GROUP AND INCOME SOURCE (2010 CONSTANT DOLLARS). DATA FOR 2010

Elderly Poverty Rates—Worrying Signs

As noted, elderly poverty rates in Canada declined noticeably in the last half of the twentieth century. Low-income rates for Canadian seniors are now among the lowest in all countries studied by the Organisation for Economic Co-operation and Development.

The pronounced decrease in Canada's elderly poverty rate can largely been attributed to the implementation of the C/QPP in 1966. Pensions as a proportion of disposable income among Canada's elderly more than doubled between 1980 and 1996, from 21 to 46 percent. The first cohort to receive full public pensions turned 65 in 1976. The generation that followed also became the first beneficiaries of private occupational pensions that were significantly expanded between the 1950s and 1970s.

Canada's system also offers a guaranteed income in the form of OAS, regardless of past participation in the labour force. The OAS has ensured a decent standard of living for our seniors, especially those most in need.

More Recent Concerns

However, after 20 years of dramatic reductions, Canada's elderly poverty rate has been rising since the mid-1990s. The biggest increase occurred in the group of elderly women. Between 2006 and 2009, nearly 128,000 more seniors were said to be living in low income, 70 percent of whom were women (Conference Board of Canada, 2013a).

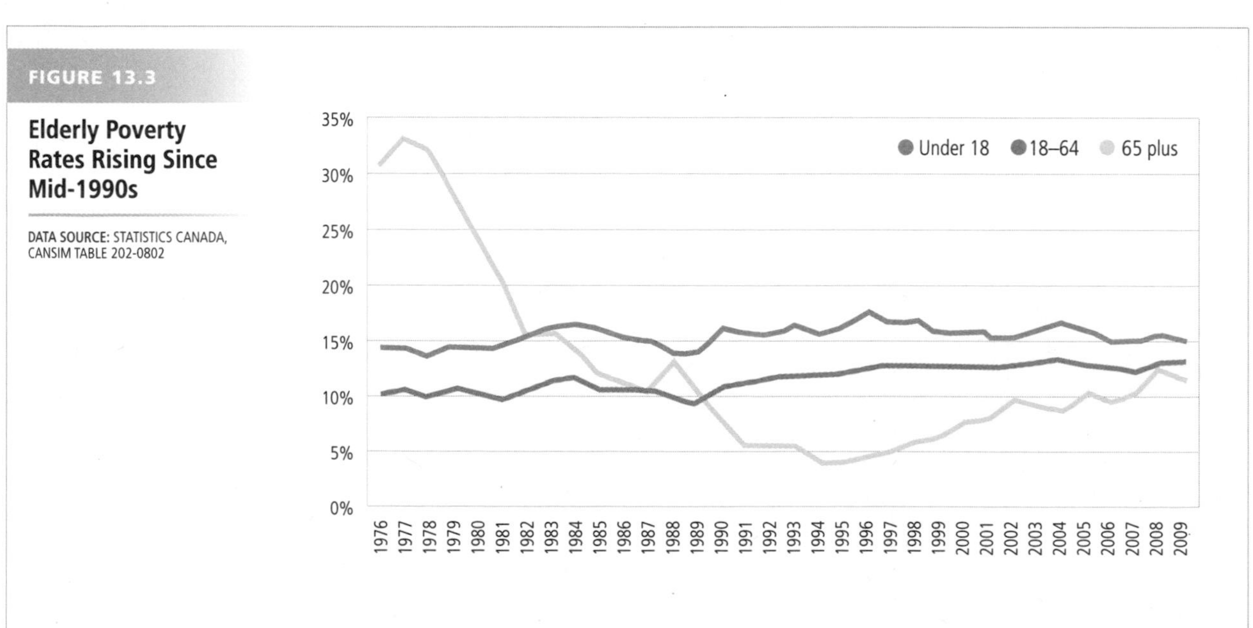

FIGURE 13.3

Elderly Poverty Rates Rising Since Mid-1990s

DATA SOURCE: STATISTICS CANADA, CANSIM TABLE 202-0802

Number of Seniors Living in Poverty Soars Nearly 25%

Joe Friesen—Demographics Reporter

The number of seniors living in poverty spiked at the beginning of the financial meltdown, reversing a decades-long trend and threatening one of Canada's most important social policy successes.

The number of seniors living below the low-income cutoff, Statistics Canada's basic measure of poverty, jumped nearly 25 percent between 2007 and 2008, to 250,000 from 204,000, according to figures released on Wednesday by Campaign 2000. It's the largest increase among any group, and as the first cohort of baby boomers turns 65 next year, could place increased pressure on families supporting elderly parents.

Economists say women make up as much as 80 percent of the increase in seniors poverty. Armine Yalnizyan, economist at the Canadian Centre for Policy Alternatives, said more women than men were living close to the poverty threshold before the financial crisis took hold in 2008, and, because their retirement savings tend to be smaller, were more likely to slip below the low-income cutoff. Men over 65 are also twice as likely as women over 65 to have a job. By January, 2009, there were 23,000 fewer women over 65 working than there were seven months earlier, while the number for men changed very little, Ms. Yalnizyan said.

"My guess is that the majority of women [who are still] working over 65 are not carrying on with their career, but trying to have a little more comfort in their lives. They were probably never too far above the poverty line, whatever line you pick. When those jobs are gone, more of them are struggling to make ends meet," Ms. Yalnizyan said.

The rise in poverty among seniors poses particular problems for their adult children, who will be expected to bridge financial gaps for their parents while supporting their own families. This so-called "sandwich generation" is often caught with the twin pressures of having children in higher education and parents requiring additional care for failing health, according to Laurel Rothman, coordinator of the Campaign 2000 report card on child and family poverty.

She said the trend is particularly hard on new Canadians who have sponsored their parents to join them in Canada. Many of those parents have been able to work for only a few years in Canada before retirement, and so receive very little in Canadian pensions.

"In Montreal, Toronto and Vancouver, ethno-racial newcomers are particularly a concern," Ms. Rothman said. "We see it all the time at Family Service Toronto, people who come here that are sponsored [by their family members]. It may be someone who puts in five or 10 years of work [in Canada] but they don't get full Canada Pension Plan. ... And their cost of living has gone up."

The jump in poverty among seniors is unusual because Canada's success in tackling this issue has been cited as perhaps its single most successful policy intervention. According to figures cited in a 2009 Conference Board report, Canada's rate of seniors poverty was as high as 36.9 percent in 1971. The government, in an effort to tackle the problem, had a few years earlier introduced the Guaranteed Income Supplement and the Canada Pension Plan. By 2007, the rate of poverty among seniors had plummeted to 4.9 percent, before rising to 5.8 percent in 2008.

The Canadian data are at odds with what's happened in the United States, where the poverty rate of 9.7 percent among seniors did not change between 2007 and 2008, despite the financial collapse. Ms. Yalnizyan said that could be explained by the time lag between the beginning of the economic upheaval in the United States and its eventual impact on Canada.

The Campaign 2000 report also says 9.1 percent of Canadian children were living in poverty in 2008, down slightly from the year before, but nowhere near the goal of eliminating child poverty set by Parliament in 1989.

SOURCE: FRIESEN, JOE (NOVEMBER 24, 2010). "NUMBER OF SENIORS LIVING IN POVERTY SOARS NEARLY 25%" THE GLOBE AND MAIL.

The Income Security of Older Women

In 2011, women comprised 56 percent of the 65-plus populations, and their proportion increases with age (Urquijo & Milan, 2011). Unfortunately, many of these elderly and retired women now find themselves living with insufficient income. There are a number of reasons for this:

- Women have tended to work in lower paying occupations and sectors, and more women work part-time or have had their careers disrupted for family reasons than men.
- Many women are unattached or single in old age: approximately 30 percent of Canadian women are widowed at age 65 and 50 percent by age 75. In 2010, 15.6 percent of unattached women aged 65 or over were living below the Canadian government's LICO (Statistics Canada, 2011).
- Fewer women are covered by their employer's pension plans than men, and as a result, a higher percentage of income for women aged 65 and over comes from government transfers.

Certainly, the current economic downturn has not helped matters for senior men and women. Unexpected downsizing, enforced involuntary retirement, and the growth in the lower-wage service sector (where many women work) lead to fewer benefits and pension coverage. This is especially the case for many older Canadian women as they approach their retirement years.

FIGURE 13.4

Seniors With Income, by Gender and Income Source

SOURCE: HRSDC. 2012. STATISTICS CANADA. INCOME OF INDIVIDUALS, BY SEX, AGE GROUP AND INCOME SOURCE (2010 CONSTANT DOLLARS). DATA FOR 2010

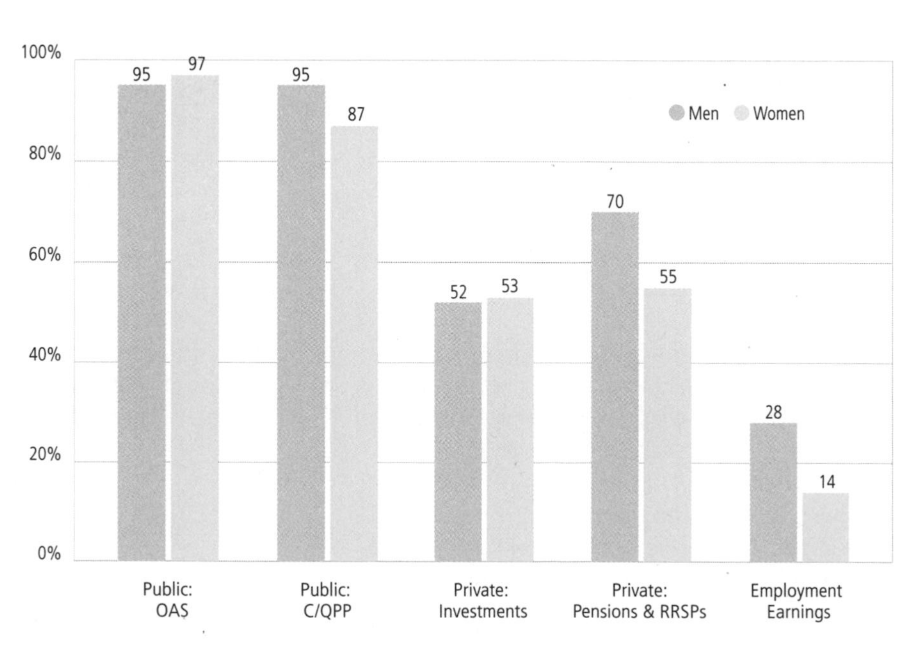

Gender Differences and Concerns

In 2010, 97 percent of Canadian women and 95 percent of men aged 65 and over received OAS benefits (roughly the same as in 1976). A smaller proportion of women (87 percent) than men (95 percent) received CPP or QPP (HRSDC, 2013). Significantly, more men than women received income from employment or private pensions and RRSPs in 2010: 28 percent of men compared to 14 percent of women had earnings, and 70 percent of men compared to 55 percent of women had income from private pensions and RRSPs. Roughly the same proportion of women (53 percent) as men (52 percent) had investment income (HRSDC, 2013).

In 2010, the median income for senior women was about a third less than that of men ($19,500, compared to $28,900 for men). The largest discrepancy was with respect to median income from private pensions and RRSPs: the $8,000 received by women was barely half of the $15,200 received by men.

Why are older women so much more likely to have low income? It is because women are more likely to have been involved with "women's work" during their careers—caring for and teaching children, nursing the sick, looking after the house and home, and serving others. Tying future income security to seemingly "gender-neutral" criteria—active labour force experience—as is currently the case, works against women. They not only have fewer sources of savings but their pension entitlements are often more limited.

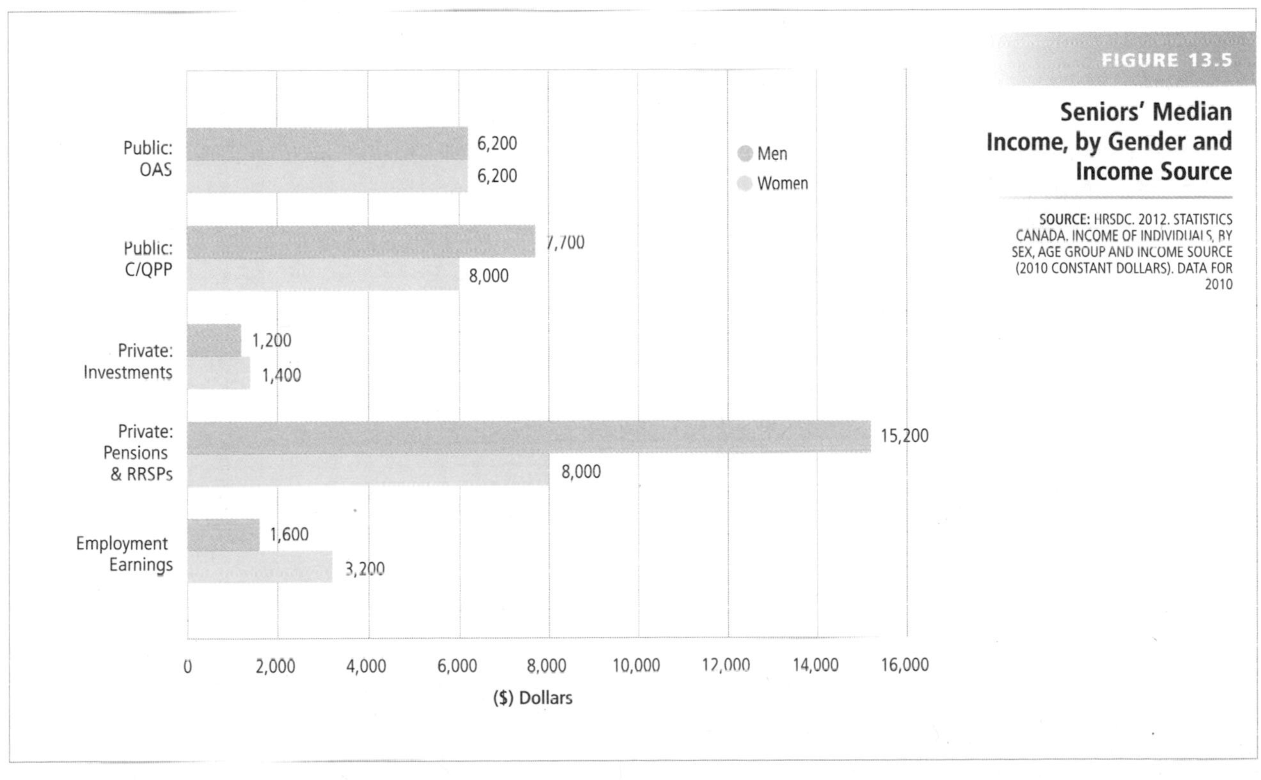

FIGURE 13.5

Seniors' Median Income, by Gender and Income Source

SOURCE: HRSDC. 2012. STATISTICS CANADA. INCOME OF INDIVIDUALS, BY SEX, AGE GROUP AND INCOME SOURCE (2010 CONSTANT DOLLARS). DATA FOR 2010

War Veterans Pensions and Allowance

Veterans' Affairs Canada (VAC) administers the *Pension Act*. It provides pensions to those suffering from disabilities related to military service, either during peace or wartime. When a disability pensioner dies, the spouse or common-law partner will receive a Survivor's Pension. Surviving children may be eligible for Orphan's Benefits following a pensioner's death. In addition, an income-tested War Veterans Allowance is available for those in financial need. It is meant to increase a minimum income to meet basic needs. Eligibility is based on wartime service, age, health, income, and residence.

History of Income Security for the Elderly and Retired

As the caring capacities of families diminished, pensions became a major issue in many industrializing countries. Denmark led the way in 1891 with its means-tested plan, and New Zealand followed in 1901. Reform-minded politicians in Canada argued that the federal government should use its new power and financial capacities to extend the pension provisions that were currently offered only to war veterans.

In 1921, a minority government was elected federally for the first time in Canadian history. The 1925 election saw similar results, and Prime Minister William Lyon Mackenzie King needed the support of the Progressive Party and the only two elected Labour members of Parliament—James S. Woodsworth and Abraham A. Heaps. Woodsworth and Heaps, in cooperation with Progressive leader Robert Forke, presented Mackenzie King with a number of initiatives, including an Old Age Pension program. In 1926, Mackenzie King won a majority Liberal government and was able to undertake reforms. This led to the first major piece of income security legislation for the elderly.

The *Old Age Pensions Act* of 1927

The *Old Age Pensions Act* of 1927 authorized the federal government to form agreements with the provinces to pay half of the costs of pensions paid under provincial legislation that met the requirements of the federal act.

Kenneth Bryden, a CCF politician and professor of economics, wrote the definitive history of Old Age Pensions (Bryden, 1974). He attributes the emergence of public pension policy in Canada to two opposing forces: the social and economic needs of an emerging urban-industrial society and the influence of a deep-rooted set of cultural values, referred to as the market ethos. He argues that the struggle between these two forces—one demanding pensions and the other resisting—led to means-tested pensions in 1927, universal pensions in 1951, and contributory pensions in 1965.

The *Old Age Security Act* and *Old Age Assistance Act* in 1951 moved the government into universal pensions. The exclusion of Aboriginal people was dropped with these acts. The *Old Age Security Act* established a universal pension for those over 70, subject only to a 20-year residency requirement. The federal government funded and administered the program. The decision to institute a universal plan was made with some reluctance by the government, but any attempts to substitute a different design were resisted by seniors. The program remained universal until 1989, and a special old age security tax was implemented to fund the program. The *Old Age Assistance Act*, on the other hand, was a provincially administered means-tested benefit with partial funding from the federal government.

Old Age Income Security

75 Years in the Making

1927: The *Old Age Pensions Act* was enacted, permitting the federal government to give assistance to provinces that provided a pension to British subjects aged 70 and older.

1952: The *Old Age Security Act* came into force, establishing a federally funded pension. It replaced the 1927 legislation that required the federal government to share the cost of provincially run, means-tested old age benefits.

1965: Amendments to the *Old Age Security Act* lowered the eligible age for the OAS pension to 65 one year at a time, starting in 1966 at the age of 69.

1966: The CPP and QPP came into force on January 1, 1966.

1967: The Guaranteed Income Supplement was established under the OAS program.

1972: Full annual cost-of-living indexation was introduced for OAS.

1973: Quarterly indexation was introduced for the OAS program.

1974: Full annual cost-of-living indexation was introduced for the CPP.

1975: The Spouse's Allowance was established as part of the OAS program.

1975: The same CPP benefits became available to male and female contributors, as well as to their surviving spouses or common-law partners and dependent children.

1975: The retirement and employment earnings test for CPP retirement pensions at the age of 65 was eliminated (a contributor can, upon application, receive his or her retirement pension the month following his or her 65th birthday, but can no longer contribute to the CPP).

1977: The payment of partial OAS pensions was permitted, based on years of residence in Canada.

1978: Periods of zero or low earnings while caring for the contributor's child under the age of 7 were excluded from the calculation of CPP benefits.

1978: CPP pension credits could be split between spouses in the event of a marriage breakdown (CPP credit splitting).

1985: Under OAS, the Spouse's Allowance was extended to all low-income widows and widowers aged 60 to 64.

1987: Several new CPP provisions came into effect, including flexible retirement benefits payable as early as the age of 60, increased disability benefits, continuation of survivor benefits if the survivor remarries, sharing of retirement pensions between spouses or common-law partners, and expansion of credit splitting to cover the separation of married or common-law partners.

1989: The repayment of OAS benefits or "clawback" was introduced.

1992: Three major amendments to the CPP came into effect: a new 25-year schedule for employer-employee contribution rates was established, children's benefits were increased, and provision was made for individuals who were denied disability benefits because of late application.

2012: In its Spring 2012 budget, the Conservative government announced changes to the eligibility for OAS and GIS. These will be gradually increased from 65 to 67 starting in April 2023, with full implementation by January 2029. The announcement was met with fierce opposition from seniors' groups, labour organizations, and opposition parties who believe the changes will have profound impacts on the lives of senior Canadians.

Canada's First *Old Age Pensions Act*

The 1927 *Old Age Pensions Act* provided a maximum pension of $20 per month or $240 per year, available to British subjects aged 70 or over who had lived in Canada for 20 or more years. As a means-tested provision of benefits, it was given only to the elderly whose income was less than $365 per year, including the pension benefits, and it excluded Status Indians.

Income Security Programs for Seniors

Canada's old age **income security system for seniors** balances public and private retirement benefits. It guarantees a minimum income for all seniors and allows Canadians to avoid serious disruptions upon retirement.

The two government-stated objectives of the retirement income system are to ensure that elderly people have sufficient income regardless of their preretirement income and to avoid drastic income reduction upon retirement. To accomplish these objectives, the government has devised a variety of income security measures. As noted earlier, these can be divided into three levels of income security:

1. **BASIC MINIMUM:** OAS, Guaranteed Income Supplement, the Spouse's Allowance, and provincial/territorial supplements
2. **SOCIAL INSURANCE:** public pensions—CCP/QPP
3. **PRIVATE PLANS:** occupational pensions and private savings

The income security of senior Canadians rests on these foundations. As the baby boom generation (1946-1976) retires, pension plan payouts will increase dramatically. Over the past few decades, successive governments have attempted to address this concern and ensure the sustainability of old age income security. Some say that the system will not be able to afford future pensions, others that retirees have been paying contributions to the plan and that these invested contributions will be sufficient to finance the benefits. Time will tell.

Unlike the OAS and GIS, which are paid out of general government revenues, the C/QPP payments are covered by contributions made by those who are retiring. This is meant to avoid an intergenerational transfer of wealth, whereby the young are working to finance the pensions of the old who are retired.

FIGURE 13.6

The Three Levels of Income Security for the Retired and Elderly

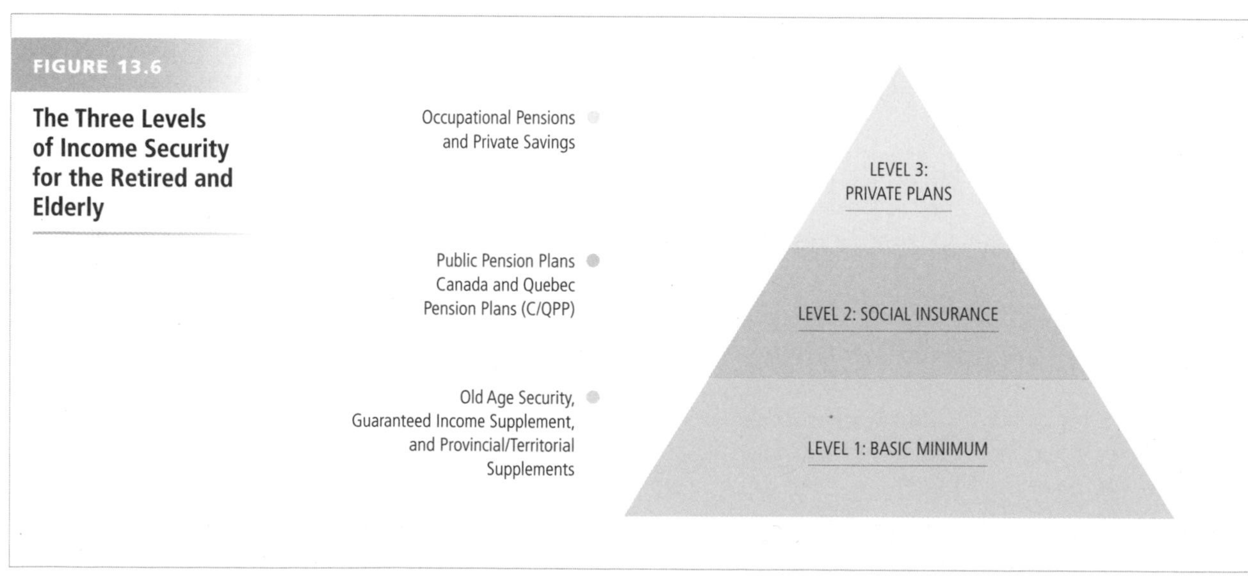

(1) The Basic Minimum—Old Age Security, Guaranteed Income Supplement, the Allowance, and Provincial/Territorial Supplements

The first level of income security for the retired and elderly comprises the following public programs:

- Old Age Security (OAS)
- Guaranteed Income Supplement (GIS)
- Allowance (previously the Spouse's Allowance)
- Provincial/territorial supplements

The **Old Age Security (OAS)** program provides a basic pension (adjusted for inflation) to virtually everyone over 65 years of age who has lived in Canada for a required length of time. It is a universal monetary benefit payable to Canadians over a specified age (though some would argue that it is no longer universal due to the clawback for higher-income Canadians). It is an income transfer program paid out of the general revenue of the federal government.

The OAS program includes the income-tested Guaranteed Income Supplement (GIS), which provides extra money to OAS recipients who have little or no other income, and the Allowance, which pays benefits to low-income spouses or partners of an OAS pensioner or widows/widowers between the ages of 60 and 64.

The OAS remained a universal program until 1989, when the Conservative government of Brian Mulroney introduced the clawback of benefits for people with higher incomes. Pensioners with an individual net income above $69,562 (as of 2012) must repay part or all of the Old Age Security pension amount. The repayment amounts are deducted from monthly payments before they are issued. Strictly speaking, the OAS is therefore no longer a universal program. The federal government insists that it is essentially still a universal program, as only about 5 percent of seniors receive reduced OAS benefits, and only 2 percent lose the entire benefit.

The **Guaranteed Income Supplement (GIS)** was implemented in 1966 as a selective, income-tested benefit for OAS recipients who had no other income. It was intended as a "guaranteed annual income" program and is the only such program in Canada; indeed, it is one of the few guaranteed income programs operating in industrialized countries. With this program, every Canadian over the age of 65, except for those who do not meet the residency requirement, have an income that is at least equal to OAS plus the maximum GIS. With this, the program guarantees a minimum income for elderly Canadians.

The federal 2012 budget introduced changes to OAS and GIS. The age for eligibility will be gradually increased from 65 to 67 starting April 2023, with full implementation by January 2029. It will not affect anyone who is 54 years or older as of March 31, 2012 (discussed later in this chapter.)

Mandatory Retirement

As of 2006, Ontarians are no longer required to quit working at age 65. Alberta, Manitoba, Quebec, Prince Edward Island, Nunavut, Yukon, and the Northwest Territories have also abolished mandatory retirement.

Many groups support this trend because it opens up options for people in their senior years. But unions warn against increasing the age at which people can qualify to collect pensions (both government and workplace), arguing that permitting people to work longer because they feel financially obligated to work does not really expand workers' options when it comes to retirement.

There has been some debate about whether or not the GIS, when taken together with the OAS, actually provides an adequate income. For example, the maximum GIS for a single pensioner was $8,867 a year in 2006, and when this was combined with the OAS, a single person would have an annual income of $15,407. This was far below the LICO. Analysis finds a similar pattern for couples, thereby showing that a poverty gap still exists for the elderly in Canada.

The other basic minimum income program, the **Spouse's Allowance (SPA)** (now called "the Allowance"), was created to deal with a hardship-creating anomaly in the OAS/GIS. The 1975 SPA intended to correct the anomaly by providing an income-tested benefit to those between 60 and 65 years of age, when one spouse is over 65. In addition, the Allowance for the survivor provides benefits for those who are 60–64 years old and whose spouse or partner has died. The Allowance for the survivor stops when a recipient remarries or lives in a common-law relationship for at least one year. The Allowance is stopped when the recipient's income reaches a certain maximum.

Federal benefits are supplemented with provincial and territorial benefits in Ontario, Manitoba, Saskatchewan, Alberta, British Columbia, Yukon, the Northwest Territories, and Nunavut. The provincial programs are generally means- or income-tested and are administered by local Social Assistance or welfare departments.

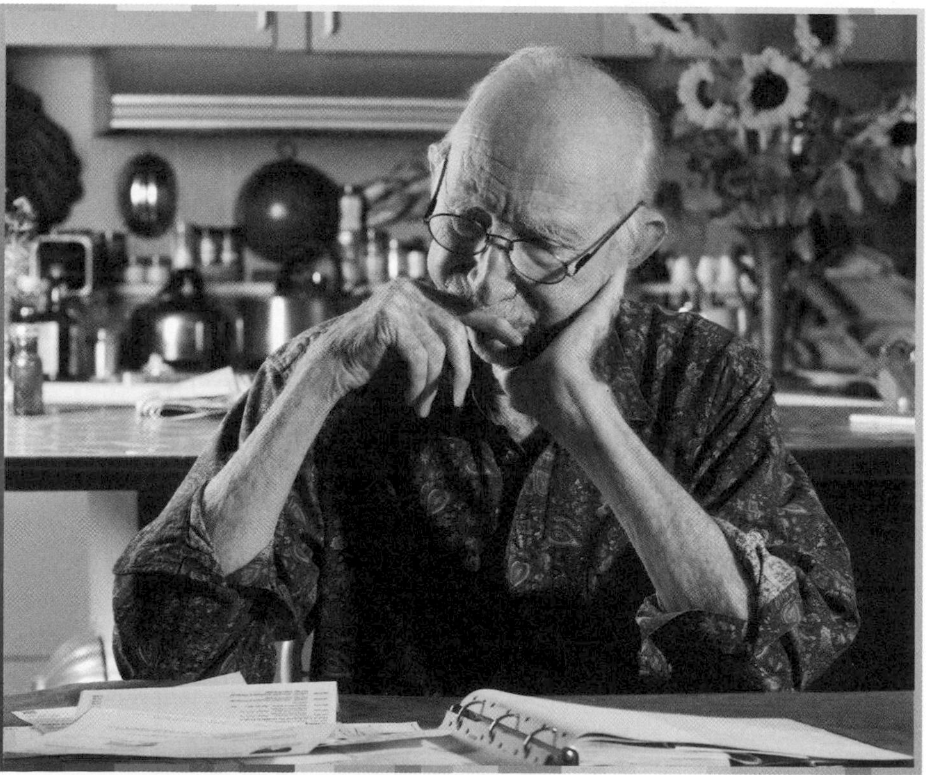

There has been some debate over whether the benefits available to seniors actually provide for an adequate income, and many believe a poverty gap still exists for the Canadian elderly population.

(2) Social Insurance: Public Pensions—Canada/Quebec Pension Plan (C/QPP)

The earnings-based **Canada/Quebec Pension Plan (C/QPP)** makes up the second level of income security for the retired and elderly. The plan provides a pension upon retirement to persons who have contributed to it. It is, therefore, a social insurance type of income security program; it insures the contributor against loss of income due to retirement.

All employed or self-employed Canadians over the age of 18 make compulsory contributions to the plan (matched by their employer) throughout their working careers. The plan also offers disability, survivor, and death benefits, as well as inflation protection. The plan is fully portable from job to job. In the 2010/11 fiscal year, 4.2 million Canadians received $31.6 billion in CCP/QPP benefits and 4.4 million seniors received OAS benefits (HRSDC, 2013).

In 1998, Parliament amended the Canada Pension Plan through Bill C-2. The changes resulted in a larger reserve fund to help ensure that the future pensions of the growing retirement population can be funded. Contribution rates were increased from the 1998 5.85 percent of contributory earnings to 9.9 percent. These changes will increase the size of the fund that is put aside to pay for future retirement pensions. The aim is to avoid a situation where younger working age Canadians are left financing the pensions of their parents.

Child Rearing Drop-Out Provision (CRDO)

The amount of the CPP benefit is based on how long and how much you have contributed. Historically, this has negatively affected women who opt to stay at home and care for newborn children. Periods when they had no earnings or their earnings were low resulted in a lower benefit. The CPP now has a special provision to prevent this. Months of low or zero earnings spent caring for children under the age of seven are excluded from the calculation of a pension.

TABLE 13.1

Old Age Security Benefit Payment Rates

Type of Benefit	Recipient	Average Monthly (Oct 2006)	Maximum Monthly Benefit	Maximum Annual Income
OAS Pension	All recipients	$467.21	$491.93	See note
Guaranteed Income Supplement	Single person	$418.87	$620.91	$14,904
	Spouse of pensioner	$261.30	$410.04	$19,728
	Spouse of non-pensioner	$406.46	$620.91	$35,712
	Spouse of recipient	$337.29	$410.04	$35,712
Allowance	All recipients	$354.69	$901.97	$27,600
Allowance for the survivor	All recipients	$559.05	$999.81	$20,064

Note: Pensioners with an individual net income above $63,511 must repay part or all of the maximum OAS pension amount. The repayment amounts are normally deducted from their monthly payments before they are issued. The full OAS pension is eliminated when a pensioner's net income is $102,865 or above.
Source: Service Canada. "Old Age Security (OAS) Payment Rates," modified 2006-10-17. Reprinted with permission

Quebec Pension Plan

www.rrq.gouv.qc.ca

Although the option of having a separate but highly linked pension plan is open to all provinces, Quebec is the only province to take the option.

Before the C/QPP was instituted, all pensions were administered by private insurance companies. A public contributory pension was a new way to provide income for retired persons. The basic-minimum programs (discussed previously) addressed the income needs of the retired by transferring income to the retired from taxes collected every year. With these programs, income is redistributed from those who are of working age to retired people. Public contributory pensions, on the other hand, help people save from their earnings during their working years and then use the accumulated funds to provide income during retirement.

As mentioned, all employed persons over the age of 18 must make compulsory C/QPP contributions while employed. Therefore, all Canadians who have participated in the paid labour force are eligible for benefits, even a person with only one contribution. Benefits are currently payable at age 65 and are equal to 25 percent of a contributor's average earnings. Benefits are adjusted downward by 0.5 percent for each month for people who begin drawing benefits before 65 years of age. The plan is fully indexed annually to the cost of living as measured by the Consumer Price Index (CPI).

The C/QPP is used as a vehicle for other non-retirement based contingencies: disability benefits, death benefits, and survivor benefits. The plan only provides disability benefits to contributors if they are unable to work due to a "severe" and "prolonged" disability—meaning that they are unable to regularly pursue any substantial gainful employment for an indefinite period. Survivor benefits are paid to the surviving spouse of a deceased contributor. Finally, a death benefit (a lump-sum benefit equal to six times the contributor's monthly pension, up to a specified maximum) is paid upon the death of a contributor.

The C/QPP began in 1966. The mandate at the time was to provide all members of the labour force in Canada and their families with retirement income and death and disability benefits. Although we discuss the plans in tandem, the Quebec Pension Plan (QPP) is a separate plan legislated by the province of Quebec—it has similar benefits and identical contribution rates to the Canada Pension Plan (CPP).

The QPP is closely associated with the CPP and is coordinated through a series of agreements between the federal government and Quebec. This ensures that Canadians who move in and out of Quebec carry all the pension benefits with them. The *Canada Pension Plan Act* allows any province to create its own program as Quebec has done. Although the option of having a separate but linked pension plan is open to all provinces, Quebec is the only province to take the option.

(3) Private Plans: Occupational Pensions and Private Savings

The **private pension plans** component of the retirement income system consists of pensions from employers and publicly supported and regulated private savings plans such as Registered Retirement Savings Plans (RRSPs), Registered Pension Plans (RPPs), and Deferred Profit Sharing Plans (DPSPs).

The federal government provides tax assistance on savings in RRSPs, RPPs, and DPSPs—taxes are deferred on the contributions and investment income in these plans until the savings are withdrawn or received as pension income. Private savings and assets also contribute to retirement incomes. As noted earlier, the tax-assisted private pension system accounts for an increasingly large share of retirement income system payments. Private **occupational pension plans** were an outcome of the escalating economy after World War II and the demand by unions for pension coverage within their collective agreements. Now, private pension capital pools are the largest in industrialized nations.

Governments are increasingly relying on private forms of savings and are raising the deductions allowed for contributors. Critics argue that these plans really only benefit those with high incomes and strongly favour men over women (see Figures 13.4 and 13.5 on pages 314–315). Over the past three decades, the proportion of seniors with private pensions, RRSPs, or C/QPP benefits has grown remarkably. The proportion with income from private pensions and RRSPs more than doubled between 1976 and 2009 (24 percent to 63 percent), due mostly to growth in RRSP savings. Private pensions still cover less than a third of the labour force.

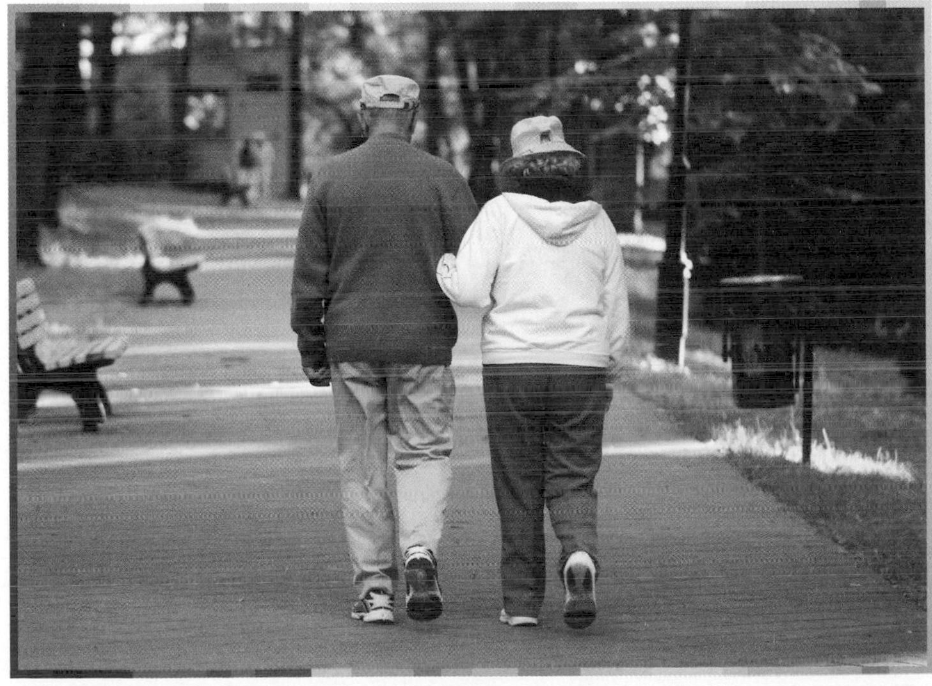

Due to longer life expectancies, the majority of Canada's elderly population is made up of women. With less consistent work histories, elderly women often have limited retirement incomes.

Canadian Association of Retired Persons (CARP)

The changes to OAS will hurt those at the lower end of the income spectrum, and they may be forced on to welfare at age 65, said Susan Eng, vice-president for advocacy for CARP, a Canadian organization for older people.

Those who have good, decent-paying jobs would likely keep working anyway, and the lack of $600 a month won't change their minds, while those who have poor, physically draining jobs will be forced to either hang on an additional two years or go on welfare, Eng said.

Changes to the Old Age Pension Eligibility

In its Spring 2012 budget, the Conservative government announced **changes to the eligibility for OAS and GIS**. These will be gradually increased from 65 to 67 starting in April 2023, with full implementation by January 2029. The changes will not affect anyone who is 54 years of age or older as of March 31, 2012. Those born on or after February 1, 1962 will have an age of eligibility of 67. Those who were born between April 1, 1958 and January 31, 1962 will have an age of eligibility between 65 and 67.

The announcement was met with fierce opposition from seniors' groups, labour organizations, and opposition parties who believe the changes will have profound impacts on the lives of senior Canadians.

OAS/GIS Changes Not "Gender Neutral"

Many seniors groups denounced the changes on the grounds that those who are most dependent on OAS/GIS income—women, those persons with disabilities, seniors with shorter residency in Canada, the lowest income groups, and the long-term unemployed—will be hardest hit by the changes.

In particular, OAS and the GIS are the only income for many women where they are guaranteed to receive the same amount as men regardless of the extent of their previous involvement in the labour force. Also, the proportion of income replaced by the OAS and the GIS is much higher for women and seniors with low incomes—about 70 percent for those with incomes of less than $15,000. For women between the ages of 65 and 69, OAS and GIS reduce poverty by 21 percentage points. For men of the same age, it is 15 percentage points. So, it is clear that rolling back the age of OAS and GIS is not "gender neutral" (Wood & Hinton, 2012).

"A False Crisis"

Announcing the changes, Finance Minister Jim Flaherty argued that raising the age eligibility was necessary to secure the long-term sustainability of the pension system in the face of aging demographics and in particular the impending retirement of the baby boomers. Opposition parties say Harper and Flaherty are creating a "false crisis," that there is no funding shortage in the OAS/GIS component.

Indeed, Canada's independent Parliamentary Budget Officer, Kevin Page, stated that the OAS/GIS system is affordable into the future without changes. In fact, Page insisted there is even some room to spare for the program. His report said "the federal government could reduce revenue, increase program spending or some combination of both by 0.4 percent of GDP annually while maintaining fiscal sustainability. This amounts to $7 billion in 2011-12." The

Congress of Union Retirees of Canada (CURC) also urged Canadians to reject the proposed changes to OAS/GIS and fight for improvements to retirement security for all (*The Advocate*, 2012).

Federal and provincial governments have recognized that the aging of Canadian society will put pressure on the Canada Pension Plan, and they have undertaken important reforms to ensure long-term sustainability. Their reforms include accelerating higher contribution rates, adopting a new investment strategy, and benefit measures that reduce the growth in benefit expenditures. The changes must also ensure that the system will be fair across generations and not place an unfair burden on contributors.

Conclusion

Canada should be applauded for the substantial gains made in the post-World War II period in relation to income security of seniors. Such gains were made largely as a result of public pressure by this increasingly large and vocal section of the population.

Nevertheless, there are signs that the gains seniors have made are coming under threat. As further pressure mounts, governments will have to make some difficult choices, and these may affect seniors. Do we break down a public system that has been recognized worldwide as exemplary, or do we make the necessary changes to maintain a viable and comprehensive public retirement system?

The challenges are many. Many older adults can still work productively past retirement age, and many want to do so. It is important that those who wish to work beyond the typical retirement age are given the opportunity to do so, while ensuring that those who have put in their time and want to retire can retire without income worries.

Of special concern are senior women, many of whom outlive their male counterparts and who, because of family responsibilities, may have not been able to build up sufficient pension entitlement.

CHAPTER 13 REVIEW

LEARNING OBJECTIVES

After completing this chapter, you should be able to:

- Describe the three main components of the income security system for the elderly and retired in Canada.
- Describe the major sources of income for Canadian seniors.
- Discuss the changing poverty rates among the elderly in Canada.
- Discuss the particular problems faced by elderly women with respect to income security.
- Provide an historical overview of the programs and policies related to the provision of income security for the elderly and retired.
- Evaluate some of the income security programs available for senior Canadians.
- Understand the important changes that are taking place with respect to old age pension eligibility.

KEY CONCEPTS IN CHAPTER

- Canada/Quebec Pension Plan (C/QPP)
- Changes to the eligibility for OAS and GIS
- Guaranteed Income Supplement (GIS)
- Income security system programs for seniors
- Occupational pension plans
- Old Age Security (OAS)
- Private pension plans
- Spouse's Allowance (SPA)

REVIEW QUESTIONS

1. What are the future demographic trends regarding aging and retirement in Canada?
2. How will demographic trends affect the old age income security system? What has the federal government done to try to ensure the sustainability of the pension system, for example?
3. Over the past 50 years of so, significant progress has been made with respect to seniors living in poverty. What factors have contributed to this progress?
4. There is a concern that some of the income security gains that seniors have made may be eroding. What is the evidence for this?
5. Briefly describe the history of income security for the elderly, beginning with the *Old Age Pensions Act* of 1927.
6. List and describe the levels of income security for old age and retirement today. Calculate the total old age security benefits for an individual earning $58,000 per year. Explain.
7. What are some of the particular issues faced by senior women in retirement? What are the reasons for these concerns? What can be done to alleviate these concerns?
8. Describe two key debates regarding old age income security reform.
9. Calculate your retirement year and, if possible, the old age security benefits you will likely be entitled to at the time. Or, if that is too far in the distance, do the same for a parent or older friend. You can find an online retirement calculator that with help with this.

EXPLORING SOCIAL WELFARE

1. The number of people over the age of 65 is projected to dramatically increase. Today, there are about six workers in Canada for every retired person. By 2020, there will be about three workers for every retired person. What do you think the implications of this will be for our social welfare programs? Which programs will be most affected? What do you think the government should do to prepare for this?
2. Explore the debates around mandatory retirement age. What are the labour unions saying about the issue, and how does this differ from the government's viewpoint? You can begin with the websites of the Canadian Labour Congress (http://canadianlabour.ca) and the Canadian Union of Public Employees (www.cupe.ca).

CRITICAL THINKING

Each of us will get old, one hopes. Think for a moment what you would like in your retirement years.

What policy changes do you think could be promoted today that would help your age cohort in their retirement years?

WEBSITES

Seniors Canada On-line
www.seniors.gc.ca
This is the official federal government website addressing seniors issues for Canadians. Seniors Canada On-line provides access to a vast amount of web-based information and services across Canada. You can select your province and get up-to-date information. There are sections on finances and pensions that provide information on income security. There is also information on federal government programs related to seniors, such as combatting elder abuse and healthy living initiatives for seniors.

Human Resources and Skills Development Canada (Seniors)
www.hrsdc.gc.ca
Go to the Human Resources and Skills Development Canada page and click on "Seniors." This link provides an overview of our retirement income system for Canadian seniors—CPP, retirement pension, Old Age Security pension, Guaranteed Income Supplement, the Allowance, and the Allowance for the survivor. The site also contains links to funding programs, research reports, and ongoing government-sponsored consultations related to seniors' issues.

CARP: Canada's Association for the Fifty-Plus
www.carp.ca
Originally known as the Canadian Association for Retired Persons, CARP is an advocacy group dedicated to improving the quality of life for Canadians as they age. With an expansive membership and strong financial support, CARP presents itself as an independent voice for seniors in Canada.

14

Globalization and Social Welfare

A Social Justice Perspective

> "Civil and political rights—the right to vote—is meaningless in the absence of having your basic needs met. An adequate standard of living is a right."
>
> — JOSEPHINE GREY, FOUNDING DIRECTOR OF LOW INCOME FAMILIES TOGETHER (LIFT)

We have entered a period of tremendous economic and political transition. The world is becoming a vast global marketplace with complex financial systems and revolutionary information technologies. Human beings need new mechanisms to protect their rights and their welfare.

As the international community becomes increasingly integrated, how can cultural diversity and integrity be respected? Is a global culture inevitable? How do global organizations like the United Nations and the World Trade Organization fit in? Can we respect cultural differences and have universal, worldwide human rights? These are some of the issues, concerns, and questions examined throughout this chapter using a social justice perspective on social welfare.

Universal Declaration of Human Rights, 1948

Human rights became an international priority for the United Nations after World War II and were addressed formally in the 1948 **Universal Declaration of Human Rights**. The UN Declaration has become a universally recognized set of norms and standards that shape our relations as individuals, within communities, and among nations. Today, there is near-universal recognition that respect for human rights is essential to achieving peace, economic development, and democracy. But achieving these priorities is proving to be difficult.

A Counterweight to Globalization

As nations compete against one another, social welfare is often sacrificed in favour of tax cuts and debt repayment. The first priority, it seems, is to be "investor friendly." Globalization has also provided an exit option—if corporations do not like what they see in a particular country, they simply up and leave. This gives these international firms more control over working conditions and indeed civil society itself.

The social welfare of people, whether nationwide or worldwide, is inseparable from the idea of human rights. Citizens and social welfare activists must hold corporations accountable to human rights standards. This chapter explores how human rights advocacy by social welfare advocates can serve as a counterweight to the pressures of economic globalization.

One-quarter of the world's population lives on less than $1 per day. The effects of global poverty include high rates of infant mortality and major health crises.

CorpWatch: Holding Corporations Accountable

www.corpwatch.org

CorpWatch investigates corporations for human rights abuses, environmental misdeeds, fraud, and corruption around the world. The goal of CorpWatch is to encourage global justice, independent media activism, and democratic control over corporations.

What Is Globalization?

Globalization means that products and services are increasingly flowing between countries and that the autonomy of territorial units such as the nation state is decreasing in importance. For example, while a car may be sold in Canada, the various parts may be produced in different countries, assembled in another country, and sold to the Canadian branch of the automobile maker. This represents a shift from production and trade between nations to globalized production and commerce.

Economic globalization refers to the growing integration of the world markets for goods, services, and finance. There are three main characteristics of economic globalization:

- **FREE TRADE AND INVESTMENT EXPANSION.** Globalization allows for expansion in the trade of goods and services between countries.
- **CONCENTRATED TNC POWER.** Economic power is increasingly concentrated in the hands of large international firms.
- **ENFORCEMENT AND TNC RIGHTS PROTECTION.** International bodies, such as the World Trade Organization (WTO), are responsible for devising policies and enforcement practices to free trade and capital investments worldwide.

Free Trade and Corporate Power

Globalization now requires the opening up of domestic markets through the removal of international trade barriers. **Free trade** refers to the lowering and dismantling of the barriers and regulations that might impede the international flow of capital and products or restrict marketplace demand. Free trade is embodied in the growing collection of free trade agreements and international trade organizations, including the General Agreement on Tariffs and Trade (GATT), the Asia-Pacific Economic Co-operation (APEC), and the North American Free Trade Agreement (NAFTA). Powerful lobbying by big corporations is behind these developments. These same forces are also encouraging the trend towards the privatization and marketization of social services and health services.

When it comes to the media (film, television, and especially the news), these transnational corporations are able to exert considerable influence over our lives in what is known as "economic fundamentalism." This influence, which previously was held more by governments for the advancement of its citizens, is now held increasingly by large international corporations for the advancement of their profits.

The Transnational Corporations

New telecommunication technologies have enabled large corporations to move capital and productive capacity quickly to anywhere in the world. They have enabled TNCs to open new operations around the world as opportunities present themselves and to execute “lean production” to ensure maximum profitability.

As the economies of individual countries become increasingly interdependent, the political sovereignty of countries is slowly diminishing. **Transnational corporations (TNCs)** are organizations that possess and control production of manufactured goods and services outside of the country in which they were established.

Calculations by the Institute for Policy Studies (IPS) indicate that the top 200 global firms account for an alarming and growing share of the world’s economic activity. The Philip Morris corporation, for example, is economically speaking believed to be larger than New Zealand, and it operates in 170 countries. Instead of creating an integrated global village, these firms are weaving webs of production, consumption, and finance that bring economic benefits to, at the most, only a third of the world’s people. Moreover, the reach and power of such TNCs is increasing at a rapid rate.

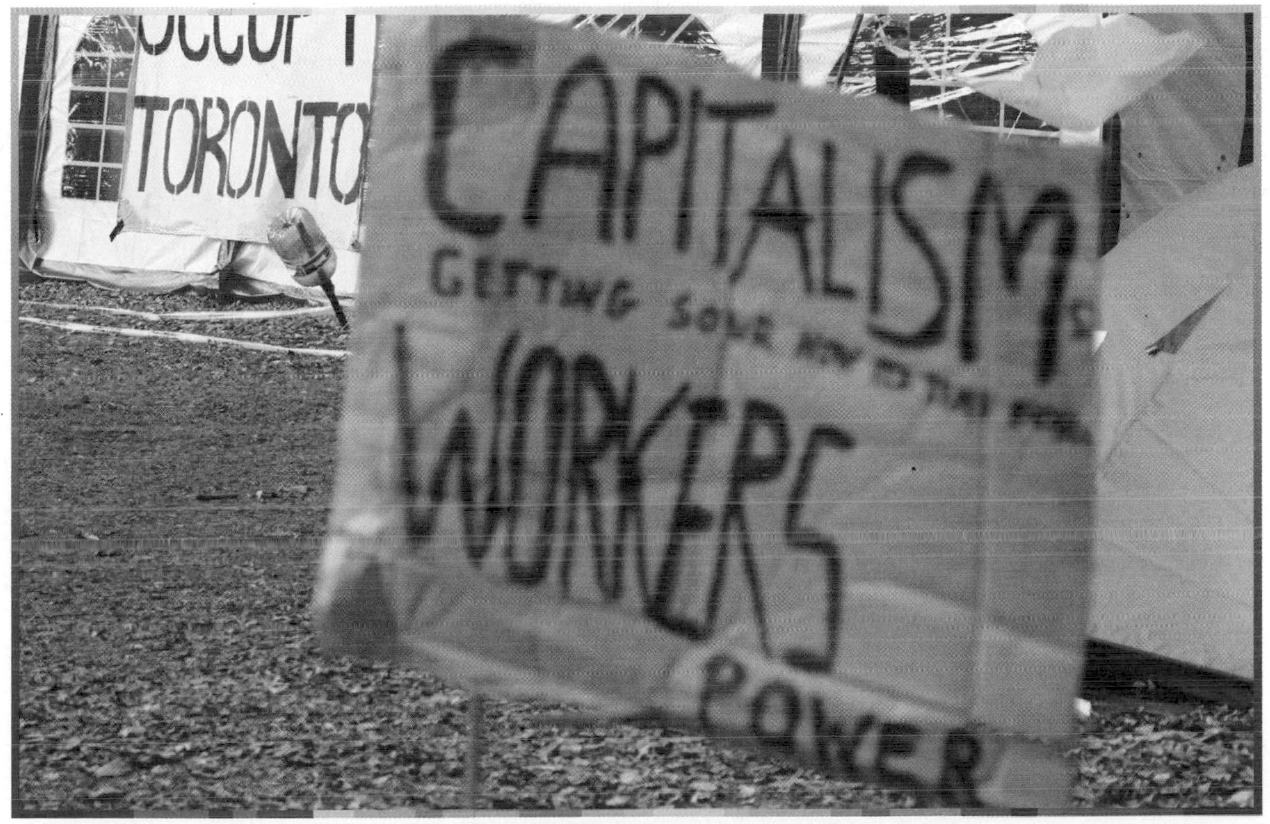

The Occupy protests, such as Occupy Toronto (pictured here), were part of a worldwide protest against global social and economic inequality.

Problems With the World Trade Organization

There are many people and organizations that object to the role and power of the WTO. The main criticisms are that:

- It operates in secret
- It promotes free trade over social and human rights
- It places priority on commercial interests
- It makes poverty and inequality worse
- It benefits large corporations and rich countries
- It dictates the ideal path to development (in conjunction with the World Bank and International Monetary Fund)
- It transforms citizens into consumers

Enforcement and Rights Protection for the TNCs

The rules governing business and finance, once made by national governments, are increasingly being made by international organizations that are not held accountable. International groups such as the World Trade Organization (WTO), the International Monetary Fund (IMF), the World Bank (WB), and the G8 are devising policies and enforcement practices that promote free trade and international financial interests. The concerns of social welfare practitioners are the last thing on the agenda.

These international institutions, along with the free trade agreements that they enforce, are increasingly determining the policy and budgetary decisions of governments around the world. Social policy professors James Rice and Michael Prince (2000, p. 21) maintain that these institutions and agreements limit the ability of local and national governments to solve social problems. In effect, they shift economic thinking, placing free trade and narrow economic concerns ahead of social policy, and thereby put limits on what local governments can do. Some have called this a post-sovereign state, meaning that the state or government is no longer free to make its own decisions.

The World Trade Organization and the United Nations

One of the primary vehicles for advancements in free trade is the **World Trade Organization (WTO)**, created in 1995. According to the WTO's website, "The World Trade Organization (WTO) is the only international organization dealing with the global rules of trade between nations. Its main function is to ensure that trade flows as smoothly, predictably and freely as possible." The WTO, for example, can rule that various environmental or social policies of countries are in violation of the WTO agreement and can mandate elimination of what would then be deemed a trade barrier.

According to critics, the WTO has ruled that every environmental policy it has reviewed is an illegal trade barrier that must be eliminated or changed. With few exceptions, the WTO has also ruled against health or food safety law it has reviewed. An organization with this type of far-reaching power certainly affects the social welfare of Canadians.

With this much global power and influence, there is an obvious need for the regulation of TNCs in order to safeguard human rights. The UN bodies currently responsible for regulating TNCs are the **UN Conference on Trade and Development (UNCTAD)** and the **Division on Transnational Corporations and Investment (DTCI)**. Until 1993, the United Nations Centre on Transnational Corporations (UNCTC) held this responsibility, and in 1998, after 20 years of discussion and redrafting, the UNCTC published the *Draft Code of Conduct on Transnational Corporations*. It was never adopted, due to extreme pressure from corporate lobby groups and Western governments.

Regulatory Vacuum

One of the last attempts to introduce international corporate regulation via the UN was at the 1992 UN Conference on Environment and Development (UNCED)—the "**Earth Summit**"—held in Rio de Janeiro. The UNCTC drafted recommendations to be included in Agenda 21 (UNCED's global plan of action) for the environmental regulation of TNCs. Again, pressure from a coalition of Western governments and corporate lobbies resulted in the removal of the recommendations.

At the present time, there is a TNC regulatory vacuum at the UN. The Bangkok Declaration and Plan of Action, adopted in 2000 at the 10th session of UNCTAD, provides the main thrust for the work of the current UNCTAD. The retooled UNCTAD has moved away from TNC regulation towards trade and investment policy. Its work now centres on analyses of economic trends and major policy issues of international concern rather than dealing with the human rights violations of TNCs (as revealed on its new website at www.unctad.org).

As noted earlier, **global social welfare** (a concern with justice, social regulation, social provision, and redistribution between nations) has already become part of the activities of various supranational organizations or international governmental organizations of the UN. Given this new era of globalization, the traditional concerns of social welfare also need to be broadened to include a concern with the issue of global human rights.

Many object to the role and subsequent power of the WTO; wherever the organization meets, there are extensive protests, like this one in Hong Kong in 2005.

The G8

The **Group of Eight** (G8), has existed for over 30 years. Since 1975, the leaders of the major industrial democracies have met annually to discuss the major economic and political issues facing their domestic societies and the international community as a whole.

France, the United States, Britain, Germany, Japan, and Italy attended the first G6 summit; Canada joined the group at the 1976 G7 summit. In 2006, Russia hosted the summit, completing its process of becoming a full member. The group is now known as the G8.

Each year the G8 selects major priorities, as set by the hosting country. When Canada hosted the summit in 2002, the major priorities included global terrorism and a new aid plan for Africa. The 2006 summit in St. Petersburg, Russia, was dedicated to energy, security, infectious diseases, and education.

Globalization in Operation

Advocates of globalization believe, or have a self-interest in believing, that freer trade will automatically benefit all countries of the world. The economic theory is that poorer countries would be able to specialize their production in areas where they have a comparative advantage, and they could export those products to richer countries. This theory may work in some cases, but in practice it tends to enrich some countries at the expense of others.

Structural Adjustment

Bananas are often cheaper than apples in Canadian cities, even though apples could have been grown in your Canadian backyard. The process of **structural adjustment**, which is commonly forced upon countries that are seeking loans, helps to explain this phenomenon. The process typically operates as follows:

1. A country needs a loan due to a currency crisis, crumbling infrastructure, or a variety of other reasons.
2. The country approaches monetary organizations such as the IMF and the World Bank.
3. The IMF and WB agree to lend money if the borrowing country agrees to undertake what is called structural adjustment. The new economic policies focus on reducing social spending and other government expenditures, increasing GDP by decreasing labour and environmental regulations, lowering any trade barriers, specializing production, allowing currency to freely trade, and encouraging foreign investment.
4. As part of the package, the country may agree to change from subsistence agriculture to monocropping. Monocropping or monoculture occurs when agricultural land is used to grow one product instead of a variety. So a country converts a large part of its agricultural production from rice to bananas and becomes dependent on one or two crops.
5. Foreign corporations purchase large tracts of land and hire former farmers to work as agricultural workers. (The new megafarms are known as agribusiness.)
6. Labourers work long days, for very low wages, under poor conditions. The very best produce is shipped for sale to foreign markets, leaving the local market with bruised bananas or no local produce.
7. Environmental deregulation leads to increased use of pesticides and health risks for labourers. Soil is rapidly spent as a consequence of monocropping and overuse. As a result, the country turns to deforestation to expose rich, unused soil.
8. Western nations are able to import cheap bananas.

Export Processing Zones

Globalization encourages people to do business wherever conditions are favourable. For large corporations, this means they can do business where their costs are minimized and profits are maximized. The deregulation of capital and freeing of trade barriers allow corporations to rapidly move their capital across international borders, making it easy for a company to set up a mobile factory in a place where labour regulations are relaxed, environmental legislation is weak, and tax laws are favourable. In fact, a country can set up and promote an "export processing zone" designed specifically for this purpose.

An **export processing zone (EPZ)** is a particular area in a country from which benefits come in the form of preferential financial regulations and special investment incentives. There are EPZs all over the world. Naomi Klein, activist and author of *No Logo: Taking Aim at the Brand Bullies*, examines how TNCs use migrant factories to move around to different EPZs in order to follow tax breaks and incentives. She calls it "zero-risk globalization" (2000, p. 287). Most EPZs employ a high proportion of women with minimal education. These women are subjected to pregnancy tests, locked out of washrooms, expected to work in conditions that strain their eyesight, forced to work overtime, paid low wages, and fired for pregnancy or joining a union (Ehrenreich & Fuentes, 1992).

International Development Research Centre (IDRC)

www.idrc.ca

Created in 1970, IDRC is a Canadian organization that helps developing countries find long-term solutions for the social, economic, and environmental problems they face. IDRC funds the work of researchers working in universities, private enterprise, government, and non-profit organizations in developing countries.

The Debt Crisis

The **debt crisis** also continues to prevent poor countries from developing their economies—debt that was often accumulated by prior rulers and dictators, many of which were supported by Western nations or by colonial governments. For example, South Africa is still paying off debts from the apartheid regime. The scale of the debt continues to rise, despite ever-increasing payments, while aid is falling. For example, the developing world now spends $13 on debt repayment for every $1 it receives in grants. For countries classified as low income by the World Bank, outstanding external debt has risen 430 percent since 1980 and now amounts to US$523 billion. For the heavily indebted poor countries, external debt has risen 320 percent since 1980 to US$189 billion (Kapoor, 2005, p. 5).

Many anti-globalization activists have called for 100 percent cancellation of multilateral debt for all countries where debt repayments are seriously hindering the country's efforts towards attaining the Millennium Development Goals (MDGs). This would entail a 100 percent debt cancellation for most low-income countries, plus significant additional resources if they are to have any hope of reaching the MDGs by 2015.

International Forum on Globalization

www.ifg.org

The International Forum on Globalization is an organization representing over 60 organizations that seek to explore the implications of economic globalization and promote alternative policies for equity, diversity, and sustainability.

Canada in the World

To this point, we have focused mainly on income security and social welfare within Canada, but it is important to understand how Canada fits into the larger global picture. We have seen how within Canada there is a great disparity in wealth, with a relatively small number of people owning a large share of the resources and obtaining a large share of total income. At the international level, the same phenomenon exists on a larger scale.

As with disparities within Canada itself, the disparities of wealth among countries are not simply a matter of entitlement—Canadians do not work harder than our Mexican neighbours, for example; in fact, the reverse may be true. Rather, our consumer-driven lifestyle at this point heavily depends upon the production of cheap goods by our poorer neighbours, and these are routinely purchased in Canada (and other advanced countries) at a price that does not represent a fair trade. This and other factors as well, ultimately creates a great disparity among nations.

Human Development Indicators

One way of understanding this economic disparity is through human development indicators. The most well-known indicator is the UN's **Human Development Index (HDI)** as part of the *Human Development Report*, launched in 1990 and released annually by the United Nations Development Programme (UNDP).

The HDI measures more than income. Clearly, deprivation should not be measured only by what people possess but also by what they are able to do. Therefore, when examining social welfare, it is important to consider access to housing, health, education, community life, and political life. The HDI does just this. It measures items that shape future opportunities, such as basic and advanced education and health, taking a social inclusion viewpoint on inequality.

The HDI compares the countries of the world according to their average achievements in three basic dimensions of human development: a long and healthy life, knowledge, and a decent standard of living. It is calculated for 177 countries and areas for which data is available. Since the first report, three additional sub-indexes have been developed by the UN: the Gender-related Development Index, the Gender Empowerment Measure, and the Human Poverty Index. See Chapter 6 for more on the UN's multi-dimensional poverty index.

The HDI takes what is called a *human development approach*. This approach values capacities—health and education—as ends in themselves, rather than simply as a means to income (as important as that is). This can be contrasted to the *human capital approach*, which views increases in capabilities such as education and health mainly in terms of the potential increase in productive capacity or income.

The UN's Human Development Index (HDI)

A Better Future for All

The United Nations' HDI is a summary measure of human development. It measures the average achievements in a country in three basic dimensions of human development: a long and healthy life (health), access to knowledge (education), and a decent standard of living (income).

To enable cross-country comparisons, the HDI is, to the extent possible, calculated based on data from leading international data agencies and other credible data sources available at the time of writing.

The HDI was created to emphasize that people and their capabilities should be the ultimate criteria for assessing the development of a country, not economic growth alone. The HDI can also be used to question national policy choices, asking how countries with the same level of income per capita can end up with different outcomes.

The concept of human development is much broader than what can be captured in the HDI or any other of the composite indices in the Human Development Report (Inequality-adjusted HDI, Gender Inequality Index, and Multidimensional Poverty Index). The HDI, for example, does not reflect political participation or gender inequalities.

Changes to the Index in 2010

The HDI remains a composite index that measures progress in the three basic dimensions—health, knowledge, and income. Under the previous HDI formula, health was measured by life expectancy at birth; education or "knowledge" by a combination of the adult literacy rate and school enrolment rates (for primary through university years); and income or standard of living by GDP per capita (adjusted for purchasing-power parity).

Health is still measured by life expectancy at birth. But the 2010 HDI measured achievement in knowledge by combining the expected years of schooling for a school-age child in a given country entering school today with the mean years of prior schooling for adults aged 25 and older.

The income measurement, meanwhile, has changed from purchasing-power-adjusted per-capita Gross Domestic Product (GDP) to purchasing-power-adjusted per-capita Gross National Income (GNI); GNI includes some remittances, providing a more accurate economic picture of many developing countries.

SOURCE: UNDP. (2013). HUMAN DEVELOPMENT REPORTS. UNITED NATIONS DEVELOPMENT PROGRAM.

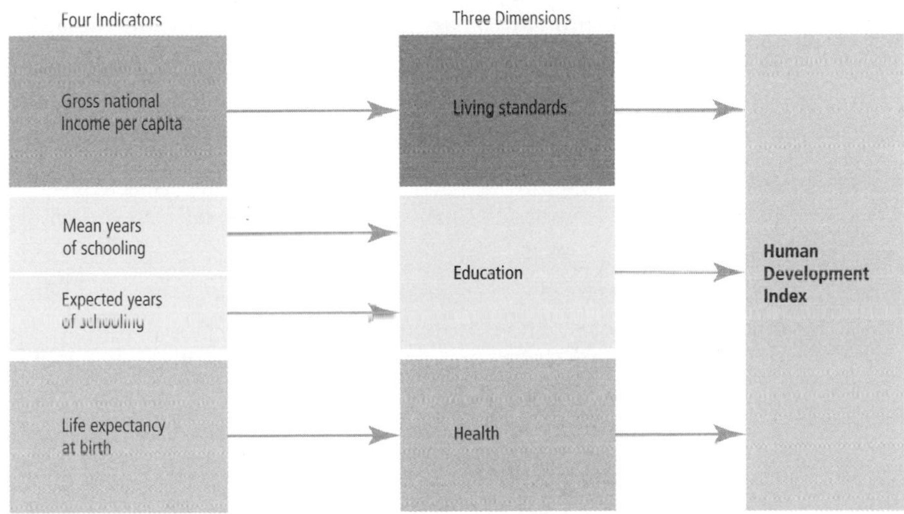

Armed conflicts are one of the common causes of human rights crises affecting children.

What Are Human Rights?

Human rights are a common standard for all peoples and all nations—they are inherent rights without which we cannot truly live as human beings. A right is a justified claim or entitlement by someone or some institution in society. Rights are not a property of a person, but rather are a reason to treat a person in a certain respectful way. Many human rights advocates and writers would agree with Ronald Dworkin's famous declaration that "rights are trumps"—a rights claim "beats" all other competing social values.

Human rights are commonly considered as being universal, indivisible, inalienable, and inabrogable (Ife, 2001, p. 12).

- *Universality* means that human rights apply to all human beings.
- *Indivisibility* refers to the conception that all human rights must be pursued and realized—we cannot pick and choose which rights are enforced and which are abandoned.
- The *inalienability* of human rights means that human rights, as a general rule, cannot be taken away. Of course, there are emergencies that may necessitate the suspension of some human rights. For example, in a medical epidemic, a quarantined infected person may find that his or her rights to freedom of movement have been suspended.
- Finally, the *inabrogable* nature of human rights refers to the idea that one cannot voluntarily give up one's human rights or trade them for special privileges.

International Human Rights Instruments

The belief that humanity has a duty to protect the universal and inalienable rights of all people is now a recognized part of the heritage of humankind. This recognition has led to international, declarations, legislation, and regulations.

The **International Bill of Human Rights** is the primary instrument of UN activities to promote, protect, and monitor human rights and fundamental freedoms. The bill comprises three texts: the *Universal Declaration of Human Rights* (1948); the *International Covenant on Economic, Social, and Cultural Rights* (1966); and the *International Covenant on Civil and Political Rights* (1966) and its two optional protocols. These instruments enshrine global human rights standards and have been the inspiration for more than 50 supplemental UN human rights conventions, declarations, bodies of international minimum rules, and other recognized principles. These have further refined international norms relating to a very wide range of issues, including women's rights, protection against racial discrimination, protection of migrant workers, and the rights of children.

Universal Declaration of Human Rights (UDHR)

The 1948 **Universal Declaration of Human Rights (UDHR)** defined the fundamental expectations for freedom and dignity in a free and just society. It stated that "disregard and contempt for human rights have resulted in barbarous acts which have outraged the conscience of mankind, and the advent of a world in which beings shall enjoy freedom of speech and belief and freedom from fear and want has been proclaimed as the highest aspiration of the common people." Accepted human rights include freedom of expression, freedom of association, freedom from fear and persecution, and freedom of religion, as well as the right to shelter, education, health, and work, among others.

The 1966 *International Covenant on Economic, Social, and Cultural Rights* and *International Covenant on Civil and Political Rights* are international legal instruments. Thus, when member and non-member states of the UN ratify a covenant and become a "state party" to it, they are wilfully accepting a series of legal obligations to uphold the rights and provisions established under the text in question.

Various committees of the UN investigate and report on states that have ratified each covenant. For example, the Committee on Economic, Social, and Cultural Rights examined and reported on Canada's compliance with the *International Covenant on Economic, Social, and Cultural Rights* (see Appendix B), which it has signed. The report is contained in Appendix C, and it outlines important areas where Canada is not in compliance with the covenant. A few items outlined in the report include:

- The low proportion of unemployed workers eligible for receiving Employment Insurance benefits
- The impact of the National Child Benefit "clawback system" on the poorest families, especially single-mother families
- The lack of affordable housing and inadequate assistance for women in abusive relationships
- The fact that Canada did not supply sufficient information regarding the standard of living possible under Social Assistance rates
- The 11.2 percent of our population that still lived in poverty
- The poverty rates that are still very high among groups such as Aboriginal peoples, African Canadians, immigrants, persons with disabilities, and single mothers

The report made numerous recommendations that are of interest for social welfare purposes.

War Child Canada

www.warchild.ca

Founded in 1999 by Samantha Nutt, Steven Hick, and Frank O'Dea, War Child Canada is assisting thousands of children and youth in some of the most devastated areas on Earth.

War Child Canada works with youth in North America to promote the awareness of human rights issues and the cause of war-affected children. War Child Canada also works closely with the music industry to help raise funds and build awareness for the cause of war-affected children and youth worldwide.

Human Rights

- **Negative rights:** civil and political rights that must be protected
- **Positive rights:** economic, social, and cultural rights that governments must ensure are realized by their citizens
- **Collective rights:** the rights held by groups of people, the most common being the right to self-determination of a cultural or ethnic group

Negative, Positive, and Collective Rights

Some rights advocates distinguish between different human rights according to whether they are negative, positive, or collective rights. Others refer to these dimensions as "generations" of human rights. The way human rights are viewed and analyzed is a topic of considerable debate, but let us consider the following three categories of human rights:

1. **NEGATIVE RIGHTS:** civil and political rights (Articles 2–21 of the *UDHR*)
2. **POSITIVE RIGHTS:** economic, social, and cultural rights (Articles 22–27 of the *UDHR*)
3. **COLLECTIVE RIGHTS:** social and international order rights (Article 28 of the *UDHR*)

Negative Rights

The first category of human rights refers to civil and political rights. These are individually based and include the right to life, the right to liberty and security of person, the right to vote, the right to freedom of assembly, the right to equality before the law, the right to presumption of innocence until proven guilty, the right to freedom of movement, and the right to own property, to name a few (Ife, 2001, p. 25). These rights are detailed in Articles 2–21 of the UDHR. They are further expounded in the *International Covenant of Civil and Political Rights*, the *Optional Protocol to the International Covenant on Civil and Political Rights*, and a wide range of other covenants that add more detail to specific rights. They address protection from torture, ill-treatment, and disappearance; the rights of women, indigenous peoples, and visible minorities; the rights of prisoners and detainees; the rights of children and juvenile offenders; the rights of employment and forced labour; and the rights of disabled persons, to name a few of the broad areas.

These are referred to as **negative rights** because their emphasis is on protection. The right is met by merely refraining from acting in a way that would violate the right. When Canadians hear the phrase "human rights," it is generally these rights that spring to mind. This category of human rights has roots in the intellectual tradition of the eighteenth-century Enlightenment and the political philosophy of liberalism. Enlightenment thinkers such as Voltaire, John Locke, and David Hume believed that human reason could be used to combat ignorance, superstition, and tyranny, and to build a better world. Their principal target was the domination of society by a hereditary aristocracy. The liberal tradition has centred on religious toleration, government by consent, personal freedom, and, especially, economic freedom. Based on these traditions, negative rights have emphasized individual liberties and freedom.

Positive Rights

The second category of human rights concerns economic, social, and cultural rights. These rights are outlined in Articles 22–27 of the UDHR. They are detailed further in the *International Covenant on Economic, Social, and Cultural Rights*. These rights refer to the various forms of social provision, such as health, education, social services, food, housing, employment, adequate wages, and the right to form trade unions.

These rights are referred to as **positive rights** because they imply that the state plays a more positive and active role in ensuring that these rights are realized. For instance, for the right to an adequate income to be realized, the state must act to provide that income to those who do not have it. These rights are pursued by means of welfare state provision: universal health care, education, social housing, and employment and labour legislation, among others.

These rights generally have their roots in social democracy, socialism, and social movements. There is less consensus in Western capitalist democracies about such rights. At times, the rights themselves seem to run contrary to models that emphasize the rule of market forces.

Collective Rights

The third category of human rights are rights held by a group of people, such as a cultural group, and are referred to as **collective rights**. They are briefly mentioned in the UDHR, Article 28. "Everyone is entitled to a social and international order in which the rights and freedoms set forth in this declaration can be fully realized." These types of rights generally have their roots in anti-colonial struggles, environmental activism, and the efforts for self-determination of indigenous peoples.

Canada's Parliament passed the *Canadian Human Rights Act* in 1977. The purpose of the act is to ensure equality of opportunity and freedom from discrimination in federal jurisdiction. In 1982, the *Canadian Charter of Rights and Freedoms* was enacted as part of the *Constitution Act, 1982*. It has sections pertaining to legal rights, democratic rights, and equality rights, but it makes no mention of social and economic rights. Each province and territory also has a human rights act that applies to businesses and organizations within its jurisdiction. For example, discrimination in housing would be brought to the provincial or territorial human rights commission.

More recently, the *Modernization of Benefits and Obligations Act* (2000) was brought about due to human rights challenges under the *Canadian Charter of Rights and Freedoms*. Sixty-eight statutes involving some 20 departments were affected. Amendments were made to statutes such as the *Income Tax Act*, the *Canada Pension Plan Act*, the *Criminal Code*, and the *Old Age Security Act*.

Social Welfare, Globalization, and Human Rights

In this era of globalization, social welfare policies aimed at protecting the poor and disadvantaged seem to be in retreat. Although the post-World War II consensus was to maintain high levels of employment and a welfare state based on a sense of social citizenship in a nation, the era of globalization has severely eroded the social safety net and undermined basic human rights.

The Future of Welfare

The post-World War II welfare state was based on general consensus between labour, civil society, and capital. It was believed that the welfare state was necessary to ensure steady economic growth and social stability. All this is changing, calling into question the future of social welfare as we know it.

In this new era of globalization, governments have increasingly taken the position that labour and everyone else should be subjected to international market forces as much as possible, like any other commodity. For their part, the TNCs generally resist policies such as minimum wages, employment insurance, and health and safety legislation—policies that protect people from the negative effects of the market.

In his book *Globalization and the Welfare State*, Ramesh Mishra refers to this as "decentring the nation state." He points to the following globalization impacts on social welfare:

- Globalization undermines the ability of national governments to pursue (Keynesian) policies of full employment and demand management.
- Globalization is increasing inequality in wages and work conditions, and high-paying unionized jobs are shrinking as non-standard and part-time work grows.
- Globalization prioritizes deficit reduction and tax cuts over systems of social security.
- Globalization shifts power to capital or corporations and away from labour and civil society, thereby weakening the support for social welfare programs.
- Globalization constrains the social policy options of national governments due to the threat of capital flight if one nation is not as "investor friendly" as another.

The logic of globalization, Mishra argues, fundamentally conflicts with the logic of community and the idea of democratic politics (Mishra, 1999). Many social welfare activists around the world agree with him and feel that unfettered globalization is eroding not only the welfare state but also the very nature of western democracy and democratic decision making.

Social Welfare as a Social Justice Issue

To meet this social welfare challenge head-on, a new approach is called for, one that involves taking a **human rights approach**. An approach to social welfare based on human rights would differ from traditional conceptualizations in several ways:

1. Programs and policies would be conceptualized as rights or entitlements rather than as needs or problems.
2. Collective rights to participation in community life would see social welfare as an investment in people.
3. The state-centric model of viewing the state or government as the exclusive provider of social welfare would have to be changed.
4. International bodies would be required to provide for global social welfare and to ensure that TNCs uphold human rights.

The traditional model of welfare puts emphasis on needs and then on the process of addressing those needs. Framing the issue as a person's right to an "adequate standard of living for his or her health and well-being" shifts income security away from a charity model, whereby only the deserving receive charity for which they should be extremely grateful, towards the idea of social justice as a right of citizenship.

The UN Millennium Development Goals (MDGs)

Sustaining Social and Economic Progress

In 2000, at the United Nations Millennium Summit, the international community adopted the **Millennium Development Goals** (MDGs).

MDGs are an expanded vision that promotes human development as the key to sustaining social and economic progress. It is the most significant and accepted commitment to the development of poor countries in history.

The MDGs recognize the importance of creating a global partnership for development and are commonly accepted as a way of measuring development progress.

The UN Secretary-General reports yearly on progress towards implementation of the Millennium Declaration, including the MDGs. The first comprehensive review was conducted in 2005. Subsequent yearly reports are available at www.un.org/millenniumgoals.

The eight goals are to:

1. Eradicate extreme poverty and hunger
2. Achieve universal primary education
3. Promote gender equality and empower women
4. Reduce child mortality
5. Improve maternal health
6. Combat HIV/AIDS, malaria, and other diseases
7. Ensure environmental sustainability
8. Develop a global partnership for development

International Council on Social Welfare (ICSW)

www.icsw.org

Founded in Paris in 1928, the International Council on Social Welfare is a non-governmental organization that now represents organizations in more than 50 countries. ICSW and its members are active in the areas of social development, social welfare, and social justice.

Social Investment Approach

Some social welfare activists go further, arguing that human rights must also be addressed through a **social investment**. This approach emphasizes the need for change in a variety of institutions, policies, and practices that directly affect social inequality in the present and in the future (see Chapter 4 for more information on social investment). Many social welfare activists advocate going beyond the provision of income security to a more dynamic improvement of citizens' well-being as well as the participation of traditionally marginalized individuals in community life.

Social activists such as bell hooks and Stephen Lewis speak about mutual respect, dignity, and compassion for each other. Their model of meeting human rights is based both on a shift in how we view the people of the world and on a shared responsibility to attaining certain agreed standards for all. As bell hooks has famously stated: "If we want a beloved community, we must stand for justice, have recognition for difference without attaching difference to privilege." (hooks, 2003).

General Agreement on Trade in Services (GATS)

However, new trade discussions at the WTO are ringing alarm bells for many social policy analysts. Since February 2000, negotiations have been underway in the WTO to expand and "fine-tune" the **General Agreement on Trade in Services (GATS)**. GATS is an international trade agreement that came into effect in 1995. It aims to gradually remove all barriers to trade in services, such as banking, education, health care, rubbish collection, tourism, and transport. These negotiations have aroused unease worldwide.

Many believe that GATS will threaten the ability of governments to provide social security and protection to citizens. It may mean the privatization of education, health care, and social insurance. It may also limit the capacity of governments to regulate health and environmental standards.

Discussions on freer trade between rich and poor nations began in 2001 in Doha, Qatar. The negotiation became known as the **Doha Development Agenda** by the WTO. In 2006, the Doha Development Agenda negotiations were suspended because gaps between the rich developed nations and under-developed nations were too wide. Developing nations blamed the failure of the talks on wealthy nations. In July 2008, negotiations broke down after failing to reach a compromise on agricultural import rules. Instead of tackling the distortions of their own subsidies, the industrialized nations demanded improved market access that would have put subsistence farmers in poor countries at risk. As of 2013, the future of the "Doha Round" remains uncertain.

Conclusion

The trend towards economic globalization has important implications for social welfare activists, not only in Canada but throughout the world. Globalization means, in effect, that national borders become less influential in many aspect of our lives. In this new era, the traditional concerns of social welfare practitioners in addressing the immediate needs of their clients now need to be broadened and "framed" in the context of globalization.

The UN's 1948 *Declaration of Human Rights* is the standard by which respect for human rights is measured around the world. Globalization has given the Declaration a new relevancy. Transnational corporations (large international business interests operating among and often even above nation states) are increasing in size and power to the point that they challenge the sovereignty of nations. Because of their economic weight, they can shape the tax system more in their favour and influence the way governments spend their money, and therefore restrict governments' ability to provide of social welfare and income security to their citizens. Indeed, in this new context, some policy analysts question whether nation states will be able to maintain the tax base necessary to support adequate social welfare programs.

TNC also operate without a great deal of limitations. International organizations set up to monitor the activities of these corporations and guarantee respect for human rights have themselves not always been able to stand up to these "corporations without borders." The result is a regulatory vacuum. In the meantime, these economic "forces of globalization" are acting to weaken, if not undermine, many of our cherished institutions and social programs.

Globalization is the new context in which social welfare activists today need to understand their work. Globalization raises new challenges and new opportunities. The defense and extension of income security and social welfare programs today is intertwined with protecting and extending the human rights of citizens, both within Canada and on a world scale. It calls for a social justice approach to social welfare that is based on the principles of equality of opportunity and human rights for all citizens.

CHAPTER 14 REVIEW

LEARNING OBJECTIVES

After completing this chapter, you should be able to:

- Appreciate the significance of the *Universal Declaration of Human Rights*, 1944.
- Explain the impact of globalization and free trade on income security in this country.
- Evaluate the effectiveness of various international trade organizations in regulating the power of TNCs.
- Explain how globalization can restrict development in the Third World.
- Explain the UN's Human Development Index and evaluate its usefulness.
- Distinguish between the three types of human rights: negative rights, positive rights, and collective rights.
- Evaluate the importance of human rights in the context of international social welfare.
- Explain what is meant by the "social investment" approach to human rights and social welfare.

KEY CONCEPTS IN CHAPTER

- Collective rights
- Debt crisis
- Division on Transnational Corporations and Investment (DTCI)
- Doha Development Agenda
- Earth Summit
- Economic globalization
- Export processing zone (EPZ)
- Free Trade
- General Agreement on Trade in Services (GATS)
- Group of Eight (G8)
- Global social welfare
- Human rights
- Human Development Index (HDI)
- Human rights approach to social welfare
- International Bill of Human Rights
- Millennium Development Goals
- Negative rights
- Positive rights
- Social investment
- Structural adjustment
- Transnational corporations (TNCs)
- UN Conference on Trade and Development (UNCTAD)
- Universal Declaration of Human Rights (UDHR)
- World Trade Organization (WTO)

REVIEW QUESTIONS

1. What are human rights? What are the three categories of human rights?
2. What is globalization, and why do some analysts see economic globalization as possibly contributing to the undermining of social welfare programs?
3. How is it possible for some developing nations to become impoverished by "structural adjustment" programs? Explain.
4. How can a human rights–based approach to social welfare act as a counterbalance to economic globalization?
5. What challenges result from a human rights–based approach?
6. What are the potential effects of globalization on the welfare states? Are they negative or positive? Can you think of any positive impacts of economic globalization?

EXPLORING SOCIAL WELFARE

1. Read Appendix C, the report by the Committee on Economic, Social, and Cultural Rights on Canada's compliance with the *International Covenant on Economic, Social, and Cultural Rights*. Pick one of the major areas where the committee has concerns about Canada's performance. Visit the website of the Office of the United Nations High Commissioner for Human Rights (www.ohchr.org) to explore your chosen issue. Write a letter to your MP, a Cabinet minister, or the prime minister to outline your concerns about Canada's lack of compliance.
2. Some critics have argued that the world needs "fair trade" and not "free trade" to address global poverty. Research this issue for yourself. Does free trade necessarily contribute to global income inequalities? If so, how does this happen? If not, why do you think global poverty remains with us? Write a short report with full APA citations.

CRITICAL THINKING

Does it make sense to pose social welfare as fundamentally a human rights issue in this era of globalization?

Reflect on why there are so many human rights abuses throughout the world.

WEBSITES

United Nations Development Programme (UNDP)
www.undp.org
Since 1966, the UNDP has been partnering to help build nations that can withstand crisis and sustain the kind of growth that improves the quality of life for everyone. The UNDP works in four main areas: poverty reduction and achieving the Millennium Development Goals (MDGs); democratic governance; crisis prevention and recovery; and environment and sustainable development. In its activities, the UNDP encourages the protection of human rights, capacity development, and the empowerment of women.

International Forum on Globalization (IFG)
www.ifg.org/
The goal of the IFG is twofold: to expose the multiple effects of economic globalization in order to stimulate debate, and to seek to reverse the globalization process by encouraging ideas and activities that revitalize local economies and communities and ensure long-term ecological stability.

The Council of Canadians
www.canadians.org
Founded in 1985, the Council of Canadians conducts research and runs national campaigns aimed at putting some of the country's most important issues in the spotlight. Look to their site for valuable information on free trade, globalization, and their effects on Canada and the world.

Appendix A

Canada Health Transfer, Canada Social Transfer and Wait Times Reduction Transfer Regulations

SOR/2004-62
Registration March 30, 2004
FEDERAL-PROVINCIAL FISCAL ARRANGEMENTS ACT
Canada Health Transfer, Canada Social Transfer and Wait Times Reduction Transfer Regulations
P.C. 2004-331 March 30, 2004
Her Excellency the Governor General in Council, on the recommendation of the Minister of Finance, pursuant to section 40[1], of the *Federal-Provincial Fiscal Arrangements Act*[2], hereby makes the annexed *Canada Health Transfer and Canada Social Transfer Regulations*.

Canada Health Transfer and Canada Social Transfer Regulations

Interpretation

1. The following definitions apply in these Regulations.
   "Act" means the *Federal-Provincial Fiscal Arrangements Act*. (*Loi*)
   "population of a province for a fiscal year" means the population of a province for a fiscal year as determined in accordance with section 2. (*population d'une province pour un exercice*)
   "taxation year" means a taxation year within the meaning of the *Income Tax Act*. (*année d'imposition*)
   "transfer payment" means payment of the Canada Health Transfer, Canada Social Transfer or Wait Times Reduction Transfer under the Act, as the case may be. (*paiement de transfert*)

SOR/2008-312, s. 2.

Determination of Population of a Province

2. For the purposes of Parts V and V.1 of the Act and for the purposes of these Regulations, the manner in which the Chief Statistician of Canada shall determine the population of a province for a fiscal year is by basing that determination on Statistics Canada's official estimate of the population of the province on June 1 of that fiscal year.

SOR/2008-312, s. 3.

Calculation of Equalized Tax Transfer

3. (1) For the purposes of clause 24.7(1)(*b*)(ii)(A) of the Act, the relevant revenue bases for a province for a fiscal year shall be determined as follows:
   (*a*) with respect to personal income taxes, by aggregating
      (i) 75% of the assessed federal individual income tax applicable to the province for the taxation year ending in the fiscal year, as determined by the Minister of National Revenue, and
      (ii) 25% of the assessed federal individual income tax applicable to the province for the taxation year beginning in

the fiscal year, as determined by the Minister of National Revenue, and

(*b*) with respect to corporation income taxes, by aggregating

(i) 75% of the aggregate of taxable income earned in the taxation year in the province, as determined by the Minister of National Revenue under subsection 124(4) of the *Income Tax Act*, for all corporations having a taxation year ending in the calendar year that ends in the fiscal year, and

(ii) 25% of the aggregate of taxable income earned in the taxation year in the province, as determined by the Minister of National Revenue under subsection 124(4) of the *Income Tax Act*, for all corporations having a taxation year ending in the calendar year that begins in the fiscal year.

(2) to (4) [Repealed, SOR/2009-327, s. 1]
SOR/2007-200, s. 1; SOR/2009-327, s. 1.

3.1 (1) For the purpose of subsection (2), "national average rate of tax" means, in respect of a revenue source for a fiscal year, the rate equal to the quotient obtained by dividing the aggregate of the federal income tax reduction for the revenue source for the fiscal year for all provinces, excluding the territories, by the revenue base for the revenue source for the fiscal year for all provinces, excluding the territories.

(2) For the purposes of the calculation under subparagraph 24.7(1.2)(b)(ii) and paragraph 24.7(1.22)(a) of the Act,

(*a*) per capita national yield of the federal income tax reduction for a revenue source for a fiscal year is determined by dividing the product of the national average rate of tax for the revenue source for the fiscal year and the aggregate revenue base of all provinces, excluding the territories, for the revenue source for the fiscal year by the population of all provinces, excluding the territories, for the fiscal year; and

(*b*) per capita yield of the federal income tax reduction, in respect of a province for a revenue source for a fiscal year, is determined by dividing the product of the national average rate of tax for the revenue source for the fiscal year and the province's revenue base for the revenue source for the fiscal year by the population of the province for the fiscal year.

SOR/2009-327, s. 2.

Interim Estimates

4. (1) The Minister

(*a*) shall make an estimate of the amount of the transfer payment related to the Canada Health Transfer and the Canada Social Transfer to a province for each fiscal year in the period beginning on April 1, 2004 and ending on March 31, 2007,

(i) before April 16 of that fiscal year,

(ii) during the period beginning on September 1 and ending on October 12 of that fiscal year,

(iii) during the period beginning on January 12 and ending on the last day of February of that fiscal year,

(iv) during the period beginning on September 1 and ending on October 12 of the first fiscal year following the end of that fiscal year,

(v) during the period beginning on January 12 and ending on the last day of February of the first fiscal year following the end of that fiscal year,

(vi) during the period beginning on September 1 and ending on October 12 of the second fiscal year following the end of that fiscal year, and

(vii) during the period beginning on January 12 and ending on the last day of February of the second fiscal year following the end of that fiscal year; and

(*a.1*) shall make an estimate of the amount of the transfer payment related to the Canada Health Transfer to a province for each fiscal year in the period beginning on April 1, 2007 and ending on March 31, 2014,

(i) during the period beginning on September 1 and ending on December 31 prior to that fiscal year, except for the fiscal year 2007–2008,

(i.1) during the period beginning on January 1 and ending on March 31 prior to the fiscal year, for the fiscal year 2007–2008,

(ii) during the period beginning on September 1 and ending on October 12 of that fiscal year,

(iii) during the period beginning on September 1 and ending on October 12 following the end of that fiscal year, and

(iv) during the period beginning on September 1 and ending on October 12 of the second fiscal year following the end of that fiscal year;

(*a.2*) shall make an estimate of the amount of the transfer payment related to the Canada Social Transfer to a province for each fiscal year in the period beginning on April 1, 2007 and ending on March 31, 2014,

(i) during the period beginning on September 1 and ending on December 31 prior to that fiscal year, except for the fiscal year 2007–2008,

(i.1) during the period beginning on January 1 and ending on March 31 prior to the fiscal year, for the fiscal year 2007–2008, and

(ii) during the period beginning on September 1 and ending on October 12 of that fiscal year;

(*a.3*) shall make an estimate of the amount of the transfer payment related to the Wait Times Reduction

Transfer to a province for each fiscal year in the period beginning on April 1, 2009 and ending on March 31, 2014, during the period beginning on September 1 and ending on December 31 prior to that fiscal year;

(*b*) shall, if there is new information available that may have a significant effect on the amount of the transfer payment related to the Canada Health Transfer or Canada Social Transfer to a province, alter an estimate of the amount of the Canada Health Transfer or Canada Social Transfer payment to be made to each province for any of the fiscal years specified in paragraphs (a) to (a.2)

(i) during the second quarter of that fiscal year,

(ii) during March of that fiscal year, and

(iii) during any period beginning on the first day of the final month of a quarter and ending on the twelfth day of the subsequent quarter, other than the periods specified in paragraphs (a) to (a.2), following the end of the fiscal year, until such time as the final computation under subsection 5(2) is completed; and

(*c*) shall, if there is new information available that may have a significant effect on the amount of the transfer payment related to the Wait Times Reduction Transfer to a province, alter an estimate of the amount of the Wait Times Reduction Transfer payment to be made to each province for any of the fiscal years specified in paragraph (a.3) during any period beginning on the first day of the final month of a quarter and ending on the 12th day of the subsequent quarter, until such time as the final computation under subsection 5(2) is completed.

(1.1) Despite subsection (1), the Minister is not required to make the estimates referred to in subparagraphs (1)(a.1)(iii) and (iv) in respect of the amount of the transfer payment related to the Canada Health Transfer for the fiscal year 2009-2010.

(2) If an estimate made under subparagraph (1)(*a*)(i), (*a.1*)(i) or (i.1) or (*a.2*)(i) or (i.1) or paragraph (*a.3*) establishes that a transfer payment is to be made to a province for a fiscal year, the Minister shall pay to the province, on account of the final payment for the fiscal year, an amount equal to one twenty-fourth of the amount so estimated on the first and third working days after the fifteenth calendar day of each month in that fiscal year.

(3) If an estimate made under any of subparagraphs (1)(*a*)(ii) or (iii), (*a.1*)(ii), (*a.2*)(ii), (*b*)(i) or paragraph (*c*) establishes that the amount payable to the province under the immediately preceding estimate in respect of that fiscal year should be revised, the Minister shall

(*a*) if any amount remains payable to the province, adjust the remaining payments referred to in subsection (2) in respect of that fiscal year in accordance with the new estimate, beginning with the first payment in the month following the month during which that estimate was calculated; and

(*b*) if an overpayment has been made to the province, recover the amount of the overpayment before the end of the fiscal year.

(4) If an estimate made under any of subparagraphs (1)(*a*)(iv) to (vii), (*a.1*)(iii) or (iv) or (*b*)(iii) establishes that

(*a*) an underpayment has been made to the province, the Minister shall pay the amount of the underpayment to the province within the four months following the month during which the estimate was made; and

(*b*) an overpayment has been made to the province, the Minister shall recover the amount of the overpayment within the four months following the month during which the estimate was made.

(5) If an estimate made under subparagraph (1)(b)(ii) establishes that the amount payable to the province under the immediately preceding estimate in respect of that fiscal year should be revised, the Minister shall

(*a*) if any amount remains payable to the province, pay to the province the amount in the month during which the estimate was made or, if the province so requests, pay the province that amount within the four months following the month during which the estimate was made; and

(*b*) if an overpayment has been made to the province, recover the amount of the overpayment in the month during which the estimate was made or, if the province so requests, recover the amount within the four months following that month.

(6) If an estimate establishes that an overpayment has been made to a province in respect of a fiscal year, the Minister may, subject to paragraph (3)(b), (4)(b) or (5)(b), recover the amount of the overpayment

(*a*) from any amount payable to the province under the Act; or

(*b*) from the province as a debt due to Her Majesty in right of Canada.

(7) For the purpose of making an estimate under subsection (1), the population of a province for a fiscal year is the population of that province on June 1 of that fiscal year as estimated by the Minister on the basis of population statistics made available to the Minister by the Chief Statistician of Canada.

(8) The requirement set out in paragraph (1)(b) does not apply to any estimate made in respect of the amount of the transfer payment related to the Canada Health Transfer for the fiscal year 2009-2010.

SOR/2007-200, s. 2; SOR/2008-312, s. 4; SOR/2009-327, s. 3.

Final Computation

5. (1) In respect of each fiscal year referred to in subsection (1.1), the Chief Statistician of Canada shall prepare and submit to the Minister, not later than the period set out that subsection, a certificate in respect of that fiscal year based on the most recent information prepared by Statistics Canada for that fiscal year, setting out, in respect of each province, the population of the province for the fiscal years required by the Act.

(1.1) The Chief Statistician of Canada shall prepare the certificate for the following transfer payments and fiscal years and shall submit the certificate to the Minister within the periods set out below:

(*a*) for the Canada Health Transfer in respect of each fiscal year in the period beginning on April 1, 2004 and ending on March 31, 2014, not later than 30 months after the end of that fiscal year;

(*b*) for the Canada Social Transfer

(i) in respect of each fiscal year in the period beginning on April 1, 2004 and ending on March 31, 2007, not later than 30 months after the end of that fiscal year, and

(ii) in respect of each fiscal year in the period beginning on April 1, 2007 and ending on March 31, 2014, not later than six months after the end of that fiscal year; and

(*c*) for the Wait Times Reduction Transfer for each fiscal year in the period beginning on April 1, 2009 and ending on March 31, 2014, not later than six months before the end of that fiscal year.

(2) Within 30 days after the receipt by the Minister of the certificate submitted by the Chief Statistician of Canada under subsection (1) in respect of a fiscal year, the Minister shall make the final computation on the basis of the information contained in that certificate of the amount, if any, of the transfer payment that is payable for that fiscal year under the Act to a province, and the Minister shall subsequently furnish each province with tables setting out the details of that computation.

(2.1) Despite subsection (2), the Minister is not required to make the final computation of the amount of the transfer payment related to the Canada Health Transfer for the fiscal year 2009-2010.

(3) If a final computation made under subsection (2) establishes that there remains an amount payable to a province for a fiscal year, the Minister shall

(*a*) in the case of the Canada Health Transfer or the Canada Social Transfer, pay to the province the amount; and

(*b*) in the case of the Wait Times Reduction Transfer, adjust the remaining payments referred to in subsection 4(2) for that fiscal year in accordance with the final computation, beginning with the first payment in the month after the month during which that final computation was calculated.

(4) If a final computation made under subsection (2) establishes that an overpayment has been made to a province in respect of a fiscal year, the Minister shall recover the amount of the overpayment

(*a*) from any amount payable to the province under the Act; or

(*b*) from the province as a debt due to Her Majesty in right of Canada.

SOR/2007-200, s. 3; SOR/2008-312, s. 5; SOR/2009-327, s. 4.

Coming into Force

6. These Regulations come into force on the day on which they are registered.

Notes

1. S.C. 1999, c. 31, s. 93.
2. S.C. 1995, c. 17, s. 45 (1).

Appendix B

International Covenant on Economic, Social and Cultural Rights

G.A. res. 2200A (XXI), 21 U.N.GAOR Supp. (No. 16) at 49, U.N. Doc. A/6316 (1966), 993 U.N.T.S. 3, entered into force Jan. 3, 1976.
[Note: This copy is for information only.]

Preamble

The States Parties to the present Covenant, considering that, in accordance with the principles proclaimed in the Charter of the United Nations, recognition of the inherent dignity and of the equal and inalienable rights of all members of the human family is the foundation of freedom, justice and peace in the world,
Recognizing that these rights derive from the inherent dignity of the human person,
Recognizing that, in accordance with the Universal Declaration of Human Rights, the ideal of free human beings enjoying freedom from fear and want can only be achieved if conditions are created whereby everyone may enjoy his economic, social and cultural rights, as well as his civil and political rights,
Considering the obligation of States under the Charter of the United Nations to promote universal respect for, and observance of, human rights and freedoms,
Realizing that the individual, having duties to other individuals and to the community to which he belongs, is under a responsibility to strive for the promotion and observance of the rights recognized in the present Covenant,
Agree upon the following articles:

PART I

Article 1

1. All peoples have the right of self-determination. By virtue of that right they freely determine their political status and freely pursue their economic, social and cultural development.
2. All peoples may, for their own ends, freely dispose of their natural wealth and resources without prejudice to any obligations arising out of international economic co-operation, based upon the principle of mutual benefit, and international law. In no case may a people be deprived of its own means of subsistence.
3. The States Parties to the present Covenant, including those having responsibility for the administration of Non-Self-Governing and Trust Territories, shall promote the realization of the right of self-determination, and shall respect that right, in conformity with the provisions of the Charter of the United Nations.

PART II

Article 2

1. Each State Party to the present Covenant undertakes to take steps, individually and through international assistance and co-operation, especially economic and technical, to the maximum of its available resources, with a view to achieving progressively the full realization of the rights recognized in the present Covenant by all appropriate means, including particularly the adoption of legislative measures.
2. The States Parties to the present Covenant undertake to guarantee that the rights enunciated in the present

Covenant will be exercised without discrimination of any kind as to race, colour, sex, language, religion, political or other opinion, national or social origin, property, birth or other status.

3. Developing countries, with due regard to human rights and their national economy, may determine to what extent they would guarantee the economic rights recognized in the present Covenant to non-nationals.

Article 3

The States Parties to the present Covenant undertake to ensure the equal right of men and women to the enjoyment of all economic, social and cultural rights set forth in the present Covenant.

Article 4

The States Parties to the present Covenant recognize that, in the enjoyment of those rights provided by the State in conformity with the present Covenant, the State may subject such rights only to such limitations as are determined by law only in so far as this may be compatible with the nature of these rights and solely for the purpose of promoting the general welfare in a democratic society.

Article 5

1. Nothing in the present Covenant may be interpreted as implying for any State, group or person any right to engage in any activity or to perform any act aimed at the destruction of any of the rights or freedoms recognized herein, or at their limitation to a greater extent than is provided for in the present Covenant.
2. No restriction upon or derogation from any of the fundamental human rights recognized or existing in any country in virtue of law, conventions, regulations or custom shall be admitted on the pretext that the present Covenant does not recognize such rights or that it recognizes them to a lesser extent.

PART III

Article 6

1. The States Parties to the present Covenant recognize the right to work, which includes the right of everyone to the opportunity to gain his living by work which he freely chooses or accepts, and will take appropriate steps to safeguard this right.
2. The steps to be taken by a State Party to the present Covenant to achieve the full realization of this right shall include technical and vocational guidance and training programmes, policies and techniques to achieve steady economic, social and cultural development and full and productive employment under conditions safeguarding fundamental political and economic freedoms to the individual.

Article 7

The States Parties to the present Covenant recognize the right of everyone to the enjoyment of just and favourable conditions of work which ensure, in particular:

(a) Remuneration which provides all workers, as a minimum, with:
   (i) Fair wages and equal remuneration for work of equal value without distinction of any kind, in particular women being guaranteed conditions of work not inferior to those enjoyed by men, with equal pay for equal work;
   (ii) A decent living for themselves and their families in accordance with the provisions of the present Covenant;

(b) Safe and healthy working conditions;

(c) Equal opportunity for everyone to be promoted in his employment to an appropriate higher level, subject to no considerations other than those of seniority and competence;

(d) Rest, leisure and reasonable limitation of working hours and periodic holidays with pay, as well as remuneration for public holidays.

Article 8

1. The States Parties to the present Covenant undertake to ensure:
   (a) The right of everyone to form trade unions and join the trade union of his choice, subject only to the rules of the organization concerned, for the promotion and protection of his economic and social interests. No restrictions may be placed on the exercise of this right other than those prescribed by law and which are necessary in a democratic society in the interests of national security or public order or for the protection of the rights and freedoms of others;
   (b) The right of trade unions to establish national federations or confederations and the right of the latter to form or join international trade-union organizations;
   (c) The right of trade unions to function freely subject to no limitations other than those prescribed by law and which are necessary in a democratic society in the interests of national security or public order or for the protection of the rights and freedoms of others;
   (d) The right to strike, provided that it is exercised in conformity with the laws of the particular country.
2. This article shall not prevent the imposition of lawful restrictions on the exercise of these rights by members of the armed forces or of the police or of the administration of the State.

3. Nothing in this article shall authorize States Parties to the International Labour Organisation Convention of 1948 concerning Freedom of Association and Protection of the Right to Organize to take legislative measures which would prejudice, or apply the law in such a manner as would prejudice, the guarantees provided for in that Convention.

Article 9

The States Parties to the present Covenant recognize the right of everyone to social security, including social insurance.

Article 10

The States Parties to the present Covenant recognize that:

1. The widest possible protection and assistance should be accorded to the family, which is the natural and fundamental group unit of society, particularly for its establishment and while it is responsible for the care and education of dependent children. Marriage must be entered into with the free consent of the intending spouses.
2. Special protection should be accorded to mothers during a reasonable period before and after childbirth. During such period working mothers should be accorded paid leave or leave with adequate social security benefits.
3. Special measures of protection and assistance should be taken on behalf of all children and young persons without any discrimination for reasons of parentage or other conditions. Children and young persons should be protected from economic and social exploitation. Their employment in work harmful to their morals or health or dangerous to life or likely to hamper their normal development should be punishable by law. States should also set age limits below which the paid employment of child labour should be prohibited and punishable by law.

Article 11

1. The States Parties to the present Covenant recognize the right of everyone to an adequate standard of living for himself and his family, including adequate food, clothing and housing, and to the continuous improvement of living conditions. The States Parties will take appropriate steps to ensure the realization of this right, recognizing to this effect the essential importance of international co-operation based on free consent.
2. The States Parties to the present Covenant, recognizing the fundamental right of everyone to be free from hunger, shall take, individually and through international co-operation, the measures, including specific programmes, which are needed:
   (a) To improve methods of production, conservation and distribution of food by making full use of technical and scientific knowledge, by disseminating knowledge of the principles of nutrition and by developing or reforming agrarian systems in such a way as to achieve the most efficient development and utilization of natural resources;
   (b) Taking into account the problems of both food-importing and food-exporting countries, to ensure an equitable distribution of world food supplies in relation to need.

Article 12

1. The States Parties to the present Covenant recognize the right of everyone to the enjoyment of the highest attainable standard of physical and mental health.
2. The steps to be taken by the States Parties to the present Covenant to achieve the full realization of this right shall include those necessary for:
   (a) The provision for the reduction of the stillbirth-rate and of infant mortality and for the healthy development of the child;
   (b) The improvement of all aspects of environmental and industrial hygiene;
   (c) The prevention, treatment and control of epidemic, endemic, occupational and other diseases;
   (d) The creation of conditions which would assure to all medical service and medical attention in the event of sickness.

Article 13

1. The States Parties to the present Covenant recognize the right of everyone to education. They agree that education shall be directed to the full development of the human personality and the sense of its dignity, and shall strengthen the respect for human rights and fundamental freedoms. They further agree that education shall enable all persons to participate effectively in a free society, promote understanding, tolerance and friendship among all nations and all racial, ethnic or religious groups, and further the activities of the United Nations for the maintenance of peace.
2. The States Parties to the present Covenant recognize that, with a view to achieving the full realization of this right:
   (a) Primary education shall be compulsory and available free to all;
   (b) Secondary education in its different forms, including technical and vocational secondary education, shall be made generally available and accessible to all by every appropriate means, and in particular by the progressive introduction of free education;
   (c) Higher education shall be made equally accessible to all, on the basis of capacity, by every appropriate means, and in particular by the progressive introduction of free education;

(d) Fundamental education shall be encouraged or intensified as far as possible for those persons who have not received or completed the whole period of their primary education;

(e) The development of a system of schools at all levels shall be actively pursued, an adequate fellowship system shall be established, and the material conditions of teaching staff shall be continuously improved.

3. The States Parties to the present Covenant undertake to have respect for the liberty of parents and, when applicable, legal guardians to choose for their children schools, other than those established by the public authorities, which conform to such minimum educational standards as may be laid down or approved by the State and to ensure the religious and moral education of their children in conformity with their own convictions.

4. No part of this article shall be construed so as to interfere with the liberty of individuals and bodies to establish and direct educational institutions, subject always to the observance of the principles set forth in paragraph I of this article and to the requirement that the education given in such institutions shall conform to such minimum standards as may be laid down by the State.

Article 14

Each State Party to the present Covenant which, at the time of becoming a Party, has not been able to secure in its metropolitan territory or other territories under its jurisdiction compulsory primary education, free of charge, undertakes, within two years, to work out and adopt a detailed plan of action for the progressive implementation, within a reasonable number of years, to be fixed in the plan, of the principle of compulsory education free of charge for all.

Article 15

1. The States Parties to the present Covenant recognize the right of everyone:
   (a) To take part in cultural life;
   (b) To enjoy the benefits of scientific progress and its applications;
   (c) To benefit from the protection of the moral and material interests resulting from any scientific, literary or artistic production of which he is the author.
2. The steps to be taken by the States Parties to the present Covenant to achieve the full realization of this right shall include those necessary for the conservation, the development and the diffusion of science and culture.
3. The States Parties to the present Covenant undertake to respect the freedom indispensable for scientific research and creative activity.
4. The States Parties to the present Covenant recognize the benefits to be derived from the encouragement and development of international contacts and co-operation in the scientific and cultural fields.

PART IV

Article 16

1. The States Parties to the present Covenant undertake to submit in conformity with this part of the Covenant reports on the measures which they have adopted and the progress made in achieving the observance of the rights recognized herein.
2. (a) All reports shall be submitted to the Secretary-General of the United Nations, who shall transmit copies to the Economic and Social Council for consideration in accordance with the provisions of the present Covenant;
   (b) The Secretary-General of the United Nations shall also transmit to the specialized agencies copies of the reports, or any relevant parts therefrom, from States Parties to the present Covenant which are also members of these specialized agencies in so far as these reports, or parts therefrom, relate to any matters which fall within the responsibilities of the said agencies in accordance with their constitutional instruments.

Article 17

1. The States Parties to the present Covenant shall furnish their reports in stages, in accordance with a programme to be established by the Economic and Social Council within one year of the entry into force of the present Covenant after consultation with the States Parties and the specialized agencies concerned.
2. Reports may indicate factors and difficulties affecting the degree of fulfilment of obligations under the present Covenant.
3. Where relevant information has previously been furnished to the United Nations or to any specialized agency by any State Party to the present Covenant, it will not be necessary to reproduce that information, but a precise reference to the information so furnished will suffice.

Article 18

Pursuant to its responsibilities under the Charter of the United Nations in the field of human rights and fundamental freedoms, the Economic and Social Council may make arrangements with the specialized agencies in respect of their reporting to it on the progress made in achieving the observance of the provisions of the present Covenant falling within the scope of their activities. These reports may include particulars of decisions and recommendations on such implementation adopted by their competent organs.

Article 19

The Economic and Social Council may transmit to the Commission on Human Rights for study and general recommendation or, as appropriate, for information the reports concerning human rights submitted by States in accordance with articles 16 and 17, and those concerning human rights submitted by the specialized agencies in accordance with article 18.

Article 20

The States Parties to the present Covenant and the specialized agencies concerned may submit comments to the Economic and Social Council on any general recommendation under article 19 or reference to such general recommendation in any report of the Commission on Human Rights or any documentation referred to therein.

Article 21

The Economic and Social Council may submit from time to time to the General Assembly reports with recommendations of a general nature and a summary of the information received from the States Parties to the present Covenant and the specialized agencies on the measures taken and the progress made in achieving general observance of the rights recognized in the present Covenant.

Article 22

The Economic and Social Council may bring to the attention of other organs of the United Nations, their subsidiary organs and specialized agencies concerned with furnishing technical assistance any matters arising out of the reports referred to in this part of the present Covenant which may assist such bodies in deciding, each within its field of competence, on the advisability of international measures likely to contribute to the effective progressive implementation of the present Covenant.

Article 23

The States Parties to the present Covenant agree that international action for the achievement of the rights recognized in the present Covenant includes such methods as the conclusion of conventions, the adoption of recommendations, the furnishing of technical assistance and the holding of regional meetings and technical meetings for the purpose of consultation and study organized in conjunction with the Governments concerned.

Article 24

Nothing in the present Covenant shall be interpreted as impairing the provisions of the Charter of the United Nations and of the constitutions of the specialized agencies which define the respective responsibilities of the various organs of the United Nations and of the specialized agencies in regard to the matters dealt with in the present Covenant.

Article 25

Nothing in the present Covenant shall be interpreted as impairing the inherent right of all peoples to enjoy and utilize fully and freely their natural wealth and resources.

PART V

Article 26

1. The present Covenant is open for signature by any State Member of the United Nations or member of any of its specialized agencies, by any State Party to the Statute of the International Court of Justice, and by any other State which has been invited by the General Assembly of the United Nations to become a party to the present Covenant.
2. The present Covenant is subject to ratification. Instruments of ratification shall be deposited with the Secretary-General of the United Nations.
3. The present Covenant shall be open to accession by any State referred to in paragraph 1 of this article.
4. Accession shall be effected by the deposit of an instrument of accession with the Secretary-General of the United Nations.
5. The Secretary-General of the United Nations shall inform all States which have signed the present Covenant or acceded to it of the deposit of each instrument of ratification or accession.

Article 27

1. The present Covenant shall enter into force three months after the date of the deposit with the Secretary-General of the United Nations of the thirty-fifth instrument of ratification or instrument of accession.
2. For each State ratifying the present Covenant or acceding to it after the deposit of the thirty-fifth instrument of ratification or instrument of accession, the present Covenant shall enter into force three months after the date of the deposit of its own instrument of ratification or instrument of accession.

Article 28

The provisions of the present Covenant shall extend to all parts of federal States without any limitations or exceptions.

Article 29

1. Any State Party to the present Covenant may propose an amendment and file it with the Secretary-General of the United Nations. The Secretary-General shall thereupon communicate any proposed amendments to the States Parties to the present Covenant with a request that they notify him whether they favour a conference of States Parties for the purpose of considering and voting upon the proposals. In the event that at least one third of the States Parties favours such a conference, the Secretary-General shall convene the conference under the auspices of the United Nations. Any amendment adopted by a majority of the States Parties present and voting at the conference shall be submitted to the General Assembly of the United Nations for approval.
2. Amendments shall come into force when they have been approved by the General Assembly of the United Nations and accepted by a two-thirds majority of the States Parties to the present Covenant in accordance with their respective constitutional processes.
3. When amendments come into force they shall be binding on those States Parties which have accepted them, other States Parties still being bound by the provisions of the present Covenant and any earlier amendment which they have accepted.

Article 30

Irrespective of the notifications made under article 26, paragraph 5, the Secretary-General of the United Nations shall inform all States referred to in paragraph 1 of the same article of the following particulars:

(a) Signatures, ratifications and accessions under article 26;

(b) The date of the entry into force of the present Covenant under article 27 and the date of the entry into force of any amendments under article 29.

Article 31

1. The present Covenant, of which the Chinese, English, French, Russian and Spanish texts are equally authentic, shall be deposited in the archives of the United Nations.
2. The Secretary-General of the United Nations shall transmit certified copies of the present Covenant to all States referred to in article 26.

Appendix C

UN Economic and Social Council Committee on Economic, Social and Cultural Rights

Thirty-sixth session
Geneva, 1-19 May 2006

Consideration of Reports Submitted by States Parties Under Articles 16 and 17 of the Covenant

Concluding observations of the Committee on Economic, Social and Cultural Rights

CANADA

1. The Committee on Economic, Social and Cultural Rights considered the fourth and fifth periodic reports of Canada on the implementation of the International Covenant on Economic, Social and Cultural Rights (E/C.12/4/Add.15 and E/C.12/CAN/5) at its 9th to 12th meetings, held on 5 and 8 May 2006 (E/C.12/2006/SR.9-12), and adopted, at its 29th meeting, held on 19 May 2006, the following concluding observations.

A. Introduction

2. The Committee welcomes the submission of the fourth and fifth periodic reports of the State party, as well as the written responses provided in advance to the Committee's lists of issues (E/C.12/Q/CAN/2 and E/C.12/CAN/Q/5). The Committee also welcomes the dialogue with the State party's delegation, composed of experts in the various fields covered by the Covenant, as well as of representatives from some provinces and territories of the State party. The Committee notes, however, that the submission of the fifth periodic report at a time when the fourth periodic report had not yet been considered did not facilitate the consideration of the situation in the State party.

B. Positive aspects

3. The Committee notes that Canada still ranks near the top of the Human Development Index of the United Nations Development Programme. On the average, Canadians enjoy a high standard of living and Canada has the capacity to achieve a high level of realization of all Covenant rights.
4. The Committee welcomes the relatively low level of unemployment in the State party, and the decrease in the proportion of persons living below the Low-Income Cut-Off (as defined by Statistics Canada) from 13.7 per cent in 1998 to 11.2 per cent in 2004.
5. The Committee notes with appreciation the reduction in disparities between Aboriginal people and the rest of the population in the State party with regard to infant mortality and secondary education.

6. The Committee welcomes the measures taken by the State party in the area of equal pay for equal work, in particular the payment of retroactive adjustments to women who had suffered discrimination.
7. The Committee welcomes the extension of maternity and parental benefits from six months to one year.
8. The Committee notes with satisfaction the numerous health programmes conducted by the State party, such as the 10-Year Plan to Strengthen Health Care and the launch of the Public Health Agency.
9. The Committee notes that Canada's level of official development assistance was raised from about 0.27 per cent of GDP in 2004 to a current estimated level of 0.33 per cent of GDP.

C. Factors and difficulties impeding the implementation of the Covenant

10. The Committee notes the absence of any factors or difficulties preventing the effective implementation of the Covenant in the State party.

D. Principal subjects of concern

11. The Committee regrets that most of its 1993 and 1998 recommendations in relation to the second and third periodic reports have not been implemented, and that the State party has not addressed in an effective manner the following principal subjects of concern, which are still relevant:
    (a) The State party's restrictive interpretation of its obligations under the Covenant, in particular its position that it may implement the legal obligations set forth in the Covenant by adopting specific measures and policies rather than by enacting legislation specifically recognizing economic, social and cultural rights, and the consequent lack of awareness, in the provinces and territories, of the State party's legal obligations under the Covenant;
    (b) The lack of legal redress available to individuals when governments fail to implement the Covenant, resulting from the insufficient coverage in domestic legislation of economic, social and cultural rights, as spelled out in the Covenant; the lack of effective enforcement mechanisms for these rights; the practice of governments of urging upon their courts an interpretation of the Canadian Charter of Rights and Freedoms denying protection of Covenant rights, and the inadequate availability of civil legal aid, particularly for economic, social and cultural rights;
    (c) The absence of a legally enforceable right to adequate social assistance benefits for all persons in need on a non-discriminatory basis and the negative impact of certain workfare programmes on social assistance recipients;
    (d) The disparities that still persist between Aboriginal peoples and the rest of the Canadian population in the enjoyment of Covenant rights, as well as the discrimination still experienced by Aboriginal women in matters of matrimonial property;
    (e) The absence of an official poverty line;
    (f) The insufficiency of minimum wage and social assistance to ensure the realization of the right to an adequate standard of living for all;
    (g) The authorization given to provinces and territories to deduct the amount of the child benefit under the National Child Benefit Scheme from the amount of social assistance received by parents on welfare.
12. The Committee is concerned that, despite the consultations and sharing of information between federal, provincial and territorial governments through the federal/provincial/territorial Continuing Committee of Officials on Human Rights, effective procedures to follow-up on the Committee's concluding observations have not been developed.
13. The Committee, while noting the State party's Court Challenges Program, regrets that this programme has not been extended to permit funding with respect to challenges to provincial and territorial legislation and policies, as previously recommended by the Committee.
14. The Committee notes with concern the cuts in financial support to civil legal aid services with regard to economic, social and cultural rights in a number of jurisdictions of the State party. This leads to a situation where poor people, in particular poor single women, who are denied benefits and services to which they are entitled to under domestic law, cannot access domestic remedies. The drastic cuts in British Columbia raise particular concern in this regard.
15. The Committee is concerned that, despite Canada's economic prosperity and the reduction of the number of people living below the Low-Income Cut-Off, 11.2 per cent of its population still lived in poverty in 2004, and that significant differences in levels of poverty persist between provinces and territories. The Committee also notes with particular concern that poverty rates remain very high among disadvantaged and marginalized individuals and groups such as Aboriginal peoples, African Canadians, immigrants, persons with disabilities, youth, low-income women and single mothers. In a number of jurisdictions, including British Columbia, poverty rates have increased among single mothers and children in the period between 1998 and 2003. The Committee is also concerned by the significant disparities still remaining between Aboriginal people and the rest of the population in areas of employment, access to water, health, housing and education, and by the failure of the State party to fully acknowledge the barriers faced by

African Canadians in the enjoyment of their rights under the Covenant.

16. The Committee, while noting that the State party has withdrawn, since 1998, the requirement for an express reference to extinguishment of Aboriginal rights and titles either in a comprehensive claim agreement or in the settlement legislation ratifying the agreement, remains concerned that the new approaches, namely the "modified rights model" and the "non-assertion model", do not differ much from the extinguishment and surrender approach. It further regrets not having received detailed information on other approaches based on recognition and coexistence of rights, which are currently under study.
17. The Committee notes with concern that the long-standing issues of discrimination against First Nations women and their children, in matters relating to Indian status, band membership, and matrimonial real property on reserve lands have still not been resolved. The Committee notes that such discrimination has had a negative impact on the enjoyment of economic, social and cultural rights of some First Nations women and their children under the Covenant.
18. The Committee notes with concern that the minimum wages in all provinces and territories of the State party are below the Low-Income Cut-Off and are insufficient to enable workers and their families to enjoy a decent standard of living.
19. The Committee is concerned that some categories of workers, such as public servants and employees of Crown corporations, public school teachers and college and university professors, are excluded from the right to strike in Canada. The Committee considers that the explanation provided by the State party that these workers provide essential services, is not satisfactory under articles 4 and 8 of the Covenant.
20. The Committee reiterates its concern that federal transfers for social assistance and social services to provinces and territories still do not include standards in relation to some of the rights set forth in the Covenant, including the right to social security. The Committee is also concerned that while the federal Government has increased its contribution to the costs of health care through the Canada Health Transfer, its support for post-secondary education, social assistance and social services through the Canada Social Transfer has not been restored to 1994-1995 levels, in spite of the sustained economic growth in the State party during these last years.
21. The Committee is concerned that the State party has not provided detailed information as to whether current provincial and territorial social assistance rates allow recipients to enjoy an adequate standard of living. It notes with concern that in most provinces and territories, social assistance benefits are lower than a decade ago, that they do not provide adequate income to meet basic needs for food, clothing and shelter, and that welfare levels are often set at less than half the Low-Income Cut-Off.
22. The Committee expresses concern about the significantly low proportion of unemployed workers eligible for receiving insurance benefits, and notes that the State party has not provided detailed responses to the Committee's previous concerns on this issue. The Committee notes with concern that in 2001, only 39 per cent of unemployed Canadians were eligible for benefits; that in some provinces, such as Ontario, eligibility rates are even lower; that the number of youth receiving employment insurance benefits has decreased; that migrant workers and many part-time workers, predominantly women, contribute to the plan but have great difficulties in accessing benefits; and that the replacement rate of income which has been reduced to 55 per cent in 1997, is the lowest ever.
23. The Committee is deeply concerned by the discriminatory impact of the National Child Benefit "clawback system" on the poorest families in Canada, in particular single-mother-led families.
24. The Committee notes with concern that low-income families, single-mother-led families and Aboriginal and African Canadian families, are overrepresented in families whose children are relinquished to foster care. The Committee is also concerned that women continue to be forced to relinquish their children into foster care because of inadequate housing.
25. The Committee regrets that domestic violence as a specific offence has not been included in the Criminal Code.
26. The Committee notes with concern that women are prevented from leaving abusive relationships due to the lack of affordable housing and inadequate assistance.
27. The Committee notes with concern that about 7.4 per cent of the population, amounting to about 2.3 million people, suffer from food insecurity in the State party, that about 40 per cent of food bank users are children and young people, and that about 51 per cent of food bank users while receiving social assistance benefits in 2005, still had to resort to food banks because of the insufficient level of these benefits.
28. The Committee, while welcoming the National Homelessness Initiative and the adoption of numerous measures on housing, regrets that the information provided was not sufficient to assess the results of such measures. In particular, the Committee is concerned that the estimated number of homeless persons in Canada still ranges from 100,000 to 250,000. The Committee, while welcoming the decrease in the proportion of households with core housing need, notes with concern that in 2001 such households still represented about

13.7 to 16 per cent of all households. The Committee is further concerned that shelter allowances and social assistance rates continue to fall far below average rental costs, and that waiting lists for subsidized housing remain very long, for example, in Hamilton and Montreal.

29. The Committee notes with particular concern that many evictions occur on account of minimal arrears of rent, without due consideration of the State party's obligations under the Covenant.
30. The Committee regrets that the State party does not recognize the right to water as a legal entitlement, which is implicitly provided for under articles 11 and 12 of the Covenant, as outlined in the Committee's general comment No. 15 (2002) on the right to water.
31. The Committee, while noting that scholarships, bursaries, loans and other types of supports are provided to disadvantaged and marginalized individuals and groups, expresses concern about the discriminatory impact of tuition fee increases on low-income persons in many provinces and territories since 1998.
32. The Committee is concerned about information that African Canadian students face difficulties in accessing education and that they experience a disproportionately high drop-out rate from secondary school.
33. The Committee, while noting the numerous programmes adopted to preserve Aboriginal languages in the State party, as well as the studies conducted in the area of the protection of traditional knowledge, regrets that no time frame has been set up for the consideration and implementation of the recommendations of the Task Force on Aboriginal Languages and Cultures, and that no concrete measures have been adopted in the area of intellectual property for the protection and promotion of ancestral rights and traditional knowledge of Aboriginal peoples.

E. Suggestions and recommendations

34. The Committee calls upon the State party to address the specific subjects of concern that date back to its second and third periodic reports and strongly reiterates that the State party should consider implementing the Committee's suggestions and recommendations in this regard.
35. The Committee reiterates its recommendation that the federal Government take concrete steps to ensure that provinces and territories are made aware of the State party's legal obligations under the Covenant, that the Covenant rights should be enforceable within provinces and territories through legislation or policy measures, and that independent and appropriate monitoring and adjudication mechanisms be established in this regard. In particular, the State party should establish transparent and effective mechanisms, involving all levels of government as well as civil society, including indigenous peoples, with the specific mandate to follow up on the Committee's concluding observations.
36. The Committee recalls that, within the limits of the appropriate exercise of their functions of judicial review, courts should take account of Covenant rights where this is necessary to ensure that the State party's conduct is consistent with its obligations under the Covenant, in line with the Committee's general comment No. 9 (1998) (see for example *Chaoulli v. Quebec - Attorney General*).
37. The Committee urges the State party to re examine its policies and practices towards the inherent rights and titles of Aboriginal peoples, to ensure that policies and practices do not result in extinguishment of those rights and titles.
38. The Committee strongly recommends that the State party resume negotiations with the Lubicon Lake Band, with a view to finding a solution to the claims of the Band that ensures the enjoyment of their rights under the Covenant. The Committee also strongly recommends that the State party conduct effective consultation with the Band prior to the grant of licences for economic purposes in the disputed land, and to ensure that such activities do not jeopardize the rights recognized under the Covenant.
39. The Committee recommends that federal, provincial and territorial legislation be brought in line with the State party's obligations under the Covenant, and that such legislation should protect poor people in all jurisdictions from discrimination because of their social or economic status.
40. The State party should take immediate steps, including legislative measures, to create and ensure effective domestic remedies for all Covenant rights in all relevant jurisdictions.
41. The Committee, drawing the State party's attention to its general comment No. 9 (1998), reiterates its recommendation that the federal, provincial and territorial governments promote interpretations of the Canadian Charter of Rights and other domestic law in a way consistent with the Covenant.
42. The Committee reiterates its recommendation that the State party extend the Court Challenges Programme to permit funding of challenges with respect to provincial and territorial legislation and policies.
43. The Committee recommends that the State party ensure that civil legal aid with regard to economic, social and cultural rights is provided to poor people in the provinces and territories, and that it be adequate with respect to coverage, eligibility and services provided.
44. The Committee recommends that the State party fully abide by its obligations under article 2, paragraph 1, of the Covenant to take all possible measures to the maximum of its available resources to ensure the

enjoyment of economic, social and cultural rights for all and reminds the State party, in line with its general comment No. 3 (1990), that steps to that end "should be deliberate, concrete and targeted as clearly as possible towards meeting the obligations recognized in the Covenant". The Committee also recommends that the State party eliminate gaps in the area of poverty as a matter of priority, bearing in mind the immediate nature of the obligations contained in articles 2 and 3 of the Covenant. The Committee further recommends that the State party assess the extent to which poverty is a discrimination issue in Canada, and ensure that measures and programmes do not have a negative impact on the enjoyment of economic, social and cultural rights, especially for disadvantaged and marginalized individuals and groups.

45. The Committee recommends that the State party, in consultation with First Nations and including Aboriginal women's groups, adopt measures to combat discrimination against First Nations women and their children in matters relating to Indian status, band membership and matrimonial property. In particular, the Committee urges the State party to repeal section 67 of the Canadian Human Rights Act, which prevents First Nations people from filing complaints of discrimination before a human rights commission or tribunal. The Committee also urges the State party to amend the Indian Act to remove any residual discrimination against First Nations women and their children.
46. The Committee recommends that the State party take into consideration the right to work of women and the need of parents to balance work and family life, by supporting their care choices through adequate childcare services.
47. The Committee urges the State party to adopt all necessary measures to ensure that minimum wages are increased throughout Canada to a level enabling workers and their families to enjoy a decent standard of living.
48. The Committee recommends that the State party take steps to ensure access to employment insurance benefits, enjoyment of trade union rights and effective protection by labour standards for workers in precarious, part-time and temporary low wage jobs in the State party, particularly women.
49. The Committee urges the State party to adopt effective measures, legislative or otherwise, to eliminate exploitation and abuse of migrant domestic workers who are under the federal Live-in Caregiver Program.
50. The Committee recommends that legislation be adopted at the provincial and territorial levels, where necessary, to ensure equal remuneration for work of equal value in both the public and private sectors. In this regard, the Committee reminds the State party that the principle of non-discrimination provided for in article 2, paragraph 2, is an immediate obligation.
51. The Committee strongly recommends that the compatibility of restrictions on the right to strike imposed at the federal, provincial and territorial levels with articles 4 and 8 of the Covenant be re-examined. Such restrictions should be eliminated where they are not strictly necessary for the promotion of the general welfare in a democratic society, for the protection of the interests of national security or public safety, public order, public health or the protection of the rights and freedoms of others, and where no other alternative can be found.
52. The Committee recommends that the State party undertake a detailed assessment of the impact of the reduction of federal transfers for social assistance and social services to provinces and territories, on the standard of living of people depending on social welfare, in particular women, children, older persons, persons with disabilities, Aboriginal people, African Canadians and members of other minorities. The Committee strongly recommends that the State party reconsider all retrogressive measures adopted in 1995.
53. The Committee urges the State party to establish social assistance at levels which ensure the realization of an adequate standard of living for all.
54. The Committee recommends that the State party reassess the Employment Insurance scheme with a view to providing greater access and improved benefit levels to all unemployed workers.
55. The Committee reiterates its recommendation that the National Child Benefit Scheme be amended so as to prohibit provinces and territories from deducting child benefit from social assistance entitlements.
56. The Committee recommends that the State party gather disaggregated statistical data in relation to the relinquishment to foster care of children belonging to low-income families, single-mother-led families, and Aboriginal and African Canadian families in order to accurately assess the extent of the problem. The Committee further recommends that, in accordance with the provisions of article 10 of the Covenant on the protection of families, the federal, provincial and territorial governments undertake all necessary measures including through financial support, where necessary, to avoid such relinquishment.
57. The Committee recommends that the State party give special attention to the difficulties faced by homeless girls, who are more vulnerable to health risks and social and economic deprivation, and that it take all necessary measures to provide them with adequate housing and social and health services.
58. The Committee recommends that domestic violence be included as a specific offence in the Criminal Code.

59. The Committee recommends that the State party ensure that low-income women and women trying to leave abusive relationships can access housing options and appropriate support services in keeping with the right to an adequate standard of living.
60. The Committee reiterates its recommendation that the State party establish an official poverty line. The Committee also recommends that the State party integrate economic, social and cultural rights in its poverty reduction strategies. In this regard, the State party is referred to the Committee's statement on poverty and the International Covenant on Economic, Social and Cultural Rights, adopted in May 2001.
61. The Committee recommends that the State party significantly intensify its efforts to address the issue of food insecurity and hunger in Canada. In this regard, the Committee reminds the State party of its core obligation to fulfil (provide) the right to food when disadvantaged and marginalized individuals or groups are, for reasons beyond their control, unable to realize these rights for themselves through all means possible at their disposal.
62. The Committee reiterates its recommendation that the federal, provincial and territorial governments address homelessness and inadequate housing as a national emergency by reinstating or increasing, where necessary, social housing programmes for those in need, improving and properly enforcing anti-discrimination legislation in the field of housing, increasing shelter allowances and social assistance rates to realistic levels, and providing adequate support services for persons with disabilities. The Committee urges the State party to implement a national strategy for the reduction of homelessness that includes measurable goals and timetables, consultation and collaboration with affected communities, complaints procedures, and transparent accountability mechanisms, in keeping with Covenant standards.
63. The Committee strongly recommends that, before forced evictions are carried out, the State party take appropriate measures, legislative or otherwise, to ensure that those affected by forced evictions are provided with alternative accommodation and thus do not face homelessness, in line with the Committee's general comment No. 7 (1997).
64. The Committee strongly recommends that the State party review its position on the right to water, in line with the Committee's general comment No. 15 (2002) on the right to water, so as to ensure equal and adequate access to water for people living in the State party, irrespective of the province or territory in which they live or the community to which they belong.
65. The Committee recommends that the State party ensure by every appropriate means that higher education be made equally accessible to all, on the basis of capacity.
66. The Committee recommends that an overall assessment of the situation of African Canadians be conducted, particularly in the area of education, in order to adopt and effectively implement a targeted programme of action to realize their rights under the Covenant.
67. The Committee recommends that the State party undertake the adoption and implementation of concrete plans, with relevant benchmarks and time frames, for the consideration and implementation of the recommendations of the Task Force on Aboriginal Languages and Cultures, as well as in the area of intellectual property for the protection and promotion of ancestral rights and traditional knowledge of Aboriginal peoples.
68. The Committee reminds the State party that, although trade liberalization has a wealth-generating potential, such liberalization does not necessarily create and lead to a favourable environment for the realization of economic, social and cultural rights. In this regard, the Committee recommends that the State party consider ways in which the primacy of Covenant rights may be ensured in trade and investment agreements, and in particular in the adjudication of investor-State disputes under chapter XI of the North American Free Trade Agreement (NAFTA).
69. The Committee requests the State party to include in its sixth periodic report, detailed information on any measures taken and progress made, particularly with regard to the suggestions and recommendations made by the Committee in the present concluding observations.
70. The Committee requests that the succeeding State party's reports focus primarily on its follow-up to the Committee's previous concluding observations, and structured by articles of the Covenant. The Committee also requests the State party to provide, in addition to information on measures adopted, details on the substantive impact of such measures on the realization of economic, social and cultural rights. In this regard, the Committee also wishes to receive comparative statistical data disaggregated by year, as well as information on percentages of budget allocations to programmes relevant under the Covenant.
71. The Committee encourages the State party to actively engage non-governmental organizations and other members of civil society in a meaningful process of discussions, at the federal, provincial and territorial levels, prior to the submission of its next periodic report to the Committee.
72. The Committee requests the State party to disseminate the present concluding observations widely among all levels of society, particularly among government officials and judicial authorities, and to inform the Committee on all steps taken to implement them in its next periodic report.
73. The Committee requests the State party to submit its sixth periodic report by 6 June 2010.

Glossary

AANDC's Income Assistance Program. Aboriginal Affairs and Northern Development Canada's Income Assistance Program provides funding for individuals and families who are ordinarily resident on reserves with basic and special needs and services similar to those provided to other residents of the province or territory. The program has four main components: basic needs, special needs, pre-employment supports, and service delivery.

Ableism. Ableism refers to the belief in the superiority of people without disabilities over people with disabilities; that is, the stigmatization of disability and prejudicial attitudes by people without disabilities towards people with disabilities.

Aboriginal Affairs and Northern Development Canada (AANDC). AANDC (initially called the Department of Indian Affairs and then known as Indian and Northern Affairs Canada) is the government department responsible for maintaining and strengthening the Government of Canada's relations with organizations representing Métis, non-status Indians, and urban Aboriginal people.

Aboriginal peoples. Aboriginal peoples are a diverse population of distinct peoples with unique heritages, languages, cultural practices, and spiritual beliefs. The Aboriginal peoples of Canada are the descendants of the original inhabitants of North America. Three groups of Aboriginal people are recognized by the *Constitution Act, 1982*: Indians, Métis, and Inuit. We now generally use the term First Nations in place of Indian except in a legal capacity, such as in the *Indian Act*.

Aboriginal self-government. Aboriginal self-government has become a major demand by Aboriginal peoples over the past several decades. Attention initially focused on constitutional reform in the 1980s and early 1990s, whereas the agenda now has shifted towards a push for policy and legislative changes. Significant developments in the direction of self-government include the Nisga'a Final Agreement (1998) and establishment of the territory of Nunavut (1999).

Absolute homelessness. Absolute homelessness is a situation in which an individual or family has no housing at all or is staying in a temporary form of shelter.

Absolute measure of poverty. The absolute measure of poverty is based on an essential basket of goods and services deemed necessary for survival (relative to cultural context). Those who cannot afford the "basket" are considered to be living in poverty. This type of measure is open for debate because people do not agree on what should be included in the "basket."

Accessibility for Ontarians with Disabilities Act (AODA). Enacted in 2005, this legislation outlines Ontario's goals to develop accessibility standards by 2025.

Accessibility. The quality of being free of or providing alternatives to barriers, both physical and systemic, that prevent full participation in society.

Active measure. AANDC funds "active measures" as a core component of its Income Assistance program. The program is a proactive approach to help First Nations individuals move to more independent and self-sufficient lives with the skills and training they need to find and hold meaningful, sustainable jobs.

Administrative eligibility. In order to qualify for Social Assistance, applicants are normally required to meet certain administrative criteria. In most provinces, this entails the completion of a formal application, providing evidence that they meet other eligibility criteria (e.g., bank books, pay stubs, or doctors' notes), agreeing to meet with a worker in order to discuss his or her situation, etc.

Agency power of business. This term refers to the fact that business interests have the capacity to organize, and do organize, to affect the overall direction of public policy and specific legislation. They do so by lobbying, through industry associations, and by funding think tanks. This is the "agency" power of business.

Anti-racist approach. This approach helps us to understand the economic roots of racism and discrimination and how these processes continue to be at play today, creating high levels of unemployment and underemployment among racialized groups.

Assembly of First Nations (AFN). The AFN is the national organization representing First Nations citizens in Canada, providing them with a national voice through their leaders, advocating for issues such as Aboriginal and treaty rights, economic development, education, languages and literacy, health, housing, social development, justice, taxation, land claims, and the environment.

Assimilation. In past federal government policy regarding First Nations, assimilation was the central pillar or goal. It was desired and expected that eventually all Indians (as they were referred to at the time) would give up their traditional customs, culture, and beliefs and become like the dominant society.

Basic Needs Lines (BNLs). In 1992, the Fraser Institute published the Basic Needs Lines (BNLs) based on the basic subsistence requirements needed for survival (an absolute approach). They were widely criticized for being below most Canadians' survival expectations.

Beveridge Report. The *Beveridge Report* came out of Britain in 1943, the same year as the subsequent Canadian *Marsh Report*. These reports established the baseline for the rapid expansion of social welfare.

Bill C-2. In 1998, Parliament amended the Canada Pension Plan through Bill C-2. The changes resulted in a larger reserve fund to help ensure that the future pensions of the growing retirement population can be funded. Contribution rates were increased from the 1998 5.85 percent of contributory earnings to 9.9 percent. These changes will increase the size of the fund of money that is put aside to pay for future retirement pensions.

Bill C-12, the Employment Insurance Act. On January 5, 1995, changes to the Employment Insurance system took effect with Bill C-12, the new *Employment Insurance Act*. The new system replaced the previous Unemployment Insurance system on July 1, 1996.

Bill C-21. The introduction of Bill C-21 in 1990 reversed several of the enhancements of Bill C-229. The bill increased the number of weeks of work required to receive Unemployment Insurance benefits, reduced the maximum duration of benefits for most regions, and reduced the replacement rate from 60 to 50 percent of insurable earnings for those who declined "suitable employment," quit "without just cause," or were fired.

Bill C-229. Bill C-229, introduced early in 1971, completed a revamped UI that followed many of the White Paper recommendations. This was part of Prime Minister Pierre Elliott Trudeau's Just Society initiative. Due to these changes, 80 percent of unemployed workers were covered by UI.

Blame the victim response. This is when a person believe that an otherwise innocent person simply "deserves what they get." An example might be a blame the victim response to a person who became ill or incapacitated as a consequence of a "sinful" lifestyle or, say, losing their job.

B/U ratio. One way to measure the extent to which unemployed Canadians are covered by Employment Insurance is to calculate the proportion of unemployed who actually receive EI benefits. This is known as the B/U ratio—the ratio of unemployed EI beneficiaries to the unemployed without benefits.

Caledon Institute of Social Policy. The Caledon Institute of Social Policy is an independent, non-profit organization that completes research and analysis to help encourage public awareness and debate on the role of social policy in Canadian society.

Campaign 2000. In 1989, the House of Commons declared its commitment to eliminating poverty among Canadian children by the year 2000. Campaign 2000, an across-Canada public education movement to build Canadian awareness and support for the 1989 all-party House of Commons resolution, reports yearly on the progress towards the goal of eliminating child poverty.

Canada Assistance Plan (CAP). In an effort to consolidate Social Assistance and other income security and social service programs, the federal government introduced a new cost-sharing arrangement with the provinces in 1966—the Canada Assistance Plan (CAP). CAP brought together a range of cost-shared income security, social services, education, and health programs into one system. It also included several national standards.

Canada Child Tax Benefit (CCTB). In 1998, a new initiative called the Canada Child Tax Benefit (CCTB) was introduced. The CCTB has two main elements: a CCTB basic benefit and the National Child Benefit Supplement (NCBS). The NCBS is an additional tax credit that adds to the CCTB and is the federal contribution to the CCTB. It provides low-income families with additional child benefits on top of the basic benefit.

Canada Health and Social Transfer (CHST). Replacing the Canada Assistance Plan (CAP) and Established Programs Financing (EPF), the 1996 CHST set the funding formula for Social Assistance, social services, health care services, and post-secondary education.

Canada Health Transfer (CHT). Replacing the CHST, the Canada Health Transfer provides federal funding to the provinces for health care services.

Canada Pension Plan Disability (CPPD) Benefit. The CPPD benefit provides a disability benefit to those with "severe and prolonged disabilities" who meet the CPP contribution requirements. It is most commonly known as providing retirement pensions to workers in Canada, but it also provides survivor, death, and disability benefits to CPP contributors and their families.

Canada/Quebec Pension Plan (C/QPP). The earnings-based Canada/Quebec Pension Plan (C/QPP) provides a pension upon retirement to persons who have contributed to it. It is a social insurance type of income security program; it insures the contributor against loss of income due to retirement. All employed or self-employed Canadians over the age of 18 make compulsory contributions to the plan (matched by their employer) throughout their working careers. The plan also offers disability, survivor, and death benefits, as well as inflation protection. The plan is fully portable from job to job.

Canada Social Transfer. Replacing the CHST, the Canada Social Transfer provides federal funding to the provinces for Social Assistance, social services, and post-secondary education.

Canada's Royal Commission on Equality in Employment, 1984. The federal government established the Royal Commission on Equality in Employment in 1983, headed by Judge Rosalie Abella. The Commission released its report in 1984. The report recognized that the social and economic patterns were changing and that, increasingly, women and minorities would form a larger part of the Canadian labour force. The Commission's recommendations directly resulted in the creation of the *Employment Equity Act* of 1986 and the Federal Contractors Program, both of which were to affect human resource and employment practice in both the private and public sectors.

Canada-U.S. North American Free Trade Agreement. The North American Free Trade Agreement (NAFTA) was signed by Prime Minister Brian Mulroney, Mexican President Carlos Salinas, and U.S. President George H.W. Bush and came into effect on January 1, 1994. The agreement facilitated a greater exchange of goods between the three countries and created the world's largest "free trade" area.

Canadian Multiculturalism Policy. Canada was the first country in the world to adopt "multiculturalism" as an official policy (in 1971). Canada's Multiculturalism Policy affirmed the value and dignity of all Canadian citizens, regardless of race or ethnic origins, language, or religious affiliation. The policy also affirmed the rights of Aboriginal peoples and the status of Canada's two official languages.

Canadian Multicultural Policy (1971). Enacted by the Trudeau government, the policy reframed ethnic or racial differences as a national agenda of "unity within diversity," recognizing the right of all cultural groups to participate within the greater Canadian society.

Capitalism. Capitalism is an economic and social system based on a monopoly of the ownership of capital rather than the ownership of land, as in the case of feudalism. Ownership of or access to capital (machinery and equipment, private property, and money) provided industrialists with the basis for employing workers at a wage.

Categorical eligibility. Categorical eligibility refers to the different types of reasons why applicants might request Social Assistance. While all applicants are presumed to be in need, different criteria for needs are considered. Criteria can depend on whether the applicant is elderly, disabled, a single parent, or otherwise employable.

Child care. Successive federal governments have done little to create a universal child care program across Canada. Indeed, federal-provincial disputes seem to have slowed the development of child care policy outside Quebec. Quebec itself introduced free public all-day kindergarten in 1997, then a subsidized day care program in 1998. The program initially offered day care for $5 per child per day (later increased to $7 per day). Recent research from the province suggests that subsidized day care pays for itself and even provides a healthy return on the investment.

Child Care Expense Deduction. The Child Care Expense Deduction was first introduced in 1971 and was originally intended for one-parent families. It was designed to offset the incremental costs of child rearing for parents in the labour force.

Child Tax Benefit (CTB). In 1993, the Government of Canada consolidated its child tax credits and the Family Allowance into a single Child Tax Benefit (CTB) that provided a monthly payment based on the number of children and the level of family income. It has now been changed to the CCTB and NCBS.

Child Tax Exemption. Income support to families with children began in 1918 with the introduction of the Child Tax Exemption in personal income tax. The exemption provided income tax savings that increased with taxable income. The after-tax benefit was of greatest absolute benefit to those in the highest tax brackets. The exemption provided no benefits to families that did not owe income tax.

Chinese Head Tax. A "tax" of $50 imposed on all incoming persons of Chinese origin, with very few exceptions, under the *Chinese Immigration Act* (1885). The tax was eventually increased to $100 in 1900 and $500 (the equivalent of two years of wages for a Chinese labourer) in 1903.

Christianization. Christianization was a process that supported the core assimilation policy. To the colonial government, the civilizing of First Nations people was synonymous with their Christianization. Aboriginal ceremonies and cultural practices were officially discouraged or outlawed. Education through church residential schools was seen as a way to destroy the social, spiritual, and cultural systems and relations of the First Nations and replace them with the beliefs of mainstream Canadian society.

Civil society organizations. Civil society organizations have an impact at various stages of the policy process and affect policy in many ways. They transform individual hardships into collective problems through forms of community organizing and mobilization. Such organizations act as sites where people come to identify shared problems and indeed are often places where new problems are identified and named. Examples might be disabilities organizations, women's organizations, and gay rights organizations.

Claim period. The claim period is the allowed amount of time you can be on EI and varies depending on the number of weeks you have worked and the local unemployment rate. The maximum claim period is 45 weeks.

Clawback rule. Programs such as EI, the NCBS, and OAS take money back from certain beneficiaries. In the cases of EI and OAS, those with income over a certain level lose the benefit. With the NCBS, people on welfare have the benefit taken away.

Collective rights. This category of human rights defines rights at a collective level. This type of rights generally has roots in anti-colonial struggles, environmental activism, and the efforts for self-determination of indigenous peoples.

Community Well-Being Index. The CWB Index was developed by Aboriginal Affairs and Northern Development Canada (AANDC) using Statistics Canada's Census population data. The Index incorporates elements from other sources, including the UN's Human Development Index (HDI). Because the CWB Index results in a single score, it can provide at-a-glance summaries of well-being in individual communities. Scores from First Nations communities can be compared to those of other Canadian communities and even across census years.

Congress of Aboriginal Peoples (CAP). CAP is an organization that represents the interests of Aboriginal people who are not legally recognized under the *Indian Act*, including non-Status Indians and Métis people.

Conservative/corporatist continental welfare states. Germany, Austria, and France typify the conservative/corporatist continental welfare state model. Welfare states following this model provide income maintenance to uphold the status quo and maintain income difference between classes. They are not concerned with eradicating poverty or creating a more egalitarian society.

Conservative ideology. The basic values of the conservative ideology are freedom, individualism, and the inevitability of inequality. According to the conservative ideology, the role of government (including its interference in the free market economy) should be limited, and the role of private property and private enterprise should be paramount.

Constitution Act, 1867. The *Constitution Act, 1867* was originally enacted as the *British North America Act, 1867* (the *BNA Act*). The Act created the federal dominion of Canada, and it defines its federal structure, the system of government, the justice system, and the taxation system. The *BNA Act* was renamed in 1982 with the patriation of the Constitution.

Consumer Price Index (CPI). The Consumer Price Index (CPI) is an indicator of changes in consumer prices experienced by Canadians. It is obtained by comparing, over time, the cost of a fixed basket of goods and services. Since the basket contains goods and services of unchanging or equivalent quantity and quality, the index reflects only pure price change. The CPI is accepted as an indicator of the change in the general level of consumer prices (or the rate of inflation).

Continuous Journey Requirement. Permitted entry to immigrants only if they arrived directly from their home country on tickets purchased before leaving the country. This policy was developed to limit immigration from the Indian subcontinent, from which a continuous journey was next to impossible.

Contributory negligence. Contributory negligence states that if the injured worker's own conduct contributed to the injury in even the slightest way, the employer completely escapes legal responsibility. This occurred up until the early 1900s, when Workers' Compensation was introduced.

Co-operative Commonwealth Federation (CCF). The Co-operative Commonwealth Federation was a political party, founded in 1932 in Calgary, Alberta, by socialist, agrarian, co-operative and labour groups. In 1944, with its provincial victory in Saskatchewan, the CCF became the first social-democratic government in North America. The CCF disbanded in 1961 and was replaced by the New Democratic Party. In the 2011 federal election, the NDP became the main federal opposition party.

Culturally biased hiring practices. Practices that favour certain skills and behaviours which can make it difficult for newcomers to find appropriate employment. For example, here in North America, "selling yourself" and your skills is not only desirable but necessary when searching for a job. Members of some cultural groups, however, see this behaviour as rude and boastful and find it uncomfortable to act with such assertiveness.

Culture. Culture is the set of ideals, norms, beliefs, and values that are shared by a group of individuals. This shapes the way people interpret the world and informs the way they live their day-to-day lives. It is important to remember that cultures shift and change over time and that members of a particular cultural group might differ from one another in terms of their specific customs and traditions.

Cyclical unemployment. Cyclical unemployment occurs due to a temporary downturn in the job market. The most common form of cyclical unemployment occurs when workers are temporarily laid off.

Demogrants. These are universal flat-rate payments made to individuals or households on the sole basis of demographic characteristics, such as number of children or age, rather than on the basis of need. The Family Allowance program, benefiting all families with children under the age of 18, was Canada's first widespread demogrant.

Department of Indian Affairs. This department was established by the federal government as the main vehicle for regulating and controlling Aboriginal movement and ways of living. It administered the reserve system and gained its authority through the *Indian Act* of 1876. Its name has changed over the years and it is currently known as Aboriginal Affairs and Northern Development Canada.

Deserving poor. A term, originating with the English Poor Laws, used to describe those not physically able to work—that is, the deserving poor or paupers. Many believe that this idea still informs much of social welfare policy towards the poor today.

Devaluation of credentials. When Canadian organizations and institutions do not recognize, or undervalue, a person's qualifications obtained in other countries.

Disability. Disability applies to a wide range of so-called impairments including sensory impairments, such as blindness or deafness, physical disabilities impairing mobility, and psychiatric, developmental, learning, and neurological disabilities.

Disability Tax Credit. The DTC is an income tax credit for individuals who have a disability that "markedly restricts" activities of daily living. A treating physician must complete a form outlining the nature of the disability.

Discouraged workers. Discouraged workers is the term used to refer to those individuals who are no longer looking for a job because they believe they will not find one. Discouraged workers are classified as not being in the labour force.

Dual-earner families. Currently, families that rely on the income of both partners predominate in Canada. This change has led to a complete revision of family obligations in a very short time and, hence, a great deal of uncertainty.

Economic class. This is an immigration category in which applicants can be either skilled workers, business owners, or entrepreneurs.

Economic efficiency. Economic efficiency refers to the existence of optimal and stable economic growth with a flexible and productive labour market.

Economic globalization. The growing integration of international markets for goods, services, and finance, characterized by free trade and investment expansion, concentrated transnational corporation power, enforcement, and rights protection.

Economic theory approach. The economic theory approach, as its name implies, focuses on the influence of economic theories. Economists have differing theories about the root causes of unemployment and poverty that generally derive from the three economic theories: Keynesian economics, monetarism, and political economy. Each body of economic theory has a different view of the role of government and the effects of social spending on the economy.

Effectiveness of Social Assistance. One way to evaluate the effectiveness of Social Assistance benefits in addressing poverty levels is to compare the welfare dollar amounts to after-tax LICO levels. The difference b is a fair indicator of the effectiveness of Social Assistance in at least ameliorating the situation of the poor in our society.

Efficiency/equity debate. The efficiency/equity debate is at the heart of many social policy discussions and debates over employment and unemployment in particular. "Economic efficiency" generally refers to economic growth with a flexible and increasingly productive labour market. "Social equity," on the other hand, refers to the existence of adequate levels of health and security for all people and a reasonably equal distribution of income and wealth.

Elder care. Canada has an aging population with a growing number of seniors requiring support and care. Most of the responsibility currently falls on families and friends, and most of the responsibility within families falls on women. Caregivers perform a range of tasks in caring for seniors, such as personal care, and help with tasks inside and outside the senior's house (transportation, medical care, and care management).

Eligibility rules. Provincial and territorial jurisdictions classify their welfare clients according to a general classification scheme. Applicants must meet the eligibility rules set out for each category of clients, depending on the category in which they are placed. The rules vary somewhat by provincial jurisdiction.

Elizabethan Poor Laws. The famous Elizabethan Poor Laws provided the bedrock of the modern welfare states in England, the United States, and Canada. In 1601, England passed the *Elizabethan Poor-Relief Act*, mainly to suppress vagrancy and begging. The act recognized the state's obligation to those in need, provided for compulsory local levies, and required work for the able-bodied poor. Institutional relief was provided by poorhouses and workhouses. The subsequent amendments of 1834 were based on the belief that pauperism was rooted in an unwillingness to work (rather than resulting from inadequate employment opportunities), and the relief provided to the poor had to be set at a level below that of the poorest labourer.

Employment. Employment includes any legal activity carried out for pay or profit. It also includes unpaid family work when it is a direct contribution to the operation of a farm, business, or professional practice owned or operated by a related member of the household. Some employed people are self-employed.

Employment Insurance (EI). This social insurance type of income security program provides a level of income replacement to those workers who are temporarily out of work and meet strict eligibility conditions.

Employment Insurance Sickness Benefits. Employment Insurance Sickness Benefits are meant to fill the gap before people become eligible for longer-term illness and disability benefits from employer-sponsored group insurance plans, private plans held by individuals, or the Canada Pension Plan Disability Benefit. Annual spending for EI Sickness Benefits in 2004/05 was $813.2 million.

Employment population ratio. The employment population ratio is the ratio of employed to the working-age population.

Employment rate. The employment rate refers to the percentage of the working-age population actively looking for work who are employed. This is not quite the same as the "employment population ratio," which represents the share of employed persons as a percentage of the total working-age population.

Enfranchisement. Enfranchisement was the method envisioned for Indians to obtain citizenship and thus be fully recognized as Canadians, a process which required the loss of Indian status. In 1966, all Status Indians gained full citizenship and the right to vote in federal elections.

Environmental policy. Environmental policy, quite simply, is any course of deliberate action taken by federal, provincial or local governments with a view to prevent, reduce, or mitigate harmful effects on nature and natural resources, and to ensure that human-made changes to the environment do not have harmful and long-lasting effects on humans themselves.

Equal pay, equal employment, other facilitating policies. These terms refer to a group of legislative changes in the post-WWII period (particularly the 1970s) aimed at improving workplace gender equality. Equal pay policies, such as pay equity were designed to improve women's pay. Equal employment policies, such as employment equity, help women's employment and promotion opportunities. Other facilitating policies, such as child care and parental leave, attempt to put women on an equal footing with men in the labour market.

Established Program Financing (EPF). Under the Canada Assistance Program (CAP) the federal government's contributions to health care and post-secondary education were funded through ETF since 1979. Both CAP and ETF were replaced with the Canada Health and Social Transfer (CHST) in 1996.

Ethnicity. Ethnicity describes a group of people who share a common descent, language, religion, and traditions. Although people might be members of the same racial grouping, they can differ in terms of ethnicity. For example, people who identify themselves racially as "black" may identify themselves ethnically as African, Jamaican, or Caribbean. Each of these ethnic groupings is linked to particular values and behaviours that differ considerably from one another, despite the perceived commonality in race.

Export processing zone (EPZ). An export processing zone is a particular area in a country from which benefits come in the form of preferential financial regulations and special investment incentives. There are export processing zones all over the world.

Family. This textbook uses the term family with some caution. Many definitions of families exclude common-law couples, most exclude lone-parent families, and pretty well all still exclude same-sex relationships. In Canada today, the term family is defined according to either structural criteria (what they look like) or functional criteria (what they do).

Family Allowance (FA). The *Family Allowance Act* of 1944 introduced the universal Family Allowance (FA), providing benefits to all Canadian families with dependent children. The FA was also popularly known as the "baby bonus." It was the first universal income security scheme. It was ended in 1993.

Family class. This is an immigration category in which applicants must be sponsored by family members who are already citizens.

Family responsibility approach. According to the family responsibility approach, parents are solely responsible for making decisions and providing for their children's well-being. The role of income security and social services is to facilitate decision making and provide support when the family's ability to provide fails.

Federalism. Federalism is a system of government in which a number of smaller states (in Canada's case, provinces and territories) join to form a larger political entity while still retaining a measure of political power.

Federal spending power. Federal "spending power" refers to the ability of the federal government to spend money outside of its immediate jurisdiction. It was on the basis of the spending power that the federal government got involved in a wide range of policies after the second world war, including social assistance, housing, social services, and disability programming. It was able to do so by offering to pay a percentage of the cost of a provincial program in a given area provided that the provincial program met certain "national standards."

Fellow servant rule. The fellow servant rule maintained that if a worker's injury was related to a co-worker's negligence, the employer was not responsible. The injured worker could sue the co-worker, but considering the income levels of workers at the time, this was an ineffective option. It also pitted worker against worker. This rule generally applied up until the early 1900s, when Workers' Compensation was introduced.

Feminization of poverty. Currently, almost 16 percent of adult women live below the Statistics Canada Low Income Cut-off, or LICO. Women are falling further and further into poverty. The term now commonly used to capture this social phenomenon is the feminization of poverty.

Feudalism. Prior to the fourteenth century, society was based largely on a system of obligations in a primarily agricultural society. This kind of social organization was known as feudalism. Feudalism was both an economic and a social system in which the owner of the property was responsible for the peasants working on the land.

Financial eligibility. To meet the financial eligibility requirement, an applicant must show the need for Social Assistance. A needs test compares the household's assets with its needs. When the cost of a household's needs is greater than its available income, Social Assistance may be granted.

First Nations. This is a term used in place of Indian. Together, First Nations, Métis, and Inuit make up the Aboriginal peoples of Canada.

Food and Agriculture Organization of the United Nations (FAO). FAO's mandate is achieving food security for all—to make sure people have regular access to enough high-quality food to lead active, healthy lives. It seeks to raise levels of nutrition, improve agricultural productivity, better the lives of rural populations, and contribute to the growth of the world economy.

Food banks and feeding programs. With cutbacks in many income security programs, Canadians are having to rely on food banks and feeding programs in order to survive. Food banks are charities that provide groceries, whereas feeding programs provide cooked meals.

Free trade. Free trade refers to the lowering and dismantling of the barriers and regulations that might impede the international flow of capital and products or restrict marketplace demand. Free trade is embodied in the growing collection of free trade agreements and international trade organizations, including the General Agreement on Tariffs and Trade (GATT), the Asia-Pacific Economic Cooperation (APEC), and the North American Free Trade Agreement (NAFTA).

Frictional unemployment. Frictional unemployment occurs when people move between jobs. This includes new labour force entrants, such as those returning to the labour force after completing school or raising children.

Full employment. In 1945, the Canadian government's White Paper on Employment and Income made a commitment to full employment, accepting that unemployment essentially results from the unregulated operation of labour markets. During the 1970s, monetarist economists, led by Milton Friedman, came up with the notion of the Non-Accelerating Inflation Rate of Unemployment (NAIRU), which refers to an "acceptable" level of unemployment (after which inflation rises). The *Unemployment Insurance Act* of 1971 established that 4 percent unemployment was henceforth to be considered "full" employment. Subsequent to this, the idea of "full" employment has been rarely mentioned in government circles in the context of Canadian social policy.

Full-time employment. Full-time employment refers to people who usually work 30 or more hours per week or to people who work fewer than 30 hours per week but consider themselves to be employed full-time.

Funnel of causality model of policy-making. A model of policy-making that provides more room for considering power and influence. In this model, the policy decision can be seen as the result of a wide range of factors—those involved and strategies employed by bureaucrats, politicians, and lobbyists, all of which directly affect the policy choice.

G8. The G8 (Group of 8) is a group of eight wealthy countries: Canada, France, Germany, Italy, Japan, Russia, the United Kingdom, and the United States. Each year, G8 leaders and representatives from the European Union meet to discuss broad economic and foreign policies.

Gender-based approach. The gender-based approach to social welfare identifies two regime types based on an analysis of the family and unpaid labour: the male-breadwinner regime and the individual earner-carer regime.

Gini coefficient. The Gini coefficient measures the degree of inequality in income distribution. Values of the Gini coefficient can range from 0 to 1. A value of 0 indicates that income is equally divided among the population, with all persons receiving exactly the same amount of income. At the opposite extreme, a Gini coefficient of 1 denotes a perfectly unequal distribution, where one unit possesses all of the income in the economy. A decrease in the value of the Gini coefficient can be interpreted as reflecting a decrease in inequality and vice versa.

Global poverty. According to the World Bank, about one-quarter of the world's population lives on less than $1 per day, and over half live on $2 per day. While some people can adequately survive on such meagre incomes given the cost of living in their home countries, many suffer with health problems, low life expectancies, high infant mortality rates, low levels of education, and malnutrition.

Global social welfare. Given the new era of globalization, the traditional concerns of social welfare will need to be broadened to include a concern with the issue of global human rights. As noted earlier, global social welfare (a concern with justice, social regulation, social provision, and redistribution between nations) is already a part of the activities of various supranational organizations or international governmental organizations of the United Nations.

Goods and Services Tax (GST). The GST is a "value added" tax (a consumption tax) first introduced in 1991 by the then Conservative government under Prime Minister Brian Mulroney. The GST was very controversial at the time. A new consumption tax, the Harmonized Sales Tax (HST), is now used in those provinces where the Goods and Services Tax and the Provincial Sales Tax (PST) are combined into a single sales tax.

Great Depression. The economic depression of the late 1920s and early 1930s was an important event in the rise of income security and social services in Canada. Public perception of the poor began to shift. Massive numbers of people were unemployed, and Canadians began to see that this could not possibly be due to individual fault but had more to do with the operation of the economy. The idea that help for the poor should be a local or family responsibility was replaced with the idea that the government should be responsible for providing relief to the unemployed.

Guaranteed Income Supplement (GIS). The Guaranteed Income Supplement (GIS) provides extra money to OAS recipients who have little or no other income.

Homelessness (absolute and relative). Simply defined, homelessness is the absence of a place to live. A person who is considered to be homeless has no regular place to live and stays in an emergency shelter, in an abandoned building, in an all-night shopping area, in a laundromat, outdoors, or any place where they can be protected from the elements. Two types of homelessness can be distinguished: absolute homelessness and relative homelessness. Absolute homelessness is a situation in which an individual or family has no housing at all or is staying in a temporary form of shelter. Relative homelessness is a situation in which people's homes do not meet the United Nation's basic housing standards.

Horizontal equity. Horizontal equity is based on the recognition that parents have heavier financial demands than childless households and single persons with the same income.

Human capital perspective. This perspective views an immigrant's attributes, specific skills, and personal resources as shaping her/his level of employment success.

Human Development Index. In 1992, Canada ranked first among all countries in the world on a composite Human Development Index (created by the United Nations Development Programme) that combined life expectancy, educational attainment, and standard of living. Canada has recently dropped on this list, primarily due to child poverty and single-mother poverty levels.

Human rights. The inherent rights without which we cannot truly live as human beings. A right is a justified claim or entitlement by someone or some institution in society, and human rights are a standard by which we define human dignity from all peoples.

Idle No More. "Idle No More" is an protest movement that originated among First Nations, Métis, and Inuit peoples and their supporters across Canada and internationally. The "Idle No More" movement, an ongoing campaign that began in 2012, was inspired by a hunger strike by Attawapiskat Chief Theresa Spence in reaction to abuses of indigenous treaty rights by the Conservative government in Ottawa.

Immigration policy. Canada's immigration policy falls into several time periods. Prior to 1967, immigrants were selected essentially on the basis of country of national origin. After 1967, a "points system" was introduced and immigrants were selected on "merit" criteria essentially related to labour force readiness (education, skill, language facility, etc.). A Family Class and Humanitarian (Refugee) Class also was created at that time. Since 2008, significant modifications have been introduced such that immigration is even more directly tied to labour market demands and employment readiness. The changes also place greater demands on immigrants prior to achieving permanent status.

Immigration policy reforms. Immigration policy reforms introduced since 2008 are fundamentally altering the nature of immigration and, with it, likely the very character of our country—for better or for worse. According to Sandra Lopes, Manager, Policy and Research of the Maytree Foundation, with its new immigration policies, the Conservative federal government is beginning to change who we select to immigrate, the supports newcomers have after they arrive, and how they can become citizens. The cumulative effect, she says, will be to change Canada as we know it.

Income redistribution. Income redistribution is a principle that underlies social welfare systems in capitalist countries. It involves "evening out" income levels somewhat across the population—taking from the rich and giving to the poor without undermining social inequality altogether.

Income security. Income security provides monetary or other material benefits to supplement income or maintain minimum income levels (e.g., Employment Insurance, Social Assistance, Old Age Security, and Workers' Compensation).

Income Security Reform (ISR). This was an INAC initiative that ended in 2003. The objective of the ISR initiative was to transform the passive on-reserve welfare system to a dynamic system that promotes opportunities and self-sufficiency.

Income supplementation. These are programs that supplement income that is obtained elsewhere, through paid employment or through other income security programs. They are not intended to be the primary source of income. The National Child Benefit Supplement (NCBS) and the Guaranteed Income Supplement (GIS) are income supplementation programs.

Indexation. Indexation is an arrangement in which periodic adjustments are made to benefits based on changes in an index of some kind, most often the Consumer Price Index (CPI). Non-indexation of benefits has the effect of reducing the benefit each year by the amount of any increases in the Consumer Price Index (CPI).

***Indian Act* of 1876.** This act provided for the government's guardianship over Indian lands. It is a piece of social legislation of very broad scope that regulates and controls virtually every aspect of Aboriginal life. The act has been amended throughout the years but remained largely intact until major changes in 1996. The *Indian Act* strictly defines who is and who is not an Indian by setting out the requirements for determining who is a Status Indian.

Individual earner-carer regimes. Individual earner-carer regimes are based on shared roles between men and women leading to equal rights. In this model, both sexes have equal rights to social entitlements as earners and caregivers. Paid work in the labour market and unpaid caregiving work have the same benefit entitlements, thereby neutralizing gender differentiation with respect to social rights. The state plays a central role in the provision of services and payments, whether it be caring for children, elderly relatives, the sick, or people with disabilities.

Individual responsibility model of the family. The individual responsibility model of the family consists of three main elements: formal gender equality, gender-neutral policies, and equalized caregiving. Within this model, the family unit is still treated as the normal unit of administration, but the husband and wife are seen as equally responsible for the economic well-being of themselves, each other, and any children.

Indoor relief. Indoor relief was provided to able-bodied men who were deemed employable. These recipients were obligated to live in a workhouse and undertake work duties in order to receive assistance. The objective was to limit relief and use work as a form of punishment.

Inequality. Inequality is linked to the differences between income groups. The way in which total income in a country is divided between households is a measure of inequality.

Institutionalization of people with disabilities. By the mid-twentieth century, many provinces had "special" residential schools for blind and deaf children and adolescents. Provincial institutions were established for people with psychiatric disabilities, and in many provinces, there were institutions for people with developmental disabilities. Specialized hospitals were established for many different disabled populations, including tuberculosis hospitals, orthopaedic hospitals, and rehabilitation hospitals. The institutionalization of people with disabilities was so widespread that it became the common belief that this was the natural order of things and that people with disabilities had always been separated from their communities.

Institutional approach. In the institutional approach, social welfare is a necessary public response that helps people attain a reasonable standard of life and health. Within this view, it is accepted that people cannot always meet all of their needs through family and work. Therefore, in a complex industrial society, it is legitimate to help people through a set of publicly funded and organized systems of programs and institutions. The institutional model attempts to even out, rather than promote, economic stratification or status differences.

Internal colonialism. In settler nations such as Canada, colonists effectively take administrative control from the colonized peoples, thereby instituting a particular type of colonialism known as internal colonialism. Internal colonialism is the term used to describe the situation of Aboriginal peoples after the European conquest.

International Bill of Human Rights. This bill is the primary basis of United Nations activities to promote, protect, and monitor human rights and fundamental freedoms. The bill comprises three texts: the Universal Declaration of Human Rights (1948); the International Covenant on Economic, Social, and Cultural Rights (1966); and the International Covenant on Civil and Political Rights (1966) and its two optional protocols.

International Labour Organization (ILO). The ILO was founded in 1919, in the wake of WWI, based on the premise that universal, lasting peace can be established only if it is based on social justice. The ILO became the first specialized agency of the UN in 1946. The main aims of the ILO are to promote rights at work, encourage decent employment opportunities, enhance social protection, and strengthen dialogue on work-related issues. The tripartite structure of the ILO is intended to give an equal voice to workers, employers, and governments.

International Monetary Fund (IMF). Created in 1945, this international organization aims to promote international monetary cooperation, exchange stability, and orderly exchange arrangements to foster economic growth and high levels of employment and to provide temporary financial assistance to countries to help ease balance of payments adjustment. Their structural adjustment programs have had many negative impacts on developing countries. At present, the IMF has $107 billion loaned out to 56 countries.

International Year of Disabled Persons. In 1976, the United Nations declared 1981 the International Year of Disabled Persons, which led to the development of Canada's action on disability.

Inuit Tapiriit Kanatami (ITK). ITK is a national organization, founded in the 1970s, that represents the four Inuit regions in Canada: Nunatsiavut (Labrador), Nunavik (northern Quebec), Nunavut, and the Inuvialuit Settlement Region in the Northwest Territories.

Investing in children approach. This approach entails building supports for families and households that enable them to attain positive outcomes for children. There is a recognition that the decisions open to families are increasingly limited and that the options for parents have narrowed insofar as most families need two incomes to adequately provide for themselves.

Job modifications. These modifications include the personal help that persons with disabilities need to participate in the labour market, such as sign language interpreters, job coaches, voice synthesizers, computers with Braille, recording equipment, and job redesign.

Job redesign. Job redesign refers to an adjustment or modification of duties, such as flexible work hours; this is a type of job modification.

Kelowna Accord. The Kelowna Accord refers to an agreement, finalized in 2005, between the federal government, the Premiers, Territorial Leaders, and the leaders of five national Aboriginal organizations. The Accord aimed to improve the education, employment, and living conditions for Aboriginal peoples. It was endorsed by the Liberal Prime Minister Paul Martin but was cancelled by his successor, Conservative Prime Minister Stephen Harper.

Keynesian. A Keynesian is a follower of the economic theory of the British economist John Maynard Keynes (1883–1946). Keynes' economic theories provided the intellectual rationale for the intervention of governments in economies and the transformation of social policy.

Labour force participation rate. The ratio of the labour force to the working-age population (age 15 and over) is referred to as the labour force participation rate.

Labour force. The official definition of the labour force is the number of people in the country 15 years of age or over who either have a job or are actively looking for one. This excludes people living on reserves, full-time members of the armed forces, and institutional residents (e.g., prison inmates and patients in hospitals or in nursing homes who have resided there for more than six months). Retired people, students, people not actively seeking work, and people not available for work for other reasons are also not considered part of the labour force, although they may be part of the working-age population.

Labour Market Agreements for Persons with Disabilities (LMAPD). Agreements between the federal government and the provinces to provide funding for employment programs for persons with disabilities.

Labour market perspective. This approach to immigrant employment suggests that characteristics of the local job market (such as the demand for certain skills and other specific qualities of the geographic location) are key factors that determine the level of unemployment or underemployment experienced by newcomer groups.

Land surrender. Land surrender is the means by which the government obtained land held by Aboriginal peoples for the settlement of non-Aboriginal people.

Liberal Anglo-Saxon welfare regimes. Liberal welfare regimes include countries such as Canada, the United States, Australia, the United Kingdom, and Ireland. "Liberal," as used here, refers to classical liberalism that is concerned with laissez-faire economics and minimal government interference.

Liberal ideology. The primary values of a liberal ideology are pragmatism, liberty, individualism, the inevitability of inequality, and humanism. Pragmatism means that, as a government or an individual, you do what needs to be done. Liberals have often been described as less ideological than conservatives, which means they are willing to do things that suit the circumstances, but may not exactly follow "liberal" principles. Liberty, individualism, and social inequality are tempered by a concern for justice for the poor. So competition and markets are tempered by a concern for people and the need for a certain basic level of social security.

Low Income Cut-off (LICO). This Statistics Canada measure of poverty is a combined relative and absolute measure often referred to as a "relative necessities" approach. It is based on the percentage of income that individuals and families spend on basic needs or necessities in comparison with the rest of Canadians. LICO is not explicitly put forth as a poverty line by the Canadian government but rather as a level of low income.

Low Income Measure (LIM). A Statistics Canada relative poverty indicator that measures low-income rates as one-half of the median income of the country. Because it is a straightforward calculation and can be collected in all nations, it allows for simple comparisons between countries.

Low-paid worker. An individual whose annual earnings are low or who works in a low-paying job. A low-paid worker may be among the working poor, depending on household circumstances.

Male-breadwinner families. Over the past 30 years, the proportion of male-breadwinner families has decreased drastically, and they now constitute less than 25 percent of the total of all Canadian families.

Male-breadwinner regimes. The male-breadwinner regime is characterized by an ideology of male privilege based on a division of labour between the sexes and resulting in unequal benefit entitlements. Men are seen as the family providers and thereby are entitled to benefits based on their labour force participation or their position as "head of the household."

Market Basket Measure (MBM). This new absolute measure of poverty calculates the amount of income needed by a given household to meet its needs based on "credible" community norms.

Market poverty. Market poverty refers to a situation in which a household remains below some measure of poverty, even though one or more members of the household earn a market income or are employed.

Marsh Report. The *Report on Social Security for Canada* by Leonard Marsh became commonly known as the *Marsh Report* and detailed the need for comprehensive and universal social welfare programs.

Maternal benefits. Under Canada's EI system, only women can claim maternity benefits, which are administered in the same way as parental leave, for 15 weeks. However, the combination of maternity and parental benefits now enables parents to receive up to one year of paid leave to care for their infants.

Maytree Foundation. Maytree Foundation is a charitable foundation that works with its many partners to fight poverty in Canada. The Foundation provides sustaining funding to partner organizations, including The Caledon Institute of Social Policy, Tamarack (An Institute for Community Engagement); the Diaspora Dialogues Charitable Society, and the Toronto Region Immigrant Employment Council (TRIEC). It provides grants, loans, and scholarships; disseminates successful local integration practices that facilitate the settlement of immigrants and refugees; and fosters leadership training programs and networking opportunities.

Medical model. The medical model views disability as a medical condition, personal tragedy, or unfortunate life event; it focuses on limitations and recommends helping the individual to adapt to their situation.

Meredith principle. The Meredith principle, also called the historic compromise, is a compromise in which workers give up the right to sue for work-related injuries, irrespective of fault, in return for guaranteed compensation for accepted claims.

Metcalf Foundation. The goal of the George Cedric Metcalf Charitable Foundation is to enhance the effectiveness of people and organizations working together to help Canadians imagine and build a just, healthy, and creative society. The Foundation works to foster sustainable communities "by creating the conditions for innovation, risk-taking, collaboration, learning, and reflection."

Mincome. This was the name given to a Guaranteed Annual Income experiment in Manitoba that would either prove or disprove the claims by conservatives that a GAI would provide disincentives for people to work. From 1974 to 1978, randomly chosen modest to low-income Manitobans received a GAI in one of three formulations combining a particular level of guaranteed income with a particular level of clawback of any income that a Mincome recipient received beyond the GAI. When social scientists later gained access to the data, they found that the impact of receiving the Mincome GAI on individuals' seeking and finding work was minimal.

Minimum income programs. This is a type of income security that provides monetary assistance to those with no other source of income. Social Assistance or welfare is a minimum income program.

Minimum wage laws. This is the lowest wage rate, by law, that an employer can pay employees to perform their work. Canada's provinces have all set a standard minimum wage.

Monetarists. The monetarists are a group of economists known for their preoccupation with the role and effects of money in the economy. Monetarist theory asserts that managing the money supply and interest rates (monetary policy)—rather than focusing on fiscal policy—is the key to managing the economy.

Mowat Centre. The Mowat Centre is a research institute based out of the School of Public Policy and Governance at the University of Toronto. The Centre seeks to "inform and revitalize Canada's public policy agenda," given new Canadian and global realities, by questioning many of the assumptions that underlie current approaches to public policy.

Multiculturalism. Multiculturalism refers to programs and policies that promote ethnic and racial diversity within a given society—individuals and groups from different ethnic and racial backgrounds coexist, and even flourish, side-by-side within a broader society context.

Multidimensional Poverty Index (MPI). The UN's new Multidimensional Poverty Index (MPI) replaces the older Human Development Index (HDI). The MPI identifies deprivations across three dimensions and shows the number of people who are "multidimensionally poor" (suffering deprivations in 33% of indicators). The MPI can be examined by region, ethnicity, and other groupings as well as by dimension, making it an ideal tool for policy-makers and for comparing countries worldwide.

NAIRU (Non-Accelerating Inflation Rate of Unemployment). A combination of frictional and structural unemployment results in what is referred to as natural unemployment or NAIRU (non-accelerating inflation rate of unemployment). According to monetarist economists, attempts to lower unemployment below NAIRU will risk the acceleration or increase of inflation.

National Anti-Poverty Organization (NAPO). Canada Without Poverty is a non-partisan organization dedicated to the elimination of poverty in Canada. Stemming from the Poor Peoples' Conference in Toronto in 1971—a national gathering of low-income citizens—Canada Without Poverty was founded later that year as the National Anti-Poverty Organization. In 2009, NAPO changed its name to Canada Without Poverty. Since its inception, the organization has been governed by people with direct, personal experience of poverty. Acting from the belief that poverty is a violation of human rights, the organization's work includes raising awareness, participating in research, and influencing public policy to prevent and alleviate poverty.

National Child Benefit Supplement (NCBS). The National Child Benefit Supplement is an additional tax credit that adds to the Canada Child Tax Benefit (CCTB). The NCBS is the federal contribution to the CCTB. It provides low-income families with additional child benefits on top of the basic benefit.

National Council of Welfare. The National Council of Welfare is a citizens' advisory body on matters of concern to low-income Canadians. It released a 1998 report entitled *Child Benefits: Kids Are Still Hungry*.

National Daycare Plan. It was the Royal Commission on the Status of Women (1970) that first proposed a national child care program for Canada. Since that time, there have been three major attempts to develop such a program: the Task Force on Child Care (1986), the Special Committee on Child Care (1987), and the Foundations Program, which was being pursued with the provinces under the Liberal government under Paul Martin. Subsequent negotiations with the provinces on a unified child care program and other matters were terminated by the new Conservative government in February 2006.

Natural unemployment. A combination of frictional and structural unemployment results in what is referred to as natural unemployment or NAIRU (non-accelerating inflation rate of unemployment). According to monetarist economists, attempts to lower unemployment below NAIRU will risk the acceleration or increase of inflation.

NCBS clawback. The distinctive feature of the National Child Benefit Supplement is that, by agreement with the provinces and territories, there is an NCBS clawback for Social Assistance recipients. Newfoundland, Nova Scotia, Quebec, Manitoba, and New Brunswick have increased Social Assistance benefits using NCBS funds. In all other provinces and territories, the supplement is clawed back from Social Assistance recipients in different ways.

NEET Generation. The "Great Recession" of 2008 along with cuts to EI premiums to the unemployed forced many middle-aged and older workers with more skills and experience to accept low-income jobs. Analysts maintain that this effectively shut many employable teens and young adults out of the job market. Indeed, many dropped out altogether—not in employment, in education, or in training (the so-called "NEET generation").

Negative rights. The emphasis of negative rights is on protection. They are rights that need to be protected rather than realized through social security or provision. These rights call for inaction on the part of the person or institution fulfilling the rights. The right is met by merely refraining from acting in a way that would violate the right.

Neo-liberalism. Neo-liberalism refers broadly to a political and economic approach to public policy that strongly favours free trade, privatization, minimal government intervention in business affairs, reduced taxes, and reduced public expenditure on social services.

New Deal. The New Deal refers to a series of economic policies enacted in the US between 1933 and 1936 under President Franklin D. Roosevelt. The spending programs were in response to the Great Depression and aimed to get the economy back on its feet. The policies focused on what historians call the "3 Rs": Relief for the unemployed and poor; Recovery of the economy to normal levels; and Reform of the financial system to prevent a repeat depression. The New Deal is widely credited for pulling the US and world economy out of the depression, though massive rearmament for WWII is also associated with helping to bring about the economic recovery.

Non-profit and for-profit welfare agencies. With government cutbacks in recent years, more and more sources of income security protection are being provided by non-profit and for-profit welfare agencies. Food banks and emergency shelters are increasingly helping people with low incomes, while people with more material means are turning to private (for-profit) pensions and insurance programs to ensure their economic security in the future.

Occupational pension plans. Occupational pension plans are linked to an employment or professional relationship between the pension plan member and the entity that establishes the plan. They may be established by employers and labour or professional associations. They are the largest pools of capital in industrialized nations.

Old Age Security (OAS). The Old Age Security (OAS) program provides a basic pension (adjusted for inflation) to virtually everyone over 65 years of age who has lived in Canada for a required length of time. It is a universal monetary benefit payable to Canadians over a specified age. It is an income transfer program paid out of the general revenue of the federal government.

Omnibus Bill (Bill C-38). The *Jobs, Growth and Long-term Prosperity Act* was introduced by the Conservative government on April 26, 2012. This piece of legislation (Bill C-38) amended or repealed 70-odd pieces of federal legislation in a single bill. Critics argued that by amending or overhauling so many pieces of legislation without allowing proper time for debate, the "Omnibus Bill," as it came to be known, undermined our democratic system of government.

Opportunities Fund for Persons with Disabilities. Funded through the Employment Insurance program, this program provides assistance to people with disabilities who have had little or no attachment to the labour force. People with disabilities who are not eligible for Employment Insurance are eligible for this program.

Organization for Economic Co-operation and Development (OECD). Founded in 1960, the Organisation for Economic Co-operation and Development (OECD) is a global organization committed to furthering democratic governments and the market economy across the globe. Canada is among the 34 member states and is one of the founding members

Outdoor relief. Outdoor relief was provided to a select category of recipients in their place of residence: the sick, the aged, the disabled, the orphaned, or the widowed—all groups that were seen as deserving of aid. The relief generally came in kind, meaning it was in the form of food, second-hand clothing, or fuel.

Parental benefits. Important changes to the *Employment Insurance Act* in 2000 increased parental leave benefits from ten weeks to 35 weeks, increasing the total maternity and parental paid leave time from six months to one year. In addition, the threshold for eligibility was lowered from 700 to 600 hours of insurable employment.

Participation and Activity Limitation Survey (PALS). The Participation and Activity Limitation Survey (PALS) was a reliable census-related survey that gathered statistics about Canadians whose everyday activities may be limited because of a condition or health-related problem. In 2010, the Conservative government announced its decision to replace PALS by a database culled from tax information, welfare rolls, and similar databanks. Disabilities activists are skeptical about whether that information will be as reliable.

Part-time employment. Part-time employment refers to people who usually work fewer than 30 hours each week. The involuntary part-time worker prefers full-time work but can only find part-time employment.

Patriarchal model of the family. This model is based on perceptions that were dominant at the beginning of the twentieth century, whereby the husband was considered the undisputed master of the family, and the wife was economically and socially beneath her husband. Children were also treated as economic dependants of the husband/father. The wife/mother was seen as responsible for providing care and services to family members without pay. Finally, divorce did not exist (although there were separations not recognized by law).

Pay equity. Legislation (in Canada since the 1970s) that ensures people receive equal pay for work of equal value.

Permanent residents. Immigrants, or "non-Canadians" who have lived in Canada legally for at least two consecutive years during any five-year period. These individuals enjoy the same rights and privileges as Canadian citizens but are not allowed to vote or hold positions in public office until they are granted citizenship.

Personal resources. Additional factors that help a person obtain and keep employment; these can include a person's ability to know where to look for work, how to write a resume, and how to prepare for an interview.

Persons with disabilities. This is considered a more humanizing, person-first term that has generally replaced the use of the term "disabled people."

Points system. This current immigration policy awards points to potential immigrants based on a variety of qualities such as education, fluency of English or French, demand for occupation, and number of relatives already in Canada. The system is intended to make the immigration system more transparent and objective.

Political economy perspective on poverty. The political economy perspective on poverty assumes a relationship between politics and economics. According to this view, the large concentration of ownership of major corporations affects the way governments operate, or fail to operate, in the regulation of industry and the labour market, wages, discrimination, etc.

Political economy theorists. Political economy theorists believe that the operation of economic markets is tied to private concentrations of ownership and is essentially exploitative. Most adherents, while not opposed to providing support to those in need, would argue that social spending serves to prop up and justify an unjust economic system. The welfare state, in their view, is one of the contradictions of capitalism: it increases well-being, but it also frustrates the pursuit of a just society. It reinforces the very institutions and values that the welfare state was established to do away with.

Political ideology approach. The political ideology approach situates social welfare in the context of economic, social, and political theory—in Canada, this is normally distinguished according to conservative, liberal, social democratic, and socialist beliefs.

Political rights model of disability (social oppression theory). The "political rights model of disability" suggests that the problems faced by people with disabilities are not the result of physical impairments alone but are also the result of the social and political inequality that exists between people with disabilities on the one hand and people without disabilities on the other. This model thus challenges the widely prevalent view that disability is essentially an individual problem requiring individual treatment and individual solutions to problems.

Poor Law Amendment Act of 1834. The rather harsh *Poor Law Amendment Act* of 1834 had three main features: it forbade outdoor relief (relief outside the almshouses) for able-bodied persons and their families, it aimed to dramatically cut relief rates, and it aimed to tighten administrative rules and clean up what it saw as abuses of the system.

Positive rights. Positive rights imply that the state plays a more positive and active role in ensuring that these rights are realized. A positive right requires action, rather than inaction, on the part of the duty-bearer or the person or institution fulfilling the right. These rights require the state to play an active role in providing income security and services.

Poverty. Poverty refers to some benchmark standard and how many people live below that standard (whereas inequality refers to the differences between income groups). In discussing how much poverty exists, three dimensions need to be considered: (1) how many people are poor (the headcount measure); (2) by how much they fall below the poverty line (the poverty gap measure); and (3) for how long they are poor (the poverty duration measure). There are three measures commonly found in the poverty literature: Low-Income Cut-Offs (LICOs); Market Basket Measures (MBMs); and Low-Income Measures (LIMs).

Poverty duration. Poverty duration refers to the length of time that people experience low income. The Statistics Canada Survey of Labour and Income Dynamics (SLID) enables analysis of the duration of poverty. SLID follows the same set of people for six consecutive years and is designed to capture changes in the economic well-being of individuals and families over time.

Poverty gap. The poverty gap is a measurement of how much additional income would be required to raise an individual or household above the LICO or some other measure of poverty. It measures the depth of poverty.

Poverty headcount. Poverty headcount measures the number and proportion of persons in poverty.

Poverty rate. A variety of measures have been proposed for measuring the rate of poverty. In discussing how much poverty exists, three dimensions need to be considered: how many people are poor (the headcount measure), by how much they fall below the poverty line (the poverty gap measure), and for how long they are poor (the poverty duration measure).

Prime Minister's Office (PMO). The PMO is made up of the Prime Minister and the Prime Minister's top political staff. The office also includes speech writers, strategists, and communications personnel, among others. The PMO is charged with advising the Prime Minister on decisions. It is arguably the most powerful single unit of decision making within the Canadian system of government. (See also, Privy Council Office.)

Principle of less eligibility. This principle is based on the idea that the amount of assistance has to be less than that of the lowest-paying job. It stipulated that the "able-bodied pauper's" condition be less eligible (that is, less desirable or favourable) than the condition of the independent labourer. The intention is to stigmatize relief.

Privately funded disability programs. Privately funded disability programs refers to programs that are provided through private insurance plans or through long-term disability plans as part of job benefits. These private income security programs are based on the amount of funding that the recipient has contributed directly to the plan or funding that has been contributed to a plan on behalf of the recipient.

Private pension plans. The private pension plans component of the retirement income system consists of pensions from employers and publicly supported and regulated private savings plans such as Registered Retirement Savings Plans (RRSPs), Registered Pension Plans (RPPs), and Deferred Profit Sharing Plans (DPSPs).

Private welfare. Private welfare can be non-profit or for-profit and provides "in-kind" benefits to those lacking income. In-kind benefits include such things as food, emergency shelter, and other bare necessities. By law, organizations that provide these benefits are often registered, and rules and regulations govern their activities.

Privy Council Office. Unlike the PMO, which is more partisan, the PCO is officially charged with providing the federal cabinet and Prime Minister with independent advice and helping to support the various government agencies and departments.

Psychological disabilities. Called mental illnesses within the health-care field, psychological disabilities are characterized by alterations in thinking, mood, or behaviour, or some combination of the three and can include conditions such as mood disorders (major depression and bipolar disorder), schizophrenia, anxiety disorders, and personality disorders.

Publicly funded disability programs. Publicly funded disability programs are those covered by federal, provincial, and municipal legislation. These include the Canada Pension Plan Disability Pension (a federal program), the Family Benefits plan (a provincial program), and the General Welfare Assistance plan (a municipal program in Ontario). These types of programs are funded through government taxation, and except for the Canada Pension Plan, do not require the financial contribution of recipients.

Public welfare. Public welfare takes place at the three levels of government: the federal or national government, the provincial and territorial governments, and the regional and municipal governments. The various levels of government fund and deliver monetary benefit programs.

Quebec Parental Insurance Plan (QPIP). In 2006, Quebec implemented the Quebec Parental Insurance Plan (QPIP). The QPIP is an expanded parental benefits plan designed to support new parents in their desire to have children and support them as they devote more time to their children in their first months. The QPIP pays benefits to all eligible workers—salaried or self-employed—taking maternity leave, paternity leave, parental leave or adoption leave. The QPIP replaced the maternity, parental, or adoption benefits previously provided to Quebec parents under the federal employment insurance plan.

Quintile income distribution. Quintiles are used to provide a window into the income levels of people at various levels of society. There are five quintiles, each measuring 20 percent of the population, usually referred to as the lowest, second, third (or middle), fourth, and highest quintiles. The quintile income distribution calculates the share of total income that goes to each quintile. If the Canadian population is divided into quintiles, the highest quintile of Canadians receives around 40 percent of the total income; the lowest fifth receives only six percent of the income.

Race. Race is defined as the observable, physical features that are shared among several people, but that distinguish them from members of other groups. For example, if we orient to skin colour and hair texture, people who are labelled "black" differ visibly from those identified as "white."

Racism. Racism is the collection of actions, attitudes, beliefs, and practices that reflect a negative view of people in particular racial groups. Individual racism describes negative attitudes that people might have about others who are members of a different racial group. Institutional racism involves the "official" policies and regulations of an organization or institution that allows people from different racial groups to be treated differently in that setting. Structural racism describes how deeply rooted inequalities in the structure of society prevent the full participation of people of colour in major social and cultural institutions.

Refugee class. This is an immigration category in which applicants are permitted to enter Canada based on the threat of persecution, torture, or cruelty in their home countries.

Refundable Child Tax Credit. Beginning in 1978, Finance Minister Jean Chrétien announced a merging of social security programs and income tax provisions. The Liberal government introduced the Refundable Child Tax Credit as a way to target families in need of government assistance. The stated goal of the benefit was to help families meet the costs of raising children. It was income tested and varied according to the number of children in a family.

Relative homelessness. Relative homelessness is a situation in which people's homes do not meet the United Nations' basic housing standards, which are that a dwelling must have adequate protection from the elements, provide access to safe water and sanitation, provide secure tenure and personal safety, and not cost more than 50 percent of total income.

Relative measures of poverty. Relative measures of poverty are based on how low one's income is relative to that of other people. Such measures reflect the differences in income between the poor and the majority of society, rather than a fixed standard.

Reserve system. The reserve system is a by-product of the land-surrender treaties. Reserves are parcels of land that have been set aside for exclusive occupation and use by Aboriginal communities.

Residential schools. This term refers to a range of historical institutions including industrial schools, boarding schools, student residences, hostels, billets, and residential schools tasked with educating Aboriginal children and the overall assimilation of Aboriginal peoples.

Residual approach. In the residual approach, social welfare is a limited, temporary response to human need, implemented only when all else fails. It is based on the premise that there are two natural ways through which an individual's needs are met: through the family and the market economy. The residual model is based on the idea that government should play a limited role in the distribution of social welfare.

Royal Commission on Aboriginal Peoples (RCAP). RCAP, in 1996, was an extensive study that focused on the current situation of Aboriginal people in Canada. It included an examination of the need for Aboriginal people to heal from the consequences of domination, displacement, and assimilation. The foundation for a renewed relationship, according to the report, involves recognition of Aboriginal nations as political entities. This report was followed by the 1998 government response: *Gathering Strength: Canada's Aboriginal Action Plan*.

Selective programs. Selective programs target benefits at those who are in need or eligible, based on a means test (sometimes called an income test) or a needs test.

Self-employment. Self-employed people rely on their own initiative and skills to generate income, and undertake the risks and uncertainties of starting and operating their own businesses.

Seniors Benefit. In 1966, the federal government proposed the Seniors Benefit. This new program would have combined the OAS, the GIS, and the Spouse's Allowance into one benefit that would be more targeted at seniors with low incomes. Due to extensive pressure from seniors and advocacy groups, the government announced in 1998 that the plans for the Seniors Benefit had been scrapped.

Seven biases with respect to families. "Seven biases" with respect to families have prevented social programs from keeping up with the changing nature of today's family, according to sociologist Margrit Eichler. These are: the monolithic bias; the conservative bias; the sexist bias; the micro-structural bias; the ageist bias.; the racist bias; and the heterosexist bias. Being aware of these societal biases helps policy-makers design social welfare programs that reflect real, existing families, not just "ideal" families.

Social Assistance (SA). When a person has no source of income, he or she is entitled to what is commonly known as Social Assistance (SA), also known as welfare. SA is a province-based minimum income program for people defined as "in need." Strict eligibility criteria, known as a needs test, are applied to determine whether people are in need. Social Assistance is a program of last resort with roots in early charity relief and the English Poor Laws.

Social citizenship. In the past few years, social policy analysts have begun to outline social welfare within a "social investment" framework. The new approach underlines the multidimensional aspect of social welfare. The goal of social investment is social inclusion. It therefore requires change at multiple levels—change that goes beyond meeting basic needs

Social democratic ideology. The key values of the social democratic ideology are social equality, social justice, economic freedom, and fellowship and cooperation. To the social democrat, social inequality wastes human ability and is inefficient in its distribution of resources. Freedom for social democrats is not only political, it is economic—the kind of freedom that results from government intervention in maintaining a stable economy and stable employment.

Social democratic welfare regimes. Social democratic welfare regimes include countries such as Sweden, Finland, and Norway. This model emphasizes citizenship rights and the creation of a universal and comprehensive system of social benefits. The model is focused on optimum conditions for the citizen—as a right.

Social equity. Social equity refers to the existence of adequate levels of health and security for all people and a reasonably equal distribution of income and wealth.

Social exclusion. Many scholars, particularly in Europe, are increasingly conceptualizing poverty in terms of social exclusion. The concept refers to marginalization—having limited opportunities or abilities to participate in the social, economic, and cultural activities of society. In short, social exclusion views poverty not as a matter of a low degree of well-being but as the inability to pursue well-being because of the lack of opportunities.

Social inclusion. This concept challenges social welfare scholars to consider the non-economic aspects of society that lead to social disadvantages or social exclusion, such as education, community life, health care access, and political participation.

Social insurance programs. The fundamental element of a modern welfare state is a social insurance scheme. You pay premiums and then have a right to benefits. Employment Insurance and Workers' Compensation are examples.

Social investment. The social investment state focuses on social inclusion by strengthening civil society and providing equality of opportunity rather than equality of outcomes. Also known as the "third way," it claims that creating jobs that are not low-paying and dead-end are essential to attacking involuntary social exclusion. Nevertheless, an inclusive society must also provide for the basic needs of those who cannot work and must recognize the wider diversity of goals that life has to offer.

Socialist ideology. Socialist ideology could be described as emphasizing freedom, collectivism, and equality. Socialists believe in equality and a society that operates to meet people's needs. Marx's saying, "From each according to their abilities, to each according to their needs," summarizes this view. In short, production should be organized according to social criteria and distributed according to need. Here, equality means the absence of special privilege.

Social justice approach. This approach aims to create systems and policies that help meet the needs of persons with disabilities. Some worry that it characterizes persons with disabilities as "charity cases" without emphasizing full citizenship.

Social model. The social model views disability within a social and environmental context, emphasizing the need for society to change so as to remove the barriers that prevent "disabled" persons from fully participating in social life.

Social policies. Social policies refer to the rules, regulations, laws, and other administrative directives that set the framework for social welfare activity.

Social problem. This is a situation that is incompatible with some standard or norm held by a significant number of people in society who agree that action is needed to alter the situation.

Social programs. Social programs are the various targeted initiatives that are created to put social policies into practice.

Social Protection Floor initiative. The UN's Social Protection Floor (SPF) Initiative is aimed at bringing together UN agencies, NGOs, development banks and other developmental organizations to support countries committed to building national "social protection floors" for their citizens. The United Nations Chief Executives Board for Coordination (UNCEB) coined the concept of the SPF. The initiative aims to make governments responsible for the promotion of essential and universal social guarantees, which in turn would set the ground for a more comprehensive social welfare system.

Social responsibility model of the family. The social responsibility model of the family directly addresses gender inequality, gender-sensitive policies, and the social dimension of caregiving. The model contains minimal gender inequality or stratification. The goal with this model shifts from moving towards a society based on equality to one where inequality is minimized.

Social safety net. This term is used to refer to the social welfare system. Income security programs and social servicees provide protection for all Canadians, if and when they need them. The social safety net has come under great stress in recent years.

Social services. Social services (personal or community services) help people improve their well-being by providing non-monetary help to persons in need. Offered by social workers, services include probation, addiction treatment, youth drop-in centres, parent-child resource centres, child care facilities, child protection services, shelters for abused women, and counselling.

Social Union Framework Agreement (SUFA). This 1999 government act affecting income security and social services aims to smooth out federal-provincial/territorial relations after the fallout from the unilateral discontinuation of CAP and the implementation of the CHST. The SUFA refers to a range of programs such as medicare, social services, and education. It also addresses how these programs are funded, administered, and delivered.

Social welfare system. The social welfare system consists of a combination of income security programs and social services.

Spouse in the house rule. Social workers and welfare advocacy groups have long been critical of the so-called "spouse-in-the-house rule." In some cities, welfare workers were trained to determine whether a person of the opposite sex had stayed overnight at a welfare recipient's home. If it was determined that there was someone staying in the home, that person could have been deemed financially responsible for the person receiving welfare support. The rule is still applied in a modified way.

Spouse's Allowance (SPA). The Spouse's Allowance (SPA) was created to deal with a hardship-creating anomaly in the OAS/GIS. In some cases, an elderly couple consisting of a woman under age 65 and an income-earning husband aged 65 would receive OAS and GIS intended for one person. When the woman reached age 65, their income would jump to the OAS/GIS amount intended for married couples. The 1975 SPA was intended to correct the anomaly by providing an income-tested benefit to those between 60 and 65 years of age when one spouse is over 65.

Stages model of policy-making. The stages model of policy-making is based on seeing policy making as a rational and incremental exercise in problem-solving that follows a predictable process. Policy moves from identifying a problem through to setting the agenda for government action by showing how policy could address the problem.

Status Indians (or Registered Indians). Status or Registered Indians are persons who are listed in the federal government's Indian Register.

Statute of Labourers. The Black Death ravaged Europe between 1347 and 1351 and brought about a serious labour shortage. English labourers took advantage of the situation and demanded higher wages. One response was the Statute of Labourers, which was issued by Edward III in 1351 and directed against the rise in prices and wages.

Structural adjustment. Structural adjustment policies (SAPs) have been imposed by the International Monetary Fund (IMF) on poor countries to ensure debt repayment and economic restructuring. With the stated goals of helping to reduce poverty and promoting economic health, SAPs have often had negative impacts.

Structural approach. The structural approach to social welfare considers the operation of economic markets to be essentially exploitative: while social welfare is necessary to assist those in need, it only further perpetuates the inherently oppressive capitalist structure, rather than forcing a chance in society.

Structural power of business. Under capitalism, firms need to make decisions with an eye to competitiveness and profitability. Social policies that affect profitability by imposing greater costs on firms (from higher taxes, wages, greater administrative oversight) are likely to lead firms to invest elsewhere, resulting in a drop-off of economic activity. The concern for business profitability is built centrally into policy-making. It is for this reason that it is called structural, because it is built into the normal workings of our economic system.

Structural unemployment. Structural unemployment is due to mismatches between the skills of the unemployed and the skills necessary for available jobs.

Tax credit. A tax credit is an amount deducted directly from income tax otherwise payable. Examples of tax credits include the disability tax credit, the married credit for individuals, and the scientific research and experimental development investment tax credit for corporations.

Tax deduction. A tax deduction is an amount deducted from total income to arrive at taxable income. Child care expenses and capital cost allowances are tax deductions. Tax deductions are worth more to people with higher incomes, as they are in a higher marginal tax bracket.

Tax expenditures. Tax expenditures are foregone tax revenues resulting from special exemptions, deductions, rate reductions, rebates, credits, and deferrals that reduce the amount of tax that would otherwise be payable.

Trade unions. Trade unions are organizations that represent those individuals working in particular industries or industrial sectors and that work to defend and advance the interests of these workers in terms of wages and working conditions, as well as broader welfare concerns.

Transnational corporations. Transnational corporations (TNCs) are organizations that possess and control the means of production or services outside of the country in which they were established.

Treaties. Treaties between the Canadian government and First Nations generally served to establish peaceful relations, institute payments, and gain the surrender of land. The treaties generally stipulated the relinquishment of the First Nations right and title to specific land and provided for the annual payment of five dollars per person (this amount has not changed and was never indexed to inflation).

Truth and Reconciliation Commission (TRC). Residential schools for Aboriginal people in Canada date back to the 1870s. Over 130 residential schools were located across the country, and the last school closed in 1996. These government-funded, church-run schools were set up to eliminate parental involvement in the intellectual, cultural, and spiritual development of Aboriginal children. Based on a similar commission set up in South Africa after the fall of the Apartheid regime, the Truth and Reconciliation Commission of Canada has a mandate to learn the truth about what happened in the residential schools and to inform all Canadians about what happened in the schools.

Types of Employment Insurance benefits. EI benefits include regular benefits, paid to people who have lost their jobs and are actively looking for work; maternity/parental benefits for new parents, including adoptive parents; compassionate care benefits for people who must leave work temporarily to care for a gravely ill family member; the family supplement for low-income families with children; and fishing benefits for self-employed persons engaged in fishing who earn insufficient earnings from that activity.

Underemployment. Underemployment occurs when the education and training required for the job are less than the education and training of the worker who is doing the job. Evidence indicates that underemployment increases as higher quality jobs become relatively fewer in number.

Undeserving poor. In early English Poor Laws, those physically able to work were considered undeserving and were forced to work by law. Today, a similar concept persists.

Unemployment rate. The unemployment rate is the percentage of the labour force that is unemployed.

United Nations (UN). The United Nations (UN) is an international organization founded after the Second World War (1945) by 51 countries committed to maintaining international peace and security, friendly relations among nations, and promoting social progress, better living standards, and human rights. Due to its unique international character, and the powers vested in its founding Charter, the Organization can take action on a wide range of issues and provide a forum for its 193 Member States to express their views through the General Assembly, the Security Council, the Economic and Social Council, and other bodies and committees.

United Nation's Children Fund (UNICEF). The United Nations Children's Fund is a United Nations program that aims to provide humanitarian and developmental assistance to children and mothers in developing countries. It was created by the UN General Assembly in 1946 to provide emergency food and health care to children in countries that had been devastated by World War II.

United Nations Educational, Scientific and Cultural Organization (UNESCO). The United Nations Educational, Scientific and Cultural Organization is an agency of the United Nations. UNESCO aim to contribute to peace and security by promoting international collaboration in the areas of education, science, and culture in order to foster universal respect for justice, the rule of law, and human rights in addition to the fundamental freedoms proclaimed in the UN Charter.

Universal Child Care Benefit (UCCB). The UCCB is a taxable $1,200 per year benefit that was introduced in 2006 and can be claimed by parents for each child under 6 years of age.

Universal Declaration of Human Rights (UDHR). The 1948 Universal Declaration of Human Rights defines the fundamental expectations for freedom and dignity in a free and just society. Accepted human rights include freedom of expression, freedom of association, freedom from fear and persecution, and freedom of religion, as well as the right to shelter, education, health, and work, among others.

Universal programs. These programs are for everyone in a specific category (such as people over age 65 or children) on the same terms and as a right of citizenship.

Urban Aboriginal Peoples Study. The *Aboriginal Peoples Study*, released in 2011, represents the first study across major Canadian cities to focus exclusively on First Nations, Métis, and Inuit Peoples living in cities. It provides a current picture of a population that has experienced substantial growth and change since the release of the RCAP report in 1996.

Vanier Institute of the Family. The Vanier Institute of the Family is a national charitable organization dedicated to promoting the well-being of Canadian families. It uses a functional definition of the family that emphasizes the activities of family members.

Veterans disability benefits. Canadian veterans are eligible for disability pension benefits if they have a permanent disability resulting from disease or injury incurred during a war or in a special duty area. Dependants of veterans are also eligible to collect the benefit.

Visible minority. A problematic term, but one that is widely used by anti-racist researchers to detect discrimination, "visible minorities" are groups that are visually distinct from the mainstream, dominant group and include people who are non-white in skin colour. According to Canada's *Employment Equity Act*, the ten visible minority groups identified are Chinese, South Asian, Black, Filipino, Latin American, Southeast Asian, Arab, West Asian, Japanese, and Korean groups. However, the term "visible minorities" is itself somewhat problematic since the obvious question is"visible minorities in relation to whom?".

Voluntary assumption of risk. This is one of the early principles used to define the relationship between employers and employees. The voluntary assumption of risk meant that the worker assumed the usual risks of the job and the rate of pay for each job was assumed to reflect its level of risk. The principle is based on the assumption that contracts between workers and their employers are the same as commercial contracts between people of equal bargaining power.

Washington Consensus. A term coined in the early 1990s that captures an approach to resolving the problems of crisis-wracked developing economies. The economic prescriptions, adopted by the IMF and World Bank among others, include macroeconomic stabilization, economic opening with respect to both trade and investment, and the expansion of market forces within the domestic economy. It is argued, essentially, that social and economic policies must encourage the free play of market forces and that the state's role should be to ensure markets work effectively.

"Weak federalism". The division of responsibilities between the federal and provincial governments affects social policy development. In areas where the provinces and territories have more autonomy and responsibility, we may see differences in the social policies across the country. This phenomenon has come to be referred to loosely as "weak federalism," though insofar as it fosters innovation it is not without some strengths as well.

Welfare fraud. Often exaggerated, fraud within the Social Assistance or welfare systems occurs when applicants are being deceptive in order to receive benefits. Almost half of the fraud cases in Ontario were instances of people collecting welfare while in prison. Many of the other reported frauds were overpayments and administrative errors or cases where documents were missing.

Welfare state consensus. The "consensus" held that economic growth and social programs could work in tandem, and that in fact the redistribution of wealth that socialists proposed could be avoided by simply growing the economic pie. That would allow those at the bottom of the income scale to achieve a bit more prosperity but not at the expense of the wealthy. The state's role then was not to redistribute existing wealth but to help industry increase overall wealth and then insure that the tendency of unregulated markets to create ever greater maldistribution of wealth was checked by government programs.

Welfare state. The welfare state is a system in which the state protects the health and well-being of its citizens, especially those in social and financial need. The key functions of the welfare state are (1) using state power to achieve desired goals (powers include government, bureaucracy, the judiciary, and political parties); (2) altering the normal operation of the private marketplace; and (3) using grants, taxes, pensions, social services, and minimum-income programs such as welfare and social insurance.

Welfare state regimes approach. The welfare state approach classifies welfare states according to how social welfare is provided in a given society. Also referred to as the welfare state approach and the welfare state models approach.

Welfare wall. The term "welfare wall" refers to disincentives that hinder the move from welfare to work because of the financial and other supports that are lost when families accept employment.

Women's suffrage. Women's suffrage refers to the right of women to vote and to stand for public office. Manitoba took the lead in extending full Canadian women's suffrage in 1916. Agnes Macphail was the first woman elected to Parliament (in 1921).

Workers' Compensation. Workers' Compensation is a collection of provincial social insurance programs for employers and workers, established to replace the tort system (the courts) in determining compensation for workplace injuries and health-related risks. It provides no-fault compensation.

Workfare. Workfare takes many different forms—it could mean that a person must take a job to get their Social Assistance cheque, or it could mean that people receive a smaller cheque if they refuse to work. It could also involve mandatory community volunteer work or self-employment.

Workhouses. Erected as private enterprises, seventeenth-century workhouses were officially called almshouses. Able-bodied applicants for poor relief were forced to report to the workhouse to complete work tasks in order to obtain assistance.

Working Income Supplement (WIS). In addition to a basic benefit, the 1993 Child Tax Benefit included a Working Income Supplement (WIS) to supplement the earnings of working poor families.

Working poor. The low-wage earners or working poor are people who are participating in the labour force through paid employment, but do not earn enough income to lift them above the poverty line.

Workplace modifications. These modifications include changes in the workplace environment for persons with disabilities, such as handrails, ramps, accessible parking, accessible elevators, modified workstations, accessible washrooms, or accessible transportation.

World Bank. The World Bank Group's mission is to fight poverty and improve the living standards of people in the developing world. It provides loans, policy advice, technical assistance, and knowledge-sharing services to low- and middle-income countries to reduce poverty.

World Trade Organization (WTO). The WTO is a global international organization dealing with the rules of trade between nations. In this new era of globalization, the rules for the global economy that were once made by national governments are increasingly being made by international organizations such as the WTO (www.wto.org).

Youth unemployment. Youth unemployment refers to Canadians under the age of 18 who are without a job but want one.

References

Chapter 1: Introducing Social Welfare

Government of Canada. (2012). *The government expenditure plan and main estimates. 2011-12*. Retrieved from: http://www.tbs-sct.gc.ca/est-pre/20112012/me-bpd/docs/me-bpd-eng.pdf.

Government of Canada. (2012). *Public accounts of Canada—Volume 1: Summary report and consolidated financial statements*. Ottawa: Minister of Public Works and Government Services Canada.

Human Resources and Social Development Canada. (2006). *Social security statistics Canada and provinces 1978-79 to 2002-03*, Table 3 *Expenditure Analyses of Social Security Programs, Canada, 1978/1979 to 2002/2003*. www.hrsdc.gc.ca/en/cs/sp/sdc/socpol/tables/table3a.shtml.

Mowat Centre. (2012). *Making It Work: Final Recommendations of the Mowat Centre Employment Insurance Task Force*. Toronto: University of Toronto.

OECD. (2012). Income tax and social security contributions: Single individual without children at income level of the average worker. June 29. Table 1: 10.1787/20758510.

Chapter 2: The History of Social Welfare in Canada

Burke, H. (1987). *The people and the poor law in nineteenth century Ireland*. Littlehampton, West Sussex: Women's Education Bureau.

Finkel, A. (2006). Paradise postponed, 1939–50: The Second World War and its aftermath. In *Social policy and practice in Canada* (pp. 125–47). Waterloo, ON: Wilfrid Laurier University Press.

Graham, J., Swift, K. and Delaney, R. (2003). *Canadian social policy: An introduction* (2nd ed.). Toronto: Pearson Education Canada Inc.

Guest, D. (1999). *The emergence of social security in Canada* (3rd ed.).Vancouver: UBC Press.

Moscovitch, A. and Albert, J. (Eds.). (1987). *The benevolent state: The growth of welfare in Canada*. Toronto: Garamond Press.

Moscovitch, A. and Webster, A. (1995). Aboriginal social assistance expenditures. In Philips, S. (Ed.). *How Ottawa spends: 1995-96: Mid-life crises* (pp. 209–236). Ottawa: Carleton University Press.

Webb, S. and Webb, B. (1927). *English local government: English poor law history*. New York: Longmans.

Chapter 3: Challenges to Social Welfare

Campbell, B. (Dec. 2011/Jan. 2012). Rising inequality, declining democracy: Canada has become more unequal as it grows less democratic. *The CCPA Monitor*, 1, 6–7.

Conference Board of Canada. (2011). *How Canada performs: A report card on Canada*. Ottawa: Conference Board of Canada.

Edmonton Journal, June 20, 1991.

Forget, E. (2011). The town with no poverty: The health effects of a Canadian guaranteed annual income field experiment. *Canadian Public Policy, 37*(3), 283–305.

Foulds, J. (2011, December 29). After Attawapiskat, what? *Toronto Star*.

Grant, T. (2011, December 5). Canada's wage gap at record high: OECD. *The Globe and Mail*.

Canadian Council on Social Development (CCSD). (2005). The disappearing just society: Fast facts. *Perception*. Spring.

Chapter 4: Social Welfare Theory

Esping-Anderson, G. (1999). *The three worlds of welfare capitalism*. Princeton, NJ: Princeton University Press.

Evans, P. and Wekerle, G. (Eds.). (1997). *Women and the Canadian welfare state*. Toronto: University of Toronto Press.

George, V. and Wilding, P. (1993). *Ideology and social welfare*. London: Routledge.

Keynes, J. M. (1936). *The general theory of employment, interest and money*. London: Palgrave Macmillan.

Mitchell, A. and Shillington, R. (2002). *Poverty, inequality and social inclusion*. Perspectives on Social Inclusion Working Paper Series. Toronto: Laidlaw Foundation.

Neysmith, S. (1991). From community care to a social model of care. In Baines, C., Evans, P. and Neysmith, S. (Eds.). *Women's caring: Feminist perspectives on social welfare* (pp. 272–299). Toronto: McClelland & Stewart Ltd.

Olsen, G. M. (2002). *The politics of the welfare state: Canada, Sweden, and the United States*. Don Mills, ON: Oxford University Press.

Sainsbury, D. (Ed.). (1999). *Gender and welfare state regimes*. Oxford: Oxford University Press.

Sörensen, K. and Bergqvist, C. (2002). *Gender and the social democratic welfare regime: A comparison of gender-equality friendly policies in Sweden and Norway*. Stockholm: National Institute for Working Life.

Titmuss, R. M. (1958). *Essays on the welfare State*. London: Allen and Unwin.

Wilkinson, R. G. and Pickett, K. (2009). *The spirit level: Why more equal societies almost always do better*. London: The Penguin Group.

Williams, F. (1989). *Social policy: A critical introduction*. Cambridge: Polity Press.

Chapter 5: Making Social Policy in Canada

Bonoli, G. (2005). The politics of the new social policies: Providing coverage against new social risks in mature welfare states. *Policy and Politics, 33*(3), 431–449.

Brooks, S. and Miljan, L. (2003). *Public policy in Canada: An introduction* (4th ed.). Toronto: Oxford.

Castles, F. G. (2004). *The future of the welfare state*. Oxford: Oxford University Press.

Farnsworth, K. and Holden, C. (2006). The business-social policy nexus: Corporate power and corporate inputs into social policy. *Journal of Social Policy, 35*(3), 473–494

Graefe, P. (2008). The spending power and federal social policy leadership: A prospective view. *IRPP Policy Matters, 9*(3), 53–106.

Grieshaber-Otto, J. and Sinclair, S. (2004). *Bad medicine: Trade treaties, privatization and health care reform in Canada*. Ottawa: Canadian Centre for Policy Alternatives.

Hudson, C.-A. and Graefe, P. (2011). The Toronto origins of Ontario's 2008 poverty reduction strategy: Mobilizing multiple channels of influence for progressive social policy change. *Canadian Review of Social Policy*, 65-66.

Korpi, W. (2003). Welfare state regress in Western Europe: Politics, institutions, globalization, and Europeanization. *Annual Review of Sociology, 29*, 589–609.

Mahon, R. and McBride, S. (Eds.). (2008). *The OECD and transnational governance*. Vancouver: UBC Press.

Smith, M. (2009). *A civil society? Collective actors in Canadian political life*. Toronto: UTP.

Smith, M. (Ed.). (2008). *Group politics and social movements in Canada*. Peterborough: Broadview Press.

Chapter 6: Canadians Living in Poverty

Bohácek, R. (2002, February 5). The efficiency-equality tradeoff in welfare state economies. CERGE-EI Working Paper No. 193. http://ssrn.com/abstract=317862 or DOI: 10.2139/ssrn.317862.

Citizens for Public Justice. (2012). *Poverty Trends Scorecard*. Ottawa: Citizens for Public Justice.

Clark, C. (1995). Work and welfare: Looking at both sides of the equation. *Perception 19*(1), 5–8

Conference Board of Canada. (2013). *Income Inequality: Is Canada Becoming More unequal?* Ottawa: Conference Board of Canada.

Diaconal Ministries of Canada. (2012). *Justice: The Working Poor*. Burlington, ON: Diaconal Ministries of Canada.

Food Banks Canada. (2012). *HungerCount2012*. Toronto: Food Banks Canada.

Gaetz, S. (2012). *The Real Cost of Homelessness: Can We Save Money by Doing the Right Thing?* Toronto. Canadian Homelessness Research Network Press.

Government of Ontario. (2002). *Ontario Welfare Fraud Control Report 2001 2002*. Toronto: Ministry of Community and Social Services.

Hughes, J. (2012). *Homelessness: Closing the Gap Between Capacity and Peformance*. Toronto: Mowat Centre.

Human Development Council. (2011). *Child Poverty Report Card, New Brunswick*. St John, NB: Human Development Council.

Human Resources and Skills Development Canada. (2013). *Indicators of Well-being in Canada*. Ottawa: HRSDC.

Laird, G. (2007a). *Shelter : Homelessness in a Growth Economy: Canada's 21 Century Paradox*. Calgary: Sheldon Chumir Foundation for Ethics in Leadership.

Laird, G. (2007b, June 26) The true cost of homelessness. *Toronto Star*.

Lefebvre, S. (2002). Housing: An income issue. *Perspectives on Labour and Income, 3*(6), 5–12.

Mitchell, A. and Shillington, R. (2004). *Federal Tax Relief for Low Income People*. Ottawa: National Anti-Poverty Organization.

National Council of Welfare. (2002). *Welfare Incomes 2000 and 2001*. Ottawa: National Council of Welfare.

National Council of Welfare. (2010). *Welfare Incomes 2009*. Winter 2010, Volume #129. Ottawa: NCW.

National Council of Welfare. (2011). *Dollars and Sense of Solving Poverty*. Volume #130. Ottawa: NCW.

Paperny, A. M. (2012, February 11). The poor in Toronto: They're working but not getting any richer. *The Globe and Mail*.

Sarlo, C. (1992). *Poverty in Canada*. Vancouver: The Fraser Institute.

Sarlo, C. (2001). *Measuring poverty in Canada*. Vancouver: The Fraser Institute.

Sarlo, C. (2009). *What is Poverty: Providing Clarity for Canada*. Vancouver: The Fraser Institute.

Stapleton, J., Murphy, B. and Xing, Y. (2012). *The working poor in the Toronto region: Who they are, where they live, and how trends are changing*. Toronto: The Metcalf Centre.

Statistics Canada. (2006a). *Income and the outcomes of children*. Ottawa: Minister of Industry. Cat. no. 11F0019MIE, No. 281.

Chapter 7: Employment, Unemployment and Worker's Compensation

Bohácek, R. (2002, February 5). The efficiency-equality tradeoff in welfare state economies." CERGE-EI Working Paper No. 193. http://ssrn.com/abstract=317862.

Canadian Union of Public Employees. (2012). "Cupe advisory: Changes to employment insurance." Ottawa: CUPE Research. Retrieved from: www.cupe.ca/updir/EI_Advisory_October 18 2012.pdf.

The Daily. (2012). *Employment insurance coverage survey, 2011*. Ottawa: Statistics Canada.

Fong, F. (2012). The plight of younger workers. Toronto: TD Economics.

Gouvernement du Quebec. 2013. *Québec parental insurance plan*. Emploi et Solidarité Social Québec. Retrieved from: http://www.rqap.gouv.qc.ca./Index_en.asp

Human Resources and Skills Development Canada. (2006a). *Employment insurance (EI) and maternity, parental, and sickness benefits*. Ottawa: HRSDC. Retrieved from http://www.servicecanada.gc.ca/eng/ei/faq/faq_special.shtml

Human Resources and Skills Development Canada. (2011). *Employment insurance monitoring and assessment report*. Ottawa: HRSDC. Retrieved from: http://www.hrsdc.gc.ca/eng/jobs/ei/reports/mar2011/index.shtml

Human Resources and Skills Development Canada. (2013). *Indicators of well-being in Canada*. Ottawa: HRSDC. Retrieved from: http://www4.hrsdc.gc.ca/h.4m.2@-eng.jsp

LaRochelle-Côté, S. and Gilmore, J. (2009). Canada's employment downturn. *Perspectives on labour and income*. *10*(12), 5–12

Marshall, K. (2012). *Youth neither enrolled nor employed*. Ottawa: Statistics Canada.

Mendelson, M., Battle, K., Torjman, S., & Caledon Institute of Social Policy. (2009). *Canada's shrunken safety net: Employment insurance in the great recession*. Ottawa: Caledon Institute of Social Policy.

Meredith, W. R. (1913). *Meredith Report*. Toronto: Legislative Assembly of Ontario.

Mowat Centre. (2012). *Making It Work: Final Recommendations of the Mowat Centre Employment Insurance Task Force*. Toronto: Mowat Centre.

Nazarik, L. (2012, November 1). Why part-time work may be the new normal. *The Globe and Mail*.

Statistics Canada. (2010). Minimum wage. *Perspectives on labour and income*. *11*(3), 14–22.

Statistics Canada. (2011) *Employment insurance coverage survey*. Ottawa: Statistics Canada.

Statistics Canada. (2012). Labour force survey estimates (LFS), duration of unemployment by sex and age group, annual. *CANSIM Table 282-0048*. Ottawa: Statistics Canada.

Statistics Canada. (2013). Labour force characteristics by sex and age group. *CANSIM Table 282-0002*. Ottawa: Statistics Canada.

Chapter 8: Women and the Family

Alexander, C. (2012). *Early childhood education has widespread and long lasting benefits*. Toronto: TD Bank.

Bella, L. (2003). Family making: A framework for anti-oppressive practice. Conference paper presented at the University of Regina.

Canadian Child Care Federation. (2003) *Child care in Canada: What does the public want—Factsheet 2*. Toronto: Child Care Advocacy Association of Canada. Retrieved from: http://www.ccaac.ca/pdf/resources/factsheets/factsheet2.pdf

Canadian Women's Foundation. (2013). *Fact sheet: Moving women out of poverty*. Toronto: CWF. Retrieved from: www.canadianwomen.org/facts-about-poverty.

Child Care Advocacy Association of Canada. (2007). *The best of all worlds: A community vision for early learning and child care in Canada*. Ottawa: CCAAC. Retrieved from: http://www.ccaac.ca/pdf/backgound_docs/Exec_Summary_Ps&Qs(3).pdf

Child Care Advocacy Association of Canada. (2012). *A strong economy needs good child care: Canada can't work without it*. Ottawa: CCAAC. Retrieved from: http://www.ccaac.ca/pdf/resources/factsheets/EconomicBackgrounder_Election08.pdf

Cranswick, K. and Dosman, D. (2008). Eldercare: What we know today. *Canadian Social Trends*. *86*(1), 49–57.

Decter, A. (2011). *Educated, employed and equal: The economic prosperity case for national child care*. YWCA Canada.

Drolet, M. (2002). Can the Workplace Explain Canadian Gender Pay Differentials? *Canadian Public Policy*, 28(s1), 41–63.

Eichler, M. (1997). *Family shifts: Families, policies and gender equality*. Toronto: Oxford University Press.

Evans, P. M., and Wekerle, G. (Eds.). (1997). *Women and the Canadian welfare state*. Toronto: University of Toronto Press.

Gunderson, M. (1998). *Women and the Canadian labour market: Transitions towards the future*. Ottawa/Toronto: Statistics Canada/ITP Nelson.

Lero, D. and Joseph, G. (2007). *A systematic review of the literature on combining work and eldercare in Canada*. Guelph, ON: University of Guelph and The Homewood Foundation.

Neysmith, S. (1991). From community care to a social model of care. In Baines, C., Evans, P. and Neysmith, S. (Eds.). *Women's caring: Feminist perspectives on social welfare* (pp. 272–299). Toronto: McClelland & Stewart.

Statistics Canada. (2012). *2011 census of population: Families, households, marital status, structural type of dwelling, collectives*. Ottawa: Statistics Canada.

Vanier Institute of the Family. (2010). *Profiling Canada's families II*. Ottawa: Vanier Institute of the Family.

Chapter 9: Children and Families in Poverty

Battle, K. and Torjman, S. (1993). *Breaking down the welfare wall*. Ottawa: Caledon Institute of Social Policy.

Battle, K. (2008a). *A $5,000 Canada child tax benefit: Questions and answers*. Ottawa: Caledon Institute of Social Policy. Retrieved from: www.caledoninst.org/Publications/PDF/669ENG.pdf

Battle, K. (2008b). A bigger and better child benefit: A $5,000 Canada child tax benefit. Ottawa: Caledon Institute of Social Policy. Retrieved from: www.caledoninst.org/Publications/PDF/668ENG.pdf

Battle, K., Torjman, S. and Mendelson, M. (2006). *More than a name change: The universal child care benefit*. Ottawa: Caldeon Institute of Social Policy. www.caledoninst.org/Publications/PDF/589ENG.pdf

Campaign 2000. (2005). *Decision time for Canada: Let's make poverty history: 2005 report card on child poverty in Canada.* Ottawa. Campaign 2000. Retrieved from: http://www.campaign2000.ca/reportCards/national/2005EngNationalReportCard.pdf

Canada Without Poverty. (2012). Poverty. Ottawa: CWP. Retrieved from: www.cwp csp.ca/poverty/

Commisso-Georgee, C. (2013, February 6). Rise in for-profit child care is a cause for concern: expert. *CTVNews.ca*. Retrieved from: http://www.ctvnews.ca/canada/rise-in-for-profit child-care-is-a-cause-for-concern-expert-1.1145270

DAWN Ontario. (2006). *National child benefit supplement (NCBS): Backgrounder*. North Bay: DAWN Ontario. Retrieved from: http://dawn.thot.net/ncbs_backgrounder.html

Friendly, M. and Beach, J. (2013). *The state of early childhood education and care in Canada 2010: Trends and analysis*. Toronto: Child Care Canada. Retrieved from: http://www.childcarecanada.org/publications/ecec-canada/13/02/state-early-childhood-education-and-care-canada-2010-trends-and-analy

Mikkonen, J., & Raphael, D. (2010). Social Determinants of Health: The Canadian Facts. Toronto: York University School of Health Policy and Management.

UNICEF. (2005). *Child poverty in rich countries, 2005: Innocenti report card no. 6*. Florence, Italy: UNICEF Innocenti Research Centre.

UNICEF. (2012). *Measuring Child Poverty*. Florence, Italy: UNICEF Innocenti Research Centre.

Chapter 10: The Social Welfare of Immigrants

Alboim, N. and Cohl, K. (2012). *Shaping the future: Canada's rapidly changing immigration policies*. Toronto: Maytree.

Bissoondath, N. (1994). *Selling illusions: The cult of multiculturalism in Canada*. Toronto: Penguin.

Dei, G. J. S., (1996). *Anti-racism education: Theory and practice*. Winnipeg: Fernwood Publishing.

Department of Justice Canada. (1995). *Employment equity act, 1995 c.44 E-5.401*. Ottawa: Department of Justice Canada. Retrieved from: http://laws.justice.gc.ca/en/E-5.401/index.html.

Isajiw, W. (1999). *Understanding diversity: Ethnicity and race in the Canadian context*. Toronto: Thompson Educational Publishing.

Kelley, N., and Trebilcock, M (1998). *The making of the mosaic: A history of Canadian immigration policy*. Toronto: University of Toronto Press.

Mahtani, M. (2004). Interrogating the hyphen-nation: Canadian multicultural policy and "mixed race" identities. *Social Identities*. 8(1), 67–90.

Ontario Ministry of Finance. (2012). Chapter 10: Immigration. In *Commission on the Reform of Ontario's Public Services*. Toronto: Ontario Ministry of Finance.

Pendakur, K. and Pendakur, R. (1998). The colour of money: Earning differentials among ethnic groups in Canada. *Canadian Journal of Economics. 31*(3), 518–548.

Picot, G. and Hou, F. (2003). *The rise in low-income rates among immigrants in Canada*. Analytical Studies Branch Research Paper Series. Ottawa: Statistics Canada.

Reitz, J. (2001). Immigrant skill utilization in the Canadian labour market: Implications of human capital research. *Journal of International Migration and Integration*. 2(3), 347–378.

Saunders, R. (2006). *Making Work Pay*. Ottawa: Canadian Policy Research Networks. Retrieved from: www.cprn.org/documents/46773_en.pdf

Chapter 11: Aboriginal Social Welfare

Aboriginal Affairs and Northern Development Canada. (2013). Income Assistance Program. Ottawa: AANDC. Retrieved from: http://www.aadnc-aandc.gc.ca/eng/1100100035256/1100100035257

Assembly of First Nations. (2006). *Royal commission on Aboriginal people at 10 years: A report card*. Ottawa: AFN

Assembly of First Nations. (2012). *Active measures community resource guide*. Ottawa: AFN, Health and Social Sector. Retrieved from: www.afn.ca/uploads/files/social/activemeasures.pdf

Canada Year Book 2011. (2011) Aboriginal Peoples. Statistics Canada: Ottawa. www.statcan.gc.ca.

CBC. (2011, May 30). Aboriginal peoples: Mapping the future: Special report on land claims across Canada. *CBC News*.

Centre for the Study of Living Standards (2012). Aboriginal Labour Market Performance in Canada: 2007-2011. Ottawa.

Government of Canada. (1996). *Royal Commission on Aboriginal Peoples*. Ottawa: Indian and Northern Affairs Canada. Retrieved from: http://www.collectionscanada.gc.ca/webarchives/20071115053257/http://www.ainc-inac.gc.ca/ch/rcap/sg/sgmm_e.html

Health Canada. (2002). *A statistical profile on the health of First Nations in Canada*. Ottawa: Health Canada.

Health Canada. (2012a). Aboriginal status. *Food and nutrition: Household food insecurity in Canada in 2007–2008. Key statistics and graphics*. Ottawa: Health Canada. Retrieved from: http://www.hc-sc.gc.ca/fn-an/surveill/nutrition/commun/insecurit/key-stats-cles-2007-2008-eng.php

Health Canada. (2012b). Are First Nations and Inuit populations more at risk? *First Nations & Inuit Health: HIV and AIDS*. Ottawa: Health Canada. Retrieved from: http://www.hc-sc.gc.ca/fniah-spnia/diseases-maladies/aids-sida/index-eng.php

Indian and Northern Affairs Canada (INAC). (2005). *Basic Departmental Data 2004*. Ottawa: Department of Indian Affairs and Northern Development. Retrieved from http://www.collectionscanada.gc.ca/webarchives/20071122094824/http://www.ainc-inac.gc.ca/pr/sts/bdd04/bdd04_e.html

Knotsch, C. & Kinnon, D. (2011). *If not now … when? Addressing the ongoing Inuit housing crisis in Canada*. Ottawa: National Aboriginal Health Organization.

Moscovitch, A. and Webster, A. (1995). Aboriginal social assistance expenditures. In Philips, S. (Ed.). *How Ottawa spends: 1995-96: Mid-life crises* (pp. 209–236). Ottawa: Carleton University Press.

National Aboriginal Health Organization. (2011). *Fact sheet: Addressing mental illness*. Ottawa: NAHO.

Ponting, J. R. (1997). *First Nations in Canada: Perspectives on opportunity, empowerment, and self-determination*. Toronto: McGraw-Hill Ryerson.

Scott, K. A. (1994). *Aboriginal health and social history: A brief Canadian history*. Unpublished. Author's personal collection.

Shewell, H. E. Q. (2004). *Enough to keep them alive: Indian welfare in Canada, 1873–1965*. Toronto: University of Toronto Press.

Statistics Canada. (2013). Aboriginal Peoples in Canada: First Nations People, Métis and Inuit. *National Household Survey, 2011*. Catalogue no. 99-011-X2011001.

Wilson, D. and Macdonald, D. (2010) *The Income Gap between Aboriginal Peoples and the Rest of Canada*. Ottawa: Canadian Centre for Policy Alternatives.

Chapter 12: Disability and Social Welfare

Bowe, F. (1978). *Handicapping America: Barriers to Disable People*. New York: Harper and Row.

Canadian Council on Social Development (CCSD). (2005). *Disability information sheet 18: Employment and persons with disabilities in Canada*. Kanata: CCSD. Retrieved from: http://www.ccsd.ca/drip/research/drip18/drip18.pdf

Frieden, L. (1980). Independent living program models. *Rehabilitation Literature. 41*, 169–173.

Hanes, R. and Moscovitch, A. (2002). Disability supports in the social union. In Allan Puttee (Ed.). *Social union and disability policy*. Kingston ON: Institute for Intergovernmental Relations.

Hanes, R. (2005). Independent living centres: An example of non government organizations for people with disabilities in Canada. Canada/China Forum on NGOs and Community Development- Beijing Institute of Technology. (Conference Proceedings)

National Council of Welfare. (2006). *Welfare incomes 2005*. Ottawa: NCW.

Oliver, M. (1990). *The politics of disability: A sociological approach*. London: Macmillan.

Oliver, M. (1996). *Understanding disability: From theory to practice*. New York: St. Martin's Press.

Social Development Canada (SDC). (2004). *Canadian attitudes towards disability issues: 2004 benchmark survey, prepared for the Office for Disability Issues*. Ottawa: Social Development Canada.

Splane, R. (1965). Review: The role of public welfare in a century of social welfare development. In Meilicke, C. A. and Storch, J. L. (1980) *Perspectives on Canadian health and social services policy: History and emerging trends*. Ann Arbour, MI: Health Administration Press.

Stapleton, J. (2012). Social assistance disability income expenditures: Why costs are going up [powerpoint slides]. Retrieved from http://www.ccdonline.ca/media/socialpolicy/social-assistance-disability-income-expenditures.zip

Torjman, S. (2002). *The Canada pension plan disability benefit*. Ottawa: Caledon Institute for Social Policy.

Williams, C. (2006). Disability in the workplace. *Perspectives on Labour and Income. 7*(2), 16–24.

Chapter 13: The Elderly and Retired

Bryden, K. (1974). *Old age pensions and policy-making in Canada*. Montreal: McGill-Queen's University Press.

Conference Board of Canada. (2013a). *Income inequality: Is Canada becoming more unequal?* Ottawa: Conference Board of Canada. Retrieved from: http://www.conferenceboard.ca/hcp/details/society/income-inequality.aspx

Conference Board of Canada. (2013b). *Elderly poverty*. Ottawa: Conference Board of Canada. Retrieved from: http://www.conferenceboard.ca/hcp/details/society/elderly-poverty.aspx

Hamilton, M., Grady, P., & Sharpe, A. (2001). The state of economics in Canada: Festschrift in honour of David Slater.

HRSDC. (2013). Indicators of well-being in Canada: Financial security—Retirement income. Ottawa: HRSDC. Retrieved from http://www4.hrsdc.gc.ca/h.4m.2@-eng.jsp

Milan, A. and Vézina, M. (2011). Senior women. In *Women in Canada: A gender-based statistical report*. Ottawa: Statistics Canada.

Office of the Parliamentary Budget Officer. (2012). *Renewing the Canada Health Transfer: Implications for federal and provincial-territorial fiscal Sustainability*. Ottawa: Office of the PBO. Retrieved from: http://www.pbo-dpb.gc.ca/files/files/Publications/Renewing_CHT.pdf

Osberg, L. (2001). *Poverty among senior citizens: A Canadian success story* (pp. 151–181). Centre for the Study of Living Standards.

Statistics Canada. (2012). *The Canadian population in 2011: Age and sex*. Catalogue no. 98-311-X2011001. Ottawa: Minister of Industry.

The Advocate: Official Newsletter of the B.C. Federation of Retired Union Members, 15(1) March, 2012.

Wood, D. and Hinton, L. (2012, September 10). Rolling back the age of eligibility for OAS and GIS is not gender neutral. *Retiree Matters*.

Chapter 14: Globalization and Social Welfare

Clarke, T. (1996). Mechanisms of corporate rule. In Madner, J. & Goldsmith, E. (Eds.). *The case against the global economy: And for a turn toward the local* (pp. 297–308). San Francisco: Sierra Club Books.

Ehrenreich, B. and Fuentes, A. (1992). *Women in the global factory*. Boston: South End Press.

hooks, b. (2003). *Teaching Community: A Pedagogy of Hope*. New York: Continuum.

Ife, J. (2001). *Human rights and social work: Towards rights-based practice*. Cambridge: Cambridge University Press.

Kapoor, S. (2005). *Paying for 100% multilateral debt cancellation: Current proposals explained*. Retrieved from: http://www.linktv.org/sitecontent/pages/01payingforrelief.pdf

Klein, N. (2000). *No Logo: Taking Aim at the Brand Bullies*. Toronto: Vintage Canada.

Mishra, R. (1999). *Globalization and the Welfare State*. Cheltenham, UK: Edward Edgar Publishing.

Rice, J. and Prince, M. (2000). *Changing Politics of Canadian Social Policy*. Toronto: University of Toronto Press.

UNDP. (2012). *Human Development Report*. New York: United Nations Development Programme. Human development Report Office.

Index

D

Photo Credits

Chapter 1. Photo background image used throughout: Oksana Telesheva/shutterstock.com / pg 2: Anton Oparin/shutterstock.com / pg 3 © Simon Fraser University / pg 4 Saskatchewan Archives R-A3256 / pg 7 © Simon Fraser University / pg 9 CP photo/Adrian Wyld / pg 11 © Simon Fraser University / pg 13 Paul McKinnon/shutterstock.com / pg 15 CP photo/Adrian Wyld / pg 16 CP photo/Darren Calabrese / pg 19 CP photo/Peter Power

Chapter 2. pg 26: Library and Archives Canada / pg 27: CP photo/ Ivan Sekretarev / pg 33 left: Image copyright Georgios Kollidas 2013 Used under license from Shutterstock, Inc. / pg 33 right: Image copyright Heartland 2013 Used under license from Shutterstock, Inc. / pg 35: Image copyright Robert J Daveant 2013 Used under license from Shutterstock, Inc. / pg 39: Library and Archives Canada / pg 42: Image copyright Simfalex 2013 Used under license from Shutterstock, Inc. / pg 43: Library and Archives Canada / pg 47: Vancouver Archives

Chapter 3. pg 54: Image copyright Vlad G 2013 Used under license from Shutterstock, Inc. / pg 57: CP photo/Paul Chiasson / pg 61: © Simon Fraser University / pg 68: Image copyright Albert Pego 2013 Used under license from Shutterstock, Inc. / pg 70: Image copyright Christopher Kolaczan 2013 Used under license from Shutterstock, Inc.

Chapter 4. pg 76 Image copyright Jaren Jai Wickland 2013 Used under license from Shutterstock, Inc. / pg 81 photo Image copyright Keith Levit 2013 Used under license from Shutterstock, Inc./ pg 83 photo Image copyright Georgios Kollidas 2013 Used under license from Shutterstock, Inc. / pg 86 CP photo/Eddie Adams / pg 88 arindambanerjee/Shutterstock.com / pg 92 Image copyright Flashon Studio 2013 Used under license from Shutterstock, Inc. / pg 95 Image copyright bikerinlondon 2013 Used under license from Shutterstock, Inc. / pg 96 Image copyright auremar 2013 Used under license from Shutterstock, Inc. / pg 97 Image copyright luxorphoto 2013 Used under license from Shutterstock, Inc.

Chapter 5. pg 102. Image copyright Pinkcandy 2013 Used under license from Shutterstock, Inc. / pg 103: CP photo/Andrew Vaughan / pg 107: SFU Library Editorial Cartoons Collection / pg 109: Komar/ Shutterstock.com / pg 111: CP photo/Mark Spowart / pg 112: Copyright © Carol Simpson CartoonWork / pg 113: CP photo/Jacques Boissinot / pg 119: CP photo/Fred Chartrand / pg 120: CP photo/Charla Jones

Chapter 6. pg 124: Image copyright joeborg 2013 Used under license from Shutterstock, Inc. / pg 133: Image copyright franco's photos 2013 Used under license from Shutterstock, Inc. / pg 138: Image copyright Jaren Jai Wicklund 2013 Used under license from Shutterstock, Inc. / pg 145: Image copyright chalabala 2013 Used under license from Shutterstock, Inc. / pg 148: CP photo/Rene Johnston / pg 151: QMI Agency

Chapter 7. pg 156: ©iStockphoto.com/David Jones / pg 164: CP photo/Editorial Cartoon by Brian Gable / The Globe and Mail / pg 167: ©iStockphoto.com/Oktay Ortakcioglu / pg 171: ©iStockphoto.com/ Valérie Brien / pg 172: ©iStockphoto.com/sturti / pg 179: Library and Archives Canada / pg 180: ©iStockphoto.com/Bart Coenders/ pg 182: ©iStockphoto.com/Eliza Snow

Chapter 8. pg 186: Image copyright Rob Marmion 2013 Used under license from Shutterstock, Inc. / pg 196: CP photo/ Deborah Baic / pg 199: V. J. Matthew/Shutterstock.com / pg 201: Image copyright V. J. Matthew 2013 Used under license from Shutterstock, Inc. / pg 202: Image copyright BlueOrange Studio 2013 Used under license from Shutterstock, Inc. / pg 203: Image copyright William Perugini 2013 Used under license from Shutterstock, Inc. / pg 209: Image copyright Brocreative 2013 Used under license from Shutterstock, Inc.

Chapter 9. pg 212: Image copyright ChameleonsEye 2013 Used under license from Shutterstock, Inc. / pg 219: Library and Archives Canada / pg 220: ©iStockphoto.com/Christopher Futcher / pg 227: Image copyright Sean Bolt 2013 Used under license from Shutterstock, Inc. / pg 230: Image copyright Gladskikh Tatiana 2013 Used under license from Shutterstock, Inc.

Chapter 10. pg 240: ValeStock/Shutterstock.com / pg 244: Sergei Bachlakov/Shutterstock.com / pg 247: CP photo/Tom Hanson / pg 249: Image copyright Darren Baker 2013. Used under license from Shutterstock, Inc. / pg 251: Image copyright digitalreflections 2013. Used under license from Shutterstock, Inc. / pg 253: Image copyright Jaimie Duplass 2013. Used under license from Shutterstock, Inc. / pg 256: Image copyright szefei 2013. Used under license from Shutterstock, Inc. / pg 258: ©iStockphoto.com/Jen Grantham

Chapter 11. pg 262: Richard Wear / DesignPics (via GetStock.com) / pg 263: CP photo/Geoff Robins / pg 267: CP photo/Ryan Remiorz / pg 271. CP photo/Andrew Vaughan /pg 272: CP photo/Nathan Denette / pg 275: CP photo/Andrew Vaughan / pg 279: CP photo/Sean Kilpatrick / pg 281: CP photo/Tom Hanson / pg 282: CP photo/Geoff Howe

Chapter 12. pg 286: Image copyright Miriam Doerr 2013 Used under license from Shutterstock, Inc. / pg 288: Image copyright Vitalinka 2013 Used under license from Shutterstock, Inc. / pg 296: Image copyright gillmar 2013 Used under license from Shutterstock, Inc. / pg 306: Image copyright Oscar C. Williams 2013 Used under license from Shutterstock, Inc.

Chapter 13. pg 310: Image copyright piotrwzk 2013 Used under license from Shutterstock, Inc. / pg 322 Image copyright Rob Marmion 2013 Used under license from Shutterstock, Inc. / pg 325 Image copyright CREATISTA 2013 Used under license from Shutterstock, Inc.

Chapter 14. pg 330: CP photo/Natacha Pisarenko / pg 331 Jan S./ Shutterstock.com / pg 333 ValeStock/Shutterstock.com / pg 335 © iStockphoto.com/EdStock / pg 340 Sam DCruz/Shutterstock.com

Other Credits

Note on Statistics Canada Material. Use of Statistics Canada data and figures does not constitute an endorsement by Statistics Canada of this product.

Chapter 4. Page 96 article: Editorial. (May 8, 2013). "An Investment in the Public Good." *The Globe and Mail* (p. A14) / Page 96-97 article: Torjman, Sherri. (May 8, 2013). "Private Money, Public Programs? There Will Always be Strings." *The Globe and Mail* (p. A15).

Chapter 5. Page 115 graphic based on data from: Curry, Bill. (August 15, 2012). "Boardroom confidential: What CEOs are Asking of Jim Flaherty." *The Globe and Mail.*

Chapter 6. The Real Cost of Homelessness (page 144): Gaetz, Stephen (2012): The Real Cost of Homelessness: Can We Save Money by Doing the Right Thing? Toronto: Canadian Homelessness Research Network Press.

Chapter 7. Case Study on page 171: Excerpt from Law Commission of Canada. 2004. Is Work Working? Work Laws that Do a Better Job. Ottawa: Law Commission of Canada, 6–7 / Box on page 179 from: *Bearing the Brunt: How the 2008-2009 Recession Created Poverty for Canadian Families* © Citizens for Public Justice 2010 www.cpj.ca

Chapter 9. Box on page 223: The National Child Benefit Progress Report: 2006, http://www.prestationnationalepourenfants.ca/eng/06/chap1.shtml, Canada Revenue Agency, 2008, Reproduced with the permission of the Minister of Public Works and Government Services Canada, 2013 / Box on page 232: Canada Revenue Agency. (2013). Child and family benefits. Retrieved from: www.cra-arc.gc.ca/bnfts/menu-eng.html / pages 233–237: Canada Revenue Agency. (2013). Provincial and territorial programs. Retrieved from: www.cra-arc.gc.ca/bnfts/rltd_prgrms/menu-eng.html

Chapter 10. Article on page 256: Chase, Steven. (May 11, 2013). "Welfare costs prompt tougher rules for immigrating parents." *The Globe and Mail.* © The Globe and Mail Inc. All Rights Reserved / page 257: text adapted from Citizenship and Immigration Canada. (2013). Family sponsorship. Retrieved from: www.cic.gc.ca/english/immigrate/sponsor/index.asp

Chapter 11. Page 282 figure: Adapted from Statistics Canada, Catalogue No. 71-588-X.

Chapter 12. Box on page 288: Adapted from Statistics Canada publication *Participation and Activity Limitation Survey* 2001. Cat. no. 89-577-XIE / page 306 box: Memo to patients and their doctors on the recent changes to the Disability Tax Credit (DTC) Certificate Form T2201 for persons with mental impairments. Fighting for Fairness, June 16, 2006, www.disabilitytaxcredit.com/news.php; and Buchanan v. Queen (2001), Tax Court of Canada, http://decision.tcc-cci.gc.ca/en/2001/html/2001tcc20001865.html

Chapter 13. Article on page 315: Friesen, Joe. (November 24, 2010). "Number of seniors living in poverty soars nearly 25%" *The Globe and Mail.* © The Globe and Mail Inc. All Rights Reserved / Box on page 319: Pension Timeline from The History of Canada's Public Pensions, 2002, www.civilization.ca © Canadian Museum of Civilization.